The European
Culture Area

D1301128

The European Culture Area

A Systematic Geography

Sixth Edition

ALEXANDER B. MURPHY,
TERRY G. JORDAN-BYCHKOV,
AND BELLA BYCHKOVA JORDAN

ROWMAN & LITTLEFIELD
Lanham • Boulder • New • York • Toronto • Plymouth, UK

Published by Rowman & Littlefield
4501 Forbes Boulevard, Suite 200, Lanham, Maryland 20706
www.rowman.com

10 Thornbury Road, Plymouth PL6 7PP, United Kingdom

British Library Cataloguing in Publication Information Available

Library of Congress Cataloging-in-Publication Data

Murphy, Alexander B., 1954–
    The European culture area : a systematic geography / Alexander B. Murphy, Terry G.
Jordan-Bychkov, and Bella Bychkova Jordan.—Sixth edition.
        pages cm
    Includes bibliographical references and index.
    ISBN 978-1-4422-2345-5 (cloth : alk. paper) — ISBN 978-1-4422-2346-2 (pbk. : alk. paper)—
    ISBN 978-1-4422-2347-9 (electronic) 1. Europe—Geography. 2. Europe—Description and
travel. I. Jordan-Bychkov, Terry G., 1938-2003. II. Bychkova Jordan, Bella. III. Title.
    D907.J67   2014
    914--dc23
                                                                        2013048229

♾™ The paper used in this publication meets the minimum requirements of American National
Standard for Information Sciences—Permanence of Paper for Printed Library Materials,
ANSI/NISO Z39.48-1992.

Printed in the United States of America

Alec Murphy and Bella Bychkova Jordan
dedicate this book to Susan N. Gary
and to the memory of Terry Jordan-Bychkov—
partners who made Europe, and so much more,
come alive for us.

Contents

List of Illustrations   xiii

Preface   xix

A Note about Place Names   xxi

1   What and Where Is Europe?   1
    Europe as a Physical Entity   1
    Europe as a Human Entity   7
    This Book's Approach   15
    Why Study Europe?   20
    Sources and Suggested Readings   23

2   Physical Geography   25
    Europe's Geomorphology and Hydrogeography   25
      Mountains   29
      Hills   33
      Plains   33
      Hydrogeography   35
    Europe's Climate   36
      Marine West Coast   39
      Mediterranean   40
      Humid Continental   41
      Minor Climate Types   42
    Vegetation and Soils   42
      Forests   43
      Treeless Areas   44
      Soils   45
    Human Alteration of the Environment   47
      Human Modification of Lands and Waters   47
       The Special Case of the Netherlands   49

Human Modification of the Atmosphere   56
Human Impacts on Forests   58
Green Europe   65
Sources and Suggested Readings   68

3   Demography   71
Population Distribution and Density   71
Population Growth Rates   75
Natural Increase   75
Migration   80
Major Influences on Population Geography   84
The Role of the Environment   85
Socioeconomic and Political Context   87
Population Policies   89
Scale Differences   90
Sources and Suggested Readings   91

4   The Pattern of Languages   93
Languages and Language Families   93
The Diffusion of Indo-European Tongues into Europe   98
The Three Major Subfamilies of Indo-European   101
Romance Languages   102
Germanic Languages   105
The Special Case of English   107
Slavic Languages   108
Other Indo-European Languages   109
Non-Indo-European Languages   113
Linguistic Decline and Revival   116
Multilingualism   118
Sources and Suggested Readings   120

5   The Geography of Religion   123
Pre-Christian Europe   124
Diffusion of Christianity   126
Christian Fragmentation   130
Roman Catholicism   131
Pilgrimages   133
Winds of Change   135
Protestantism   136
Eastern Orthodoxy   140
The East–West Divide   142
Uniate and Armenian Churches   144
Dechristianization   145
Sects and Cults   147

Non-Christian Minorities   147
  Islam   147
  Judaism   153
Conclusion   155
Sources and Suggested Readings   156

6 The European State System   159
  The General Picture   159
  The Emergence of the European State Pattern   161
  The Twentieth-Century European State   168
  Case Studies   171
    France: The Quintessential Unitary State   172
    Germany: Federalism in the European Core   174
    The United Kingdom: Core–Periphery Tensions 176
    Italy: Roman Legacy   177
    Spain: A Multiethnic State   179
    Switzerland and Belgium: Astride a Language Divide   180
    Fragmentation in the Balkans: Yugoslavia and Its Successor States   184
    Russia: Nation-State or Empire?   186
    Ukraine: From Border Province to Independent State   188
  Challenges to the Territorial State   189
  Sources and Suggested Readings   194

7 Land and Life in the Rural Sector   197
  Traditional Agriculture   197
    Mediterranean Agriculture   199
    Three-Field Farming   203
    Hardscrabble Herder-Farmers   204
    Shifting Cultivation of the North   204
    Nomadic Herding   205
  Traditional Land Divisions and Settlement Patterns   207
  New Crop Introductions   214
  Modern Agricultural Systems   215
    Market Gardening   217
    Dairying   217
    Cattle/Hog Fattening   219
    Sheep Raising   220
    Cash Grain Farming   220
    Reindeer Ranching   220
    Fishing and Fish Farming   221
  Land Tenure in the Modern Era   221
  Production Patterns in the Modern Era   225
  Rural Depopulation   228

Preserving Rural Landscapes   229
Sources and Suggested Readings   230

8   Manufacturing and Industry   233
    Historical Overview (Pre–Eighteenth Century)   233
        Traditional Manufacturing Systems   235
    The Industrial Revolution   236
    Diffusion of the Industrial Revolution   240
        Spreading beyond the Coalfields   242
    Impacts of Industrialization   244
        Social Impacts   245
        Environmental Impacts   246
        Impacts on Transportation Infrastructure   248
            Roads   248
            Railroads   255
            Waterways   258
            Pipelines   263
            Air Transport   264
    Deindustrialization   264
    Industrial Rejuvenation   268
    Contemporary Patterns   271
    Sources and Suggested Readings   271

9   The Postindustrial Economy and the Quest for European Integration   275
    The Nature of Europe's Service and Information Economy   275
    Communications   278
    Energy Production   279
    Tourism   281
    Retailing and Governmental/Social Services   287
    The Quaternary Sector   287
    The Trajectory of Integration   289
    Economic Impacts of Integration   294
    Sources and Suggested Readings   297

10 The European City   299
    The Rise of the European City   299
    The Medieval City   303
        City Sites   305
        City Attributes   309
        Medieval Urban Morphology   311
    Renaissance–Baroque Urban Development (1500–1800)   313
    The Industrial City   314
    Characteristics of the Mid-Twentieth-Century European City   317
    The Late/Postindustrial European City   320
        The Preindustrial Core   323
        The Preindustrial Periphery   324

The Industrial Suburbs   325
The Postindustrial Suburbs   326
Regional Variations   326
The Modern Urban Pattern   336
Sources and Suggested Readings   338

11   Europe's Changing Social and Ethnic Geography   343
Patterns of Social Well-Being   346
Health   351
Employment   354
Education   355
The Role of Women   357
Ethnic Patterns   360
The Traditional Social Model in Transition   367
Macroeconomic Challenges   367
The Demographic Challenge   370
The Immigration Challenge   375
Sources and Suggested Readings   376

12   Whither European Integration?   379
Impetuses for Integration   383
Globalization   383
The Changing Geopolitical Order   383
Relationships with Surrounding Regions   385
Heightened Interaction   386
Economic Advances   387
The "Irrationality" of the Pattern of States   388
Ethno-regionalism   390
Impetuses for Fragmentation   390
Globalization   390
The Changing Geopolitical Order   391
Nationalism   392
Bureaucratization   394
Differences over Widening and Deepening   394
Heightened Interaction   395
Ethno-regionalism   396
Where from Here?   398
Sources and Suggested Readings   401

Glossary   403

Index   413

About the Authors   431

Illustrations

Figure 1.1.   World map drawn by the Ancient Greek geographer Hecataeus   2
Figure 1.2.   World map of the Roman geographer Pomponius Mela   3
Figure 1.3.   Two versions of the medieval European "T in O" map   4
Figure 1.4.   The Ural Mountains   5
Figure 1.5.   Proposals for defining Europe physically   6
Figure 1.6.   Areas in Eurasia where one, two, or all three of the following human traits are predominant: Indo-European language, Christian beliefs, Caucasoid racial characteristics   9
Figure 1.7.   A measure of "European-ness"   11
Figure 1.8.   The Europeanization of the world   14
Figure 1.9.   Proposed culture-based borders of Europe   16
Figure 1.10.   Member states of the European Union   18
Figure 1.11.   Sources of selected European concepts and inventions   21
Figure 2.1.   Terrain regions   26
Figure 2.2.   Tectonic plates   27
Figure 2.3.   Glaciers in Europe during the height of the most recent glaciation   28
Figure 2.4.   The dramatic Dolomite mountains of northeastern Italy   30
Figure 2.5.   A branch of the Sognefjord   31
Figure 2.6.   Earthquakes, volcanism, and tsunamis in Europe   32
Figure 2.7.   Hydrogeographic features   36
Figure 2.8.   Climate regions   38
Figure 2.9.   Floristic provinces   43
Figure 2.10.   Soil regions   46
Figure 2.11.   Evidence of abandoned terraces on hillsides in Croatia   48
Figure 2.12.   How the Netherlands would look without human intervention   50
Figure 2.13.   An ancient *terp* in the Dutch coastal province of Friesland   51
Figure 2.14.   Humans at work modifying the Dutch coastline, 1200–1950   52
Figure 2.15.   The Zuider Zee Project   54
Figure 2.16.   The Delta Project   55

Figure 2.17.   Percentage of forest area damaged or dead by the late 1990s   57
Figure 2.18.   Deforested, rocky landscape on the Aegean island of Patmos   59
Figure 2.19.   Percentage of land forested   61
Figure 2.20.   The retreat of woodland in central Europe, 900–1900 CE   62
Figure 2.21.   Stages of forest clearance   63
Figure 2.22.   Logs floating to Joensuu, Finland   64
Figure 2.23.   Reduction of heath   65
Figure 2.24.   Soviet-era coal-burning power plant in southwest Poland   67
Figure 3.1.   Europe forms one of the major clusters of "continuous"
               settlement in the world   73
Figure 3.2.   Population density in Europe   74
Figure 3.3.   Diagram of the demographic transition   75
Figure 3.4.   Advent of sustained fertility decline in Europe   76
Figure 3.5.   Annual natural population change   77
Figure 3.6.   Percentage of population aged 60 or older   78
Figure 3.7.   Population pyramids for Germany and Albania   79
Figure 3.8.   Emigration from Ireland, 1846–1851   81
Figure 3.9.   Migration within and to continental western Europe
               during the 1960s and 1970s   83
Figure 3.10.   Diffusion of the Bubonic Plague, 1347–1351   86
Figure 3.11.   Population loss owing to warfare and disease in central
               Europe, 1618–1648   87
Figure 3.12.   War memorial in the French commune of Limeuil   88
Figure 3.13.   Concentration of settlement in the Rhône Valley, Swiss Alps   90
Figure 4.1.   Languages and selected dialects of modern Europe   94
Figure 4.2.   The Indo-European language tree   96
Figure 4.3.   Maximum extent of the Roman Empire   97
Figure 4.4.   Origin, diffusion, and fragmentation of the Indo-European
               languages   100
Figure 4.5.   Number of Arabic and Arabized topographic names   103
Figure 4.6.   An archaic language border in Germany   106
Figure 4.7.   Retreat of the Celtic languages   110
Figure 4.8.   Defacing of English language   112
Figure 4.9.   The non-Indo-European lands of Europe   114
Figure 4.10.   Galician-language graffiti   117
Figure 4.11.   Bilingual French-Breton   118
Figure 4.12.   Ability to speak English   119
Figure 5.1.   Religious groups in Europe   124
Figure 5.2.   Templed promontories of the ancient Aegean   125
Figure 5.3.   Proportion of pilgrimage shrines dedicated to the Virgin Mary   126
Figure 5.4.   Kildrummy Church   127
Figure 5.5.   Diffusion of Christianity   128
Figure 5.6.   Diffusion of Protestantism   130
Figure 5.7.   St. Peter's in Vatican City   132
Figure 5.8.   Pilgrimage shrines in Western Europe   134

Figure 5.9.   Pilgrims at Santiago de Compostela   135
Figure 5.10.   A rural Lutheran church   136
Figure 5.11.   Neo-Protestant church in southern Sweden   137
Figure 5.12.   A Methodist chapel in the Lleyn Peninsula of Celtic Wales   138
Figure 5.13.   On the Protestant–Catholic divide, in Belfast,
               Northern Ireland   139
Figure 5.14.   A splendid Eastern Orthodox church in Sarajevo, Bosnia   141
Figure 5.15.   The Cathedral of Christ the Savior in Moscow   142
Figure 5.16.   The great monastery at Pechory   143
Figure 5.17.   Population in European countries that is secular (percentage)   145
Figure 5.18.   Muslim population in European countries (percentage)   148
Figure 5.19.   The Giralda   151
Figure 5.20.   The Grand Mosque of Paris   152
Figure 5.21.   The non-Christian periphery and former Jewish diaspora   154
Figure 6.1.   The independent countries of Europe   160
Figure 6.2.   Types of states in Europe based on their territorial and
               ideological foundations   162
Figure 6.3.   Core areas and the evolution of European states   163
Figure 6.4.   Europe in the eighteenth century   164
Figure 6.5.   Main post roads in Europe, 1850   166
Figure 6.6.   Europe at the end of World War I   167
Figure 6.7.   Types of independent states, based upon unitary versus
               federal governments   169
Figure 6.8.   Swedish–Norwegian border near Torsby, Sweden   170
Figure 6.9.   Inheritance systems and land fragmentation in the German
               province of Hessen, 1955   171
Figure 6.10.   France: Selected geopolitical features   173
Figure 6.11.   Germany   174
Figure 6.12.   The United Kingdom   177
Figure 6.13.   Italy   178
Figure 6.14.   Spain   180
Figure 6.15.   Switzerland: Territorial development and ethnic diversity   181
Figure 6.16.   Belgium   183
Figure 6.17.   The disintegration of the former Yugoslavia   185
Figure 6.18.   Territorial evolution of Russia   187
Figure 6.19.   Areas of separatism or significant ethno-cultural difference
               within states   190
Figure 6.20.   NATO expansion, 1949 to present   193
Figure 7.1.   Neolithic origins and the diffusion of agriculture in Europe   198
Figure 7.2.   Ancient and traditional types of agriculture   200
Figure 7.3.   Intertillage of wheat and olives in an alluvial valley in Greece   201
Figure 7.4.   Cork newly stripped   202
Figure 7.5.   Finnish farmers in the interior of their country   205
Figure 7.6.   Sami man in traditional dress with one of his reindeer in
               northern Norway   206

Figure 7.7.   Field patterns exhibiting Roman influence   208
Figure 7.8.   Fragmented, long-lot landholdings in Lorraine   209
Figure 7.9.   Forms of rural settlement   210
Figure 7.10.   Major types of rural settlement in Europe   211
Figure 7.11.   Traditional rural building materials   212
Figure 7.12.   Bergerac, in Aquitaine, France   213
Figure 7.13.   Danish half-timbered houses   214
Figure 7.14.   Specialized types of agriculture in modern Europe   216
Figure 7.15.   Wine grape monoculture near Sadillac, in southwestern France   218
Figure 7.16.   A collective farm in the Hungarian Basin   222
Figure 7.17.   A commercial sunflower farm in southwest France   223
Figure 7.18.   Production of all grains per hectare   227
Figure 7.19.   Percentage of workforce employed in agriculture   228
Figure 8.1.   Guild houses on the central square in Brussels   236
Figure 8.2.   The concentrations of primary industry and traditional heavy
               manufacturing, about 1960   238
Figure 8.3.   The Ruhr industrial district, Germany, about 1950   241
Figure 8.4.   Selected patterns of environmental pollution   247
Figure 8.5.   The Roman roads in Europe   249
Figure 8.6.   Automobiles per person   251
Figure 8.7.   Controlled access, divided highways   252
Figure 8.8.   Motorable highways, kilometers per 1,000 square kilometers   253
Figure 8.9.   Road traffic bottlenecks and choke points   254
Figure 8.10.   Railroad density and gauge   255
Figure 8.11.   Diffusion of the railroad in nineteenth-century Europe   256
Figure 8.12.   The European master plan for twenty-first-century
               high-speed railroads   258
Figure 8.13.   The Channel Tunnel, providing a railroad link between
               England and France   259
Figure 8.14.   Templed promontories of the ancient Aegean   260
Figure 8.15.   Containerized port of Bremerhaven   262
Figure 8.16.   Gas pipelines   263
Figure 8.17.   Zones of deindustrialization and of new manufacturing
               growth, 1960–2010   266
Figure 8.18.   Percentage unemployed in Europe   268
Figure 9.1.   Percentage of labor force employed in the service industries   276
Figure 9.2.   Internet connections, proportional to population, 2012   278
Figure 9.3.   The geography of electrical energy   280
Figure 9.4.   Major tourist destinations in Europe   282
Figure 9.5.   Tourism in Europe, 2011–2012   283
Figure 9.6.   Traditional farmsteads in Stockholm's pioneering open-air
               museum known as Skansen   284
Figure 9.7.   Major centers of producer service industry   288
Figure 9.8.   The European Union   290
Figure 9.9.   Schengen Agreement countries, 2013   292

Figure 9.10.   The Eurozone in 2013   293
Figure 9.11.   Government debt as a percentage of GDP, 2012   295
Figure 10.1.   Urban population as a percent of total population and
                distribution of large metropolitan areas in the early
                twenty-first century   300
Figure 10.2.   Diffusion of the city   301
Figure 10.3.   Cities of the Roman Empire   303
Figure 10.4.   Distribution of important cities, about 1500 CE   304
Figure 10.5.   Toledo, in the central Meseta of Spain   306
Figure 10.6.   The city of Sion/Sitten, in the Swiss Canton of Valais/Wallis   307
Figure 10.7.   The skyline of Bruges, Belgium   310
Figure 10.8.   Ávila, on the Castilian Meseta of interior Spain   310
Figure 10.9.   The central market square in Lübeck, Germany   311
Figure 10.10.   Street plans of medieval towns in Germany   312
Figure 10.11.   Survival of the Roman grid pattern in Pavia, Italy   313
Figure 10.12.   Central part of Palmanova, Italy   315
Figure 10.13.   The Champs Elysées in Paris   316
Figure 10.14.   Munich (München), Germany, and Milwaukee, Wisconsin   318
Figure 10.15.   Paris, looking westward from the Tour Montparnasse   319
Figure 10.16.   Urban redevelopment in Duisburg, Germany   323
Figure 10.17.   La Défense   325
Figure 10.18.   Distribution of European city types   327
Figure 10.19.   The preindustrial core of the small Hessian city of Weilburg   328
Figure 10.20.   War damage to housing in Hamburg, Germany   329
Figure 10.21.   A stylized scheme of modern Budapest   330
Figure 10.22.   Models of the typical Spanish and southern Italian city   332
Figure 10.23.   The northern periphery of Moscow   333
Figure 10.24.   The urban landscape in contemporary Moscow   334
Figure 10.25.   Oulu, a Nordic city of Finland   335
Figure 10.26.   Development of Randstad Holland   337
Figure 10.27.   European megalopolises   338
Figure 11.1.   Effective tax rates for selected major countries   344
Figure 11.2.   Percentage of GDP devoted to social welfare programs
                (excluding education)   348
Figure 11.3.   Differences in GDP per capita in Europe and surrounding areas   349
Figure 11.4.   GDP per capita in first-order substate regions of the
                European Union and European Free Trade Association
                member states, relative to the EU average (percentage)   350
Figure 11.5.   Levels of socioeconomic well-being in the Paris
                metropolitan area   351
Figure 11.6.   SDR, chronic liver disease, and cirrhosis per 100,000 people   353
Figure 11.7.   One of the book's authors in front of the former main entrance
                to the public primary school he attended in 1964–1965   356
Figure 11.8.   Percentage of women occupying seats in the parliaments of
                EU countries, 2012   358

Figure 11.9.   The gender pay gap within the European Union, 2011   359
Figure 11.10. The absolute gender employment gap within the
               European Union, 2011   360
Figure 11.11. Areas of separatism or significant ethno-cultural difference
               within states   361
Figure 11.12. Percentage of the population that is foreign born in
               European countries   363
Figure 11.13. Evidence of Middle Eastern immigrants in Brussels   364
Figure 11.14. The geography of the 2005 riots in the Paris metropolitan area   365
Figure 11.15. Containers being loaded onto a ship in the Copenhagen harbor   369
Figure 11.16. Total fertility rates in first-order substate regions in the EU   371
Figure 11.17. Park in Paris's 13th Arrondissement   373
Figure 12.1.   Attitudes toward European integration in 2011   381
Figure 12.2.   Trust in the European Union among EU member states
               and applicant countries, 2011   382
Figure 12.3.   The Nordic vote on European Union membership, 1995   384
Figure 12.4.   Areas benefiting from European Union regional
               development funds   387
Figure 12.5.   Future development scenarios within the European Union   389
Figure 12.6.   Degree of identification with states, the European Union,
               or a combination of the two, 2013   393
Figure 12.7.   Gross domestic product per capita in the EU, 2011–2012   397
Figure 12.8.   European Union border regions eligible to participate in
               the EU's INTERREG III program   400
Figure 12.9.   Regions participating in the Four Motors Agreement   401

Preface

The sixth edition of *The European Culture Area* is the latest incarnation of a book begun in 1973 by the distinguished cultural-historical geographer Terry Jordan. Terry's original idea was to write a text on Europe reflecting geography's rich humanistic tradition—one that sought to situate economic, social, and political circumstances within the broader story of the region's evolution over time. Terry carried that tradition through four editions, but unfortunately succumbed to cancer before a fifth edition could be launched. He left the fifth edition in the hands of his fourth-edition coauthor and a new lead author. For that edition we endeavored to stay true to Terry's original vision, but we expanded the coverage of political, economic, and social developments to give the book more contemporary relevance.

The sixth edition of the book comes in the wake of a major financial crisis and significant political and demographic shifts that are having profound impacts on Europe. Capturing these developments required more than updating statistics and introducing contemporary examples. We needed to make substantial revisions to reflect the changing European scene. The present edition reflects the results of those efforts. The book continues to present geographic patterns and processes against the backdrop of changing arrangements and ideas over time, but recent developments shaping the geography of Europe are emphasized as well.

Our fundamental goals in creating this edition were several. We sought to situate Europe within the wider world—focusing attention on how the region's interactions with the rest of the globe have affected its development. We also wanted to build on the book's tradition of providing a wealth of historical and contemporary maps and photographs aimed at facilitating understanding of the material in the text; 57 new maps and photographs appear in this edition of the book. Finally, we wanted the book to speak forcefully to many of the political, economic, and social issues of the day.

In tackling this edition, we were able to draw on extended past experiences in Europe, as well as on our own research and writing on European themes. Our endeavor was also greatly aided by others. Several University of Oregon graduate students contributed substantially to the project. Anna Moore provided thoughtful input on areas that needed revision, as well as invaluable research assistance. She also drafted two of the new maps. Eric Stipe undertook the task of researching and creating some two-dozen new or revised maps for this edition, and Nicholas Perdue designed and crafted another dozen maps. The sixth edition continues to build on the assistance provided by former University of Oregon graduate students as well, particularly Corey Johnson, who contributed substantially to the chapter on social and ethnic geography, and Matthew Derrick, many of whose maps and graphs for the fifth edition continue to appear in original or revised form in this edition. Some of the book's cartography still bears the imprint of Dr. John Cotter, who created the maps for early editions of *The European Culture Area*.

Beyond the individuals who contributed directly to this book, Alec has benefited from being part of a community of colleagues and students at the University of Oregon who have shared ideas about Europe over the past twenty years. Among colleagues, special acknowledgment goes to Ronald Wixman, whose insights encouraged new and important ways of thinking about Europe's geographical character, and to Everett Smith, who shared his perspectives on the European city during a team-taught seminar many years ago. General thanks also go to a number of former and present Oregon graduate students with European interests who have shared ideas and insights: David Keeling, George White, Amber Kemp, Dominique Salliard, Anne Hunderi-Eli, Nancy Leeper, Sara Press, Anthea Fallen-Bailey, Joanna Kepka, Robert Kerr, Roberto Serralles, Minna Pavulans, Kyle Evered, Hunter Shobe, Adam Lake, Megan Dixon, Mahmood Khan, Vincent Artman, Emma Slager, and Douglas Foster. On a more personal level, Alec would like to acknowledge his partner, Susan Gary, and his sons, Richard and George, whose presence has enriched multiple explorations of Europe, and who provided encouragement and support during the preparation of this edition of the book.

Bella Jordan owes a deep debt of gratitude to her esteemed colleague and scholar of Balkan history and geography Dr. Mary Neuburger, the director of the Center for Russian, East European, and Eurasian Studies at the University of Texas at Austin. Dr. Neuburger shared her extensive knowledge of the region and provided unwavering support throughout the revision process. Thanks also go to University of Texas graduate students Roxana Popan from Romania and Vladyslav Alexander from Ukraine, whose comments and insights were of great help in revising the chapters on language and religion.

The authors owe a special debt to the team at Rowman & Littlefield—most particularly Susan McEachern, whose belief in this project and gentle but persistent encouragement was essential to bringing it to fruition. Thanks also to Carolyn Broadwell-Tkach, who was in charge of the art program, and to Alden Perkins, who oversaw production. Their efforts and professionalism are much appreciated.

A Note about Place Names

Decisions about how to render toponyms are complicated, and our general preference is to defer to indigenous forms. Since most readers of this book will be English speakers, however, we have decided to use the English forms of place names in cases where an English variant is in wide use (e.g., Naples instead of Napoli and Flanders instead of Vlaanderen). The danger in this approach is that it can lead to confusion. One American tourist bound for the wonders of Florence reportedly refused to get off the train at the station bearing the placard "Firenze," convinced that the conductor intended to cheat him! But the indigenous names of some places in Europe are not well known to most English speakers (Hrvatska, as opposed to Croatia), and most readers—including those of a variety of languages other than English—are more likely to identify with Vienna than Wien. Moreover, using the English term provides a convenient way of designating geographic features that extend across international and linguistic boundaries (e.g., the Danube, which is, at various places along its course, known as Donau, Duna, and Duanrea).

As for the names of independent countries, we have opted for commonly used anglicized short forms rather than formal country names (Germany instead of Federal Republic of Germany or Bundesrepublik Deutschland). The one case that might be less familiar to readers concerns the Czech Republic. Increasingly one hears the short form Czechia. Even though that name is not as widely known as other truncations (e.g., Slovakia for the Slovak Republic), we have decided to use Czechia for consistency and to reflect its growing use in the country itself.

Finally, when we capitalize the adjective in the compound terms Western Europe and Eastern Europe, we are referring to the two distinct parts of Europe that were a product of the geopolitical division that existed from the late 1940s through 1989. When the adjectives are not capitalized in these compounds, the intent is to refer to general parts of Europe without invoking Europe's post–World War II partitioning. Thus "western Europe" does not denote a precise territory with a particular geopolitical and temporal association, but the western portion of the European landmass.

CHAPTER 1

What and Where Is Europe?

The title of this chapter raises a complicated question because Europe represents, in the words of Norwegian geographer Leif Ahnström, "an elusive notion." Anyone who has followed the debate over the geographical limits of the European Union knows there is little consensus as to what constitutes Europe. Yet the term has deep historical roots and we use it all the time. One of the core concerns of the discipline of geography is to make sense of how the world is organized—both on the ground and in our minds—so it is appropriate to begin a study of Europe by considering what we mean by Europe, and where Europe is located.

Europe as a Physical Entity

Most people regard Europe as a **continent**. Continents are usually thought to be distinct, sizable landmasses standing more or less separate from other landmasses. North and South America, connected by the narrow Isthmus of Panama, form continents, as do Africa, linked to Asia only by the severed land bridge at Suez. Australia and Antarctica clearly qualify, as they are fully separated from other landmasses by surrounding seas.

Europe, however, does not satisfy the most common definition of a continent since it is not a separate landmass. To be sure, the Mediterranean Sea provides a separation from Africa in the south, while the Atlantic and Arctic Oceans define Europe's western and northern limits. But in the east the notion of continentality founders. Only the beginning of a water separation appears in the southeastern fringe, where an arm of the sea reaches northward from the Mediterranean, through the Aegean, Dardanelles, and Bosporus to the Black Sea, and still beyond to the Sea of Azov. There the division ends, for to the north stretches the vast East European Plain. Instead of a narrow isthmus similar to Panama or Suez, the map reveals a wedge of land broadening steadily to the east, welding Europe and Asia into one large continent called **Eurasia**. A glance at a map of the Eastern Hemisphere reveals Europe as simply one rather

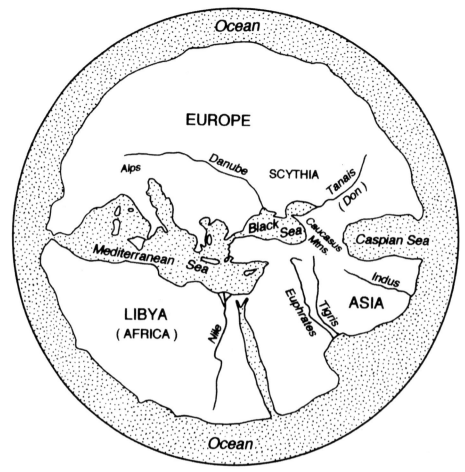

Figure 1.1.   World map drawn by the ancient Greek geographer Hecataeus about 500 BCE. He erroneously linked the Caspian Sea to the open ocean so that Europe and Asia joined only at the Caucasus isthmus. *Source:* Adapted from Parker 1960.

small appendage of Eurasia, merely a westward-reaching peninsula. At most, Europe forms only one-fifth of the area of Eurasia.

The belief that Europe possesses the characteristics of a continent can be traced to the civilizations of the ancient Mediterranean, in particular those centered on Greece and Rome (fig. 1.1). The Greco-Roman worldview, in turn, owed much to older cultures. One theory concerning the origin of the words Europe and Asia ties them to the Semitic Assyrian-Phoenician words *ereb* ("sunset") and *acu* ("sunrise"). Living along the eastern shores of the Mediterranean, the Assyrians were aware of two different cultural realms located in the direction of the sunrise and the sunset; it would have made sense for them to refer to these cultural realms by their geographical positions in relation to the rising and setting sun. Another theory has it that an ancient mythological ruler of Sidon in Phoenicia had daughters named *Europa* and

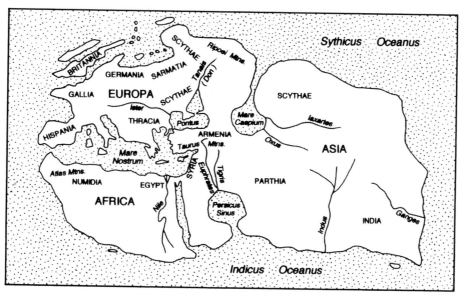

Figure 1.2. World map of the Roman geographer Pomponius Mela, drawn in 43 CE. The Caspian Sea is still depicted as an arm of the ocean, but Russia has also been narrowed to form an isthmus. *Source:* Adapted from Parker 1960.

Asia. The legendary Europa married the Greek king of gods, Zeus, and accompanied him back to the Aegean, whereas her sister remained in the east.

Whatever the origins of the words may have been, the ancient Greeks, from their vantage point on the northeast shores of the Mediterranean, perceived a world divided into three parts—one to the north and west (Europe), one to the south and west (Africa—then called Libya), and one to the east (Asia). Greece was long a nation of seafarers, and its sailors from the time of Ulysses and earlier had charted the marine separation between Europe and Africa. In addition, the classical Greeks knew of the division of Africa and Asia because the Phoenicians before them had circumnavigated the African continent. The Argonauts and other Greek explorers had probed into the Black Sea, founding trading colonies as far away as present-day Ukraine. Intrepid Greek merchants went beyond the Black Sea to the shores of the landlocked, saltwater Caspian Sea. Certain Greek scholars evaluating the information brought back by traders assumed that the saline Caspian was part of the ocean. They assumed the isthmus between the Black and Caspian seas was the only land bridge connecting Europe and Asia (fig. 1.1). Little did they know that the Caspian was an inland sea, with no opening to the ocean, and that to the north of the Caspian stretched a huge expanse of land. The Romans carried on this view. Their maps whittled down the expansive Russian plains to a narrow land bridge (fig. 1.2).

As time went on, the three-continent concept passed to monastic scholars of the medieval period. Religious-inspired cartography based on Greco-Roman representations of the world led to the creation of the famous "T in O" map. The church simplified the map of the known world in such a way that the pattern of land and seas formed the letters T, for *terrarum* ("earth"), and O, for *orbis* ("circle")—suggesting

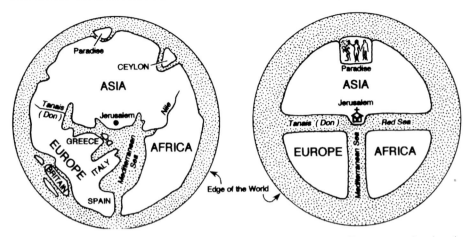

Figure 1.3.   Two versions of the medieval European "T in O" map. Europe remained, as in classical times, a separate continent. *Source:* Adapted from Woodward 1985.

that God had shaped the world in a sort of Latin shorthand. The Mediterranean Sea represented the lower bar of the T, and the top of the map was east rather than north. The Nile River (or Red Sea)–Aegean Sea–Black Sea–Don River line formed the horizontal bar of the T (fig. 1.3). On many such maps, the center of the world was the holy city of Jerusalem, while the lost Garden of Eden lay far out in the inaccessible reaches of Asia. We should not judge "T in O" maps by modern standards because their purpose, as interpretative art, was to depict religious mysteries and offer a stylized stage for the Christian drama, rather than to picture the world accurately. These maps played an important role, though, in perpetuating the pre-Christian notion of a clear distinction between Europe and Asia.

Even after the European **Age of Discovery** produced more precise understandings of the physical configuration of the earth's surface, the idea of Europe as a distinct continent persisted. This idea had to be sustained against the backdrop of maps showing that, instead of a relatively narrow land bridge separating the western and eastern portions of Eurasia, a 2,000-kilometer-wide wedge of land lay between the White Sea to the north of Russia and the Sea of Azov in the south. Discarding a 2,000-year-old basic belief does not happen easily, however. In the absence of an isthmus, geographers began looking for other environmental features that might mark Europe's eastern border.

Attention soon fell upon the Urals, a low mountain range running in a north–south direction across the heart of Eurasia (fig. 1.4). These mountains had never represented a significant barrier to west–east movement, but they served the purpose of suggesting a divide in the physical environment. To this day many publications treat the Urals as the border between Europe and Asia. Farther to the south, the more impressive snow-capped Caucasus Mountains, stretching between the Black and Caspian Seas, provided another link in the effort to bound Europe. The problem is that many different physical features could be—and have been—proposed as markers of the border between Europe and Asia (fig. 1.5). The Don, the Dnieper, and the Ural

Figure 1.4.   The Ural Mountains, long regarded by many as the eastern border of Europe. The view here is in the far north, near the Arctic Ocean, on the eastern boundary of Russia's Komi Republic. The month is June, but snow still caps the northern Urals. Farther south, the Urals did not act as a major barrier to east–west movement. Photo by T. G. J.-B., 1997.

Rivers have all been advanced as demarcators of Europe's eastern edge; other scholars have proposed that only those lands drained by streams flowing into the Atlantic Ocean, Baltic, Mediterranean, and Black Seas (as opposed to the Arctic and Indian Oceans) should qualify.

The difficulty of specifying an eastern land boundary for Europe led some scholars to propose a climatic approach to demarcating Europe—casting it as a region characterized by temperate, well-watered lands flanked by deserts, steppes, and frigid subarctic wastes. In the early twentieth century, the geographer Herbert Louis suggested that Europe reached only as far north and east as those lands having at least two months averaging +15° Celsius or warmer and a total of four months above +10°C—a limit judged critical for grain cultivation (fig. 1.5). Some scholars suggested excluding from Europe the steppe grasslands that intrude from Asia north of the Black Sea, regarding them as alien in appearance.

Of what value are these diverse proposals for an environmentally constrained Europe? Why, in fact, has the concept of "Europe" survived so long after its continentality, in the conventional sense, has been disproven? Why do we teach courses in the geography of Europe, instead of Eurasia? Why is there a "European Specialty Group" within the Association of American Geographers? Indeed, why do the Europeans themselves continue to believe that a separate and distinct Europe exists? Clearly the answers do not lie in the contrived and discordant physical boundaries

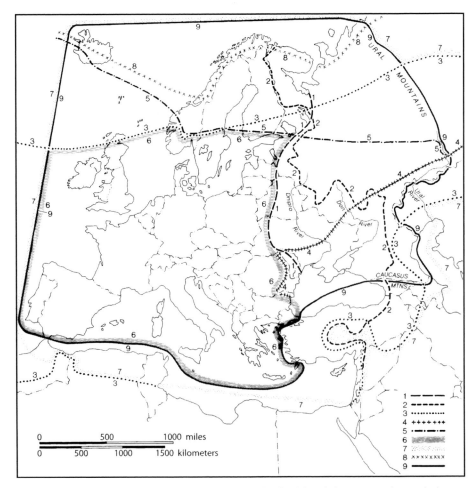

Figure 1.5. Proposals for defining Europe physically. Mountain ranges, rivers, drainage basins, terrain patterning, and climatic traits have all been suggested. Borders: **1** = eastern border of small discrete terrain regions, beyond which lie boundless plains; **2** = western border of interior–Arctic–Indian Ocean drainage; **3** = Louis's borders, based on warmth and rainfall; **4** = northern limit of the steppe grasslands; **5** = northern limit of temperate climates; **6** = Europe narrowly defined, including lands accepted by all who seek to bound Europe on a physical environmental basis; **7** = Europe most broadly defined, including lands accepted by at least one scholar seeking a physical boundary; **8** = southern border of Arctic tundra; **9** = most widely accepted border of Europe today. Europe, environmentally, thus becomes a temperate, well-watered land of variegated terrain. Louis oddly extended it far into southern Siberia, off our map. *Sources:* Hahn 1881, plate 3; Louis 1954, map following p. 80; Wolf 1982, 31; Parker 1953; Parker 1960.

that have been identified in an effort to find order where there is none. As the Russian geographer E. M. Murzayev put it, "any attempt to divide Europe from Asia on a systematic physical-geographical basis is doomed to fail." Addressing these questions, then, requires us to look elsewhere.

Europe as a Human Entity

The main alternative to viewing Europe in environmental terms is to see it as a distinct **culture area**. As conventionally understood, a culture area comprises a set of people who hold numerous beliefs, behaviors, and overall ways of life in common, including ways of thinking, technology, social institutions, and material possessions. Adopting this definition, geographer W. H. Parker long ago argued that Europe represents "a cultural concept" because "its eastern limits have been cultural and never long stable." Europeans, following this way of thinking, belong to a cultural community rooted in a Judeo–Christian–Hellenic heritage.

Viewing Europe in this way has deep historical roots. As we have already seen, the ancient view of Europe and Asia as distinct realms reflected the generally accepted idea that the peoples lying to the east and to the west of the eastern Mediterranean were fundamentally different. By the Middle Ages, a common belief was that those living in "Europe" could be distinguished from peoples living farther to the east because the former were descendants of Japheth, one of the sons of the biblical Noah. Europe also came to be seen as synonymous with "Christendom." By 1571, the pope revealingly referred to "Europeans, or those who are called Christians." Europe acquired a specific cultural meaning, and Europeans could be thought of as peoples who had a distinctive worldview based in a vivid, distinctive self-image.

Of course parts of what we now consider to be Europe did not fall within the Christian realm during the late Middle Ages. Islam held sway in parts of the Iberian Peninsula (until the late fifteenth century), and Christianity had not fully taken root in parts of northern Scandinavia. Moreover, Christianity coexisted with other belief systems in what is now commonly referred to as eastern Europe, Islam was expanding in southeastern Europe, and Judaism was present in many places in the European east and west. As such, Europe as Christendom was less a precise territorial demarcation than a geographically loose conception. Moreover, the official division of Europe between the Western and Eastern Churches in 1054 formalized a rift in the key cultural attribute that supposedly gave Europe its distinctiveness. For those living in the western parts of the "continent," that split gave birth to the idea that those oriented toward the Western Church were the true Europeans, whereas the Eastern Orthodox realm was a zone of transition (an idea that is alive and well today).

Beginning in the fifteenth century, western Europe's engagement with the rest of the world took the form of a globe-girdling colonial project that furthered the idea of Europe as a distinct cultural realm. Other parts of the world were cast as backward and culturally inferior—and therefore open for the taking and in need of domination and control. This way of thinking was underwritten by a strong sense of racial superiority, as Europeans encountered peoples who looked different from them. The idea took root of a world divided among three races—termed Caucasoid, Negroid, and Mongoloid—with explicit geographical connotations attached to each (respectively, European, African, and Asian). Religion joined race, custom, and socioeconomic status as constitutive ingredients of the European culture area.

Even in the contemporary secular era, religion has not disappeared as a way of thinking about Europe. In 1991, a pope in Rome exhorted Europe to return "to its Christian roots." In that same year, the president of Turkey, frustrated at the failure of his dominantly Muslim country to be accepted as a member of the European Union (EU), lamented that "some people maintain that the EU should be a Christian club." A few years later, a British periodical described "a Muslim crescent curling threateningly around the southern and eastern edges of Europe" (*Economist*, 6 August 1994).

In the early 2000s a vigorous debate developed over whether the preamble to a proposed constitution for the European Union should include reference to the area's Christian heritage. Although not ultimately accepted, the debate revealed the degree to which there remains at least a historical sense of Europe as a Christian realm. Moreover, religious differences are still sources of tension in Europe, affecting relations between Spaniards and Arabs, Greeks and Turks, Russians and Chechens, Serbs and Bosnian Muslims. Even in the very heart of Europe, and within the past century, religion served as a sufficiently potent focus of identity to bring on a reign of terror against those of Jewish descent.

Since the nineteenth century an additional cultural trait has sometimes been used to define Europe as a human entity: language. The great majority of Europeans speak tongues belonging to the **Indo-European** language family—an extended family of related languages with common historical roots. The term itself highlights the language family's European (and South Asian) credentials. Flanking the Indo-Europeans are speakers of other language families, including Uralic, Altaic, Caucasic, and Afro-Asiatic, all of which extend far beyond most people's conceptions of what constitutes Europe, and are therefore sometimes viewed as extra-European.

Even though religion, race, and language represent the three most common ways Europe has been historically thought about as a human entity, these traits are no more helpful than physical characteristics in delimiting Europe geographically. As figure 1.6 suggests, there is no boundary in the east separating areas where these three characteristics predominate—and of course such a small map covering a wide area hides areas in western Eurasia where, for example, Islam is the dominant religion.

The historical territorial record is of no more help than the distribution of overt cultural attributes in delimiting Europe. Some 2,000 years ago, many thought of Europe as coinciding with the territorial extent of the Roman Empire, a considerable expansion from the nucleus of 1000 BCE. Yet the passage of another millennium, to about 1000 CE, brought dramatic areal changes. As already mentioned, the Arabs, driven by the evangelical spirit of a new religion, Islam, had spread across all of North Africa, through the larger islands in the Mediterranean Sea, and into most of Iberia. The Arabs eventually reached into central western France, where they were turned back on the battlefield of Tours. Horsemen from the East, the Magyars, penetrated as far as southern Germany, where a major battle was fought on the Lechfeld in 955 CE. After long years of raiding, these mounted warriors eventually abandoned all but the grasslands of Hungary, where their linguistic descendants remain today.

The territorial ebb and flow of Europe continued into the present millennium. Spaniards and Portuguese, gripped by a religious fervor reminiscent of the earlier

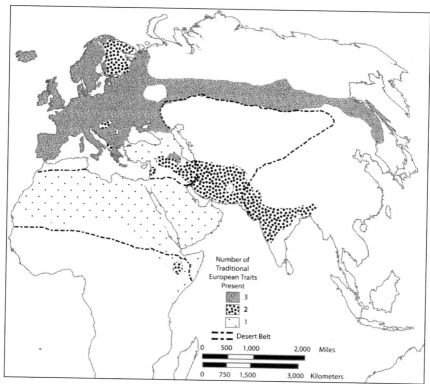

Figure 1.6.   Areas in Eurasia where one, two, or all three of the following human traits are predominant: Indo-European language, Christian beliefs, Caucasoid racial characteristics. These formerly common traits that were thought to characterize Europe are of little help in delimiting the eastern boundary of the "continent."

Muslim expansion, drove the Arabic Moors from Iberia, a reconquest that was completed in 1492. In the east, a major Slavic expansion overland, accomplished by the Russians, busily pushed "Europe" deep into the heartland of Eurasia and beyond to the Pacific shore. In the southeast the Muslim Turks overwhelmed the Greeks and seized the center of eastern Christendom, Constantinople, which they renamed Istanbul. From there the Turks spread northward to occupy most of the Balkan Peninsula. Repeatedly, an alliance of warriors gathered to turn the Turks back from the gates of Vienna (Wien) and also at Lepanto off the Greek coast. The Turkish tide gradually receded, but not without leaving significant Muslim populations in the Balkans and a Turkish bridgehead on the north shore of the Dardanelles and Bosporus around Istanbul. Even the most persistent efforts by Europeans failed to destroy this bridgehead.

As the twentieth century unfolded, Europe both tore itself apart in major conflicts that drew in significant parts of the rest of the world, and saw territorial integration initiatives that shaped people's conceptions of Europe. In the aftermath of World War II, an East–West geopolitical split divided the European realm into two parts—leading many in the West to view "Western Europe" as the only true Europe.

The latest political-territorial configuration to influence thinking about Europe is the EU, which expanded to the east with the collapse of the Cold War order. That entity does not include all states in the world region conventionally labeled Europe, however, and its boundaries have steadily shifted over time.

With culture and history providing limited help in determining what constitutes Europe, some commentators focus attention on social and economic indicators that distinguish Europe from surrounding areas.

1. *A well-educated population.* More than 95% of the population is literate, and in some places it is illegal not to be. In Germany, for example, 99% of the population can read and write, and in Spain the proportion is 98%. By contrast, as close a neighbor as Morocco, along the southern shore of the Mediterranean, has a literacy rate of just over 56%.

2. *A healthy population.* The population enjoys a far-above-average life expectancy—well in excess of 70 years in many countries. Perhaps an even better measure of health is provided by the **infant mortality rate**—the number of children per thousand who do not survive to the age of 1 year. For much of what is universally viewed as Europe, the rate stands below 10, whereas across the Aegean and Mediterranean Seas one encounters rates such as Turkey's 20, Algeria's 21, and Egypt's 22.

3. *Low population growth rates.* The population is scarcely growing at present, and it is declining in Romania, Ukraine, Serbia, Moldova, Latvia, Hungary, Georgia, Germany, Estonia, Croatia, Bosnia-Herzegovina, and Belarus. By contrast, most countries in neighboring North Africa, as well as in Africa and Asia at large, experience annual natural increases close to, or in excess of, 1%.

4. *A wealthy population.* Standards of living are comparatively high, as judged by standard socioeconomic indicators, with 14 of the world's top 20 countries in terms of per capita gross national product lying in what is conventionally thought of as Europe. In adjacent areas to the south and east, significant numbers of peoples achieve a bare subsistence.

5. *An urbanized population.* The vast majority of the population lives in cities and towns of 10,000 or more people, and in some countries the proportion exceeds 80%. By way of comparison, only 31% of the people in India, 51% in China, 43% in Egypt, and 57% in Morocco are urbanites.

6. *An industrialized or postindustrial economy.* All sectors of industry, especially the service sector, are well developed in what is conventionally defined as Europe, and they collectively employ the vast majority of the labor force. By contrast, agriculture remains the dominant form of economic activity in many regions lying to Europe's south and east.

7. *Freely elected governments.* Democracy is the dominant political form throughout what is conventionally termed Europe. Competing ideologies are tolerated, and considerable deference is given to the rights of individuals. Forms of political governance are much more diverse in areas lying to the south and east.

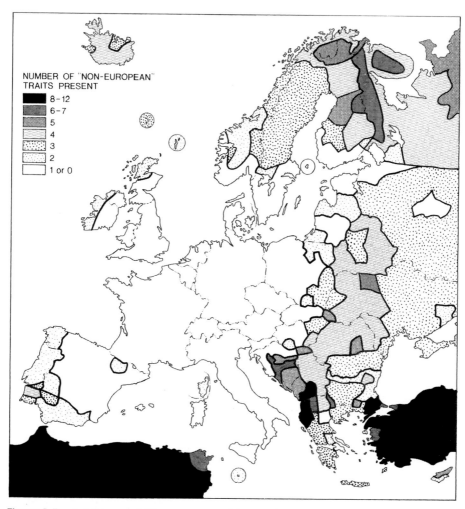

Figure 1.7. A measure of "European-ness," by province, based upon 12 traits that have historically been associated with Europe. A pronounced core–periphery pattern is revealed— a pattern we will encounter repeatedly in subsequent chapters. **1** = over 80% Christian or of Christian heritage; **2** = over 80% Indo-European speakers; **3** = over 90% Caucasian; **4** = infant mortality rate below 12; **5** = per capita gross domestic product is at least 40% of the European Union average; **6** = over 90% of people literate; **7** = 300 or more km of highway per 100 square km of territory; **8** = less than 25% of workforce employed in agriculture; **9** = over 50% of people live in towns and cities; **10** = less than 0.5% annual natural population increase; **11** = lies inside the European zone of continuous settlement (see fig. 3.1); and **12** = no substantial restrictions on democracy today.

Although the foregoing attributes draw attention to some broad distinctions between "Europe" and surrounding areas, no neat lines can be drawn around them that help us understand where Europe ends and the rest of the world begins. Instead, when socioeconomic variables are mapped along with characteristics such as language and religion, a broad transitional zone emerges. From a core in central and north-

Table 1.1.   European Self-Identity: A Checklist

Category	Europe/Self	Non-European/Alien
Physical Habitat	Marine	Continental
	Occident	Orient
	Temperate	Extreme
	Rimland	Heartland
	Northern	Southern
Religion	Christian	Non-Christian
	Roman Catholic	Orthodox Christian
	Secular	Believer
Race	Fair complexion	Dark complexion
Ideology/politics	Democratic	Authoritarian
	Uniting	Dividing
	Postnational	Nationalist
	Social democracy	Communism
	Peace/stability	War/turmoil
Culture	Civilization	Nature/barbarism
	Reason	Emotion
	Teacher	Pupil
	Progress	Stasis
	Cosmopolitan	Parochial
	Tolerance	Intolerance
	Wisdom	Immaturity
	Postmodern	Traditional/modern
Economy	Postindustrial	Industrial/agrarian
	Tertiary	Primary/secondary
	Core	Periphery
	Developed	Colonial

Source: Adapted, with modifications and addenda, from Painter 2000.

western Europe, where all the defining traits are found, the presence of these traits declines gradually to the peripheries, especially in the east and south (fig. 1.7). "But," you might protest, "how could Greece—the widely accepted birthplace of Europe— display fewer than half of the European traits?" Such an observation nicely highlights the difficulties and controversies surrounding efforts to define Europe in sociocultural terms.

It is also important to recognize that, in some respects, the sociocultural approach to defining Europe represents the continuation of a process of **othering** (i.e., defining Europe in opposition to other areas) that is centuries old (table 1.1). The attributes at the heart of this type of othering process are reflected in the work of historian David Gress, who refers to European culture as "a synthesis of democracy, capitalism, science, human rights, . . . individual autonomy, and the power of unfettered human reason." Gress's formulation casts Europe as the crucible of the elusive concept known as Western Civilization.

There are three problems with thinking about Europe largely in these terms, however. One is that the criteria used to highlight European difference (such as those listed above) are highly selective—focusing primarily on matters widely viewed as positive. Inevitably, Europe's character and legacy is much more complex. Racism, colonial domination, and genocide are also part of the European story. A second problem is that the reasons why Europe has a comparatively wealthy, well-educated population can easily be obscured. Europe's prosperity is not just the product of European innovation; it also resulted from Europe's highly unequal encounters with other parts of the world. Most obviously, Europe's colonial empires were integral to its extraordinary economic success. A third problem is that Europe's current character has been fundamentally influenced over time by developments, ideas, and practices coming from other places.

The second and third problems raise a geographical issue of fundamental importance. No region can be understood in isolation. The interconnections among places often run deep, both in extent and in time. Even before the Age of Discovery, Europe's encounters with regions to the east and south shaped its character, and Europe's makeup and destiny became increasingly intertwined with distant places from the fifteenth century onward. Germanic-speaking peoples, in particular the English, created overseas Europes in Anglo-America, Australia, New Zealand, and South Africa, while Spaniards and Portuguese transplanted much that is European to Central and South America. Great tropical colonial empires were established by the Spaniards, Portuguese, British, French, Dutch, Belgians, and Germans in the eastern hemisphere. In the entire world, only China, Japan, Thailand, Iran, Arabia, and Turkey avoided falling under direct European imperial rule at some time between 1500 and 1950, and even they were profoundly influenced by Europe's colonial project.

Europeans, in short, carried their practices and ideas throughout the world, transplanting them to thinly occupied lands or grafting them onto societies too firmly rooted to be dislodged (fig. 1.8). In the process, many native peoples were subjugated or destroyed, and the imprint of Europe became truly global. India has a railroad system founded by the British, Haitians speak a form of French, and Filipinos adhere to the Roman Catholic faith. Even those few areas never ruled from Europe felt its cultural impress. Japan embraced the Industrial Revolution, China adopted Marxist socialism, and Turkey replaced Arabic script with the Latin alphabet.

It is important to remember, however, that other parts of the world also helped to shape Europe. Influence flowed both ways, and the European way of life was profoundly altered in the process. Prior to 1500 CE, Europe could best be regarded as peripheral to the great culture centers of the eastern hemisphere, receiving far more than it gave. Even Christianity, the traditional basis for much of Europe's distinctiveness, originated in the so-called Middle East and attained its first major foothold in what was long called Asia Minor (i.e., modern-day Turkey). African Arabs taught Iberians some of the navigational secrets that permitted the Age of Discovery, and Muslims preserved and advanced much ancient Greco-Roman knowledge during Europe's lengthy Dark Age. Agriculture originally reached Europe from a western Asian hearth, and the later introduction of American Indian crops, such as the potato, tomato, tobacco, and maize, greatly altered the European agrarian system.

Much more recently, Europe has been profoundly influenced by cultural and economic innovations coming from former colonies—artistic ideas from Africa, cul-

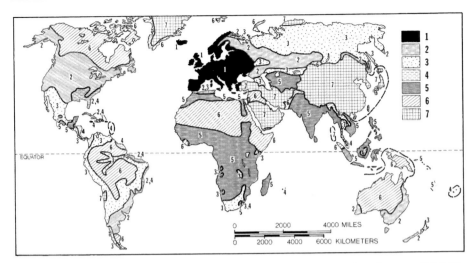

Figure 1.8.   The Europeanization of the world. Key: **1** = European hearth area, 1500 CE; **2** = neo-European areas: population and culture almost wholly of European derivation; **3** = mixed European and aboriginal areas, but culture strongly influenced or dominated by European practices; **4** = plantation culture; small European-derived minority traditionally dominated a large non-European labor force; **5** = exploitive or custodial occupation by Europeans in colonial era, minute numbers of Europeans implanted some durable customs and artifacts; **6** = loose, ineffective, or brief European control and impact; and **7** = eastern border of the European Union, which is now often used to delimit Europe. The border shown as **8** is the one most commonly used when defining Europe for statistical purposes throughout this book. *Source:* Modified from Wilbur Zelinsky, *A Prologue to Population Geography* (Englewood Cliffs, NJ: Prentice Hall, 1966), 74–75.

tural and technological innovations from North America, foods from South and Southeast Asia, to name just a few. Moreover, recent immigrants have played a key role in sustaining the European economy in the contemporary era. Contemporaneously, Europe's global influence has declined in some arenas—fueled in places by rising resistance to Europeanization. In Africa, Islam rather than Christianity is the fastest-growing religious faith, and Asia's rapidly expanding economies have eclipsed Europe in key sectors. Falling birth rates also mean that Europeans form an ever-smaller part of the world population.

What is clear is that Europe's fortunes cannot be understood by looking at internal developments alone. When that reality is considered alongside the ambiguous nature of Europe's territorial reach, one might reasonably question whether there is any sense in singling out "Europe" as a place to be studied. Yet there are strong reasons for seeking to make sense of Europe—not least because Europe is widely *thought of* as a distinct geographical realm. That conception makes it an important object of analysis because how we think the earth's surface is organized can profoundly influence what we do and what happens. Why is there a European Union? In part because Europe is widely considered to be a distinct geographic realm. Nonetheless, as we focus our geographical lens we should not forget that behind the seeming simplicity of the place name lies an uncontestable verity: Europe is a constantly shifting, much disputed geographical idea.

This Book's Approach

Given the obvious complexities of defining Europe for a book such as this, what geographical space should be the focus of analysis? As we have seen, there is no good answer to this question. Nonetheless, it makes more sense to look toward cultural than physical factors in delimiting Europe, as the very notion of European distinctiveness is a cultural product. But considering the perceptions of Europeans about what constitutes Europe hardly provides clarity. Consider the following revealing, if sometimes inflammatory or bigoted, comments:

- "Africa begins at the Pyrenees." (Alexandre Dumas, Frenchman, nineteenth century)
- "We were once, and will be again, Europeans." (Latvia's prime minister, 1991)
- "Russians: a European people or some mongrel Asian one?" (Steven Erlanger, 1995)
- "All throughout Europe a new reality is rising: entire Muslim neighborhoods where very few indigenous people reside or are even seen. And if they are, they might regret it." (Far-right Dutch politician Geert Wilders, 2012)
- "Turkey [has] a different culture, a different approach, a different way of life . . . its capital is not in Europe, 95% of its population live outside Europe. It is not a European country." (French presidential candidate Valéry Giscard d'Estaing, 2002)
- "With our mother country Croatia behind us, we will unite not with the barbaric hordes, but with Europe." (Kresimir Zubac, Bosnian Croat politician, 1996)
- "You're thinking of Europe as Germany and France. I don't. I think that's old Europe." (US Defense Secretary Donald Rumsfeld, 2003, in response to a reporter's question)

Such remarks are suggestive of the intensity of the debate over what constitutes Europe. The status of Turkey is particularly contested, as is Russia and its immediate neighbors. One member of the Ukrainian parliament recently distinguished the "Europeanized Slavs" in the western part of his country from the "Russo-Slavs" of the eastern region. Witold Orlowski, a Pole, suggesting that his country would soon lie at the eastern edge of Europe proper, declared that "Europeans are drawing the borderline of Europe for the next 50 years and don't care about Ukraine, Belarus, and Russia."

Yet we should not forget that Mikhail Gorbachev, the former Russian leader, coined the term "our common European home." Historically, many geographers have drawn the border of Europe *through* Russia, claiming the western part of it—**Eurorussia**—for the European culture area (fig. 1.9). These examples show that seeking a sharp cultural border for Europe is futile, especially in the east. As long ago as the 1920s, geographers had "largely emancipated themselves from the hypnotic effect

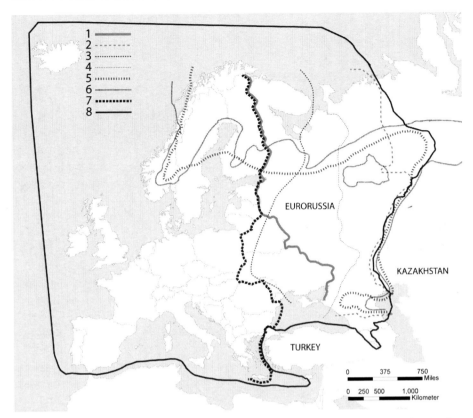

Figure 1.9.   Proposed culture-based borders of Europe. 1 = western border of Russia; **2** = eastern border of Europe proposed by the Russian geographer Murzayev, based upon internal administrative units; **3** = border proposed by the German geographer Banse, 1912; **4** = border proposed by the French geographer Thevet, 1575; **5** = border of the "European space economy," according to geographer Andrew Dawson, 1993; and **6** = borders of "sedentary agricultural Europe," proposed by the Frenchman Delaisi, 1929. The border shown as **7** is the eastern border of the EU, and **8** is the one used when defining Europe for statistical purposes throughout this book. *Sources:* Parker 1960; Francis Delaisi, *Les Deux Europes* (Paris: F. Payot, 1929), 24–25; Hahn 1881, plate 3; Murzayev 1964; Andrew Dawson, *A Geography of European Integration* (London: Belhaven, 1993).

of terms like Europe and Asia," wrote the geographer Marion I. Newbigin, stressing instead the gradual transition from European to non-European.

Yet we cannot let the complexities surrounding what constitutes Europe stop us from an effort to understand it, for however much we might debate its geographical extent and meaning, Europe *is* a significant idea and place. With that in mind, this book starts from the premise that Europe's contested areal extent is one of its interesting geographical features. We proceed under the assumptions that (1) there is wide consensus that Europe at least encompasses the western portions of the area mapped in figure 1.9, and that the consensus diminishes as one moves east, and (2) that Europe is not a product simply of internal developments, but has been constantly reinvented in relation to other places near and far.

This approach still leaves open the question of what territory will be the focus of attention. In some places a relatively sharp border is simple to draw, as is true in the Arctic Sea, the Atlantic Ocean, and the Mediterranean Sea. Even in these seas, however, delineation is not as straightforward as it might initially seem. In the Atlantic, Iceland and Greenland present questions. We have included Iceland in the mix, given its close connections with Europe, but we focus relatively little attention on more distant Greenland—a semi-autonomous territory of Denmark—because addressing the many remaining overseas territories and possessions of European countries would stretch the analysis too thin. The Mediterranean includes places such as the island of Cyprus, which is divided between Greek and Turkish sectors that are reflective of different cultural-historical influences, and Malta, which has been shaped by influences coming from the north and the south over the centuries. It makes sense to include these islands in our study, however, since they are members of the EU.

Beyond the Mediterranean the picture becomes even more complicated. Not only are there no clear physical or cultural boundaries that provide much guidance; in recent times conflicts have raged over the cultural and political status of areas at the eastern edges of Europe, as happened in Bulgaria, where expulsions of ethnic Turks flared in the 1980s; in Azerbaijan, where the Armenian Christian minority in Nagorno–Karabakh Province rebelled; in Georgia, where Abkhazi Muslims seceded amid civil war in 1993; and in the Russian Caucasus, where elements in Islamic Chechnya continue to struggle for independence.

The most convenient, albeit necessarily limiting, approach to the problem of boundary definition in the east is to follow the lead of those who view the EU as a loose approximation of Europe, but only with reference to the EU's eastern border so as to avoid the problem of ignoring states farther west that are not EU members (see fig. 1.10). This approach makes some sense given that almost all states lying to the west of the EU's eastern border see themselves—and are regarded by most others—as fundamentally European and they now have extensive economic and political interconnections with other parts of Europe because of the EU. With that in mind, the authors of this book have chosen to focus principal attention on those areas lying to the west of Russia, Belarus, Ukraine, Moldova, and Turkey. In recognition of the artificiality of this approach, however, whenever possible our maps and generalizations about Europe reflect a more expanded notion of the region to the east. We hope that this approach, together with periodic discussion of developments taking place in lands bordering the EU to the east, will serve as reminders of the inevitable messiness associated with the geographical concept of Europe.

In substantive terms, the goal of this book is to give the reader an appreciation not just of Europe's character as a place, but of the nature and significance of a geographical perspective on the region. Many people associate geography with memorizing lists of capital cities, mountains, and rivers. This way of thinking often comes from elementary and secondary school classrooms where cursory attention (at best) is given to where things are located—and then only as background to discussions of social, historical, or environmental issues. Geography too often comes across as a dry, boring backdrop to questions of interest.

Figure 1.10.   Member states of the European Union. From its founding in the 1950s as an economic organization involving six countries, the European integration project has expanded to encompass 28 states and a range of issues beyond the strictly economic (migration, environmental change, infrastructure, foreign aid, etc.).

Yet it is no more accurate to see place-name memorization as the essence of geography than it is to treat the memorization of dates as the essence of history. Place names provide a vocabulary that allows us to talk about the world, and they can sometimes provide interesting insights into past cultural influences on places. But geography's real interest and importance comes from the insights that can be gained from exploring not just *where* various attributes can be found, but *why they are there*, and by exploring how particular geographical arrangements and patterns reflect and influence the world around us.

Geography is an integrative discipline concerned with the nature and significance of the patterns, places, and landscapes that make up the earth's surface. What can shifting vegetation patterns tell us about climate change? Why have migrants from

North Africa ended up in some parts of Europe more than others? How does the changing character of the French–German political boundary along the upper Rhine affect people's sense of place and their approach to common problems? Questions such as these are at geography's core—and are the ones that make studying Europe from a geographical perspective such an interesting and important endeavor.

This book, then, is concerned not just with where questions, but with "why there" and "so what" considerations. Europe is a complex amalgam of physical, demographic, cultural, political, economic, and social arrangements and processes—each influencing the other. The goal of the book is to facilitate understanding of the region through investigation of the geographical patterns—physical and sociocultural—that have shaped Europe's character and landscape through time. Toward that end, the book treats various aspects of Europe's geography like the layers of a cake. We begin with the physical setting—looking at the patterns and processes that help explain the physiographic, climatic, and vegetative complexes found in Europe. We then move to basic demographic issues, looking not just at underlying patterns and processes, but at how they relate to the physical geographic issues presented earlier. We then add further layers to the cake—turning to language and religion, to the evolution of the region's political pattern, and to economic and social arrangements. By the end of the book the reader should have at least an introductory understanding of many of the key geographical arrangements and processes that have shaped, and continue to shape, this fascinating part of the world.

The advantage of taking this approach is that it allows us to cut across many of the usual topical categories that are the focus of academic attention. We will look not just at the physical environment or at demographic dynamics or at political forces, but at how those are interrelated in space. Constructing our multilayered cake allows us to treat layers not just as isolated phenomena but as interrelated parts of a whole. With the background provided in this book, a reader should be able to cut down through the layers of the European cake in different places and see how the interaction of forces have shaped their pasts and will influence their futures.

The principal limitation of this approach is that it requires us to tackle a wide array of subject areas. To deal with them in a modest-length book, we necessarily have to operate at a fairly high level of generalization. Each of the topics discussed in the book has been addressed extensively by geographers and others. The bibliographies at the ends of chapters provide an entrée into deeper exploration of individual topics.

Finally, it is worth noting that our fundamental approach to discussing and explaining Europe's geographical character is cultural-historical. Many geographical studies of world regions focus on the characteristics of contemporary spatial structures and arrangements—with a particular emphasis on economic and demographic matters. We are interested in these, but our emphasis is on how and why spatial structures and arrangements came to be, which means directing central attention to how they evolved over time. To put it another way, our book consistently explores how cultural-historical processes—many of which are deeply intertwined with economic and political processes—have given rise to the geographical patterns and landscapes that are at the heart of contemporary Europe. This approach is certainly not the only one that could be taken, but we believe it provides telling insights into *why* the patterns and processes discussed in this book have taken the forms that they have.

Why Study Europe?

Before launching into the substance of the book, it is worth pausing for a moment to consider why Europe is a region worthy of study. The most obvious answer is that the western part of Eurasia is a place that, for better or for worse, has had an impact on the world that is greatly disproportionate to its size. As such, studying this region can provide important insights into developments of global import.

To appreciate the degree to which Europe has shaped the contemporary world, consider how many influential concepts and inventions of the last millennium trace their origins to this region (fig. 1.11). The concept of democracy came from classical Greece. It reappeared in medieval Iceland, in the infant Switzerland, in the Magna Carta of England, and in the Teutonic city-states of the Middle Ages, before bursting forth over much of Europe in the late 1700s and 1800s. The European Age of Discovery, primarily the product of Italian and Iberian Europeans, allowed Europe to discover (from its perspective), and in many cases to dominate, much of the remainder of the world.

The printing press employing moveable type, a gift from the artisans of the German Rhine Valley, had a tremendous impact in most parts of the world, revolutionizing people's means of communication. The concept of the earth's sphericity, developed by the classical Greeks, was revived by Italians and Iberians in the Age of Discovery; the Polish astronomer Nicolaus Copernicus was the first to proclaim the heliocentric concept that the earth revolves about the sun. If Copernicus dealt a first great blow to human ego by removing the earth from the center of the universe, his fellow European Charles Darwin struck another in his theory of evolution by proposing that humans were animals with traceable biological ancestry. Gregor Mendel provided the basis for genetic science, and Sigmund Freud, born a short distance from Mendel in Czechia, founded modern psychology, the scientific study of the mind.

The Englishman Isaac Newton, in his laws of motion and gravity, established modern physics, whereas the German-born Swiss resident Albert Einstein, through his theory of relativity, greatly enhanced our understanding of the universe. Discovery of bacterial and viral causes of disease, the beginning of modern medicine, was the work of the German country doctor Robert Koch and the Frenchman Louis Pasteur. Marie Sklodowska Curie, a native of Poland and citizen of France, pioneered the study of radioactivity with her husband Pierre (the word *curie* became the unit of measurement for this property), ushering in the atomic and nuclear age. The Russian Dmitry Mendeleyev developed the periodic table of chemical elements, working in St. Petersburg in the 1890s. Dutch and Italian inventors perfected the first microscope and telescope, allowing humans for the first time to inspect objects too small or too distant to be studied with the naked eye.

Perhaps Europe's most far-reaching impact resulted from the **Industrial Revolution**, the invention of diverse machines and the harnessing of inanimate power that

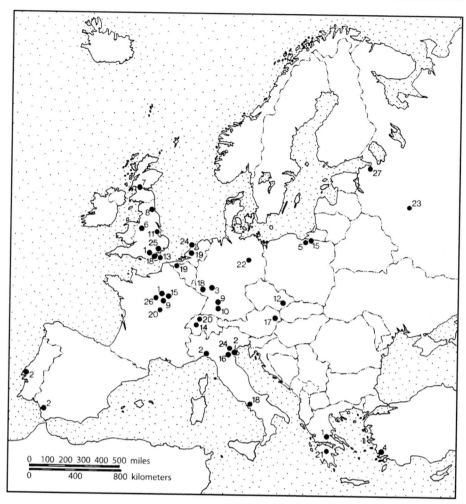

Figure 1.11.   Sources of selected European concepts and inventions. Key: **1** = democracy (Ancient Greece, French Revolution, Magna Carta); **2** = Age of Discovery (Genova, Venèzia, Cádiz, Lisboa); **3** = printing press (Gutenberg, at Mainz); **4** = concept of the spherical earth (classical Greeks at Miletus, now in Turkey); **5** = concept of heliocentric solar system (Copernicus in Frombark); **6** = Industrial Revolution (English Midlands); **7** = steam engine (Watt in Glasgow); **8** = railroad (northeast England); **9** = internal combustion engine (Lenoir in Paris, Otto and Daimler in Germany); **10** = automobile (Daimler and Benz in Germany); **11** = laws of motion and gravity, providing the basis of modern physics (Newton in England); **12** = science of modern genetics (Mendel in Morava); **13** = theory of evolution (Darwin in England); **14** = theory of relativity (Einstein in Bern); **15** = discovery of bacterial and viral causes of diseases (Koch in Ostpreussen and Pasteur in Paris); **16** = radio (Marconi in Bologna); **17** = modern study of the mind (Freud in Vienna); **18** = socialism (Marx in Trier and London, Campanella in Italy); **19** = productive capitalism (Holland and Flanders); **20** = nationalism (Switzerland and France); **21** = nation-state (Greece); **22** = expressways (Germany); **23** = orbital satellites and manned space flight (Russia); **24** = microscope and telescope (Lippershey and Janssen in Holland; Galileo in Padua); **25** = digital computer (Babbage in England); **26** = early research on radioactivity (Curie in France); and **27** = periodic table of chemicals (Mendeleyev in St. Petersburg).

began in Great Britain in the 1700s. It led to countless crucially influential inventions, including the steam engine, railroad, internal combustion engine, automobile, expressway, radio, orbital satellites, manned space flight, and digital computer, to mention but a few (fig. 1.11). Prometheus was unbound, and it was Europeans who loosened his bonds. **Modernity** and the concept of progress, quintessentially European, sprang into being. Europe rose to become the dominant global economic power by the nineteenth century, and it continues to play a major economic role in the world of the early twenty-first century. The rapid ascent of China has grabbed the headlines recently, but the economy of the EU is considerably larger than that of China. Europe is the principal trading partner of the United States as well as most countries in Africa.

Other cornerstones of modernity were also laid in Europe, including capitalism, socialism, nationalism, and the modern state. Capitalism, distinguished by the application of capital to innovation in order to elevate levels of production, spread from an early nucleus in the Low Countries, and soon "overtly commercial values" permeated European civilization, leading to an economic boom that spread material prosperity through a larger segment of the population than ever before in world history. When linked to the Industrial Revolution, capitalism reshaped the world. Socialism arose in Europe as a movement to spread prosperity still more widely and to prevent the migration of great wealth back into the hands of the few. Rooted in Italian Tommaso Campanella's 1602 *City of the Sun*, socialism appeared as a fully developed ideology in the nineteenth-century works of Karl Marx, a German. A modified form of socialism produced the enviable quality of life achieved in the Scandinavian welfare states, but it also underlay the economic and political deprivations of Russian Communism.

Nationalism, in which citizens transferred allegiance from the monarch to the state, began perhaps in medieval Switzerland and later appeared more forcefully in revolutionary France. Still later came another European innovation, the **nation-state** idea, in which nationality became conceptually linked to a common language and/or religion in a sovereign political territory. The nation-state idea was subsequently spread throughout the world.

Collectively, the impact of these diverse European concepts and inventions has been prodigious. Try to imagine a world never touched by them. Pointing out Europe's influence, though, does not mean embracing the Eurocentric conclusion that European culture is superior. As we have seen, many European inventions came about because of Europe's encounters with other parts of the world. Moreover, some of the region's innovations proved malevolent and destructive, in some cases threatening the very existence of the human race. Europe gave us fascism, religious inquisitions, imperialism, colonialism, and mechanized total warfare. Europeans developed a complex, sophisticated culture, but it could not, in the final analysis, prevent them from committing unspeakable atrocities in the German heart of Europe, nor does it allow them to control the powerful technology they unleashed.

Still, the importance of Europe remains uncontestable and profound. It is thus vital that we understand something about it. Moreover, many readers of this book will be North Americans—a place that cannot be understood without reckoning with Europe's imprint. The extensive interconnections across the Atlantic help to explain the extraordinary flow of visitors each year who travel from North America to Europe. Many readers of this book will visit Europe at some point during their lives, if they have not done so already. The matters discussed here can, at a minimum, help enrich a traveler's experience in Europe. And they might even provide a foundation on which new transatlantic understandings and insights can be built. So let us turn our attention now to a geographical analysis of this comparatively small but highly influential corner of the planet.

Sources and Suggested Readings

Ahnström, L. 1993. Europe: Culture Area, Geo-ideological Construct or Illusion? *Norsk Geografisk Tidsskrift* 47 (2): 57–67.

Barzini, L. G. 1983. *The Europeans*. New York: Simon and Schuster.

Berezin, M., and M. Schain. 2003. *Europe without Borders: Remapping Territory, Citizenship, and Identity in a Transnational Age*. Baltimore: Johns Hopkins University Press.

Blaut, J. M. 1993. *The Colonizer's Model of the World: Geographical Diffusionism and Eurocentric History*. New York: Guilford Press.

Cuisenier, J. 1979. *Europe as a Cultural Area*. The Hague: Mouton.

deBlij, H. 2012. *Why Geography Matters More Than Ever*. Oxford: Oxford University Press.

Delamaide, D. 1994. *The New Superregions of Europe*. New York: Dutton.

Dodgshon, R. A. 1992. The Role of Europe in the Early-Modern World-System: Parasitic or Generative? *Political Geography* 11 (4): 396–400.

Fells, J., and J. Niznik. 1992. What Is Europe? *International Journal of Sociology* 22 (1/2): 201–7.

Fischer, E. 1943. *The Passing of the European Age: A Study of the Transfer of Western Civilization and Its Renewal in Other Continents*. Cambridge, MA: Harvard University Press.

Graham, B., ed. 1998. *Modern Europe: Place, Culture, and Identity*. London: Arnold.

Gress, D. 1998. *From Plato to NATO: The Idea of the West and Its Opponents*. New York: Free Press.

Hahn, F. G. 1881. Zur Geschichte der Grenze Zwischen Europa und Asien. *Mitteilungen des Vereins für Erdkunde zu Leipzig*, 83–104.

Hay, D. 1968. *Europe: The Emergence of an Idea*. History, Philosophy and Economics 7. Edinburgh: Edinburgh University Press.

Hebbert, M., and J. C. Hansen, eds. 1990. *Unfamiliar Territory: The Reshaping of European Geography*. Aldershot, UK: Avebury.

Heffernan, M. 1998. *The Meaning of Europe: Geography and Geopolitics*. London: Arnold.

Jönsson, C., S. Tägil, and G. Törnqvist. 2000. *Organizing European Space*. London: Sage.

Judt, T. 1996. *A Grand Illusion? An Essay on Europe*. New York: Hill and Wang.

Kormoss, I. B. F. 1987. The Geographical Notion of Europe over the Centuries. In *Europe: Dream—Adventure—Reality*, ed. H. Brugmans, 81–94. New York: Greenwood Press.

Kuus, M. 2004. Europe's Eastern Expansion and the Reinscription of Otherness in East-Central Europe. *Progress in Human Geography* 28 (4): 472–89.

Lewis, M. W., and K. Wigen. 1997. *The Myth of Continents: A Critique of Metageography*. Berkeley: University of California Press.

Louis, H. 1954. Über den Geographischen Europabegriff. *Mitteilungen der Geographischen Gesellschaft in München* 39:73–93.

Lyde, L. W. 1926. *The Continent of Europe*. London: Macmillan.

McNeill, D. 2004. *New Europe: Imagined Spaces*. London: Arnold.

Meinig, D. W. 1969. A Macrogeography of Western Imperialism. In *Settlement and Encounter*, eds. F. Gale and G. H. Lawton, 213–40. Melbourne: Oxford University Press.

Murphy, A. B. 2005. Relocating Europe. In *Engaging Europe: Rethinking a Changing Continent*, eds. E. Gould and G. Sheridan, 81–101. Boulder, CO: Rowman & Littlefield.

Murzayev, E. M. 1964. Where Should One Draw the Geographical Boundary between Europe and Asia? *Soviet Geography: Review and Translation* 5:15–25.

Pagden, A., ed. 2002. *The Idea of Europe: From Antiquity to the European Union.* Woodrow Wilson Center Series. Washington, DC: Woodrow Wilson Center Press; Cambridge: Cambridge University Press.

Painter, J. 2000. Transnational Citizenship and Identity in Europe. Ninth Congress of the International Geographical Union, Seoul, South Korea.

Parker, W. H. 1953. Europe and the New Civilization. *Canadian Geographer* 3:53–60.

———. 1960. Europe: How Far? *Geographical Journal* 126:278–97.

Strahlenberg, P. J. v. 1738. *An Historico-Geographical Description of the North and Eastern Part of Europe and Asia.* London: J. Brotherton et al.

Unwin, T., ed. 1998. *A European Geography.* Essex: Pearson.

Whittlesey, D. S. 1949. *Environmental Foundations of European History.* New York: Appleton-Century-Crofts.

Wintle, M. J., ed. 1996. *Culture and Identity in Europe: Perceptions of Divergence and Unity in Past and Present.* Perspectives on Europe, Contemporary Interdisciplinary Research. Aldershot: Avebury.

Wolf, E. R. 1982. *Europe and the People without History.* Berkeley: University of California Press.

Woodward, D. 1985. Reality, Symbolism, Time, and Space in Medieval World Maps. *Annals of the Association of American Geographers* 75 (4): 510–21.

CHAPTER 2

Physical Geography

Europe's human drama has been acted out on a small peninsula composed of many even smaller peninsulas attached to the western extremity of Eurasia. In this chapter we consider Europe's physical geography. The goal is to provide insight into fundamental environmental features and forces that have shaped the region over time. Since Europeans have massively altered that environment, however, humans must be part of the picture. To the geographer, environment, people, and place are inextricably intertwined.

At the broadest level of generalization, several features of Europe's physical geography are particularly notable. First, Europe has a very long coastline in relation to its landmass. Only in the east can one find land that lies more than 600 kilometers from a coast. The vast majority of Europeans live within less than 200 kilometers of a coast.

Also of great importance is Europe's position at the western edge of a continent in the Northern Hemisphere—abutting a large ocean. Moreover, Europe does not have a major north–south trending mountain range near its western edge. Instead, its higher mountains tend to be oriented in a west–east direction. As we will see, these characteristics have important implications for the region's climate.

A final notable aspect of Europe's physical geography is its northern location. Many Americans mistakenly think that Europe sits astride the same latitudes as does the United States. Yet Europe is considerably farther north. Rome lies on roughly the same latitude as New York City. If Brussels were in North America, it would lie along the southern shores of Hudson's Bay. With these overarching features in mind, we are in a better position to understand three basic aspects of Europe's physical geography: its **geomorphology** and related **hydrogeography**, its climate, and its vegetation.

Europe's Geomorphology and Hydrogeography

The European land is highly varied, ranging from high, rugged mountains to featureless flat plains. Focusing on the basic forces that have shaped the region through time helps explain the general patterns shown in figure 2.1. One of those is the movement

Figure 2.1.   Terrain regions. *Sources:* Raisz 2000; Embleton 1984.

of tectonic plates. As figure 2.2 shows, Europe lies near the western edge of the vast Eurasian plate, just north of the African plate. One of the dominant influences on Europe's landscape has been the movement of the Eurasian plate. Between c. 280 and 240 million years ago, a huge supercontinent known as Pangea was formed when prior amalgamations of tectonic plates crunched together. What came to be Europe lay on the northeastern part of the supercontinent, and the enormous stresses and strains associated with its formation caused tremendous folding and faulting—particularly in the western and northwestern parts of what was to become Europe. This long-ago mountain-building period is called the **Hercynian period** in Europe.

Pangea began to break up about 225 million years ago, and folding and faulting continued, albeit at a less intense level. Gradually, the higher Hercynian-era moun-

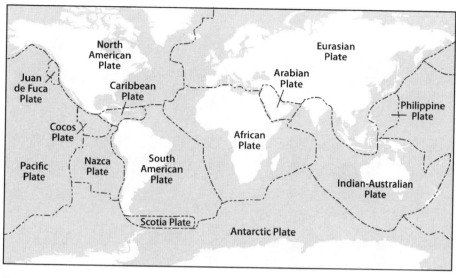

Figure 2.2. Tectonic plates. No plate bisects Europe. Instead, the plate boundaries lie at Europe's southern and western edges. As a result, earthquakes and volcanic activity are common in the Mediterranean and in Iceland, but not elsewhere.

tains were reduced in elevation by erosion—many taking on a more rounded, hilly look. But then between c. 100 and 60 million years ago, the African plate began pushing up against the Eurasian plate from the south, initiating an intensification of faulting and folding in a different part of Europe. This period of tectonic activity, sometimes called the **Alpine period,** led to substantial mountain building in a west–east direction at a location somewhat inland from Europe's southern edge. These more recently uplifted mountains have had much less time to erode—and in some places they continue to grow. Europe's highest peaks are associated with these relatively recent uplifts.

Faulting and folding in conjunction with the movement of tectonic plates is not the only major influence on Europe's landscape. The other is erosion, and no source of erosion has been quite as dramatic as the advance and retreat of glaciers. Since at least the beginning of the Pleistocene some 1.65 million years ago, the earth has been in an **ice age** characterized by multiple cold periods, called glacials, interrupted by periodic warmer periods known as interglacials. The Serbian astronomer Milutin Milankovitch came up with the most widely accepted explanation for these oscillations, attributing them to cyclical changes in (1) the shape of the earth's orbit, (2) the earth's tilt on its axis, and (3) the earth's orbital position at the time of the equinox. Each of these cycles has a different periodicity, but they interact with one another to produce irregular colder and warmer periods known as the **Milankovitch cycle.**

The general character of the modern European landscape was greatly influenced by the most recent glacials, during which enormous ice sheets built up in northern Europe and glaciers colonized the taller mountains farther south (fig. 2.3). The ice sheets scraped off and ground up most surface materials in the north—depositing

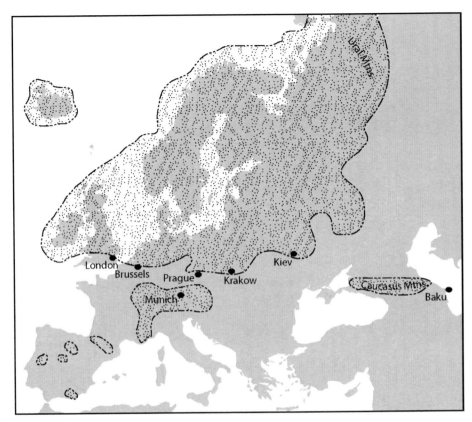

Figure 2.3.   Glaciers in Europe during the height of the most recent glaciation. Far northern Europe lay under thick layers of ice. All of Europe's climate zones were shifted significantly to the south.

them at the feet of the glaciers as they retreated or grinding them into fine particles that were distributed by wind throughout Europe's middle section. In the mountainous areas glaciers carved craggy peaks and created U-shaped valleys as they wound their way down from the upper elevations. With a significant percentage of the earth's water locked up in ice sheets that developed on the land, sea levels were much lower during glacial periods, and U-shaped valleys could extend far into areas that are now below water. When the ice melted and sea levels rose, the U-shaped valleys below current sea level filled with water, creating what are known as **fjords**.

Europe entered the current interglacial period some 10 to 12 thousand years ago, although it experienced a return to somewhat colder temperatures between c. 1200 and 1850 in what is sometimes termed the Little Ice Age (a misleading term because the temperature shift was not nearly as great as that associated with major glacial advances). With the melting of the ice sheet, Europe's northern bedrock was exposed and the area of glacial deposits farther south could start supporting significant vegetation. The retreat of the glaciers exposed highly sculpted tall mountains and considerable sculpting of some shorter mountains with Hercynian roots, particularly in Norway.

Armed with these insights, we can begin to make sense of the general character of Europe's terrain: the pattern of mountains, hills, and plains shown in figure 2.1.

MOUNTAINS

Europe's taller mountains lie largely in the southern half of the "continent," and most ranges are oriented in a west–east direction. This concentration can be explained by the Alpine-era tectonic forces described above. Moving from west to east, the Bética Mountains parallel the south coast of Spain and consist of several ridges, including the Sierra Nevada. The Bética stretch from the Rock of Gibraltar to the vicinity of Valencia, where they disappear beneath the sea, only to emerge again to the east as the Balearic Islands. The Bética area, which includes peaks of more than 3,350 meters, served as the final stronghold of the Moors (Arabs originally from North Africa). The southernmost ridge of the Bética range fronts on the Mediterranean Sea, creating a rocky and picturesque coast.

Central Iberia is bisected by the Central Sierras, and along the north coast lies the Cantabrian Mountains (Cordillera Cantabrica), reaching 2,600 to 2,750 meters at the highest. The steepest face of this fault-block range faces north, to the Atlantic, producing a rocky coast with numerous small, protected bays long used as fishing harbors. Extending to the east are the high Pyrenees that run along the border between Spain and France.

Moving farther east, the Alps, the highest and most famous European mountains, stretch from the French Riviera in an arc eastward through Switzerland to Vienna on the bank of the Danube (fig. 2.4). The western Alps form the highest and most spectacular part of the range, with deeply incised valleys and impressive remnant glaciers. Mont Blanc, towering 4,813 meters above sea level, is the highest in Europe. (For comparison, Mt. Whitney in California, the tallest peak in the contiguous 48 American states, is 4,421 meters above sea level.) Deep, sheer-sided, U-shaped valleys sometimes have floors 2,750 meters lower than the adjacent peaks.

While impressive in appearance, the southern and western Alps never served as a true barrier to human movement. So many low passes exist through which invaders can move that the Italians, who live south of the mountains, used to refer to the range as the "magnificent traitor." The Carthaginian general Hannibal successfully moved a cavalry of elephants and 30,000 men through the southern Alps to attack Italy. Centuries later came various Germanic peoples from the north, who slipped through to deal a deathblow to the Roman Empire. The ease of access through the western Alps is attributable to low passes and streams that provide access into the heart of the range as they flow into the plains and hills beyond the Alps.

The Apennine Mountains, the backbone of the Italian Peninsula, branch out from the southern Alps in the Riviera region, arc gently to approach Italy's Adriatic shore, and then return to the western coast to form the toe of the Italian boot. Structurally,

Figure 2.4.   The dramatic Dolomite mountains of northeastern Italy. These formidable southern extensions of the Alps were heavily fought over during World War I. Photo by A. B. M., 2008.

they reappear in the island of Sicily. The Apennines, narrow and of modest height, offer many easy passes and have never presented much of a barrier to movement.

To the east of the Adriatic, the Dinaric Range begins where Italy, Slovenia, and Austria meet and stretches southeastward along the Adriatic coast through the western Balkan Peninsula, continuing through to Greece. While not unusually high, the Dinaric Range is in many sections rugged and difficult to traverse, especially in areas of **karst topography**, where water filtering down from the surface dissolved permeable limestone, forming numerous large sinks or troughs that are used for farming. One of the few easy passages through the Dinaric Range is found in the extreme north, near the juncture with the Alps, where Pear Tree Pass made it relatively easy for Hunnic and Gothic warriors to attack the Roman Empire. To the south, about midway through Albania, the Dinaric Range becomes more open and accessible, a condition that persists through Greece.

Just east of Vienna, across the Danube River in Slovakia, the Carpathian Mountains begin, almost as a continuation of the Alps. Their directional course inscribes a huge mirror image of the letter *C* through southern Poland, a corner of Ukraine, and Romania, ending on the shores of the Danube. The southern part of the Carpathians in Romania bears the name Transylvanian Alps. High elevations rarely occur in the Carpathians—few peaks are over 2,500 meters—and they form a narrow range with

Figure 2.5.   A branch of the Sognefjord and an inhabited *vik* at its head. In the Norwegian Kjølen Range, only small agricultural areas occur. The fjords provide an excellent transportation facility. Photo by T. G. J.-B., 1981.

numerous low passes. To the east, the Crimean Mountains occupy the southern side of a large peninsula jutting into the Black Sea in Ukraine and shelter the famous resort of Yalta from the east European winter.

Elsewhere in Europe, the mountain range that bears the greatest resemblance to the mountains of the European south is the Kjølen Range, which forms the spine of the Scandinavian Peninsula in Norway and western Sweden. With Hercynian roots, this range is not particularly high. But its northern position meant that it was heavily glaciated during recent glacial advances, giving it an Alpine look. The range's western edge is deeply indented by fjords. The Kjølen Range supports very few permanent dwellers, but at the upper end of most fjords, a small patch of flat, unflooded land known as a *vik* can be found, backed by a steep headwall and flanked by nearly perpendicular valley sides (fig. 2.5). Long ago the inhabitants derived their very name, Vikings ("people of the inlet"), from these small plains. Encouraged by the local terrain to look outward, down the fjord to the sea, the Vikings became famous as traders and sea raiders.

Not surprisingly, the earthquakes, volcanism, and tsunamis found in contemporary Europe (fig. 2.6) are concentrated near tectonic plate boundaries (fig. 2.2). Huge losses of life sometimes accompany European earthquakes, as was the case when 60,000 Sicilians died in an early twentieth-century disaster and when 25,000 Armenians lost their lives in 1988. The fatalities were often caused by the collapse of stone houses and tiled roofs, both common in southern Europe.

Volcanoes can also bring grief. The eruption of Vesuvius near Naples in 79 CE destroyed the Roman city of Pompeii. On Sicily over 500 recorded eruptions of Etna,

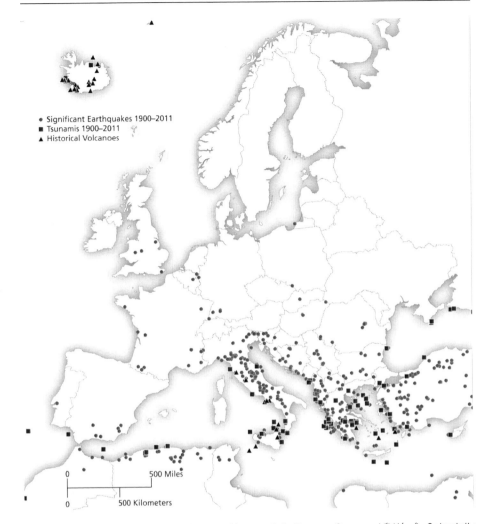

Figure 2.6.   Earthquakes, volcanism, and tsunamis in Europe. *Sources:* Vít Kárník, *Seismicity of the European Area* (Dordrecht: D. Reidel, 1971); Tom Simkin et al., "This Dynamic Planet: World Map of Volcanoes, Earthquakes, and Plate Tectonics" (Washington, DC: Smithsonian Institution, 1989); data supplied by U.S. Geological Survey, National Earthquake Information Center website, http://earthquake.usgs.gov/.

the largest continental volcano in the world, have claimed an estimated one million lives over the past 2,500 years. A perpetually active volcano called Stromboli lies in the Aeolian Isles, north of Sicily. The most violent and powerful volcanic eruption ever known in Europe occurred on the small Greek Aegean Island of Santorini, today merely a shattered, sea-flooded caldera. The island erupted and collapsed with incredible force about 1625 BCE. The noise was likely heard as far away as Scandinavia and central Africa; a huge tsunami, perhaps 200 meters tall, crashed against the shore of nearby islands; and the sky was blackened with falling volcanic debris. Parts of the large nearby island of Crete (Kriti) may have become temporarily uninhabitable as volcanic ash killed vegetation. Altogether, some 54 cubic kilometers of material were removed in the explosion, and most likely gave rise to the legend of the lost continent of Atlantis.

On the mountainous island of Iceland, astride a tectonic plate divide at the opposite territorial extremity of Europe, volcanism and earthquake activity occur frequently. Iceland, with 30 volcanic systems, has experienced over 250 eruptions in the past 1,100 years. In the 1960s, a new island—Surtsey—appeared as a volcanic peak off Iceland's southern shore, and a massive eruption occurred on a nearby, older island, creating a natural harbor. In 2010, a massive ash cloud from one of Iceland's volcanoes brought transatlantic air travel to a halt for six days—grounding over 95,000 flights. Small wonder that this northern island is called "the land of fire and ice."

HILLS

A second terrain category includes the major hill areas of Europe. Hills dominate the European west and midsection (fig. 2.1), where faulting and folding connected with the formation and breakup of Pangea were concentrated. Moving from west to east, hills dominate the west and north of the British Isles, confining the English Scarplands to the southeastern part of Great Britain. Cornwall is the hilly peninsula reaching southwest to Land's End, and the Cambrian Mountains occupy the larger part of the province of Wales. The Pennine Chain forms the spine of Great Britain, blending into the Scottish Highlands to the north.

Moving to the mainland, among the more important hilly districts are Brittany (Bretagne) in western France, the Massif Central to the southeast, and a complex of Hercynian-era hills extending from northeast France and southern Belgium through central Germany and into Czechia. The hills of this area carry different names, including the Ardennes of Belgium and Luxembourg, the Vosges of eastern France, the Schwarzwald (Black Forest) of Germany, and the Jura of Switzerland. Scattered among these hills are numerous small plains that long served as population clusters. The weblike gateways linking them have been routes of trade and invasion.

PLAINS

Europe's plains are concentrated in the north and east (fig. 2.1). A large, compartmentalized lowland extends from the foot of the Pyrenees in southwestern France, bending northward and eastward along the coast through Germany and Poland as far as the Baltic states. Many different sections can be distinguished, from the Basin of Aquitaine in the southwest (home to France's famous Bordeaux wines), through the Paris Basin and the communal delta of the Rhine, Maas, Schelde, and Ems in the Low Countries, to the vast North and East European Plains. In places, the retreating glaciers left behind relatively infertile, poorly drained areas, but they also helped form some of the most fertile parts of these lowlands. Winds sweeping down from the ice mass picked up fine particles of earth and carried them to the southern edge of the plain, where the lowlands give way to a zone of hilly terrain. The forced ascent blunted the velocity of the winds, causing them to drop at the foot of the hills much of their load of dust. These wind-deposited, fine-textured parent materials, known as **loess**, weathered into fertile and easy-to-work soils.

Across the English Channel in the southeastern part of the island of Great Britain lies the English Scarplands. This area is in many respects simply a continuation of the Paris Basin. Just as the Paris Basin served as the nucleus of the French state, so the English Scarplands witnessed the initial nation-building by the Saxon invaders of Britain.

Europe's north is dominated by the Fenno-Scandian Shield. Massively glaciated and underlain by ancient rocks, some of which lie exposed at the surface, the shield is centered in Finland and Russian Karelia. Two great **moraine** walls, formed at the foot of a retreating glacier, parallel the south coast of Finland and serve to dam up much of the interior, producing an intricate system of connecting lakes. The Finns and Karelians long used these waterways to move around, but in the age of highways, roads follow sinuous **eskers**—ridges of sediment left behind from ancient rivers beneath glaciers.

All other European plains lie in the south, wreathed by mountain ranges. Most are small, but some are of great economic significance. Again moving from west to east, the mountain ranges of Iberia divide that peninsula into a series of separate plains, each of which is home to people of a distinct subculture. The narrow Portuguese Lowland, which fronts the Atlantic coast of Iberia, and the Ebro Valley in northeastern Spain are economic heartlands for Portugal and Spain, respectively. The interior plains of Iberia differ from others in Europe because they are elevated plateaus rather than lowlands, standing about 800 meters above sea level. The Central Sierras divide the plateau into two parts, Old and New Castile—homelands of the people who have traditionally dominated and ruled Spain.

Proceeding east, France's gateway to the Mediterranean is the Languedoc Plain, a narrow coastal lowland reaching from the Pyrenees to the Riviera. In Italy, the Po–Veneto Plain is the one sizable plain area in the country. Glaciers moving down into the fringe of the Po–Veneto Plain from the north deposited moraines, which dammed up the mouths of tributary Alpine valleys, creating a chain of beautiful natural lakes, including Como, Maggiore, Lugano, Iseo, and Garda. South of the moraine dams is an infertile outwash plain, beyond which lies the greater part of the Po–Veneto Plain, an area of fertile, river-deposited soils. At the juncture of alluvium and outwash, the groundwater table reaches the surface, resulting in an east–west line of springs called **fontanili**. From ancient times, the fontanili attracted human settlement. Today a row of cities, including Torino and Milano, traces the course of the spring sites. Still another line of cities, including Parma, Modena, and Bologna, lies along the southern edge of the plain, at the foot of the Apennines. The western, uppermost part of the plain served as the political nucleus of Italian unification in the nineteenth century; today the same area contains the industrial heart of the nation.

An exception to the small scale of most southern European plains is the Hungarian Basin in the east, surrounded by the Alps, Carpathians, and Dinaric Range. The Black Sea lies beyond the so-called Iron Gate on the Danube, where the river severs the Carpathians. The diverse ethnic makeup of the Hungarian Basin today, including German, Hungarian, Slav, and Romanian, is a testament to its economic and strategic significance.

To the southeast, the Valachian Plain is a smaller lowland reaching eastward into the Balkan Peninsula from the Black Sea. Valachia has witnessed the comings and goings of a great variety of invaders and migrating peoples, including the Huns, Slavs, Magyars, and Mongols. Today, the Valachian Plain is the heartland of the Romanians, who have managed to preserve a language derived from the Roman armies, perpetuating an isolated eastern bastion of Romance speech.

Outside the North European Plain, compartmentalization is a recurrent trait in the terrain makeup of Europe. The segmentation into numerous peninsulas and islands helps create this image, but it is heightened by the distinctive characteristics of individual terrain units. The Basin of Aquitaine differs from its neighbor, the Paris Basin, and the western Alps is not like the eastern Alps.

HYDROGEOGRAPHY

With most of Europe lying close to a sea or ocean, only eight sizable independent countries in Europe lack a coastline. Europe's flanking seas, named on figure 2.7, are linked by numerous strategic straits, facilitating the movement of people and goods around the perimeter of Europe. Control over the connecting straits has long been the goal of competing European powers, and many of these waterways have been militarily contested. The Bosporus and the Dardanelles, two narrows that join the Black and Aegean Seas, have alternately been controlled by the seagoing Greeks, most notably in the period of the Byzantine Empire, and by the land-based Turks, who presently control these strategic straits. Similarly, Arabs and Spaniards contested Gibraltar—a small part of the southern part of the Iberian Peninsula adjacent to the strait bearing the same name—before it fell to the British, who hold it as a vestige of their sea-based empire.

On the Atlantic front of Europe, the most crucial strait is at Dover. Briefly, this white-cliffed passage and the adjacent English Channel served as the core of a Norman French state, but ultimately it became a natural moat and trade route for the British. Instead of joining the mainland to Britain, Dover came to separate them. Since 1994 France and the United Kingdom are linked by the Channel Tunnel, or "Chunnel," which passes under the English Channel between Calais and Dover.

The great navigable rivers of Europe lie disproportionately on the North and East European Plains. Flowing in a southeast-to-northwest direction, each has a major port city at its juncture with the sea. Canals interconnect these streams, providing a splendid waterway system. Most of eastern and southeastern Europe drains to the Black Sea, in particular through the great Danube, which, rising in southern Germany, passes through or borders nine independent states and is known by five different names along its course. The rivers of southern Europe, not being navigable, generally lack port cities at their mouths. The most important European Mediterranean rivers are the Ebro, Rhône, and Po.

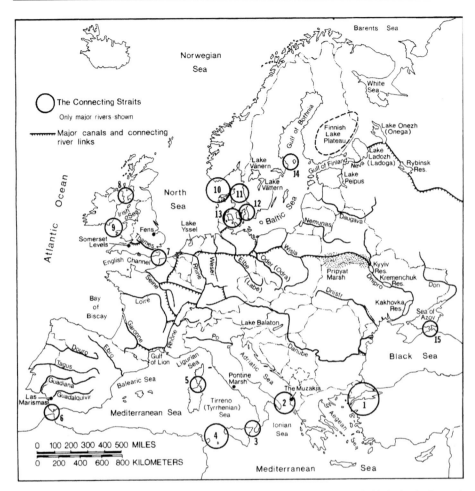

Figure 2.7. Hydrogeographic features. Europe is characterized by a highly indented coast-line of surrounding seas and connecting straits. Key to connecting straits: **1** = Bosporus–Dardanelles, **2** = Otranto, **3** = Messina, **4** = "waist" of the Mediterranean, **5** = Bonifacio, **6** = Gibraltar, **7** = Dover, **8** = North Channel, **9** = Saint George's Channel, **10** = Skagerrak, **11** = Kattegat, **12** = Øresund, **13** = the Belts, **14** = Åland, **15** = Kerch.

Europe's Climate

Europe's climate is generally humid and mild, considering the rather high latitudes involved. Temperate, moist conditions favored the development of large population concentrations and helped Europe become one of the major homelands of humanity.

Why is Europe's climate predominantly humid and mild and why does the mild-ness and humidity extend as far inland as it does? The basic answers to these ques-tions lie in four characteristics of the natural environment: the **Gulf Stream**, the **North Atlantic Drift**, the configuration of the European landmass, and the seasonal movement of the **Azores anticyclone**.

Despite Europe's northerly location, moderate waters lie off Europe's coast due to the clockwise rotation of ocean currents in the Northern Hemisphere. This rotation happens because anything moving in a straight line north of the equator is deflected to the right due to the rotation of the earth (the **Coriolis effect**). As the waters in the Atlantic Ocean move, then, they tend to be drawn into a clockwise rotation that moves water from the warm Caribbean to the north and east—an ocean current known as the Gulf Stream. As the Gulf Stream moves through the northern Atlantic, it divides; the North Atlantic Drift is the divide of the Gulf Stream that moves water toward the European coast. The waters arriving on Europe's shores, then, are fairly moderate—arriving as they do from farther south and west.

The moderate waters washing Europe's shores have a significant impact far into the "continent" because of the dominant west-to-east movement of air masses in the Northern Hemisphere. The so-called westerlies coming off the Atlantic Ocean move in the direction that they do because, in the northern hemisphere, air circulates from the equatorial regions toward the poles and is deflected to the right (as seen from above) by the Coriolis effect. Not too cold in winter and not too hot in summer, the westerlies bring unsettled conditions into a significant part of Europe year-round.

The configuration of the European landmass also comes into play. Unlike in North America, there is no north–south trending mountain range that causes milder, moister air coming off the adjacent ocean to rise and lose much of its moisture, and then descend and create dry conditions to the east of the mountains. As a result, moderate, moist air coming off the Atlantic penetrates far into Europe. Europe's peninsular character helps as well. Waters surround Europe well to the east of its western edge (the Mediterranean, the North Sea, the Baltic); it is only in Europe's eastern reaches that the moderating influences of these waters drop off.

There is, however, a significant north–south divide in Europe's climatic makeup. Those areas lying to the south of the Cantabrians, Pyrenees, Alps, and Dinaric Mountains are shielded from the effects of the westerlies during the summer months by the northward migration of a high-pressure ridge, the so-called Azores anticyclone (the fourth fundamental force influencing Europe's climate). The Azores anticyclone is a product of global air circulation patterns that tend to produce downward drafts of air—zones of high pressure—at the northern and southern edges of the tropics that keep unstable, moist air masses at bay. These zones are where the great deserts of the earth can be found.

The high pressure ridge that lies off the northwest coast of Africa is called the Azores high, or Azores anticyclone—named after the islands found there. The Azores anticyclone is not stationary throughout the year. Instead, it migrates north in the summer months and south in the winter in keeping with the seasons. The Azores anticyclone never moves far enough north to allow significant unstable air to penetrate into the Sahara Desert of northern Africa, but it does move far enough to keep the southern part of Europe quite dry during the summer months. As it retreats to the south in the winter, however, moister, more unstable air finds its way into areas bordering on the Mediterranean Sea.

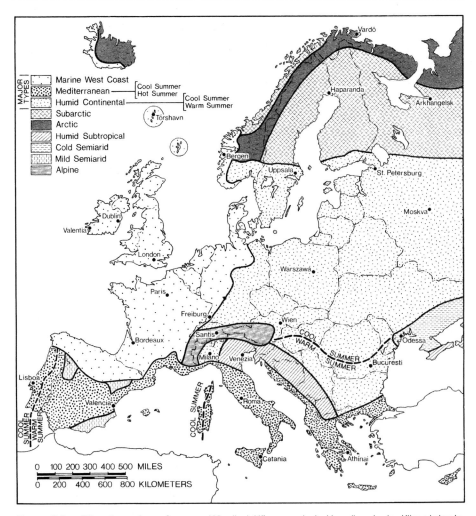

Figure 2.8. Climate regions. *Sources:* Wladimir Köppen et al., *Handbuch der Klimatologie*, (Berlin: Borntraeger, 1930–1936); Wallén 1970; Hermann Flohn and Roberto Fantechi, eds., *The Climate of Europe: Past, Present and Future* (Hingham, MA: D. Reidel, 1984).

The interaction of these influences shapes Europe's basic climate pattern. In broad brush, Europe is characterized by a zone of moderate, humid conditions to the north of the Pyrenees and Alps in the west—gradually giving way to more extreme conditions as one moves east and north. To the south of those mountain ranges, moderate, somewhat humid conditions dominate during the winter months, but hot, dry conditions are found in the summer.

Mapping Europe's climate patterns requires grouping climatic conditions into generalized regions. A common way of accomplishing this task is shown in figure 2.8, which provides the basis for the discussion that follows.

MARINE WEST COAST

Dominating Europe's western reaches to the north of the Pyrenees and Alps is the *marine west coast climate* region. The name describes both the region's location and an important property governing its character: the role of maritime air masses. As we have seen, the latter are moisture-laden and mild in winter and not too hot in summer. They penetrate deep into Europe—giving the marine west coast climate zone a significant eastward penetration. Temperatures remain mild all year, with cool summers and relatively pleasant winters. The coldest month averages above freezing and generally below 7°C. Temperatures do not differ greatly between winter and summer. Dublin, Ireland, averages only 10°C warmer in July than in January. The majority of January nights in London do not have frost. Even in the Shetland Islands, far to the north, snow is relatively rare.

Occasional bitter cold waves do occur in the marine west coast climate. London has recorded –16°C, and in one severe cold spell in February 1929, the temperature remained constantly below freezing for 226 hours in the British capital. A bitter cold spell struck western Europe again in December 1996 and January 1997, causing more than 200 deaths and freezing over the River Thames above London. Still, the appearance of a few palm trees at places along the southwest Irish coast suggests the overall mildness of the winters. It was not always so. During the colder climatic phase known colloquially as the Little Ice Age (1200 to 1800 CE), the winters were more severe. The canals of Holland often froze over, permitting the ice-skating shown in the paintings of some of the Dutch masters.

Marine west coast summers are cool, with July averages generally below 21°C, and sweaters feel comfortable on many days. Heat waves, with temperatures above 32°C, do occur occasionally in parts of the marine west coast area. The record high temperature at Paris is 38°C. A number of severe heat waves have occurred in the marine west coast region in recent years. During an August 2003 outbreak of hot weather, in excess of 14,000 mainly elderly people were estimated to have perished in France of heat-related illnesses. During the summer of 2006, the British Isles endured an extended period of temperatures in the high 30s Celsius, and judges in the Royal Courts were allowed to remove their wigs in light of the heat. (Most buildings in this region do not have air conditioning.)

Because the marine air masses contain great amounts of moisture, the climate is quite humid, with regular precipitation all year round. Normally between 50 and 100 centimeters fall each year, although relatively little precipitation typically falls on any given day. Gentle showers or drizzles are the rule. The cool temperatures retard evaporation, as does prevalent cloudiness, and precipitation is adequate to produce humid conditions. Stations situated at the western edge of hills and mountains receive considerably more precipitation as humid air masses moving from the west rise over hill and mountain barriers. In rising, the air mass cools, lowering its ability to hold moisture in an evaporated state. The excess is precipitated on west-facing slopes, a process known as the **orographic effect**.

In the marine west coast climate region, winds are generally gentle, although blustery conditions occur frequently in some coastal areas. In a few cases winds come so regularly and from predictable directions as to have names. One of the best known is the **föhn** of southern Germany, a warm, dry wind from the south that results when a cyclonic storm north of the Alps in the winter draws in its wake drier, warmer winds over the mountains from the Mediterranean lands. A föhn blowing in midwinter can produce a sudden false springtime, with fair skies and pleasant temperatures, a delightful though short-lived respite from dreary, damp winter conditions.

MEDITERRANEAN

Most of southern Europe, in particular the three southward-reaching peninsulas of Iberia, Italy, and Greece, lies in the *Mediterranean climate* zone (fig. 2.8). In this zone, precipitation is concentrated in the winter season, with notably dry summers—a product of the seasonal movement of the Azores anticyclone. Generally, less than one-tenth of the annual precipitation falls in the quarter-year comprising the summer months of June, July, and August, and the month of July is almost totally rainless. Occasionally the summer drought expands to include the entire year, causing serious water shortages. Southern and central Spain suffered such a prolonged drought in the 1990s. Even the olives—hardy trees able to endure dry conditions—began to die. During the summer of 2007, Greece endured an unprecedented period of hot and dry conditions, culminating in the worst fire season in many decades. At one point, forests were ablaze in half of the country, and many ancient ruins, including the site of the first Olympic games, were threatened by flames. The fires sparked an emotional debate over who was to blame for the extensive destruction: the government and its weak response in fighting the flames, or those who perennially set forest land on fire to free up land for farming. Winter precipitation usually occurs as rainfall in the small lowland plains, but snow is common in the numerous mountain ranges found in the Mediterranean climate region. Accumulated snow in the highlands is of crucial importance to farmers because the runoff in spring and summer provides a source of irrigation water during the drought season.

Temperatures in the Mediterranean climate zone are warmer than those of the marine west coast area because of the former's more southerly location and its lower incidence of cloudiness. Summers are hot, with July averages usually in the 24° to 28°C range. Because the relative humidity in summer tends to be low, fairly rapid nighttime cooling occurs. A cool-summer subtype of the Mediterranean climate also appears in places, confined to the Atlantic **littoral** of Portugal and certain other windward coastlines (fig. 2.8). In these areas, warmest-month averages do not exceed 22°C because of the moderating influence of the adjacent ocean.

Throughout the Mediterranean climate area, except in the mountain ranges, winters remain mild, and extended periods of frost are unknown. Groves of citrus dot the lowlands of the Mediterranean, a good indicator of the absence of severe cold. Cloudiness is at a minimum, particularly in the summer, a striking contrast to the marine west coast region. Parts of Italy receive more than 2,500 hours of sunshine per year, almost twice as much as the British Isles.

The local winds of the Mediterranean reflect its location between the marine west coast and the desert. Winter storm centers moving through the basin draw cold, damp winds down from the north, including the **mistral** and the **bora**. The mistral blows with fury down the Rhône–Saône corridor into the Mediterranean coastal fringe of France and on beyond to the islands of Corsica and Sardegna, whereas the bora strikes the eastern coast of Italy from across the Adriatic Sea. From the opposite direction, dry, hot **sirocco winds** are drawn up from the Saharan region by cyclonic storms to afflict southern Italy and Greece. In Italy, the sirocco blows from 30 to 50 times annually, lasting 80 to 120 days per year and occurring most often from March through May and again in November. The Saharan winds are least common in summer, but when they do happen in that season, the searing heat is brutal and can be damaging to crops and orchards.

HUMID CONTINENTAL

A *humid continental climate* dominates the eastern part of Europe, from southern Scandinavia to the eastern Balkans and deep into Russia (fig. 2.8). Here, as the climate's name implies, continental air masses, borne over the vast Eurasian interior and frozen Arctic Ocean, prevail over those of marine origin. These air masses display a great annual range of temperature, becoming very cold in the winters and surprisingly warm in the summers, producing a climate given to seasonal extremes. In particular, the winters are colder and become progressively bitterer toward the east. The disasters that befell the armies of Hitler and Napoleon in Russia were in no small part the work of numbing cold. January averages in the humid continental area range from about –12°C up to freezing, and low readings below –20°C are not uncommon. A blizzard in February 1999 produced heavy snowfall that cut off more than 200 villages and towns in Hungary. January 2006 saw another cold spell, with Moscow recording the longest stretch of days with temperatures dipping below –30°C since 1950.

The difference between January and July averages runs double or more the annual range of many marine west coast locations. Winter temperatures are low enough to cause a durable snow cover to develop, with usually at least one month in which the ground remains blanketed. In more eastern areas, the continuous snow cover can last for three or four months. Rivers, lakes, and shallow ocean inlets freeze over, including the Baltic Sea. Occasionally during winter in the East European Plain, the heart of the humid continental climate zone, cloudy and mild spells of weather occur.

Summer temperatures are remarkably similar to those in the marine west coast zone. The July average at Moscow and Warsaw is identical to that at Paris, and most stations fall in the 16° to 21°C range for the warmest month average. Only in the southern extremity of the humid continental area, in the Balkans and in an outlier in the upper Po–Veneto Plain, does a warm-summer subtype of the humid continental climate occur (fig. 2.8). In this region, July averages exceed 22°C, and some summer days are unpleasantly hot. Throughout the humid continental climate area, precipitation is adequate if not abundant at all seasons, owing in part to the low evaporation rate associated with cool and cold weather. Between 48 and 65 centimeters of precipitation can be expected each year at typical humid continental stations, only slightly less than is the norm in marine west coast areas.

MINOR CLIMATE TYPES

The greater parts of Sweden and Finland lie in the *subarctic climate* zone, more severe than the humid continental (fig. 2.8). Only one to three months average over 10°C, and the proximity to the pole in a continental location means bitter, dark winters. In January 1987 a temperature of −45°C was recorded in Norway's Kjølen Range. The precipitation total is modest and comes mainly as snow, but the resultant climate is humid, due to very low evaporation. At these high latitudes, darkness prevails in the winter months and daylight is fleeting. One of every ten Finns suffers Seasonal Affective Disorder (SAD), a depression caused by the prevailing darkness, and extravagant use of public lighting is employed to offset the problem.

Still more severe is the *arctic climate* zone, a region largely devoid of trees (fig. 2.8). It lacks a summer altogether, and the warmest month averages below 10°C. Interestingly, the adjacent Barents Sea, part of the Arctic Ocean, does not freeze in winter, and the entire Norwegian coast and the Russian Arctic port of Murmansk remain open to shipping, thanks to the influence of the easternmost branch of the North Atlantic Drift.

The Dinaric Range and coastal portion of the Po–Veneto Plain are characterized by a *humid subtropical climate*, similar to the Mediterranean climate in temperature but lacking the pronounced summer drought. Here the summers are hot with high humidity, and the July visitor to Venice may well be reminded of New Orleans or Brisbane.

Nearly all of Europe receives considerable precipitation, even if it is seasonal as in the Mediterranean. The principal exceptions are some peripheral semiarid regions (fig. 2.8). In these places, the great desert belts of Africa and Eurasia gently touch Europe. The lands immediately north of the Black and Caspian seas have a cold *semiarid climate*, with bitter continental winters, made all the more fierce by the absence of trees to block the wind. Southeastern Spain has a mild semiarid climate, sharing the temperatures of the Mediterranean winter but lacking its precipitation because the area is in the rain shadow of the Bética, Ibérica, and Cantabrica ranges.

The final minor type, the *Alpine climate*, occurs to some extent in all the mountain ranges of Europe, though shown in figure 2.8 only in the Alps (because of the scale of the map). The key causal factor is elevation above sea level. Mountain heights cause the climate to be colder. The Alpine climate varies greatly from valley to valley and slope to slope.

Vegetation and Soils

Because climate has a major influence on plant life, Europe's vegetation pattern (fig. 2.9) closely mirrors its climate regions. People have so massively altered the veg-

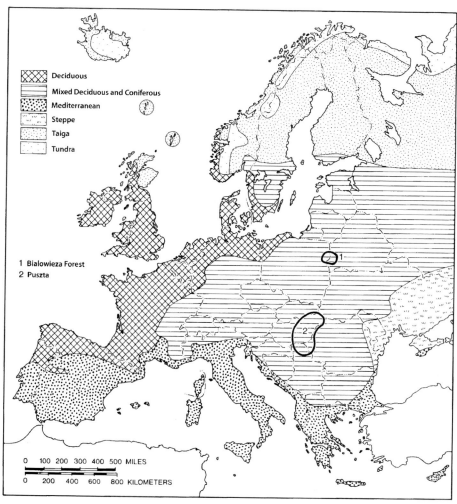

Figure 2.9. Floristic provinces. *Sources:* Jaako Jalas and Juha Suominen, *Atlas Florae Europaeae* (Helsinki: Suomalaisen Kirjallisuuden Kirjapaino Oy, 1972–1976); Oleg Polunin and Martin Walters, *A Guide to the Vegetation of Britain and Europe* (Oxford: Oxford University Press, 1985).

etative cover that we cannot know precisely what Europe's biotic provinces were like in a natural state. As a starting point, though, it is useful to sketch out the general types of vegetative cover that would likely be found in Europe if humans were not present. We will then turn later in the chapter to the impacts of humans on Europe's biogeography.

FORESTS

The part of Europe corresponding to all but the eastern and northern fringes of the marine west climate zone was once mostly covered by a *broadleaf deciduous forest,* consisting of trees that drop their leaves during the dormant season in winter. Oaks served as the dominant species; other common trees included the ash, linden, beech, and birch. Elms, maples, willows, and hornbeams were also well represented among the canopy trees. In the vegetative understory of these Atlantic forests grew yews, hollies, and hazel shrubs, beneath which lay a groundcover of ivy, heather, anemone, ferns, bracken, primrose, and wild strawberry.

As one moves to the east and north, the broadleaf deciduous forest zone gives way to a *mixed broadleaf and coniferous forest*. Here the beech was long a dominant species, with many oak, larch, and hornbeam, but there were also abundant coniferous needle-leaf evergreen trees such as fir, spruce, and the Scottish pine, especially in hilly, mountainous, and sandy regions. The understories were similar to those in Atlantic forests, and orchids and sedges also abounded.

The most impressive remnant of the original Central European woodland is the Bialowieza Forest on the eastern margin of the North European Plain, straddling the border between Poland and Belarus (fig. 2.9). It encompasses some 127,000 hectares; about 4% is preserved as a national park in Poland. Earlier, it enjoyed royal protection. The Bialowieza Forest houses at least 4,000 plant species, including immense specimens of hornbeam, spruce, and oak. Here, and only here, one can glimpse the great forest of the European heartland in something resembling its pristine condition, but access is carefully regulated.

The *taiga* zone, sometimes called the boreal forest, lies in the European north. This is where the great coniferous evergreen woodlands are found. Dominant species include the Norway spruce, Scottish pine, and various firs. The downy birch, a broadleaf deciduous tree, also abounds, as does the gray alder and larch. In poorly drained places, abundant due to the heavy hand of glaciation, peat bogs and mires support a growth of mosses, grasses, and shrubs, while some hilly areas have heaths. The taiga is thinly populated and a refuge for peoples speaking non-Indo-European languages.

In the European south, generally corresponding to the climate region of the same name, lies the *Mediterranean forest* zone. In its natural state this is an area of relatively open forests of broadleaf evergreen live oaks and olives, as well as Aleppo and stone pines, chestnuts, myrtles, walnuts, cypresses, and, in the mountains, firs. The dominant tree is the holm oak. Beneath and between the trees is an evergreen shrub layer of juniper, honeysuckle, heather, and spiny broom. The groundcover includes various grasses, especially esparto, as well as spurge and spleenwort.

This vegetative cover must withstand the pronounced summer drought of the Mediterranean region. Most trees and shrubs exhibit **sclerophyllous** features—an exceptional development of protective external tissue, as in the thickening of leaves and bark, in order to retard evaporation. Examples include the deeply fissured bark of the cork oak and the stiff, leathery leaf of the olive. Also, leaves are small, and the upper side is shiny, further retarding evaporation.

TREELESS AREAS

Few significant native open grasslands existed within the original central European woodland. The prairies of the Hungarian basin, called Puszta (fig. 2.9), are a possible exception, but they are more likely a product of fires and grazing. Nonetheless, a fair amount of woodland survives in the Puszta.

Farther south, the semiarid areas of Ukraine and southern parts of Eurorussia were traditionally areas of tallgrass prairie. The prairie represents an extension of the expansive steppe grasslands that dominate the heart of Asia, reaching eastward to Mongolia and beyond. Pointed like an extended finger toward Europe, Eurasia's steppe corridor served repeatedly as a natural route of invasion by mounted nomad-warriors from the east, who found the treeless country suited to their mode of warfare and the abundant grasses excellent for their flocks and herds. For a thousand years and more, wave after wave of people passed this way—Hun, Bulgar, Magyar, Avar, Tartar. Some left, but most remained. The great prairie that led the Asian nomadic tribes into Europe has largely vanished. The steppe proved too fertile to escape the plow, and today domesticated grasses, mainly wheat, grow in place of the natural grassland.

Places such as the British Isles and Denmark have large expanses of treeless **moor** and **heath**. As a general rule, "heath" is the term used for hilly areas or undulating plains, whereas "moor" describes level surfaces. Both are covered with a variety of low shrubs, including heather, juniper, and gorse (a reed-like plant with abundant yellow flowers). Peat bogs abound. Some of these areas never had trees because they were insufficiently well drained. But there is evidence that some of them came about when human-set fires, used to create pastureland, produced a more open landscape.

Another treeless area that is fairly widespread is the **tundra**, which occupies lands north of the tree line along the Arctic coast of Scandinavia and Russia, Iceland, in the higher elevations of the Kjølen Range, and above the limit of forest growth in certain mountain ranges such as the Alps. Tundra vegetation consists largely of lichens, mosses, sedges, rushes, dwarf beech and birch, stunted or creeping evergreen shrublets, and some grasses. Rarely do these plants exceed 30 centimeters in height, though in the transition zone between the tundra and taiga, scrub birch forests grow somewhat taller. The brief Arctic summer brings an outburst of flowery plants of unique coloring and beauty. Permafrost, or permanently frozen subsoil, occurs in some places, causing water logging of the upper layers and a variety of surface soil hummocks. As a result, walking across the tundra in summer can be very difficult. The European tundra is an area of low population densities. It serves as a homeland for the Sami people and other Finnic minorities.

SOILS

Climate, vegetation, and geomorphic parent materials combine to yield a variety of soil types in Europe, varying greatly in texture, depth, and fertility. For our purposes, it is important simply to understand the basic distribution of soils of varying fertility (fig. 2.10).

Highly fertile soils encompass those derived from several different parent materials, including loess—wind-borne materials ground up by glaciers, alluvium, and volcanic ash. Over the millennia, loess has weathered into a dark-colored, fertile, fine-textured, and deep soil known as **chernozem**, or "black earth." The organic matter of

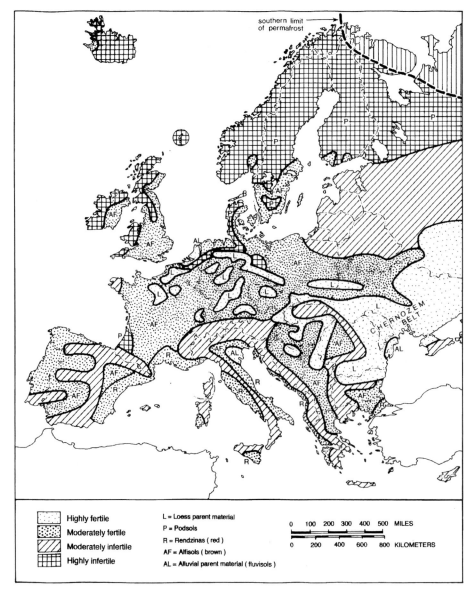

Figure 2.10.   Soil regions. This simple classification conceals an incredibly complex pattern. Note the core–periphery pattern of fertility and infertility. *Sources:* F.A.O. UNESCO, *Soil Map of the World*, vol. 5 (Europe) (Paris: United Nations, 1981); F.A.O. UNESCO, *Soil Map of the World: Revised Legend* (Rome: United Nations, 1988); Alice Garnett, "The Loess Regions of Central Europe in Prehistoric Times," *Geographical Journal* 106 (1945): 301–27.

decaying prairie grasses has added to its fertility. Rich **alluvial soils** dominate the Low Countries and also occur in smaller pockets elsewhere, as in broad river valleys and certain Mediterranean lowlands. Dark volcanic soils, called **andosols**, occur too locally to be revealed on a general map of Europe, but they are highly fertile and attract dense agricultural populations to the environs of volcanoes in Italy and Greece.

Moderately fertile soils are found on parts of the plains in northern and eastern Europe. Limestone has also weathered into moderately fertile soils in the Mediterranean region. Highly infertile soils lie mainly in northern Europe. These **podsols**, meaning "white earth" or "ash-colored soils," are highly acidic and humus-starved because of leaching—the downward movement of plant nutrients to lower soil layers. Sandy areas such as outwash plains are also highly infertile.

Human Alteration of the Environment

Humans have profoundly affected Europe's vegetation, soils, waters, and even the land itself over the millennia. Indeed, the impact of humans on the natural environment is so profound that it is sometimes difficult to know what Europe's physical geography would have been like if humans had not been part of the picture.

HUMAN MODIFICATION OF LANDS AND WATERS

An unmistakable feature of many hills and mountain slopes in southern Europe is the presence of existing or abandoned terraces—a testament to the role of humans as agents of geomorphic change. The ancient practice of terracing, probably derived from the mountain fringe of the Fertile Crescent in southwest Asia, comes out of the effort to "level" mountains for agricultural use. In the Mediterranean lands, where level terrain is in short supply, terraced hillsides are common, especially in Greece (fig. 2.11).

People also build hills. To cite just two examples, the Teufelsberg, or "Devil's Mountain," stands on the North European Plain near Berlin. Building material for the Teufelsberg came from the rubble of the war-destroyed German capital. The peak reaches sufficient height to provide a modest ski slope in winter. In eastern Ireland, there are numerous small hills called **motes**, erected as fortifications by invading Normans in the Middle Ages. If people build, they also excavate, forming open-pit mines that scar the landscape in many regions.

Many European rivers have been greatly modified by human action, both deliberate and accidental. Some streams, such as the Dnieper River, have had their character greatly altered by dam and reservoir construction. The Drin, a minor river of northern Albania, has been completely transformed from a gorge-cutting mountain stream to a stair step of three lakes, now open to boat traffic. Many rivers of the North European Plain have been channelized and canalized. In some cases, massive amounts of earth have been moved to build canals and locks that connect rivers. The Maine–Danube canal in southern Germany (discussed in Chapter 8) provides a particularly dramatic

Figure 2.11.   Evidence of abandoned terraces on hillsides in Croatia. Photo by A. B. M., 2009.

example. In other places, rapids have been dynamited away to facilitate river trans-port, as happened at the Iron Gate of the Danube, where the river cuts through at the Carpathian–Stara Planina juncture. Moreover, riverbanks along many streams are manicured and lined with facing stones, giving them an artificial appearance.

Water pollution has also affected Europe's rivers. One of the region's most severely polluted major river is the Vistula, which is laced with heavy metals such as lead and mercury, coal-mine salts, and organic carcinogens. Groundwater pollution is also widespread. Chemical fertilizers and pesticides used in agriculture have found their way into subsurface waters, raising nitrogen levels significantly. In many heavily industrialized areas, toxic substances have migrated downward through overlying soils. Since the drinking water of three-quarters of the European population comes from groundwater, the pollution of subsurface waters represents a significant environ-mental *and* human health challenge for Europe.

Marshes were once common in many parts of Europe, but the majority of wet-lands have been drained and converted to agriculture. The Fens in the English Scarp-lands disappeared in this way. Some marshes were created by human action, as in the Val di Chiana in Toscana, Italy. There, Etruscan forest removal in ancient times led to **siltation**, which in time clogged the valley's drainage system, forming a large malarial marsh. Later, farmers drained the Val di Chiana marshes and made them agriculturally productive. Human modification of marshes is common in Europe as it is elsewhere in the world, but converting marshland can have negative consequences. First, marshes act as natural sponges during wet periods; their water storage capacity can prevent intense, rapid flooding of streams, which can cause erosion and loss of property. Second, marshes and other wetlands are good storage sinks for sediment. The small particles that cause streams to be murky also provide the habitats for many species of fish, and marshes and other wetlands act as natural filtration for the hydrologic system.

Coastal silting represents another device by which Europeans have modified Europe's physical character, especially on the three Mediterranean peninsulas. As a result of deforestation and certain types of agriculture, bays have silted up, rivers have become unnavigable, ports have been made landlocked, and islands near the coast have been joined to the mainland. Many of these changes have unfolded over long periods of time. The Greek geographer Strabo, writing some 2,000 years ago, noted that the Adriatic tides reached to Ravenna in northern Italy, a city 10 kilometers inland today. Palos de la Frontera on the Odiel River, from which Columbus departed on his voyage of discovery in 1492, is now silted up for 1.5 kilometers below the former docks. Even more impressive is the silting that occurred near Monte Circeo, a mountain on the western coast of Italy. According to the Homeric epic *Odyssey*, Monte Circeo formed an island in preclassical times, and it retained that status even as late as 300 BCE. Several centuries later, siltation joined it to the Italian mainland. Where Ulysses once sailed, farmers labor today in fertile fields.

The Special Case of the Netherlands

Nowhere has the scale and scope of human modification of lands and waters been greater than in the Netherlands, where the Dutch live on the "wrong" end of a huge geomorphological seesaw. Their deltaic homeland has been gradually sinking, at the rate of about 20 centimeters per century, coincident with an increase in the elevation of lands lying along the northern shores of the Baltic Sea. The elevation increase in the north is due to a process known as **isostatic rebound**, wherein a segment of the earth's surface that was depressed by the weight of an ice sheet gradually returns to its former elevation after the ice melts. As northern Europe rebounded after the last glacial retreat, adjacent areas were pulled downward, including the Netherlands. Since about 10,000 BCE, the coastal fringe of the Netherlands has sunk some 20 meters. Silt brought in and deposited by the Rhine, Maas, and Schelde rivers has partially offset the sinking of the land, but without active human efforts, the coastline would be dramatically different from what it is today (fig. 2.12).

Before encroachment by the sea began, the ancient Dutch coast had few indentations and was paralleled by a protective wall of sand dunes. The only breaks in the dunes occurred where the many distributaries of the Rhine, Maas, and Schelde cut through to reach the North Sea. As thousands of years passed and the level of some lands on the inland side of the dunes fell below sea level, parts of the Low Country flooded. Driven by storms, the North Sea broke through the sand dune barrier in the northern and southwestern Netherlands and permanently inundated large areas. This deterioration can still be seen today, especially in the north. The Friesche Islands, which

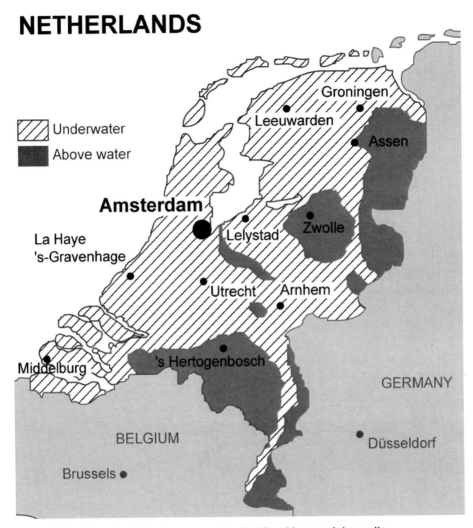

NETHERLANDS

Underwater

Above water

Groningen

Leeuwarden

Assen

Amsterdam

Lelystad

Zwolle

La Haye
's-Gravenhage

Utrecht   Arnhem

Middelburg

's Hertogenbosch

GERMANY

BELGIUM

Düsseldorf

Brussels

Figure 2.12.   How the Netherlands would look without human intervention.

lie in an east–west string along the northern coast, represent all that remains of the sand dune wall in that sector, and the shallow saltwater Waddenzee, which separates the islands from the coast, was once dry land. Besides the Waddenzee, the other major marine incursion helped create a huge flooded river mouth, or estuary, where the Rhine, Maas, and Schelde rivers came to the sea on the southwestern coast.

As coastal deterioration proceeded, parts of the coastal margin of the Low Country fragmented into marshy tidal islands, and numerous lakes formed in depressions. From time to time storm tides broke through to join some of these lakes to the sea. When the Romans came to this region, they found a large freshwater lake just south of the Waddenzee, fed and drained by a distributary of the Rhine. Centuries later that lake had became a saltwater embayment of the North Sea after a

Figure 2.13.   An ancient terp in the Dutch coastal province of Friesland. This artificial mound dates from the earliest period of the Dutch battle against the sea and today contains a church, house, and cemetery. Before the era of dike building, the countryside all around the *terp* was subject to periodic inundation by the waters of the sea. Photo by A. B. M., 2004.

series of storms about 1200 CE cut through the ribbon of dry land separating it from the Waddenzee. A new saline sea, the Zuider Zee ("southern sea"), replaced the Roman "Flevo Lacus."

Another type of deterioration involved the slow eastward migration of what remained of the sand dune barrier. The prevailing westerly winds gradually moved the dunes inland, and the sea followed close behind. A fortress built during the Roman occupation on the landward side of the dunes was covered by drifting sands, disappeared, and was soon forgotten after the legions left, only to reappear in 1520 on the *seaward* side of the dune wall. Soon thereafter the ruins were flooded by the advancing North Sea.

Human efforts to resist the incoming sea go back more than 1,500 years. At first, the early Dutch inhabitants did nothing more than pile up mounds of earth upon which they built their homes. These mounds, called **terpen** (in Dutch), can be seen today in parts of the Low Country and are often still inhabited (fig. 2.13). During periods of high water, terpen temporarily became little islands protecting the people clustered in dwellings on top. These mounds, 4 to 12 meters high, varied in area from 1.5 to 16 hectares. Terpen were built mainly from the third to the tenth centuries CE, and the remnants of some 1,500 of them still survive. Somewhat later, in the

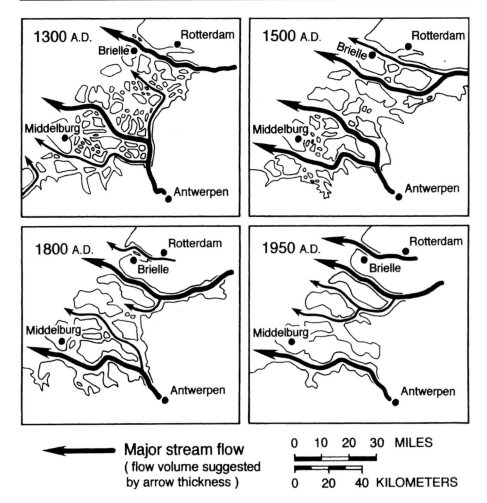

Figure 2.14. Humans at work modifying the Dutch coastline, 1200–1950. Both the advance of the North Sea and the subsequent work of humans to keep the North Sea at bay are evident in these maps of the Rhine–Maas–Schelde Estuary in the Zeeland province of the Netherlands. The Delta Project is not shown. *Source: Westermanns Atlas zur Weltgeschichte* (Braunschweig, Germany: Georg Westermann, 1963), part 2, 97.

900s, the Dutch began placing obstructions along the coast to catch and hold accretions of sand and silt, and they built walls to trap silt being washed down the rivers. In the process they induced island building in the delta (fig. 2.14).

Dike building began about 900 CE in tidal marsh areas. **Dikes** protected lands above the low-tide level that were subject to periodic flooding, and sluice gates were opened at low tide to allow gravity discharge of the water that had accumulated through seepage. Such protected areas became known as **polders**, a term first used in 1138 in Flanders. Dike building and poldering spread northward into the province of Holland, where Count William "the Diker" directed poldering in an area of peat bogs, lakes, and marshes south of Amsterdam in the early 1200s. A peak of dike construction occurred in the 1300s to protect cropland from the unpredictable seas, lakes, and rivers.

The development of polders in areas too low to be drained by gravity at low tide awaited the invention of a mechanical water lifter. The windmill, known in the area at least since the late 1100s, initially served only as a grinder of grain, but in the year 1408 the windmill was first employed as a water lifter and by the 1600s it had achieved general use for this purpose. The same westerlies that pushed the waters against the Dutch shores and caused the retreat of the protective sand dunes were harnessed to reclaim the land. Within several centuries nearly all the marshes and bogs had been converted into polders, with a resultant increase in population and food production.

Drainage of the numerous freshwater lakes dotting the coastal fringe of the Low Country represented the next advance in Dutch reclamation technology. Two centuries of experimentation with the windmill convinced engineers that sizable water bodies could be converted to agricultural use. Between 1609 and 1612, the combined work of 49 windmills laid dry a 7,300-hectare freshwater lake. Other small lakes were drained in quick succession. More powerful water lifters were needed to allow reclamation of large lakes and oceanic inlets; for these the Dutch had to wait until the nineteenth and twentieth centuries, when steam- and, later, electric-engine pumps became available. Between 1840 and 1846, a dike was built around the 60-kilometer circumference of the freshwater Haarlemmer Lake, covering 17,800 hectares west of Amsterdam. Then three British-built steam-engine pumps worked continually for five years, from 1847 to 1852, to drain the lake. Haarlemmer was the largest water body yet to surrender to the Dutch at that time, but the greatest projects still lay in the future.

The treacherous Zuider Zee had been a menace to the Low Country ever since its formation. Its waters needed only a strong wind to send them raging against the vulnerable sea dikes protecting the polderland to the south, and over the years the Zee had claimed many victims. A severe flood in 1916 finally prompted the Netherlands' government to take action on the Zuider Zee Project. The key to the project was a huge sea dike called the Afsluitdijk, which was constructed between 1927 and 1933. The dike cut off the mouth of the Zuider Zee from the ocean and greatly reduced the amount of protective dike exposed to the open sea by shortening the coastline (fig. 2.15). The streams flowing into the Zee soon flushed it clean of salt water, creating the freshwater Lake Yssel. The dike included sluices to allow for outflow of water and locks to accommodate shipping. The name Zuider Zee disappeared from the map. Perhaps the only group of people who mourned its demise were the saltwater fishermen, mainly Frisians, whose livelihood was destroyed. The highway and railroad built on the new dike provided greatly shortened transport links between western and eastern parts of the Netherlands.

The second part of the project involved the diking and draining of four large polders from the floor of the old Zuider Zee. The Wieringer Polder in the far northern part was actually drained before the entire sea dike was finished, becoming dry in 1931. Experimentation established the best sequence of crops to remove salinity from the soils, and soon the Wieringer Polder was colonized by Dutch farmers. Settlement

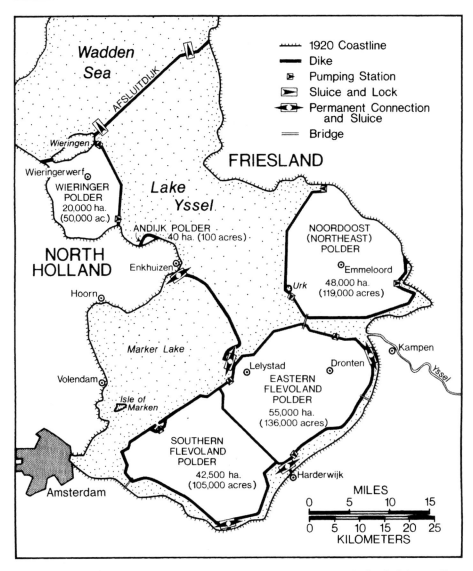

Figure 2.15.   The Zuider Zee Project produced a dramatic change in the Dutch coastline, as well as converting what remains of the old saltwater Zee into the freshwater Lake Yssel.

was completed in 1941, and today the area is a fully integrated part of the Netherlands, largely indistinguishable from surrounding districts. The other major polders include the Noordoost, drained by electric pumps in 1936–1942 and colonized by the early 1960s; Eastern Flevoland, named for the ancient Roman lake and laid dry in 1957; and Southern Flevoland, pumped free of water in 1968 and today absorbing suburban spillover from the adjacent cities of Holland, as well as providing parkland. The remainder of Lake Yssel remains undrained, serving as a freshwater supply and recreational area.

With the Zuider Zee Project, the Dutch turned back the major marine encroachment on their northern coast. The other principal danger area lies in the southwestern province known as Zeeland, where the Rhine–Maas–Schelde estuary passes through six large gaps in the old sand dune barrier. This delta country was no stranger to storm floods from the sea, but the attention of the Dutch government was finally attracted by an especially severe disaster in 1953. Between January 31 and February 2, 160-kilometer-per-hour winds from the northwest pushed river water back up into the estuary, breaking down dikes and spilling into the farmlands and towns of the islands in the estuary. More than 80 breaches were made in the dikes, and some 150,000 hectares were flooded with seawater. Approximately 1,800 persons drowned, 100,000 were evacuated, and damage reached enormous proportions. The storm could easily have been even more catastrophic than it was. A strategic dike along the north bank of the Rhine–Maas channel called the Nieuwe Waterweg, protecting the densely settled heartland of Holland to the north, held—barely. Had it collapsed, the homeland of three million people would have been inundated and many more persons drowned.

To prevent such an occurrence in the future, the government approved the Delta Project (fig. 2.16). Four large new sea dikes closed off most of the mouths of the Rhine–Maas–Schelde estuary, with a freshwater lake on the landward side. The Nieuwe Waterweg remained open so as not to disrupt Rhine River shipping, but elaborate new water-diversion systems and storm-surge barriers directed the flow of

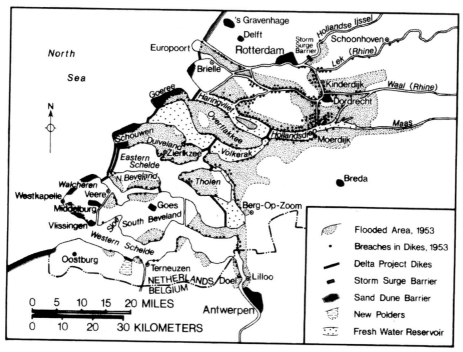

Figure 2.16. The Delta Project was designed to protect the southern Dutch coast and prevent another catastrophic flood like the one in 1953. *Sources:* Wagret 1968; van Veen 1962.

the Rhine and Maas into the adjacent lake in case a storm tide backs up the river as it did in 1953. The lake can absorb the river flow for several days without spilling over its dikes, and the excess water can then escape through sluices to the sea when the storm subsides. The western Schelde estuary also remains open since it serves the major Belgian port of Antwerp, but dikes along the estuary shore were raised and strengthened. Little land reclamation occurred in the Delta Project, only about 16,200 hectares, for the goal was preservation rather than expansion.

More than any other part of Europe, the Netherlands has been human-made. Under the circumstances, the Dutch saying seems appropriate: "God made the world, but the Dutch made Holland." Without the effort of the inhabitants, the seacoast would lie far to the interior, and some of Europe's richest farmland and largest cities would be underwater.

HUMAN MODIFICATION OF THE ATMOSPHERE

Europeans have significantly altered the atmosphere, both on a local scale and more broadly. Turning first to local-scale impacts, Europeans live preponderantly in cities, each of which, in some measure, suffers from air pollution and experiences altered temperatures attributable to humans.

London's climate has been studied for centuries, and we know a great deal about the human-induced changes there. As early as 1661, John Evelyn wrote in reference to London that "the weary traveler, at many miles distance, sooner smells, than sees the city." When the coal smoke poured through myriad chimneys, "London resembles the face rather of Mount Etna, the Court of Vulcan, Stromboli, or the suburbs of hell than an assembly of rational creatures." On October 15, 1880, the *New York Times* concluded that "the fate of London is obvious and inevitable. It will be smothered in its poisonous and sooty fogs, while New York, which burns anthracite coal and never indulges in mixed fogs, will become the chief city of the earth." Some of the city's air pollution problems have abated in the face of new technologies and economic shifts, so in recent times attention has turned to London's **heat island**—the consistently higher temperatures found over the built-up portion of the city as opposed to the surrounding rural greenbelt. Minimum nighttime temperatures are at times 7°C higher over the central portion of London than in the greenbelt, and daytime maxima are also higher. The heat island results from the retention of heat by paved streets and buildings; the inability of heat radiation from surfaces to penetrate the pollution haze that hangs over the city; and the heat produced locally by fuel combustion in vehicles, factories, and homes.

Human activity also influences rainfall and humidity characteristics of the London area. More thunderstorms occur over the city, more precipitation, and a distinctly higher absolute humidity than in adjacent rural areas. The causes include greater thermal convection resulting from more surface heating and heightened levels of microscopic particulate matter associated with air pollution. Drops of condensation are built around such nuclei. A decrease in coal burning has lessened the degree of air pollution in London since about 1960, but the heat island persists. This same

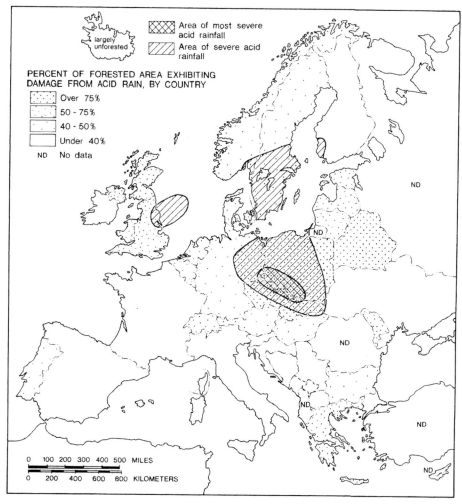

Figure 2.17.   Percentage of forest area damaged or dead by the late 1990s. Acid precipitation is a significant contributor to forest disease. Subnational data are shown only for Germany. *Source: Statistical Yearbook 1999 for Foreign Countries* (Stuttgart: Metzler-Poeschel), and various national statistical yearbooks.

effect can be detected in many other areas of Europe. In fact, every city has a heat island, and significant air pollution remains a problem in many urban areas.

At a larger geographic scale, the corridor of worst air pollution lies in the humid continental climate zone, along the southern margins of the North European Plain, and in the Bohemian Basin, from eastern Germany and Czechia into Poland. This corridor, not coincidentally, also has the worst concentration of **acid precipitation**, more commonly referred to as acid rain (fig. 2.17). Acid rain has a higher level of acidity because of a chemical reaction between water in the atmosphere and industrial pollutants. Its most dramatic impact is on forests (discussed below), but acid rain can also diminish soil fertility, poison fish, and damage a wide range of plants.

Also found on a wide scale is a pan-European warming of climate—a regional reflection of global climate change. According to the European Environment Agency (EEA), the global mean temperature has increased by 0.8°C since the mid-nineteenth century, and by slightly more than that in Europe itself. Moreover, warming is accelerating. Eleven of the 12 years between 1995 and 2006 rank among the 12 warmest in Europe since records have been kept (1850), and the decade from 2002 to 2011 was the warmest on record. The EEA concludes, along with virtually all of the environmental agencies and climate research institutes in the world, that human activity—particularly the release of greenhouse gases such as CO_2—is responsible for this warming.

Reflecting the warming trend, extreme weather events are becoming more common; 2012 was the wettest year on record for the United Kingdom since record keeping began, resulting in significant flooding. The following year, devastating floods struck parts of central Europe. Atlantic cyclones have taken more northerly tracks, and sirocco-type winds off the Sahara have increased in frequency and duration. Melting glaciers also attest to the warming climate. Alpine glaciers have lost a third to a half or their ice mass in the twentieth century. The Aletsch glacier in Switzerland retreated almost two kilometers and lost around 100 meters of thickness in the 1900s. In contrast, the Icelandic and Kjølen glaciers have grown since 1950, but this growth is not inconsistent with climatic warming, since a hotter world is also wetter in places—providing some northern glaciers more snow while still not increasing temperatures to the melting point.

At lower latitudes, where Alpine glaciers are found, snowfall has decreased markedly since the 1970s, not just in the Alps but throughout the temperate zone in Europe. The glaciers of the Caucasus have also retreated. Climate change entails a variety of impacts on the habitats of plants and animals, as well as on human activities. The EEA predicts that the ecosystems in Europe especially threatened by warming are mountain zones (due to the melting of glaciers and lower snowpack) and coastal zones, particularly coastal wetlands (largely due to sea level rise). Species are forced to adapt or migrate. Some climatologists, for example, predict that climate change will likely raise the elevation of reliable snow conditions in Switzerland from its current 1,200 meters to 1,800 meters, which would make 56% of the country's famed ski areas unavailable for skiing during the winter. Sea level rise driven by melting ice sheets and glaciers also threatens low-lying parts of the Netherlands and Belgium and the Po River delta region of Italy, as well as Venice.

HUMAN IMPACTS ON FORESTS

We sometimes think of massive human alteration of the environment as a product of the industrial age, but the destruction of the Mediterranean evergreen forest goes back millennia—and is virtually complete. Alteration began in prehistoric times; the initial effect was probably to produce a parkland-like landscape in which live oaks were scattered in a grassland. Stretches of this sort of vegetation can still be seen in Extremadura, on the Meseta of southwestern Spain.

Figure 2.18.   Deforested, rocky landscape on the Aegean island of Patmos. Thousands of years of grazing, accidental fires, and the need for lumber have left this Greek hillside denuded of forest, with much exposed rock. Tall stone fences have been built to separate adjacent herds of goats and sheep. Most of the Greek islands were once much more forested than they are today. Photo by T. G. J.-B., 1971.

Large-scale decimation of the Mediterranean forest (fig. 2.9) was well under way by Homer's time, some 3,000 years ago. He wrote of ongoing forest removal, both accidental and purposeful. In the rainless summers, "fierce fire rages through the glens on some parched mountainside, and the deep forest burns. The wind driving it whirls the flames in every direction." Shipbuilding also took a heavy toll, including the "thousand" ships launched for the sake of fair Helen of Troy. Timber also provided charcoal for smelting, particularly after the use of iron replaced bronze. The construction of buildings, including temples and palaces, demanded still more lumber, until finally a shortage of wood forced acceptance of stone as the primary Mediterranean building material. Considerable damage had already occurred by the 400s BCE, prompting the classical Greek writer Plato to compare deforested, eroded Attiki to "the skeleton of a sick man, all the fat and soft earth have been wasted away, leaving only the bare framework of the land" (fig. 2.18).

People, then, using both fire and ax, assaulted the Mediterranean woodlands in ancient times and continued the destruction for many centuries. Unfortunately, the forest proved unable to reestablish itself after having been cleared, for two major reasons. First, most of the Mediterranean open forest occupied steep slopes, for mountainous terrain dominates southern Europe. With the trees removed from the slopes, the soil washed away with the winter rains, stripping the mountains to bare rocky skeletons unfit for reforestation. The second retarding factor in woodland regeneration was the lowly goat, a domestic animal of great importance to most Mediterranean rural people. Quite at home in the rugged terrain, the goat devours the tender young shoots of trees newly broken through the soil. Still, much timber survived in the classical period, as is indicated by the writings of numerous scholars of the time. Destruction continued in postclassical times. Venetian and Genovese merchant fleets and Byzantine, Spanish, and Portuguese imperial navies made the same demands on the forests as had their Greek and Roman predecessors. The craftsmen of Firenze (Florence), Toledo, and Byzantium (modern Istanbul) needed charcoal, as had their classical forerunners, and the ever-present herdsmen and farmers continued to regard the woodland as an enemy to be conquered.

Expanses of bare rock devoid of vegetation today represent the most extreme result of human activity in the Mediterranean (fig. 2.18). More common, however, are regions covered with thickets of evergreen shrub growth a meter or more in height. Such thickets served as hiding places for the French underground in World War II. Some limited **afforestation** (the replanting of forests) has been accomplished in the Mediterranean, but often with exotics such as Australian eucalypts, now especially widespread in Portugal. Given that scientists have identified the Mediterranean zone as one of the ecosystems most threatened by climate change, it is likely that the nature of forests will continue to change dramatically in the future as current flora struggle to adapt to warmer, dryer conditions.

Significant deforestation in the deciduous broadleaf forest zone (fig. 2.9) began somewhat later than in the Mediterranean and has been less all-encompassing (fig. 2.19). Nonetheless, the forests of northwestern and central Europe are pale reflections of their former selves. Germanic peoples began clearing significant areas for agricultural use about 500 CE. Charcoal burners also exacted a toll on the Atlantic woodlands, as in the Belgian province of Brabant, where in the place of the once great Forest of Carbonnière (charcoal makers), an unwooded plain meets the eye today. This devastation by farmers and burners continued unabated into the 1300s, when pestilence and warfare greatly reduced the human population. The Hundred Years' War between France and England proved so destructive of human life in the Basin of Aquitaine that it gave rise to the local folk saying that "the forests returned to France with the English."

Following this respite, the broadleaf deciduous forests were subjected to a renewed attack by ax wielders. Population decline proved to be temporary, and a final phase in the clearing occurred in the 1500s and 1600s. To the renewed demands of an expanding farm population were added the needs of English, French, and Dutch shipbuilders, as well as other artisans. By 1550 England suffered from acute timber shortages, and France reached the same predicament a century later. Both came to rely on their American colonies to supply much-needed lumber. Considerable forests remained in Ireland during the late 1500s, for contemporary documents mention the difficulty of conducting military campaigns against Irish rebels in their woodland refuges. It seems likely that the English felled many Irish woods to destroy these hideouts. Profit-hungry landlords completed the process of deforestation in Ireland in the 1600s, selling the timber abroad. By the year 1700, woodlands

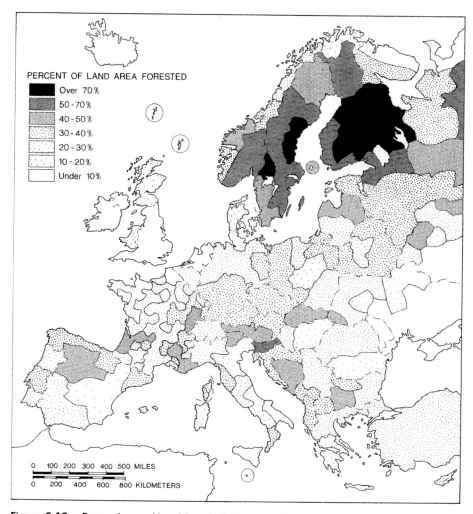

Figure 2.19. Percentage of land forested. Deforestation is greatest in the west and south.

had vanished from the Irish scene, and oak virtually disappeared from the pollen record after that time. In England, similarly deforested, the word *wold* (as in Cotswold), which originally meant "forest," came to mean instead "an upland area of open country."

So catastrophic was the assault on the woodland that in several countries lying within the broadleaf deciduous forest zone, less than 10% of the land bears a forest cover today, and much of this meager woodland results from twentieth-century afforestation. Hill districts of the British Isles have been the scene of some of the most impressive afforestation projects, especially the Scottish Highlands and islands. However, trees planted in these projects tend to be commercially valuable exotics such as Douglas fir and Sitka spruce. The soil must be regularly limed, often by helicopter drop, to counteract natural acidity so that the desired exotic trees will survive.

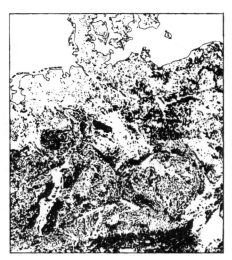

Figure 2.20. The retreat of woodland in central Europe, 900–1900 CE. *Source:* Otto Schlüter, as reproduced in Darby 1956.

Only scattered patches of forest containing native Atlantic trees remain. Some owe their existence to royal protection, as for example England's Sherwood Forest. In places, rough terrain, unattractive to farmers, sheltered a remnant of woods. The tiny vestiges of Atlantic woodland are today carefully tended, with heavy penalties for unauthorized cutting. Often these tidy groves resemble parks more than natural woodlands, particularly to the American eye. Western Europeans value remnant forests as recreational areas and have laid out a splendid network of hiking trails; one rarely finds a forest area not open to the public.

While less catastrophically influenced by human activity, the mixed deciduous/coniferous forest of central Europe (fig. 2.9) has also been greatly altered. Germanic farmers engaged in a great era of forest clearance during the Middle Ages to create new farming colonies (fig. 2.20). Often, evidence of the initial clearing survives in the present-day village and town names. In Germany, the common suffixes *-rod*, *-rot*, *-reuth*, and the like, as in Wernigerode, Heiligenroth, and Bayreuth, are all related to the modern German verb *roden*, which means "to root out," or "to clear." The German suffix or prefix *brand* indicates that the original clearing was accomplished by burning, for it derives from a Germanic root word meaning "fire."

Germanic forest removal typically began with small clearings. As population grew, the settlers worked communally to push the perimeter of farmland outward at the expense of the forest, until finally the clearings of adjacent villages joined, sometimes leaving small isolated groves of trees at points farthest from the settlements (fig. 2.21). From the Germans, extensive clearance of the Central European forests spread east to the Slavs, who had already made modest inroads before 500 CE. Slavic forest removal is indicated by place names containing the word elements *kop*, *lazy*, and *paseky*, all of which specifically indicate "clearing."

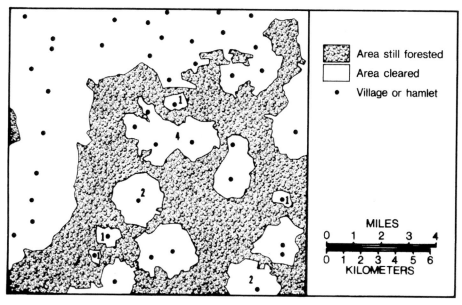

Figure 2.21. Stages of forest clearance in the southeastern outskirts of Munich, Germany, showing typical Teutonic clearance at almost every stage curiously preserved to the modern day. The smaller clearings (#1) are suggestive of the early stage, while those marked #2, almost perfectly circular, reflect a somewhat later stage. #3 (between the two areas shown as cleared near the bottom of the map, just to the left of center) indicates the earliest phase of coalescence of adjacent clearings, whereas #4 illustrates more mature coalescence. To the north and west, more complete clearing occurred. *Source:* Jean Brunhes, *Human Geography* (Chicago: Rand McNally, 1920), 81.

A conservation movement arose in time to rescue substantial wooded areas in central Europe. As in the west, the nobility, anxious to preserve recreational hunting grounds, took the lead. An example, rare because it stands in the middle of a great city, is Berlin's Tiergarten, literally "animal garden," long the royal hunting preserve of the Hohenzollern family. It survived until the winter of 1945–1946, when desperate inhabitants of the destroyed capital cut the trees for firewood. The Tiergarten has since been replanted and offers Berliners and tourists a peaceful respite from the urban bustle that surrounds it on all sides.

Much of the woodland standing in central Europe today consists of artificially planted tree farms. The science of forestry arose in eastern Germany in the late 1700s, but the result was single-species commercial forests. When traveling in Germany, it is common to see tree stands that have been planted in orderly rows, and the North American visitor is often struck by the lack of debris on the forest floor. This landscape reflects an approach to trees as cultivatable crops, particularly in the western part of Germany. Vast stands of trees of a single species have not fared well over the long term, however. Since the 1980s, efforts to introduce sustainable forestry practices have resulted in more mixed-species forests and unevenly aged stands, as scientists became aware that monocultural woodlands lack biodiversity and are not ecologically rich.

Figure 2.22.   Logs floating to Joensuu, Finland, in the taiga region of the Fenno-Scandian shield. The great needle-leaf evergreen forests of the European north provide the basis for a large-scale wood-processing industry, dealing in lumber and pulp. Photo by T. G. J.-B., 1985.

The fate of the remnant woodlands of Europe, whether natural or artificial, has also been affected by acid precipitation. Around 1975, forestry experts began to notice tree damage, especially in needle-leaf species. Then in the 1980s, as if some critical threshold had been crossed, the percentage of trees exhibiting damage increased rapidly. In western Germany, only 8% of the forest showed visible damage in 1982; by 1984 that figure rose to 50%. In Switzerland's forest, damage rose from 17% in 1984 to 40% by 1988 and 65% by 1998 (fig. 2.17). In Czechia, well over two-thirds of the woodland exhibited damage by 1988, a proportion that rose to 96% a decade later. Controls on sulfur emissions have helped to alleviate the problem over the last two decades, but acid rain continues to have a deleterious impact on forest health in parts of Europe.

Deforestation in the taiga region (fig. 2.9) has been less severe. Much of the land retains a forest cover, as in Finland, which is 73% wooded (fig. 2.19). The taiga represents the last substantial forest in Europe and is the focus of a large lumbering and paper-pulp industry (fig. 2.22). As a result, most of the taiga is no longer a natural forest but instead is planted and regularly harvested. Nor does this represent a new industry. For centuries the northern lands have supplied lumber for the European core countries.

Before leaving the subject of human impacts on vegetation, it is worth nothing that those areas of Europe dominated by heaths and moors have also come under human attack. As we have seen, afforestation projects are partly responsible; one can still see the rock fences that once enclosed Scottish sheep pastures zigzagging through new forests of spruce and fir. In other cases, especially in Denmark, heath has been converted to agricultural use, especially improved pastures for dairy cattle (fig. 2.23). In other words, people first removed the forests in ancient times to produce rough

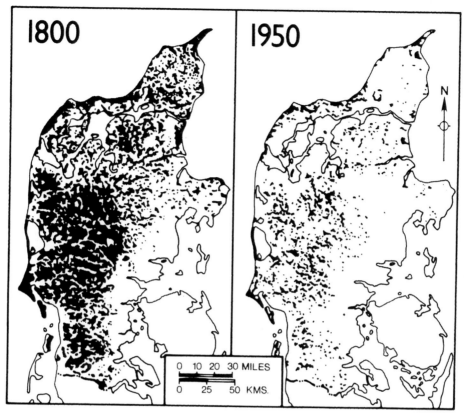

Figure 2.23. Reduction of heath in the Jylland Peninsula of Denmark, 1800–1950. The land was reclaimed for agricultural use. *Source:* Thorpe 1957, 88.

pasture of heath, and then much later they destroyed the heath to obtain a better grassland.

The human impact on soils has been great. Deep plowing mixes soil layers—called horizons—and irrigation can cause surface deposits of salt or other sediments to accumulate. Soil erosion has also occurred widely, especially in the dry-summered Mediterranean where steep slopes and limited vegetative cover can leave soils vulnerable. In Spain, about half of all farmland in some provinces is severely eroded, prompting land abandonment in places. Some Spanish fields have lost up to a meter of soil through erosion. Clearly, the concept of a natural ecosystem is largely alien to Europe.

Green Europe

The history of human–environment alteration notwithstanding, over the past few decades Europe has moved to the forefront of global efforts to address environmental issues. Europe's efforts in this regard have been facilitated by its high level of socioeconomic development and by social and political pressures stemming from the impacts of environmental degradation on the lives of Europeans. The term "Green Europe" is often used to highlight the region's environmental activism.

The EU has emerged as a particularly significant supranational player in the environmental governance arena. Climate change provides a case in point. In 2007 the European Commission set an ambitious 20–20–20 target for reducing carbon emissions: a 20% reduction in carbon dioxide emissions and a 20% share of the region's energy usage to come from renewable sources by the year 2020. The EU also created the world's largest carbon emissions cap-and-trade scheme, creating a market for companies to trade carbon offsets to emitters exceeding allotted carbon-output levels.

To curb biodiversity loss and protect ecosystem services, the EU established Natura 2000, a network of protected areas across the region. Launched in 1992, Natura 2000 now encompasses some 18% of the European landmass and nearly 4% of its seas. Extensive taxes on energy, transportation, and pollution help cover the costs for environmental programs, with most EU member states generating revenue from environmental taxes equivalent to between 2 and 3% of GDP. EU environmental expenditures largely go toward waste and wastewater management, and the protection of the atmosphere.

At the national scale, many European states are pursuing aggressive environmental agendas. Germany, which is at the forefront of Green Europe, leads the world in solar power generation and ranks second in wind energy—falling behind the much larger United States only a few years ago. The Netherlands is investing heavily in the infrastructure necessary for electric plug-in vehicles and is promoting the use of electric cars through free parking, tax breaks, and special leases for new owners. Recycling is also common, particularly in northern and western Europe, with Belgium, Denmark, and the Netherlands leading the way.

Iceland serves as a particularly notable example of clean energy production. Renewable geothermal sources provide a large majority of the country's power and all its electricity needs. In fact, the population of 300,000 uses just 17% of the electricity generated by geothermal technologies. This cheap energy source could potentially supply a sizable chunk of the European electrical grid, but first the region must find an efficient way to transport the energy 1,500 kilometers to mainland Europe.

On a smaller geographic scale, one German town has emerged as a global model for renewable energy and self-sufficiency. Feldheim, a village some 60 kilometers southwest of Berlin, started its own energy grid and generates all its electricity and heating needs through local, renewable sources. Wind turbines and a biogas plant were installed over the last decade. Feldheim now attracts visitors from all over the world seeking to replicate its green efforts.

Despite such successes, Green Europe has its critics, and some claim it is a myth. Critics point to the high energy costs that have accompanied green energy initiatives (solar- and wind-powered energy alternatives still need substantial tariffs and subsidies to be commercially competitive), and some people claim that the region's move toward renewable energy is undermining economic vitality. Many in the latter camp are promoting hydraulic fracking to extract natural gas—a practice that is expanding despite its potentially deleterious environmental consequences. Those who argue that

Green Europe is a myth point to the expansion in fracking as well as the impacts of the economic downturn that began in 2009 on the Green agenda. In recent years, cash-strapped states have cut back renewable energy investment, and coal is being reintroduced as a cheaper alternative to costly natural gas and renewables. In Spain, for example, environmental advances associated with the closure of one of the country's most polluting industrial coal plants in 2011 were offset by a growth in coal use by 15% between 2011 and 2012 alone.

Despite these setbacks, environmental problems in the European west tend to be less severe than in eastern Europe, where controlling environmental pollution was not a priority during the communist era, and where economic circumstances have worked against aggressive environmental remediation since then. Coal still provides nearly 90% of Poland's energy supply. The area around Katowice, an industrial town in southern Poland's brown-coal belt, is known as the "Black Triangle" because of the pollution problems there (fig. 2.24). In sprawling eastern European cities—among them Prague, Bucharest, and Warsaw—poor infrastructure and weak institutional governance are responsible for waste management problems and, in places, leaky sewage systems.

The strict environmental mandates that come with EU membership are beginning to help. Countries must commit to an environmental agenda of some 200 provisions covering water and air quality, waste management, nature protection, industrial pollution, chemicals and genetically modified organisms, and noise and forestry.

Figure 2.24. Soviet-era coal-burning power plant in southwest Poland. Efforts are being made to upgrade these types of power plants, which have been a source of considerable environmental pollution. Photo by A. B. M., 1997.

Compliance with these demands requires significant investment, and progress is carefully monitored. The European Commission has been active in penalizing member states that fail to meet or fall below environmental benchmarks.

Continuing progress on the environmental front is important given Europe's high population densities, global impact, and fragile ecosystems. Europe's physical environment has been conducive to the development of large concentrations of people (the subject of the next chapter) and great agricultural and industrial wealth (Chapters 7–9). Nurturing that environment is a challenge and an imperative for the European future.

Sources and Suggested Readings

Alexander, D. 1984. The Reclamation of Val-Di-Chiana (Tuscany). *Annals of the Association of American Geographers* 74 (4): 527–50.

Allen, H. D. 2001. *Mediterranean Ecogeography*. New York: Prentice Hall.

Behre, K. 2005. Meeresspiegelbewegungen, Landverluste und Landgewinnungen an der Nordsee. *Siedlungsforschung* 23:19–46.

Bennett, C. F. 1975. Human Influences on the Ecosystems of Europe and the Mediterranean. In *Man and Earth's Ecosystems: An Introduction to the Geography of Human Modification of the Earth*, ed. C. F. Bennett, 121–44. New York: Wiley.

Berz, G. 2006. Globaler Klimawandel: Werden Die Alpen Zum Katastrophengebiet? *Jahrbuch des Vereins zum Schutz der Bergwelt* 71:51–60.

Brázdil, R., P. Dobrovolný, J. Luterbacher, A. Moberg, C. Pfister, D. Wheeler, and E. Zorita. 2010. European Climate of the Past 500 Years: New Challenges for Historical Climatology. *Climatic Change* 101 (1–2): 7–40.

Cerdan, O., G. Govers, Y. Le Bissonnais, K. Van Oost, J. Poesen, N. Saby, A. Gobin, A. Vacca, J. Quinton, K. Auerswald, A. Klik, F. J. P. M. Kwaad, D. Raclot, I. Ionita, J. Rejman, S. Rousseva, T. Muxart, M. J. Roxo, and T. Dostal. 2010. Rates and Spatial Variations of Soil Erosion in Europe: A Study Based on Erosion Plot Data. *Geomorphology* 122 (1–2): 167–77.

Chandler, T. J. 1965. *The Climate of London*. London: Hutchinson.

Cioc, M. 2002. *The Rhine: An Eco-Biography, 1815–2000*, Weyerhaeuser Environmental Book. Seattle: University of Washington Press.

Darby, H. C. 1956. The Clearing of the Woodland in Europe. In *Man's Role in Changing the Face of the Earth*, ed. W. L. J. Thomas, 183–216. Chicago: Published for the Wenner-Gren Foundation for Anthropological Research and the National Science Foundation by the University of Chicago Press.

———. 1968. *The Draining of the Fens*. 2nd ed. Cambridge University Press Library Editions. London: Cambridge University Press.

de Moel, H., J. C. J. H. Aerts, and E. Koomen. 2010. Development of Flood Exposure in the Netherlands during the 20th and 21st Century. *Global Environmental Change* 21 (2): 620–27.

Embleton, C. 1984. *Geomorphology of Europe*. New York: Wiley.

Endlicher, W., and N. Lanfer. 2003. Meso- and Micro-Climatic Aspects of Berlin's Urban Climate. *Erde* 134 (3): 277–93.

European Environment Agency (EEA). 2012. Climate Change, Impacts, and Vulnerability in Europe 2012. Available at http://www.eea.europa.eu/publications/climate-impacts-and-vulnerability-2012.

Goudie, A. 1990. *The Landforms of England and Wales*. Oxford: Basil Blackwell.

Grove, J., and M. Grubb. 2000. *Climate Change and European Leadership: A Sustainable Role for Europe.* Boston: Kluwer Academic.

Heine, K., and H. P. Niller. 2003. Human and Climate Impacts on the Holocene Landscape Development in Southern Germany. *Geographia Polonica* 76 (2): 109–22.

Hulme, M., and E. Barrow. 1997. *Climates of the British Isles: Present, Past, and Future.* London: Routledge.

Ives, J. D. 1991. Landscape Change and Human Response during a Thousand Years of Climatic Fluctuations and Volcanism: Skaftafell, Southeast Iceland. *Pireneos* 137:5–50.

Jalas, J. 1999. *Atlas Florae Europaeae: Distribution of Vascular Plants in Europe.* Helsinki: Committee for Mapping the Flora of Europe.

Jeftic, L., J. D. Milliman, and G. Sestini, eds. 1992. *Climatic Change and the Mediterranean.* New York: Routledge.

Jones, A., L. Montanarella, R. Jones, and E. Akça. 2005. *Soil Atlas of Europe.* Luxembourg: Office for Official Publications of the European Communities.

Jordan, A. J., and C. Adelle, eds. 2012. *Environmental Policy in the European Union: Contexts, Actors and Policy Dynamics.* London: Earthscan.

Koster, E. A., ed. 2005. *The Physical Geography of Western Europe.* Oxford Regional Environments Series. Oxford: Oxford University Press.

Lambert, A. M. 1985. *The Making of the Dutch Landscape: An Historical Geography of the Netherlands.* 2nd ed. London: Academic Press.

Peterson, D. J. 1993. *Troubled Lands: The Legacy of Soviet Environmental Destruction,* A RAND Research Study. Boulder, CO: Westview Press.

Pryde, P. R., ed. 1995. *Environmental Resources and Constraints in the Former Soviet Republics.* Boulder, CO: Westview Press.

Raisz, E. 2000. Physiography of Europe. In *Goode's World Atlas,* eds. J. C. Hudson and E. B. Espenshade, 150–51. Skokie, IL: Rand McNally.

Roth, D., and J. Warner. 2007. Flood Risk, Uncertainty and Changing River Protection Policy in the Netherlands: The Case of "Calamity Polders." *Tijdschrift voor Economische en Sociale Geografie* 98 (4): 519–25.

Ryan, W. B. F., and W. C. Pitman. 2000. *Noah's Flood: The New Scientific Discoveries about the Event That Changed History.* 1st ed. New York: Simon & Schuster.

Scott, J. C. 1998. *Seeing Like a State: How Certain Schemes to Improve the Human Condition Have Failed,* 11–51. New Haven, CT: Yale University Press.

Seager, R. 2006. The Source of Europe's Mild Climate. *American Scientist* 94:334–41.

Sigurdson, H., et al. 1985. The Eruption of Vesuvius in A.D. 79. *National Geographic Research* 1:332–87.

Svenning, J., and F. Skov. 2005. The Relative Roles of Environmental and History as Controls of Tree Species Composition and Richness in Europe. *Journal of Biogeography* 32 (6): 1019–33.

Thorpe, H. 1957. A Special Case of Heath Reclamation in the Alheden District of Jutland, 1700–1955. *Transactions and Papers (Institute of British Geographers)* (23): 87–121.

Tockner, K., C. T. Robinson, and U. Uehlinger, eds. 2009. *Rivers of Europe.* London: Elsevier.

van Veen, J. 1962. *Dredge, Drain, Reclaim: The Art of a Nation.* 5th ed. The Hague: Nijhoff.

Wagret, P. 1968. *Polderlands.* Translated by M. Sparks. London: Methuen.

Wainwright, J., and J. B. Thornes. 2004. *Environmental Issues in the Mediterranean: Processes and Perspectives from the Past and Present.* Routledge Studies in Physical Geography and Environment. London: Routledge.

Wallén, C. C. 1970. *Climates of Northern and Western Europe.* Amsterdam: Elsevier.

———. 1977. *Climates of Central and Southern Europe.* Amsterdam: Elsevier.

Zwingle, E. 2006. Meltdown: The Alps under Pressure. *National Geographic* 209 (2): 96–115.

CHAPTER 3

Demography

Hominids began arriving in Europe from Africa as much as a million or more years ago. By 130,000 years ago, a distinctive hominid known as **Neanderthal** had taken up residence throughout much of the region. About 30,000–40,000 years ago, the Neanderthal faced another Homo species arriving from Africa: **Homo sapiens**. For reasons that continue to be debated, the Neanderthals disappeared by c. 24,000 years ago, leaving Homo sapiens as the sole hominid in Europe. With northern Europe still under ice produced by the most recent glacial advance (known in Europe as Würm and in North America as Wisconsin), these early Stone Age peoples settled in the southern and central parts of Europe. The paintings they left behind on the walls of caves in southern France and Spain provide the earliest evidence of the artistic creativity of modern humans in Europe.

After the onset of the current interglacial period (known as the **Holocene**) a little over 10,000 years ago, Europe saw a gradual expansion of its human population, the movement of people into northern Europe, and the arrival of new peoples from the east and south. Between 8,000 and 5,000 years ago, agricultural communities started to develop—setting the stage for expanding populations in different parts of Europe and the rise of the classical civilizations of the Mediterranean. We will look at some of the cultural, social, and environmental legacies of these developments later in the book, but we begin our exploration of Europe's human geography by examining the region's basic demographic characteristics and the forces that produced them. We make reference to certain qualitative influences on Europe's demography (e.g., health, social circumstances), but central consideration of such variables will be deferred until later in the book (especially Chapter 12).

Population Distribution and Density

Europe plays host to one of the greatest concentrations of people in the world. Some 710 million people live in Europe (including Eurorussia, Ukraine, Moldova, and Belarus)—more than any "continent" other than Asia and Africa. If Eurorussia,

Ukraine, Belarus, and Moldova are subtracted, the remaining total, 540 million, is still almost one and three-quarters times the population of the United States.

A number of individual European states have substantial populations. Five have populations in excess of 50 million, including Germany, 82; France, 64; the United Kingdom, 63; and Italy, 61. Eleven other European countries have at least 10 million inhabitants. Eurorussia, if separate, would form the 12th most populous country in the world.

Even more remarkable than absolute numbers is the density of the European population. The 540 million people in Europe west of Eurorussia, Ukraine, Belarus, Moldova, and the Caucasus are crammed into just under 3.5% of the world's land area, giving the European core a population density of 116 people per square kilometer. This is one of the highest population densities on earth. At the global scale it is rivaled only by parts of South and East Asia and a limited area along the eastern seaboard of the United States.

The distribution and density of Europe's population has changed dramatically over the last two millennia. At the beginning of the Christian Era, about 33 million people lived in Europe, broadly defined, and most were concentrated in southern Europe. The disruptions associated with the collapse of the Roman Empire caused the total population to fall to only 18 million by the year 600. The Medieval Age witnessed significant population growth, to about 70 million by 1340, as well as the development of much higher densities in areas favorable for human settlement north of the Alps and Pyrenees. The ravages of the Black Death led to another population decline in the fourteenth century, but there was a rapid rebound after about 1450. The European population reached 100 million by 1650, 200 million by shortly after 1800, 400 million by about 1900, and 600 million by 1960.

Despite its expanding population, Europe's share of the world's population has declined dramatically over the last 100 years. At the beginning of the twentieth century, more than 20% of the world's people lived in Europe; that figure has now fallen to just over 10%. This decline shows that Europe's population growth has fallen far below many other parts of the world during the course of the last 100 years.

As for the distribution of people within Europe, if everyone presently living west of the Urals and north of the Mediterranean were evenly distributed across the countryside, each square kilometer would contain about 75 persons. But this figure conceals the fact that population density varies greatly from one part of Europe to another, ranging from the totally uninhabited glaciers of interior Iceland to more than 500 per square kilometer in some districts. Among independent states, densities range from Iceland's three persons per square kilometer to Malta's 1,262 and Monaco's 17,703.

One way to gain an understanding of population distribution is to map areas of continuous and discontinuous settlement, the former including all areas in which habitations and transport routes form a dense network (fig. 3.1). Defined in this manner, Europe stands somewhat apart, bounded by sparsely settled deserts and subarctic areas, which serve to separate it from the peoples of Sub-Saharan Africa and those of South and East Asia.

Measured and mapped in another way, as the number of persons per square kilometer, a core–periphery pattern can be discerned (fig. 3.2). Most densely populated

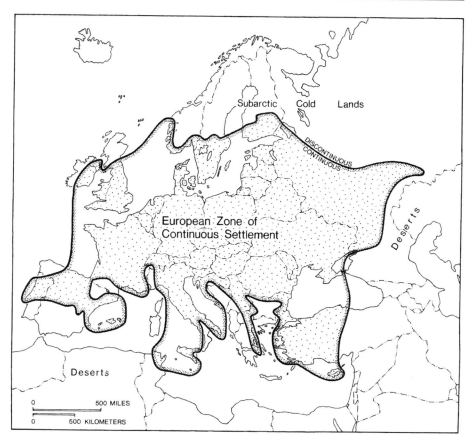

Figure 3.1.   Europe forms one of the major clusters of "continuous" settlement in the world. "Continuous settlement" means that all habitations lie no more than five kilometers from other habitations in at least six different directions and that roads/railroads lie no farther than 16 to 32 kilometers away in at least three directions. In other words, the term describes a densely inhabited land, served by a transport network. *Sources:* Adapted from Kirk H. Stone, 1993, personal communication and Stone, "The World's Primary Settlement Regions," *GeoJournal* 2 (3) (1978): 196.

districts—those having 200 or more persons per square kilometer—lie far from the edges, whereas regions of sparse settlement, with fewer than 25 or 50 persons per square kilometer, usually appear around the perimeter, forming the transition into the deserts and boreal forests that border Europe.

What explains the variable density of the population revealed in figure 3.2? No one factor provides a complete answer, but there is a relatively good correlation between areas of high population density and **arable land**. Put simply, people settled historically where they could produce the food they needed, and the inertia of that settlement pattern is still evident today. Thus, at the continental scale, the areas with the highest population concentrations are generally in the parts of the European plains with good soils and ample rainfall, and in major river basins. Thus, unusually dense settlement can be found across the North European Plain into England. Other

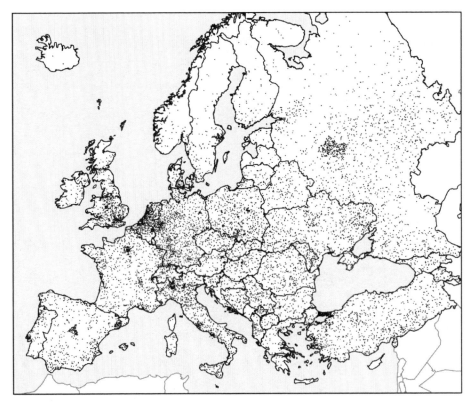

Figure 3.2.   Population density in Europe. A distinct core–periphery pattern is evident. A core area of over 200 persons per square kilometer reaches southeast from the Anglican Plain through the Low Country and Germany to Sicily, forming an English–Rhenish–Italian axis of dense population. Peripheral regions, especially the subarctic north, are far more sparsely settled. *Sources:* ESRI data acquired from Michael Bauer Research GmbH and EuroGraphics.

areas of dense settlement include the river valleys of the Po, Rhone, Ebro, and Tagus. By contrast, European mountain ranges stand out as zones of sparse settlement. Also, settlement is much less dense in colder climates; the northern border of continuous settlement in Scandinavia follows very closely the line between the humid continental and subarctic climate types.

The concentration of particular natural resources of value to humans can affect population distribution as well. It is no surprise that in earlier times, humans concentrated around water sources, at places where game was abundant, or in areas where they had access to a valuable raw material. More recently, a shift in the distribution of England's population occurred in the early phases of the Industrial Revolution as economic opportunities opened up areas with accessible coal deposits in northern England. Since then technological advances have altered the relative advantages of locations as places to live and work. For example, southeast England has recently experienced significant growth at the expense of older industrial areas in the north, as new economic opportunities have developed in the vicinity of London.

Population Growth Rates

A fundamental influence on any region's demographic structure is population growth over time. Population growth is a function of natural increase (the difference between the numbers of births and deaths) and migration. Let's look at how each of these components of growth has played out in Europe over time.

NATURAL INCREASE

The natural increase of a population is the difference between the numbers of births and deaths during a given time period. Throughout the medieval and early modern periods in Europe, the death rate and the birth rate were both high, meaning that the rate of natural increase was low. It was even negative at times. But with improvements in diet and hygiene—most notably the use of soap—people began living longer. As a result, the death rate came down, but the birth rate remained high, leading to a rapid expansion in the size of the population. Then birth rates went through a gradual, persistent fall as well, producing what has come to be known as the **demographic transition** (fig. 3.3). The European population explosion had ended, ushering in a period of slow growth.

Europe's demographic transition occurred at different times in different places. Sustained fertility decline first appeared in France about 1820 (fig. 3.4). Ethnic minorities in France and people in other countries were initially slow to follow the

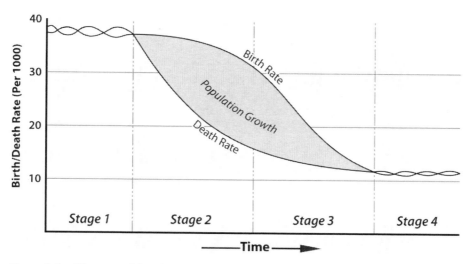

Figure 3.3.   Diagram of the demographic transition. All of Europe was in Stage 1 throughout the Middle Ages and Early Modern period. By the nineteenth century, parts of western Europe started to move into Stage 2, with most of the rest of Europe following by the end of the century—and western Europe beginning to move into Stage 3. By the closing decades of the twentieth century, most of Europe was moving into Stage 4, which is where almost all of Europe lies today.

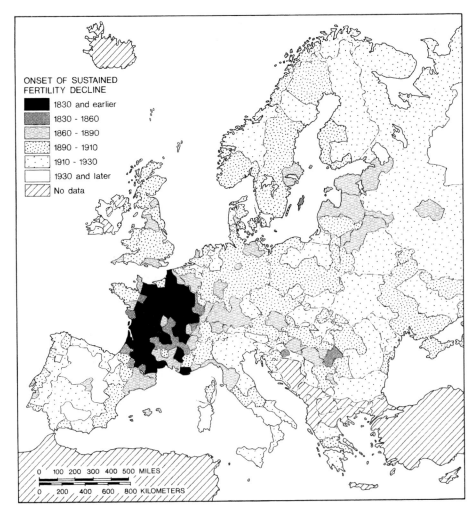

Figure 3.4. Advent of sustained fertility decline in Europe. The French-speaking part of France provided the prototype for diminished fertility. People in other countries were slow to emulate the French, but diffusion to the various peripheries of Europe eventually occurred. Today, all areas have birth rates well below the world average. *Source:* Adapted from Coale and Watkins 1986, 484 et seq.

French example, with the result that France fell behind major neighboring countries' population size. In the 1700s, one of every six Europeans was French, and even as late as 1850, the French outnumbered the Germans, Italians, and British; by 1970 the French had become the smallest of these four nations.

Eventually, sustained fertility decline spread. By 1900 about half of all European provinces had been affected (fig. 3.4), and today birth rates have become remarkably low throughout Europe. Sustained fertility decline came last to the eastern areas of Europe, but a major decline in fertility began there after 1990. In Russia, for example, the annual birth rate fell from 17.2 per thousand inhabitants in 1987 to only 13 in 2012. Czechia's birth rate declined from 11.1 in 1990, at the time of reunification,

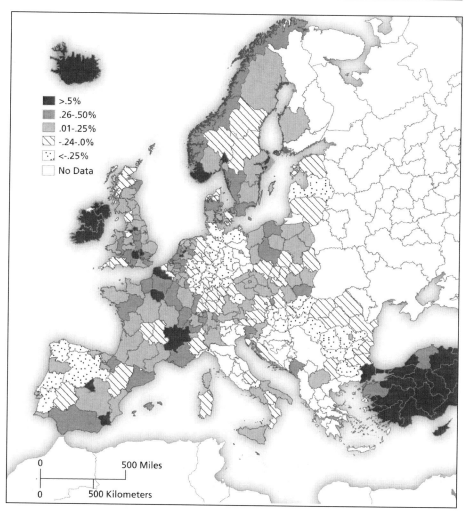

Figure 3.5. Annual natural population change, as a percentage of total population, by province. This rate is achieved by comparing the number of births and deaths in a year, calculating the difference (either + or –), and taking it as a percentage of population. Faint core–periphery and east–west patterns can be detected. Gains or losses through migration are not reflected here. *Source:* Eurostat 2009.

to 5.1 in 1993, though by 2012 the number had rebounded to 10. There are some areas currently experiencing modest positive annual natural population change, such as Iceland, the Arctic fringe, and Ireland (fig. 3.5). The more general picture, though, is one of fertility decline.

A variety of explanations exist for the decline in natural growth rates over the past two centuries. The single most important factor was the growing prosperity and urbanization of the European population, which produced social and economic circumstances that were less conducive to large families. Other factors played a role as well, including the invention of modern contraception. In addition, abortion, first achieved with various folk medicines and later at modern, state-supported clinics, served to depress growth rates. During the Communist period, abortion was particularly common in Eastern Europe. The number of abortions is declining throughout much of that region, but the annual number of abortions still exceeds live births in Russia.

The **total fertility rate** (TFR) of a population is a statistic indicating the number of children born to women of childbearing age. Without immigration, a TFR of 2.1 is needed to keep a population stable over time. In Europe, the TFR has fallen to around 1.6, a startling contrast to Sub-Saharan Africa's 4.7. The TFR in Europe as a whole had fallen to 1.69 as early as 1985 and in western Germany to 1.28. Russia experienced the latest phase of the demographic transition with surprising rapidity; deaths exceeded births by 200,000 there in 1992 and by 800,000 the following year, by which time the TFR had declined to only 1.4, where it remains today. Not one single European country today except Ireland has a TFR as high as 2.1. In fact, Euro-

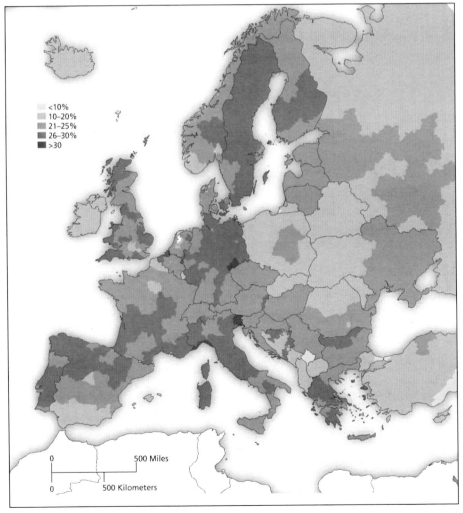

Figure 3.6. Percentage of population aged 60 or older. Europe's population is far older than the world average. *Source:* Eurostat 2011.

pean states account for seven out of the ten lowest fertility rates in the world, including Moldova. Latvia, tied with Taiwan, is the lowest with a TFR of 1.1.

The decline of the European population has made Europe's population among the world's oldest. All but one of the 20 countries in the world having the greatest proportion of people aged 60 or older lie in Europe, led by Italy, Germany, Finland, and Sweden. In many provinces, especially in the EU, people over 60 account for 22% or more of the total population (fig. 3.6). The basic problem is that Europe has a low **potential support ratio** (PSR)—a measure of the number of persons aged 15 to 64 years for every older person aged 65 years or older. In the early 2000s, the global average PSR was 9; in Europe it was 4. Germany, Italy, and Sweden have a PSR of 3.

The PSR challenge can be illustrated graphically by looking at population pyramids (fig. 3.7). Germany, like many other European countries, has an inverted popu-

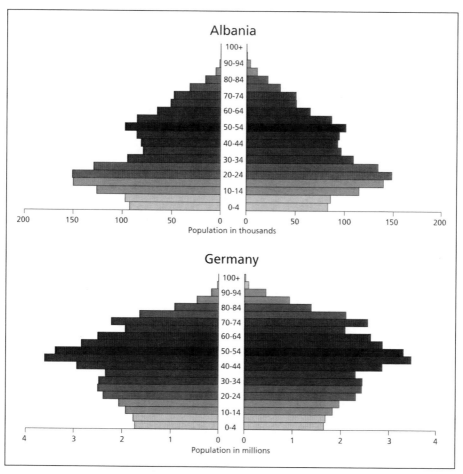

Figure 3.7. Population pyramids for Germany and Albania. The German pyramid is fairly typical for Europe. The bulge representing the greatest number of people of a particular age appears in the late 40s and early 50s. By contrast, the pyramid for Albania shows a bulge at a younger age range—a situation more typical of areas surrounding Europe, but not of Europe itself. *Source:* U.S. Census Bureau.

lation pyramid, with elderly retirees making up a larger segment of the population than younger workers. Albania's more classic looking pyramid, in contrast, is unusual for Europe. Small wonder that terms such as "demographic crisis" are heard in Europe today; these demographic circumstances are placing major strains on health and welfare service (see Chapter 12). In some countries efforts are being made to increase fertility through family-friendly policies. They are having some impact, but the primary offset to fertility decline is migration: the second major component of population growth.

MIGRATION

Over the past few centuries, Europe's population has been influenced by different types of migration. Viewed historically, the principal dynamic at work during the sixteenth to nineteenth centuries was **external migration**. A great many "push" and "pull" factors work to prompt the decision to leave one's home and seek another. From about 1500 to 1950, many millions of Europeans departed for Anglo-America, Central and South America, Australia, New Zealand, South Africa, Israel, Siberia, and Algeria. Iberians began the exodus in the 1500s. Between 1600 and 1880, this tremendous emigration involved mainly northwestern Europeans of Germanic and Celtic background seeking better economic opportunity abroad. After about 1870 the exodus spread to southern and eastern Europe.

Some countries lost substantial parts of their total populations in the process, causing major changes in densities. The island of Ireland provides a good example. In 1841 the census listed more than 8 million Irish, a density of nearly 100 per square kilometer. By the middle of the decade, the Irish population had reached an all-time high of almost 8.5 million. Then came the great famine of the mid-1840s, bringing death to hundreds of thousands, and in its wake a massive and persistent out-migration to Great Britain and overseas. In a five-year span from 1846 to 1851, some 800,000 Irish starved or perished from disease, and another million emigrated to foreign lands. Hardest hit was interior Ireland, where one county lost more than 20% of its population through emigration (fig. 3.8). A century later, a little more than half as many people resided in Ireland as in 1841. By the early twenty-first century, nine times as many people claiming Irish ancestry lived in the United States as remained in Ireland.

Germans, too, departed their native land in enormous numbers, settling mainly in the United States but also in southern Brazil, Canada, and South Africa. Persons of German ancestry constitute the largest national-origin group in the United States, numbering some 43 million in 2010, more than half of the present population of Germany. Sweden and Norway experienced huge proportional losses. Between 20 and 25% of the total population of those two Scandinavian countries emigrated overseas in the nineteenth century.

By the second half of the nineteenth century, another migration dynamic was at work that was to greatly transform the European demographic picture. That was rural-to-urban migration, an **internal migration** process that greatly accelerated in

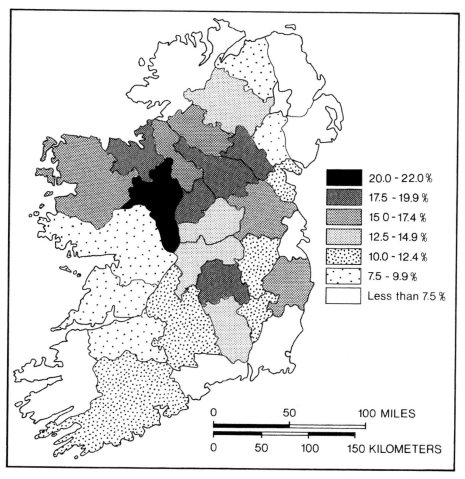

Figure 3.8.   Emigration from Ireland, 1846–1851, as a percentage of the 1841 population. *Source:* After S. H. Cousens, "The Regional Pattern of Emigration During the Great Irish Famine, 1846–51," *Institute of British Geographers, Transactions and Papers* 28 (1960): 121; see also James H. Johnson, "The Distribution of Irish Emigration in the Decade Before the Great Famine," *Irish Geography,* 21(2) (1988): 78–87.

the twentieth century and has not yet fully run its course everywhere. In 1900, the United Kingdom was the only country in Europe in which more than 50% of the population lived in cities. Now all European countries are dominated by urban dwellers. And as cities grew and transportation technology improved, urbanites began building new settlements around cities—giving rise to a wave of suburbanization in the second half of the twentieth century (see Chapter 10).

A disturbing piece of the story of internal European migration over the past 100 years has been forced migration. Most dramatically, in the short span of about 35 years between 1920 and 1950, an astounding 33 million Europeans were forced to leave their homelands without the right of return—violating what Albert Schweitzer called "the most basic of human rights." Dramatic changes in population density and cultural patterns resulted. The first step came in the early 1920s, following Greek liberation from Turkish rule. More than one million Greeks left Turkey in exchange for hundreds of thousands of Turks, Pomaks, and other Muslims. The next series of forced population transfers was carried out at the instigation of Nazi Germany. Contrary to what one might expect, some of the people involved were ethnic Germans who left Italy, Estonia, Latvia, Lithuania, eastern Poland, Croatia, Romania, and Hungary to move to the "homeland." The Nazis expelled even greater numbers of Jews, Poles, Russians, and other groups from their territories, and a great many of them perished in concentration camps. In the process, the Nazis brought about an immense restructuring of the ethnic geography of east-central Europe.

As the Third Reich collapsed, large eastern territories were annexed by Poland and Russia. Between 1944 and 1951, in the largest forced migration ever to occur, nine million people were expelled from these areas, amounting to 90% of the total population in an area the size of Pennsylvania. The effects on population density persisted for decades. Contemporaneously, three million Germans were expelled from Czechoslovakia, and exchanges of Slovaks and Hungarians and of Poles and Russians occurred. More recently, 260,000 Greeks and Turks suffered **ethnic cleansing** in Cyprus in the 1970s. The Balkan war of the 1990s brought renewed ethnic cleansing to Europe. Bosnians and Croats suffered most in this latest episode of forced migration, with the number of refugees totaling as many as one million.

The last 60 years have also seen significant population shifts as a result of migration spurred by differential economic opportunities in and around Europe. The initial flow of people was from periphery to core. Its prototype was perhaps the large-scale movement of Irish to Great Britain in the nineteenth century. Of far greater magnitude was the south-to-north migration in the period from 1950 to 1975. Spain, Portugal, Italy, Greece, Croatia, and Slovenia became the major senders, with destinations lying mainly in France, Germany, Belgium, the Netherlands, and the Alpine countries (fig. 3.9). Some 5 million people took part in this migration, including 1.7 million Italians, mainly from the impoverished southern part of that country, and 1.1 million Portuguese. As recently as 1970 in Germany, Yugoslavs and Italians ranked as the two largest immigrant groups. Portugal and Spain contributed disproportionately to France, and the Low Countries also received large contingents of Spaniards. Many Greek Cypriots came to the United Kingdom. Numerous southern European emigrants eventually returned to their native lands. The northern periphery of Europe, far more thinly populated than the south, could not send mass migration to the core. Even so, a sizable proportion of the northerners went south, most notably Finns from subarctic districts who sought employment opportunities in central and southern Sweden.

The most important European migration story of the last half century is immigration from outside Europe. As early as the late 1950s, Europe's booming economy began attracting workers from other realms. Moreover, growing affluence left many Europeans unwilling to engage in menial jobs and actively seeking cheap labor to fill those jobs. Among the immigrants drawn into Europe at this time were West Indians, Africans, and Asians, who came mainly to the United Kingdom, France, and the Netherlands. Many came at the invitation of national governments, which saw them

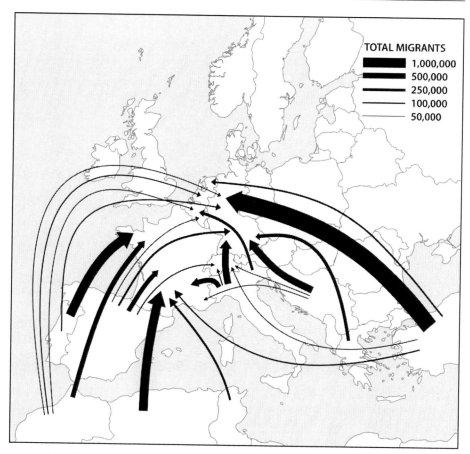

Figure 3.9   Migration within and to continental western Europe during the 1960s and 1970s. Prior to 1950, Europe lost more people through migration than it gained. Since then western Europe has become an immigration zone. The bases of the arrows on the map are located in sending countries and the points of the arrows are in receiving countries. The thickness of the arrows roughly corresponds to numbers of migrants. *Source of underlying data:* Rosemarie Rogers, "Post–World War II European Labor Migration: An Introduction to the Issues," in *Guests Come to Stay: The Effects of European Labor Migration on Sending and Receiving Countries*, ed. R. Rogers, 4–11 (Boulder, CO: Westview Press, 1985).

as temporary laborers who would eventually return to their home countries. Hence, they came to be known as **guest workers**.

These extra-European guest workers were followed by some one million Muslims from the formerly French-ruled Maghreb countries of North Africa—Morocco, Algeria, and Tunisia (fig. 3.9). Following on the heels of numerous ethnic French fleeing Algeria after that country overthrew rule by France in 1962, the Maghreb Muslims came mainly to France. In addition, many Moroccans went to Belgium and the Netherlands. The Maghreb immigration to France peaked in the 1970s, after which Italy and Spain became their major destinations. Paralleling the Maghreb immigration, another two million persons or more entered Europe from Turkey prior to 1990;

three-quarters of them headed to Germany (fig 3.9). Turks also became the largest non-European immigrant group in Switzerland and Sweden.

Since about 1990, this mass immigration has changed in character. The sources are now more diverse, reaching into Sub-Saharan Africa and South Asia, though the Maghreb and Turkey remain important. Germany and Switzerland are among the favored destinations of legal and illegal immigrants alike. Some 20% of Switzerland's population now consists of foreign-born persons, about twice the proportion in the United States. Germany houses about 16 million people descended from foreigners who immigrated over the past 50 years.

As we will discuss later, an anti-immigrant backlash has developed in many of the major destination countries. Certain right-wing political parties, such as France's National Front, Austria's Freedom Party, Belgium's Vlaams Belang, the Netherlands' Party for Freedom, and the Swiss People's Party, openly oppose immigration. By the latter half of the first decade of the twenty-first century, more than 100,000 illegal immigrants were entering the EU each year—many arriving at places such as Gibraltar and the Italian island of Lampedusa. The influx of migrants—both illegal and legal—has declined recently, but with immigrants continuing to arrive and with birth rates among recent immigrants well above Europe's norm, some Europeans fear being overwhelmed by masses of poor people from other regions. German speakers have coined the word *Überfremdung* ("overforeignization") to describe this perceived threat. Less stigmatized is another type of immigration. After the collapse of the Soviet Union in 1991, ethnic Russians and Germans residing in the former Central Asian Soviet Republics, particularly Kazakhstan, began moving to Russia and Germany, reversing a centuries-old diaspora and overwhelming the supply of jobs, housing, and social services for a time.

More recently, workers from countries in eastern Europe have moved to the west. Long kept in the East by the Iron Curtain and Cold War, an avenue of westward mobility opened up in the 1990s. Dire predictions of uncontrollable mass migration soon appeared, including speculation that as many as 40 million Russians might seek to move west. Initially a wave of immigrants came into western Europe from the east, but the predicted tidal wave of east-to-west migration has not materialized. The proportion of the workforce from eastern Europe is below 2% in all western and central European countries, and the percentage exceeds 1% in only two of those countries: Austria and Ireland. Poland is the largest labor-exporting country, but many eastern European states have a larger volume of immigration than emigration. Barring a major economic crisis, east-to-west migration seems unlikely to zoom out of control.

Major Influences on Population Geography

As the foregoing discussion suggests, a variety of factors can influence population density, distribution, and growth. Focusing on a few of the most significant of these can provide insight into important aspects of Europe's demographic makeup.

THE ROLE OF THE ENVIRONMENT

As we have already seen, environments suitable for agriculture have favored the development of substantial population concentrations, as has the location of valuable natural resources. Looking across the broad sweep of history, climate change clearly influenced the gradual diffusion of Homo sapiens northward in Europe thousands of years ago. Later, the expansion of population in northern and western Europe was facilitated by the **Medieval Warm Period** (sometimes called the Medieval Optimum), which brought milder conditions between the ninth and twelfth centuries. Agricultural areas increased, and Norse seafaring developed. Populations became sufficiently well established north of the Alps and Pyrenees that they were able to withstand the temperature downturn associated with the so-called Little Ice Age (c. 1200–1800), although far northern areas and Iceland experienced significant population losses during this period as a consequence of the increasingly inhospitable environment there.

For all the importance of the environment, however, its impact on demography needs to be understood against the backdrop of human factors, particularly culture and technology. Dietary and lifestyle preferences, social structures, and opportunities for trade with others all influence whether a given environment becomes an important settlement node for a given cultural group. And that group's level of technological development is fundamental to its capacity to exploit different environmental niches. Moreover, culture and technology continue to influence the environment–demography link right down to the present. In today's affluent Europe, a noticeable shift in population has taken place in response to the perceived advantages of living in warm, dry climates. Higher population densities in favorable spots along the Mediterranean are a product of wealthy Europeans from farther north moving to what they regard as pleasant environments. As for technology, infrastructural and mechanical advances, and new synthetic materials, have allowed humans to expand into increasingly marginal areas—sometimes with deleterious long-term consequences.

Disease is a different kind of environmental factor that has notably influenced demography over time. Humans greatly influence the spread of disease, of course, so it is not a purely environmental influence. But its roots are environmental, and its demographic consequences can be great. Consider, for example, the bubonic plague of the Middle Ages. Arriving in Constantinople (modern Istanbul) from the east in 1347, the plague spread quickly to Crete, Genoa, and southern France (fig. 3.10). In 1348 the bubonic plague made major inroads in southern Europe, and it spread north the following year. Scandinavia and eastern Europe felt its effect by 1350, and epidemics recurred through much of the remainder of the fourteenth century. Some experts believe the bubonic plague (sometimes called the Black Death) claimed 25 million victims in the 1300s, including two-thirds of the people living in parts of Italy. The English population is said to have declined from 3.7 million in 1350 to only two million by 1377. Graphs of population numbers throughout most of Europe show a noticeable downtick during the second half of the fourteenth and the early fifteenth century.

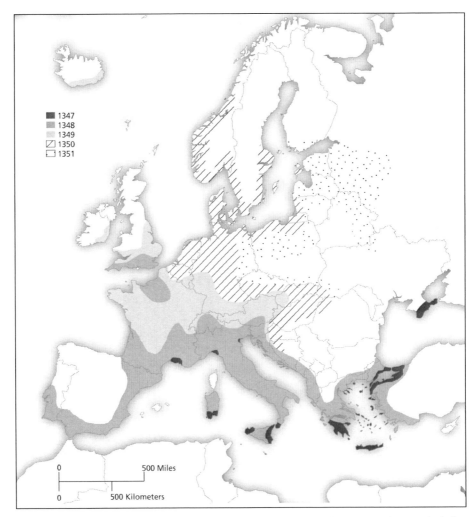

Figure 3.10.   Diffusion of the Bubonic Plague, 1347–1351. Before the century ended, the disease had killed perhaps 25 million persons in Europe, causing a major population decline. The political borders shown are modern. *Sources:* Adapted from Norman J. G. Pounds, *Hearth and Home* (Bloomington: Indiana University Press, 1989), 225; E. Charpentier, "Autour de la peste noire," *Annales: Economies/Sociétés/Civilisation* 17 (1962): 1062–92; Colin McEvedy, "The Bubonic Plague," *Scientific American* 258 (2 February 1988): 121.

No disease in more recent times has rivaled the plague in its impact, although malaria had a significant impact in parts of southern Europe in the 1600s and 1700s. Malaria has been largely eradicated in Europe, but a major flu pandemic struck western Europe in 1918, causing the greatest loss of life in Europe from disease over a short period of time since the Black Death. A more recent plague of sorts has come in the form of HIV/AIDS, with noticeable demographic impacts in localized areas. Infection rates in the eastern part of Europe are of particular concern, with some estimates suggesting that half a million Europeans may be carrying HIV. The social and personal consequences of HIV/AIDS are great, but the overall demographic impact has been small in comparison with earlier pandemics. Not surprisingly, the leading causes of death in contemporary Europe are circulatory and respiratory diseases, and cancer.

SOCIOECONOMIC AND POLITICAL CONTEXT

As we have seen, demographic characteristics are influenced by socioeconomic conditions, levels of urbanization, and political purges. At least until recently, population growth in Europe has tended to be greatest in areas of political stability and economic sufficiency. By contrast, warfare has had a particularly negative demographic impact. The Thirty Years' War, which raged from 1618 to 1648 in central Europe, saw the population of some German districts decline by two-thirds or more (partly as a result of out-migration); major losses of life occurred in Bohemia as well (fig. 3.11). Warfare has remained a source of demographic decline into the modern era. Well over a million French and almost two million Germans died in World War I. The French toll in World War II was lower, but German casualty figures were much higher

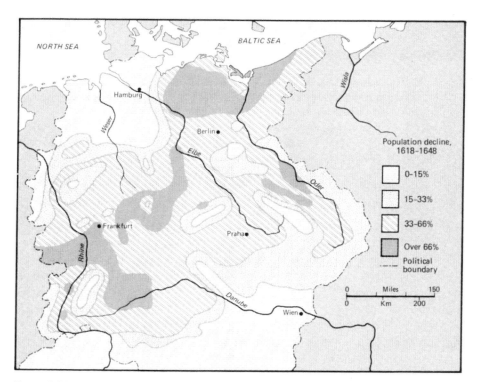

Figure 3.11.   Population loss owing to warfare and disease in central Europe, 1618–1648. The Thirty Years' War and associated epidemics drastically reduced the number of people in parts of Germany and Bohemia, producing a major change in population density and distribution. *Source:* After Franz and Keyser in *Westermanns Grosser Atlas zur Weltgeschichte* (Braunschweig, Germany: Georg Westermann, 1956), 107.

Figure 3.12.   War memorial in the French commune of Limeuil. Like every small town and commune in France, Limeuil (population just over 300) has its monument to local citizens who lost their lives in World Wars I and II. The list of names for World War I in particular is often staggeringly long. Photo by A. B. M., 2009.

(fig. 3.12). The Soviet Union suffered even more, losing some 20 million of its citizens, a figure representing about 10% of the country's inhabitants. Yugoslavia was deprived of fully 11% of its population, some 1.7 million persons.

Wars remain a source of demographic decline, but the role of socioeconomic and political factors has changed in the contemporary era. As already noted, over the past century and a half the percentage of the population working in the agricultural sector has shrunk dramatically, people have moved into cities, general prosperity has increased, and birth rates have fallen dramatically. Thus, currently, the areas with greatest political stability and economic prosperity tend to have particularly *low* population growth rates.

The reasons why development and urbanization produce declining birth rates are complex and a matter of some debate. Some demographers point to the fact that children are more of an economic advantage in rural settings than in urban settings, but there is much to suggest that the decision to give birth is not simply an exercise in utility maximization. Instead, the decline of birth rates in prosperous urban areas is likely the result of a complex of economic, cultural, and psychological factors that come with living in a radically different material and social context.

POPULATION POLICIES

As the discussion of the effort of European governments to attract foreign guest workers illustrated, laws and policies can have an important influence on demographic circumstances as well. In some cases these influences have deep historical roots. Southern Europe's legal systems were heavily influenced by Roman law. Under the Roman system, landholdings and possessions were divided equally among all heirs. As a result, farms became smaller over the generations—a circumstance that helped to promote dense rural settlement. In northern Europe, in contrast, Germanic law supported the principle of **primogeniture** or some other means of undivided inheritance. Land passed intact from parent to one child—usually the oldest son. The landless children often emigrated or, in more recent times, moved to cities—depressing population growth rates in rural areas dominated by Germanic law traditions.

In more recent time, the main story is the rise of strong state governments seeking to advance specific demographic agendas. There are dark times in Europe's recent history when governments pursued policies of forced migration and extermination that changed the demographic picture. During the Nazi period, government policies of eugenics in Germany were designed to steer natural evolution by means of forced sterilization of the mentally or physically handicapped, and incentives were offered for racially "pure" couples to have children.

In a more benign vein, governments have more recently sought to promote heightened natural growth rates. Governmental encouragement of large families in Eastern Europe during Communist times retarded the decline of birth rates for a time, especially in Romania. Farther west, France in particular has been engaged in an active effort to increase its birth rate. In the 1970s French President Valéry Giscard d'Estaing called on his countrymen to have "un troisième enfant pour la France" (a third child for France). It took some time before his call was answered, but by 2012 France's TFR had increased to 2.08—second only to that of Ireland in western Europe. Some of this increase is due to relatively high fertility rates among immigrants, but as we will see in Chapter 11, France's social policy is likely playing a role as well. That policy provides for long maternity leaves, allowances for parents, and government-supported childcare. Such policies are unlikely to alter current demographic trends in any dramatic way, but they can have an impact. Britain introduced French-style measures in 2001 and had its highest birthrate in 13 years by 2006.

Governments can also influence demographic trends through policies that promote better medical care. Access to high-quality, affordable medical care remains the rule in Europe. Doctor–patient ratios are low; the traditional epidemic and endemic diseases have been banished; and life expectancy, with a few eastern European exceptions, exceeds 70 years. Only Russia and Moldova, where life expectancy is 69 years, fall below this level. San Marino, Italy, Spain, Sweden, and Switzerland rank highest, at 82 years.

Scale Differences

So far we have focused on population patterns and processes at the European and national scales. An important geographic principle holds that the scale of analysis influences both what we see and the explanations we derive. A few examples of localized influences on demography illustrate the different kinds of forces that shape demography at smaller geographic scales.

Figure 3.13, a historical settlement map from a Swiss valley, reveals a completely different impact of the environment on demography from what we have seen at the European scale. In the Alps of Switzerland, northern Italy, and Austria, south-facing slopes receive much more sunlight than do shadowy north-facing slopes. The local inhabitants long recognized this contrast and tended to cluster in the areas most warmed by the sun. In some instances social distinctions developed between those living on the sunnier side of the river and those on the shadier—complete with senses of superiority and even taboos against intermarriage. Elsewhere in Europe, other types of environmental influences on population geography are evident, ranging from the clustering of settlements in the hills of Tuscany away from malarial-ridden lowlands to the abandonment of areas threatened by volcanism in Iceland and Sicily.

Turning to population growth and migration, focusing solely at the European and national scales obscures local variations that can be both demographically signifi-

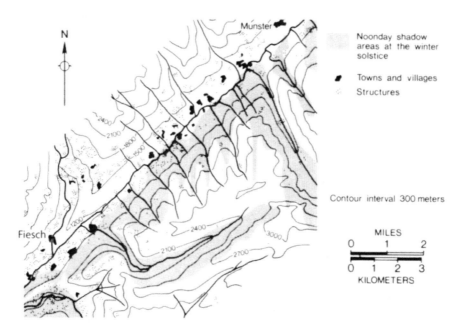

Figure 3.13.   Concentration of settlement in the Rhône Valley, Swiss Alps. The shaded area is in shadow at noon at the winter solstice. Villages and scattered dwellings are shown in black. Elevations are shown in meters. *Source:* After Alice Garnett, "Insolation, Topography, and Settlement in the Alps," *Geographical Review* 25 (4) (1935): 601–17.

cant and politically volatile. Some of the immediate suburbs around Paris have large immigrant populations with much higher rates of natural population increase than does the central city or more far-flung suburbs. These differences affect population densities and place strains on infrastructure and housing supply. They are also highlighted by those seeking to draw attention to the growing presence of immigrant populations in France.

Population patterns close to political boundaries provide an example of the impacts of political-economic circumstances on demography at the local scale. Particularly in places where borders are closed or difficult to cross, economies tend to stagnate and people move out. In the former West Germany, the zone bordering Czechoslovakia and East Germany experienced steady population decline during the decades immediately after World War II. Only recently have these areas begun to rebound.

Armed with a basic understandings of Europe's demographic circumstances, we are now in a position to begin fleshing out the human picture by turning our attention to cultural, political, economic, and social aspects of the European scene. We begin with the first of these in the next two chapters.

Sources and Suggested Readings

Anderson, B. A. 2002. Russia Faces Depopulation? Dynamics of Population Decline. *Population & Environment* 23 (5): 437–64.

Bade, J. J. 2003. *Migrations in European History*. Oxford: Blackwell.

Carter, F. W., and W. Maik. 1999. *Shock-Shift in an Enlarged Europe: The Geography of Socio-Economic Change in East-Central Europe after 1989*. Aldershot, UK: Ashgate.

Casado-Diaz, M. A., C. Kaiser, and A. M. Warnes. 2004. Northern European Retired Residents in Nine Southern European Areas: Characteristics, Motivations and Adjustment. *Ageing and Society* 24 (3): 353–81.

Coale, A. J., and S. C. Watkins, eds. 1986. *The Decline of Fertility in Europe*. Princeton, NJ: Princeton University Press.

Coleman, D. A., and S. Dubuc. 2010. The Fertility of Ethnic Minorities in the UK, 1960s–2006. *Population Studies* 64 (1): 19–41.

Cromley, E. K. 2010. Pandemic Disease in Russia: From Black Death to AIDS. *Eurasian Geography and Economics* 51 (2): 184–202.

Demko, G. J., G. V. Ioffe, and Z. A. Zaonchkovskaia, eds. 1999. *Population under Duress: The Geodemography of Post-Soviet Russia*. Boulder, CO: Westview Press.

Dorbritz, J. 2007. Demographischer Wandel in Mittel- und Osteuropa. Krisenreaktion oder Einstellungswandel? *Geographische Rundschau* 59 (3): 44–51.

Feldman, G. 2012. *The Migration Apparatus: Security, Labor, and Policymaking in the European Union*. Stanford, CA: Stanford University Press.

Grigg, D. 1995. The Nutritional Transition in Western Europe. *Journal of Historical Geography* 21 (3): 247–61.

Hamilton, K. A., ed. 1994. *Migration and the New Europe*. Washington, DC: Center for Strategic and International Studies.

Johnson, J. H. 1990. The Context of Migration: The Example of Ireland in the 19th Century. *Transactions of the Institute of British Geographers* 15 (3): 259–76.

King, R., ed. 1993. *The New Geography of European Migrations*. London: Belhaven Press.

————, ed. 2001. *The Mediterranean Passage: Migration and New Cultural Encounters in Southern Europe*. Liverpool Studies in European Regional Cultures 9. Liverpool: Liverpool University Press.

Leitner, H. 1997. Reconfiguring the Spatiality of Power: The Construction of a Supranational Migration Framework for the European Union. *Political Geography* 16 (2): 123–43.

Lesthaeghe, R., and P. Willems. 1999. Is Low Fertility a Temporary Phenomenon in the European Union? *Population and Development Review* 25 (2): 211–28.

Livi-Bacci, M. 1999. *The Population of Europe: A History*. Oxford: Blackwell.

Lynch, J. 2009. The Political Geography of Mortality in Europe. *Perspectives on Europe* 39 (2): 13–17.

Monzini, P. 2007. Sea-Border Crossings: The Organization of Irregular Migration to Italy. *Mediterranean Politics* 12 (2): 163–84.

Oberhauser, A. M. 1991. The International Mobility of Labor: North African Migrant Workers in France. *Professional Geographer* 43 (4): 431–45.

Ogden, P. E., and R. Hall. 2004. The Second Demographic Transition, New Household Forms and the Urban Population of France during the 1990s. *Transactions of the Institute of British Geographers* 29 (1): 88–105.

Penninx, R., M. Berger, and K. Kraal. 2006. *The Dynamics of International Migration and Settlement in Europe: A State of the Art*. Amsterdam: Amsterdam University Press.

Pounds, N. J. G., and C. C. Roome. 1971. Population Density in Fifteenth-Century France and the Low Countries. *Annals of the Association of American Geographers* 61 (1): 116–30.

Rodriguez, V., G. Fernandez-Mayoralas, and F. Rojo. 1998. European Retirees on the Costa Del Sol: A Cross-National Comparison. *International Journal of Population Geography* 4 (2): 183–200.

Rothenbacher, F. 2002. *The European Population, 1850–1945*. Basingstoke, UK: Palgrave Macmillan.

Samers, M. 2004. An Emerging Geopolitics of "Illegal" Immigration in the European Union. *European Journal of Migration & Law* 6 (1): 27–45.

Thorarinsson, S. 1961. Population Changes in Iceland. *Geographical Review* 51 (4): 519–33.

Thumerelle, J. 1992. Migrations Internationales et Changement Géopolitique en Europe. *Annales de Géographie* 101:289–318.

Usher, A. P. 1930. The History of Population and Settlement in Eurasia. *Geographical Review* 20 (1): 110–32.

Vandermotten, C., G. Hamme, and P. Medina Lockhart. 2005. The Geography of Migratory Movements in Europe from the Sixties to the Present Day. *Belgeo* (1–2): 19–34.

Velikonja, J. 1958. Postwar Population Movements in Europe. *Annals of the Association of American Geographers* 48 (4): 458–72.

Wild, T., and P. N. Jones. 1994. Spatial Impacts of German Unification. *Geographical Journal* 160 (1): 1–16.

CHAPTER 4

The Pattern of Languages

Language, like religion, is a basic element of culture. Language plays a central role in the way most people construct their identities—often serving to set them apart from "outsiders." And ethnic and national divisions frequently follow linguistic divides. Language is so fundamental to the way we view society that the common origin of most of the major languages of Europe has served to bolster the idea that Europe is a distinctive culture area.

In this chapter, we explore the many different languages spoken (or once spoken) in Europe, their distribution, and the relationships among them. We also look at the social and political implications of language divisions.

Languages and Language Families

In Europe, including Eurorussia, nearly 100 recognizably separate, mutually unintelligible languages are spoken, plus countless local dialects. Moreover, the region's complex linguistic geography is ever changing. Over the centuries and millennia, some languages spread and grew, others retreated to refuge areas and became "isolates" (examples include Icelandic and Faeroese). Still others vanished, leaving behind only a few words adopted into surviving tongues or perhaps merely a sprinkling of place names (fig. 4.1).

To grasp the essentials of the European language pattern, we need to understand how languages are defined and organized. Defining a language is no easy matter. We often think of languages as sets of mutually understood words and phrases that allow people to communicate with one another. **Dialects**, following this reasoning, are variants of languages. In practice, however, we generally refer to Chinese as a language even though there are at least five major variants of spoken Chinese that are mutually unintelligible. At the same time, we typically think of Norwegian and Danish as distinct languages even though a Dane could understand most of what was being said by someone speaking the form of Norwegian found in Oslo. Or consider another example. Many inhabitants of northern Switzerland think of themselves as

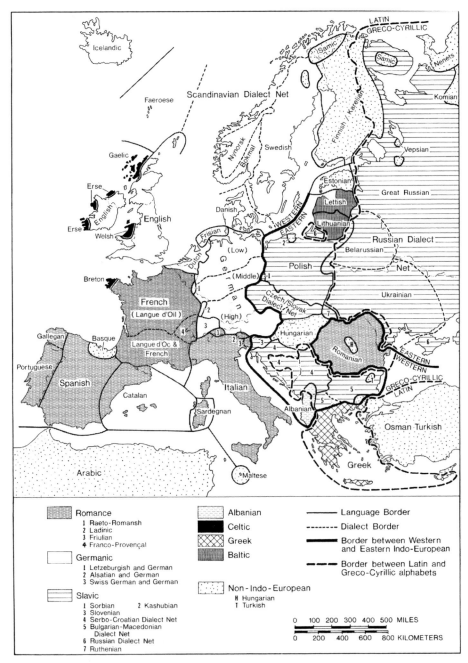

Figure 4.1. Languages and selected dialects of modern Europe. Many forms of speech normally considered separate languages, such as Swedish or Ukrainian, are perhaps better regarded as dialects enmeshed in nets. *Sources:* Straka 1979, Alinei et al. 1983, Mackenzie 1994, and Murphy 1998.

speaking a separate language, *Schweizerdeutsch* (Swiss German), or as the Swiss people say, *Schwyzerdütsch*, *Schwiizertüütsch*, and *Schwizertitsch*, as these major varieties of spoken Swiss German are prevalent in three geographical regions within the country. These three language variants are further divided into 21 subdialects, some of which are spoken in small clusters of villages in the Alps. These dialects and subdialects vary so greatly from the German of northern Germany that someone from Hamburg would be hard pressed to converse with someone speaking any variant of Swiss German. Yet most Germans consider Swiss German to be a dialect of German, and most language maps take the same position, perhaps because written Swiss German is standard German.

These examples show that there is no neat distinction between a language and a dialect. What we generally refer to as a language is a dialect or set of dialects that has achieved recognition as such, often as a result of political events. Hence, it is only partly in jest that one can describe a language as a dialect with an army behind it. This general point is a good illustration of why geography matters. Language cannot be understood in isolation from the sociopolitical and environmental context in which it is situated.

When we seek to describe the language pattern of an area, we need to consider the relationships among languages and dialects. To do this, linguists look at the way languages are structured and their vocabularies. Those languages that share broad similarities are grouped together into **language families**. Even greater similarities provide the basis for identifying broader and then narrower subfamilies and eventually individual languages. This approach means that language families can be diagrammed in tree form with the trunk representing the language family, the major branches representing broad subfamilies, and so on outward until one ends up with individual small branches representing discrete languages (fig. 4.2).

When one looks at the European linguistic kaleidoscope in these terms, it becomes clear that most of the major languages of Europe belong to a single language family, **Indo-European**. The linguistic kinship of the various Indo-European languages can be illustrated by comparing their vocabularies, especially words that describe commonplace things encountered in everyday life. Consider, for example, the word for *three* in various Indo-European tongues: *tre* or *tri* in Erse, Albanian, Italian, Swedish, Russian, Czech, and Serbo-Croatian; *tría* in Greek; *tres* in Spanish; *trei* in Romanian; *thrír* in Icelandic; *trzy* in Polish; and *trys* in Lithuanian. Contrast these to the words for *three* in non-Indo-European languages, such as *uç* in Turkish, *kolme* in Finnish, *három* in Hungarian, or *sahn* in Chinese.

Vocabularies are not a completely reliable guide to linguistic relationships because groups can borrow words from very different languages. Hence, linguists also look for similarities and differences in word order and the linguistic alterations that are made when, for example, a singular noun becomes plural. Indo-European languages generally employ the sentence structure of subject-verb-object. For example, "Jamie threw the ball." By contrast, languages in the Sino-Tibetan family employ a different word order, which is often verb-subject-object. Forming the plural of a word in an Indo-European tongue involves changing the ending. *Apple* becomes *apples*. In Swahili, however, one adds a prefix to form the plural.

Figure 4.2.   The Indo-European language tree. The trunk of the tree represents the language family, the major branches are the principal subfamilies, and the limbs are the major languages.

Classifying languages is only a beginning. As geographers, we want to understand why a particular pattern of languages came into being. **Geolinguistics** is the study of language change over space and through time. Language families are thought to begin with a proto-language, or set of closely related tongues in a given area. Geolinguists use a combination of archaeological evidence and words for animals and plants that languages in a language family share in common to figure out where the language family began. The next task is to understand the process of language diffusion. Geolinguists infer that major language subfamilies arise when groups of speakers move away from the area where the proto-language developed. Over time, the language of the separated groups evolves with the general assumption that greater distance and time apart yields greater differences.

The pattern of particular languages that follows geographical separation can be fundamentally influenced by writing, technology, and political organization. Writing is critical because texts are the primary means by which the evolution of language is slowed. Technology is important because it influences both the production of written texts and their dissemination. Political organization is key because it affects what people have access to and which areas are in close contact with one another.

Armed with these insights, we can begin to make sense of the circumstances that produced a language pattern such as that found in Europe. First, various peoples speaking languages that were part of the dominant language family diffused into Europe. Then, the rise of larger-scale, more technologically sophisticated literate societies allowed certain languages to spread over larger areas. Most notably, by 2,000 years ago, Latin had successfully diffused over a significant part of Europe (fig. 4.3). Latin spread rapidly because it was associated with a sophisticated political system that knit together large swaths of territory. When the Roman Empire collapsed, however, linguistic divergence took place.

Given the importance of writing, technology, and politics for the diffusion of languages, two developments in the late Middle Ages were of particular importance to the emergence of the modern language pattern: the invention of the printing press and the rise of relatively large states. The printing press was invented in Germany in

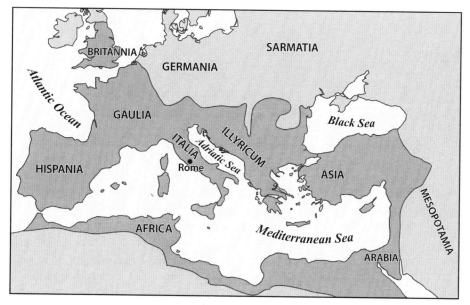

Figure 4.3. Maximum extent of the Roman Empire. The Roman Empire collapsed more than 1,500 years ago. In some places, little can be found today to remind us of the empire, but its cultural imprint remained strong in the parts of continental western Europe where it held sway.

1588, and during the succeeding century, it spread to other parts of Europe and beyond. The printing press allowed for the mass production and dissemination of materials that helped to spread particular forms of what became the major languages of Europe. The form of writing and speech promoted by elites to foster communication across broad areas is known as the **standard** (or standardized) **language**. Many of the early printed texts that promoted standardization were religious. The Luther Bible played this role for German, as did the King James Bible for English. In later centuries, the media and schools played key roles in language standardization.

It follows that the spread of political authority was important to the rise of standard languages, for political leaders have a strong interest in fostering integration by bringing peoples together and exposing them to common linguistic influences. Thus, language became a tool through which the leaders of early European states such as England and Spain sought to consolidate their power (see Chapter 6). The expansion of political authority also explains why some European languages spread far beyond Europe. As the states with colonial empires expanded their influence, certain languages came to be spread over vast portions of the earth's surface (fig. 1.9).

To move beyond these generalities, we need to look at the circumstances that brought speakers of different language families into Europe. We begin with the region's dominant language family, Indo-European. After examining the pattern of Indo-European subfamilies and languages that emerged, we turn our attention to the pockets of non-Indo-European speech that also are (or were) found in Europe.

The Diffusion of Indo-European Tongues into Europe

The Indo-European language family is thought to have originated somewhere in the region of the Caucasus Mountains around 12,000 years ago. Archaeological evidence suggests that its speakers were among the first farmers—that is, the people who initially domesticated plants and animals. Indo-European-speaking agriculturalists moved out of this area, both to the southeast and to the west, absorbing indigenous hunter-gatherers and producing a swath of Indo-European speech stretching from the Atlantic coast of Europe through South Asia. Great linguistic divergence occurred as speakers of the proto-language lost contact with one another, coined terms for new things they encountered, and borrowed words and phrases from other peoples. But recognizable similarities can still be found between the French spoken in northwestern Europe, the Farsi (Persian) spoken in Iran, and the Urdu spoken in Pakistan and India.

Indo-European speakers probably began moving out of the area around the Black Sea about 8000 BCE. As they became separated, different dialects developed due to linguistic drift and mixing with non-Indo-European peoples. A **dialect net**, a linguistic continuum in which the speakers of each dialect could understand the neighboring ones but not those spoken farther away in regions with which they had no regular contact, formed. Further fragmentation into separate, mutually unintelligible tongues seems to have occurred whenever the dialect net was torn. That likely happened where the farming frontier, spreading slowly west and north from Turkish Anatolia at the rate of about a kilometer every 20 years, encountered physical geographic obstacles. Indo-European pioneer farmers branched around these obstacles. Some went one way; some went the other. When that occurred, the two groups lost contact with each other for centuries, and their speech drifted apart. Generations later, when they coalesced beyond the obstacle, they could not understand each other.

The first such tear of significance to Europe probably occurred about 6000 BCE when one group of Indo-Europeans spread westward from Anatolia into the Aegean Isles and beyond onto the Greek mainland, while the other went north along the Black Sea's western coast (fig. 4.4). The split between western and eastern divisions of Indo-European may have been induced by the catastrophic creation of the Black Sea about 5600 BCE. Scientists recently determined that, prior to then, the Black Sea was a much smaller, interior drainage lake, lacking a connection to the Aegean and standing 120 meters below sea level (see the book by William Ryan and Walter Pitman, *Noah's Flood*, in the Chapter 2 bibliography). The sea suddenly burst through the natural dam at what is today the Bosporus, spilling in and enlarging the Black Sea to its present size. In the process, the large lowland plain adjacent to modern Bulgaria, Romania, and Turkey was inundated, which very possibly gave rise to the story of the great biblical flood. The Indo-European farmers living in these lowlands fled in different directions. Some went toward Turkey and Greece; others went into the Balkans, likely ripping the dialect net. Whether caused by the Aegean water barrier or the Black Sea flood, this tear produced the divide between Western and Eastern (formerly called *Centum* and *Satem*) Indo-European. This divide would later extend all the way to the Baltic Sea.

Fragmentation continued. The Eastern branch perhaps divided at the Stara Planina, with **Thracian** developing to the south among flood refugees in the Maritsa Valley (see fig. 2.1). In the north, even beyond the corridor of steppe grasslands on the margin of the East European Plain, the ancestral Balto-Slavs, descendants of others who fled the waters, arose. In their continued northward migration, they apparently divided around the Pripyat Marsh, separating the ancient **Baltic** and **Slavic** languages. The Slavs moved east and north, eventually populating a wedge between the 120-day growing season to the north and the steppes to the south, pushing agriculture as far as their prehistoric technology would allow (fig 4.4).

Equally profound tears in the dialect net happened at obstacles in the west. From Greece, where **Hellenic** speech developed, some Indo-Europeans migrated across the Strait of Otranto to Italy, giving rise to the Italic-speaking group, while about the same time, others seem to have pressed north through the Vardar–Morava rift valley, a narrows that restricted contact with the Hellenes to the south. Emerging into the Hungarian Basin, they became the Danubian people. Later, at the northern foot of the Alps, the proto-**Celtic** culture evolved from the Danubian parent, and it eventually spread to dominate most of central and northwestern Europe. Other Danubians went north into Scandinavia by way of the Jutland Peninsula of modern Denmark, crossing the infertile outwash plain and following a narrow strip of fertile land along the fjord-strewn east coast of Jutland (fig. 4.4). Those venturing north along this route after about 3500 BCE became the **Germanic** peoples.

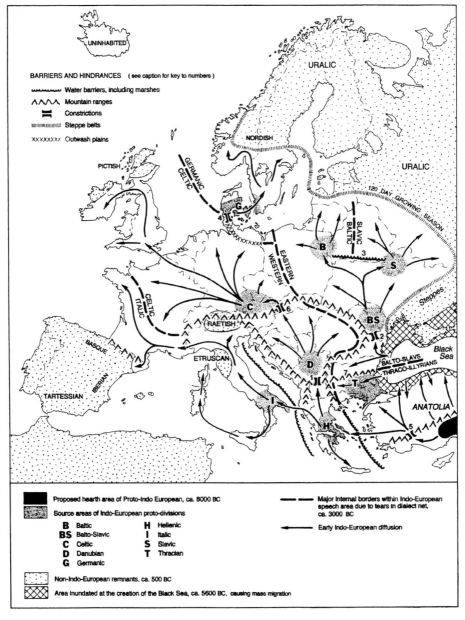

Figure 4.4. *(See figure legend on facing page).*

What happened in the Iberian Peninsula is less clear. The substantial survival of non-Indo-European languages there into historic times suggests a different linguistic order prevailed. Perhaps farmers speaking Afro-Asiatic tongues, belonging to a different language family, spread across North Africa, entered Iberia at Gibraltar, and continued northward until they met their fellow agriculturists, the Indo-Europeans, at the Pyrenees. Basque, an indigenous language unrelated to either Indo-European or Afro-Asiatic (see below), could have survived along the contact zone of the two immigrant farming peoples (fig. 4.4).

Many geolinguistic changes have occurred in Europe since 3000 BCE when the Indo-European diffusion had largely run its course. Yet some features have displayed remarkable durability, such as the western–eastern divide and the tenacious survival of minorities such as the Basques. One of the most notable changes, however, has been the continued tearing of several dialect nets to form the language subfamilies and individual languages of contemporary Europe.

The Three Major Subfamilies of Indo-European

At the dawn of the Roman Empire, much of western and central Europe was dominated by Celtic-speaking peoples, with a zone of Italic speech in what is now Italy and southern and western France and some non-Indo-European languages in the periphery. Over the ensuing 2,000 years, the situation fundamentally changed. Celtic speech was reduced to a small periphery as two major subfamilies of western Indo-European speech spread across western and central Europe, and one subfamily came to dominate the east. Now over 90% of all Europeans are accounted for by three Indo-European subfamilies: Germanic, Slavic, and Romance. Each of these, however, encompasses multiple languages (fig. 4.1).

Figure 4.4.   Origin, diffusion, and fragmentation of the Indo-European languages, 8000 to 3000 BC E: a geographical speculation. The dialect net was "torn" whenever the advancing Indo-European farmers split around an obstacle or fled a catastrophe, losing contact with their former neighbors. Such tears soon produced separate languages, due to linguistic drift in isolation. It is possible that other, now extinct Indo-European groups developed in southern France and the British Isles, due to the Alpine and English Channel obstacles. Residual non-Indo-European speakers survived best in border areas between languages and in harsh environments marginally suited to agriculture. Much of the map is speculative. Key to groups: **B** = proto-Balts; **BS** = proto-Balto-Slavs; **C** = proto-Celts; **D** = Danubic; **G** = proto-Germanic; **H** = proto-Hellenes; **I** = proto-Italic; **S** = proto-Slavs; **T** = proto-Thraco-Illyrians. Key to possible obstacles to migration: **1** = Vardar–Morava rift valley; **2** = constriction between Carpathians and steppes; **3** = Pripyat Marsh; **4** = Jylland narrows, a wedge of good land between marshes and outwash plains on the west and south and the Schlei Fjord on the east; **5** = Cilician Gate, a passage through the Taurus Mountains; **6** = Danube water gap; **7** = Stara Planina. *Sources:* Krantz 1988; William Ryan and Walter Pitman, *Noah's Flood* (New York: Simon & Schuster, 1998); Renfrew 1988, 1989, and personal communication 1999, all with very substantial modifications.

ROMANCE LANGUAGES

The **Romance** languages, western Indo-European in affiliation, today dominate the western and southern edges of Europe (excluding the British Isles). Romance languages derive from the ancient Italic division of Indo-European (fig. 4.4). One Italic tongue, Latin, originally spoken only in the district of Lazio (Latium) around Rome, rose to dominance and achieved a remarkable dispersal. When a language successfully expands in this manner, its speakers possess some cultural or technological advantage. In the case of Latin speakers, this advantage came in the form of a highly developed political organization and technological sophistication, which permitted empire-building. Latin was the language of the Roman Empire. It spread with Roman victories. By about 100 CE the Roman Empire, with its Latin language, reached its greatest territorial extent (fig. 4.3). Latin was heard on the banks of the Thames, Rhine, and Danube rivers, as well as in North Africa. Few of the cultural groups ruled by the Roman Empire successfully resisted linguistic assimilation, though the Greeks did because of their written language tradition and the respect the Romans accorded to it. In fact, many Greek words found their way into Latin. The Etruscans, a highly developed non-Indo-European civilization just north of Rome, succumbed linguistically to Latin, but not before they gave the parent words for *people, public, military*, and *autumn*. In Iberia, the Romans likely achieved the decisive introduction of Indo-European, wresting it away from the Afro-Asiatic peoples and a scattering of Celts.

Even before the Roman Empire collapsed, Latin was mixing with other tongues throughout the empire to form different variants. Romance languages are the result of the continued linguistic fragmentation that occurred in succeeding centuries. All had roots in Latin, but their vocabularies and forms of pronunciation evolved in different directions.

The fall of the Roman Empire led to some decline in the use of Romance tongues, but they survived remarkably well throughout the core of what had been the Roman Empire. Nonetheless, Germanic invaders brought their own language to Britain, the west bank of the Rhine, and the Alps (see below), while Slavs and Magyars surged into the Balkans, leaving a lonely linguistic outpost in Romania and Moldova as a reminder of the former eastern extent of the Romans (fig. 4.1). In these forfeited areas, only place names survive today as remnants of the Latin tongue. In England for example, *-caster* and *-chester* suffixes, as in Lancaster or Manchester, derive from *castra*, Latin for "military camp." Later, when the Moors invaded Iberia beginning in the eighth century, the Afro-Asiatic languages, especially Arabic, regained a foothold there, though the Latin-derived Mozarabic tongue survived as the language of Christians under Moorish rule. The subsequent defeat of the Moors by the Spaniards and Portuguese reclaimed nearly all of Iberia for the Romance languages and completely extinguished Arabic. Only abundant place names and numerous loanwords survive as reminders of the former Arabic presence. Thus Gibraltar got its name from *Jebel Tariq* ("Mountain of Tariq"), a Moorish general who led the invasion of Iberia in 711, and the major river of Spain, the Guadalquivir, means "Great Valley" (from *al-wadi-al-kabir*) (fig. 4.5).

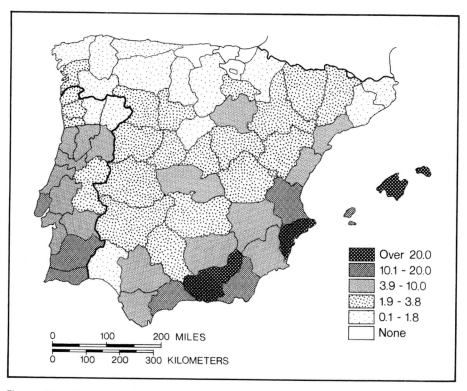

Figure 4.5. Number of Arabic and Arabized topographic names per thousand square kilometers in Iberia. "Africa begins at the Pyrenees," according to a traditional French saying, a reflection of the fact that, a thousand years ago, the Moors (Arabic-speaking Muslims from North Africa) were the dominant presence south of the Pyrenees. The subsequent Indo-European, Christian "reconquest" of Iberia led to their expulsion. A reminder of their presence is the many place names derived from the Arabic tongue. *Sources:* After Lautensach 1954 and Sopher 1955.

The fragmentation of Latin into many separate languages proceeded rapidly after the political and social institutions that had bound the Roman Empire together ceased to exist. All of the surviving Romance tongues in modern Europe represent the fragmented legacy of Latin, but they solidified and spread as Europe's political geography took shape. Today, the Iberian Peninsula is home to three of these languages. Dominating the nation of Spain from the Meseta interior is Castilian Spanish, which some 30 million people speak as a mother tongue. Speakers of the Catalan language, numbering close to 7 million, are found in the eastern coastal fringe of Spain, the Balearic Islands, a corner of southern France, and Andorra, and they also have a foothold on the Italian isle of Sardinia. Catalan is now the dominant tongue in Barcelona and all of Catalonia, an autonomous region in Spain. Even France, which historically extended few rights and privileges to linguistic minorities, permits bilingual French-Catalan road signs in its southern region, where Catalan is spoken. The Atlantic front of Iberia is home to Portuguese/Galician, a dialect net with almost 13 million speakers. The survival of Portuguese was historically guaranteed by political independence, and Galician has achieved legal status in the autonomous Spanish province of Galicia, where it is the habitual language of daily use of a considerable majority of the population.

Northward from Iberia, beyond the Pyrenees, French is spoken by the large majority of France's population as well as by the southern Belgians, or Walloons; the western Swiss; and residents of the Valle d'Aosta in northwest Italy. All in all, it encompasses a total of some 63 million persons. The southern form of the two principal French tongues, *langue d'oc*, has gradually retreated before *langue d'oïl*, which was originally found only in the Parisian north. Occitan is the principal dialect in the *langue d'oc* region, and it is now being taught in some schools, ending two centuries of government suppression. French is an official language in Monaco, Belgium, Switzerland, Luxemburg, and the Channel Islands of Jersey and Guernsey.

Italian, at 60 million speakers, is spoken not only in Italy but also on the island of Corsica, which belongs to France; Canton Ticino in southern Switzerland; and parts of the Nice district on the French Riviera. The Tuscan dialect has become standard Italian speech, a heritage of the cultural significance of Florence. Due to the late unification of Italian polities (Chapter 6), many regional dialects persist on the Apennine peninsula. Italian has the third largest number of speakers among the languages of Europe.

Along the northern fringe of Romance speech, sheltered in Alpine valleys, are found several minor tongues with diminishing numbers of speakers: Romansh with 40,000 speakers and two main dialects in eastern Switzerland; Ladinic in Italian South Tirol; and Friuli in the easternmost end of the Po–Veneto Plain. Collectively, these three constitute the Raeto-Romanic group. With about 1,850,000 speakers, Sardinian, distinct from Italian, survives on that Mediterranean island.

Romanian, an eastern outlier of the Romance languages, is separated from the larger western area by the interposed South Slavs. This language, spoken by over 22 million persons in Romania and adjacent Moldova, has survived in spite of invasions by Slavs, Magyars, and other groups, though the vocabulary is infiltrated with Slavic words. Closely related to Romanian is Vlakh, presumably derived from Valachia in southern Romania. Today, it is spoken by a few nomadic herding tribes in interior northern Greece and adjacent countries. The Vlakhs are descended from Romanians who migrated southward after the collapse of the Roman Empire to find refuge in the Dinaric–Pindhos mountain region. The seasonal shelters of Vlakh nomads may be seen at the foot of Mount Ólimbos in Greece and elsewhere.

The northern border of the Romance languages today, stretching from the English Channel to the head of the Adriatic Sea (fig. 4.1), displays a diverse character that relates to physical geography. Generally, where the border crosses plains, as in Flanders and the upper Rhône Valley of Switzerland, it tends to be unstable and mobile. French has advanced against Dutch in the former and retreated before German in the latter. But where the language border follows mountain ridges, as in the St. Gotthard Pass region in the western Alps, it has remained unchanged for more than a thousand years. To cross St. Gotthard going north today, as in the Early Middle Ages, is to leave Romance speech and enter the Germanic lands.

GERMANIC LANGUAGES

The second of the three major Indo-European subfamilies, also belonging to the western division, consists of the **Germanic** languages. These languages dominate in west-central and northern Europe (fig. 4.1).

The Germanic branch probably arose, as described earlier, in the isolation of Jutland (fig. 4.4), and, from there, it spread through the Danish Isles and into northern Scandinavia, absorbing a non-Indo-European race of hunters and fishers. They are sometimes referred to as *Nordish*. From them, the early Germanic people apparently adopted a sizable vocabulary, with the result that perhaps one-fourth or even one-third of all Germanic words today are not Indo-European in origin. *Bear* provides an example, for the parent Indo-European word for this animal was *urse*. (Compare modern French *ours* or Spanish *oso*.) The Germanic speakers, in the process, also took on some of the modes of livelihood of the indigenous hunter-fishers, including their seagoing practices. In the colder conditions of the north, their grain crops developed into faster-maturing varieties to accommodate the shorter growing season, but the Germanic advance halted at about the northern limits of the humid continental and marine west coast climates. (Compare figures 2.8 and 4.4.)

There, in the north, the Germanic people remained for millennia on the outer margins of the agricultural, Indo-European world. Then, about 500 BCE, the climate of Scandinavia became colder, in a deterioration that continued to the beginning of the Common Era. Their response was remarkable. Nearly all Germanic people evacuated the north, boarding longboats and crossing the seas to resettle in the river valleys of northern Germany. These valleys, due to a pattern of springtime flooding that delayed planting and effectively shortened the growing season, had remained largely uncolonized by the resident Celtic Indo-Europeans. The Germanic folk, with their fast-ripening grains, could occupy this riverine environment. Their southward advance continued, eventually displacing the Celts from Germany, leaving behind only a scattering of Celtic place names such as *Alp* (mountain), *Halle* (salt), and *Rhine* (river). With the collapse of the Roman Empire, Germanic tribes such as the Franks, Goths, Burgundians, and Lombards pressed far into Romance territory, but they usually failed to achieve a permanent implantation of their languages.

Elsewhere, the Germanic invasions continued, bringing Anglo-Saxons to England, and, after warmer climatic conditions resumed, they accomplished much agricultural recolonization in Scandinavia. From there, Viking longboats eventually reached the Faeroes, Iceland, Greenland, and Newfoundland. For 1,500 years, Germanic longboats assisted the dispersal of these peoples.

In central Europe, about 700 CE, the Germans developed an innovative, more intensive form of agriculture known as the three-field system (see Chapter 7) and an effective system of organized government, the **feudal system**. Deploying those new arrangements to their advantage, they began expanding east at the expense of the Slavic peoples in about 800, pushing the German language frontier well into present-day Poland as well as eventually creating the eastern diaspora of Germans that eventually returned to Germany. Only a residue of Slavic place names survived in some

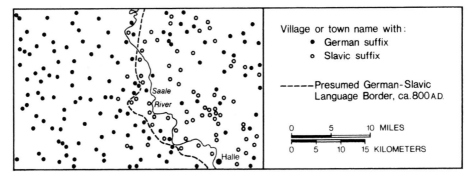

Figure 4.6. An archaic language border in Germany. About the year 800 CE, the Germanic–Slavic boundary in central Europe lay roughly along the line of the Elbe and Saale rivers. German-speaking settlers, in the 800–1300 period, surged eastward across this border, changing the linguistic pattern as they carried their speech far into Slavic territory. But even today, evidence of the old border remains in the form of Slavic place names. Villages with name suffixes such as *-itz*, *-in*, and *-zig* are of Slavic origin. Europe abounds with such archaic linguistic features.

parts of the North German Plain and Danube Valley as reminders of their former presence (fig. 4.6).

The single most important Germanic language, both in terms of the population of speakers and the number of countries where it serves as a mother tongue, is German. Close to 90 million people speak this language, including majorities not just in Germany but also in Austria, Switzerland, Liechtenstein, and Luxembourg. In addition, German-speaking provinces can be found in Italy (South Tirol or Alto-Adige), eastern Belgium, and France (Alsace). German has the second-highest number of speakers in Europe, surpassed only by Russian. Until very recently, large German minorities remained in many eastern European countries, especially Russia, Hungary, Romania, and Poland, though all of these groups have been greatly depleted by recent **return migration** to Germany after an absence of centuries. During the six-year span from 1986 through 1992, the peak of the migration, over 1.5 million ethnic Germans departed from lands east of the former Iron Curtain, including the former Soviet Union, and went to Germany, where automatic citizenship awaited them. Romania's German minority dwindled from 360,000 in 1977 to only 17,000 by 1998. The German diaspora in eastern Europe has, for all practical purposes, ceased to exist, though many remain in Russia.

A standardized form of German based on Luther's Bible translation is understood and spoken throughout the German language region, but many dialects survive, some of which have become proper languages, unintelligible to speakers of standard German. Most notable are *Letzeburgish*, which is gaining increased usage in Luxembourg; Alsatian, the declining German dialect of eastern France; and several variants of Swiss German, spoken by the majority in Switzerland.

Dutch, spoken by 20 million in the Netherlands, northern Belgium, and extreme northern France, also developed as a separate language out of the former German dialect net in the northern German region, but the difference is that its speakers never adopted standard German. Another offshoot is the Frisian language, spoken by about 300,000, mainly in the northeastern Netherlands.

The northern part of the Germanic language region is dominated by the Scandinavian dialect net (fig. 4.1). The standard language maps suggest that separate Danish, Norwegian, and Swedish languages exist, but, in fact, these are mutually intelligible dialects, even in the standard forms promoted by the three governments. For example, some 64% of Norwegians understand "all but a few words" of standard Swedish, and the same is true of 58% of all Danes concerning the Bokmål form of Norwegian, one of two government-recognized dialects in that country (fig. 4.1). In local areas along international borders within Scandinavia, mutual intelligibility is virtually universal. **Isoglosses**, or boundary lines between linguistic features (word usage, pronunciation, and the like), crisscross Scandinavia without regard to political borders.

Only Icelandic, where the Scandinavian dialect net was torn by the intervening sea, is a separate language if mutual intelligibility is the criterion. The Scandinavian dialect net encompasses a little over 20 million speakers, and Icelandic includes about 300,000 speakers. Faeroese, spoken in a small island group between Iceland and Norway, should perhaps also be regarded as a separate Scandinavian language, but long rule by Denmark has altered the local speech to the extent that Faeroese probably fits better in the Scandinavian dialect net.

The Special Case of English

English, the closest Germanic relative of Frisian, is also a Germanic language, but with a twist. As a result of the Norman French conquest of England almost a thousand years ago, English absorbed a great many Romance words, totaling perhaps 30% of the present English vocabulary. This mixing of Germanic and Romance, with the resultant richness of vocabulary, made English a **composite language**, one whose form was taken from more than one language. Of course, almost all languages are composite in the sense that they are influenced by other tongues, but, in the case of English, the influence was particularly dramatic.

The story of English begins in Britain in the beginning of the fifth century. The Roman Empire was losing its grip, and the ensuing vacuum facilitated the arrival of new Germanic-speaking peoples from farther east, including Jutes, Angles, Saxons, and Frisians. Within a couple of hundred years, the languages of the new arrivals came to dominate significant areas in Great Britain, particularly in the fertile Anglican Plain of the southeast where an Anglo-Saxon mix (referred to as Old English) held sway.

When the Norman French leader William the Conqueror arrived on the southern coast of England in 1066, he encountered a largely Germanic-speaking population. He and his successors came to control much of southern Great Britain. The Norman French conquerors were too small in number to change the essential character of the Germanic tongues that they encountered, but they introduced a new language that coexisted—and ultimately blended—with those tongues. As a result, English developed two words for many objects and actions. In English people are tired (Germanic root) or fatigued (Romance root). They seek help (Germanic root) or aid (Romance root). The animal in the field is called a cow (Germanic root), whereas the meat from that animal that is consumed at the dinner table is called beef (Romance root). These examples tell us something about the social structure of Norman England. Words that refer to basic things, for example, tired, help, and cow, reflect the language history of those at the lower ends of the social and political hierarchy.

The so-called Middle English that evolved from the Germanic–Romance mixture was still fairly different from the English of today. One strand of Middle English centered in London evolved to the point where it began to take on a form more like modern English, and that strand came to be widely disseminated because it was institutionalized as the principal tongue of culture and government. Publications in the late sixteenth and early seventeenth century, such as the King James Bible and Shakespearean plays, played key roles in the standardization of English. The language continued to evolve, but more slowly. To this day, we can read works from that period with only modest difficulty.

The extraordinary reach of the British Empire brought the English language to the far corners of the globe. In some places—for example, parts of North America and Australia—it became the dominant tongue. In other areas, it provided a **lingua franca**, a common language that could be used as a means of communication among speakers of diverse tongues. Over the last 150 years, the rising power of the United States and the continued global influence of the United Kingdom have made English an increasingly common lingua franca around the world, including in Europe itself. French occupied that role throughout much of Europe in the seventeenth and eighteenth centuries, and especially in the Age of Enlightenment, when it became closely associated with learnedness, cultural sophistication, and diplomacy. The use of French is still common in the international arena—at sessions of the United Nations, during Olympic games, and in international diplomatic exchanges. But today English is the usual language of choice when Europeans who do not speak each other's language communicate with one another.

SLAVIC LANGUAGES

The third (and largest) of the three major Indo-European divisions consists of the **Slavic** languages, which belong to the eastern branch of the family. Slavic speech dominates throughout much of the eastern half of Europe.

The origins of the Slavic languages probably lie somewhere on the margins of the Pripyat Marsh (fig. 4.4) in dim prehistory. The proto-Slavs, who called themselves *Sorby*, established agricultural communities on the central section of the East European Plain. Slavic might have remained a minor and peripheral linguistic group if its speakers had not invented a new type of curved-blade plow in about the year 200 CE. Equipped with a moldboard, it lifted the topsoil and turned it over. Mounted on wheels and pulled by multiple teams of oxen, this plow allowed the cultivation of heavy clay soils for the first time, and greatly increased crop production. With this innovation, the Slavs expanded west and south, entering the rich prairie regions of the North and East European Plain (fig. 2.1). When the Roman Empire collapsed, Slavic peoples pushed deep into the Balkans.

The Slavic region today is separated into a large northern part and a much smaller southern area, divided by a corridor of non-Slavic languages (fig. 4.1). In the north, Polish claims about 42 million speakers, the Czech/Slovakian dialect net 16 million, and the Russian dialect net about 165 million inside Europe. Most sources recognize Ukrainian, Belarusian, and Russian as three separate languages, and they are now being promoted as such for nationalistic purposes, but, linguistically, they are part of a single multiethnic Russian dialect net that encompasses virtually the entirety of the East European Plain. In 2005, the Russian component, formerly strewn widely through the Soviet Union, included about 12 million persons living outside Russia in newly independent European countries, more than two-thirds of them in Ukraine. Another 6 million or so Russian speakers still live in the former Soviet Central Asian republics, plus Azerbaijan.

A substantial return migration of Russian speakers to Russia from the former Soviet republics is occurring. Between 1989 and 1996, over two million people took part in this mass migration, and the flow continues, though at a lower volume. Many additional ethnic Russians departed Siberia, the Asian part of Russia, to return to Eurorussia in the 1990s. Today Russian speakers constitute the largest linguistic community in Europe.

Stretching from the Adriatic to the Black Sea in the Balkan Peninsula, the three southern Slavic languages are Slovenian with 2 million speakers, the Serbo-Croatian dialect net with some 20 million speakers, and the Bulgarian-Macedonian dialect net with close to 11 million speakers. Further complicating the pattern of Slavic languages is an alphabet divide, a fundamental cultural boundary in Europe that separates users of the Latin characters from those employing Greek or Greek-derived Cyrillic letters (fig. 4.1). This literary divide cuts right through the Slavic lands, both northern and southern.

Other Indo-European Languages

All of the other Indo-European tongues present in Europe are spoken by relatively small numbers of people, generally in peripheral locations. Some have experienced retreat, and a few face the possibility of extinction. The Celtic division of Western Indo-European clings to refuges on the hilly, cloudy coasts of northwestern Europe (figs. 4.1 and 4.7). According to the 2011 census, some 562,000 speakers, or 19.0% of residents of Wales, were able to speak and read Welsh. As recently as 1911, Welsh had almost a million speakers, and the subsequent decline has caused some to predict "a land where children will not be able to pronounce the names of the places where they live." Indeed, most Celtic languages have been in retreat over the last century and a half, including Cornish in Cornwall and Gaelic in Scotland; Manx on the Isle of Man became extinct. Recently, Cornish has shown tenuous signs of revival, leading the authors of UNESCO's 2008 *Atlas of World Languages* to change its designation for Cornish from "extinct" to "critically endangered." Still, the UK census shows only

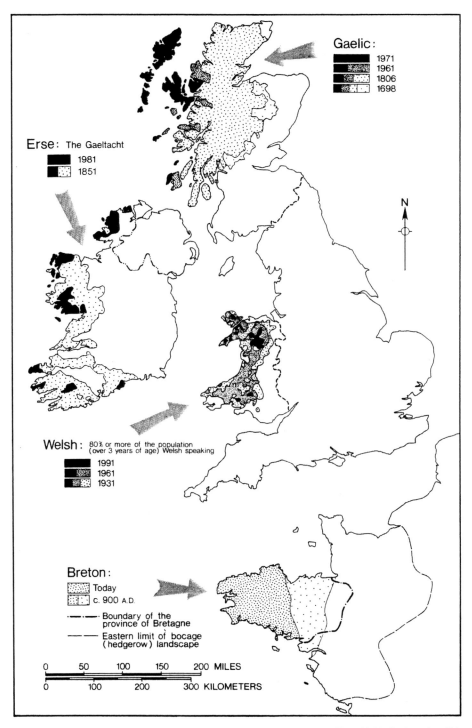

Figure 4.7.   Retreat of the Celtic languages, as represented by Erse (Irish), Breton, Scottish Gaelic, and Welsh. The rural refuge areas fragmented as the decline progressed. Today all but Scottish Gaelic are experiencing a revival, centered in the towns and cities, not in the rural refuges. *Sources:* After Withers 1984, 47, 81, 233, 234; Hindley 1990; Aitchison and Carter 1999.

557 people declaring Cornish to be their language. In an attempt to educate a new generation of native speakers, the first *crèche* (Cornish language day care center) opened in 2010.

In the case of Welsh, the obituary seems to have been premature. The Welsh Language Act of 1993 gave the language legal equality with English, and the Welsh elite began insisting that their children study the ancestral tongue. It is a required language in state schools. The number of speakers stabilized and then began to increase. Welsh newspapers, radio broadcasts, and television channels are now available. Folk song competitions are widespread in North Wales, and the proportion of children under four who are educated in Welsh has increased considerably. Indeed, many young people are now able to text and twitter in their native tongue.

Breton, the Celtic language of western France that is closest to Cornish, retains a population of relatively fluent speakers estimated to be somewhere between 172,000 and 200,000. A Breton elite has mounted a linguistic revival movement in recent decades. In the 1990s, 34 Breton-only schools opened, a radical departure from the not-too-distant past, when French officials banned the language altogether in education and the number of speakers declined. It is not clear, however, that the revival is producing much growth in the number of Breton speakers, as only 35,000 people use Breton in everyday life, whereas 11% of Bretons do not know the language at all. Some scholars predict that by 2017 the number of speakers will be as low as 122,000, 29–30% lower than in 2012.

The situation of Gaelic in the *Gaidhealtacht* refuge of the northern highlands and islands of Scotland is tenuous. Bilingual Gaelic/English road markers conceal the fact that only a little over 58,000, mainly elderly, speak the language (less than 1% of the 5.3 million residents of Scotland). Erse, or Irish Gaelic, has enjoyed governmental protection and support since the independence of Ireland in the 1920s, but it declined in the 1980s when the mandatory teaching of Erse in schools ceased. In 2011, only 77,000 persons still used Erse as the language of the household, though anywhere from 613,236 to 1.7 million reputedly have at least limited ability in the language. Some *Gaeltacht* residents protest by defacing the English parts of bilingual signs (fig. 4.8). An Erse revival of sorts is under way in the cities of Ireland, all of which lie outside the Gaeltacht. The first Erse television station began operating in 1996, and a few all-Erse primary schools were opened. Still, just over 2% of Ireland's population uses Erse frequently in conversation. In Northern Ireland the use of so-called Ulster Irish has increased slightly, with 11% of the population claiming at least partial knowledge of the language.

The ancient **Hellenic** branch of the Indo-European languages is parent to Modern Greek, which is spoken by a little over 10 million people in Greece and Cyprus. Minorities can be found in surrounding countries, such as Albania. While a minor tongue, accounting for less than 1.5% of all Europeans, Greek is not an endangered language. Greeks celebrate their tongue and take pride in the cultural achievements of their ancient ancestors. Greek Orthodox Christianity has also played a major role in the survival and vigor of Greek culture. Self-pride allowed the Greeks to preserve their language even during lengthy periods of rule by the Romans and Turks. Modern

Figure 4.8.   Defacing of English language on highway signs in the Connemara *Gaeltacht*, Republic of Ireland. The official bilingual policy of the republic is unpopular in both English and Erse areas. Photo by T. G. J.-B., 1974.

Greek is spoken in almost precisely the same region as in the Mycenean Age (1300 BCE) and the area where the tearing in the dialect net apparently produced proto-Hellenic some 8,500 years ago. Since then, the language changed significantly, and Modern Greek is roughly as different from Classical Greek as Italian is from Latin, but it remained astoundingly stable geographically.

Neighbors to the Greeks are the speakers of **Thraco-Illyrian** tongues, today represented only by Albanian. They number over six million and reside mainly in Albania and Kosovo, though they also have a sizable presence in Macedonia and Italy, where Albanian is recognized as a minority language. A scattering of Albanian villages can also be found in southern Italy and Greece. The ancestral Thraco-Illyrian linguistic subfamily, belonging to the Eastern Indo-European division, perhaps originated in the Maritsa Valley of Bulgaria (figs. 2.1 and 4.4), but the ancient geographical development remains poorly understood. Apparently, Thraco-Illyrian speakers were a mountain people, diffusing through the Stara Planina and Rodopi Range. This may have happened as early as the time of the Black Sea flood. They went over into Illyria, in the Dinaric Range, the present seat of the Albanian language. Eventually, Thraco-Illyrian died out altogether in the eastern Balkans, and modern Albanian occupies a refuge not unlike that of Celtic.

Another minor Eastern Indo-European group consists of the **Baltic** languages, Lettish (Latvian) and Lithuanian, spoken in two small independent states on the eastern shore of the Baltic Sea (fig. 4.1). Together, these languages have a little over four million speakers. Baltic speech survives close to its presumed area of origin, west of the Pripyat Marsh (fig. 4.4). Territory was later lost to both Germanic and Slavic languages, but the Balts have held out in a northern refuge. The achievement of political independence by Latvia and Lithuania bodes well for these two relatively small languages.

Romany, the Eastern Indo-European speech of many or most of the seven million or more Roma (or gypsies as they are popularly called), is spoken widely, especially in eastern Europe, though not in contiguous or sizable areas. Romania with around a million, Spain with 750,000, and Bulgaria with 310,000 Roma house the largest numbers, though sizable minorities are found throughout the EU. Romany is split into three separate languages and 13 dialects, due to the wide distribution of the group and the largely oral status of the tongue. The Roma apparently entered Europe in the fourteenth century as a caste of itinerant Hindu peddlers from the Indus Valley of present-day Pakistan. In almost every European country, they are the objects of discrimination. With high rates of illiteracy and limited prospects for social advancement, the Roma are among the poorest groups in Europe.

Non-Indo-European Languages

Non-Indo-European languages are rare, accounting for only 5% of the population, and generally peripheral in location (fig. 4.9). On the northeastern margins of Europe live speakers of the **Uralic** language family, an indigenous group whose ancestors retreated to cold, marshy refuges as the Indo-Europeans advanced. Today, they live in a chain of independent countries and autonomous regions from Finland and Estonia eastward through the Karelian and Komi republics of Russia, among others, as far as Mordvinia (fig. 4.9). These are peoples of the taiga. Many, particularly the speakers of Estonian (around 910,000) and Finnish-Karelian (4.8 million), adopted agriculture from the Indo-Europeans in ancient times and carried it into the taiga, but cer-

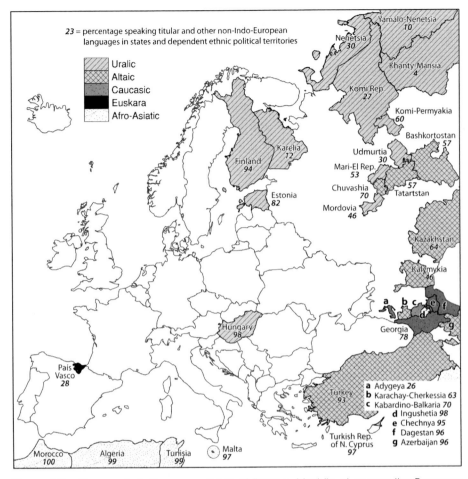

Figure 4.9.   The non-Indo-European lands of Europe. Most lie at or near the European periphery, with the exception of Hungary.

tain other Uralic groups, such as the Sami (or Lapps), with a present population of around 80,000, never became farmers. The Uralic peoples were historically closely connected to the forest, and their graveyards often take on a wooded, wild appearance. A formidable belt of marshes marks the Uralic–Indo-European border along the present Estonia–Latvia boundary, a line beyond which the Baltic speakers apparently never progressed.

Among the Uralic speakers, only the Hungarians, or Magyar, do not live in a peripheral area. Instead, 13.5 million strong, they occupy the heart of the structural basin that bears their name, close to the center of Europe (fig. 4.9). Most live in Hungary, but sizable minorities can also be found in Romania, Slovakia, Slovenia, northern Yugoslavia, and western Ukraine. By their own tradition and historical evidence, the ancient Hungarians, a herding people of the east, entered Europe as invaders in 895 CE and found a permanent foothold in areas where prairie vegetation had been created by earlier human activity in the central European biotic province. They largely replaced the Slavic peoples who had moved into what came to be known as the Hungarian Basin, completing the break between northern and southern Slavic.

On the southeast, the Indo-Europeans border the **Altaic** language family, mainly Turkic groups. The Osman Turks of Anatolia long ago attained footholds in Cyprus and north of the Bosporos–Dardanelles. In addition, the long rule of the Balkans left behind minorities in countries such as Bulgaria, where perhaps one in ten persons speak Turkish, in spite of three attempts in the past 150 years to expel them, most recently in 1989. Another 2 million Osman Turks reside as immigrants in Germany, and an additional 700,000 German citizens are of Turkish descent. Tatar, also a major Turkic language, is centered in Tatarstan, Bashkortostan, and, as a minority, Crimea, the peninsular part of Ukraine (fig. 4.9). Altogether, about 6 million Tatars live in Europe. In small pockets of Moldova, Bulgaria, and southern Ukraine live over 200,000 Gagauz speakers, who are Christians and belong to the Oguz branch of Turkic. Europe abounds with such tiny minorities, most of which have not been mentioned here.

The **Caucasic** language family, including most notably Georgian, also bounds Indo-European on the southeast (fig. 4.9). To the south, across the Mediterranean Sea, **Afro-Asiatic** languages such as Arabic and Maltese mark the edges of Europe as conventionally defined.

The non-Indo-European periphery of Europe is completed by Basque, or Euskera, in the southwest, on the Pyrenean borders of Spain and France (fig. 4.9). With a little over 800,000 speakers, Basque long suffered decline, but a vigorous revival is presently under way, and today it enjoys the status of a semiofficial EU language along with Catalan and Galician. In Spain, establishment of the Basque Autonomous Province (Pais Vasco) offers hope for the future of this unique language that faced considerable repression during much of the twentieth century. That repression served as a catalyst for a resistance movement that has pushed for independence for the Basque country—sometimes employing violence in support of its cause. The autonomous status of the Basque country has blunted the more extreme forms of Basque nationalism, but tensions remain between the Basques and the Castilian Spanish.

Closer inspection, then, reveals that at Europe's core three major Indo-European divisions prevail, surrounded by an inner periphery of smaller Indo-European groups and an outer periphery of altogether different tongues. Moreover, east–west linguistic contrasts are reflected in the major, most ancient division within the Indo-European family and two different alphabets. The Romance–Germanic divide and the split of Slavic into two geographically separate areas provide a significant north–south patterning.

For centuries, many smaller languages declined, and some perished, but recent decades have witnessed the revival of many endangered tongues. It is instructive to look more closely at these opposing trends.

Linguistic Decline and Revival

Why do some languages decline or even die? Why do revivals occur? Geographer Charles Withers, studying Scottish Gaelic, listed four basic processes, each directly or indirectly spatial, for decline. First is a *clearance model*, or decline caused by emigration of speakers to places outside the refuge area, leaving behind a smaller population to perpetuate the language. Second, a *changeover model* describes reduced linguistic viability due to the immigration of an alien population. A third process encouraging linguistic simplification is the *economic development model*. New modes of production, particularly industrialization, accompanied by urbanization, can break up the social structure needed to perpetuate a language. The transition from subsistence farming to working in a factory, even if made within the ethnic area, could be quite destructive in the linguistic sense, particularly if the language of the workplace was not that of the farm. In this context, geographer Keith Buchanan referred to the decline of the Celtic tongues as an example of "liquidation" carried out by the English in order to produce a loyal and obedient workforce for the mines and factories. Finally, a *social morale model* describes the process by which an ethnic minority, over time, loses pride in its language and voluntarily abandons it. An educational system using solely the majority language produced bilingualism and, indirectly, fostered illiteracy in the minority tongue. Depriving the language of legal and religious status helped convey the same message—that is, the minority tongue is inferior, and its use is socially degrading. Denying the language access to printed and broadcast media can hasten the process. All four of these processes were at work until the late twentieth century to diminish or destroy many lesser languages in Europe.

Recent decades have witnessed the opposite process—the revival of endangered languages. Welsh and Breton provide examples, as do numerous languages of the former Soviet Union. Partly, these revivals accompanied the collapse of the Soviet Empire, and have seen migration patterns reverse, counteracting the earlier clearance and changeover models. Russian speakers since 1990 emigrate from Latvia, for example, while Lettish speakers immigrate back to it. The social morale model is reversed as newly independent governments promote languages such as Lettish and stigmatize Russian.

But more is at work in linguistic revival than simply imperial collapse. The rise of a global economy and progress toward a united Europe also contribute. The more globalized and uniform European civilization becomes, the more people seem to want to anchor themselves in a regional or even local culture. An identity with place and region counteracts the trend toward oneness. Ethno-linguistic resurgence occurs.

Resurgence invariably has political consequences (see Chapter 6) and is a **postindustrial** phenomenon (see Chapter 9) (fig. 4.10). Indeed, the rapid deindustrialization of Wales after about 1965, which witnessed the widespread closure of mines and factories, coincided with the Welsh revival movement. Buchanan's linguistic liquidation collapsed when the Celtic workforce became unemployed. Whatever the exact causal forces may be, modern Europe is witnessing the widespread rejuvenation of small languages as well as regional dialects (fig. 4.11). In the Netherlands, for example, radio broadcasts in the Limburgs dialect of the southeast can now be heard.

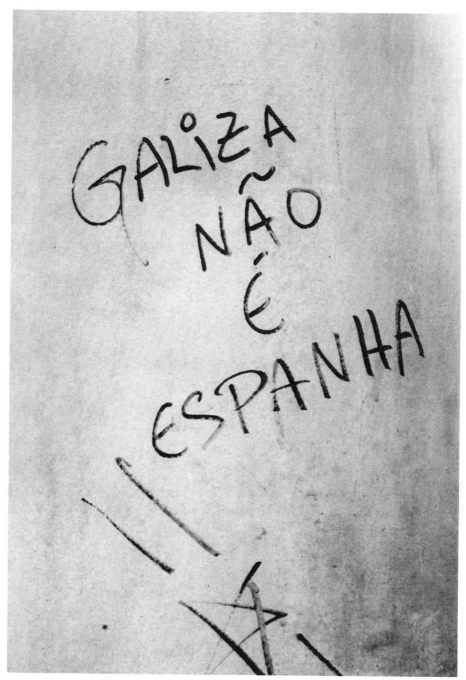

Figure 4.10.   Galician-language graffiti greets the visitor to the pilgrimage town of Santiago de Compostela in the Spanish autonomous province of Galicia. Galician is undergoing a modest revival, following repression under the Franco dictatorship. The message is political— "Galicia is not Spain." Photo by T. G. J.-B., 1999.

Figure 4.11.   Bilingual French-Breton sign in Brittany, France. Breton "hid" in isolation behind hedgerows like the one seen here, for a thousand years, gradually retreating before French, but today this Celtic language is enjoying a modest revival. Photo by T. G. J.-B., 1999.

Multilingualism

Europe is a region of many languages, and the EU is officially committed to preserving multilingualism across the "continent." That commitment dates from the early period of European unity when a declaration was adopted guaranteeing the equal status of the national languages of member states. This guarantee is still in place, meaning that there are now 24 official languages in the 28-member EU, including Erse, Maltese, and Estonian, which are each spoken by fewer than one million people. The EU has embraced a number of initiatives aimed at maintaining linguistic diversity and protecting the language rights of minorities—drawing on the Swiss model for inspiration. But the costs of maintaining such programs are high, and some advocates of closer economic and social integration suggest a "pragmatic medium of a common language." What that language might be, however, raises difficult issues. English is a logical candidate, but as we will see, there is much controversy over the growing role of English in Europe, and there are only two EU countries where English is the dominant tongue.

Multilingualism can be a personal, not just a regional, attribute. Given the presence of many languages in Europe in close proximity to one another, it is not surprising that many Europeans place a high value on being able to speak more than one language. Recent surveys show that well over half of those living in the EU are able to hold a conversation in a language other than their mother tongue, and the figure rises to over 90% in countries such as Luxembourg, Slovakia, and Latvia. Perhaps even more remarkably, a little more than a quarter of the citizens of the EU claim they can carry on a conversation in two languages other than their mother tongue.

Nonetheless, multilingualism is much more advanced in some parts of Europe than in others. Most generally, those speaking major international languages (e.g., English, Spanish, French) are less likely to know another language than those speaking tongues with less international standing (e.g., Swedish, Finnish, Slovak). It is important to note, however, that even among people who speak another language, most are anxious to preserve and protect their native tongues.

As noted above, English is increasingly becoming Europe's lingua franca. In countries such as Sweden and the Netherlands, over half of the population speaks

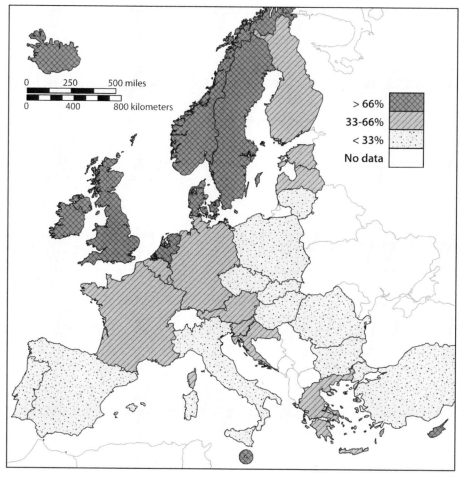

Figure 4.12. Ability to speak English, as a percentage of total population, by national units and selected dependent territories. *Sources:* Eurobarometer and selected national statistical yearbooks.

English as a second language (fig. 4.12). In almost all EU countries, students are far more likely to study English as a second language than German, French, Spanish, or Italian. Even in Eastern Europe, Russian and German have been overshadowed by English. This development has raised some concerns, particularly in France, where the government has taken steps to purge the French language of English vocabulary. In other parts of Europe, serious questions are being raised about what might be lost if languages lose standing or are radically changed by the rush toward English. Others, however, see this as merely the latest phase in a process of linguistic evolution that is as old as humanity itself.

Controversies over multilingualism are also present in states with significant populations speaking more than one language. Despite the role of the state in spreading and standardizing languages, there are many places in Europe where the political and language boundaries do not coincide. As we have seen, some of these cases involve relatively small language groups fighting for their survival. In other cases, speakers of one major language spill across the border into adjacent countries (e.g., French speakers in northwest Italy, German speakers in Belgium and Italy). In yet other cases, a substantial population (more than 5%) in a state speaks a minority language (e.g., Catalan speakers in Spain, Hungarian speakers in both Romania and Slovakia, Swedish speakers in Finland). Given that states have historically sought to foster a common identity based on a single language, these situations are fraught with controversy. In many cases, active ethnolinguistic movements have developed that seek to ensure not just language rights but some degree of political autonomy (see Chapter 6).

Multilingualism is a particularly important issue in Switzerland and Belgium, where sizable populations (greater than 30%) speak two or more languages in different parts of the country. Both states are officially multilingual, and the central governments have little say over language matters. Switzerland has a long tradition of multilingualism and an internal administrative structure that vests substantial power in cantons, units that are even smaller than language regions. Hence, language has not been a source of great controversy there. Belgium, by contrast, developed initially as a French-language state despite its majority Dutch/Flemish-speaking population, because the ruling elite in the nineteenth century was largely French-speaking. The legacy of attempting to create a single-language state, combined with an internal administrative structure that gives each major language group a single region, has turned language into a major source of social friction in that country. Controversies over relations between the country's two major ethnolinguistic groups have intensified to the point that some are questioning whether Belgium can hold together as a state.

Arguments over language serve as an important reminder that cultural phenomena are a product of the ideas and practices that develop in different places. They are, in other words, influenced by their geographical situation. If that is true of language, it is certainly true of religion—the topic of the next chapter.

Sources and Suggested Readings

Aitchison, J. W., and H. Carter. 1999. Cultural Empowerment and Language Shift in Wales. *Tijdschrift voor Economische en Sociale Geografie* 90:168–83.

Alinei, M., et al. 1983. *Atlas Linguarum Europae*. Vol. 1. Assen, the Netherlands: van Gorcum.

Bellwood, P. 2005. *First Farmers: The Origins of Agricultural Societies*. Malden, MA: Blackwell.

Beynon, E. D. 1941. The Eastern Outpost of the Magyars. *Geographical Review* 31:63–78.

Blomkvist, Y. E. 1985. Settlements of the Eastern Slavs. *Soviet Geography* 26:183–98, 268–83.

Buchanan, K. 1977. Economic Growth and Cultural Liquidation: The Case of the Celtic Nations. In *Radical Geography: Alternative Viewpoints on Contemporary Social Issues*, ed. R. Peet, 125–43. Chicago: Maaroufa.

Chinn, J., and R. Kaiser. 1996. *Russians as the New Minority*. Boulder, CO: Westview.

Cogo, A., and J. Jenkins. 2010. English as a Lingua Franca in Europe: A Mismatch between Policy and Practice. *European Journal of Language Policy* 2 (2): 271–93.

Coluzzi, P. 2006. Minority Language Planning and Micronationalism in Italy: The Cases of Lombardy and Friuli. *Journal of Multilingual & Multicultural Development* 27 (6): 457–71.

Cornish, V. 1936. *Borderlands of Language in Europe and Their Relations to the Historic Frontiers of Christendom*. London: Sifton.

Cvijic, J. 1918. The Geographical Distribution of the Balkan Peoples. *Geographical Review* 5:345–61.

Dominian, L. 1917. *The Frontiers of Language and Nationality in Europe*. Special Publication 3. New York: American Geographical Society.

Dugdale, J. S. 1969. *The Linguistic Map of Europe*. London: Hutchinson University Library.

Fernández-Armesto, F., ed. 1994. *The Times Guide to the Peoples of Europe*. London: Times Books.

Geipel, J. 1969. *The Europeans: An Ethnohistorical Survey*. London: Longmans.

Goetschy, H., and A.-L. Sanguin, eds. 1995. *Langues Régionales et Relations Transfrontalières en Europe*. Paris: Harmattan.

Gordon, R. G. 2005. *Ethnologue: Languages of the World*. 15th ed. Dallas: SIL International.

Greenberg, J. H. 2000. *Indo-European and Its Closest Relatives: The Eurasiatic Language Family*. Stanford, CA: Stanford University Press.

Grüll, J. 1965. Entwicklung und Bestand der Rätoromanen in den Alpen. *Mitteilungen der Österreichischen Geographischen Gesellschaft* 107:86–103, 117.

Hindley, R. 1990. *The Death of the Irish Language: A Qualified Obituary*. London: Routledge.

Jones, P., and M. T. Wild. 1992. Western Germany's "Third Wave" of Migrants: The Arrival of the Aussiedler. *Geoforum* 23:1–11.

Kirk, J. M., S. F. Sanderson, and J. D. A. Widdowson, eds. 1985. *Studies in Linguistic Geography: The Dialects of English in Britain and Ireland*. London: Croom Helm.

Kjaer, A. L., and S. Adams, eds. 2011. *Linguistic Diversity and European Democracy*. Farnham, UK: Ashgate.

Krantz, G. S. 1988. *Geographical Development of European Languages*. New York: Peter Lang.

Lautensach, H. 1954. Über die Topographischen Namen Arabischen Ursprungs in Spanien und Portugal. *Die Erde* 6:219–43.

Lundén, T. 1988. Language, Geography and Social Development: The Case of Norden. In *Language in Geographic Context*, ed. C. H. Williams, 47–72. Clevedon, UK: Multilingual Matters.

MacGiolla Chríost, D., and J. W. Aitchison. 1998. Ethnic Identities and Language in Northern Ireland. *Area* 30:301–9.

Mackenzie, J. L. 1994. Western Europe. In *Atlas of the World's Languages*, ed. C. R Moseley and R. E. Asher, 245–61. London: Routledge.

Makkay, J., and J. Jamieson. 2003. An Archeologist Speculates on the Origin of the Finno-Ugrians. *Mankind Quarterly* 43 (3): 235–72.

Mallory, J. P. 1989. *In Search of the Indo-Europeans: Language, Archaeology, and Myth*. London: Thames & Hudson.

Murphy, A. B. 1988. *The Regional Dynamics of Language Differentiation in Belgium: A Study in Cultural-Political Geography*. Geography Research Paper 227. Chicago: University of Chicago.

———. 1998. "European Languages." In *A European Geography*, ed. T. Unwin, 34–50. Harlow, UK: Addison Wesley Longman.

Nash, C. 1999. Irish Placenames: Post-Colonial Locations. *Transactions of the Institute of British Geographers* 24:457–80.

O'Luain, C. 1989. The Irish Language Today. *Europa Ethnica* 46 (1): 1–10.

Orton, H., and N. Wright. 1974. *A Word Geography of England*. London: Seminar Press.

Pryce, W. T. R. 1975. Migration and the Evolution of Culture Areas: Cultural and Linguistic Frontiers in North-East Wales, 1750 and 1851. *Transactions of the Institute of British Geographers* 65:79–108.

Renfrew, C. 1988. *Archaeology and Language: The Puzzle of Indo-European Origin*. Cambridge: Cambridge University Press.

———. 1989. The Origins of Indo-European Languages. *Scientific American* 261 (4): 106–14.

Sanguin, A.-L., ed. 1993. *Les Minorités Ethniques en Europe*. Paris: Harmattan.

Sopher, D. E. 1955. Arabic Place Names in Spain. *Names* 3:5–13.

Straka, M. 1979. Karte der Völker und Sprachen Europas unter besonderer Berücksichtigung der Volksgruppen. Graz: Akademische Druck- u. Verlagsanstalt.

Studer, P., and I. Werlen. 2012. *Linguistic Diversity in Europe: Current Trends and Discourses*. Berlin: De Gruyter Mouton.

Vanhaeren, M., and F. d'Errico. 2006. Aurignacian Ethno-linguistic Geography of Europe Revealed by Personal Ornaments. *Journal of Archaeological Science* 33 (8): 1105–28.

Wilkinson, H. R. 1951. *Maps and Politics: A Review of the Ethnographic Cartography of Macedonia*. Liverpool: University Press.

Withers, C. W. J. 1984. *Gaelic in Scotland, 1698–1981: The Geographical History of a Language*. Edinburgh: Donald.

———. 1988. *Gaelic Scotland: The Transformation of a Culture Region*. London: Routledge.

Wixman, R. 1980. *Language Aspects of Ethnic Patterns and Processes in the North Caucasus*. Research Paper 191. Chicago: University of Chicago, Department of Geography.

———. 1981. Territorial Russification and Linguistic Russianization in Some Soviet Republics. *Soviet Geography* 22:667–75.

CHAPTER 5

The Geography of Religion

Of all the human traits mentioned in Chapter 1 that have been used to define "Europe," the one that stands out most prominently across the sweep of time is religious affiliation. In the centuries preceding the Age of Exploration, Europe and Christianity were viewed as nearly synonymous. Christian Europeans had been engaged in armed conflict with Muslims in the Mediterranean for centuries, strengthening their sense of collective identity based on religion. European colonialism led to the diffusion of Christianity to the far corners of the globe, but the idea of Europe as the center of Christianity was never lost. Pope John Paul II, in 1982, claimed that European identity "is incomprehensible without Christianity," that the faith "ripened the civilization of the continent, its culture, its dynamism, its activeness, its capacity for constructive expansion on other continents." That same impulse led some of the framers of a draft constitution for the European Union in the early 2000s to call for a reference to Europe's Christian heritage in the document's preamble. They were unsuccessful, but the proposal and the debate that ensued provided a clear reminder of the historical role of Christianity in Europe's development.

From the perspective of the early twenty-first century, the foregoing point is easy to overlook because a dramatic turn toward secularism has occurred in Europe. Yet it is important to remember that Christianity is at the heart of much of what came out of Europe—both good and bad. Much of its great art, literature, music, and philosophy were inspired by Christianity. One cannot imagine European culture devoid of the magnificent cathedrals, altarpieces, crucifixes, and religious statuary. The *Commentaries* of Saint Thomas Aquinas, Leonardo da Vinci's *Last Supper*, Michelangelo's *David* and Sistine Chapel, orthodox churches inside the Kremlin in Moscow and the cathedral at Chartres, Dante's *Inferno*, and Milton's *Paradise Lost* were all products of Christianity. Yet some of Europe's most intractable wars, its genocides, inquisitions, and colonial endeavors, were also inspired by Christianity.

However one views the Christian legacy, it is important to understand its foundations and geographical expression. This means focusing attention on the diffusion of Christianity in Europe and its fragmentation into different branches (fig. 5.1). It

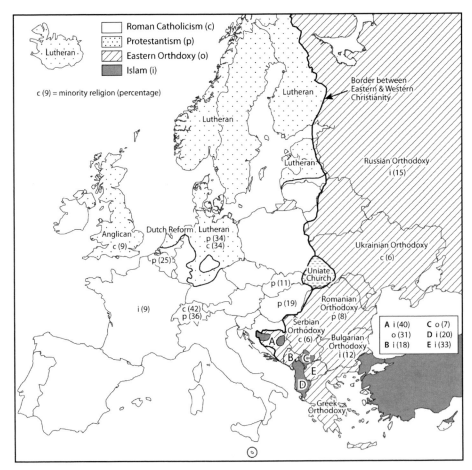

Figure 5.1. Religious groups in Europe. Significant minority religions within each country are shown by small letter abbreviations (c = Catholic, o = Orthodox, p = Protestant, i = Islam) followed by the percentage of adherents to the minority religion found in each country. The figures for Russia are for Eurorussia, as defined in the preface. *Sources:* Eurobarometer, Eurostat, and various national statistical yearbooks.

also means situating Christianity within the context of other religious traditions that have been part of Europe's story.

Pre-Christian Europe

Christianity was not native to Europe. In pre-Christian times, European religions were principally **polytheistic**—worshipping multiple divinities. Most groups practiced **animism**, which imbued objects such as rocks, heavenly bodies, mountains, forests, and rivers with souls. The Ancient Greeks and Romans were followers of elaborate forms of **paganism** that involved a pantheon of supreme beings and lesser deities overlooking life on earth. A bewildering array of gods, goddesses, and spirits

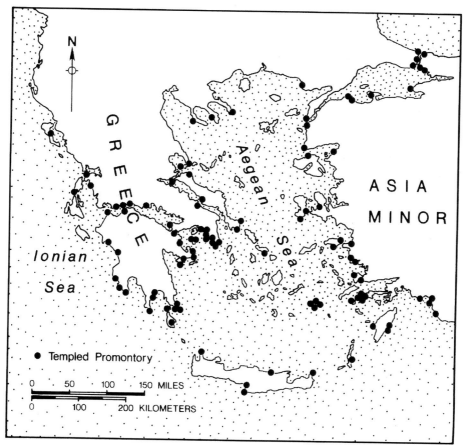

Figure 5.2. Templed promontories of the ancient Aegean. The seagoing Greeks placed great importance upon promontories, both as hazards to sailing and as landmarks. Temples both heightened the visibility of the promontories and allowed placation of the relevant gods. *Source:* Semple 1927.

ruled over war, fertility, woodlands, high places, caves, harvests, death, lightning, navigation, earthquakes, volcanoes, moon, sun, winds, and a hundred other domains. The Greek goddess Artemis facilitated hunting, her sister Aphrodite governed love and fertility, and the Roman Mars assisted in warfare. Thousands of shrines and altars dedicated to these divinities dotted the ancient landscape of Europe, many of which remain today as ruins (fig. 5.2). Some pre-Christian deities achieved more importance than others, often gaining acceptance over fairly large areas. A mother-fertility-love goddess, referred to by the Romans as *Magna Mater*—the great mother—was widely venerated throughout the Mediterranean lands, and *Mithras*, a male god originating in Persia, achieved widespread worship among the Roman military class. Especially strong in Greece, the *mystery cults* had a main center at Eleusis near Athens. In the western and northern fringes of Europe, astronomy-based religions of early Indo-European origin held sway, leaving us megalithic ruins such as Stonehenge, which is believed to have been a rather sophisticated observatory.

In other words, pre-Christian Europe was religiously divided and complex. That most of Europe should have been converted to a radically different, **monotheistic** faith—Christianity—seems amazing. Originally, the worship of a single male divinity had been confined to Afro-Asiatic nomadic herders of the southwest Asian deserts.

Diffusion of Christianity

The key figure in the remarkable diffusion of Christianity to Europe, the Apostle Paul, bridged the Semitic and Greek cultures; he presented monotheism in terms that were understandable and appealing to Europeans. Throughout the centuries of conversion, Christianity also proved adept at absorbing elements of the native religions of Europe. *Sun*day, devoted to a Roman god of the sun, became the Christian Sabbath;

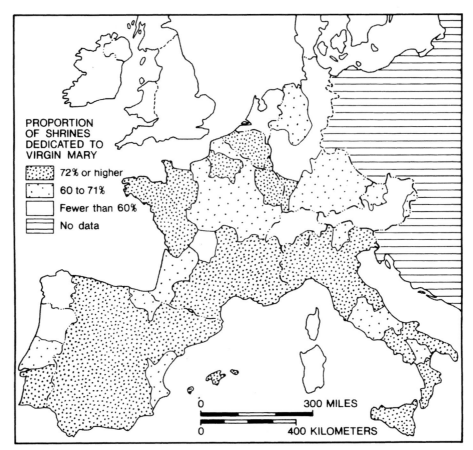

Figure 5.3. Proportion of pilgrimage shrines dedicated to the Virgin Mary in modern Europe. Marian devotion is greatest in the Mediterranean lands, where the Magna Mater was venerated in pre-Christian times. Spain alone has some 22,000 Marian shrines. Catholic shrines dedicated to Christ and various saints are most common in the North and Alpine lands. *Source:* Nolan and Nolan 1989, 121.

many of the old multiple divinities survived as saints; the Virgin Mary annexed the devotion afforded to the Mediterranean Magna Mater; Jehovah replaced the old king of the gods, Zeus/Jupiter/Odin; and the mystery cult promise of eternal life was honored by Christianity. The veneration of Mary remains strongest in the Mediterranean lands even today (fig. 5.3).

Pagan places of worship typically became Christian shrines and churches. For example, a rural church in Scotland stands atop a prehistoric artificial mound venerated since ancient times; the Alvestra monastery in south-central Sweden abuts standing stones dating from pre-Christian antiquity; and Canterbury Cathedral, seat of the Church of England, rests on the foundations of a solar-oriented pagan temple (fig. 5.4). Sacred groves from pagan times still stand protected alongside Greek monasteries, and springs holy to the pre-Christian Irish continue to be pilgrimage sites today.

Christianity largely destroyed the animistic belief that humans were part of nature, replacing it with the doctrine that God had given his people dominion over the environment. By removing the animistic sacredness of nature, some people believe that Christianity opened the way for the massive environmental modification that has so altered Europe's physical environment. Others, however, see these changes largely as the product of modernization and industrialization.

Initially, Christianity spread from city to city in the Roman Empire, leaving the intervening rural areas pagan. (The Latin word *pagus*, meaning "rural district," is the root of both the word *pagan* and the word *peasant*.) Similarly, the isolated, unconverted

Figure 5.4.   Kildrummy Church, positioned atop an ancient artificial mound in the northern Scottish Highlands where pagans worshipped. Such juxtapositions occur frequently in all parts of Europe. Photo by T. G. J.-B., 1992.

dwellers of the heaths gave rise to the word *heathen*. Christianity in Europe was, at first, an urban faith.

Perhaps one key to the concentration of the first European Christians in the cities of the Roman Empire lies in the Jewish **diaspora**. Early in the Christian era, the Romans dispersed most Jews from Israel in an attempt to quell their rebellions against imperial authority. Jews came as refugees to almost every Roman city throughout the empire, and they clustered in ethnic neighborhoods. Evidence now suggests that those very neighborhoods often housed the first Christian congregations. In other words, certain Jewish people in their diaspora, already monotheists whose holy scriptures formed half the Christian Bible, may have become the earliest Christians in Europe, though many or even most Jews did not convert.

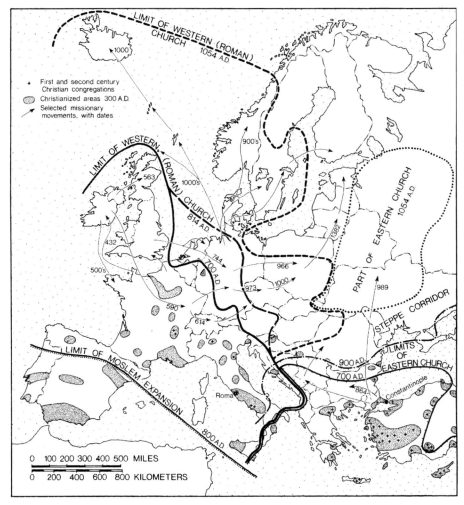

Figure 5.5. **Diffusion of Christianity** to 1400 CE. The faith spread in the early centuries by moving from city to city while bypassing rural areas.

Whatever the case, the spread of Christianity remained slow until 313 CE, when the Roman emperor Constantine issued an edict of toleration for Christianity, which led eventually to its status as a state religion. In the centuries that followed, two major centers directed the diffusion of Christianity into Europe from its Mediterranean base: Latin Rome and Greek Byzantium (later Constantinople, and now Istanbul). The Roman Church spread rapidly in the western Mediterranean during the fourth and fifth centuries CE. Before the fall of the empire, significant areas in what are now Italy, France, and Spain became converted, and many members of the Germanic tribes who subsequently overran these areas quickly accepted Christianity. From the western Mediterranean core, Roman missionaries spread far to the north. Patrick arrived in Ireland in 432, and a major cultural flowering occurred among the Celtic converts there. Many of the peoples of Britain, missionized from both Ireland and the continent, converted from the 400s through the early 600s CE (fig. 5.5).

Christianity lost ground in parts of western Europe with the disintegration of social and political institutions following the fall of the Roman Empire. However, missionary activity—often from peripheral locations in the British Isles and what we now call France—began to reclaim territory for the religion. The pagan tribes of Germany received missionaries beginning in the early 600s, and the Germans in turn carried the church to Scandinavians and Slavic Poles by about 1100. The pivotal event in Poland occurred in 966, when the principal local ruler allowed himself to be baptized, an event duplicated in Hungary in 973. The European work of Roman missionaries ended in 1386 with the conversion of the Balts in distant Lithuania. In carrying Christianity to the north, missionaries also took the Latin alphabet, and the zone of Roman mission work is fairly well indicated even today by the use of Latin characters.

The impressive gains in the north were partially offset by losses to Islam in the south. North Africa, where the Christian church had been well established, became permanently Muslim in the 700s, and much of Iberia fell under the control of Muslims for many centuries. The Moors (Islamicized Arabs) who came into Iberia respected those religions that possessed a written book of beliefs, so Christianity survived.

Greek Christians, centered in the Byzantine Empire, initially converted the Slavic tribes that had spread south of the Danube River into imperial territory. Mission work north of the Danube was hindered by repeated invasions of Asiatic tribes entering Europe through the steppe corridor and Valachian Plain between 550 and 1050 CE (fig. 5.5); but finally, in 988, Ukrainians and Russians became Christian. Missionaries working among the Slavs developed the Cyrillic alphabet, derived from Greek characters, and the distribution of this script today, with some exceptions, parallels the extent of their church in Europe. Greek Christianity, like its Roman counterpart, lost ground in the south while winning converts in the north. Soon after 1200, the Byzantine Empire collapsed under Turkish pressure, eventually causing the loss of Asia Minor, and even the Christian center at Constantinople, to Islam.

Christian Fragmentation

Europe may appear to have been unified by Christianity, but this façade conceals major internal contrasts. Monolithic Christianity never existed in Europe. Early Christian theology and practices in the Hellenistic part of the Roman Empire embodied elements of mysticism from neighboring cultures to the south and east, whereas a more pragmatic and politically oriented church arose in the center of the empire. The claim of the Latin bishop of Rome to leadership of all Christendom never gained unqualified acceptance by the Greeks and the bishop of Byzantium. The subsequent split of the empire into western and eastern halves presaged a major religious schism. In a separation made formal in 1054 CE, the western church became Roman Cathol-

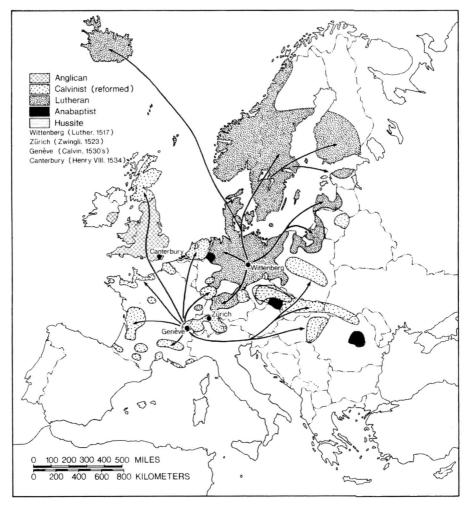

Figure 5.6. Diffusion of Protestantism to 1570 CE. The Reformation spread from several different nuclei to influence most of northern and central Europe.

icism, whereas the Byzantine Church became Eastern Orthodoxy. The dividing line between Catholicism and Orthodoxy (fig. 5.1) has changed little in a thousand years and provides the basis for important contrasts between west and east in Europe.

The second great schism occurred in the 1500s, when western Christianity split, the southern lands remaining Catholic and the north becoming Protestant (fig. 5.6). Protestantism arose in different places over several centuries in an attempt to bring about reforms within the Roman church. The pivotal event, the challenge to the church issued by Martin Luther at Wittenberg, Germany, in 1517, evolved into successful secession. The new church quickly spread through northern Germany and the Scandinavian lands, supported by the rulers of individual states. John Calvin furthered the Protestant cause in the mid-1500s from his base in Switzerland, dispersing a set of ideas that gave rise to Puritanism in England, Presbyterianism in Scotland, the Reformed Church in the Netherlands and Germany, and the Huguenot faith in France, as well as lesser groups of Calvinist followers in eastern Europe. Also in Switzerland, Ulrich Zwingli led a Protestant movement in the German-speaking cantons. A number of Anabaptist Protestant sects also arose, including the Mennonites in the Netherlands. These people rejected infant baptism and offered the rite only to adult believers. An additional breakaway from Roman Catholicism came in 1534, when King Henry VIII created the Church of England, also known as the Anglican Church.

Henry VIII's initiative was not simply a matter of differing beliefs; it reflected a desire on the part of the English monarch to free himself and his domain from the influence of Rome. This same desire led political leaders in other parts of northern Europe, including some states within the German Empire, to adopt Protestantism as the official religion. The spread of Protestantism was not simply a product of individual conversion, then; in many cases it was imposed from above by state leaders. To this day, many northern European countries have an official state religion, even though freedom of religious practice is guaranteed.

The Protestant breakaway reinforced a significant north–south cultural divide in Europe. The religious border between Catholicism and Protestantism had pretty much stabilized by 1570, though the dreadful Thirty Years' War between Catholics and Protestants still lay ahead (compare figs. 5.1 and 5.6). As a result of the two Christian schisms, Europe acquired three major religious regions: a Roman Catholic region, a Protestant region, and an Eastern Orthodox region.

ROMAN CATHOLICISM

About 277 million Europeans are practicing or nominal Roman Catholics today, roughly 32% of the total population. **Roman Catholicism** is practiced across a huge region, stretching from Iberia and Italy in the south to Lithuania in the north, and from Ireland in the west to Croatia and Hungary in the east. In some countries, such as Spain, Catholicism is overwhelmingly prevalent, but many regions, particularly along the contact zones with Protestantism and Orthodoxy, exhibit considerable denominational variety.

Figure 5.7.   St. Peter's in Vatican City, the papal seat and center of European and world Catholicism. The Catholic Church retains a viable central authority, based here in a small independent state. Photo by A. B. M., 2001.

Roman Catholicism remains a relatively united church oriented toward the papacy, and Vatican City is the seat of a highly centralized administration (fig. 5.7). At the same time, regional differences exist. Irish Catholicism is not the same as Italian or Lithuanian Catholicism, and the church has encouraged national patron saints and other regional qualities to persist. Individual districts and valleys often boast their own patron saints and shrines. For example, in the Bética mountains south of Granada in Spain lies the highly distinctive region of Las Alpujarras, where the town of Ugijar proudly houses the sanctuary of Our Lady of the Martirio, "patroness of Las Alpujarras." In this manner, Catholicism heightens, and draws strength from, a local sense of place.

Catholicism has certainly shaped the landscape over time. Geographers speak of **cultural landscapes**—the visual, varied trace of human presence as revealed in the assemblage of tangible physical and human characteristics making up an area. Significant parts of Europe can be said to display a Catholic landscape. Among the most obvious religious contributions to the landscape are sacred structures, especially church buildings. Europe exhibits many regional contrasts in church size, building material, and architectural style. In Catholic areas, church structures tend to be large and visually inspiring, in part because the Roman church places great value on visible beauty. Catholic landscapes gain additional distinctiveness from the numerous roadside shrines and chapels that dot the countryside. Catholicism also influenced the names people gave to places and physical features. In Catholic countries, the custom of naming towns for Christian saints was common. Often, saintly suffixes were added to preexisting settlements, as in Alcazar de San Juan in Spain. The frequency of such sacred names decreases to the north in Europe, and they are rarely found in Protestant lands. In Germany, some three-quarters of the towns and villages bearing the saintly prefix *Sankt* lie in the Catholic-dominated southern part of the country, including 21% in the province of Bavaria alone. Cross the religious divide into Protestant Germany, and saints largely disappear from place names.

Catholicism has also left a distinctive economic imprint on its part of Europe. For example, the Catholic tradition of avoiding meat on Friday and on numerous church holidays greatly stimulated the development of the fishing industry. The church encouraged the use of fish during periods of fasting and penitence, as well as on Friday. Seashore Catholics, such as Basques, Bretons, Galicians, and Portuguese, are among the greatest fishing peoples of Europe. Saint Peter, the original Christian fisherman, holds a place of special veneration in the fishing villages of Catholic Europe. The importance of the Catholic Church to fishing is suggested by the economic crisis in English fishing communities when Catholic dietary restrictions ended as a result of the Anglican breakaway in the 1500s. Many fishermen were obliged to become sailors, perhaps leading to the great era of English naval exploration, piracy, and overseas colonization.

Pilgrimages

An even more profound economic influence of Catholicism results from the Church's enduring practice of religious pilgrimages. Favored holy sites have long derived considerable financial benefit. In Catholic Europe, tens of millions of pilgrims travel to

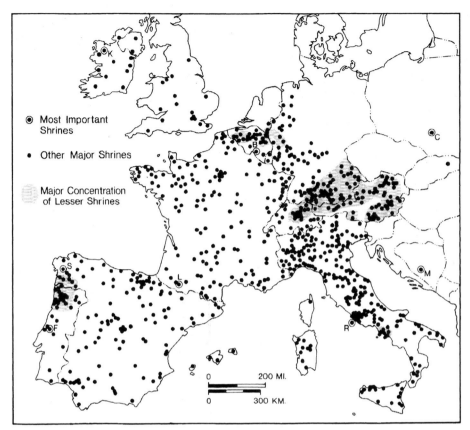

Figure 5.8.   Pilgrimage shrines in Western Europe. Each dot represents a shrine that is the most important in its diocese or draws at least 10,000 pilgrims per year. In the shaded areas, remarkable concentrations of lesser shrines occur. Pilgrimage is largely a Catholic phenomenon, as the distribution suggests. Only a small selection of eastern European shrines is shown. Key to symbols for most famous shrines: B = Beauraing; C = Czestochowa; F = Fátima; K = Knock; L = Lourdes; M = Medjugorje; R = Rome; S = Santiago de Compostela. *Source:* In part from Nolan and Nolan 1989, 29, 31, 32.

thousands of holy places each year. Pilgrimage sites vary in importance, ranging from small shrines that attract only the faithful from the immediate surroundings to internationally known places sought out by Catholics from all over Europe and the Americas. Pilgrimage sites are unevenly distributed in Europe, even within Catholic areas (fig. 5.8). In France, for example, pilgrimage sites devoted to the Virgin Mary lie mainly in the south and west, with a few isolated clusters elsewhere in the country (fig. 5.3).

Vatican City draws millions of Catholic visitors to Rome each year, adding to the already important tourist trade based on antiquities. As recently as the 1700s, most long-distance travel of people within Europe involved pilgrims going to Rome and a few other religious centers. Many roads developed mainly for pilgrim traffic, complete with hospices at difficult places such as mountain passes. Monks built bridges along these routes.

Figure 5.9.   Pilgrims at Santiago de Compostela, the greatest of the shrines in Spain and a goal of pilgrims since the Middle Ages. It lies in Galicia. Photo by T. G. J.-B., 1999.

The major present-day pilgrimage sites, in addition to Rome, include Lourdes, a French town at the foot of the Pyrenees in the Basin of Aquitaine where the Virgin Mary supposedly appeared in a vision; Fátima, north of Lisboa in Portugal; Czestochowa, where the greatest icon of Polish Catholicism, the miraculous Black Virgin, is housed; Medjugorje, in the Croatian Catholic district of Bosnia-Herzegovina, where the faithful believe the Virgin Mary appeared repeatedly beginning in 1981; and Santiago de Compostela in Spanish Galicia, a medieval site associated with St. James (figs. 5.8 and 5.9). Fátima alone attracts over five million pilgrims annually, as does Lourdes. In the centennial year of the miracle at Lourdes in 1958, an astounding eight million visitors came to the area. Small wonder that this small provincial town ranks second in France only to Paris in number of hotels.

Winds of Change

The Roman Catholic Church remains the largest Christian denomination in the world with 1.2 billion followers. In 1910, two-thirds of all Catholics in the world were Europeans, but a century later less than 24% lived in Europe. Today over 66% of the world Catholics are non-European, with 41% residing in Latin America. A testament to the significance of this demographic and geographic shift came in 2013, when the first non-European pope ascended to the papacy in 500 years: Francis, a former cardinal from Argentina. Unlike his predecessors John Paul II and Benedict XVI, Francis has sought to open the church to wider participation, while emphasizing service to the poor and underprivileged. As Austrian theologian Father Zulehner put it, "the Eurocentric era (for the Church) is clearly over."

Within Europe, the gap between traditional church teachings and postindustrial life is widening. Fewer people attend mass (only one out of five Spaniards report doing so on a regular basis), and the positions the Church has taken on issues such as abortion, same sex marriage, and the role of women in the priesthood have alienated a good number of younger Roman Catholics. Interestingly, Spain and Portugal, once considered the bastions of traditional Catholicism, have moved away from traditional Church teaching in some respects, legitimizing gay marriage, for example, in open defiance of the Vatican stand on this issue.

PROTESTANTISM

Protestantism is the traditional faith of the European north, centered in the lands around the shores of the North and Baltic seas (fig. 5.1). Some 110 million Protestants live in Europe, forming roughly 15% of the total population.

Figure 5.10.   A rural Lutheran church in west-central Norway. This modest structure is typical of the Protestant cultural landscape in Scandinavia. Photo by A. B. M., 2010.

In marked contrast to Catholicism, the most profound geographical feature of European Protestantism is its fragmentation into separate denominational regions, a splintering present from the very first due to the work of multiple Reformation leaders (fig. 5.6). Lutheranism has the largest geographical distribution, including the Scandinavian countries, Iceland, Estonia, Finland, Latvia, and half of Germany (figs. 5.1 and 5.10). No central Lutheran authority exists in Europe, and the faith is divided into a series of independent national churches.

The Anglican denomination remains the official established church in England, with lesser branches in the other British provinces, as well as in Ireland; and Presbyterianism, derived from Calvinism, enjoys the status of the official Church of Scotland, with some two million adherents. The United Kingdom also has an array of so-called free churches, which lack official status but are nevertheless traditional denominations of long standing. The largest of these is Methodism (with some 800,000 adherents), with lesser numbers of Baptists and many others. The Dutch Reformed Church, another Calvinist-derived body, is centered in the northern Netherlands. In 2004 it merged with the Evangelical Lutheran Church to form the Protestant Church in the Netherlands—with some 2.3 million adherents. In Switzerland, the Protestant majority belongs to a church that combines Calvinist, Lutheran, and Zwinglian influences. About all that remains of the work of Jan Hus, the first Reformation leader, is a community of some 120,000 Brethren in Czechia.

All of these traditional Protestant groups in Europe have experienced sharp declines, particularly since 1900. Neo-Protestantism provides an exception. In the

Figure 5.11.   Neo-Protestant church in southern Sweden. The church buildings are humble in appearance. Evangelical Christians have won many converts in Scandinavia and Finland. Photo by T. G. J.-B., 1989.

past several decades, evangelical groups, many based in the United States, have begun actively missionizing Europe, both in the Protestant north and the formerly Communist east (fig. 5.11). Pentecostals, Jehovah's Witnesses, Seventh-Day Adventists, and Baptists have been especially active. Ethnic minorities, such as the Sami of the far north and South Asians in the United Kingdom, have been particularly attracted to neo-Protestantism, but the phenomenon is widespread. Cultural links with Latin America brought charismatic Evangelical groups to Roman Catholic Spain. These neo-Protestant communities are predominantly concentrated in urban centers. Romania, perhaps typical of Eastern Europe, now has about 550,000 followers. The Romani, a large ethnic minority of Romania, are among the most enthusiastic converts from Eastern Orthodoxy; almost every fifth Romani belongs today either to the Pentecostal church or to one of the neo-Protestant "charismatic" churches. In Russia and Ukraine, neo-Protestantism won many new members after the collapse of the Soviet Union.

As a result of the diversity of European Protestantism, no single religious landscape has been produced. As a rule, however, Protestantism is less visible than Catholicism. Church buildings tend to be smaller and less ornate, pilgrimage places are absent, and no wayside shrines line the roadsides (fig. 5.10). Some Protestant groups traditionally rejected all visible ostentation, rendering their presence almost invisible. For example, the modest Methodist chapels of Wales, lacking steeples and stained glass, often prove difficult for the uninitiated even to identify as places of worship (fig. 5.12).

Figure 5.12.   A Methodist chapel in the Lleyn Peninsula of Celtic Wales reflects the architectural simplicity preferred by British "free" churches. Photo by the T. G. J.-B., 1974.

Instead, Protestant influences manifest themselves in other aspects of European culture. Individualism, so central a trait in modern European culture, may have its roots in the Protestant Reformation. The far-reaching **Industrial Revolution** (see Chapter 8), which so profoundly reshaped European culture, also has ties to Protestantism. Some scholars argue that the inherently dynamic character of Protestantism, the willingness of its adherents to accept change and strive for self-improvement, coupled with the Protestant ethic of hard work and the rejection of Catholic restrictions on lending money for interest, provided necessary social precedents for the Industrial Revolution. Modern industrialism arose in Protestant lands and only belatedly spread into Catholic and Orthodox areas, though nonreligious factors such as the location of coal deposits help explain the origin and dispersal of industry. Earlier historical developments played a role as well. In the late seventeenth and early eighteenth centuries, Catholic persecution of French Calvinists (or Huguenots) and Protestant Flemings, including many skilled artisans, led to an emigration of many craftsmen to England, northern Germany, and Holland. The Protestant countries thereby gained a valuable industrial impetus, while the Catholic lands, particularly France, lagged behind.

Given such attitudinal and cultural contrasts, it is not surprising that the Protestant–Catholic border, helping divide Europe into north and south, witnessed much strife over the centuries. The Thirty Years' War (1618–1648), a Protestant–Catholic contest for possession of the core of Europe, devastated large areas of Germany and Czechia and caused enormous loss of life. Two centuries earlier the Hussite war, a similar contest, also caused much grief. Most of the religious border has since fallen quiet, and the two groups learned to live in peace. Only in Northern Ireland, where the population is fairly evenly divided between Protestants and Catholics, does the feud persist—a circumstance that has as much to do with

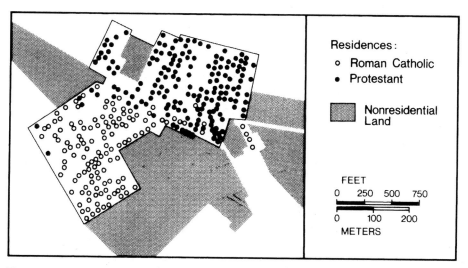

Figure 5.13. On the Protestant–Catholic divide, in Belfast, Northern Ireland. Only here does strife continue on the great north–south religious border in Europe, with the result that people have become residentially segregated along denominational lines. *Source:* Frederick Boal, "Territoriality on the Shankill-Falls Divide," *Irish Geography* 6 (1969): 37.

nationalism as it does with religion. An intrusive British-Protestant conquest and colonization occurred in Northern Ireland in the 1600s, followed by centuries of overlordship and attempted conversion of native Irish Catholics by the Protestants. During the second half of the twentieth century, the province suffered from terrorist activity by extremists of both religious groups, with the result that Protestants and Catholics became increasingly segregated (fig. 5.13). Over the past two decades a set of agreements between the British and the Irish have served to reduce tensions, and in 2006 significant powers were formally given to a Northern Ireland Assembly (seated in 2007) with representation from both communities. Nonetheless, residential segregation remains high, particularly among the middle and lower classes, although public spaces and institutions are becoming more integrated.

EASTERN ORTHODOXY

As its name implies, **Eastern Orthodox** Christianity prevails in the eastern part of Europe, especially in Greece, most of the Balkans, Ukraine, Belarus, Georgia, and Russia (fig. 5.1). Some 150 to 200 million Europeans profess this faith, roughly 20–28% of the total population of Europe. The eastern Church, steeped in mysticism and communalism, retains more of the qualities of the original Christianity, unaltered by the Renaissance, Reformation, and Enlightenment.

The patriarch of Constantinople, nominal leader of Orthodoxy, enjoys none of the central authority of the Roman papacy. Orthodoxy long ago began splintering into an array of national churches, including Greek, Serbian, Bulgarian, Romanian, Russian, Cypriot, Estonian, Georgian, and two Ukrainian Orthodox groups. The leadership at Constantinople, or Istanbul, was permanently weakened when this capital of eastern Christendom fell to the Turks in 1453. Only a few thousand Christians remain in Istanbul today. In 1996, the Russian Orthodox Church severed all ties to the patriarch.

Splintering extended still further. In Russia, the ultraconservative Old Believers separated from Orthodoxy in the late 1600s, and some 10 million followers lived in different parts of Russia by 1910. Today, only about 70,000 remain, centered in Belarus, Latvia, Lithuania, and Russia, though a revival appears to be under way. Another conservative splinter group, the *Molokans*, dating from the 1700s, once had over a million followers; today surviving parishes can be found in the Caucasus, south Russia, Ukraine, and Moldova. In 1991, the splintering continued when the Free Orthodox Church broke away from established Russian Orthodoxy.

The Orthodox religious landscape shares with that of Catholicism a beauty and vividness, while at the same time being both highly distinctive and regionally varied. Balkan church buildings, borrowing from the colorful and decorative Byzantine architectural style of the south, attract the eye with abundant reds and yellows (fig. 5.14). Russian churches and monasteries display their own style, often built of wood with distinctive onion-shaped domes.

The Orthodox Church today is experiencing something of a revival in the Slavic north, after eight decades of governmental oppression. In Russia and Ukraine, hundreds of churches and cathedrals have been restored or built anew. A mass campaign

Figure 5.14.   A splendid Eastern Orthodox church in Sarajevo, Bosnia. Eastern Orthodoxy produces distinctive regional religious landscapes. Photo by A. B. M., 2009.

Figure 5.15.   The Cathedral of Christ the Savior in Moscow. The massive church was completed in 2000. Photo by A. B. M., 2013.

was organized throughout Russia to rebuild the cathedral of Christ the Savior in downtown Moscow, which was razed on Stalin's orders in 1931. During the 1990s, when the Russian economy was in shambles and people were struggling to eke out a living, almost one billion dollars was collected from Russian citizens for the restoration of this spectacular structure, which now occupies a significant place in the cityscape of the Russian capital (fig. 5.15).

The contemporary Orthodox Church in Russia encompasses a range of beliefs and practices, but a close tie has developed between one wing of the Church and ardent Russian nationalists. Many nationalists believe that Orthodoxy is at the heart of Russian culture and has played a fundamental role in the development of the Russian state. Some worry that the Orthodox Church will come increasingly under the sway of the more extreme variants of Russian nationalism.

The East–West Divide

The western border of Orthodoxy continues to represent a fundamental internal cultural divide in Europe. In the Orthodox realm, east of this line, individualism, personal freedom, and materialism are less well developed, whereas communalism is strong. By contrast, democracy and capitalism have deeper historical roots in the west.

Figure 5.16.   The great monastery at Pechory, in far western Russia, is an Orthodox outpost on Europe's main religious divide. Photo by T. G. J.-B., 1999.

The border between eastern and western Christianity has long been stable in location and is well marked on the cultural landscape. Perhaps the best place to observe this ancient divide is the small Russian town of Pechory, situated directly on the Estonian border, a remarkable outpost of the Greco-Russian religious world. An impressive and beautiful Orthodox monastery, itself a pilgrimage destination, dominates Pechory, announcing visibly this perimeter of the Orthodox realm (fig. 5.16). A scant few kilometers away lies Estonia, belonging to the Western Christian tradition.

A very short distance from Pechory stands the ruined stone fortress of Izborsk, built over a millennium ago to fend off invaders from the west. Just beyond Izborsk, toward the provincial city of Pskov, is the venerated place where the Russian hero-prince Aleksandr Nevsky met and crushed a German Catholic military order, the Teutonic Knights, on the ice of frozen Chudskoye Lake in 1242—a victory commemorated by a huge statue and monument. Nevsky's defiant words, "Who comes here bearing a sword will die by the sword," are still remembered by Russians.

For a thousand years and more, then, this segment of the great European cultural divide has been marked and defended. All who would understand the multiplicity of European culture should come to this place. Go stand on this same line much farther south, in the Balkans. Listen, with author Michael Ignatieff, to a Serbian militia-man—a representative of the Orthodox east—as he explains how the neighboring Catholic Croats (who speak the same language, Serbo-Croatian) differ from Serbs. "Those Croats, they think they're better than us. Think they're fancy Europeans." The guns of war fell silent over a half-century ago at Pechory, but in the Balkans the east–west conflict flared anew at the end of the twentieth century.

Uniate and Armenian Churches

A fourth, minor division of European Christianity consists of the **Uniate Church**, centered in western Ukraine and adjacent parts of Romania, Slovakia, Hungary, and Poland. Also referred to as Greek Catholic or Ukrainian Catholic, this church claims about six million adherents. It is that rarest of hybrids—an attempted merging of eastern and western Christianity along the religious divide. The Uniate Church derives from the long Catholic Polish and Austrian rule of an Orthodox area. The Catholic monarchs demanded that their Orthodox subjects acknowledge the authority and supremacy of the Roman pope. Beneath that façade of Catholicism, the Uniate Church retained most Orthodox rites and practices, such as a married priesthood. When Polish and Austrian rule ended, Uniate Christians suffered persecution by Russian czarist Orthodoxy and, later, Communists. When freedom of religion was restored in 1990, the church reemerged vigorously in the western part of Ukraine, becoming one statement of national identity. Some 2,000 parishes reopened, and the future of the revitalized Uniate Church seems secure.

The **Armenian Orthodox Apostolic Church**, founded by apostles Thaddeus and Bartholomew, is officially a branch of eastern Christianity. Yet it has an independent status because it never acknowledged the supremacy of the patriarch at Constantinople. Instead, Armenian Christianity diverged theologically from its neighbors as early as the beginning of the fourth century. Its liturgy is still infused with Latin rites, but priests below the rank of bishop can marry before ordination. This **autocephalic** (i.e., self-governing, from Greek "cephalous," meaning a head) ethnic church, with about two million adherents, is one of the oldest branches of Christianity and today survives in independent Armenia, at Europe's southeastern edge.

Dechristianization

A substantial part of the European population is secularized. Terms such as ***dechristianization*** and *post-Christian* have been used to describe modern Europe. More than a quarter of Europe's total population does not profess belief in any religion. The geographical pattern of dechristianization is complicated (fig. 5.17). In some

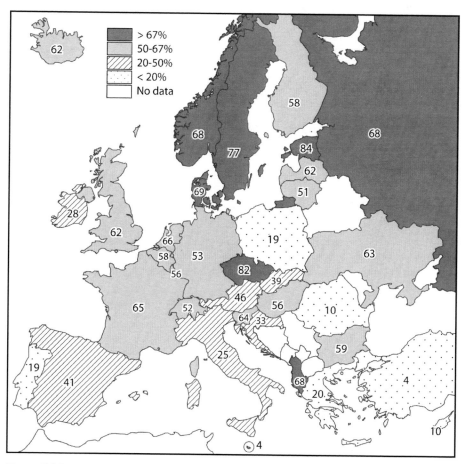

Figure 5.17. Population in European countries that is secular (percentage). *Secular* is defined as a combination of those who regard themselves as "atheist," "agnostic," "unreligious," "no religious faith," and "never attend church." *Sources:* Eurobarometer 2005, U.S. Department of State, *International Religious Freedom Report,* 2005.

regions, especially in the north and east, over half of the population is secularized, as in most of Scandinavia, Eurorussia, the United Kingdom, the Netherlands, and Czechia. Eastern Germany—the formerly communist area—is thoroughly dechristianized, as are significant parts of France and Bulgaria. If measured by national units, the most thoroughly secular countries are Estonia, with over 72% of its population claiming to be unreligious, agnostic, or atheist; Czechia 60%; Russia 50%; France 48%; Denmark 42%; the Netherlands 41%; Germany 29%; and the United Kingdom 23.2% (fig. 5.17). Attendance at mass among Catholics has declined drastically just within the last three decades, to only 10% in the Netherlands, 12% in France, 15% in Germany and Austria, 18% in Spain, and 25% in Italy. Of course, attendance at religious services does not indicate a lack of religious belief. In Russia, 66% of those who identified themselves as "believers" have never attended a religious service. But the trend away from religion is marked. Even in Ireland, once a bastion of Catholic strength, more than 40% of the population today claims no religious faith.

Within Eurorussia, the northern regions are clearly the most disaffected. By contrast, refuge regions of surviving Christian vitality include a belt from Poland through western Ukraine to Romania, nearly all of Greece, southern Italy, western Iberia, the Irish west, and an area overlapping parts of the Alps and the Po–Veneto Plain. In Greece, 98% of the people claim to be religious, and in Portugal 85% claim to be. Moreover, active efforts are being made to promote religion in some areas. For example, in the German province of Bavaria, part of the Alpine zone of religious intensity and a center of Catholicism, the parliament in 1995 passed a law requiring crucifixes to be hung in all school classrooms, defying a Supreme Court ruling against this practice and citing "the historical and cultural character of Bavaria."

The decades-long persecution of the church under Communist regimes in the east clearly helps explain the dechristianization pattern there, though it does not address the issues of how Polish Catholicism, Romanian Orthodoxy, or the Ukrainian Uniate Church so successfully resisted that oppression, or why Scandinavia and Britain are so secular. Of the three main divisions of Christianity, Catholicism clearly resisted secularization most successfully, whereas Protestantism has suffered the greatest losses. In formerly Lutheran-dominated Latvia, only 5% of the people claim to be actively involved in a church, while in the United Kingdom some 40% of the adult population never attends church.

Some dechristianization may be a reaction against established churches, particularly since these churches often have official status and are supported by tax revenues. It can work the other way, too. Professed devotion to the church can be a reaction to governmental suppression, as happened in Poland during the Communist era. For these reasons, a better measure of secularization in a Christian realm might be the proportion of the population that prays at least once a week. By this measure, Poland at 74% and Portugal at 66% appear fairly religious, but not as much as one might expect. By contrast, religiosity as measured by regular prayer appears to be quite low in Sweden (17%) and Czechia (15%).

Though many Europeans hold secular views, the influence of a Christian heritage still permeates the culture of Europe. An entire mindset, a way of thinking and viewing the world, was shaped by Christianity. That cornerstone of European culture is unlikely to disappear. And in more pragmatic terms, church organizations are deeply interwoven in the very fabric of the society despite high degrees of secularization. Indeed, many nonprofit organizations, charities, and welfare service organizations have church affiliations.

True, some say that secularized Europe lives on "old capital" inherited from Christianity, its basic institutions supported only by inertia, but others counter that agnostic intellectual freedom, unfettered by religious dogma, represents the logical culmination of the European experiment in reason and individualism.

Sects and Cults

Dechristianization during the twentieth century has left the door open to other ideologies. Some argue that Communism spread as rapidly as it did because it was positioned to fill the void. Indeed, Communist ideology incorporated some precepts associated with Christianity, such as the victorious proletariat ("the meek shall inherit the earth"), spreading the Revolution (missionizing the world), and the almost godlike status of Marx and Lenin (presented as new Russian icons, or holy images). For others, nationalism became the new faith, as in Nazi Germany.

Others have turned to New Age sects and cults. In Britain, Druids have reappeared and now make regular pilgrimages to ancient sites such as Stonehenge. Nearby Glastonbury has become the focus of several New Age cults. The French government has identified 172 sectarian movements with some 400,000 followers. Their activities have sometimes raised concerns. In the mid-1990s, the Order of the Solar Temple, active in both Switzerland and France, conducted two mass suicides. In response, French authorities tightened their scrutiny and regulation of sects, but these initiatives have raised concerns about religious freedom in some circles. Religious freedom is also an issue in Germany, where Scientologists claim to be the object of discrimination and oppression. Germany does not recognize Scientology as a religion, and the governments of both France and Germany have brought legal charges against the group for fraud and tax evasion.

Non-Christian Minorities

ISLAM

The diffusion of Christianity through Europe proved almost complete, leaving little in the way of minority religions. Today, the only substantial non-Christian presence consists of Muslims, or **Islamic** peoples. For the past 1,200 years, the Christian–Muslim religious divide in southern Europe has shifted back and forth in the face of frequent warfare (fig. 5.1). With the migration of substantial numbers of Muslims to western and northern European cities in recent times, the divide has taken on socioeconomic meaning—reflecting differences in prosperity, living standards, and population growth rates. These differences have worked together with growing extremism

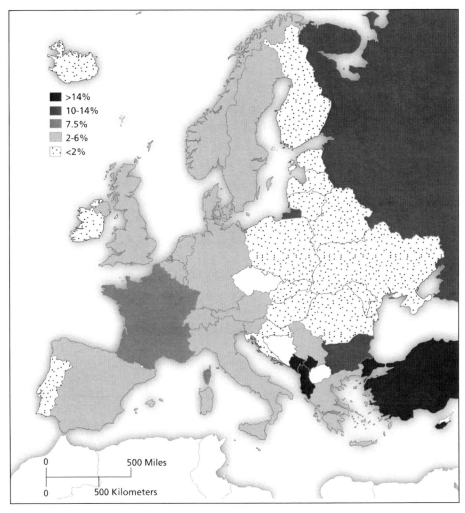

Figure 5.18.   Muslim population in European countries (percentage). Europe's Muslim population has swelled in recent decades, first as guest workers came at the invitation of state governments, and then as their families and other immigrants followed.

on both sides of the divide to produce an increasingly pronounced "us versus them" dynamic between those of Christian and Muslim heritage in Europe.

As is true of nearly every cultural border, there is no sharp geographic divide between Christians and Muslims. Only the Strait of Gibraltar offers a relatively clear-cut division, achieved by systematic ethnic cleansing centuries ago. Nearly 24 million Muslims reside in modern Europe, and an additional 15 to 20 million Islamic adherents can be found in Russia. Most of Europe's Muslims live in ancient homelands, including parts of Bosnia, Albania, Kosovo, southern Bulgaria (the Pomak area), Macedonia, the Caucasus (Chechens, Ingushis, Dagestanis, Karachai, Balkaris, Cherkessians, Abkhazis, and Adzhars), and on the southeastern margins of Russia's East European Plain and the Crimean Peninsula of Ukraine (fig. 5.18).

Of the countries with long-standing Islamic populations, Islam is most notably on the rise in Russia. Between 1991 and 2003, the number of Islamic communities increased from 914 to 3,445. Since the fall of the Soviet Union, the number of mosques has increased from a mere 90 to some 4,000. These are concentrated mainly in the republics of Tatarstan and Bashkortostan, and the North Caucasus. Kazan, the capital of Tatarstan, located on the confluence site of the Volga and Kama rivers, was one of the first places where a grandiose Muslim mosque arose after the collapse of the Soviet Union. The mosque stands in the very heart of the Kazan Kremlin—hovering above the sixteenth-century Russian Orthodox Church built by Ivan the Terrible in commemoration of the Russian defeat of the Kazan khan. In 2008 Russian president Putin participated in the dedication ceremony of the largest mosque in Russia and Europe in Grozny, the capital of Chechnya, in a symbolic gesture of reconciliation between Moscow and the former breakaway republic.

Looking farther west, some 12 million Muslims are the product of recent immigration streams to western Europe, particularly from Turkey, North Africa, and Pakistan (fig. 5.18). France has approximately 6.1 million Muslims, largely Arabs from the Maghreb; Germany has between 3.8 and 4.3 million, mainly Turks and Kurds; and Great Britain has 1.6 million, mainly from the Indian subcontinent. The French port of Marseille, the country's second largest city, has 250,000 Muslims in its population of over 8,560,000, as well as some 50 mosques. In 2009 a permit was issued for the construction of one of the largest mosques in all of France—the Grande Mosque de Marseille—a structure designed to accommodate up to 14,000 followers.

Europe's immigrant Muslims have faced considerable prejudice, hatred, and worse. In countries such as Hungary and Greece, the rising popularity of extremist groups and far-right political parties with anti-immigrant platforms represents a threat to the traditional European values of democracy and tolerance (see Chapter 11). In other places Muslims have been attacked, and some mosques have been targets of vandalism, including the large Paris mosque in 2005. Even though two-thirds of the North African Muslims in France no longer practice the faith and only 10% are devout, the government in 1999 banned Islamic headscarves for schoolgirls. One French political extremist declared Islam to be "incompatible with our civilization and our laws." Turks and Kurds face similar prejudice in Germany.

Sensitivities surrounding the Islamic presence in Europe were very much on display in 2006 when Pope Benedict XVI made reference to the comments of a fourteenth-century Byzantine emperor who described Islam as "evil and inhuman" and argued that jihad was "contrary to God's plan and to reason." Even though the pope's apparent motive was to show how Islam had been viewed in the past rather than to endorse the Byzantine view, his words aroused strong reactions. Islamic communities were outraged that the pope would draw attention to such views, while the European ultra-right applauded. The Italian prime minister at the time, Silvio Berlusconi, weighed in with a comment that incited passions further—calling Benedict's remarks "an open, a positive provocation, and so for this reason he is a great pope, with a great intelligence."

Hostility toward Islam in Europe is directed not just toward recent immigrants but also toward Muslim peoples living in their ancestral homelands. Catholic Croats and Orthodox Serbs battered Bosnian Muslim enclaves in the 1990s with a ferocity reminiscent of the Crusades. On Europe's southern cultural frontier, Armenians recently warred against Muslim Azeris, Georgians against Abkhazis, and Greek Cypriots against Turkish Cypriots. Muslim Chechens have defied Russian rule during the past two decades, but at great human cost, and other Caucasus Islamic minorities could follow Chechnya's example. Serbian leaders tried to cleanse Kosovo of Albanian Muslims; and Bulgaria, in 1989, expelled hundreds of thousands of Muslim Turks, most of whom later returned. Earlier, in 1877–1878, many Muslims were expelled from Bulgaria, causing it to become a Christian majority country. Tensions between Orthodox Greece and Muslim Turkey never completely relaxed, and the two countries fought a war in the 1920s. Clearly, Islam has given focus to European cultural identity over time, even as many today see it as a threat to that identity. Against this backdrop, it is not difficult to see why Turkey's application to join the European Union has met such resistance (see Chapter 12).

Of course hostility does not run in only one direction. Europe has been a seedbed for Islamic extremism. Terrorist cells in Germany were implicated in the September 11, 2001, attacks on the United States, and in the early 2000s Europeans faced major terrorist bombings by self-described Islamic militants in London and Madrid. Some mosques in Britain, Spain, and Germany have been recruiting grounds for disaffected Muslims, who are encouraged to think of Europeans of Christian heritage as the enemy. All of these developments fuel a widening divide along religious lines.

Contrary to the popular perception of some, Islamic fundamentalism and revival have generally not caught hold among most European Muslims. Indeed, Bosnians and Albanians had become secularized even before the arrival of Communism in the 1940s. Incredibly, recent history has seen dechristianized Europeans battling secularized Muslims in the name of religious heritage and identity.

There are some hopeful signs, though. In recent years, a growing number of Islamic religious leaders in Europe have spoken out against terrorism and extremism. On the other side of the equation, the European Agency on Fundamental Rights has released reports drawing attention to the challenges faced by Muslims in Europe. Efforts to educate people about the nature and diversity of Islam are being actively pursued, and in some instances legal protections have increased. Nonetheless, prejudice persists. As the French sociologist Jocelyn Cesari has pointed out, during the last two decades an increasing number of Europeans have come to view Muslim immigrants as opponents of modernization and integration; in some circles they are associated not only with terrorism but with general criminality and hate crimes. Such views are not shared by the majority of Europeans, but there is evidence of relatively widespread unease about the cultural and political implications of Islam's growing presence in Europe.

Islam's expanding imprint on the European landscape has fueled that unease. Islam has long been part of the landscape in southeastern Europe, where the minarets of mosques pierce the sky as aggressively as the spires of Christian churches. In Iberia, reminders of the past Islamic presence are found in mosques that were converted into churches (fig. 5.19). But in other parts of western Europe, mosques were relatively

Figure 5.19.   The Giralda, a tower on the Roman Catholic cathedral at Seville in southern Spain, was originally the minaret of the Great Mosque when the city was Arabic and Muslim. After the Christian "reconquest" and forced expulsion or conversion of the Muslims, victorious Christians added the bell chamber to the top. In this manner, a Muslim element was retained in the religious landscape. Photo by T. G. J.-B., 1986.

Figure 5.20. The Grand Mosque of Paris. The mosque was erected after World War I as a sign of gratitude for the Muslim military recruits from French colonies in North Africa who had fought alongside the French during the war. Photo by A. B. M., 2000.

scarce before the 1960s, although the Grand Mosque of Paris, which opened in 1926, was long a notable exception (fig. 5.20).

New mosques have sprung up in western Europe over the last several decades as a consequence of the influx of migrants from North Africa and Southwest Asia. Some of these have caused much controversy. The city of Cologne (Köln) witnessed a heated debate about plans to build the largest mosque in Germany. Home to the largest number of Muslims in the country, Cologne already had 30 small mosques, but the local Muslim community chose a prestigious place in the very center of the city—just across the Rhine from Cologne's grandiose, world-renowned, 700-year-old Gothic cathedral. As expected, strong opposition to the idea came from ultra-right political groups, but the plan caused a stir in the broader community. The German Jewish writer Ralph Giordano called the project "an expression of creeping Islamicization of our land." Mosques have been erected in major German cities such as Berlin, Manheim, and Duisburg, but the scale of the new Islamic structure in Cologne with its 55-foot-tall minarets marks a dramatic change in the traditional European cityscape.

The Swiss have taken the most dramatic step to limit the Islamic imprint on the cultural landscape, voting in 2009 in favor of a ban on the construction of new minarets in their country. The vote reflects a more widespread concern among many Europeans that a "parallel Muslim society" is developing in which new generations of immigrants opt not to assimilate but to create their own detached, if not always antagonistic, society (see Chapter 11). Such thinking is echoed by journalist Henryk Broder, who argues that "a mosque is more than a church or a synagogue. It is a political statement."

In an effort to counter such concerns, the Islamic community in some places has sought to keep landscape changes to a minimum. When a former Methodist church in the small town of Clitheroe, Lancashire, was sold to a local Muslim community to serve as a mosque, the cross was taken down, but no minarets were added so that the familiar silhouette of a Christian edifice would remain a part of the town's historical landscape. As the leader of the local Muslim community explained, "There will be no external call to prayer. What matters is what goes on inside."

For all the tensions between ethno-religious groups, it is important to keep in mind that in some places relations between Muslims and non-Muslims are good. The northeastern French town of Roubaix, for example, is a place where Muslim residents feel comfortable wearing traditional garb, including head coverings that were outlawed in 2004 by the French principle of **laïcité** mandating a strict separation of church and state. Muslims comprise up to one-fifth of the population in this city, which houses six mosques and a Muslim section in the town cemetery. One of the leaders of French Union of Muslim Associations, Muhammad Henniche, recently expressed hope that Roubaix might serve as a model of multicultural harmony for other French cities.

JUDAISM

The other sizable religious minority in Europe consists of adherents to Judaism, today numbering only about 1,500,000. Their fate at the hands of Europeans in the twentieth century is a grim reminder of the devastation human communities can visit on one another. As recently as 1939, Europe was the world's principal Jewish home, and the population stood at 9,700,000—about 60% of all Jews. In 1880, prior to the great Jewish migration to America, some 90% of all Jews in the world resided in Europe. Not only was Europe the principal home of Judaism, but Jews such as Albert Einstein, Felix Mendelssohn, Benjamin Disraeli, Sigmund Freud, and Heinrich Heine had contributed greatly to European history and civilization. It mattered little. Jews, in the mindset of Nazis, were not permitted to be Europeans and were murdered by the millions. Only 3,900,000 remained in Europe by the end of World War II—over half of whom have since emigrated.

France has more Jews in its population today (just under 500,000) than any other European country, having received 220,000 Jews from Morocco and Algeria when those French colonies became independent in the 1950s and 1960s. French Jews live mainly on the Mediterranean coast and in Paris. The United Kingdom has just under 300,000 Jews, most of whom reside in greater London. Russia and Ukraine together retain only about 300,000 Jews. The number of Jewish religious communities, including synagogues and rabbinic schools, increased from 34 to 262 between 1991 and 2003, but the Jewish population in Ukraine has shrunk due to emigration. Remarkably, many of these Jews go to Germany, whose Jewish population has risen from 30,000 in 1970 to 115,000 today, in spite of the fact that anti-Semitic crimes continue to occur with some regularity. In 2006, the country's first and only rabbinic seminary after the Holocaust opened in Potsdam.

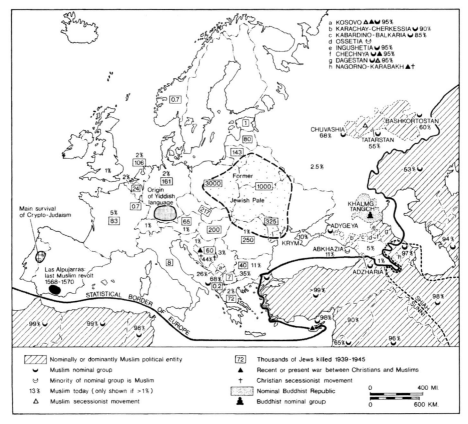

Figure 5.21.   The non-Christian periphery and former Jewish diaspora. Islam and Judaism both present Europe with a perceived challenge to the very essence of its culture. Both minorities have faced prejudice and marginalization. *Sources:* Cecil Roth, *A History of the Marranos*, 4th ed. (New York: Hermon Press, 1974), 368–73; Robert D. King, "Migration and Linguistics as Illustrated by Yiddish," in *Reconstructing Languages and Cultures*, ed. Edgar C. Polomé and Werner Winter, 419–39 (Berlin: de Gruyter, 1992).

The Jewish presence in Europe, now so horribly diminished, had ancient roots. Jews reached Mediterranean Europe in Roman times, after their forced dispersal from Palestine. One major early concentration developed in Muslim Arabic Iberia, where Judaism won toleration, flourished, and eventually claimed perhaps one-fifth of the population. These Iberian Jews, or **Sephardim**, later faced eviction or forcible conversion to Roman Catholicism after the Christian reconquest, leaving behind only "secret Jews" (*Marranos*) and empty *judarias* (ghettoes). Their synagogues became churches or were destroyed. To the present day, in certain mountain towns of northern Portugal, Marranos still practice Jewish ritual while outwardly adhering to Roman Catholicism (fig. 5.21). Many Sephardic Jews fled Iberia and found new homes, particularly in Protestant countries such as Britain and the Netherlands.

Another major Jewish concentration developed in medieval times in western and southern Germany, where the German-derived Yiddish language originated. These became known as the **Ashenazim**, the second major division of European Jewry. In the late Middle Ages, Ashkenazic Jews, responding to an edict of tolerance and invitation to settle by the Kingdom of Poland, began the migration that created the great concentration in Eastern Europe. This "Jewish Pale," as it came to be called after Russia annexed it and forced the Jews to remain within set borders, became the principal focus of Jewish life and culture in the entire world (fig. 5.17). The Lithuanian city of Vilnius, within the Pale, was at one time the unrivaled center of Jewish culture, the "Jerusalem of the North," with 100 synagogues, libraries, and a population that was 40% Jewish. The Nazis utterly destroyed the Pale and its inhabitants. Sadly, anti-Semitism is not just a thing of the past. During the past two decades, Jewish cemeteries and synagogues have been desecrated in France and Germany, and hate crimes are not infrequent. In one particularly dramatic incident in March 2012, three children and a teacher were gunned down by a Muslim militant in a Hebrew school in Toulouse (southern France).

At the same time, many Europeans speak out fervently against anti-Semitism. In 2005, a German cardinal, Walter Kasper, addressed the Organization on Security and Cooperation in Europe with the following admonition: "Anti-Semitism cuts through the roots of Christianity and has no place in the Church. The struggle against it means a struggle for human rights and engagement for peace." But when the larger Jewish experience in Europe is taken into consideration, it becomes clear that this small, creative religious minority has faced extraordinary intolerance. Any self-claim of Europe's cultural superiority—and these are not hard to find—must be measured against the treatment Europeans have afforded religious minorities over the centuries.

Conclusion

European Christianity faces many dilemmas in the twenty-first century. The traditional Christian churches have lost their mass appeal and are facing dwindling attendance and memberships. The *European Values Study*, a large-scale project undertaken from 1981 to 2008, found that only one-fifth of western Europeans regard religion as something that is "very important" to them. And many Europeans practice so-called "believing without belonging," characterized by "church-free spirituality" and eclectic worldviews.

The parts of Europe that have experienced the highest degree of secularization are not just in the east, where religious practice was suppressed for decades, but also in the Protestant north, as well as significant parts of Catholic Europe. At the same time, new trends are afoot, including the growing popularity of charismatic Evangelical or Pentecostal denominations, especially among the younger generations, and the resurrection of historic denominations and religious communities in Russia, Ukraine, Moldova, and other former communist states.

Europeans today have to deal with increasingly pluralistic, multicultural, and multifaith realities. The growing Muslim presence is presenting particular challenges. According to some public polls, Europeans have begun to address differences with their Muslim compatriots bluntly, especially as they relate to issues such as gender equality and free speech. Yet the events of 9/11, and the subsequent bombings in London and Madrid, have fostered feelings of distrust and fear. Immigrants from North Africa and Turkey and their descendants were long thought of as ethnic minorities; today, many think of them first and foremost as Muslims. In the process, a religious divide has once again become a significant cultural fault line in Europe. Differences between Muslims and non-Muslims were highlighted in the early 2000s when a Danish newspaper published cartoons that cast the founder of Islam, Muhammad, in an unfavorable light. Many Europeans of Christian heritage saw this as an act of free speech. Yet one Belgian woman who is married to a Muslim man commented that "no amount of explanation about free speech could convince her husband that the publication of cartoons lampooning Muhammad in a Danish newspaper was in any way justified."

Still, efforts to encourage interreligious and intercultural dialog are growing. In 2004, more than 2,000 Christian, Muslim, and Jewish leaders met with European Union officials in Russia to discuss ways of promoting constructive interaction among faiths in the aftermath of the massacre of schoolchildren in Beslan, North Ossetia. That same year, six Balkan presidents met in Albania and called for the "celebration of people's religious heritage" as a profound part of their identities. Such meetings and their resolutions remind us that, even as Europe has played host to appalling interfaith conflicts, hope lies in the humanistic values of European civilization: human rights, democracy, pluralism, and equality.

Europe, then, reveals sharp, ever-changing religious contrasts. These contrasts have been shaped through time by social forces but also by the political organization of space. It thus makes sense to turn in the next chapter to the evolution of the European political pattern.

Sources and Suggested Readings

Anderson, J. 1980. Regions and Religions in Ireland: A Short Critique of the Two Nations Theory. *Antipode* 11:44–53.

Bäckström, A., et al. 2010. *Welfare and Religion in 21st Century Europe.* Vol. 1. Surrey, UK: Ashgate.

Boyer, J.-C. 1996. La Frontière Entre Protestantisme et Catholicisme en Europe. *Annales de Géographie* 105:119–40.

Connell, J. 1970. The Gilded Ghetto: Jewish Suburbanization in Leeds. *Bloomsbury Geographer* 3:50–59.

Davie, G. 2006. Religion in Europe in the 21st Century: The Factors to Take into Account. *European Journal of Sociology* 47 (2): 271–96.

de Planhol, X. 1962. L'Islam dans la Physiognomie Géographique de la Péninsule Iberique. *Revue Géographique des Pyrénées et du Sud-Ouest* 33:274–81.

Derrick, M. 2013. The Tension of Memory: Reclaiming the Kazan Kremlin. *Acta Slavica Iaponica* 33 (1): 1–26.

Doherty, P. 1989. Ethnic Segregation Levels in the Belfast Urban Area. *Area* 21:151–59.

———. 1993. Religious Denomination in Northern Ireland, 1961 to 1991. *Irish Geography* 26:14–21.

Donkin, R. A. 1978. *The Cistercians: Studies in the Geography of Medieval England and Wales.* Toronto: Pontifical Institute of Medieval Studies.

Duocastella, R. 1965. Géographie de la Pratique Religieuse en Espagne. *Social Compass* 12:253–302.

Gay, J. D. 1971. *The Geography of Religion in England.* London: Duckworth.

Girardin, P. 1947. Les Passages Alpestres en Liaison avec les Abbayes, les Pèlerinages et les Saints de la Montagne. *Geographica Helvetica* 2:65–74.

Gitelman, Z. Y. 2001. *A Century of Ambiguity: The Jews of Russia and the Soviet Union, 1881 to Present.* Bloomington: Indiana University Press.

Greely, A. M. 2003. *Religion in Europe at the End of the Second Millennium: A Sociological Profile.* New Brunswick: Transaction.

Gustafsson, B. 1957. *Svensk Kyrkogeografi, med Samfundsbeskrivning.* Lund: Gleerup.

Hannemann, M. 1975. *The Diffusion of the Reformation in Southwestern Germany, 1518–1534.* Research Paper 167. Chicago: University of Chicago, Department of Geography.

Hard, G. 1965. Eine Topographie der Pilgerwege von Deutschland nach Santiago in Spanien aus dem 15. Jahrhundert. *Erdkunde* 19:314–325.

Hellyer, H. A. 2009. *Muslims of Europe: The "Other" Europeans.* Edinburgh: Edinburgh University Press.

Hunter, S. T., ed. 2002. *Islam, Europe's Second Religion: The New Social, Cultural, and Political Landscapes.* Westport, CT: Praeger.

Ignatieff, M. 1998. *The Warrior's Honor: Ethnic War and the Modern Conscience.* New York: Henry Holt.

Jouret, B. 1968. L'influence du Protestantisme dans l'Économie Douroise. *Revue Belge de Géographie* 92:61–74.

Jurkovich, J. M., and W. M. Gesler. 1997. Medjugorje: Finding Peace at the Heart of Conflict. *Geographical Review* 87:447–67.

Knippenberg, H. 2005. The Netherlands: Selling Churches and Building Mosques. In *The Changing Religious Landscape of Europe*, ed. H. Knippenberg, 88–106. Amsterdam: Het Spinhuis.

Knudsen, J. P. 1986. Culture, Power and Periphery—The Christian Lay Movement in Norway. *Norsk Geografisk Tidsskrift* 40:1–14.

Kotin, I. Y., and A. D. Krindatch. 2005. Religious Revival in a Multi-Cultural Landscape. In *The Changing Religious Landscape of Europe*, ed. H. Knippenberg, 145–73. Amsterdam: Het Spinhuis.

Lambert, E. 1943. Le Livre de Saint Jacques et les Routes du Pèlerinage de Compostelle. *Revue Géographique des Pyrénées et du Sud-Ouest* 14:5–33.

Lehmann, S. G. 1998. Inter-Ethnic Conflict in the Republics of Russia in Light of Religious Revival. *Post-Soviet Geography and Economics* 39:461–93.

Luxmoore, J., and J. Babiuch. 2005. *Rethinking Christendom: Europe's Struggle for Christianity*. Leominster: Gracewing.

Martyniuk, J. 1993. Religious Preferences in Five Urban Areas of Ukraine. *Radio Free Europe/Radio Liberty Research Report* 2 (15): 52–55.

Newman, D. 1985. Integration and Ethnic Spatial Concentration: Changing Spatial Distribution of Anglo-Jewish Community. *Transactions of the Institute of British Geographers* 10:360–76.

Nolan, M. L. 1983. Irish Pilgrimage: The Different Tradition. *Annals of the Association of American Geographers* 73:421–38.

Nolan, M. L., and S. Nolan. 1989. *Religious Pilgrimage in Modern Western Europe*. Chapel Hill: University of North Carolina Press.

Richard, J. 1996. Géographie Religieuse et Géopolitique en Biélorussie du XVIe Siècle a Nos Jours. *Annales de Géographie* 105:141–63.

Rinschede, G. 1985. The Pilgrimage Town of Lourdes. In *Geographia Religionum*, Vol. 1, *Grundfragen der Religions-Geographie*, ed. M. Buttner et al., 1–61. Berlin: Dietrich Reimer.

———. 1992. Pilgerzentrum Fátima/Portugal. *Geographie Heute* 106:15–22.

Semple, E. C. 1927. The Templed Promontories of the Ancient Mediterranean. *Geographical Review* 17:353–86.

Sidorov, D. 2000. The Resurrection of the Cathedral of Christ the Savior in Moscow. *Annals of the Association of American Geographers* 90:548–72.

Stanislawski, D. 1975. Dionysus Westward: Early Religion and the Economic Geography of Wine. *Geographical Review* 65:427–44.

Triandafyllidou, A., ed. 2012. *Muslims in 21st-Century Europe: Structural and Cultural Perspectives*. London: Routledge.

Walker, E. W. 2005. Islam, Territory, and Contested Space in Post-Soviet Russia. *Eurasian Geography and Economics* 46:247–71.

Waterman, S., and B. Kosmin. 1988. Residential Patterns and Processes: A Study of Jews in Three London Boroughs. *Transactions of the Institute of British Geographers* 13:79–95.

Whelan, K. 1983. The Catholic Parish, the Catholic Chapel, and Village Development in Ireland. *Irish Geography* 16:1–15.

———. 1988. The Regional Impact of Irish Catholicism, 1700–1850. In *Common Ground: Essays on the Historical Geography of Ireland*, ed. W. J. Smyth and K. Whelan, 253–77. Cork: Cork University Press.

CHAPTER 6

The European State System

In the previous chapters, we looked at a variety of maps that provide insight into Europe's physical and human characteristics. When people think of Europe's geography, however, they rarely think of those maps. Instead, they tend to think of a map showing France, Germany, Poland, and so forth. In one sense this tendency is odd, for most of the units on the typical political map of Europe did not exist 200 years ago, and none of them was around a thousand years ago. Yet the social and economic significance of the modern state has become so great over the past two centuries that it now dominates the geographical imagination. For every question that is asked about what is going on in the North European Plain or the Douro River Basin, thousands are asked about Germany, France, Spain, and Portugal.

The European state system has been such a dominant force in the modern era that it is important to understand its emergence before turning to developments in the rural and urban sectors. There is a certain awkwardness to this ordering, because consideration of topics such as rural land use and urbanization require us to reach farther back in time than the emergence of the modern state system. Yet it is impossible to carry the discussion of those topics forward without some appreciation of the partitioning of Europe into states. The European state is now being challenged to some degree by the rise of the EU—a development we take up in some detail later in the book (Chapter 9). Yet the state continues to merit attention, for it remains a fundamental forces shaping how people define their identities and lead their lives.

The General Picture

Europe is splintered into no fewer than 47 independent states (fig. 6.1). These formally independent countries, in turn, contain many autonomous regions and territories, some of which harbor separatist sentiments. Geographer Richard Griggs has counted 130 culturally distinct peoples in Europe, only some of whom have a state of their own.

Figure 6.1. The independent countries of Europe, with selected dependent territories. Excluding Turkey, Europe now encompasses almost 50 independent states.

To gauge the magnitude of fragmentation, consider that Europe, broadly defined, contains almost exactly the same amount of land area as the United States. Imagine the complexity that would exist if every state within the United States were independent. At the Russian border, this fragmentation abruptly gives way to the largest territorial state in the world—a circumstance that fuels debate over whether Russia is a European country or not.

So severe is the political splintering of Europe that a number of microstates exist, some so small as to be invisible on a map of Europe as a whole. These include Andorra, Liechtenstein, Monaco, San Marino, and Vatican City. Most ministates have sought to capitalize on their size, offering services not always available in their larger neighbors (gambling in Monaco, duty-free shops in Andorra, postage stamp sales in San Marino, and low-tax business arrangements in Liechtenstein). The European map is also populated by islands with different political statuses. Malta and Cyprus in the Mediterranean are independent countries, though the latter is partitioned into two political regions: a

Turkish-controlled region in the north and the Greek-Cypriot-controlled Republic of Cyprus in the south. Corsica and Sardinia are parts of France and Italy, respectively, and have a status similar to other regions in those countries. Greenland and the Faeroe Islands are formally part of the Kingdom of Denmark, but they are largely autonomous and self-governing. The Isle of Man is a British Crown Dependency in the Irish Sea; the British monarch is the official head of state, but the island's citizens control their own affairs.

Not only is Europe territorially fragmented; it has become more so over the past century. In the year 1900, Europe exclusive of Turkey encompassed 23 independent states; in 1930, 31; in 1985, 34; and by 1993, 46—double the total at the beginning of the century. The breakup of several great imperial states as a result of World War I, most notably the Austro-Hungarian and Ottoman Turkish empires, yielded many new countries. The collapse in 1991 of Europe's last surviving empire, the Soviet Union, coupled with the subsequent disintegration of two smaller multiethnic states, Yugoslavia and Czechoslovakia, produced many more independent European states. The reunification of Germany was the only development countering this trend.

Nor has fragmentation necessarily run its course. Separatist movements of widely differing levels of intensity continue in Europe (see Chapter 11). Before we turn to such matters, however, it is important to gain some understanding of how the pattern of European states came into being, and the role that pattern has played in the creation of patterns of identity in Europe.

The Emergence of the European State Pattern

During the Middle Ages, political territories were complex and overlapping throughout much of Europe. Few people had a sense of identity that was broader than a local commune or fief. The exception were members of a small ruling elite, most of whom functioned in royal or ecclesiastical territories with indistinct, frequently changing boundaries.

By the late Middle Ages, the feudal order began to erode. Increasingly autonomous cities sprang up in northern Italy and in Flanders (see Chapter 10), and rulers in the far western part of Europe began to consolidate power over larger territories—most notably in what we now call northern France and southern England. As these early states grew, they came into conflict with one another. (England controlled significant territories in what is now France—a legacy of the Norman invasion of England.) These conflicts, in turn, gave rise to larger-scale senses of identity. The concept of the **nation** was born. Many people now think of the terms *nation* and *state* as synonymous, but nation originally did not refer to a politically organized territory. Instead it referred to a group of people with a shared sense of culture and history, and a desire to control its own affairs. In early modern Europe, the growing French and English states served as incubators for the development of national sensibilities, as did the states on the Iberian Peninsula that came into being in the wake of the expulsion of the Moors. England, France, Spain, and Portugal are thus sometimes considered to be the original **nation-states** (in the literal sense of the term, i.e., states associated

Figure 6.2. Types of states in Europe based on their territorial and ideological foundations. The different political-territorial circumstances that produced Europe's political pattern unfolded over many hundreds of years, but most modern European states are less than 200 years old.

with particular ethnic nations) (fig. 6.2). Of course these early nation-states encompassed many minorities, but each was based on the idea that the state was the homeland of a particular nation.

These early states grew up around a core area, which served as a power center and a crucible for the cultural norms that came to dominate the state (fig. 6.3). Such core areas possessed some measure of natural defense against the encroachments of rival political entities, a fairly dense population (at least in comparison to surrounding regions), and a prosperous agricultural economy that produced a surplus capable of supporting a sizable military establishment. Perhaps most important of all, the core area required a government headed by ambitious leaders, skilled in the military and diplomatic arts, and bent on territorial aggrandizement. During the process of territorial accretion, the core often retained its status as the single most important area in the state, housing the capital city and the cultural and economic heart of the nation.

Figure 6.3. Core areas and the evolution of European states. Many modern independent countries evolved gradually from core areas. Others celebrate an area deemed to be the historic heartland of a national culture, even if it did not play a direct role in the creation of the modern state. The Osman statelet was the core area of the Ottoman Empire and modern Turkey. *Sources:* Based in part upon Pounds and Ball 1964 and McManis 1967.

An example would be Paris and the Île de France, which lie nearly in the middle of France. But in some instances, territorial accretion occurred mainly in one direction, leaving the core in a peripheral location. Wessex, the nucleus of England, became eccentric, as did the region in Spain from which the **reconquista** was mounted.

The European state system is grounded in two fundamental territorial concepts. One we have already introduced: the nation-state. The other is **sovereignty**—a concept that emerged out of developments within the German Empire of the sixteenth and seventeenth centuries. During that time, the German Empire comprised hundreds of small states or principalities. The Wars of Religion (see Chapter 5) brought these entities into intense conflict with one another. A settlement, known as the Peace of Westphalia, was finally reached in 1648. Under the terms of the agreement, the ruler of each of the states making up the German Empire had the right to choose the religion of the territorial unit over which he ruled (Catholic or Protestant)—and each state agreed not to interfere with the religious choices made by the rulers of other states. This arrangement gave birth to the idea that states should be able to control their own affairs without outside interference.

The Peace of Westphalia ushered in a period of stability within the German Empire that lasted almost a century. By the middle of the eighteenth century, the German Empire was still carved up into multiple units, although internal conflicts had begun to develop. Elsewhere in Europe, the modern political pattern had only taken shape at the western edges of Europe (fig. 6.4). The original nation-states continued to function as relatively large-scale, autonomous political units—and they had grown increasingly powerful as a result of their colonial activities. The northern provinces of the Low Countries had also successfully thrown off external rule, giving rise to another independent state: a confederation of provinces that came to be known as the Netherlands. That state too set itself up as an early colonial power and developed financial and trading networks that gave it a position of enormous influence by the seventeenth century.

Outside of Europe's western fringe, the political map did not look much like the one we know today. What we now call Belgium was controlled from outside. The territories occupied by the modern states of Italy, Germany, and Austria were frag-

Figure 6.4. Europe in the eighteenth century. Only at Europe's western edge does the eighteenth-century political pattern look like that of today.

mented. To the east and north of the German and Italian realms, empires were the norm. The Kingdom of Hungary represented a partial exception, as a statelike entity had come into being there—albeit in a territory that was considerably larger than the present state of Hungary. Another exception was in the Alps, where a set of cantons had developed a loose alliance in an effort to ward off outside influence, giving rise to the political entity we now call Switzerland.

The rulers of the mix of political territorial units found in eighteenth-century Europe were primarily hereditary monarchs. However, the idea of the nation that had been forged in the early western European states gave rise to a growing sense that rulers should serve the interests of the nation (i.e., the people), not vice versa. Spurred on by the excesses of the monarchy, this idea gained particular potency in France. It eventually led to the violent French Revolution of 1789, which was undertaken in the name of **nationalism** (a notion rooted in the glorification of a particular ethnic nation and an insistence on the right of that nation to control its own affairs). The French Revolution ushered in Europe's Age of Nationalism, a period during which the ideal political form was seen to be a sovereign nation-state.

France was the key catalyst for the Age of Nationalism. The country entered a tumultuous period in the wake of its revolution, but order was restored for a time when Napoleon Bonaparte took control of the state in the name of the French nation. Napoleon's expansionist policies helped to spread the concept of the sovereign nation-state throughout the region—giving rise to a long century of independent state formation (from c. 1815 to 1925) that brought into being the modern political map of Europe. The states that emerged came about primarily as a result of two types of nationalism: **unification nationalism** and **anti-empire nationalism**—although the territorial cores of the dismantled empires also became states (fig. 6.2).

Unification nationalism was the product of an effort to bring together, within a single state, peoples who ostensibly shared a common culture and history. Unification movements developed in both Germany and Italy (fig. 6.2). The German and Italian domains encompassed considerable cultural diversity as a result of centuries of political fragmentation, but the ideas of a German nation and an Italian nation were of sufficient appeal that the movements eventually were successful. Germany and Italy emerged from core areas (fig. 6.3), but only in the German case did the core become the power center of the newly independent state.

The different relationships between nation and state in the original nation-states, as opposed to the states that were the products of unification nationalism, are suggested by figure 6.5, a map of Europe's main post roads in 1850. France is easy to find on the map because of the road pattern. All roads lead to Paris—a reflection of a centuries-long project in which the political organization of territory promoted a growing sense of being French among relatively diverse peoples. The territory helped to create the nation (in the original sense of the term). In contrast, it is difficult to find Germany on the map because it had no history of unity. In the German case, an idea about the existence of a German nation led to the creation of the territory.

Anti-empire nationalism occurred in places where a sense of nationalism took root among peoples who considered themselves to be under the control of outsiders. Peoples with a distinctive sense of culture and history wanted a sovereign nation-state of their own. Anti-empire nationalism took two forms. In some cases peoples with a

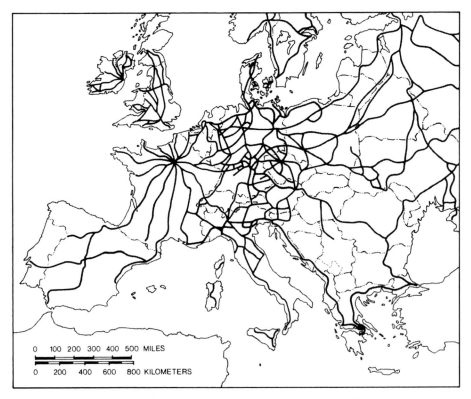

Figure 6.5.   Main post roads in Europe, 1850. Note the highly centralized pattern in France and the lack of a dominant focal point in central Europe. This map clearly shows that France had functioned as a single territorial unit for some time, whereas Germany had not yet been unified. *Source:* George W. Hoffman, ed., *A Geography of Europe,* 3rd ed. (New York: Ronald Press, 1969), 107.

distinct cultural-territorial identity sought to split off from states they viewed as empires that had wrongfully expanded into their territory. The classic examples of states that emerged from the first kind of anti-empire nationalism are Ireland and Norway, both of which split away in the early twentieth century from countries that had come to rule them (the United Kingdom and Sweden, respectively) (fig. 6.2).

A second type of anti-imperial nationalism is associated with the disintegration of the explicitly multiethnic European empires of the nineteenth and twentieth centuries: the Ottoman Empire, the Austro-Hungarian Empire, and the Russian Empire. The former two began to disintegrate late in the nineteenth century, and they were fully dissolved at the end of World War I. Most of the states that emerged from these empires had a clear ethno-nationalist base, even if their borders did not necessarily correspond very precisely with ethnic distributions (fig. 6.2). Under the guise of the Soviet Union, Russia expanded its territorial reach during the twentieth century, but by the end of the century anti-empire nationalism led to the creation of independent states at the edges of that empire as well.

With the dismantlement of Europe's empires, their political-territorial centers also became part of the political map (fig. 6.2). Sweden was the old core of the Swedish Empire, Russia of the Russian Empire, and Turkey of the Ottoman Empire. Austria and Hungary each went its own way—a reflection of political-territorial arrangements in preimperial times.

Even though the Age of Nationalism saw the disintegration of Europe's internal empires, that period also saw the solidification and expansion of the overseas colonial ventures of various European powers. In an atmosphere of increased competition among European states anxious to establish themselves as major powers, efforts to control resources and territory outside of Europe intensified. Long-standing colonial states such as France, the United Kingdom, the Netherlands, and Portugal were joined by Belgium, Germany, and Italy in a land grab in Africa that led to the partitioning of that continent near the end of the nineteenth century. Colonial control was also solidified over interior areas of Asia and on selected islands and territories in other parts of the globe. Colonialism entered its most ruthless stage, with devastating impacts on many colonized areas. Within Europe, power disparities grew as some colonial countries successfully exploited the system at the expense of other colonial powers and noncolonial countries.

Figure 6.6. Europe at the end of World War I. The breakup of the Ottoman and Austro-Hungarian empires produced a map of states that, for the first time, looked much like the one that exists today.

The Age of Nationalism culminated in a conflict of global proportions in 1914. The immediate catalyst for World War I was a contest over territory and influence in southeastern Europe. In many senses, the war represented the high-water mark for nationalism in the region—one that took an enormous human toll. Out of the ashes came a political pattern that bears a strong resemblance to the contemporary map of European states (fig. 6.6). There were exceptions. The area that came to be known as Yugoslavia (called the Kingdom of the Serbs, Croats, and Slovenes until 1929) was a multiethnic mix, and Czechoslovakia brought together two increasingly self-conscious ethnic nations and several smaller groups within one state. Both would break up in the closing decade of the twentieth century. Moreover, Germany controlled significant territories in the east—territories that were lost after the second horrendous European conflict of the twentieth century ended in 1945.

The Twentieth-Century European State

The European state that emerged in the early twentieth century was very much a product of the historical and geographical circumstances described above. However messy the ethnic pattern might have been, most states regarded themselves as true "nation-states." Indeed, the link between nation and state became so naturalized that the two terms started to be seen as interchangeable—a troubling development for the many ethnic minorities within European states. Moreover, the idea of territorial sovereignty was widely accepted, although in some places sovereignty had come to mean the right of regimes to do whatever they wanted, including (if seen to be necessary to protect the national interest) intervene in the affairs of other states. This notion of sovereignty was at the heart of Nazi expansionism at the end of the 1930s but was largely abandoned after the horrors of World War II in favor of a notion of sovereignty more in keeping with the principles set forth in the Peace of Westphalia.

Internally, states sought to integrate their territories economically and socially; they encouraged commitment to national norms through the expansion of state-funded education. The majority of states were **unitary** in administrative structure, with power concentrated in a central government (fig. 6.7). Many of the capital cities of these states were also **primate cities**—ones that contained by far the largest populations and greatest concentrations of economic and cultural functions (e.g., Paris and Athens). Many of these capital cities were in the original core areas of states, but not all. In some cases the capital was relocated to the frontier of most active territorial expansion. Sofia replaced Bulgarian capitals farther to the east as that state expanded south and west at the expense of the Turks; Lisbon and Madrid displaced northern capitals as the Portuguese and Spaniards pushed the Moors southward in Iberia. Similarly, capitals were sometimes relocated to take advantage of commercial and cultural contacts. St. Petersburg replaced Moscow as the Russian capital for a time, when the czars desired closer cultural contacts with Europe; and Oslo replaced Trondheim in Norway as a result of its closer proximity to Sweden and Denmark, which ruled Norway for centuries.

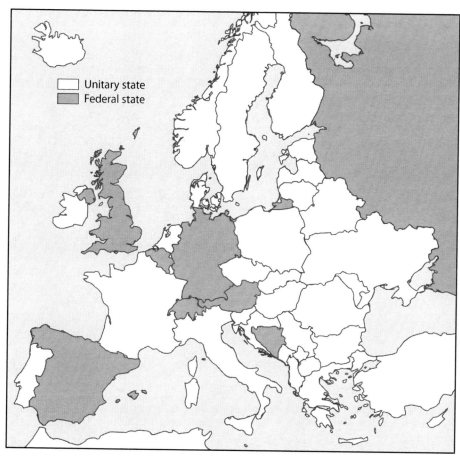

Figure 6.7.   Types of independent states, based upon unitary versus federal governments.
In those states shown as federal, all powers that are not explicitly granted to the central government reside with the units that make up the state.

An alternative to the unitary state is the **federal state**, in which internal states or provinces retain considerable power, or even autonomy. Europe had few of these early in the twentieth century, but the number has grown (fig. 6.7) as states such as Spain, Belgium, Russia, and the United Kingdom have looked to federalism to accommodate the demands of regional ethnic minority groups for greater control over their own affairs. Switzerland represents the most disaggregated form of federalism; the country did not even have a national capital until the mid-nineteenth century.

Modern states are also characterized by international borders. Many of these borders are declining in significance (see Chapter 9), but they are still marked in some way. Even the peaceful, uncontested Sweden–Norway boundary is represented by a swath cut through the forest and by diverse official signs of varying age (fig. 6.8). The first acts of newly independent Estonia and Latvia included severing many connecting rural roads with trenchers, erecting street barriers within border towns, and establishing

Figure 6.8.   Swedish–Norwegian border near Torsby, Sweden. The border is clearly marked by a strip cleared through the Finnskog, or "Finns' Forest." Photo by T. G. J.-B., 1985.

manned crossing points. Their mutual border, previously a largely invisible line between Soviet republics, became part of the visible landscape.

The policies and legislation of independent states often have a homogenizing effect within their borders, with the result that significantly different economic, social, and material landscapes can be found on either side of some borders. An example is the Rhine River border between France and Germany. On the French side lies the province of Alsace, and on the German side, Baden. Both Alsace and Baden are traditionally German-speaking and predominantly Roman Catholic, and yet clear differences developed between the two provinces. Prosperous Baden underwent rapid industrialization after 1945, absorbing numerous refugees from ceded eastern German territories, while Alsace stagnated economically. In part, the economic malaise of Alsace was caused by repeated boundary changes as the province passed back and forth from German to French rule in 1871, 1918, 1940, and 1945. Yet the province also lay far from Paris in a state with a highly centralized form of government with priorities focused elsewhere. Baden, as part of a much less centralized federal state, fared better. Federal funds generously assisted resettled refugees in Baden, causing a boom in housing construction and renovation. Rural population density is now much lower on the Alsatian side, and the prosperity of Baden causes many French citizens to commute to jobs on the German side of the Rhine. The two provinces also differ in the configuration of rural village suburbanization. Partly as a result of differences in national planning legislation, the suburbs being added to villages in Baden tend to be compact, with apartment dwellings most common, whereas Alsatian villages sprawl more loosely across the countryside due to the prevalence of freestanding, single-family suburban houses.

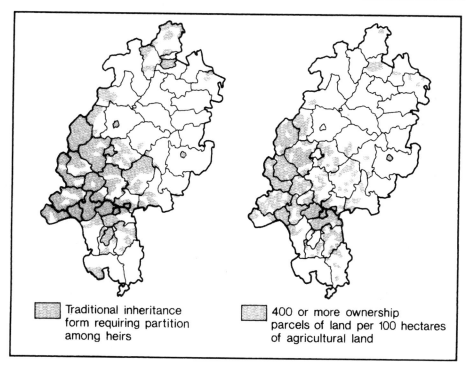

Traditional inheritance form requiring partition among heirs

400 or more ownership parcels of land per 100 hectares of agricultural land

Figure 6.9. Inheritance systems and land fragmentation in the German province of Hessen, 1955. In the southern and western parts of Hessen, the tradition, dating to Roman times, was to divide the farms among the various heirs. As a result, the farms there became ever smaller over the centuries, with excessive fragmentation of the holdings. Northern and eastern Hessen, by contrast, clung to the ancient Germanic custom of primogeniture, by which the farm passes intact to the eldest son. *Source:* Adapted from Eckart Ehlers, "Land Consolidation and Farm Resettlement in the Federal Republic of Germany," in *Man, Culture, and Settlement*, ed. Robert C. Eidt et al., 124 (New Delhi: Kalyani, 1977).

The differentiating effect of borders can be seen even where borders themselves no longer exist. The northern border of the Roman Empire ran through the modern German state of Hessen. As we saw in Chapter 3, the Roman system of law required that inheritances be divided among all heirs, in contrast to the tradition of the neighboring German tribes, which favored primogeniture. After the empire collapsed and the political border ceased to exist, the boundary separating the different inheritance systems persisted into the modern era (fig. 6.9).

Case Studies

Beyond the general forces and trends that shaped the European state system lies a multitude of particular circumstances at play in individual cases. To gain some appreciation of the historical and geographical differences that have shaped the European state system, as well as the ethnic diversity that lies behind the nation-state concept, it is useful to look at some specific cases.

FRANCE: THE QUINTESSENTIAL UNITARY STATE

Though linked by language and religion to the Mediterranean, France owes both its origin and name to a Germanic tribe, the Franks, which moved into the power vacuum created in the area after the collapse of the Roman Empire. The Franks established a short-lived Frankish Empire, which fragmented in 843 CE after the death of Charlemagne. The westernmost part—a loose feudal federation known as the Kingdom of the West Franks—became the embryonic France.

After about 1000 CE, the kings of France, based in Paris, began a program of conquest and annexation to convert the federation, over which their rule was largely ceremonial, into an integrated territory under royal domination. In the process, the so-called Île de France—the original, small domain of the kings in the center of the Paris Basin—served as the core area of the evolving unitary state (fig. 6.10). The Île de France enjoyed splendid natural defensive advantages, sheltered behind **cuesta** escarpment walls.

From their Paris Basin fortress, the French kings undertook three prolonged campaigns of expansion: southward to reach the Mediterranean and the Pyrenees; westward to dislodge the English from the Atlantic coast, where they ruled Normandy and Aquitaine; and eastward, at the expense of Bourgogne and other German states, to the banks of the Rhine. By 1650, France had reached more or less its present territorial limits. The city of Paris, the Île de France, and the Paris Basin never lost their early dominance. A unitary state with a powerful central government was in the making.

Most of France's territory was easily accessible from the fairly centrally located capital, and belts of mountains and hills paralleled the border in many places, including the Pyrenees, Alps, Jura, Vosges, and Ardennes (fig. 6.10). Still, the resultant France was no nation-state in the original sense of the term. As late as 1790, half the population spoke a language other than the Parisian form of French. In 1793, the government mandated elimination of regional languages and dialects. This policy met with considerable success, but even today ethnic minorities are found in many of France's peripheral regions (fig. 6.10). These include the German-speaking Alsatians in the east, the Dutch speakers around Dunkerque in the north, the Celtic Bretons of Bretagne, the Basques of the western Pyrenees, the Catalans of the south, and the Italian-speaking Corsicans. In addition, France had the task of uniting a more Germanized north with a Mediterranean south. The northern French descended in large part from Germanic tribes—not only the Franks, but also Normans (Vikings), Burgundians, and others. While these tribes abandoned their ancestral languages and adopted French, they remained Germanic in many other ways. Their houses, villages, and farm field patterns are Teutonic in appearance and origin; their Germanic diet relies heavily on bovine dairy products, including butter for cooking; and their dialect of French, *langue d'oïl*, is distinctive.

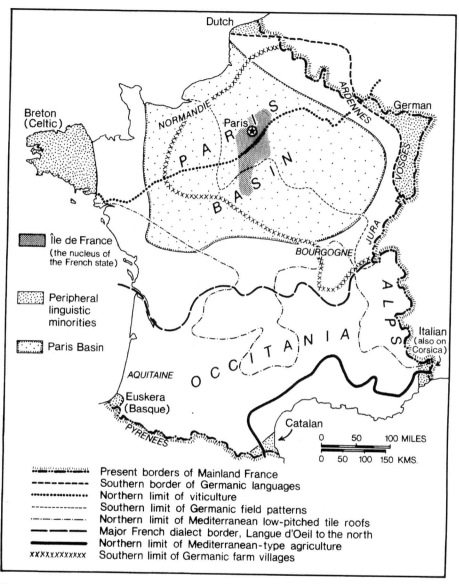

Figure 6.10. France: Selected geopolitical features. Growing from the Île de France, a core area in the Paris Basin, France attained a hexagonal shape and "natural" borders such as the Alps and Pyrenees, but annexed numerous peripheral ethnic areas in the process, as well as the more Romanized south.

The lands annexed in the south, sometimes called *Occitania*, retain a much stronger Roman and Mediterranean imprint, with minimal Germanic influence. A deeply rooted, distinctive southern regional culture took root, which is manifest, for example, in the cultivation of grapes for wine, the use of olive oil in cooking, and the presence of a distinctive tongue known as *langue d'oc*.

The French reaction to the challenges of ethnic peripheries and regional culture was to develop an all-powerful unitary state, based in Paris, and to impose the will and culture of the north on both the south and the restive peripheries. This strategy largely succeeded. Over the past 30 years, France has devolved some power to its outlying regions, but no province has a substantial degree of autonomy from Paris.

GERMANY: FEDERALISM IN THE EUROPEAN CORE

Just as France represents the legacy of the collapsed Frankish Empire in the west, Germany descends from the east Frankish Kingdom of 843 CE. For the initial millennium of its existence, the German realm, unlike France, remained a loose federation of states with an emperor who had little authority outside his home statelet. Federalism, verging on virtual disunity, has been the German norm. Potential core areas from which ambitious emperors might have forged a unitary state certainly existed, such as the fertile Börde beyond the Ruhr River on the North European Plain, or the hill-ringed Upper Rhine Plain between Frankfurt-am-Main and Basel, but no such process developed. By the 1600s, the Holy Roman Empire of German-speaking principalities encompassed some 300 virtually independent states.

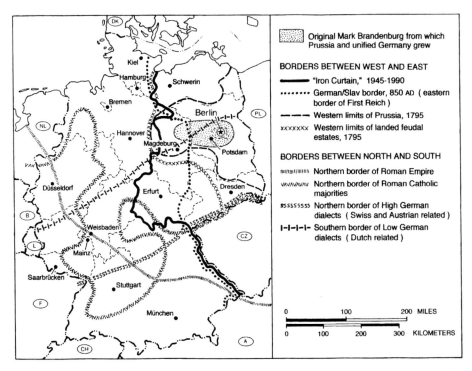

Figure 6.11. Germany, occupying much of the European core, has always struggled to unite north and south, east and west, lying astride these two European cultural fault lines.

The loose-knit German Empire did succeed in expanding eastward, into ancestral Slavic tribal lands, following the path of German agricultural colonists and forest clearers spreading east on the North German Plain and along the Danube. In each of these two lobes of eastern expansion, a powerful state and ambitious royal family arose: Prussia (German *Preussen*) in the North European Plain, which grew from a core area in Brandenburg, and Austria, which expanded from the *Ostmark* (Eastern March) around Vienna. These two new states both continued to function as part of the empire, even though some of the territories they annexed lay beyond its bounds. Once they consolidated their holdings in the east, Prussia and Austria (by then called *Österreich*, or the "Eastern Empire") began competing with one another for control of the original, politically fragmented western part of the empire. This contest lasted for centuries, but a union of Prussia and the western German states eventually was forged in the second half of the nineteenth century. The Prussian capital, Berlin, was named the imperial capital, and the Prussian kings became the German *kaisers*. The newly independent Germany was federalist in form, but constituent territorial units such as Bavaria and Sachsen retained their own monarchs and postal systems for a time (fig. 6.11). Austria, the defeated rival, found itself excluded from Germany.

In the 1930s the Nazis seized power and imposed the first dictatorship Germany had known. Unitary rule quickly replaced the traditional federalism; not merely Germany, but all of Europe, felt the dire consequences. Modern Germany emerged in the wake of World War II, but it was not until 1990 when the German Democratic Republic of East Germany, the old Russian occupation zone, became part of the Federal Republic. In 1999, Berlin regained its status as the capital of Germany.

An essential feature of the German state—one that helps explain its repeated fragmentation—is that it straddles major east–west and north–south cultural divides in Europe. The north–south divide is ancient, going back 2,000 years to the time when southern Germany was part of the Roman Empire while the north was controlled by various Teutonic tribes. Rome placed its cultural imprint on the south, and such influences never completely disappeared, even after many centuries. Indeed, the German south remains Roman Catholic, whereas the north is Protestant (Chapter 5). The country is home to some 24,500,000 Protestants and 25,000,000 Catholics—about as even a split as could be imagined. Dialects of the German language also separate south from the north.

The east–west division within Germany is also deeply rooted. A thousand years ago and more, German peoples lived only in lands west of the Elbe and Saale rivers. Slavic tribes possessed what is now eastern Germany. Teutonic peoples only gradually spread east, absorbing the Slavs. This colonial eastern German culture remained feudal, its landless peasants working on manorial estates owned by the aristocracy. Prussia, the political expression of eastern German culture, remained entirely confined to the east as late as the 1790s. When German unification was realized in the 1870s with the Prussian royal family in charge, the east–west contrast remained strong.

The distinctiveness of eastern Germany was powerfully reinforced between 1945 and 1990, when it fell under communist Russian domination. In spite of reunification in 1990, the old "Iron Curtain" border has not disappeared, and *Ossis* ("easterners") and *Wessis* ("westerners") still differ. Average incomes in the east lag behind those in the west, though the gap is narrowing, and local tax revenues in eastern provinces are just 60% of those in the German west. In an effort to mitigate these problems, the German government annually transfers billions of euros into the eastern provinces, but these transfers fuel resentments, particularly in poorer towns and cities in the west. Thus, the long-standing struggle to create an increasingly integrated state in Germany is alive and well.

THE UNITED KINGDOM: CORE–PERIPHERY TENSIONS

If Germany's quixotic task has been to bridge east, west, north, and south, the United Kingdom has struggled to link together peoples with diverse histories and cultures. Ultimately, this union proved untenable, and the Republic of Ireland broke away in the 1920s—the culmination of a revolt that had endured for centuries. The Irish secession occurred along one of several natural and cultural dividing lines that cut across the country's territory (fig. 6.12).

The United Kingdom traces its roots to Germanic tribes, particularly the Saxons, Angles, and Normans, who came as waves of invaders from across the North Sea and English Channel, eventually mixing with indigenous groups and each other to become the English people. Their new state, England, arose in Wessex, in the lowland plains that form the southeastern part of the island of Great Britain (fig. 6.12). Once the English had unified the lowlands, they turned to the second great task— conquering and annexing the hilly lands on the west and north, inhabited by the Celts. One by one these Celtic refuges—Cornwall, Wales, and Scotland—fell to the English. Even before these conquests were completed, the English began their third, and final, major expansion—into Ireland, another Celtic land, lying across a narrow sea to the west. In this way, the two British Isles came to be a single country, the United Kingdom, ruled by the English from their base in London and the surrounding lowlands.

While outwardly successful, the expanded United Kingdom never fully absorbed the conquered Celts. The country has had to cope with an environmental divide between fertile lowlands and barren hills and the separation into two major islands, and divisions between Anglo-Saxons and Celts, Protestants and Catholics, rich and poor, and industrial and rural. It was along the Protestant/Catholic divide that the United Kingdom fragmented, though the divide was really more about different ethno-national loyalties than religious practices. Northern Ireland remained in the UK but faced enormous internal struggles for decades. Recent power-sharing agreements have raised hope for a more stable future, but the situation remains fragile.

On the larger island, Great Britain, other divides continue to plague the United Kingdom. The Scots in 1999 established their own separate parliament, as did the Welsh, and a movement seeking complete independence for Scotland has significant support. "Rise up and be a nation again" implore bumper stickers in Scotland, a message carried forward by the Scottish Nationalist Party. The United Kingdom is an ancient and largely stable state, but the balance is delicate in a state that has extended its reach into areas where it was not always welcome.

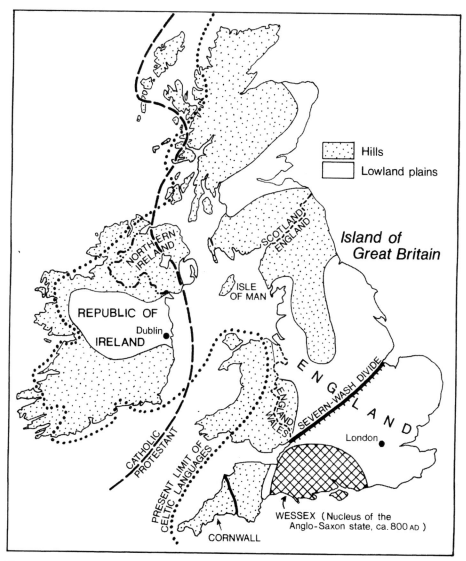

Figure 6.12.   The United Kingdom, originating as the Saxon state of Wessex, early came to encompass the Scarpland plains and began to claim territory in the Celtic refuges. At its peak, the UK ruled all the British Isles.

ITALY: ROMAN LEGACY

Like the United Kingdom, Italy struggles to unite segments of the European core and periphery. Unlike Britain, Italy is a relatively new state by European standards, though it rests upon the memory of ancient greatness. The Roman Empire collapsed long ago, and what is now Italy became politically fragmented. Yet the memory of Roman glory and unity persisted. In the nineteenth century, a unification movement successfully reassembled Italy from an array of weak, small states ruled by feudal

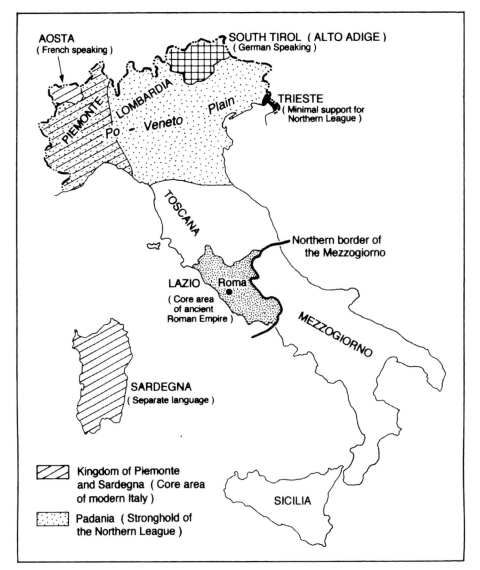

Figure 6.13.   Italy, though seemingly provided with a natural framework by the peninsula and the Alps, consists of very different regions. A prosperous north contrasts with the Mezzogiorno.

lords, princes, and popes. Although the unification movement originated in the north, the ancient legacy demanded that Rome be the capital (fig. 6.13).

Despite the unifying potential of the ancient Roman legacy, the peninsula was and is very culturally diverse. To unify Italy over 2,000 years ago, the tribes of *Latium* (modern Lazio)—a district surrounding Rome and the origin of the word "Latin"— had to conquer in the north both the Etruscan peoples of Tuscany and the Celts of the Po–Veneto Plain, then called Cisalpine Gaul. Then they had to annex the Greek-inhabited lands of south Italy.

These ancient minorities never completely vanished. To complicate matters more, new invaders settled the peninsula after the fall of the Roman Empire. Germanic tribes, especially the Lombards, seized the Po–Veneto Plain, while Arabs, Crusaders, and Catalans ruled much of the south, including the large island of Sicily. Then, in the 1400s and 1500s, northern Italy gave birth to a great awakening of culture—the Renaissance—and with it an era of prosperity based in trade and manufacturing, while the south—the Mezzogiorno—remained mired in a feudal system that impeded economic growth.

The modern Italian state has struggled to hold the north and south together. Some of the resultant internal pressure was relieved by the mass migration of poor southerners to factory jobs in the north after 1950. In addition, the central government transfers enormous amounts of northern wealth to the south as subsidies, relief, and developmental funds. But tensions persist. Many prosperous northerners express disdain for southern Italians, and some even speak of *Padania*—an independent northern Italy (fig. 6.13). A political party, the Northern League, has promoted greater autonomy, and even secession. In addition, inhabitants of the German-speaking part of Alpine Italy—the South Tirol or *Alto Adige*—have agitated for a half century for autonomy.

SPAIN: A MULTIETHNIC STATE

Spain, like Italy, has historically struggled to hold together north and south, but its internal stresses are far more complicated than this simple twofold division. The Spanish state had its beginnings in far northern Iberia in the Christian resistance against the Moors, who had invaded from Africa in the 700s CE (see Chapter 5). In particular, two Christian statelets, Castilla and Aragon, led the resistance, and when they united in the 1400s, Spain was born (fig. 6.14). The defining deed of Spanish national identity was successful warfare against the Arabs, pushing them southward back into Africa, a process completed only after 700 years, in 1492.

The resultant Spanish state included the greater part of the Iberian Peninsula, excluding only Portugal in the far west. In common with Italy, the peninsula housed diverse peoples, speaking different languages and possessing strong regional allegiances. Portugal was one of these and soon succeeded in escaping Spanish rule. Others were incorporated, more or less against their will. The Castilians—the people of central Meseta—built and ruled Spain, establishing the capital city, Madrid, in the center of the elevated interior plains. Ethnic minorities in the peripheries—Basques, Catalans, and Gallegans—were dominated by the Castilians in a unitary state. Too, the cultural legacy of the Moors and Africa remained strong in southern Spain, particularly in the province of Andalucía. Southern distinctiveness is still evident in higher levels of poverty than the Spanish norm, aristocratic landed estates, lower levels of religiosity, and socialist political leanings (fig. 6.14).

Internal divisions almost tore Spain apart in a civil war in the 1930s, but the outcome was a Castilian-run fascist dictatorship that endured into the 1970s, perpetuating the traditional strong-handed rule from Madrid. In a radical shift, Spain then

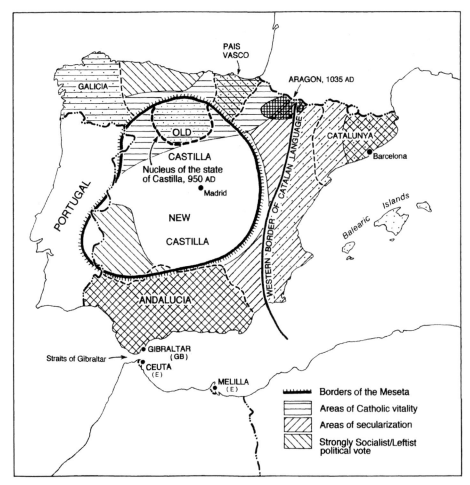

Figure 6.14. Spain, though a very old state, encompasses restive ethnic peripheries and other internal contrasts.

adopted a federalist democracy and extended sweeping freedoms to the provinces and ethnic minorities. These initiatives helped to quell strong anti-Spanish sentiments, but they have not proven entirely successful, as both Basques and Catalans continue to exhibit strong separatist tendencies.

SWITZERLAND AND BELGIUM: ASTRIDE A LANGUAGE DIVIDE

One of the most important language borders in western Europe separates the Romance-speaking south from the Germanic-speaking north (Chapter 4). Switzerland and Belgium both straddle this border, but only the Swiss have achieved relative stability.

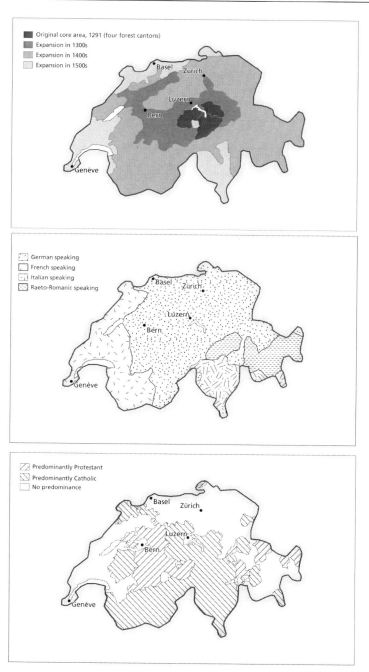

Figure 6.15.   Switzerland: Territorial development and ethnic diversity. The Swiss state is a classic example of gradual expansion from a core area. It includes a mixture of Roman Catholics and Protestants and four major linguistic groups. *Sources:* H. J. Fleure, "Notes on the Evolution of Switzerland," *Geography* 26 (1941): 169–77; and Karl Schib, "Territoriale Entwicklung der Eidgenossenschaft," in *Atlas der Schweiz* (Wabern-Bern: Verlag der eidgenossischen Landestopographie, 1965–1970), 21.

Switzerland has enjoyed considerable success in joining different linguistic and religious groups in a multinational country. Almost two-thirds of the Swiss speak German, 18% French, and one-tenth Italian, in addition to a tiny Romansh minority. Religiously, Switzerland is 39% Catholic and 29% Protestant (fig. 6.15); the remainder include those following a different religion and those professing no religion (about 20% of the population). The Alps cut directly through the country, dividing much of Switzerland into separate valleys, each with its own identity and desire for autonomy. In spite of these challenges, Switzerland has existed for over 700 years as an independent state.

The origins of the Swiss state can be traced to a core area in the 1200s around the eastern shores of the *Vierwaldstättersee* (Lake of Four Forest Cantons or Lake Luzern), at the northern approach to St. Gotthard Pass, the principal land route between Italy and Central Europe in the Middle Ages. Feudal lords banded together there in 1291 for mutual defense, and gradually over the centuries increased their autonomy within the loose-knit German Empire, strengthened by their control of the strategic pass (fig. 6.15). In its formative stage, the state remained wholly German in speech, Catholic in faith, and centered on the lake that afforded easy communication among the member cantons. From the first, Switzerland formed a very loose federal state, or *confederation*, a framework that successfully accommodated subsequent linguistic and religious diversity as the country continued to grow from its tiny core area.

In the 1400s and 1500s, the confederation seized control of other strategic Alpine passes and also Rhine River crossings, in the process incorporating Italian and French-speaking districts. In more recent times, Switzerland achieved prosperity and demonstrated an isolationist ability to avoid wars, accomplishments that greatly enhanced the value of Swiss citizenship.

Switzerland has faced its share of internal problems over the centuries, including at least five civil wars and, recently, ethnic tensions that led the French-speaking part of Canton Bern to break away and form Jura, a new Francophone canton. But all things considered, Switzerland must be regarded as an astounding success in an improbable setting. It helps that much of the power is held at the cantonal level, and that there are multiple cantons where the majority speak one of the major languages or practice one of the major religions. As a result, the competing positions that cantonal authorities take on national issues are usually viewed as representative of local interests, not large-scale ethno-cultural divides.

Belgium, also astride the Germanic–Romance linguistic border, encompasses the Dutch (Flemish) speakers of Flanders in the north and the French speakers of Wallonia in the south—as well as a small German-speaking area in the east (fig. 6.16). A much newer state than Switzerland, Belgium dates only from 1830, when its Catholic population, with approval and encouragement from the Great Powers of Europe, broke away from the Protestant-dominated Netherlands. At its inception, the Belgian state was not viewed as a union of two major language regions. The term *Wallonia* was not even coined until later in the nineteenth century, and in 1830 Flanders meant the old medieval Flanders (the western part of present-day Flanders and adjacent parts of the Netherlands and France). Moreover, there were significant dialecti-

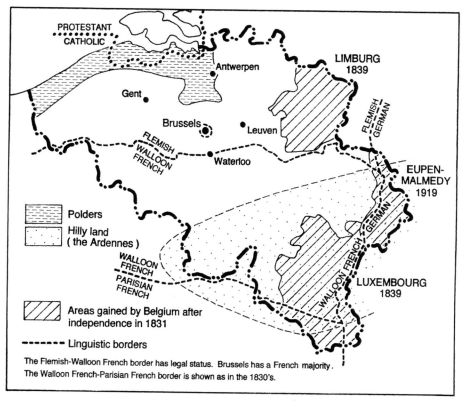

Figure 6.16.   Belgium. The ethnolinguistic divide between north and south has raised growing questions about the viability of the Belgian state in the twenty-first century.

cal divisions, particularly in northern Belgium. No one at the time conceived of the north and south as discrete ethnic territories.

Language came to be politicized in Belgium as a result of the decision to construct a unitary state in which French was to be the language of power and governance. The effort to impose French as the dominant language led to a reaction that brought together the diverse dialectical communities of northern Belgium. As tensions grew between the two linguistic groups, the pressure to decentralize Belgium mounted. Belgium's struggle with that pressure during the middle of the twentieth century led to the establishment of an internal political structure that reflected emerging senses of ethnolinguistic identity. Significant powers were devolved to Flanders and Wallonia, as well as to Brussels—an officially bilingual third administrative region. Eventually Belgium became a loose federation made up of regions based explicitly on ethnolinguistic criteria.

Other paths to federalism could have been followed. Powers could have been given to the old provinces, in which case northern and southern Belgium would each have had four or five administrative regions. Each region would have had a single dominant language, but decisions on cultural, economic, and social issues would have produced different alignments of regions, which could have shifted attention away from the country's linguistic divide. The decision to partition Belgium along ethno-linguistic lines, however, guaranteed a constant reinforcement of the idea that Belgium is made up of two ethnolinguistic communities. As a result, Belgium's viability as a state continues to be tenuous. It took 353 days after the June 2010 elections for the different sides to agree on the formation of a new government.

The contrast between Switzerland and Belgium highlights the importance of viewing political geography as more than the memorization of place names. The different internal political-geographic arrangements that took shape within these two countries have profoundly influenced their internal cultural and political development.

FRAGMENTATION IN THE BALKANS: YUGOSLAVIA
AND ITS SUCCESSOR STATES

Belgium's problems astride a major cultural divide pale in comparison to the geopolitical fate of Yugoslavia, the "land of the South Slavs." Formed following World War I when peacemakers appended various territories to previously independent Serbia (fig. 6.6), the new state joined shards of diverse former empires—Roman, Byzantine, Turkish, Austrian, and Hungarian—each of which had left indelible cultural residues. Largely Serbo-Croatian in speech, Yugoslavia inherited three major faiths—Catholicism, Orthodoxy, and Islam; two alphabets; and a territory running from the Hungarian Basin to the Adriatic coast, but split by the rugged Dinaric Range.

The Serbs dominated Yugoslavia from the first. Belgrade, the Serb capital, became the national capital, and street signs there remained exclusively in the Cyrillic alphabet. No meaningful steps toward federalism were taken in the 1920s and 1930s. Serbs saw themselves both as defenders of the Orthodox faith and of European civilization at large. Catholic Slovenes and Croats, as well as the Muslim Bosnians, though fellow south Slavs, became second-class Yugoslav citizens. Croats took advantage of the German occupation during World War II to contest their status, but also committed various atrocities against the temporarily weakened Serbs.

In addition, major economic disparities developed among the various provinces of Yugoslavia, with Slovenia and Croatia becoming relatively prosperous while Macedonia and parts of Serbia fell behind (fig. 6.17). When one considers that both Croatia and Bosnia-Herzegovina harbored memories of medieval independence, the challenges that faced this multiethnic state become clear.

The state was held together by a charismatic leader, Josip Tito, in the post–World War II era, but the rise to power of an uncompromising Serbian nationalist leader in the late 1980s sealed its fate. In the early 1990s, four provinces seceded from Yugoslavia and achieved independence—Slovenia, Croatia, Macedonia, and Bosnia-Herzegovina (fig. 6.17). In the early 2000s, Montenegro split off as well. Later in the decade, Kosovo, a quasi-autonomous region within Serbia inhabited by an overwhelming majority of Albanians, followed Montenegro's lead. The dismantling of Yugoslavia was accomplished only with great bloodshed on all sides—primarily in Serbia, Croatia, and Bosnia-Herzegovina. The Serbian leadership undertook a program of ethnic cleansing in its territory. Croatia expelled hundreds of thousands of

Figure 6.17. The disintegration of the former Yugoslavia. Seven successor states emerged in the 1990s and 2000s: Slovenia, Croatia, Bosnia and Herzegovina, Macedonia, Montenegro, Serbia, and Kosovo.

ethnic Serbs from its territory. And multiethnic Bosnia-Herzegovina was drawn into the vortex and disintegrated into a long civil war.

Traditionally in the Balkans people had identified with territories, regarding themselves as "Bosnians," "Kosovars," "Herzegovians," "Dalmacians," and such. In other words, they had regional rather than ethnic identities. In those nuclei, nation-states developed beginning in the late nineteenth century, and as each expanded, ethnically mixed populations were annexed. As identity shifted from region to ethnicity, the stage was set for conflict. Political boundaries rarely matched ethnic borders, and most districts had a high degree of mixing. The nation-state principle, applied to such a situation, fueled the tragic ethnic cleansing that took place.

Of the successor states to the former Yugoslavia, Slovenia is in the strongest position since it stood aside from the subsequent troubles and, in any case, had only a tiny Serb minority. Croatia, confronting an awkward territorial configuration and significant minorities, made matters worse by opting for a French-style unitary state that could not easily accommodate minority rights. Even some ethnic Croatian districts grew restive. In Istria, the westernmost part of Croatia, many people feel a greater loyalty to province than to state.

Landlocked Macedonia is a mere fragment of the former territory by that name, which laps over into Greece and Bulgaria and once housed a population of Bulgars,

Pomaks, Turks, Greeks, and Albanians. Even the remnant independent Macedonia retains sizable Albanian and other Muslim minorities.

Bosnia-Herzegovina was, upon becoming independent, almost as diverse as the former Yugoslavia at large. The partition that ended the civil war produced the Srpska Republic, now populated and ruled predominantly by Serbs. Its territory is awkwardly shaped, with two areas barely joined at the strategic Posavina Corridor (fig. 6.17). The remainder of Bosnia-Herzegovina is made up of the "Muslim-Croat Federation."

The condition of the remnant core of Yugoslavia—Serbia—was no more stable. Serb atrocities in Kosovo during the mid-1990s led its dominantly Albanian-Muslim population to declare independence in 2008. Many countries soon recognized Kosovo as an independent state, but Serbia rejected the claim. Nonetheless, after years of tension, in 2013 Serbia entered into an agreement with the Kosovo government accepting the latter's authority over the territory in exchange for an autonomous status for the Serbs living in the northern part of the country. Vojvodina, the northernmost province of Yugoslavia, has a mixed population including many ethnic Hungarians, whose loyalty to a Serb-dominated nation-state is tenuous. Also potentially troublesome is the Sandzak region on the border with Montenegro, peopled predominantly by 250,000 Slavic-speaking Muslims. The Yugoslav case shows that dismantlement of multiethnic states does not guarantee stability, as people are rarely distributed in ways that make line drawing easy, and minorities are found almost everywhere.

RUSSIA: NATION-STATE OR EMPIRE?

In many respects, Russia presents a political anomaly in Europe. It is the only state to exert effective control over a sizable portion of Europe for a period of decades within the last millennium—giving rise to significant political and economic differences between western and eastern Europe. Even in its greatly diminished post-Soviet size, Russia remains by far the largest independent state in Europe—indeed in the entire world—while retaining aspects of empire long after the collapse of Europe's other imperial powers.

Muscovy—modern Moscow—was one of many competing principalities to emerge from an expansive Kiev-centered East Slav Kingdom, which collapsed in the thirteenth century in the wake of Tatar-Mongol invasions (fig. 6.18). Decisive in Muscovy's development as the political focus of Russia was a succession of leaders who skillfully cooperated with the Tatar-Mongols against competing Russian princedoms. Muscovy grew from its core area to dominate the East European Plain—traditionally called European Russia or Eurorussia—and facing no natural barriers to the east, expanded unabated into Siberia in the sixteenth and seventeenth centuries, and then into the Caucasus and Central Asia. Following the Russian revolution and civil war, the Bolsheviks managed to reassemble much of the Czarist Empire by promising many important non-Russian populations territorial autonomy within the new communist state.

When the Soviet Union disintegrated in 1991, Russia faced a difficult transition. An empire traditionally under despotic, unitary rule, post-communist Russia faced wrenching adjustments. In the polity that emerged from the collapse, some 80% of the

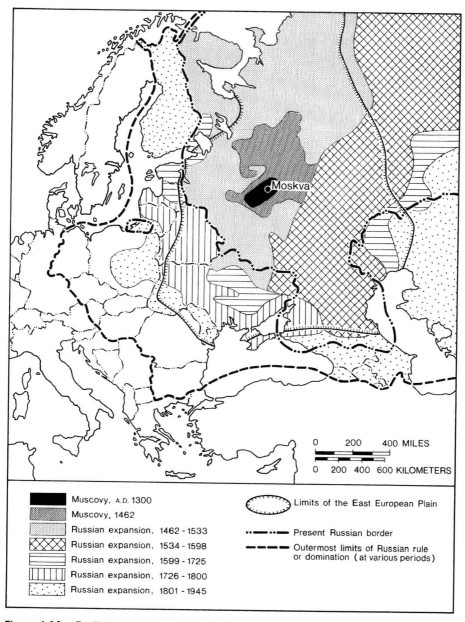

Muscovy, A.D. 1300
Muscovy, 1462
Russian expansion, 1462 - 1533
Russian expansion, 1534 - 1598
Russian expansion, 1599 - 1725
Russian expansion, 1726 - 1800
Russian expansion, 1801 - 1945

Limits of the East European Plain
Present Russian border
Outermost limits of Russian rule or domination (at various periods)

Figure 6.18.   Territorial evolution of Russia. Russia grew from a core area, the Principality of Muscovy around Moscow, to encompass a huge empire, which only collapsed in 1991. Its influence has at times extended deep into Europe and even more profoundly into Asia, but the East European Plain has always provided the spatial and physical focus of Russia.

people were Russian, and no single ethnic minority made up even 4% of the population. Increasingly, Russian nationalists have come to regard the country as a nation-state and emphasize its Eurasian—as opposed to European—character.

Russia's federalist form aims to accommodate ethnic minorities in autonomous republics. Yet the country's territorial integrity has been tested as various Turkic, Caucasic, and Muslim minorities have sought, with greater or lesser fervor, autonomy or independence. Chechnya declared independence in 1991 and since then has undergone two periods of warfare with Moscow. Oil-rich Tatarstan, a Turkic Muslim republic lying on and beyond the Volga River in the southeastern reaches of the East European Plain, declared "sovereignty" in 1990 and enjoyed considerable autonomy for the remainder of the decade. So did neighboring Bashkortostan, also Turkic and Muslim. In recent years, amid Moscow's recentralization of the Russian Federation, these aspirations have been muted.

Other republics and districts pose an array of challenges. Karelia, in the northwest, is a republic designated as the historic homeland of a Finnish-speaking people, but ethnic Russians form the large majority of its population. The Kaliningrad District, on the Baltic Sea, presents a special problem to Russia. This territory was never a part of Russia before 1945, when it was taken from a defeated Germany, nor did any Russians live there. The German population was expelled and replaced by Russians. Moreover, Kaliningrad is an exclave, separated from the rest of Russian territory. In some ways, Kaliningrad is beginning to function like a separate Baltic republic, based on its status as a free-trade zone and smugglers' haven.

Another issue confronting Russia is the status of Belarus, one of the Soviet republics that became an independent state in 1991. Belarus did not actively seek independence, achieving that status by default when the USSR's central government was abolished. Many Belarusians identify as Russians, but there is a cultural-historical basis of Belarusian ethnicity. The Belarusian language, though closely related to the Russian tongue and spoken by only a minority in Belarus, is usually regarded as a distinct language. "Belarusian" often—but inaccurately—is translated as "White Russian," implying that they are a sub-ethnic group of a greater Russian people. But Belarusians also have much in common with Poles and Lithuanians, who controlled the isolated marshlands inhabited by the Belarusians until the late eighteenth century. Poverty-stricken and burdened with a corrupt, strong-armed dictator, Belarus represents a potential liability for Russia.

UKRAINE: FROM BORDER PROVINCE TO INDEPENDENT STATE

Ukraine, the second largest country in Europe in land area and the sixth largest in population, resembles Belarus in some ways. Its independence occurred in the same manner as that of Belarus (i.e., not as the result of a separatist movement). At the time of independence, more than eight million of Ukraine's inhabitants identified themselves as ethnic Russians, and many opposed independence. In recent years a substantial number of ethnic Russians have reidentified themselves as Ukrainians, but internal unity remains a challenge.

Unlike Belarus, Ukraine contains substantial areas of fertile soils and large mineral deposits, especially coal, though it is now wracked by political difficulties, both internal and external. The strongest nationalist sentiment in Ukraine is found in the western half of the country. Long ruled by Poland and Austria-Hungary, the western Ukrainians came under the influence of Roman Catholicism, giving rise to the Uniate Church (see Chapter 5)—a hybrid of the Catholic and Orthodox faiths. The revived Uniate Church provides one major basis of Ukrainian nationalism today.

The eastern part of Ukraine, more heavily Orthodox and Russian, is different. The peninsula of Krym, jutting into the Black Sea and peopled predominantly by Russians and Crimean Tatars, recently was granted the status of autonomous republic in an effort to defuse separatist sentiment. The most heavily Russian district north of the peninsula, Kharkov (now renamed *Karkhiv* by Ukraine), is also restive. The westernmost part of the country, the Zakarpats'ka District, lies west of the Carpathian Mountains and has no history prior to 1945 of belonging to Ukraine. There, too, Ukrainian nationalism has not taken root, though no separatist sentiment has arisen.

A potential problem for Ukraine also exists in Transdnistria, a fertile, dominantly Slavic sliver of adjacent Moldova. A separatist movement exists there, but Transdnistria is small and unlikely to emerge as an independent state. Were it to secede from Moldova, the area might logically join Ukraine, but such a transfer might lead to a major boundary dispute, involving also Romania, which regards itself as Moldova's protector, given the two countries' shared language and Latinized culture.

Challenges to the Territorial State

As many of the cases we examined in the prior section make clear, there remains in Europe a tension between the nation-state idea and an ethno-national reality characterized by a lack of correspondence in many places between the pattern of states and the pattern of ethnic nations. In other words, states have not been entirely successful in forging single nations out of disparate peoples. Even leaving aside the complexities introduced by recent streams of migrants, Europe does not consist solely of Spanish, French, Belgian, and Dutch peoples; it also encompasses Galicians, Basques, Catalans, Walloons, Flemings, Frisians, and many more.

Most of Europe's historically rooted ethno-cultural groups occupy discrete regions and live in uneasy tension with the dominant political-territorial order (fig. 6.19). It is difficult to generalize about the socioeconomic situation of these groups. Some are located in areas of significant economic prosperity (Basques and Catalans in Spain, Flemings in Belgium), whereas others are found in more economically marginal regions (Galicians in Spain, Bretons in France, Walloons in Belgium). What they share in common is some desire to maintain distinctiveness from the "nation-state" in which they live.

In pursuit of that desire, many members of Europe's long-standing ethno-regional minority communities seek some degree of autonomy from the state in which they are situated, and in some instances the call is for complete independence. The degree of radicalization is directly related to the extent to which state authorities

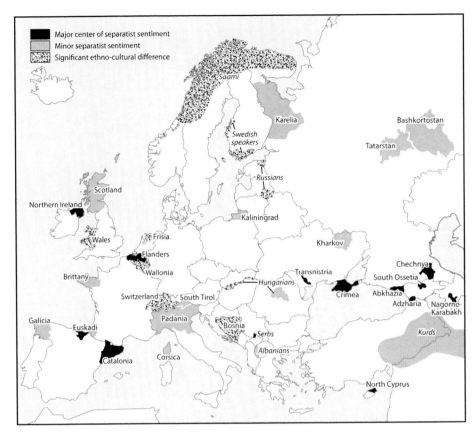

Figure 6.19.   Areas of separatism or significant ethno-cultural difference within states. This map shows only areas that are the object of separatist sentiment or where significant ethno-cultural minorities can be found. More than a dozen new recognized independent states have appeared as a result of separatist movements since 1980, and several others, such as Turkish North Cyprus and Abkhazia, have achieved de facto independence.

seek to impose a single ethno-national norm throughout the territory. When states are actively engaged in such efforts (e.g., Franco's Spain), radicalization usually follows. On the other hand, when states take a more conciliatory and inclusive attitude toward ethno-cultural minorities (such as Finland toward its Swedish-speaking minority, or the Netherlands toward the Frisians), there is less incentive to demand a high degree of autonomy or independence.

Of course, Europe's ethnic diversity is not just a function of these longer-standing ethno-cultural differences. Many European countries have been destinations for migrants coming from other parts of the world. We will look at the some of the principal issues presented by these newer waves of migrants in Chapter 11. But their arrival in Europe is symptomatic of another challenge to the territorial state—one that comes from above, not below. That challenge is associated with the accelerating globalization of recent decades. Since we have not yet focused attention on the fundamentals of Europe's economic system, it is premature to analyze globalization's impacts in any depth (see Chapter 9), but it clearly has had a significant influence on the functions and capacities of the territorial state. States have had to make major adjustments in the face of increasingly powerful international economic institutions, global financial and capital flows, influential transnational corporations, unprecedented movements of peoples across international boundaries, technologies that allow instantaneous communication across vast distances, and much, much more. Some of their traditional powers have been devolved downward to local or substate regional governments, whereas others have been ceded to authorities above the scale of the state.

Europe has gone further on the latter front than any other part of the globe in part because globalization has played out against the backdrop of a set of cultural-historical circumstances that set the stage for the development of a far-reaching supranational organization: the EU. At the end of World War II, Europe found itself in ruins after a second devastating conflict in less than 50 years. Many Europeans thought the only hope for the future lay in making some fundamental adjustments to the way Europe functioned politically. Yet the concept of the nation-state and the supporting doctrine of nationalism were deeply embedded principles in the European geographical imagination. Moreover, when the war ended, many leaders of European states focused their attention internally, adopting protectionist measures to help rejuvenate their national economies. Even as the political map of Europe had been changed somewhat by the war, it looked for a time as if the principles underlying the prewar political-geographic order would reemerge unscathed.

Nonetheless, a group of visionaries began calling for change—promoting the idea of a more integrated Europe. Few were ready to consider proposals for a United States of Europe, but by the 1950s the leaders of a set of core countries were willing to entertain tearing down some of the economic barriers that divided one country from another. The catalysts for moving forward were several. First, there was a recognition that it would be harder for countries with closer economic links to go to war with one another. Second, the increasing solidification of Soviet control over Eastern Europe prompted concerns about fragmentation in the West; only by presenting a more united front, it was thought, could Western Europe hope to stand up to the increasingly unified and potentially threatening East. Third, the United States, which flooded Europe with redevelopment assistance under the Marshall Plan, pushed Western Europe toward a more unified stance in an effort to head off further internal conflict and promote solidarity in the face of the Soviet-dominated East. Finally, there was a sense within Europe that the world was increasingly being dominated by large superpowers. During the course of the prior 50 years, Europe had gone from being a major global player to an increasingly weakened and fragmented region. Only by working together, it was argued, could Europe regain some of its former standing.

Inspired in part by the Benelux Customs Union, a free-trade area previously created by Belgium, the Netherlands, and Luxembourg, in 1951 France, West Germany, and Italy joined the three Low Countries in an agreement to create a "common market" in coal and steel: the European Coal and Steel Community (ECSC). By 1957, these same six countries decided to broaden greatly the scope of what they were doing—establishing the European Economic Community (EEC), which was designed to bring into being a common market in agricultural and industrial goods. These countries also founded a cooperative agency focused on nuclear energy: the European Atomic Energy Community (EURATOM).

Of the three "communities"—ECSC, EEC, and EURATOM—the EEC was clearly the largest and most important. Hence, the roots of the European unity project are often traced to the EEC and the 1957 agreement that brought it into being: the Treaty of Rome. (European treaties are often named after the place where they are negotiated and signed.) What started with six countries expanded in subsequent decades to include nine, then ten, then 12, then 15, then 25, then 27, and most recently 28 countries (fig. 1.10). Moreover, the scope and significance of the integration project has also grown over time. That growth is reflected in changes to the name given to the formal European integration project. The EEC became the EC (the European Community), which in turn became the EU (European Union).

We will defer more detailed consideration of the EU's development and current prospects until after we have examined Europe's economic foundations. For present purposes, the important thing to note is that Europe has taken far more significant steps toward integration than any other region in the world. The EU has become, in some important respects, a unified economic space, although there are certainly aspects of the economy—especially labor—that do not move seamlessly across national borders. Perhaps more remarkably, European integration has done something that would have seemed unthinkable 75 years ago: create a political and social environment that makes warfare between member states almost unimaginable. Despite its successes, Europe's experiment with integration is facing significant challenges, with many Europeans opposing the increasing concentration of powers in EU institutions, resenting the bureaucratization that has come with an expanding EU, and contesting the fiscal transfers that have occurred from richer to poorer member states. At their core, these challenges serve as a reminder that state nationalism is far from dead in Europe. The EU has changed Europe's political geography in far-reaching ways, but the state continues to be the principal focus of identity for the majority of Europeans. With concerns over European integration mounting, that situation is unlikely to change anytime soon.

Before leaving our review of supranational challenges to the European state, it is useful to consider the impacts of the changing organization of military and security matters in Europe. Until the middle of the twentieth century, such matters were handled on a state-by-state basis. In the wake of World War II, however, the North Atlantic Treaty Organization (NATO) became an increasingly important part of the western European security landscape. Founded in 1949, NATO was effectively an American-dominated military alliance confronting the Soviet-dominated Eastern Bloc (fig. 6.20).

With the collapse of the Soviet threat after 1990, NATO expanded into several former Soviet satellite states. Poland, Czechia, and Hungary joined in 1999, followed by Estonia, Latvia, Lithuania, Slovenia, Slovakia, Bulgaria, and Romania in 2004, and Albania and Croatia in 2009 (fig. 6.20). A number of other European countries have expressed interest in joining, including Macedonia, Georgia, Montenegro, and Ukraine. The purpose of NATO has also changed. It has become a military force

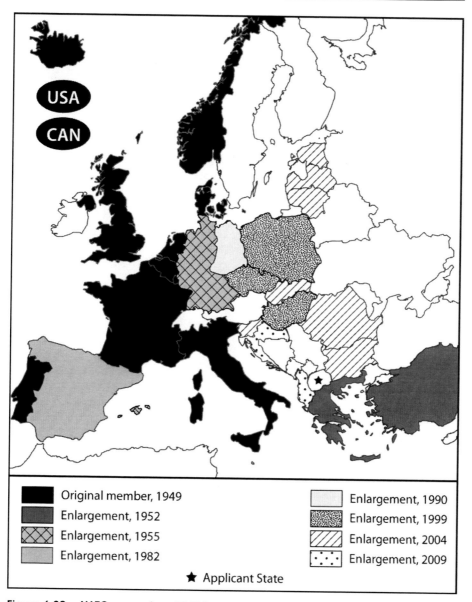

USA

CAN

■ Original member, 1949		▨ Enlargement, 1990	
■ Enlargement, 1952		▨ Enlargement, 1999	
▨ Enlargement, 1955		▨ Enlargement, 2004	
▨ Enlargement, 1982		⋰ Enlargement, 2009	

★ Applicant State

Figure 6.20.   NATO expansion, 1949 to present. Long dominated by the United States, NATO is a holdover from the Cold War searching for a new raison d'être. Some applicant countries fear a revival of Russian imperialism.

employed to intervene in local and regional conflicts. In Bosnia-Herzegovina, NATO forces served as peacekeepers. In Kosovo, the alliance undertook an eleven-week bombing campaign against the former Yugoslavia. NATO also played a leading role in the 2011 air campaign against the Qaddafi regime in Libya, with Europeans taking the lead.

In the wake of the terrorist attacks on the United States on September 11, 2001, and the subsequent invasion of Afghanistan, NATO took command of the International Security Assistance Force (ISAF) in that country. Tensions between parts of Europe and the United States over the U.S.-led invasion of Iraq and U.S. efforts to build a missile defense system in Europe have raised growing questions in Europe about the region's role in an organization that is widely seen as being dominated by the United States. In response, the EU has developed an increasingly significant foreign policy wing, and the member states are represented collectively in many international bodies. Moreover, efforts have been made to develop a robust European Security and Defense Policy and to create a military force that can deal with European crises. An important step was taken in 2004 when a European Union Force (EUFOR) took over leadership of the mission in Bosnia and Herzegovina from NATO. However, foreign policy differences among EU states regularly complicate EU efforts to serve as a unified geopolitical actor. As a result, individual states continue to be the most important players in the military arena—particularly the United Kingdom and France, the two leading military powers in Europe.

There is much more to say about Europe's changing political geography, but let us turn first to the ways Europeans have carved out a living, and the landscapes and socioeconomic patterns they have created in the process. We begin our exploration in the rural sector—the focus of the next chapter.

Sources and Suggested Readings

Agnew, J. 1995. The Rhetoric of Regionalism: The Northern League in Italian Politics, 1983–94. *Transactions of the Institute of British Geographers* 20:156–72.

———. 2003. Territoriality and Political Identity in Europe. In *Europe without Borders*, ed. M. Berezin and M. Schain, 219–42. Baltimore: Johns Hopkins University Press.

Anderson, J. 1986. Nationalism and Geography. In *The Rise of the Modern State*, ed. J. Anderson, 115–42. Brighton: Wheatsheaf Books.

Berezin, M., and M. Schain. 2003. *Europe without Borders: Remapping Territory, Citizenship, and Identity in a Transnational Age.* Baltimore: Johns Hopkins University Press.

Clem, R. S. 2006. Russia's Electoral Geography: A Review. *Eurasian Geography and Economics* 47 (4): 381–406.

Dahlman, C. T., and T. Williams. 2010. Ethnic Enclavisation and State Formation in Kosovo. *Geopolitics* 15:406–30.

Elden, S. 2010. Land, Terrain, Territory. *Progress in Human Geography* 34 (6): 799–817.

Habermas, J. 1996. The European Nation-State: Its Achievements and Its Limits. In *Mapping the Nation*, ed. G. Balakrishnan, 281–94. London: Verso.

Heeg, S., and J. Ossenbrugge. 2002. State Formation and Territoriality in the European Union. *Geopolitics* 7:75–88.

Heffernan, M. 1997. *Twentieth-Century Europe: A Political Geography.* New York: John Wiley.

Hudson, R. 2000. One Europe or Many? Reflections on Becoming European. *Transactions—Institute of British Geographers* 25 (4): 409–26.

Johnson, C. M. 2011. Mezzogiorno without the Mafia: Modern-Day Meridionalisti and the Making of a "Space of Backwardness" in Eastern Germany. *National Identities* 13 (2): 157–76.

Johnson, C. M., and G. White. 2011. Traces of Power: Europe's Impact on the Political Organization of the Globe. In *Engineering Earth: The Impacts of Mega-Engineering Projects*, ed. S. Brunn, 2139–58. London: Kluwer/Springer Academic.

Jones, A. 1994. *The New Germany: A Human Geography*. Chichester, UK: John Wiley.

———. 2006. Narrative-Based Production of State Spaces for International Region Building: Europeanization and the Mediterranean. *Annals of the Association of American Geographers* 96 (2): 415–31.

Kaplan, D. H., and J. Hakli, eds. 2002. *Boundaries and Place: European Borderlands in Geographical Context*. Lanham, MD: Rowman & Littlefield.

Klemencic, V., and R. Genorio. 1993. The New State of Slovenia and Its Function within the Frame of Europe. *GeoJournal* 30:323–33.

Kolossov, V. A., and A. Treivish. 1998. The Political Geography of European Minorities, Past and Future. *Political Geography* 17:517–34.

Kuus, M. 2011. Policy and Geopolitics: Bounding Europe in EUrope. *Annals of the Association of American Geographers* 101 (5): 1140–55.

Lefebvre, E. L. 2003. Belgian Citizenship: Managing Linguistic, Regional, and Economic Demands. *Citizenship Studies* 7 (1): 111–34.

McManis, D. R. 1967. The Core of Italy: The Case for Lombardy-Piedmont. *Professional Geographer* 19:251–57.

Mikesell, M. W. 1983. The Myth of the Nation State. *Journal of Geography* 82 (6): 257–60.

Murphy, A. B. 1988. *The Regional Dynamics of Language Differentiation in Belgium: A Study in Cultural-Political Geography*. Chicago: University of Chicago Geography Research Series.

———. 1996. The Sovereign State System as Political-Territorial Ideal: Historical and Contemporary Considerations. In *State Sovereignty as Social Construct*, ed. T. Biersteker and C. Weber, 81–120. Cambridge: Cambridge University Press.

———. 2008. Rethinking Multi-level Governance in a Changing European Union: Why Metageography and Territoriality Matter. *GeoJournal* 72 (1–2): 7–18.

Paasi, A. 2002. Regional Transformation in the European Context: Notes on Regions, Boundaries and Identity. *Space & Polity* 6 (2): 197–201.

Painter, J. (2002). Multi-level Citizenship, Identity and Regions in Contemporary Europe. In *Transnational Democracy: Political Spaces and Border Crossings*, ed. J. Anderson, 93–110. London: Routledge.

Perepechko, A. S., V. A. Kolossov, and C. ZumBrunnen. 2007. Remeasuring and Rethinking Social Cleavages in Russia: Continuity and Changes in Electoral Geography 1917–1995. *Political Geography* 26 (2): 179–208.

Pounds, N. J. G., and S. S. Ball. 1964. Core-Areas and the Development of the European States System. *Annals of the Association of American Geographers* 54:24–40.

Sassen, S. 2006. *Territory, Authority, Rights: From Medieval to Global Assemblages*. Princeton, NJ: Princeton University Press.

van der Wusten, H. 2004. The Distribution of Political Centrality in the European State System. *Political Geography* 23:677–700.

Walters, W. 2004. The Frontiers of the European Union: A Geostrategic Perspective. *Geopolitics* 9 (3): 674–98.

Weber, E. 1976. *Peasants into Frenchmen: The Modernization of Rural France, 1870–1914*. Stanford, CA: Stanford University Press.

White, G. 2004. *Nation, State, Territory: Origins, Evolutions, and Relationships*. Lanham, MD: Rowman & Littlefield.

Williams, C. H. 1980. Ethnic Separatism in Western Europe. *Tijdschrift voor Economische en Sociale Geografie* 71:142–58.

Wixman, R. 1991. Ethnic Nationalism in Eastern Europe. In *Eastern Europe: The Impact of Geographic Forces on a Strategic Region*, 36–47. Washington, DC: U.S. Government Printing Office.

CHAPTER 7

Land and Life in the Rural Sector

The vast majority of Europeans today are urban dwellers, but until recently most people lived in rural areas and made their living by farming, herding, fishing, and harvesting natural resources. These are all examples of **primary economic activities**, meaning those involved in extracting resources from the land and seas. Because agriculture is the most important primary economic activity, we will emphasize it in this chapter, but we will also focus on the types of land divisions and settlement patterns found in rural Europe.

Traditional Agriculture

The origins of European agriculture lie in prehistory in the same hearth from which Christianity and Indo-European speech spread into Europe. The domestication of plants and animals—the **neolithic revolution**—occurred in the Near East and entered Europe later, apparently borne by proto-Indo-Europeans. For that reason, the maps of linguistic and agricultural diffusion largely match (compare figs. 4.4 and 7.1). Both language and agrarian technology advanced from southeast to northwest over a period of about four millennia. Agriculture came first to Greece and arrived last in the lands beyond the North and Baltic seas.

The advent of agriculture seems to have occurred in two ways. In southeastern and central Europe, agriculture made a sudden intrusion, producing a sharp break in the archaeological record, as hunters were displaced by farmers (fig. 7.1). Elsewhere, the advent of farming occurred more gradually. The Etruscans in Italy and Uralic speakers in the north may have adopted agriculture to avoid being displaced or absorbed. Transitional economies based upon both farming and hunting/gathering became typical, blurring the distinction between mesolithic and neolithic.

The earliest neolithic crop complex included wheat, barley, lentils, peas, and flax. Other crops came later, after the neolithic diffusion had reached Europe. Europe's garden vegetables and orchard trees belong among these later introductions from the

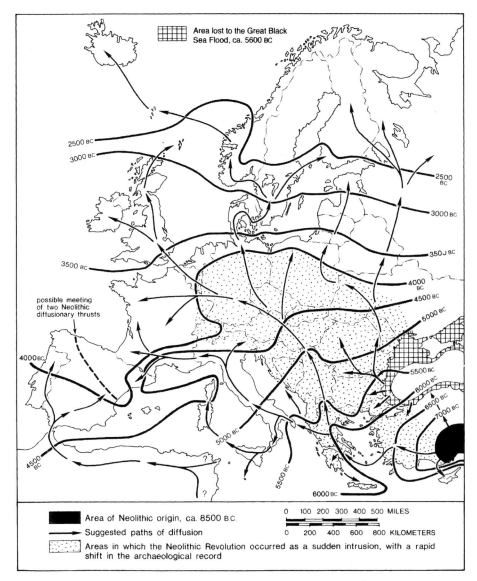

Figure 7.1.   Neolithic origins and the diffusion of agriculture in Europe. Domesticated plants and animals reached Europe from the Near East. This map is based on archaeological finds but nevertheless remains speculative and controversial in detail. *Sources:* John Chapman and Johannes Müller, "Early Farmers in the Mediterranean Basin," *Antiquity* 64 (1990): 128; Peter Breunig, *14C-Chronologie des vorderasiatischen, südost-und mitteleuropäischen Neolithikums* (Köln: Böhlau, 1987); João Zilhão, "The Spread of Agro-pastoral Economies across Mediterranean Europe," *Journal of Mediterranean Archaeology* 6 (1993): 5–63; Renfrew 1989 and Krantz 1988 (both cited in Chapter 4); Ryan and Pitman 2000 (cited in Chapter 2); Robert Sokal et al., "Genetic Evidence for the Spread of Agriculture in Europe by Demic Diffusion," *Nature* 351 (1991): 143–45; Thorpe 1996.

Near East by way of Anatolia. Grapes may first have been made into wine in Georgia, in the Caucasus region.

Domestic herd animals also came from the Near East. Cattle, pigs, sheep, goats, donkeys, and horses all first entered Europe by way of Anatolia, as did poultry. The basic tools of agriculture, such as the hoe and plow, the technique of terracing, and irrigation technology also came from the Near East. In the formation of early agriculture, then, Europe borrowed from higher civilizations to the east and south.

Spreading through Europe, and adjusting to different environments and cultures, agriculture fragmented into traditional regional types. The major ancient and traditional agrarian systems were the following: (1) Mediterranean agriculture; (2) three-field farming; (3) hardscrabble herding/farming; (4) shifting cultivation; and (5) nomadic herding (fig. 7.2). The basic characteristics of Europe's physical geography outlined in Chapter 2 help explain why different agricultural activities came to dominate in different parts of Europe.

MEDITERRANEAN AGRICULTURE

The rural peoples of Cyprus, Greece, the eastern Adriatic coast, peninsular Italy, the Languedoc Plain, and southern Iberia traditionally practiced a distinctive agrarian system, appropriately referred to as **Mediterranean agriculture**. This system came more or less unaltered from the neolithic hearth to the east. Agriculture had arisen in an eastern extension of the Mediterranean climate zone, and the southern European peninsulas offered a sufficiently similar setting such that few adaptive changes were necessary.

By the time of classical Greco-Roman civilization, Mediterranean agriculture consisted of a threefold system of field agriculture, horticulture, and pasture, beautifully adapted to the unique climate and rugged terrain of southern Europe. The Mediterranean climate has a long summer drought and mild, rainy winters. The field was devoted to the winter cultivation of small grains. These thrived in the cool, wet season without irrigation. Wheat and barley, sown with the arrival of the first autumnal rain showers, grew slowly through the winter months and reached maturity in the warm, sunny days of late spring. Harvesting occurred before the annual drought tightened its grip on the land. The great harvest festivals of the Mediterranean people accordingly came in the spring rather than the fall. Farmers typically employed a two-field rotational system, cultivating the land only every other year to prevent soil exhaustion. Wheat was generally the more important of the two grain crops, but barley achieved greater importance in drier areas with poor soils since it is hardier than wheat. In the middle 1900s, wheat and barley still accounted for 40% of all tilled land in Italy and 50% in Greece. Many classical farmers also raised millet, a hardy grain that tolerates heat, drought, and poor soils.

Horticulture provided the second element of the traditional Mediterranean agricultural trinity. Of particular importance were orchards and vineyards of drought-resistant perennials native to the Mediterranean region and able to withstand the summer dry season. From the vineyard, Mediterranean farmers derived table grapes, raisins dried after the late summer harvest before the onset of rain, and wine. Southern

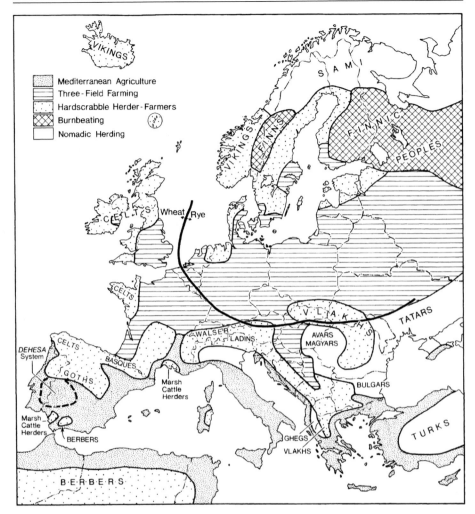

Figure 7.2.   Ancient and traditional types of agriculture. The division between wheat and rye as the dominant bread grain occurred around 1900 CE. Ancient and traditional systems gave way at widely different periods in the various parts of Europe.

Europeans have a long and close relationship with wine. About 1000 BCE, in the Greek lands, a cult devoted to the god Dionysus arose, in which alcoholic intoxication served to aid religious experiences. The cult, not surprisingly, became very popular among the common folk, and by the sixth century BCE it had gained governmental approval. Dionysus and wine spread to the western Mediterranean with the Greek colonists, and the Romans subsequently accepted the cult, renaming the wine god Bacchus. After Christianization of the Roman Empire, wine retained its ancient Dionysian sacredness by finding a place in the Eucharist as the symbolic blood of Christ. Vineyards grow both on terraced hillsides and on alluvial valley floors. The vine produces a crop of high value on a wide variety of surfaces and soils, including steep slopes, without irrigation.

The olive is another important element of Mediterranean horticulture. Olive trees are long lived and drought resistant, but not tolerant of a hard frost. The olive tree yields a crop only in alternate years, blossoming in the first year and bearing fruit in the next. Harvesting is accomplished by hitting the branches with a pole. While Mediterranean peoples eat many olives, the principal value of the olive tree, both in ancient times and today, is as a source of cooking oil. Butter has never been produced in southern Europe, so olive oil provides a needed substitute.

Other orchard trees of the classical Mediterranean included the fig, which is also drought resistant, native to the area, and suited to hillsides; the pistachio; the carob; and the pomegranate. While horticulture and field agriculture typically occupied different areas within the village lands of the Mediterranean, intertillage also occurred. In this system, wheat and barley were sown among the widely spaced orchard trees (fig. 7.3). While not technically an element of horticulture, the cork oak also played an important role in some Mediterranean regions. Every eight to ten years, the outer bark of this wild tree can be stripped, producing a commercially valuable item of trade (fig. 7.4).

The third element of traditional Mediterranean agriculture was the pasture. Village herders raised mainly small livestock, particularly sheep, goats, and swine. These animals survived on the scanty forage offered by the rugged highland pastures and mountain oak forests of southern Europe. Goats and sheep moved with agility through

Figure 7.3. Intertillage of wheat and olives in an alluvial valley in Greece. Two typical Mediterranean crops share the same field on the island of Crete. The wheat has only recently been reaped by hand and tied into bundles to be carried in for threshing. Intertillage is common in traditional Mediterranean agriculture. The month is May, the time of grain harvest before the drought of summer. Olives from these young trees will be ready for harvest in autumn. Photo by T. G. J.-B., 1971.

Figure 7.4.   Cork newly stripped from the trunks of cork oak trees in Portugal. It takes about ten years for the bark to regenerate to a point where the tree can be stripped again. The numbers on the tree correspond to the last digit of the year in which the trunk was stripped. Photo by A. B. M., 1986.

the rocky landscape, and pigs thrived in the native live oak forests. Sheep, the most numerous livestock, provided wool, hides, and some meat—though the Mediterranean diet remained heavily vegetarian. Goats yielded mohair, milk, and hides, and to a certain extent they took the place of dairy cattle in southern Europe. The cheeses produced in Mediterranean districts come from goat's milk or, more rarely, from sheep's milk, as in Roquefort.

The Mediterranean pasture remained largely divorced from field agriculture and horticulture. No crop harvests were used as feed or fodder for the herds, and animal manure was not collected as fertilizer for the fields or orchards. In fact, livestock often ranged far from villages, under the care of migrant shepherds and swineherds. In the dry, hot summer, sheep and goats moved to high pastures in the mountains, where grass grew more abundantly. During the winter they migrated down to marshy parts of the alluvial lowlands. The herders went with them, in a system called **transhumance**, and often months passed between the herders' visits to the home village. The beast of burden of the traditional Mediterranean agriculture was the donkey—though some farmers did not own one, making do instead with human labor.

All three of the basic classical agricultural enterprises were practiced on most farms, though one or another might have been emphasized. From the diverse unspecialized trinity of small grains, vine and tree crops, and small livestock, nearly all of life's necessities could be obtained, including woolen and leather clothing, bread, beverages, fruit, cheese, cooking oil, and even a cork for the leather wine container.

THREE-FIELD FARMING

North of the Mediterranean, in fertile lands beyond the mountains and centered in the Great and East European plains and the Hungarian Basin, a second traditional agricultural system once prevailed: **three-field farming** (fig. 7.2). In this system, found mainly among Germanic and Slavic peoples living in the marine west coast and humid continental climate regions, grains were raised on a three-field rotation. In year one, farmers would plant a summer crop on one part of their land, a winter grain on another, and another part would lie fallow. Farmers would then rotate land uses in years two and three—returning to the original pattern in year four.

The grains grown in this system differed from place to place. In southern and western areas, including England, France, and northwestern Iberia, wheat was the principal bread grain. Rye, the second great bread grain, dominated the north, in Germany, Scandinavia, Poland, and Russia, where dark bread was preferred. Poland and Russia together produce nearly half of the world's rye today. Rye has greater resistance to cold and more tolerance for acidic, sandy soils than does wheat, allowing it to succeed better in northern and eastern regions. Oats share the hardiness of rye and grow usually as a summer grain throughout the three-field area, providing oat-cakes, gruel, and—most important—the major livestock feed grain of the system. The fourth major grain, barley, was used in beer, the northern substitute for wine, but was raised primarily as a feed grain.

Oats and rye apparently joined the ancient Indo-European agrarian system as it spread north into colder lands. Earlier, these two grains had apparently grown only as weeds in the wheat and barley fields of early agriculturists in the south and east. Rye and oats may be the only crops domesticated within Europe. Flax, one of the original Near Eastern crops, made the transition northward to find an important place in three-field farming as the major fiber crop in the three-field system. Linen garments are made from flax. Still today, the old three-field countries, led by Russia, produce much of the world's flax.

Horticulture also survived the northward diffusion into colder lands, though a different array of fruit trees from those of the Mediterranean prevailed. In place of the olive, almond, fig, and pomegranate came the apple, pear, peach, cherry, and plum, all of Asian origin but also able to grow in the north. The grapevine eventually strug-gled northward, but reached its climatic limits roughly along the line of the Seine, Rhine, and Danube rivers. There, it thrived best on south-facing, sunny slopes.

Another basic part of three-field farming, the cutting of hay from meadowland, provided additional sustenance for livestock during the winter season. During much of the winter season, livestock remained in stalls and consumed hay and feed grains. At the opposite season, they grazed fallow fields, pastures, and remnant forests, which usually lay toward the periphery of village lands.

Livestock played a much greater role in three-field farming than in Mediterra-nean agriculture, supplying a larger part of the rural diet. Cattle, the dominant ani-mals, provided meat, dairy products, manure for the fields, and, as oxen, power to pull the bulky plow characteristic of the Germanic and Slavic lands. In more moun-tainous areas, transhumance was practiced. In much of Central Europe, including

Germany and Poland, swine were a more important source of meat than cattle, and pork is still a mainstay of the diet there. The unique value of swine is their ability to convert even the least savory garbage and waste into high-quality meat.

Perhaps the key difference between three-field farming and Mediterranean agriculture was the close relationship in the former between crops and livestock. The Mediterranean farmer raised both plants and animals, but there was little or no tie between the two, and animal husbandry remained separate from tillage. In the three-field system, crops and livestock were inseparable, for the animals provided the manure used to maintain soil fertility and the power for plowing the fields. In turn, much of the produce of the cropland, particularly the barley and oats, went to feed the livestock, and meadow and pasture occupied extensive acreage.

HARDSCRABBLE HERDER-FARMERS

Separating and surrounding the favored lands of the three-field farming and Mediterranean agriculture lay **hardscrabble belts**, afflicted with broken terrain, much cloudiness, or sterile soils (fig. 7.2). In these regions, open-range livestock herding constituted the dominant traditional activity, with crop farming minor and secondary in importance. From ancient times, stable village-dwelling farmers of the Mediterranean and Germano-Slavic lands both vilified and romanticized the herders of the peripheries—Celts, Vikings, Basques, Berbers, Vlakhs, and others.

In common with Mediterranean shepherds, the herder-farmer hardscrabble folk relied heavily upon transhumance, shifting their herds seasonally. While these shifts usually occurred between highlands in the summer and lowlands in the winter, other patterns also developed. For example, in Las Marismas, the great marsh at the mouth of the Guadalquivir River in Spain, Iberian longhorn cattle entered the core of the wetlands in the dry summer and then retreated to the peripheries of the marsh as the floods of winter turned the area into a huge lake.

Cattle were the favored animals of the herder-farmers, and a milking culture-complex characterized most of these areas. Alpine areas, even before the beginning of the Common Era, exported cheese, and by about 1100 CE, a distinctive high-mountain system of dairy cattle herding developed among the Walser people there, involving transhumance, hay cutting, winter stall-feeding, milk products, and sheep raising. (Think of the lifestyle depicted in the famous story of Heidi.) Sheep dominated most of the other hill and mountain areas and were the favored animal of the Vlakhs, Basques, and Dinaric folk. In response to the demands of late medieval and Renaissance woolen textile industries, as well as the mechanized woolen mills of the Industrial Revolution (discussed in Chapter 8), many highland herding areas shifted from cattle to sheep.

SHIFTING CULTIVATION OF THE NORTH

In the subarctic expanse of taiga with poor soils, Finnic peoples of the forests practiced another traditional farming system called **shifting cultivation** (fig. 7.2). They cut

Figure 7.5.   Finnish farmers in the interior of their country practicing a traditional form of shifting cultivation that required the repeated clearing and burning of woodland. The fields were used only for one or two years before being abandoned. Photo by T. G. J.-B., 1985, at the Kuopion Museum in Kuopio, Finland.

down trees in small clearings, allowed the dead vegetation to dry, burned it, and then sowed rye and barley in the fertile ashes among the stumps (fig. 7.5). After a year or two, shifting cultivators (or burnbeaters as they were sometimes known) abandoned the clearing and made another. Shifting cultivation made the infertile, acidic soils of the virgin taiga productive for one crop year. Farmers cut or girdled trees in the early spring of the first year and allowed the wood to dry until midsummer of the third year and then set fire to the clearing. They then planted rye, which came to harvest in the fourth summer, after which the field was abandoned. The system must have offered the spectacular sight of flaming tree trunks being rolled over the ground by soot-blackened men and women. Shifting cultivators also kept cattle herds in the woods, and many relied as much on hunting and fishing as upon agriculture for livelihood. So successful was their system that the Swedish crown introduced Finnish shifting cultivators into interior Scandinavia as colonists after about 1575. In the long run, however, population pressures made shifting cultivation untenable in northern Europe, and it has not been practiced since about 1920.

NOMADIC HERDING

In the outermost peripheries of Europe, cold, soil infertility, and aridity worked against the introduction of agriculture. In the dry Asian steppe, only the herd animals, not the crops of the ancient Near East agricultural hearth, were part of the mix.

Figure 7.6. Sami man in traditional dress with one of his reindeer in northern Norway.
Large herds once roamed the Scandinavian north. The formerly nomadic system has evolved into ranching today—and a draw for tourists. Photo by A. B. M., 2010.

The Asiatic herders moved from place to place, seeking fresh pastures for their animals. The steppe corridor of the southeast and the Hungarian Puszta received wave after wave of such **nomadic herders**, who raised horses, sheep, goats, and cattle. Among them were the Magyars, Avars, Bulgars, Tatars, and many others, driving their flocks and herds westward in a competition for land.

A unique group of nomadic herders, the Sami, inhabited Sapmi (Lapland) in the far north. None of the Near Eastern herd animals could survive in the arctic tundra, but the Sami observed their linguistic cousins, the Finns, herding cattle. Following that example, they or some neighboring tundra people domesticated the reindeer, which became the sole basis of their herding system (fig. 7.6). The Sami had no other animals and no crops at all. Like the Finns, they also engaged in hunting and fishing, but Sami herders acquired many of the necessities of life from the reindeer: meat for food, skins for housing and clothing, and bone for tools and instruments. They spent the summer herding stock on the tundras of the hilly interior and northern Scandinavian coastal fringe, including some islands off the coast of Norway. In wintertime, the reindeer migrated into the protective coniferous forests adjacent to the tundra, which afforded shelter from the bitterly cold winds of the open tundra. Autumn and spring were spent en route to and from the summer pastures on the tundra. The Sami had no awareness of international boundaries and moved freely through what is today Norwegian, Swedish, Finnish, and Russian territory.

Traditional Land Divisions and Settlement Patterns

Before the modern era, a landed aristocracy dominated a tenant peasantry in both the Mediterranean and the three-field farming regions of Europe. Most agriculture was carried out on small plots. It was unspecialized and subsistence based—designed to produce the basic necessities of life. The fields of the Mediterranean region were divided into countless block-shaped parcels, forming a complicated patchwork of fragmented holdings. In districts colonized during Roman times, a more rigid checkerboard pattern survives in places, a legacy of the imperial land survey system (fig. 7.7). The Roman period also saw the establishment of some large grain farms in fertile parts of Sicily, northern Italy, and more far-flung areas to serve the needs of the expanding empire. Once the empire came to an end, however, the nobility took over control of large estates—called **latifundia**—which were divided into small units and farmed by indentured peasants. Because of a shortage of flat land in the Mediterranean, terraces were built on the hillsides of slopes throughout the region. Many of these continued to be farmed through the nineteenth and into the twentieth centuries, but most have now been abandoned.

As in the Mediterranean farming region, the lands devoted to three-field farming were controlled by an aristocracy that dominated a tenant peasantry. Nonetheless, field patterns north of the Alps and Pyrenees were quite different from their counterparts to the south. In most cases the land was divided into long, narrow strips (fig. 7.8). The strip field accommodated the massive moldboard plow of the three-field farmers, a device that cut deeply into the earth and turned the soil over, creating a furrow. Invented by the Slavs and later adopted among the Germanic peoples, the moldboard plow was pulled by teams of oxen. It was difficult to turn around. By laying the fields out in long, narrow strips, the number of times the plow and team needed to be turned was minimized.

An additional north–south difference in the traditional European agricultural landscape was produced by the different inheritance systems of Germanic and Roman Europe discussed in Chapter 3. Here the important dividing line was not the Alps and Pyrenees but the northern limit of where traditions developed during Roman times held sway. In the southern part of the three-field farming area and the Mediterranean region, the traditional Roman practice of dividing the land equally among offspring resulted in a high degree of land fragmentation over time (fig. 7.8). By contrast, where the Germanic tradition of primogeniture dominated, larger land parcels tended to remain intact because the oldest son of each generation would inherit the entire parcel.

Turning to settlement patterns, most rural inhabitants lived in clustered or semiclustered villages and hamlets (fig. 7.9). The farmers then traveled to their fields. Clustering was a response to social needs and family ties during a time when transportation was limited to walking or a cart pulled slowly by an animal. Clustering was perpetuated under the manorial system of feudalism. In areas of limited water availability, it was also encouraged by the need to live in close proximity to sources of

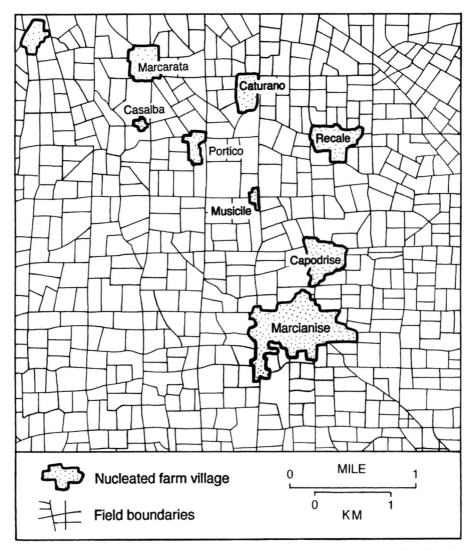

Figure 7.7. Field patterns exhibiting Roman influence, in the Campania north of Naples, Italy. Fields in the Mediterranean areas, dominated by use of the small plow, take on a rectangular shape. In this instance, the rectangularity has been made even more pronounced by the survival of the Roman rectangular survey system. *Source:* After Meitzen 1895.

water. It served defensive needs as well in areas where outlaws, raiders, or political instability made the countryside a dangerous place.

Throughout much of Europe's southern and western areas, clustered villages were highly irregular in form. These villages grew, without planning, over many centuries, and often in places with defensive advantages (fig. 7.9). Paths chosen for convenience gradually solidified into streets bordered by houses built close to the streets for ease of access (fig. 7.10). To stroll through them is to walk the streets of antiquity.

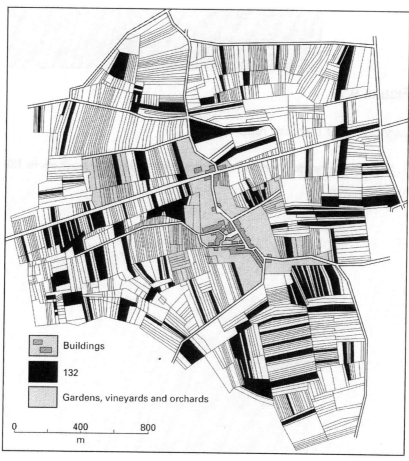

Figure 7.8.   Fragmented, long-lot landholdings in Lorraine. Small strip fields typical of three-field farming survived in the irregular clustered village of Seichamp, near Nancy in northeastern France, into the twentieth century. The 132 separate strips belonging to one sample farm are shown. *Source:* Albert Demangeon, *La France* (Paris: Armand Colin, 1946), with modifications.

In parts of eastern and northern Europe, farmers lived in villages of a more regular layout. Whenever regularity is a feature of the landscape, some kind of planning took place. The most widespread form of regularity can be found in **street villages**, in which the farmsteads lay on either side of a single road (fig. 7.10). These were probably of Slavic origin, linked to cultural preferences and offering transportation efficiencies; they are found throughout much of eastern Europe—including eastern Germany where groups of German agricultural settlers moving eastward beyond the Elbe and Saale rivers after 800 CE abandoned the irregular clustered village form they had known and adopted the Slavic street village. A less common form of irregular settlement, the **green village**, developed in parts of the North European Plain, from lowland Britain to Poland (figs. 7.9 and 7.10). The houses in these villages were grouped around a central green or commons that served as a marketplace, a festival

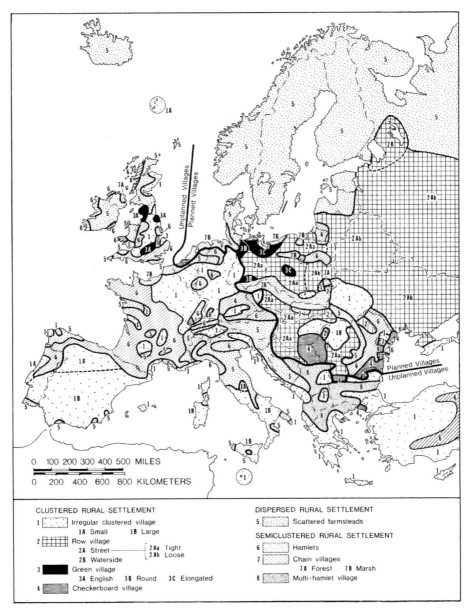

Figure 7.9. Forms of rural settlement. *Sources:* Uhlig 1961; Schröder and Schwarz 1969; Roberts 1979; Thorpe 1961; Demangeon 1939; Otremba 1961; Wagstaff 1969; Wilhelmy 1936.

ground, and a protected enclosure for livestock. In districts colonized during Roman times, a more rigid rectilinear pattern survives in some **checkerboard villages**, a legacy of the imperial land survey system (figs. 7.9 and 7.10).

Although clustered rural settlement is the norm in the more populous parts of Europe, dispersed settlement is found in the north, in mountainous areas, and in scattered agriculturally marginal regions. Dispersal tends to be found in areas where

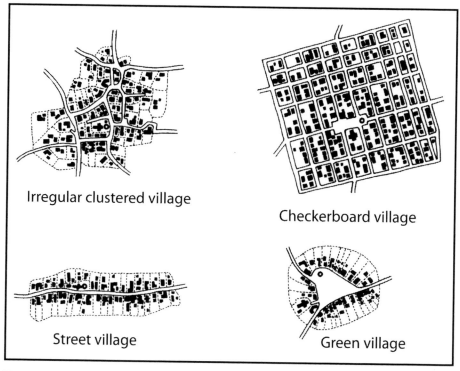

Irregular clustered village

Checkerboard village

Street village

Green village

Figure 7.10.   Major types of rural settlement in Europe. For the distribution of these types, see figure 7.9. *Sources:* Wilhelmy 1936; Demangeon 1939; Mayhew 1973; Schröder and Schwarz 1969; Thorpe 1961.

there is the following: (1) insufficient productive arable land to support groups of people living in close proximity to one another, (2) a widespread availability of water (so that people do not need to cluster near water sources), (3) an absence of the need for defense, and (4) no political obstacles to colonization by individual pioneer families. These are the conditions that prevailed in places such as the Alps, northern Scandinavia, and interior Ireland (fig. 7.9).

The traditional building styles evidenced in various parts of Europe very much reflect available building materials (fig. 7.11). The typical Mediterranean farmstead was built of stone or, less commonly, mud-brick and covered with a heavy tile roof. Because of deforestation, wood for construction was scarce, leaving earth and rock as principal building materials. In plan, the Mediterranean farmstead was multistoried, with the ground level and cellar devoted to food storage and cheese- and wine-making. The upper stories contained the living quarters. Many such farmsteads survive to the present day, as do the venerable villages in which they are found, lending a traditional charm to the southern European countryside (fig. 7.12).

In place of the stone farmsteads of the south, wooden buildings dominated the three-field region. Where wood was particularly plentiful (in the north and east), buildings were made of logs or sawn lumber. In transitional areas farther to the west,

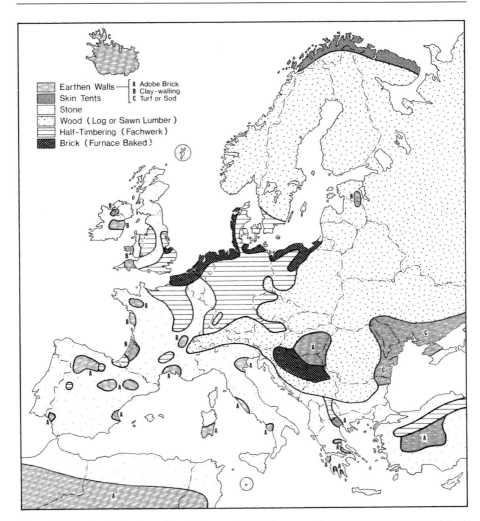

Figure 7.11.   Traditional rural building materials. *Sources:* Paul Vidal de la Blache, *Principles of Human Geography* (New York: Henry Holt, 1926); Gwyn Meirion-Jones, *The Vernacular Architecture of Brittany: An Essay in Historical Geography* (Edinburgh: Donald, 1982); Peter Smith, *Houses of the Welsh Countryside: A Study in Historical Geography*, 2nd ed. (London: Her Majesty's Stationery Office, 1988).

half-timbering was common. Half-timbering consists of a heavy framework of oaken beams, bound together and left exposed as the skeleton of the structure (fig. 7.13). The spaces between the beams are filled in with brick or, more commonly, with wattle-and-daub, a composite of sticks daubed with clay, straw, or animal dung. The folk architecture of these farmsteads was also distinctive. Typically, the stead consisted of multiple buildings, grouped tightly around a central courtyard, a type closely associated with the Franks, a Germanic tribe influential in spreading both the farmstead and three-field farming itself.

Figure 7.12.   Bergerac, in Aquitaine, France. Narrow streets and traditional buildings made out of local stone are common in the villages and towns of southern France. Photo by A. B. M., 2009.

Peoples living in certain areas closer to the European periphery used building materials that were easily available and useful. In parts of southeastern Europe, constructions made of turf, sod, and adobe brick were common (fig. 7.11). Along the southern shores of the North and Baltic seas, soils rich in clay favored the use of bricks in construction. The Sami of the far north lived in skin tents. The British Isles played host to several different types of construction. Half-timbering was popular in the southern, more productive agricultural lowlands, whereas stone construction was common in the mountains and in northerly or poorly drained areas.

Today only remnants of traditional agricultural systems survive. Those systems have been radically altered by changes in the types of crops raised, land tenure, field systems, levels of commercialization and specialization, intensity of land use, and the proportion of the population working in agriculture.

Figure 7.13.   Danish half-timbered houses. Houses of this sort were once common features of the rural landscape in northern Europe. Photo by A. B. M., 1985.

New Crop Introductions

Two enormously significant diffusions brought exotic crops to Europe during the past two millennia, radically altering agriculture in the process. The first wave came from the Arabic Muslim lands across the Mediterranean, bearing the citrus fruits, which had apparently been unknown to the classical Greeks, though the eleventh labor of the mythical Hercules had been to obtain the "golden apple" from the Garden of the Hesperides, a probable reference to the orange. Hercules' quest took him into the warm lands to the south, where the orange in fact grew in the irrigated gardens of Arabia. He failed to get the job done properly, but the Arabs brought citrus into Europe when they conquered Iberia and parts of Italy in the Middle Ages. Citrus quickly became a basic part of Mediterranean horticulture, though these fruits lacked drought resistance and required extensive development of irrigation. The Arabs also introduced apricots and sugar cane, as well as sorghum, cotton, and rice.

The second revolutionary introduction of crops came from the Americas as a result of the **Columbian Exchange**, which occurred in the wake of Columbus's voyage to the New World. In the decades after 1492, a massive exchange of plants, animals, people, germs, and ideas transformed the western and eastern hemispheres alike. For the Americas, the most dramatic (and tragic) impact of European contact was the introduction of diseases that decimated the indigenous population. One of the greatest impacts for Europe was benign: the introduction of new crops.

Two distinct agricultural diffusions occurred. The first involved the Mesoamerican food complex of maize (corn), chili peppers, squash, beans, and pumpkins, to which was appended the turkey and the tomato. Improbably, this food complex did not reach Europe directly, by way of the Spaniards in Mexico. Instead, the complex of Mexican domesticates accompanied the Portuguese around Africa to India and from there to Turkey, gaining acceptance at every stop. All spread into Balkan Europe with the Turkish conquests, and adoption of the Mesoamerican complex remains greatest there, even to the present day. Taste the paprika in Hungarian food, observe the expansive tomato fields of Bulgaria, watch stick-wielding Peloponnesian women drive flocks of turkeys through the streets, see the festival corn decorations of the South Slavs, consider that cornmeal mush served as a main Romanian food staple, and you will grasp the extent to which southeastern Europe's agriculture has been reshaped in a Mesoamerican image.

Andean Indians of highland South America provided the other major New World crop, the potato. It spread to Europe by an altogether different route. Arriving in Spain from Peru in 1565, the potato quickly reached Spanish-ruled Belgium. Within two centuries it gained acceptance throughout most of the three-field farming region and the herder-farmer hardscrabble periphery, completely revolutionizing both. The potato provided four times as much carbohydrate per hectare as wheat and became the principal food crop of most people living north of the Alps and Pyrenees. It yielded large amounts of food from small fields, even in a cloudy, cool climate. Temporarily, at least, the potato ended famines wherever it gained acceptance. Hunger returned again only when the potato itself became blighted in the 1840s.

Modern Agricultural Systems

Even more radical changes in European agriculture occurred after about 1850 as a result of the urbanization and industrialization of Europe. Farmers moved away from subsistence agriculture, no longer content merely to provide their own needs and have a small surplus left over to sell. Instead, the large urban markets prompted them to focus on production of commodities for sale.

Subsistence breeds diversity, whereas market orientation usually leads to **specialization**. No longer would the Mediterranean farmer pursue a threefold system; no longer would three-field agriculture retain its multiplicity of crops and livestock. Specialization

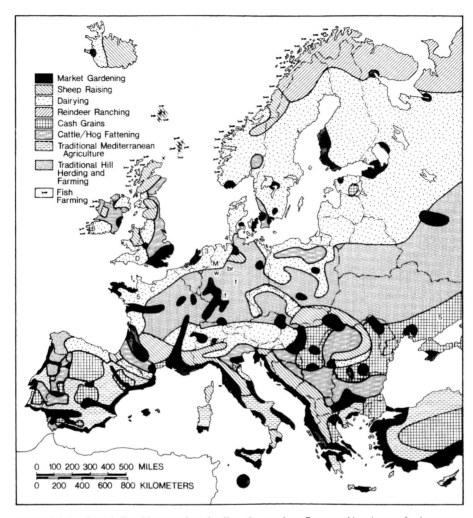

Figure 7.14. Specialized types of agriculture in modern Europe. Numbers refer to source regions of selected dairy breeds: **1** = Guernsey and Jersey, **2** = Ayrshire, **3** = Friesian, **4** = Holstein, **5** = Maine-Anjou, **6** = Kerry. Capital letters refer to the place of origin of selected generic cheeses: C = Camembert, D = Cheddar, M = Muenster, T = Tilsit. Lower-case letters refer to the origin of selected generic meat products: b = bologna, br = braunschweiger, f = frankfurter, t = thüringer, w = westphalian ham. *Sources:* Modified from Kostrowicki 1984; Fry 1971.

remains an ongoing process in Europe, increasing decade by decade. As a result, the map of agricultural types in Europe has been almost totally redrawn, with a focus on individual cash products replacing the older, multifaceted systems (fig. 7.14). In Mediterranean Europe, specialization was usually achieved by elevating horticulture as the primary agricultural pursuit. Grain fields and pastures shrank, crowded out by the expansion of orchards, vineyards, and vegetable fields—often made possible by expanded irrigation. The result was a modern, specialized type of agriculture called **market gardening** or truck farming.

MARKET GARDENING

Mediterranean specialization centered not merely on horticulture, but on specific elements within it. Entire districts came to be focused on a single product. The Languedoc Plain, for example, became one huge sea of grapevines stretching as far as the eye can see; the irrigated *huertas* of eastern coastal Spain developed specialized citrus cultivation and gave the name to the Valencia orange; whereas Andalucía, the Adriatic coast of Italy, and the Riviera achieved fame for their olives. Northern Sicily and the area around Naples also became noted for citrus, and the valley of the Douro River in Portugal expanded production of the famous port wines.

The older, diversified Mediterranean system has not completely disappeared. Rougher, interior districts, poorly endowed with irrigation water or sufficient flat land, retain relicts of the older system. Fine examples of traditional Mediterranean agriculture can be seen in such districts as the southern flank of the Pyrenees in Spain, in the mountains of Crete in insular Greece, or in the Cinque Terra area along Italy's northwest coast. In effect, two quite different agricultural types developed in southern Europe, one preserving the traditional system and the other evolving into market gardening.

Market gardening also emerged north of the Alps, mainly in small pockets of the old three-field region. Each sizable city there acquired a surrounding "halo" of farms producing fruit and vegetables for the nearby urban market (fig. 7.14). Other local districts of northern market gardening appeared in climatically favored places where one or another crop thrived particularly well. For example, Bretagne in France today specializes in apples and cider, nearby Picardie produces potatoes, Holland is a center for flowers and bulbs, Bulgaria is known for tomatoes, and cherries thrive on the shores of the Bodensee in southern Germany. Modern technology has facilitated the expansion of market gardening even into areas where the climate is not conducive to the production of fruits and vegetables. One example is hothouse market gardening near Reykjavik in Iceland, where all sorts of warmth-loving crops such as bananas grow beneath glass.

The most impressive and lucrative example of market gardening outside the Mediterranean is found in the wine-producing vineyards of the Bordeaux region, Champagne, Bourgogne, the middle Rhine Valley, Austria's Weinviertel (wine region) north of Wien (itself named for wine in Roman times), and certain other favored districts (fig. 7.15). Traceable to monastic settlements of the fourth century, founded to produce sacramental wine, viticulture expanded rapidly to supply growing urban and export markets.

DAIRYING

Milk cows enjoyed importance in several traditional agricultural systems, especially in the three-field system and highland herding-farming of Scandinavia, the Alps, the Celtic fringe, the Massif Central, and the Pyrenees. When specialization and commercialization became popular, many of these districts elevated bovine dairying to

Figure 7.15.   Wine grape monoculture near Sadillac, in southwestern France. The specialization and commercialization of European agriculture produced such landscapes. Photo by A. B. M., 2009.

their only major activity. Cropland was converted to pasture and meadow, herd size increased on each farm, and an elaborate network of milk processing plants, creameries, cheese factories, and milk transport systems developed. As a result, the great European dairy belt took shape around the shores of the North and Baltic seas, including much of northern Russia, the British Isles, coastal France, the Low Country, northern Germany, and the Scandinavian lands. An outlier exists to the south, in the Alps of Switzerland and Austria (fig. 7.14). The dairy belt occupies the cloudiest, coolest part of northwestern Europe, a land better suited to pasture and the raising of hay than to field crops such as wheat. Similarly, the rugged mountain terrain of the Alps is more easily adapted to the raising of grasses, and hay can be mown on the steep slopes where crop tillage would be difficult.

The trend toward specialized dairying can be traced to the Middle Ages in some parts of northern Europe. In England, the counties of Essex and adjacent East Suffolk, on the North Sea coast northeast of London, became known for dairying in the late Middle Ages. In the 1600s, the shires of Hertford and Buckingham north of the British capital adopted the same agricultural specialty, as did certain districts in the English Midlands. Generally, the more peripheral dairy areas produced cheese, which was less perishable. Also in the 1600s, the French provinces of Normandie on the English Channel and Brie near Paris became famous as dairy areas, as did parts of the Low

Country. In the nineteenth century, commercial dairying spread to its present limits, displacing grain farming in countries such as Denmark. Dairying now enjoys overwhelming importance in the belt devoted to it. In Finland, for example, milk production accounts for 40% of the total agricultural income of the country, while meadow, pasture, and silage crops cover a third of the arable land.

Every major breed of dairy cattle in the world today derives from the European dairy belt, and the breeds bear names indicative of their origin. The Jersey and Guernsey commemorate the names of two of the Channel Islands, which lie between France and England; the Ayrshire breed reminds us of a Scottish county; the Holstein-Friesian comes from Friesland in the Netherlands and the north German province of Holstein; the Brown Swiss was originally bred in the canton of Schwyz in central Switzerland; the Maine-Anjou breed honors two old provinces of western France; and the Kerry breed reveals its Irish county of origin. The famous cheeses and butters of the world often have the names of towns, cities, or provinces in the European dairy belt, including Edam (Netherlands), Münster (Germany), Camembert (Normandie), Gruyères (Switzerland), Cheddar (English Somerset), and many others. In Russia, "Vologda" butter, bearing the name of a province north of Moskva, is synonymous with the highest quality product.

CATTLE/HOG FATTENING

Another element of traditional three-field farming that survived into the modern age of commercialization and specialization is the breeding and fattening of cattle and hogs. Most of the protein in the Germanic and Slavic diet comes from these sources. As a result, an elongated belt of commercial cattle/hog-fattening farms now stretches from the Paris Basin through Germany, Poland, and Ukraine into Russia (fig. 7.14). Specialization began at least as early as the 1600s in parts of England, particularly in East Anglia northeast of London and Leicestershire in the Midlands. Similar developments occurred about the same time in parts of Germany and the Netherlands, but most such developments awaited the growth of urban markets in the 1800s.

Throughout the cattle/hog-fattening belt, more land is devoted to livestock feed than to crops for human consumption. A pronounced regional contrast developed in the choice of crops, however. South of a rather sharp line across the neck of the Balkan Peninsula, the Alps, and on through central France, maize is the principal feed crop used to fatten livestock, as in the American corn belt, but north of the line small grains and root crops dominate, including barley, oats, potatoes, and sugar beets. In Germany, 70% or more of the potato harvest goes for livestock feed.

Despite the dominance of livestock feed, the modern period has brought a significant expansion of selected cash crops for human consumption in the cattle/hog-fattening belt. An example is rapeseed, which has become the world's third largest source of vegetable oil. Its bright yellow spring flowers have become a distinctive presence in some areas north of the Alps. Wheat has come to dominate the former nomadic herding region in the steppes of Ukraine and Russia, forming Europe's greatest wheat belt.

SHEEP RAISING

A great portion of the hardscrabble regions originally devoted to herding with secondary crop farming is now engaged in specialized sheep raising. The Celtic fringes of the British Isles, Massif Central, Dinaric Range, Carpathians, and Iceland all contain important sheep-raising districts today (fig. 7.14). The market that prompted this specialization lay in the woolen textile districts, especially in Great Britain. In the 1700s and 1800s, landlords in the British highlands converted the far greater part of their estates to sheep pasture. Raising sheep required only a small resident population of herders. Most of the tenant farmers pursuing the traditional agricultural system became superfluous and found themselves cruelly evicted from the land in a long series of "clearances," their houses pulled down stone by stone and their stored food destroyed to make sure they could not return. Many perished. Others fled to Australia or North America, leaving behind hilly homelands devoted almost solely to sheep raising. Cattle largely disappeared from these areas, as did crops.

CASH GRAIN FARMING

Wheat is the most important cash grain crop (fig. 7.14). Large wheat farms are found in parts of the Castilian plateau and in the Paris Basin, where fields are harvested by migratory crews using giant American-made combines. Tall grain elevators now compete visually with Castilian church spires in local market towns, and much of the landscape has taken on the appearance of Kansas or Saskatchewan. The modern period in Europe has also brought a significant expansion in the growth of crops that can be used as biofuels.

REINDEER RANCHING

Not even the Sami, in the remotest northern fringes of Europe, have been immune to the far-reaching changes in the agricultural economy. Traditional nomadic herding by the Sami has been destroyed. Beginning in 1852, border closings forced the Sami to accept citizenship in one or another country and disrupted many routes of seasonal movement. An agreement allowed some Swedish Sami to use summer tundra pastures in Norway in exchange for the use of Swedish forests for winter refuge by Norwegian Sami, but border crossings became rare. Another significant change involved range fencing, separating the herds of adjacent groups and ending the traditional open-range system. The Sami have lost large areas that once belonged to them, particularly in Finland, where dairy farmers pushed far to the north. Moreover, commercial lumbering, utilizing large machines and clear-cutting techniques, damaged woodlands that once supported large herds. Those who remain herders have adopted new, different methods. Snowmobiles replaced skis in reindeer herding, and the stock receives less frequent attention nowadays, owing to the fencing of ranges and the reduction of predators. Herders now belong to cooperatives, which operate much like collective farms. Most Sami abandoned herding altogether, accepting employment in fishing, mining, and other industries.

FISHING AND FISH FARMING

In the seas that flank Europe on the south, west, and north, a great variety of commercially valuable fish is found. These are exploited in part by peoples of the less-industrialized periphery of Europe, particularly Norwegians, Icelanders, Færoese, Portuguese, Greeks, Dalmatian Croats, and Basques. Norway, with one of the smallest populations in Europe, accounts for 2.5% of the total world catch of fish each year. Iceland is also a major fishing country.

The types of fisheries vary from one peripheral sea to another in Europe. Mediterranean fishermen go after tuna, sardines—which are named for the Italian island of Sardinia—and sponges, found particularly in the Aegean Sea. The Black and Caspian seas yield sturgeon, from which caviar is obtained, while the North Sea, Arctic Ocean, and Norwegian Sea fishers specialize in cod, herring, mackerel, and haddock. The less saline Baltic Sea is important for flounder and eels, in addition to cod and herring. Oysters and sardines provide the principal take in the Bay of Biscay and other Iberian Atlantic waters.

An issue of growing concern in Europe is the depletion of fish stocks in the surrounding seas. More than 80% of Mediterranean fish stock is suffering from overfishing, as is more than 60% of Atlantic fish stock. In response, the EU has revamped its fishing policy to place limits on catches, block "discards" (the practice of dumping dead fish back into the sea to avoid exceeding quotas), and promote aquaculture (fish farming). The latter is of growing importance. In the past four decades, northern Scotland, parts of Ireland, western Norway, and the Færoe Islands have become fish-farming centers (fig. 7.14). Fish farming focuses mainly upon salmon, raised in anchored cages moored in the saltwater inlets, bays, and channels of peripheral northwestern Europe. In the same region, trout grow to maturity in freshwater ponds, often providing a second income on sheep farms. These valued fish find a ready market in the urban areas of Europe and now offer significant competition for the fishing industry.

Land Tenure in the Modern Era

The modernization of the rural sector has involved more than new crop introductions and the rise of specialized, market-oriented pursuits. Radical changes in land tenure have also taken place. The history of farm fragmentation in significant parts of Europe put European farmers at a distinct disadvantage in producing cash crops. As a result, governments took steps to bring about **land consolidation**, redrawing property lines to reduce or eliminate the fragmentation of holdings.

Land consolidation began in the United Kingdom, where the process was completed by the late 1700s. Scandinavian countries followed the British example, and in

Figure 7.16.   A collective farm in the Hungarian Basin. Many such large-scale farms were broken up after the fall of Communism, but some were taken over by large agricultural concerns and run as modern, commercialized farms. Photo by A. B. M., 1973.

the twentieth century most other western European countries followed suit. The process was slow, however. In western Germany, only half of all agricultural land had undergone consolidation by the middle 1970s, but there are increasingly few vestiges of the old system. Eastern Europe experienced an altogether different process in the elimination of fragmented holdings. Under Communism, large fields suited to **collective agriculture** abruptly replaced private farms, radically and suddenly altering the rural landscape (fig. 7.16).

In recent decades, land consolidation in western Europe has not been driven by government policy, but by the rise of large-scale **agribusiness**. The commercialization of agriculture and the opening of markets have favored large-scale production. Corporate agricultural concerns have emerged that buy up adjacent smaller holdings to put together megafarms (fig. 7.17). These are particularly common in the agriculturally productive lowlands of Europe found in parts of France, the Low Countries, and Germany.

As for farm ownership, traditionally almost all of rural Europe belonged to a landed aristocracy. The peasantry labored as tenants, required to pay a share of their produce as rent (this practice is called **sharecropping**). Only the shifting cultivators and nomadic herders escaped this pervasive bondage. In a few regions, large landed estates survive to the present day, as in southern Iberia, parts of southern Italy, and some British Highland areas. Elsewhere, agrarian **land reform** took place. In most of western Europe, a steady move toward peasant landownership occurred between about 1650 and 1850, with a gradual elimination of the landed aristocracy. This

Figure 7.17.   A commercial sunflower farm in southwest France. Small French farms can still be found in parts of France, but large concerns now control a significant portion of French agriculture. Photo by A. B. M., 1991.

transition occurred in various ways, but the sequence of events in the Po Valley of northern Italy is illustrative. Landlords there by law had to pay outgoing peasant tenants for any improvements made during their terms as renters; failure to do so forced the owner to renew the lease at no increase in rent. These improvements included clearing of woodland, marsh drainage, or even irrigation development, for which the landlords were hard pressed to pay. Hence, they typically allowed the lease to be renewed. The rent thus remained constant while inflation lowered its relative cost, until eventually the peasant could buy the land. In Greece, the successful rebellion against Turkish rule had the side effect of destroying the landed aristocracy, composed primarily of Turks. Typical of present conditions is the Greek island of Kriti, where 96% of the farmers owned their land by 1960.

In eastern Europe the landed aristocracy persisted, and few farmers gained possession of the fields they worked. Some aspects of medieval bondage even survived into the 1900s in Slavic Europe and eastern Germany. A more drastic and violent solution came there: liquidation of the landed aristocracy under Communist rule. Typically, the Communists won early peasant support by promising the farmers land-ownership. In 1946, for example, such a campaign occurred in Soviet-occupied East Germany under the slogan "aristocrats' lands in farmers' hands." After a brief period of peasant ownership, the state confiscated the land and established collective and state farms. Collectives involved farmers operating as a unit, more or less in business for themselves as a group, paying rent to the state and splitting profits. In the less-common state-farm system, the farmers labored as salaried state employees for a fixed wage on huge super-farms, turning all produce over to the government. Collective and state farms became dominant in most Communist countries.

Since the collapse of Communism, land tenure has once again undergone fundamental changes in former Eastern Europe. Every previously Communist country has seen privatization of the agricultural sector, with differing results and rates of progress. Some commonalities exist. In the majority of countries, most state and collective farms have been replaced with cooperative farms, owned and operated by the workers, who no longer answer to state planners. The ancient peasant collectivism of eastern Europe replaced the state-owned enterprises. In the process, almost everywhere, production levels fell, and many farm workers left the land.

In Russia, some collectives made the transition directly to agribusiness, when farm directors from the Soviet era seized ownership and became capitalistic entrepreneurs. Even so, private farms have grown in number, and by 2003 private farms accounted for 14.4% of Russia's total grain production. The greatest strides toward privatization occurred in the fertile black-earth belt of southern Eurorussia. Farm production declined in the 1990s, and today nearly half of all food grown in Russia comes from garden lands, especially in the urban peripheries, where many city dwellers own or rent plots of land.

Ukraine possesses the richest farmlands of Europe. Until recently all land was tilled by private farmers who were not allowed to control more than 100 hectares each—too little to be commercially viable. Recent reforms are beginning to change the picture, but inefficient private collectives persist. Estonia, a Baltic republic, made the transition to private farm ownership, but in the process agricultural production fell by 56% between 1990 and 1997, and only slowly rebounded thereafter. In all of Estonia, only a few farms are operating at a competitive level. Neighboring Latvia seems to have made the transition to private, family-operated farms more smoothly, and agricultural production began to increase again in the middle 1990s, following an abrupt decline. In Latvia, the vast majority of all farms are now privately owned.

In Romania, nearly half of all parcels had passed into private hands as early as 1991, but the average size of such farms today is around three hectares. Most are seriously undercapitalized and unable to achieve more than a subsistence production. The state-owned cooperative farm, a compromise between socialistic and capitalistic enterprise but retaining far more of the old system, remains important. Neighboring Bulgaria allowed each state collective to oversee its own dissolution, dividing land and fixed assets as fairly as possible.

By contrast, in Czechia, Slovakia, and Hungary, most land reverted to private ownership but was then promptly pooled into cooperatives or rented to agribusiness enterprises. Many people own land while the number of renters is small. Hungary reached a similar solution, allowing the old collectives to survive as cooperatives. About a third of Hungarian farmland in cooperatives is privately owned, with most of the balance collectively owned. Slovakia has favored cooperatives over agribusiness enterprises.

In the former East Germany, yet another solution was found. The 4,500 state-owned farms in 1990, at the close of the Communist period, gave way to some 20,000 corporate and private enterprises by 1993. Corporate agribusiness now owns more than 80% of all East German livestock. In the process, the farm population has plummeted. The restoration of rural property to private owners is complete, but most East German landowners are absentee and lease their property to corporate agribusinesses.

Production Patterns in the Modern Era

The commercialization of European agriculture over the past two centuries was part of a larger move toward industrialization and modernization that we will examine in the next chapter. It was fueled by the dominant position Europe came to play in the developing world economy, which in turn was a product of its colonial and imperial reach. Increased intensity of land use in the European core began in England in the 1700s and then spread to adjacent parts of the continent. One of its first victims was the traditional three-field system. Fallowing one year in three disappeared from the three-field rotation. Fallowing had always been something of a problem, because the field quickly became choked with grass and weeds in the idle year unless the farmers continually cultivated it. In many areas, turnip crops replaced the fallow, with repeated hoeing employed to keep the weeds out. The amount of pastureland declined, and many old grazing areas became cropland. The net result of the changes was a marked increase in the amount of feed available for livestock, and the numbers of animals rose accordingly. Stall-feeding became widespread. Increased confinement of animals allowed a more complete collection of manure, which in turn aided the elimination of fallowing. The changes occurred in a spiral: the elimination of fallowing, an increase in yield of feed crops, more livestock per farm, more manure per farm, increased fertility of fields, increased yields of feed crops, and so on. Chemical fertilizers, invented by the Germans, assisted the upward spiral, as did agricultural machinery of various kinds. Later, in the twentieth century, pesticides further enhanced productivity. Increased attention to selective breeding produced better-quality livestock and hybrid seeds.

The two world wars during the first half of the twentieth century set back European agriculture, and food shortages were common. Hence, one of the early goals of the European Economic Community was to ensure a stable food supply. The chief policy instrument for achieving that goal was the Common Agricultural Policy (CAP). Begun in the late 1950s, the CAP was designed to boost productivity by subsidizing farmers to produce specific crops. The CAP contributed to specialization and also greatly boosted productivity. By the 1980s, however, the CAP had led to large surpluses of certain products and charges were made that certain countries—particularly France with its large agricultural sector—were receiving a disproportionate share of the benefits.

Significant reforms to the CAP have been introduced over the past two decades. Farmers are no longer paid simply to produce certain crops. They now receive aid but must look more to the market in making production decisions. Also, the CAP began offering special supports for environmentally friendly farming and has become an instrument that is used to encourage broad-based regional development initiatives.

The program remains somewhat controversial, however, as it is expensive and its benefits go disproportionately to states with a significant agricultural sector. When most of the countries in eastern Europe joined the EU, vast amounts of new agricultural land were added to the CAP. Instead of extending to a new member such as Slovakia the same benefits that, for example, an Austrian farmer might receive (just across the border), the EU has curtailed benefits for recently joined states. There have also been benefit cuts in places such as France and Germany to subsidize the added cost of the CAP in an expanded EU. As in many places, agriculture as a way of life is a cultural issue in Europe. Some see the CAP in its new form as something that continues to push Europe in the direction of large-scale commercialized agriculture and away from smaller-scale, potentially more sustainable farms. Not surprisingly, then, the CAP has come in for significant criticism.

Whatever the merits of such criticisms, postindustrial Europe has seen a revitalization of its agriculture sector. In Spain alone, the number of hectares of cultivated farmland rose 18.5% between 1999 and 2009, and most countries have experienced productivity gains in recent years. Europe is now one of the leading agricultural exporters in the world, particularly of processed food items. (Beverages, cereals, fats and oils, fruits and vegetables, and meat dominate the export picture.) At the same time, Europe is a major importer of agricultural products, many coming from former colonies in Africa, Asia, and South America, as well as the United States, Canada, Japan, Australia, and New Zealand. Europe is thus in a powerful position to influence global prices for agricultural products and to shape the global exchange of agricultural goods.

Within Europe, agricultural productivity follows a rather pronounced core–periphery pattern. Various statistical measures can be used to demonstrate the agrarian core–periphery pattern of Europe, including grain productivity per hectare, percentage of land cultivated, livestock density, amount of fertilizer applied per hectare, value of agricultural produce per capita, and the distribution of economically distressed rural regions (fig. 7.18).

At the scale of the state, a few countries dominate the European agricultural picture. In the east, Ukraine and Russia have vast agricultural lands, and crop production represents an important element of their economies. Romania and Hungary also have significant agricultural sectors; those and other recently admitted EU states in central and eastern Europe have benefited from agricultural technology transfer from the European west. In western Europe, the amount of arable land differs greatly from country to country. France leads the list with over 18 million hectares. Spain, Poland, and Germany are next with around 12 million hectares. Then comes Italy at 8.7 million and the United Kingdom at 5.4 million. All other western European EU countries fall below 3.5 million. When productivity and crop value are taken into account, France, Spain, and Italy emerge as western Europe's agricultural superpowers.

Some of the environmental and health consequences of agricultural intensification—including nitrogen-infused groundwater, declining organic matter in the soil, and soil erosion—have led to the development of significant organic production and consumption in Europe. Organic farming avoids the chemical additives, pesticides, and fertilizers common in industrial agriculture operations. In the period between

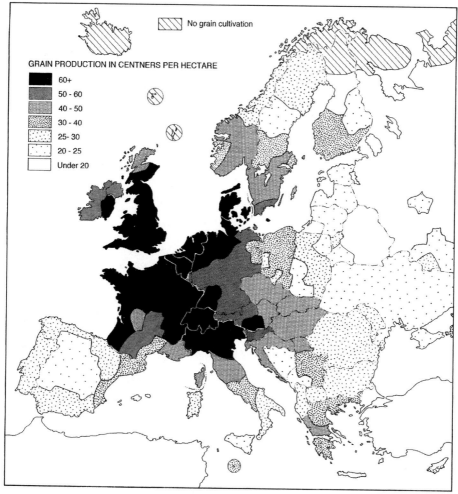

Figure 7.18.   Production of all grains per hectare. A classic core–periphery pattern is revealed, a recurring geographical configuration in Europe. Anomalies include the cultivation of irrigated rice in some small Mediterranean districts and maize in the Balkans, which yields far more per unit of land than the European small grains. *Sources:* Eurostat and national statistical yearbooks.

2000 and 2008, the amount of land devoted to organic production expanded at an average rate of 20% per year in many western European countries. The contrasts between west and east are striking, however. Less than 1% of all agricultural production is organic in Bulgaria and Romania, whereas more than 12% of Austria's farmland produces organic crops. In absolute terms, Spain, Italy, Germany, the UK, and France lead Europe in the number of hectares devoted to organic produce.

Europeans have also been instrumental in the rise of the slow food movement, an appreciation for good, clean, and fair food provided by small-scale harvesters. Like the organic sector, slow food followers seek to opt out of the global food production

system, which increasingly distances consumers from producers. The slow food movement has become especially appealing to many Italians, who place enormous value in
heritage crops and food preparation using traditional ingredients. The move toward
organics and a reappreciation for local foods have made modern genetically modified
crops—sometimes disparaged as "Frankenfoods"—unwelcome in much of Europe.
Germany, Austria, and Hungary have banned many GMO crops, although Sweden
has allowed one: a modified potato used to make paper.

Rural Depopulation

Another profound agricultural change in Europe during the past two centuries has
been the flight of people from the land. Today only a small minority of Europeans
still work in agriculture, constituting in some districts less than 2% of the labor force

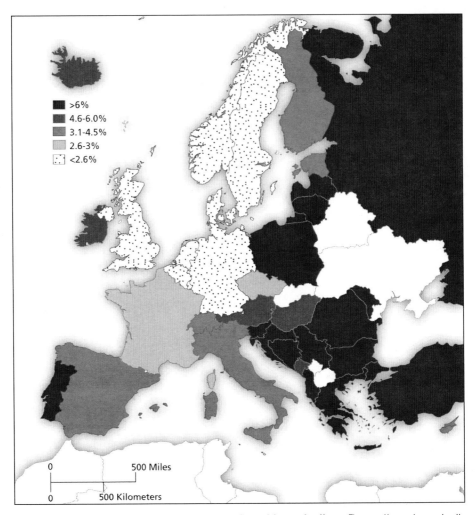

Figure 7.19. Percentage of workforce employed in agriculture. The pattern shows both
west–east and core–periphery contrasts. *Source:* World Bank 2011.

(fig. 7.19). The decline of the farm population has been absolute as well as proportional, and flight to the cities continues today.

In large part, economic circumstances explain the emigration of rural people. Europe's small farms simply could not effectively compete on the world market when the commercialization of agriculture occurred. Moreover, mechanization reduced the need for labor on larger farms. At the same time, growing cities offered jobs at salaries allowing a higher standard of living. Among the criteria defining economically depressed regions in Europe today is a higher-than-average proportion of the workforce in agriculture. Those who remain in farming often take second jobs to augment their income. Increasingly, people left in the countryside are elderly. Aging of the agricultural population guarantees that the numbers engaged in farming will continue to dwindle.

The map showing the proportion of the labor force working in agriculture reveals several basic geographical patterns that should by now be familiar. A core–periphery arrangement appears, in which the lands bordering the North Sea rank lowest in percentage employed in farming (fig. 7.19). North–south and east–west contrasts are also evident.

Emigration from the countryside caused both a decline in the number of farms and an increase in their size. In West Germany, for example, the number of farms declined by 57% between 1949 and 1986, and by half in Finland between 1960 and 1990. A third of all French vineyards have disappeared since 1960. In every country, the agricultural contribution to the national economy has declined sharply. Some countries, most notably Norway, provide subsidies designed to keep people working the land, with results readily visible when one crosses the Norwegian–Swedish border, but the trend nevertheless continues.

Partly as a consequence of rural depopulation, farmland of marginal quality has gone out of production. Recreational land uses have taken over much of Europe's abandoned farmland, a trend likely to continue. Many Europeans own second homes in the countryside, often converted farmhouses purchased cheaply from departing agriculturists. Others who have stayed in rural areas commute to cities for work. As a consequence, the distinction between rural and urban has significantly eroded.

Preserving Rural Landscapes

As European agriculture changes, the venerable villages, hamlets, and farmsteads that provide beauty and charm to the countryside stand at risk. Were the traditional landscape to disappear, Europe could lose much of its aesthetic appeal. Europeans in many countries have responded to the endangerment of their rural landscapes with effective, subsidized preservation programs. In the Netherlands, for example, some 43,000 features of the cultural landscape were listed and protected by the middle 1980s, including 5,300 farm buildings, 1,000 mills, and an array of other objects such as wayside shrines. In various countries, rigorously enforced building codes restrict the demolition of traditional structures and regulate their renovation. Beneath the façade of a seventeenth-century farmhouse may lie a modern suburban home equipped with central heating and modern appliances. New buildings often must be architecturally compatible with traditional ones. In short, many countries have inventoried their rural landscapes, passed protective legislation, implemented preservation, aggressively resorted to rural land-use zoning, and subsidized these enterprises with tax monies.

In this chapter we have emphasized the primary economic activities that are at the heart of rural life. But some manufacturing has always accompanied farming, fishing, and lumbering. Throughout much of European history, **secondary economic activities** such as weaving, blacksmithing, and grain grinding had only modest impacts on the landscapes of rural Europe, but they laid the foundations for a set of economic developments that gave rise to the urbanization of Europe and, in more recent times, served to break down the distinctions between rural and urban. We turn to these developments in the next chapter.

Sources and Suggested Readings

Alix-Garcia, J., T. Kuemmerle, and V. C. Radeloff. 2012. Prices, Land Tenure Institutions, and Geography: A Matching Analysis of Farmland Abandonment in Post-socialist Eastern Europe. *Land Economics* 88 (3): 425–43.

Andrews, J. 1993. Diffusion of Mesoamerican Food Complex to Southeastern Europe. *Geographical Review* 83:194–204.

Boyazoglu, J., and J.-C. Flamant. 1990. Mediterranean Systems of Animal Production. In *The World of Pastoralism*, ed. J. G. Galaty and D. L. Johnson, 353–93. London: Belhaven.

Clout, H. 1991. The Recomposition of Rural Europe. *Annales de Géographie* 100:714–29.

Crowley, W. K. 1993. Changes in the French Winescape. *Geographical Review* 83:252–68.

Demangeon, A. 1920. L'habitation Rurale en France: Essai de Clasification des Principaux Types. *Annales de Géographie* 29:352–75.

———. 1939. Types de villages en France. *Annales de Géographie* 48:1–21.

European Commission, Director-General for Agriculture and Rural Development. 2010. *An Analysis of the EU Organic Sector*. Brussels: European Commission. Available from http://ec.europa.eu/agriculture/organic/files/eu-policy/data-stat istics/facts ¥en.pdf.

Fry, V. K. 1971. Reindeer Ranching in Northern Russia. *Professional Geographer* 23:146–51.

Gardner, B. 1996. *European Agriculture: Policies, Production, and Trade*. London: Routledge.

Hoggart, K., H. Buller, and R. Black. 1995. *Rural Europe: Identity and Change*. London: Arnold.

Horlings, L. G., and T. K. Marsden. 2012. Exploring the "New Rural Paradigm" in Europe: Eco-economic Strategies as a Counterforce to the Global Competitiveness Agenda. *European Urban and Regional Studies* doi:10.1177/0969776412441934.

Hoskins, W. G. 1957. *The Making of the English Landscape*. London: Hodder & Stoughton.

Ioffe, G., and T. Nefedova. 2000. *The Environs of Russian Cities*. Lampeter, UK: Edwin Mellen.

Jonasson, O. 1925–1926. The Agricultural Regions of Europe. *Economic Geography* 1:277–314; 2:19–48.

King, R. L., and L. Took. 1983. Land Tenure and Rural Social Change: The Italian Case. *Erdkunde* 37:186–98.

Kostrowicki, J. 1984. The Types of Agriculture Map of Europe. 9 sheets, scale 1:2,500,000. Warsaw: Institute of Geography and Spatial Organization, Polish Academy of Sciences.

Mayhew, A. 1973. *Rural Settlement and Farming in Germany*. New York: Barnes & Noble.

Meitzen, A. 1895. *Siedlung und Agrarwesen der Westgermanen und Ostgermanen, der Kelten, Römer, Finnen und Slaven*. 3 vols. and atlas. Berlin: Wilhelm Hertz.

Millman, R. N. 1975. *The Making of the Scottish Landscape*. London: Batsford.

Otremba, E. 1961. *Die deutsche Agrarlandschaft*. 2nd ed. Wiesbaden: F. Steiner.

Overton, M. 1985. Diffusion of Agricultural Innovations in Early Modern England, 1580–1740. *Transactions of the Institute of British Geographers* 10:205–21.

Roberts, B. K. 1979. *Rural Settlement in Britain*. London: Hutchinson.

Rose, R., and Y. Tikhomirov. 1993. Who Grows Food in Russia and Eastern Europe? *Post-Soviet Geography* 34:111–26.

Schacht, S. 1988. Portuguese Agrarian Reform and Its Effects on Rural Property and Agricultural Enterprise Conditions. *Erdkkunde* 42:203–13.

Schröder, K. H., and G. Schwarz. 1969. *Die ländlichen Siedlungsformen in Mitteleuropa*. Bad Godesberg: Bundesforschungsanstalt für Landeskunde und Raumordnung.

Semple, E. C. 1928. Ancient Mediterranean Agriculture. *Agricultural History* 2:61–98, 129–56.

Stanislawski, D. 1975. Dionysius Westward: Early Religion and the Economic Geography of Wine. *Geographical Review* 65:427–44.

Thorpe, H. 1961. The Green Village as a Distinctive Form of Settlement on the North European Plain. *Bulletin de la Société Belge d'Ètudes Géographiques* 30:93–134.

Thorpe, I. J. 1996. *The Origins of Agriculture in Europe*. London: Routledge.

Uhlig, H. 1961. Old Hamlets with Infield and Outfield Systems in Western and Central Europe. *Geografiska Annaler* 43:285–312.

Valdes, A., C. Csaki, and A. Fock. 1998. Estonian Agriculture in Efforts to Accede to the European Union. *Post-Soviet Geography and Economics* 39:518–48.

Vogeler, I. 1996. State Hegemony in Transforming the Rural Landscapes of Eastern Germany. *Annals of the Association of American Geographers* 86:432–58.

Wagstaff, J. M. 1969. The Study of Greek Rural Settlements. *Erdkunde* 23:306–17.

Wilhelmy, H. 1936. Völkische und koloniale Siedlungsformen der Slawen. *Geographische Zeitschrift* 42:81–97.

CHAPTER 8

Manufacturing and Industry

Primary economic activity lies at the heart of rural life, but Europe's modern urbanized landscape is first and foremost a product of the secondary sector. That sector—traditionally termed manufacturing—is concerned with processing the materials collected by primary industries into finished products. Ore is converted to steel, fibers made into cloth, textiles and steel become clothing, automobiles, machines, and the like. The importance of the secondary sector has declined in recent years as manufacturing has moved overseas, but the story of modern Europe's rise as a global economic and political power is inextricably tied to the development of large-scale secondary industries.

Historical Overview (Pre–Eighteenth Century)

The origins of Europe's secondary sector lie in prehistory, in the same Near Eastern culture hearth that gave Europe agriculture, Christianity, Indo-European speech, the city, and the political state. Initially, secondary industries were centered in Mediterranean Europe, particularly in Ancient Greece during its golden age. The cities of Athens and Corinth led in manufacturing, boasting cloth makers, dyers, leather workers, potters, weapon makers, jewelers, metalworkers, stonemasons, and shipwrights to keep the great Greek merchant fleets and navies afloat. The Hellenic leadership in artisanry passed for several centuries to the Romans, only to return to the Byzantine Greeks. Constantinople (modern Istanbul) was in time rivaled by Moorish Spain, where Toledo developed a reputation for high-quality steel and Cordoba produced fine leather goods.

Then came the rise of northern Italy as a center of manufacturing and of Mediterranean **mercantilism**. Above all, the Italian blossoming resulted from the dominant position achieved by its merchants, who ranged from China to England. Cities such as Genoa, Milan, Florence, and Venice acquired widespread fame for their silks and other textiles, cloth dying, brassware, weaponry, glass, and shipbuilding. At its peak, Venice housed 16,000 shipwrights who turned out an average of one galleon per day, using prefabricated parts in an early form of assembly-line production. By 1300, artisans of the city of Florence produced 100,000 pieces of cloth per year, and Milan became the chief European center of weaponry manufacture. A system of free, prosperous craftsmen facilitated the northern Italian achievement, a major departure from the classical tradition of slave artisans.

The most important manufacturing district of the north lay in Flanders, where the first major developments can be traced back to the 1100s. Flanders, like northern Italy, acquired its manufacturing importance partly as a result of a favorable trade location. A fortunate concentration of river, road, and marine trade routes allowed the inhabitants of the region to achieve the same dominance in northern Europe that the Italian towns had in the Mediterranean. Cloth making was centered at Ypres, Ghent, and Bruges, which drew on the wool of England and Spain as the primary raw material. In the 1400s, linen joined wool as a major product of the Flemish towns and attained an importance that persisted into the nineteenth century.

Carried by emigrant artisans, the influence of Flanders was instrumental in the industrial development of the Netherlands beginning in the 1400s. Flemish tradesmen skilled in woolen-textile manufacture also migrated to England, particularly Yorkshire, as early as the 1300s. The Netherlands rose to commercial dominance in the seventeenth century, and northern Germany experienced growth as well. The wealth and influence of this part of the world was rooted in an economic system characterized by several distinct features: the right of manufacturers to own (and by extension buy and sell) the property and materials that were part of the production process, the payment of wages to laborers, and the right of individuals to hold and reinvest the profits that came from selling goods. These, of course, are the foundations of modern **capitalism**.

The gradual northward shift of secondary economic activity and a corresponding decline in southern Europe meant that manufacturing became increasingly identified with Germanic, Protestant areas and less with Roman Catholic, Romance-language countries. Some commentators have suggested that certain social characteristics of Protestantism, including approval of change and veneration of work, proved more conducive to economic development. Persecution and expulsion of Huguenot merchants and artisans by the Catholic-backed French government and similar pressure on Protestant Flemings by the Spanish rulers contributed materially to the rise of the Netherlands, northern Germany, and England as manufacturing centers.

Advances in manufacturing facilitated the development of far-flung trade routes, which in turn paved the way for the era of European **colonialism**. Europe's ties to the wider world began to change in a fundamental way beginning in the early fifteenth century, when Portuguese traders started sailing south along the coast of Africa, establishing bases and developing trade networks. Not wanting to be left behind, the government of Spain soon got in on the act—most dramatically sending an expedition across the Atlantic in 1492 that opened up vast new areas to European influence. Aided by more effective weaponry and the devastating impacts of the diseases they brought, the Spanish and the Portuguese were able to bring much of Central and South America under their control by the end of the sixteenth century.

The Portuguese and Spanish established the template, and the English, French, and Dutch carried it on—eventually to be joined by the Germans, Belgians, Italians, and Russians. It is beyond the scope of this book to tell the story of European colonialism, but the establishment of European bases and the penetration of European economic interests into South and Southeast Asia, the Middle East, and Africa led to an extraordinary globe-girdling power arrangement in which a small number of modest-sized European countries controlled the better part of the earth's land surface (fig. 1.8).

The significance of these developments for Europe's economic development is hard to overstate. Were it not for the accumulation of wealth that came from the very unequal political and economic relations Europe established with the rest of the world, preindustrial manufacturing would likely not have developed nearly to the extent that it did. And once industrialization began, the profits derived from colonial empires put European governments and individuals in a financial position to nurture, and ensure the expansion of, large-scale industries.

TRADITIONAL MANUFACTURING SYSTEMS

Within Europe, industrial transformation took place against the backdrop of two different preindustrial manufacturing systems: **guild** and **cottage**. Guilds were based in towns and cities, whereas cottage industries were largely rural. Guilds were professional organizations of free artisans skilled in a particular craft. The skills were passed from generation to generation through an apprenticeship system. A boy served as apprentice, for example, to a cooper, potter, mason, ironworker, glassblower, silversmith, sculptor, or master weaver and worked for years as a helper. At the end of apprenticeship, the young man demonstrated his skill before an examining board composed of members of the particular guild. Approval allowed the apprentice to be a member of the guild and begin practicing the trade on his own. In larger cities, each major guild had a house on the main municipal square; some of these survive today in well-preserved towns such as Ghent, Bruges, and Antwerp in Belgium (fig. 8.1).

Many relics of the guild system can be found in Europe today. Craft shops, for example, are still surprisingly numerous, even in highly industrialized countries such as Germany. In that country scores of registered crafts exist, represented by thousands of local guilds, including tailors, bakers, knifesmiths, sausage makers, and others. The same high standards for membership typical of medieval times survive to the present day.

A much more common traditional system of manufacturing, the cottage industry, was generally practiced as a sideline to agriculture. A village might have a cobbler, weaver, miller, and blacksmith who spent part of the time farming and the remainder, during slack periods in the fields, working at the household trade. The abundance of people today with surnames such as Smith, Miller, Potter, and Weaver suggest the former abundance of village crafts. Little formality surrounded the passing on of skills. Sons most commonly learned from fathers and daughters from mothers simply by observing the work being done. Cottage trades survive today in some parts of Europe, particularly if they attract buyers from beyond the village community. On islands off the west coast of Scotland, for example, women still weave the famous Harris Tweed on looms in their individual cottages.

Figure 8.1.   Guild houses on the central square in Brussels. The elegance and location of these buildings attests to the importance of guilds in the preindustrial city. Photo by A. B. M., 2000.

The Industrial Revolution

In Britain during the 1600s, some skilled craftsmen began moving to rural areas to escape the confining, formal control of the urban guilds, which acted to keep membership and production low, while the quality of goods and prices remained high. By fleeing to villages and small towns, they acquired the freedom to increase output and cheapen products, thereby enlarging the market. Simultaneously, some workers engaged in cottage industries began increasing their output and selling wares in a larger territory, abandoning farming altogether. Among such proto-industrial villagers—fugitive guildsmen and, particularly, cottagers—in a small corner of England, a series of revolutionary manufacturing innovations occurred in the 1700s that forever changed England, Europe, and the entire world.

Both guild and cottage manufacturing systems were fundamentally altered by this **Industrial Revolution**. Collectively, the associated inventions represent the most rapid and pervasive technological change in the history of the human race. Two fundamental modifications accompanied the revolution. First, machines replaced human hands in extracting primary resources and in fashioning products. The word *manufacturing* ("made by hand") became technically obsolete. No longer would the weaver sit at the hand loom and painstakingly produce each piece of cloth; instead, huge mechanical looms were invented to do the job faster and more economically. In many industries, mechanization eventually made possible the use of interchangeable parts and the assembly line. A second change involved the rise of inanimate power, as humans harnessed water, steam, and later electricity, petroleum, and the atom. The new technology did not appear overnight, but in bits and pieces over many decades and centuries. Nearly all of the interconnected developments of the formative stage of the Industrial Revolution, from about 1730 to 1850, occurred in backcountry Great Britain. That is, the Industrial Revolution arose in a peripheral part of Europe. Innovations often occur in such peripheries, where orthodox thinking and behavior are weaker. It was much more likely that the Industrial Revolution would emerge out of the relatively informal environment of northern England than in cities under the tight control of guilds.

The textile industry first felt the effect of the Industrial Revolution. Beginning in the 1730s, major advances led to mechanical spinning and weaving devices driven by waterpower and operated by semiskilled labor. These technological breakthroughs occurred in village and small-town areas, where cottagers had long favored quantity of goods over quality and low price over high. The lower price of goods expanded the market available for manufactured cloth. The textile revolution unfolded in the small towns and villages of dominantly rural areas in England such as Lancashire, Yorkshire, and the Midlands (fig. 8.2). New mechanized factories soon appeared wherever waterfalls and rapids could power the machine looms, particularly on the eastern and western sides of the Pennines, where some traditional textile making had long been centered. In Yorkshire, on the eastern flank, a woolen textile center since late medieval times, the same streams that had long provided the soft water for cleaning wool now turned the waterwheels that drove the new machine looms. Lancashire, on the western Pennine flank, applied the power loom to cotton textile manufacture. To a lesser extent the Midlands and, somewhat later, the Scottish Lowlands shared the water-powered textile boom. By 1830, the tiny island of Great Britain produced some 70% of the world's cotton textiles.

Waterpower dominated the early textile phase of the Industrial Revolution, but not for long. James Watt and others perfected the steam engine in the 1760s, and the first steam-powered cotton textile mill went into operation shortly thereafter. General acceptance followed in the 1790s. The steam engine required fuel, but Great Britain, a largely deforested land, had an inadequate supply of wood. The island fortunately possessed an even better fuel: coal. The mining of coal represented the second major industry to be affected by the Industrial Revolution. Coal presented a problem, though. It was bulky and expensive to transport any great distance, especially at the turn of the nineteenth century, before the railroad, internal-combustion engine, and bulk-carrying ships had been developed. Consequently, the industries that relied upon coal as fuel were drawn to the coalfields, just as the earlier factories had been attracted to waterfalls and rapids. The Midlands, Lancashire, and Yorkshire, as well as the Scottish Lowlands, possessed noteworthy coal deposits, allowing a smooth transition from water to thermal power with a minimum of factory relocations. In addition, substantial reserves of coal occurred along the coastal fringe of southern Wales and in the region of Newcastle on the North Sea coast near the Scottish border (fig. 8.2).

A distinctive trait of the Industrial Revolution had become evident: the spatial concentration of industries in areas close to the natural resources used in production.

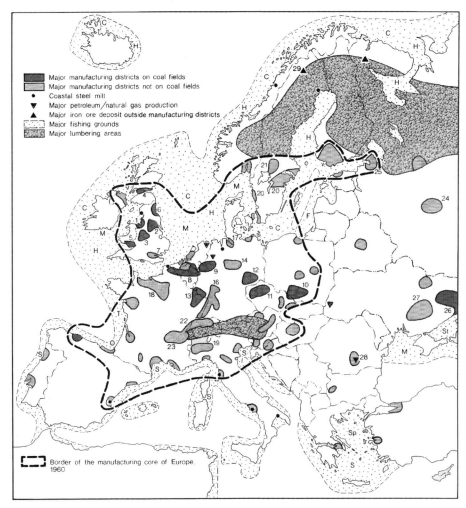

Figure 8.2.   The concentrations of primary industry and traditional heavy manufacturing, about 1960. Major manufacturing districts: 1. Lancashire, 2. Yorkshire–Humberside, 3. English Midlands, 4. Scottish Lowlands, 5. South Wales, 6. Newcastle–Tyneside–Tees, 7. Greater London, 8. Sambre–Meuse–Lys, 9. Ruhr, 10. Upper Slask, 11. Bohemian Basin, 12. Saxon Triangle, 13. Saar–Lorraine, 14. Lower Sachsen, 15. Randstad Holland, 16. Upper Rhine Plain, 17. Greater Hamburg, 18. Paris–Lower Seine, 19. Upper Po Plain, 20. Swedish Central Lowland, 21. Bergslagen, 22. Swiss Plateau–Jura, 23. Rhône–Alps, 24. Greater Moskva, 25. Greater St. Petersburg, 26. Donets Basin–Lower Don, 27. Kryvyy Rih–Dnipro Bend, 28. Ploësti, and 29. Kiruna–Gällivare. Key for the fishing areas: C = cod, F = flounder, H = herring, M = mackerel, O = oysters, S = sardines, Sp = sponges, St = sturgeon, and T = tuna.

Mechanized production focused on a small number of cities and districts, which attracted large populations. Gravitation to the coalfields accelerated the spatial concentration of industry, causing great increases in population in favored districts and substantial emigration elsewhere.

Metallurgical industries, including the making of iron and steel, also felt the effects of the Industrial Revolution. Throughout most of history, the smelting of iron remained a primitive process, and few who practiced it had any valid understanding of what happened chemically. Iron ore was simply heated over a charcoal fire, and the charcoal's carbon combined with the ore's oxygen to free the iron. The Industrial Revolution brought major changes. The pivotal early developments occurred in Coalbrookdale, a small principality in west-central England near the Welsh border (fig. 8.2). There, in 1709, coke (purified coal that burns at a high temperature) was first substituted for charcoal in smelting, a process that caused steelmaking to become cheaper and permitted the use of lower-grade ores. By 1790, Coalbrookdale produced almost 50% of Britain's iron. Acceptance of coke drastically changed the geographical distribution of steelmaking. The industry abandoned countless scattered small forges and, out of necessity, relocated in the coal districts, where coke could be obtained most cheaply. Iron and steel thus contributed to the accelerating **nucleation** of industries in small coalfield districts.

Other technological changes in steelmaking followed. The traditional hammer and anvil gave way to the rolling mill, blast furnaces supplanted small ovens, and metallurgical science arose. Through such innovation and change, the steelmakers of Britain achieved world leadership in the nineteenth century. In other developing British manufacturing areas where both ore and coal occurred, additional concentrations of steel mills soon developed, as in the Newcastle–Tyneside–Tees district, where the legendary coal of Newcastle supplemented iron ore from the nearby Cleveland Hills, in South Wales, and in the western part of the Scottish Lowlands (fig. 8.2).

Another industry forever changed by the Industrial Revolution was the ancient and honored craft of shipbuilding. Traditionally, ships had been small, wooden, and powered by wind or oars. The Industrial Revolution created demands for larger, faster ships to transport bulky raw materials and finished products, and provided the technology needed to produce such vessels. Iron barges first appeared in the late 1700s, and experimental steam navigation began about the same time. Steam-powered steel ships arose in the 1830s, and wooden sailing vessels disappeared a generation later. By the 1890s, British shipyards produced 80% of the world's seagoing tonnage, and Britannia ruled the waves.

Textiles, coal mining, steelmaking, and shipbuilding formed the core of the Industrial Revolution, but other industries were also involved. The shift to machinery gave rise to an entire new engineering industry specializing in the manufacture of machines and machine tools. As machines became more numerous and complex, the industry that supplied them grew steadily.

Yet another basically new industry arose—one devoted to the large-scale manufacture and processing of various chemicals, including dyes, paints, fertilizers, drugs, explosives, soap, and, eventually, products such as synthetic fibers. Many such items could be salvaged from by-products of the coking process, and, partly for this reason, many chemical factories developed in the coalfields. Other industries besides shipbuilding and machine making used finished steel as a raw material, and these often located near steel mills: manufacturers of cutlery, surgical instruments, locks, locomotives, automobiles, and weaponry. Similarly, textile-using industries, such as the making of clothing, found it advantageous to be situated near the textile factories.

The snowballing accumulation of a great variety of industries in the coalfield districts of Britain caused hundreds of thousands of people to migrate there, seeking factory employment. In short order, the British population massed in a small number of clusters. These concentrations in turn attracted still other manufacturers, primarily those that needed to be close to the consumers of their products, such as bakers, brewers, meatpackers, and other food processors.

The importance of coal as a locational factor in the formative stages of the British Industrial Revolution was so great that all but one of the major industrial districts developed on the coalfields. London provided the only exception (fig. 8.2). Remote from coal deposits, it had no significant natural resources other than a navigable river, yet London developed into the largest single industrial center in the United Kingdom. Its advantages were several. First, London had already accumulated a large population before the Industrial Revolution, reaching perhaps a half million by the late 1600s. This population offered both market and labor supply when industrialization came. Second, London served as the center for commerce and trade of the country, handling in its harbor three-quarters of the nation's overseas trade by 1700. As a result, a concentration of banks, insurance firms, and shipping brokerage houses developed, which in turn stimulated the process of growth. Industries that depended on foreign areas either as suppliers of raw materials or as consumers of finished products found advantage by locating in London. Third, the large, well-to-do merchant class of the city controlled a huge amount of capital that was needed for investment in industrial activities. Consequently, London thrived in the Industrial Revolution. Its diverse industries eventually ranged from clothing and food processing to oil refining, various engineering and electronic industries, printing, and automobile and aircraft manufacture.

On a far more modest scale, coastal Northern Ireland—the part of the island settled by Protestants from Great Britain—followed London's example and industrialized in the absence of coal (fig. 8.2). Linen textiles and shipbuilding became the principal industries of cities such as Belfast and Londonderry.

Diffusion of the Industrial Revolution

As in Britain, manufacturing on the European mainland tended to concentrate in small coalfield districts. The first mainland area to feel the effects of the British innovations, the Sambre–Meuse–Lys valley, straddled the Belgian–French border (fig. 8.2). Long before the Industrial Revolution, textile manufacture was well established there, especially in the basin of the Lys River. Even before 1800, British textile technology began to be adopted. Traditional metalworking industries had long lined the region's rivers, and in the Middle Ages copper, brass, and iron came from towns such as Dinant, Namur, and Huy. Around Namur in the mid-1500s, 120 forges and furnaces supported the activities of 7,000 charcoal burners in the surrounding forests. A district of adjacent Brabant became known as the "forest of the charcoal makers."

Coal in the Sambre–Meuse area occurs at the foot of the belt of Hercynian hills, in this case the Ardennes. Some use was made of the coal as early as the 1500s, but large-scale mining activities awaited the nineteenth century. A coke-fired blast furnace operated at Liège by 1823; within two decades 45 of 120 furnaces used coke. Expansion of coke production outstripped any other mainland industrial district. Sambre–Meuse craftsmen served as leaders in adopting British techniques, remaining ahead of better-endowed districts in Germany until the mid-1860s. Textile production became centered in Lille, France, known for cottons, linens, and woolens; in Verviers, Belgium, where woolens dominated; and in the southern Netherlands.

One mainland manufacturing district, the Ruhr in Germany, eventually surpassed all the others in importance and even eclipsed the British parent districts (fig. 8.2). Also situated at the juncture of the Great European Plain and the Hercynian regions to the south, it lies in an area underlain by huge deposits of accessible high-grade coal (fig. 8.3). Small amounts of coal had been chipped away from surface outcroppings in the Ruhr valley at least as early as the thirteenth century—mainly to provide heat for local houses. In medieval times, a significant iron and steel industry developed at the town of Solingen. Linen textiles made from locally grown flax were similarly well established. As late as 1800 the textile weavers and steelmakers continued to function in the traditional way. Little or no suggestion of the Industrial Revolution sweeping Britain was visible in the Ruhr, with the minor exception of steam pumps installed in 1801 to combat water seepage in some of the small coal mines. Urban growth had not been rapid, and guilds still dominated the manufacturing system.

Major changes came in the middle of the nineteenth century. Mechanized, steam-powered textile mills arose by 1850 in Krefeld and the twin cities of Mönchen-Gladbach, west of the Rhine. The textile guilds and cottage weavers rapidly gave way to the new technology. These early industrial developments paved the way for a radical change that, by the end of the 1800s, made the Ruhr area the most important European industrial center. Annual coal production increased by 33 times. The mines grew from small enterprises scratching at the surface of the earth to sizable establishments employing hundreds or thousands of workers and utilizing sophisticated mining

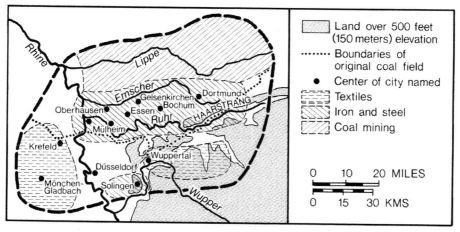

Figure 8.3.   The Ruhr industrial district, Germany, about 1950. The southern part of the coalfield had been largely mined out, and mining migrated steadily northward. Steel mills remained concentrated between the Ruhr and Emscher rivers, whereas textiles were manufactured at Wuppertal and in the cities west of the Rhine. *Source:* Norman Pounds, *The Ruhr: A Study in Historical and Economic Geography* (London: Faber, 1952).

machinery. The manufacture of iron and steel shifted primarily to the coalfield, and large plants using coke supplanted the charcoal-burning guilds of Solingen. The small, local iron-ore deposits proved inadequate to supply the demand, and the Ruhr reached out to Sweden, Spain, and Lorraine for additional ore, exporting, in exchange, large amounts of coking coal. The Rhine River forfeited much of its romantic character to become the major transport route linking the Ruhr to the rest of the world.

The population of the Ruhr exploded, as towns became sprawling industrial cities. A line of urban centers developed from Dortmund in the east through Bochum, Essen, and Oberhausen to Duisburg on the Rhine in the west (fig. 8.2). Essen, which had a population of only 4,000 within its medieval town walls in 1800 and still only 10,000 at midcentury, became a city of 200,000 by 1900. The local agricultural population proved inadequate as a labor supply, and workers immigrated from other parts of Germany, as well as from Belgium, the Netherlands, Italy, and the Slavic lands of the east. A melting pot of peoples assembled, giving the Ruhr a distinctly different ethnic character from the rest of Germany. A gray pall of smoke settled over the district, blackening buildings and human lungs, and blotting out the sun. With the smoke, however, came a prosperous, powerful Germany, which, by the turn of the twentieth century, rivaled Great Britain as an industrial and military powerhouse.

During the second half of the nineteenth century, industrialization spread to other parts of Europe that had the advantage of accessible coal deposits and the ability to obtain raw materials either locally or by use of Europe's waterways. Among the key areas to industrialize were the Upper Slask, an area in what is now southern Poland, where the North European Plain joins the hills and mountains of Central Europe; the Saxon Triangle, with apexes at the cities of Chemnitz (the "Saxon Manchester"), Halle, and Dresden; the Saar–Lorraine area, which straddles the present border between Germany and France, and also including parts of southern Luxembourg; the northern part of the province of Cechy that became the core of the modern Czech Republic; and far to the east the Donets Basin in eastern Ukraine, where a combination of coal and iron ore deposits permitted development of one of Europe's most important centers of heavy industry (fig. 8.2). Many of these places had been centers of smaller-scale manufacturing in the preindustrial period, and governments played a key role in bringing industrialization to all of them.

SPREADING BEYOND THE COALFIELDS

In most areas not endowed with coal deposits, the nineteenth century witnessed slow industrial growth, or even decline in the face of competition from the coal-rich areas. Some urban centers with sizable populations in the pre–Industrial Revolution period imitated the success of London in attracting industries on the basis of a large, ready-made labor force and market. In this category were places such as Paris, Hamburg, Vienna, and Rotterdam. Paris, for example, developed two basic industries: high-quality luxury items such as fashion clothing, cosmetics, and jewelry, distributed in small workshop factories around the city; and engineering industries, dominated in the present century by automobile manufacture and concentrated in the suburb towns.

A few areas in a strategic position to capture trade also became targets of industrialization. The Upper Rhine Plain of southwestern Germany and French Alsace, including cities such as Mannheim and Frankfurt-am-Main, is a prime example (fig. 8.2). This area lies on an ancient route between the Mediterranean coast and the North European Plain, and many cities had a heritage of guild industries. In the 1800s, new industries moved here, especially those producing textiles and chemicals. Ludwigshafen, founded in the nineteenth century on the Rhine River, became the site of the famous Farben chemical works, and the Frankfurt suburb of Höchst developed a similar industry. In the twentieth century, the Upper Rhine and nearby Neckar Valley acquired important automobile factories, including the Daimler-Benz works at Stuttgart and the Opel plant at Rüsselsheim near Frankfurt. Alsace played host to early textile mills, which developed at waterpower sites along the foot of the Vosges.

Hydropower, converted into electricity, helped revive the former industrial greatness of northern Italy, particularly in the area between Milan and Turin in the upper reaches of the Po River Plain (fig. 8.2). Milan became the first European city to have electric lights, in 1883. The government provided added subsidies and incentives to industrialization, and a sizable workforce of cheap labor was assembled from among the peasantry of the adjacent Alpine fringe and southern Italy. The diverse industries eventually included iron and steel, based on imported raw materials; automobile manufacture, including the Fiat plant at Turin; and textiles. The district is served by the port of Genoa, across the Apennines on the Mediterranean coast—a city that acquired sizable iron and steel mills and shipbuilding yards of its own. Once-proud Venice profited less than might be expected from the rise of the Po Valley industries, for the Adriatic Sea remained a backwater, leading away from the major markets and suppliers of raw materials, until petroleum from the Middle East became an important energy source in the twentieth century.

The industrial portion of Switzerland, lying to the north of the Alps on the Swiss Plateau and in the hilly Jura, developed industries adapted to a scarcity of raw materials (fig. 8.2). The Swiss relied on highly skilled labor to produce quality goods with a high value added in the manufacturing process. Hydroelectric power brought a major expansion of industry in the twentieth century. Watchmaking, concentrated in numerous small towns and cities of the Jura, is a typical Swiss industry, retaining a pre–Industrial Revolution geographic dispersal and veneration for craftsmen. St. Gallen in the east became the major textile center, producing such items as luxury silks, laces, and ribbons, while Basel in northwestern Switzerland evolved into an important chemical center at the head of barge navigation on the Rhine. Other industries specialized in the production of various kinds of machinery or food processing, including milk chocolate.

Several small areas in northern Spain also felt the effects of the Industrial Revolution, particularly the Barcelona area on the Mediterranean shore and the Bay of Biscay coast around Bilbao and San Sebastian (fig. 8.2). In the latter area, major iron ore deposits and minor coalfields supported a local steel industry, which in turn provided raw material for shipbuilders.

Despite very early industrial beginnings, Sweden had become a poor country by the late 1800s. Though endowed with iron ore and copper deposits, which had been mined since the Middle Ages, Sweden lacked coal deposits and could not share in the early Industrial Revolution. Its steelmakers, known for the high quality of their product, continued to use charcoal. Adoption of hydroelectric power finally permitted the modernization of Swedish industry around 1900, eventually creating extraordinary economic well-being. Hydropower fueled electric furnaces employed in steelmaking, and while Sweden's output of steel never rivaled Germany or Britain, the quality was unsurpassed, including various steel alloys. A variety of local engineering industries rely on this steel, including manufacturers of machines, automobiles, ball bearings, electrical equipment, aircraft engines, bicycles, diesel motors, armaments, and ships.

Finland, also late to industrialize, relied upon its abundant forests to develop a manufacturing complex in the southwest and far-flung primary industry in the woodlands. On that precarious base, the Finns, too, achieved an enviable level of economic development. Wood products remain a specialty in Finland.

By the year 1900, all of the European industrial districts combined accounted for about 90% of the world's manufacturing output, an overwhelming dominance. The power and prosperity of the Germanic industrial core reached unprecedented heights. The period 1900–1960 witnessed other efforts to industrialize the European peripheries. Ties to raw material sites weakened with improved transportation. Ports became favored new places for steelmaking because ore and coal could be shipped by sea. As a result, coastal steel mills developed at seaports such as Valencia in eastern Spain and Piombino, Genova, Taranto, and Naples in Italy.

As European industrialization kicked into higher gear in the later nineteenth century, the relationship between Europe and the rest of the world was fundamentally transformed. Colonies moved from sites that could supply specialty goods and slave labor to resource sinks. By the early twentieth century, many of the colonies were fueling Europe's industrial growth, as colonial governments established plantations and large-scale extractive enterprises that were worked by locals who were often paid very little and had to endure terrible working conditions. Europe was the world's great economic power in the late nineteenth and early twentieth centuries, but it achieved that position not just by developing internally. Europe's primacy reflected an unequal, exploitative relationship with much of the rest of the world. Even though the colonial empires have now been largely dissolved and much industry has moved to other parts of the world, the impacts of the disparities that came out of Europe's colonial era are still very much with us.

Impacts of Industrialization

As industrialization unfolded, its impacts were so pervasive that few corners of Europe remained untouched by it. Large-scale industrial establishments were built, cities mushroomed in size, and rural places were gradually pulled into the vortex. In human geography terms, the greatest impact of all may well have been the explosive growth of cities, a subject we will examine in some detail in Chapter 10. As we have seen, industrialization also produced some important demographic shifts, as workers flowed into newly industrializing regions, but even these impacts represent only the tip of the proverbial iceberg, however. Industrialization brought with it sweeping social and environmental changes, and fostered transportation innovations that fundamentally altered the activity patterns and life prospects of Europeans.

SOCIAL IMPACTS

Europe's early industrialization raised the standard of living of many Europeans and made Europe a global power, but it also brought with it sweeping social changes. Those changes can be most clearly grasped by considering the contrasts between life in a guild-dominated and a heavy-industry-dominated community. In the former, disparities between rich and poor were significant, but not nearly as great as in the latter, which spawned an industrialist class that controlled enormous wealth. Moreover, in a preindustrial guild setting, the percentage of the population involved in the secondary sector was relatively low. Those involved in manufacturing would spend years developing the skills to produce something of high value. They would be involved in the production process from beginning to end, and those who stayed the course would, over time, have more and more influence within the guild. In a community dominated by large-scale heavy industry, a much higher percentage of the population would be involved in the secondary sector, but most people working in that sector would hold low-skill jobs with little prospect of advancement. They would participate in only one small aspect of the manufacturing process, and they would have little prospect of ever having a say over what the business did. They would, in the words of Karl Marx, have a different "relationship to the means of production" than would someone working in a guild.

The name Karl Marx is associated in many people's minds with the rise of authoritarian regimes in places such as the Soviet Union. Marx's writings spawned a variety of political movements with a distinctly checkered record, but his observations about the social changes he saw unfolding during the middle of the nineteenth century made him one of the most influential social commentators of the modern era. It is no surprise that Marx grew up in Germany; lived in Paris and then Belgium, where he penned (along with Friedrich Engels) the *Communist Manifesto*; and then moved to England, where he wrote his greatest work, *Das Kapital*. He spent his life in the places most clearly associated with the early era of industrialization. Whatever one might think of **Marxism** as a political project, Karl Marx unquestionably provided penetrating insights into the profound economic and social costs of industrial capitalism.

Many nineteenth-century champions of industrialization argued that, in critiquing industrial capitalism, Marx overlooked the poverty and social distress that was the lot of many Europeans in the preindustrial era. They had a point, but so did Marx, for industrial capitalism led to the concentration of wealth in a few hands and gave leading industrialists unprecedented power over the lives of workers, who were virtually powerless in the new system. Marx also argued that industrial capitalism was setting in motion a drive toward accumulating ever more money and goods that would eventually undermine social stability. That idea gained credence as industrial areas developed where workers were paid little, were subjected to abominable working conditions, and were unable to gain access of basic health care and other necessities of life.

In the face of deteriorating social conditions, by the later nineteenth century the early-to-industrialize countries began adopting regulations aimed at promoting public health, ensuring better conditions for workers, and putting some restraints on the ability of a small group of individuals to exert complete control over certain industries. Such initiatives set the stage for the rise of the European welfare state (see Chapter 11) and came to be the focus of political debates that are still very much in evidence today: what is the appropriate balance between policies that promote entrepreneurship and those that regulate what can be done in the name of the public interest?

ENVIRONMENTAL IMPACTS

Not surprisingly, the Industrial Revolution and the prosperity it brought exacted a terrible environmental cost. No part of Europe has been exempt from this damage, but the highly industrialized core has suffered most, as suggested in the discussion of human-environment impacts in Chapter 2. Nor was the damage limited to the natural environment. The graceful, humanized landscapes of preindustrial Europe—the fine old towns and aesthetically pleasing rural landscapes—also suffered greatly. Industrial activity altered or obliterated many of the places that endow Europe with its special human character, prompting geographer Douglas Porteous to coin the word **topocide**—the deliberate obliteration of a place—to describe the fate of his native Howdendyke in Yorkshire. The "Faustian bargain" that industrialized Europe made exacted its price.

Such warnings came very early. After a brief initial period of optimism about industrialization in the period before 1775, the more sensitive Europeans—poets and artists—sensed that something was amiss. They expressed their alarm in the form of paintings and poems, beginning in the last quarter of the eighteenth century. The Scottish poet Robert Burns visited an iron foundry "lest we gang to Hell, it may be nae surprise," and many artists of the period left paintings of the industrialized districts that convey a sinister, foreboding landscape. Such warnings continued over the following centuries. Charles Dickens's descriptions of London and Paris in *A Tale of Two Cities* (1859) highlight some of the squalid environmental and social conditions industrialization produced in these cities. Meanwhile, Käthe Kollwitz chronicled through her paintings and etchings the miseries of working-class women and children of German cities such as Berlin during the early twentieth century. More recently, the Welshman Richard Llewellyn penned the poignant novel *How Green Was My Valley* (1939), a classic lament of the economic oppression of his people and the ravaging of their countryside by industrialization.

The culprits of environmental alteration were many. Smoke and soot from the burning of coal and wood darkened both the sky and the buildings below. Chemicals also entered the atmosphere, and carbon dioxide levels increased. The dumping of industrial wastes into rivers and oceans fouled Europe's surface waters, and seepage of industrial waste introduced noxious chemicals into the groundwater. And then there were the industrial sites themselves—cleared of natural vegetation and often containing hazardous dumps and chemical-infused ponds of water.

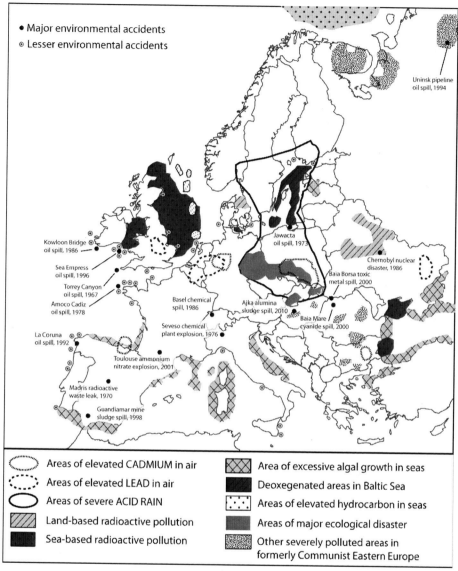

Figure 8.4.   **Selected patterns of environmental pollution.** The core of Europe has been most disastrously affected, but the peripheries have not escaped, due to the discharge of polluted rivers, the practice of dumping toxic wastes in the sea, and oil spills in the transport lanes. *Sources:* François Carré, "Aperçu sur la pollution de la mer du Nord," *Hommes et Terres du Nord* 3 (1992): 142; *The Economist Atlas of the New Europe* (New York: Henry Holt, 1992), 203, 210; *Geographica Polonica* 59 (1962): 51; Dan Ionescu, "Romania: The A to Z of the Most Polluted Areas," *Report on Eastern Europe* 2, n. 19 (1991): 20–25; Richard Petrow, *In the Wake of the Torrey Canyon* (New York: David McKay, 1968), frontispiece; *Concise Statistical Yearbook of Poland, 1991* (Warsaw: Central Statistical Office, 1992), 25; Hugh Clout et al., *Western Europe: Geographical Perspectives*, 2nd ed. (Harlow, UK: Longman, 1989), 182; G. E. Vilchek et al., "The Environment in the Russian Arctic," *Polar Geography* 20 (1996): 22–23.

Laws and regulations gradually began to curtail the worst environmental abuses, but these were slow in coming in many places—particularly in the former Eastern Europe. The greatest concentration of environmental damage in the twentieth century occurred in the Black Triangle, the borderland between eastern Germany, Czechia, and southern Poland (fig. 8.4). Visits to ravaged industrial towns in eastern Germany until quite recently provided a sobering experience for any sensitive person, although dramatic improvements have been made in recent years. The city of Bitterfeld, near Leipzig, is practically synonymous with environmental destruction and is known for its smokestacks, chemical refineries, and horrific pollution. Since 2000, the countryside around Bitterfeld has undergone a striking transformation. The area called Goitzsche, known for its moon-like landscape of slag heaps and shallow coal-mining pits, was cleaned up and flooded, and is now a chain of attractive lakes used for recreation and restored animal habitat.

In spite of such success stories, there are plenty of places in eastern and western Europe where one can still observe the long-term imprints of industrialization on the landscape. Russia's Kola Peninsula is plagued by nuclear wastes and the by-products of nickel smelting. Bulgaria's fishing industry has been devastated by die-offs of mackerel, sturgeons, and anchovies. Serious industrial accidents have occurred in recent decades at Seveso in northern Italy (1976), at Basel in Switzerland (1986), at Toulouse in France (2001), and at Glasgow in Scotland (2004) (fig. 8.4). The human consequences of such disasters can be profound. The chemical factory explosion at Seveso produced a dioxin cloud that led to elevated rates of leukemia, lymphoma, and liver cancer in the area.

IMPACTS ON TRANSPORTATION INFRASTRUCTURE

Transportation innovations went hand-in-hand with the development of manufacturing and industry. Creating the infrastructure and vehicles associated with advances in the transportation system contributed greatly to Europe's secondary economy, and the results of transportation-related production greatly facilitated the furthering of industry. Given Europe's leading role in industrialization, it is no surprise that the western part of the Eurasian continent developed a system of transport that is one of the most advanced and efficient in the world. Still, disparities exist, and there is pressure for more flexibility and reliability. Moreover, the transport system in the core region, good as it is, cannot at present handle the demand at peak times. A look at the historical and present character of several major facets of Europe's transportation infrastructure provides insights into the ways transport innovations have reflected and shaped the region's changing economic geography.

Roads

Europe's roads have played a crucial economic and political role since the time of the Romans. Desiring to rule more than the Mediterranean shores, the Romans built a truly astounding network of stone-paved roads connecting all parts of their

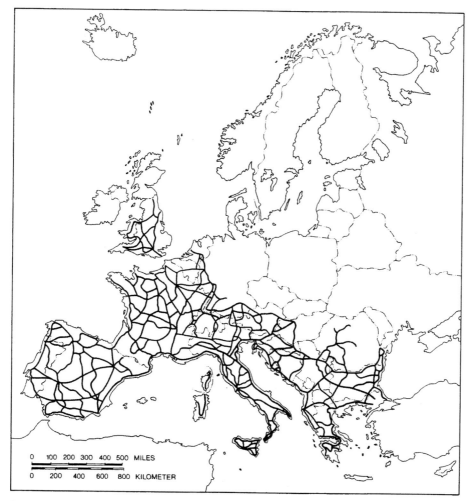

Figure 8.5.   The Roman roads in Europe. The political borders are modern. *Source: Westermanns Grosser Atlas zur Weltgeschichte* (Braunschweig: Georg Westermann, 1956).

empire within Europe (fig. 8.5). They constructed some 320,000 kilometers of highway in the empire as a whole, some of which, astoundingly, remain in use today. Construction on the oldest of these Roman roads—the Appian Way from Rome southeast to Brindisi on the Adriatic coast—began in 312 BCE. Laid out by surveyors in long, straight stretches where terrain permitted, the Roman highways offered an overland mobility previously unknown to merchants, the military, and the common folk. Roman engineers even bridged major streams such as the Rhône; some of these splendid stone spans remain in use today after 2,000 years of traffic, flood, and warfare. Among them are the bridges over the Tejo River at Alcántara and the Guadiana at Mérida, both in southwestern Spain. Contrary to the popular saying, not all roads led to Rome (fig. 8.5). Indeed, the network had few major focal points.

The decline of trade after the fall of the Roman Empire curtailed the use of roads, as did political fragmentation. A rebirth of major mercantile activity in medieval times, coupled with greater internal security provided by the feudal system, renewed the demand for roads. The new routes hardly rivaled their Roman predecessors. Pavement was a rarity. Numerous streams remained unbridged, and as a consequence, river-ford sites typified many emerging towns. In time, new road patterns emerged. Regions that had undergone political unification and were in the process of industrializing, such as France and the United Kingdom, developed highly centralized road patterns by the mid-nineteenth century, with the major routes radiating out from the national capital (fig. 6.5). Paris was the all-important hub of French roads, and Dublin served a similar function within Ireland. Moreover, some new routes unused in earlier times arose. St. Gotthard Pass through the Alps, ignored by the Romans, emerged as the great north–south route between Italy and the Rhine Valley in the Middle Ages, supplanting Splügen Pass to the east. The importance of the Gotthard route survives to the present.

Improvements in the wake of industrialization came slowly. A major step was taken in 1779 when Abraham Darby III built the first bridge out of cast iron over the Severn River near Coalbrookdale. The bridge helped to advance the Industrial Revolution and inspired such people as Thomas Telford, who went on to build hundreds of bridges, including the 1826 Menai Strait Bridge—a steel suspension bridge linking the large island of Anglesey to the coast of Wales. Another major transportation innovation of the time came from John McAdam. He built all-weather highways in England in the early 1800s, paved with several thin layers of tightly packed crushed rock, covered by water, and compacted by a heavy roller.

Continued improvement and elaboration of Europe's highway system occurred in the 1900s, largely because of the automobile. Before long, a pronounced west–east contrast developed. Western Europe's middle class gained the financial ability to purchase cars after the middle of the twentieth century. In 1950, only 6,100,000 private automobiles existed in non-Communist Europe, about one for every 48 persons; but by 1970 the total had increased tenfold, and by the middle 1980s the total was 112,400,000, so that one western European in three owned a car. The proportion is now approaching one in two (fig. 8.6). Truck traffic also increased rapidly in the western part of Europe. Since 1990, trucks have carried some two-thirds of all freight, as contrasted to less than half as late as 1970.

The European east long remained a region of far lower rates of automobile ownership, much less truck usage, and sparser highway networks (fig. 8.6). Highway infrastructure in Soviet-dominated Eastern Europe was less well developed than in the West. One of the first major tasks undertaken by east-central European governments in 1990 involved upgrading roads. Automobile ownership is increasing rapidly today in countries to the east of the old Iron Curtain, even in the poorest countries such as Albania, where the number of passenger cars rose from 3,000 to almost 300,000 between 1985 and 2010. The gap between east and west is closing.

Private automobiles now account for well over 80% of all passenger kilometers in western Europe, and around half in the east. Trucks and vans dominate goods transport. The rise of private automobile and truck transport caused a major boom in

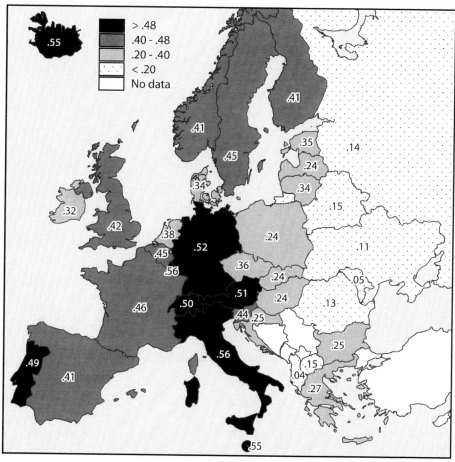

Figure 8.6.   Automobiles per person. Private car ownership remains more common in western Europe, and is generally much higher in Europe than in adjacent parts of Africa and Asia. *Sources:* Eurostat and various national statistical yearbooks.

highway construction that continues to the present in most parts of Europe. An already dense network has become even denser. Controlled-access expressways have proliferated since 1970, building upon the prototype of Germany's autobahn system, the origins of which date to the Nazi era (fig. 8.7). As the highway network has expanded, many new bridges have been erected, some of which rank as grand works of art. One of the most ambitious recent projects is a bridge linking Denmark and Sweden, just north of Copenhagen.

While east–west contrasts remain in highway transportation, the more compelling and vivid contrast is between European core and periphery (fig. 8.8). The densest network exists in the center, whereas the peripheries have a sparser pattern. Some settlements in Norway, for example, remain unconnected to the country's highway system, though an ambitious program of road, tunnel, and bridge construction has linked even some sparsely settled offshore islands to the road network.

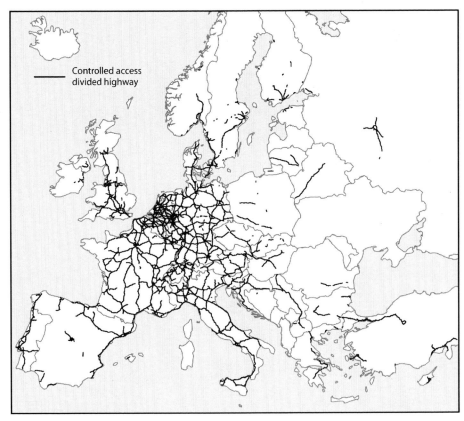

Figure 8.7. Controlled access, divided highways. Germany built the prototype of such expressways in the 1930s, and they remain a trait of the European core.

Efforts to integrate Europe's highway system have progressed for decades, with the aim of more effectively meshing together the various national networks of roads. The "European highway" designation is one result. In addition to having a national number, these routes also have a standard E designation. For example, the E8 highway runs from Gravenhage eastward through Hannover, Berlin, Poznan, Warsaw, and Minsk to Moscow. The E1 extends from Sicily in the far south to Rome, Genoa, Lyon, Paris, Le Havre, and, after a ferry connection, to London. New routes of this type include the Via Baltica, an upgraded highway from Tallinn to Riga, Vilnius, and into Poland. Efforts to create an integrated European highway system have not translated into full harmonization of automobile travel in Europe. England, Scotland, Wales, and Ireland continue to have a right-hand drive system (i.e., they drive on the left side of the road), whereas drivers in continental Europe conform to the international norm of the steering wheel on the left-hand side. Incidentally, differences in what is viewed as the "correct" side for travel extend beyond roads. Trains travel on the left-hand track on British and Irish railways. Curiously, most Belgian and French railways also use the left track because they were originally built by British engineers, even though cars in both of those places conform to the right-hand model.

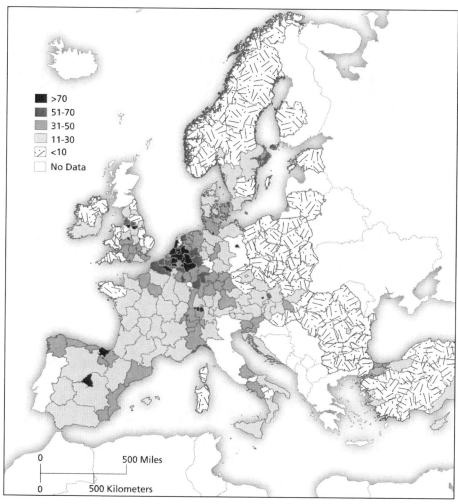

Figure 8.8.   Motorable highways, kilometers per 1,000 square kilometers. The European road density exceeds that of any other sizable part of the world. A pronounced core–periphery pattern exists. *Source:* Eurostat 2009–2011.

In spite of the ambitious programs of highway and expressway construction, the road network of the European core has become overwhelmed by the volume of automobile and truck traffic. Bottlenecks have formed at natural obstacles such as the Alps and sea channels, and major traffic jams develop on some expressways. Germans regularly endure the *Autobahnstau*—"expressway dam," when freeway traffic comes to a halt even in the countryside. Many international borders also produce jams (fig. 8.9). Within cities such as Paris, London, and Milan, traffic congestion is an acute problem as well. In London, where population growth brought inner-city traffic to a nearly perpetual standstill, a system of tolls ("congestion charges") has been introduced to limit traffic inside London's inner ring road. This system has been proposed in a number of other global cities facing constant gridlock, including New York.

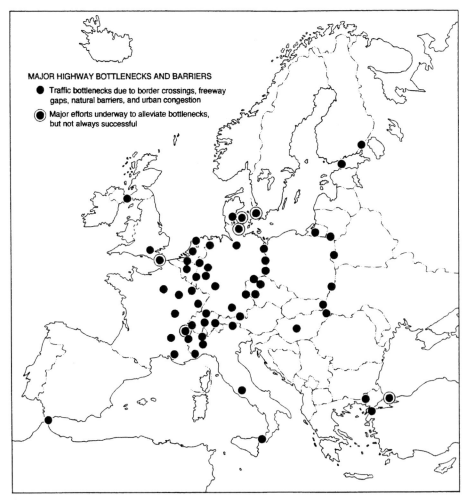

Figure 8.9.   Road traffic bottlenecks and choke points. Europe has a splendid network of highways, but its large population, high automobile ownership rate, indented coastline, and numerous international borders, coupled with the position of the Alps in the central core, create many choke points.

As John Whitelegg noted two decades ago, high levels of motorization constitute a major source of "disturbance, nuisance, health hazards, land-take, and ecological disruption," not to mention an appalling death rate from accidents and frequent grid-lock traffic jams on the freeways. Germany, the epicenter of these problems, has seen picturesque towns such as Idar-Oberstein mutilated by highway construction and watched forests die from automobile exhaust, while suffering over 300,000 traffic accidents annually resulting in death or significant injury. As a result, public opinion has begun to turn against additional road building in Germany. Switzerland heavily taxes transit trucks to reduce traffic, noise, and pollution.

Efforts to relieve some of the bottlenecks have been partially successful. Perhaps most ambitious have been the bridge/tunnel between Denmark and Sweden and the

English Channel tunnel, through which cars and trucks move by rail (see below). In the final analysis, however, the road congestion problem cannot be solved short of a radical shift away from automobiles. Europe has too many people, too many vehicles, too many barriers, and not enough space.

Railroads

Europeans invented the railroad, just as they did the all-weather highway. Thus it is not surprising that Europe possesses almost one-third of the world's rail tracks by length. Railroad network density is greatest in a band stretching from England across northern France, the Low Countries and Germany, and into Czechia and western Poland (fig. 8.10). Outlying islands such as Iceland, the Shetlands, Malta, and Cyprus

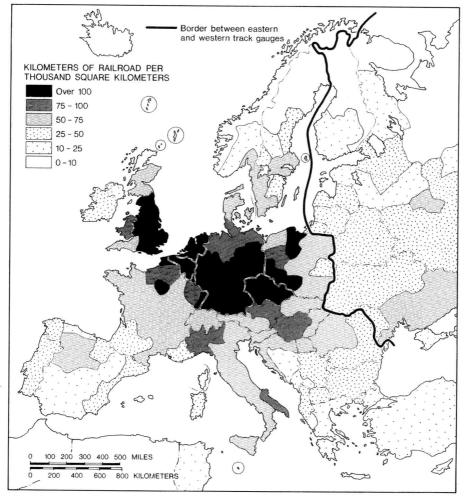

Figure 8.10. Railroad density and gauge. A core–periphery contrast is obvious, and the gauge difference adds an east–west component to the pattern. The western gauge is typically 1.64 meters and the eastern 1.74 meters.

have no railroad lines, nor do the northernmost provinces of Norway. European rail-roads are state-owned or semi-privatized rather than wholly private, with the result that relatively little duplication of routes has developed.

The European railroad system derives from the English Industrial Revolution. In 1767 a British ironworks cast the first rails, initially for use by horse-drawn trams. A crude steam locomotive appeared by 1804, and ten years later, a locomotive first pulled a train. By 1825 the British opened regularly operated railroad service connecting the industrial towns of Darlington and Stockton on the River Tees in northeastern England. The British invention, prompted by increased demands for bulk transport, spread rapidly to mainland Europe, reaching France by 1832, Belgium and Germany by 1835, Austria-Hungary by 1838, Italy and the Netherlands by 1839, and Switzerland by 1844. By midcentury, a railroad network had developed in England, and sig-

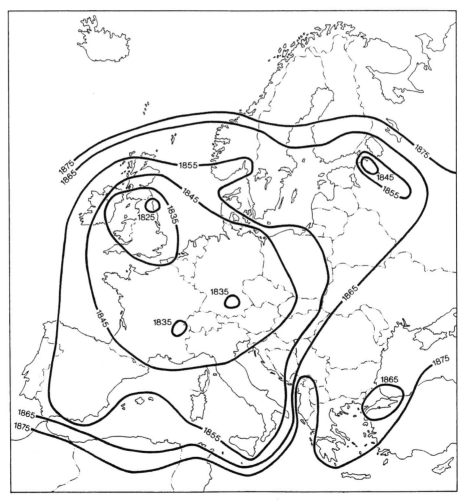

Figure 8.11.   Diffusion of the railroad in nineteenth-century Europe. A striking core–periphery pattern appears. Political borders shown are modern.

nificant beginnings had been made in the Paris Basin, Belgium, and northern Germany (fig. 8.11). The great era of rail construction ended by 1900 in Europe, by which time much of the present network existed. Albania, the final country to join the railroad age, built its first line in 1947.

The rise of motorized highway transport caused a notable shrinkage of the railroad network in the twentieth century, particularly in western Europe. As early as the 1920s, over 700 kilometers of line had been abandoned in Great Britain. In western Germany, the number of passenger rail cars on the *Bundesbahn* (Federal Railroad) declined from 22,600 in 1958 to 18,700 as early as 1967, and the volume of riders decreased in almost every western country. The downward trend ended in the early 1990s, and since 1995 the number of passengers traveling by rail has inched up. Nonetheless, the growing number of passengers traveling by train has not kept pace with increases in automobile ridership.

Freight movement by rail has historically been less important in Europe than passenger movement. Rail freight also experienced a decline between 1970 and 1990. After 1990 rail freight began to grow again, but the rate of growth has been modest, and like passenger service, it has not kept pace with increases in freight movement by road. This trend reflects in part the move toward smaller and more frequent deliveries that have accompanied the shift away from heavy industry to the manufacture of high-quality and luxury goods (see below). Another problem the railroads faced was that, until very recently, no real Europe-wide network existed. Instead, a series of patched-together national systems with different gauge widths was the norm.

Nonetheless, Europeans have by no means given up on either freight or passenger rail transport. Indeed, rail transport is far more important in Europe than it is in the United States. For every 1,000 passengers using a car in Europe, 80 use a train. In the United States the ratio is 1,000 to 3. Moreover, throughout much of Europe, rail transport is well organized and efficient—a reflection of government oversight and subsidies. Finally, the European railroad network is becoming faster and is increasingly well integrated across national boundaries. The first step came in the late 1950s, when the international Trans-Europ Express was introduced. The service attracted business travelers by offering luxurious rolling stock and quicker service. Then, in the early 1980s, France led the way in ultra-high-speed passenger rail service (TGV), followed a decade later by Germany with its ICE.

Expansion of high-speed passenger rail transport now has top priority in the EU, and enormous sums are being spent. A master plan for a Europe-wide network is being implemented (fig. 8.12). When completed, this high-speed system will extend to all corners of Europe. High-speed trains operating in Europe today travel at 230 to 320 kilometers per hour. They compete successfully, time- and cost-wise, with many airline connections. (However, as noted below, the rise of low-cost air carriers is changing the calculus in some places.)

The most compelling evidence of Europe's future commitment to rail transport is provided by the completion of the 50-kilometer English Channel Eurotunnel, or "Chunnel," which links England and France by railroad (fig. 8.13). Trains move through the tunnel at speeds of up to 160 kilometers per hour carrying freight, passengers, and ferried automobiles. The Eurotunnel project has faced financial chal-

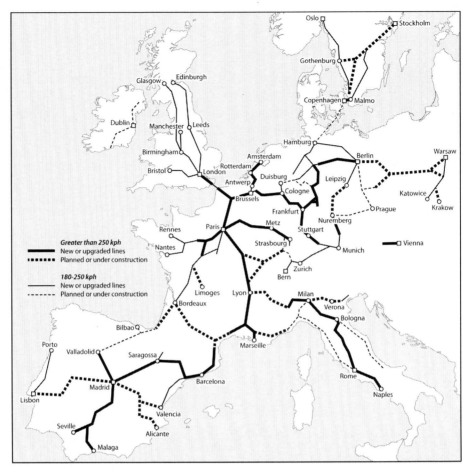

Figure 8.12. The European master plan for twenty-first-century high-speed railroads. This plan will be difficult to implement, especially in the Balkans and east. Part of the system, particularly in the west, is already operational. *Source:* European Commission.

lenges, but ridership has increased, and the outlook for the future looks reasonably bright. Once a major hindrance to land transport, the English Channel can now be crossed in less than 30 minutes.

Waterways

Complementing the road and rail systems is an intricate network of navigable waterways. It consists of Europe's rivers and peripheral seas, connected by a series of canals (see fig. 2.7). The interconnected oceans and seas flanking Europe on three sides provide a splendid opportunity for transportation. The outline of Europe shows deep indentations on all shorelines, with the result that no place lies very far from the sea;

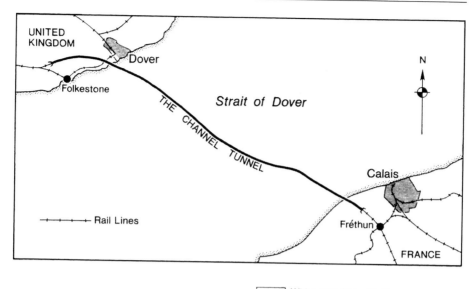

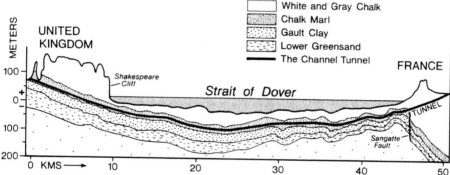

Figure 8.13. The Channel Tunnel, providing a railroad link between England and France.
Completed in the 1990s, it links Britain directly to the high-speed rail system of the mainland. The Chunnel, or Eurotunnel as it is also called, transports both passengers and automobiles.

small wonder that Europeans have long taken advantage of the pattern of peripheral seas to move their commodities from place to place.

The Mediterranean, the first sea used extensively for transportation, proved admirably suited to early navigators, who needed few advanced marine skills because ships could sail about its waters without ever losing sight of land. High, rocky coasts, with promontories made even more visible by the erection of temples and shrines atop them, guided the sailors of Ancient Greece, as did the many mountainous islands (fig. 8.14). By "coasting" parallel to the shore or keeping island landfalls in sight, the sailors overcame much of the danger of sea transport. At a remarkably early date, Mediterranean seamen ventured out beyond Gibraltar, as far as Cornwall in Great Britain, attracted by tin mines. Still, at the time depicted in the Homeric epics, about 1200 BCE, the Greeks apparently remained ignorant of even the western part

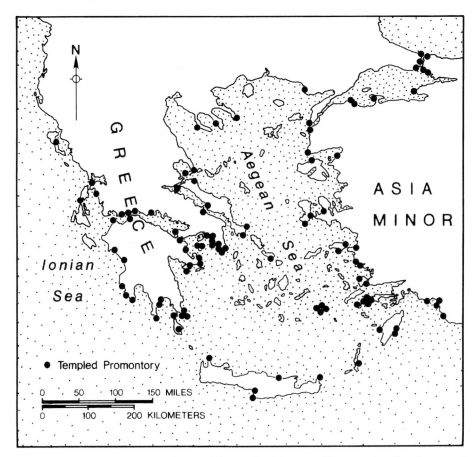

Figure 8.14. Templed promontories of the ancient Aegean. The seagoing Greeks placed great importance upon promontories, both as hazards to sailing and as landmarks. Temples both heightened the visibility of the promontories and allowed placation of the relevant gods. *Source:* Semple 1927.

of the Mediterranean. Ulysses' relatively short voyage to western lands such as Malta and Tunisia placed him in unknown waters, where fear and imagination led him to people the shores with one-eyed cannibalistic giants and sorceresses who changed men to swine. In later centuries, the Greeks searched out every bay and cove around the Mediterranean and used the sea as the highway of their far-flung commercial empire. The Romans succeeded the Phoenicians and Greeks. They in turn gave way to other great Mediterranean seafaring peoples, including the Byzantine Greeks and Venetians.

The use of the North and Baltic seas for trade came later. By the eighth century, a trade in furs, slaves, and amber developed in the Baltic, while merchants in the North Sea handled cloth, wine, and wool. The Middle Ages saw the emergence of the **Hanseatic League**, or Hansa, a trading union of many towns, in countries around the shores of the North and Baltic seas. With the Age of Discovery, the Atlantic assumed its present position as the major trade route of Europe.

Complementing the peripheral seas are numerous navigable rivers, improved through dredging, removing rapids, constructing locks, and digging connecting canals. Only after the commercial focus of Europe shifted north of the Alps did river traffic become important. The North European Plain is drained by a series of parallel navigable rivers trending from the southeast to the northwest, most of which rise in the hills and mountains south of the plain. Some achieved major use by the 1100s and 1200s, and feudal lords who resided along the banks of such streams as the Rhine collected tolls from ships passing beneath their strongholds. In modern times, many rivers have been internationalized, and the countries through which they flow cannot charge unnecessary tolls or restrict traffic.

The navigable rivers of Europe became bound together early by canals. The building of canals predated railroad construction, beginning in earnest in the late 1700s and reaching a peak in the first half of the nineteenth century. Most canals connected the different rivers on the North European Plain. The English led the way in canal building as well as railroads, and by 1790 they had established a good network. Some 8,000 kilometers of canals existed in the United Kingdom by the middle 1800s, and the Industrial Revolution experienced a "canal phase." Inland waterways became the prime carriers of bulky products with a low per-unit value, particularly raw or semi-processed materials. Canals and rivers provided the most important linkages for early industrial districts.

By the end of the great era of European canal building, barges could cross the entire Great European Plain, from France to Russia (fig. 2.7). The densest concentration of canals anywhere in the world lay in the region from the Seine and English Scarplands eastward to the Oder River. That link remains open today, part of which is Germany's Mittelland Canal. Other major water linkages included the Kiel Canal, shortening the distance between the Baltic and North seas, and the Canal du Midi through the Gap of Carcassonne. Russia long ago linked the headwaters of the Volga, Don, and Neva rivers with canals to allow movement through the East European Plain.

After the great age of canals ended, many became derelict, bypassed by railroads and highways. Once-famous waterways such as the Göta Canal of Sweden became largely recreational routes used by vacationers. Canals experienced a decline even more profound than that afflicting the railroads. By 1948, some 6,500 kilometers of the British waterway system had been abandoned. Usage continues to decrease; inland waterways carried 12.5% of Europe's freight tonnage in 1970 but only a little over 3% by the early 2000s, though the actual tonnage decline was slight. Waterways are now primarily used for bulk transport, as well as for tourism.

Even so, several European countries have continued to upgrade their waterways for transport use, most notably Germany and France. Canalization of the Mosel/ Moselle River with 14 locks between Thionville in Lorraine and Koblenz in Germany, where it joins the Rhine, greatly enhanced the navigability of the river in the 1960s. Romania opened the Danube–Black Sea Canal in 1984, shortening the route by avoiding the river delta, and in 1992 Germany completed the extraordinary Main–Danube Canal, linking the Rhine River and North Sea with the Black Sea by way of Nürnberg. The canal uses a series of locks to traverse the 175-meter-high continental divide and can accommodate huge "Eurobarges" carrying as much freight as 90 truck trailers or 60 rail freight cars.

The elaborate network of seas, rivers, and canals focuses on Europe's numerous port facilities, most of which lie at the transshipment points between inland waterways and the open ocean. A string of major ports lines the shores of the North and Baltic seas, at the mouths or on the lower courses of the rivers of the Great European Plain. These include, from west to east, Bordeaux on the Garonne, Nantes on the Loire, Le Havre and Rouen on the Seine, London on the Thames, Antwerp on the Schelde, Rotterdam-Europoort on the Rhine, Bremerhaven on the Weser, Hamburg on the Elbe, Szczecin on the Oder, Gdansk on the Vistula, Riga on the Daugava, and St. Petersburg on the Neva (fig. 2.7). In contrast, most major ports of southern Europe, including Barcelona, Genoa, and Naples, are generally not riverine, but instead lie some distance removed from the silted river deltas. An exception is Marseille, where a major port, Fos, operates west of the city at the mouth of the Rhône, at the southern access to the core of Europe. Traffic volume at Marseille/Fos increased enormously since World War II, and it now ranks as one of Europe's larger ports. Europoort, serving Rotterdam and the rest of the Randstad Holland, as well as the European industrial heartland, ranks as the greatest port of Europe, reflecting the huge volume of traffic carried by the Rhine and Maas rivers. Rotterdam began to grow rapidly in the last three decades of the nineteenth century, coincident with the rise of the Ruhr and other industrial areas along the Rhine. By 1938, the Dutch port

Figure 8.15.   Containerized port of Bremerhaven, at the mouth of the Weser River in Germany. Ships are quickly loaded and unloaded, and the standardized containers can be put on trucks or railroad cars. Photo by T. G. J.-B., 1999.

ranked as the largest in Europe in terms of tonnage handled, and in 1962 it became the leading tonnage port in the world, surpassing New York City. Europe's seaports are all containerized, handling freight in standard-sized rectangular containers that are easily stacked in ships or moved by truck and railroad flatcar (fig. 8.15). Hamburg's port, meanwhile, has benefited greatly from the opening of central European trade since the fall of communism, and it is now the second busiest in Europe.

Pipelines

During the second half of the twentieth century, Europe shifted steadily away from coal as its primary energy source, adopting instead petroleum and natural gas. In the process, a network of pipelines was built. Most lines connect the European core area, where industry is centered, to peripheral and external sources. One major supplier consists of oil and gas fields in Russia's East European Plain and beyond, in western Siberia and Central Asia. Oil and gas pipelines operated by Russia's state-owned Gazprom bring these fossil fuels westward to Europe (fig. 8.16). Much of the oil has long flowed through a pipeline that crosses southern Russia and Belarus to Ukraine, and on into the heart of Europe. This antiquated line could handle only about 1.25 million barrels of petroleum per day, so new pipelines linking Russia and Germany via the North Sea were constructed in 2011 and 2012. The push to build new pipelines stems in part from disputes between Russia and Ukraine, which led to Russia cutting off gas supplies flowing to Europe several times between 2006 and 2009. There is general unease that Europe is becoming overly dependent on Russian natural gas—particularly in light of Russia's new strength and concerns that it is moving in a more authoritarian direction. Plans for several major new pipelines in and around the Black

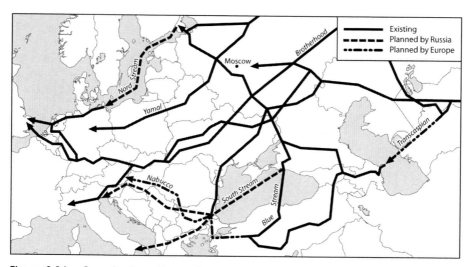

Figure 8.16. Gas pipelines. The main sources lie in the east, in Siberia and Central Asia, while the principal consumers are in the European core region. *Source:* Based on a map in the *Economist*, January 26, 2008.

and Caspian Seas and into southeastern Europe do little to alleviate these concerns, since the source of most of the pipelines is in Russian territory.

The Middle East remains Europe's largest supplier of petroleum. To accommodate this oil, pipelines lead northward from the Mediterranean, beginning at Trieste and Genoa in Italy, Marseille in France, and Málaga in Spain. Two of these lines cross the Alps to the German city of Ingolstadt, a major refining center. The pipeline from Marseille passes north through the Rhône–Saône Corridor, Belfort Gate, and Upper Rhine Plain, reaching Karlsruhe in southwestern Germany and the Lorraine area of France. Since virtually all pipelines have been built since 1950, their routes reflect international planning.

Air Transport

Europe has a dense network of air routes and a large number of airlines that started as national carriers, including Lufthansa (Germany), Alitalia (Italy), Air France, Swissair, KLM (Netherlands), British Airways, Aer Lingus (Republic of Ireland), and SAS (Sweden, Denmark, and Norway). Many intercity air connections within the European core carry well over one million passengers annually. The numbers have grown rapidly over the past two decades, due to an explosion in budget carriers that now make it possible to buy a roundtrip ticket from southeast England to southern France for the cost of a nice meal back in England.

The largest volume of passenger traffic in Europe moves through London's Heathrow Airport, followed by Charles de Gaulle at Paris, Frankfurt International Airport, Schiphol at Amsterdam, Madrid's Barajas International Airport, and London's Gatwick Airport. As for cargo, Paris's Charles de Gaulle is in the lead, followed by Frankfurt, Amsterdam, and London Heathrow. Congestion at some of these airports, notably London Heathrow, has prompted airport enlargements and the construction of new airports. Competition has also arisen. Munich now rivals Frankfurt with its splendid facility, situated in the virtual center of Europe.

When travel restrictions between East and West loosened after 1990, airlines proved better able than any other mode of passenger transport to exploit the demand for increased movement within Europe. It is a decades-long process to upgrade railroad and highway infrastructure sufficiently to allow ease of movement, but airline connections are already in place. Even eastern cities formerly difficult to reach by air, such as Riga, now enjoy much enhanced airline linkages.

Deindustrialization

Despite the economic impetus that came from the development of the EEC (see Chapters 6 and 9), beginning in the mid-1960s the most important mass-production industries in Europe went into severe and irreversible decline, prompting use of terms such as ***deindustrialization*** and *industrial crisis*. Once-prosperous industrial districts became, within no more than two decades, "derelict," "pauperized," and eligible for economic assistance. The blue-collar labor force in a single generation deteriorated into "a dispirited people who reflected a growing passivity to their plight," to use the words of geographer Shane Davies. Entire working-class communities became devastated and dependent upon unemployment relief.

The statistical evidence of deindustrialization tells the story. In the United Kingdom, birthplace of the Industrial Revolution, the labor force employed in manufacturing plummeted from 9,119,000 in 1966 to 5,172,000 by 1987. In the Midlands district, where the modern coal and steel industry was born, manufacturing employment fell by 55% during that two-decade span. In Wales, "its spirit and wealth now broken," employment in mining dropped from an all-time high of 270,000 to only 24,000 by 1982. All of Great Britain could claim only 31 coal mines, with 12,000 employees, by 1994. In the half century after 1930, some 400,000 people emigrated from the South Wales industrial area. The Newcastle–Tyneside–Tees district of northeastern England saw its last operating shipyard and deep coal mine closed in 1994. Manchester in Lancashire and Belfast in Northern Ireland, once prosperous industrial cities, suffered particularly severe decline. Even London was not spared. Its manufacturing workforce declined by 40% in the brief period between 1975 and 1982, and an additional 300,000 industrial jobs were lost in greater London during the decade ending in 1991.

Mainland industrial districts fared little better. The peak year of coal production in the Saar–Lorraine was 1957; 20 years later it was labeled a "problem region," as were the Ruhr and Sambre–Meuse–Lys regions. In western Germany, the workforce employed in coal mining dwindled from 600,000 in 1955 to 95,000 by 1995. The Ligurian coast around Genoa in Italy and the Bay of Biscay coast of northern Spain also joined the list of severely stricken industrial regions (fig. 8.17). Turin in the Po Valley suffered particularly severe manufacturing decline. In France, which had 190,000 coal miners in 1948, the number shrank to 6,000 a half century later, and the government ended all coal mining in 2005.

The crisis began in the primary sector—in particular, coal mining. A steadily decreasing demand for coal, principally the result of a shift to alternative energy sources, especially petroleum, brought depression to mining. Also contributing to the decline of the mining sector was the depletion of minerals such as iron ore. Saar–Lorraine ore peaked in output in 1960, and even in Sweden, Europe's leading iron ore producer, the reserve is now small and yield falls.

But the problem was not just declining resources in Europe. The global political and economic picture was changing in a way that worked against European industry. By the mid-1960s, Europe had lost most of its colonies. At the same time, an industrial boom was taking place in eastern Asia, introducing a new source of competition for European industry. Two interrelated factors were of paramount importance: the declining cost of transportation and growing wage differentials between workers in Europe and those in the less developed world. Technological innovations and the economies of scale made possible by the expansion of shipping, airline, and railroad industries greatly reduced the cost of transporting goods across large distances. As a result, it became less important to locate industries near raw

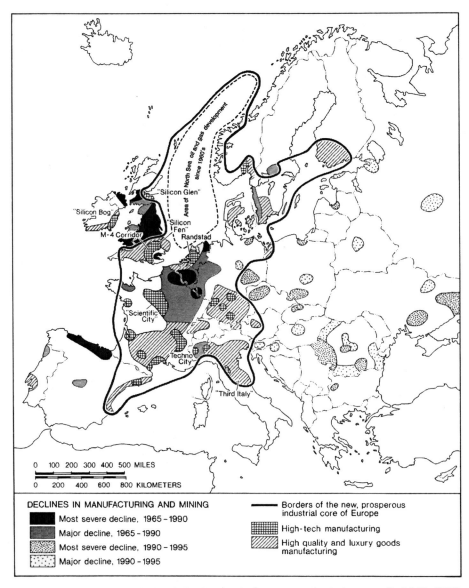

Figure 8.17.   Zones of deindustrialization and of new manufacturing growth, 1960–2010.
Decline and growth remain largely separate geographically, though often in close proximity.
The emerging economic core, based on high-tech, crafts, and, to a lesser extent, petroleum,
favors the European west.

materials and consumer markets. Instead, earning a good profit meant controlling
expenditures on what had become the single greatest contributor to the cost of
many finished products: labor. The less industrialized world offered a great advantage in this regard, and it became increasingly difficult for European industry to
compete.

Some industries declined earlier than others. Britain's position in the textile industry began to slip as early as the late nineteenth and early twentieth centuries; its share of world cotton textile production dropped from 56% in 1870 to 38% in 1915. A more extreme example of decline is provided by the linen industry of Northern Ireland. Between 1950 and 1970, the labor force and number of factories in the Belfast area fell by half, a critical decline in the local economy since a fifth of the labor force had been employed in the linen industry. Shipbuilding declined even more catastrophically. As recently as 1948, the United Kingdom produced almost half of the world tonnage launched, but by 1980 its share had fallen to only 4%. The 1960s witnessed the most rapid decline. The plight of shipbuilding is illustrated by the Clydeside district in the Scottish Lowlands. Local shipyards began their rise to world importance in the 1830s, only to find prosperity arrested a century later. Clydeside ship tonnage peaked in 1913. Foreign competition, particularly from Japan, sent the Clydeside region into severe depression after the middle 1950s. In short, deindustrialization struck hardest at the traditional mass-production enterprises that had formed the core of the Industrial Revolution—textiles, steel, coal mining, shipbuilding, and chemicals—and at the districts specialized in these pursuits. Textile towns such as Troyes in France and mining centers like South Wales suffered most.

In Eastern Europe, traditional mass-production industries remained free of competition in the absence of a market economy before 1990. Many of these industries were inefficient, but that did not translate into decline as long as the Communist system of central planning and state subsidization survived. As a result, deindustrialization came both late and very abruptly to the east, largely running its course in the first half of the 1990s and causing massive economic problems and social dislocations (fig. 8.17). Industrial collapse better describes what happened in the eastern parts of Europe.

In Russia, oil production declined to 68% of the 1990 level by 1997 and iron ore output to 59%, while coal production declined 66% in the 1990–1995 period. Russian manufactures likewise plummeted; by 1997, chemical production stood at 46% of the 1990 output, iron and steel at 59%, and machinery and metalworking at 40%. The declines ended by the turn of the twenty-first century, and output in some industries has risen over the last ten years.

Elsewhere in formerly Communist Eastern Europe, deindustrialization took a similar toll. In Romania, the labor force declined by 7% in just two years, from 1989 to 1991. The East German industrial city of Plauen in the Saxon Triangle lost a third of its total population between 1990 and 1994, and the east German textile workforce plummeted from 320,000 in 1990 to only 20,000 by 1999.

In both eastern and western Europe, deindustrialization led to high rates of unemployment, particularly in the old, decayed heavy industry districts. Persistent governmental efforts had little impact on the unemployment problem for some time. The mid-2000s showed some improvements as European economies adjusted to new realities, but the global economic downturn that began late in 2008 reversed these gains in most places. Unemployment skyrocketed in many parts of Europe, and the old, decayed industrial districts were hit particularly hard (fig. 8.18). We look at the unemployment issue in more depth in Chapter 11.

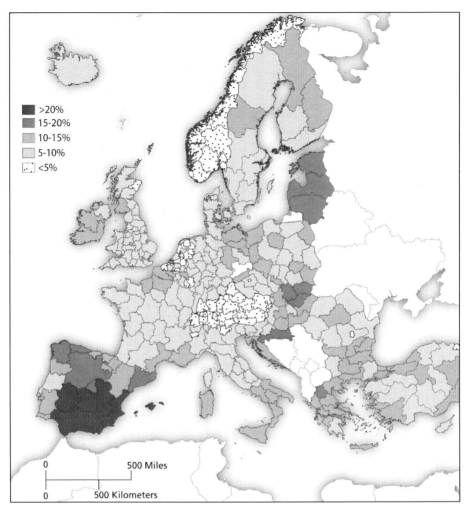

Figure 8.18.   Percentage unemployed in Europe, 2010. Patterns at the subnational level are available for most European Union countries. Note particularly the pockets of unemployment in former East Germany, Poland, Slovakia, Greece, and southern Spain. *Source:* Eurostat 2010.

Industrial Rejuvenation

The impacts of deindustrialization were variable across Europe. While many major industries and districts descended into crisis, others did not, and some even grew. In the primary sector, the collapse of coal mining and the decline of iron ore production occurred simultaneously with the development of the great North Sea oil and natural gas field—a submarine deposit shared by the United Kingdom, Norway, Denmark, Germany, and the Netherlands (fig. 8.17). The northern forests of Sweden, Finland, and Russia, a renewable primary resource, continued to yield their sizable harvests.

These three northern European countries still provide more than 20% of the world's sawn lumber exports and some 15% of the wood pulp and paper.

Even more important than these primary industries to Europe's efforts to cope with deindustrialization was the shift to the manufacture of high-quality goods requiring a skilled labor force, ongoing innovation, and sophisticated technology. A number of Europe's regions—particularly in the west—successfully moved from an emphasis on mass-produced goods requiring large factories and minimally skilled labor to a focus on labor-intensive skilled operations producing items of high value, often in small workshops.

The most high-profile of these new enterprises can be grouped under the much-used term *high tech*. Properly speaking, these include industries manufacturing high-technology products, such as electronic and microelectronic devices, data processing equipment, robotics, telecommunications apparatuses, and the like. To these should be added firms that make preponderant use of high-tech products—particularly the computer—in the manufacturing process. These include pharmaceutical firms, pesticide makers, and automobile assembly plants. All such manufacturers invest heavily in research and development in order to foster the innovations that drive the volatile **high-tech industry**, though these innovations more often than not spawn new companies. Research and development activity constitutes a service industry and as such will be considered in the next chapter. While much is made of high-tech manufacturing—and several European countries have tied their industrial future to such activity—these firms employ far fewer people than the old, low-tech ones. Their rise has thus had only a marginal impact on problems associated with deindustrialization.

In some places the effects of deindustrialization were lessened by the expansion of enterprises focused on the manufacture of high-quality expensive luxury goods, mainly for export. Factories devoted to this type of manufacturing tend to operate as labor- and design- (rather than technology-) intensive craft industries and represent, in fact, a revival of guildlike manufacturing. Indeed, the apprenticeship system has survived from guild times, under government protection in countries such as Germany. The highly skilled workforce enjoys good wages, job security, and the satisfaction of laboring in "a positive culture of work." Creativity, skill, and craftsman pride are all essential components. Factories tend to be small, and the workplace pleasant. Typical products include ceramics, pottery, decorative glassware, fine clothing, jewelry, quality leather goods such as shoes, well-crafted wood products, and luxury automobiles. Such manufacturing survived in Europe even during the heyday of heavy industry, especially in non-coalfield districts such as the Swiss Plateau–Jura, but a major expansion occurred after 1970. High-quality craft industries have one great potential weakness—their dependence upon a high level of prosperity among consumers, many of whom reside outside Europe. As such, these industries can be vulnerable in the fact of the type of economic downturn that hit Europe at the end of the first decade of the twenty-first century (see Chapter 9)—though the upsurge in consumer spending in China at the time helped to blunt the impact.

Geographically, deindustrialization and rejuvenation occurred in distinct European regions, with relatively little overlap (fig. 8.17). The high-tech and craft-industry districts were often close enough to the old industrial areas to have been positively affected by their former prosperity, but not so close as to have to confront the enormous challenges of deindustrialization. Geographer Allen Scott gave these districts the name "new industrial spaces." Southern England, southern Germany, southern France, and northern Belgium eclipsed the northern parts of those countries as centers of manufacturing, while the eastern part of the Po–Veneto Plain has surpassed the older Milan–Turin manufacturing zone.

High-tech industry, which tends to be drawn to universities, major airports, suburbs, small towns, and medium-sized cities, has concentrated in places such as the "M4 Corridor," a crescent-shaped area west of London; "Silicon Glen" in the Lothians near Edinburgh; "Scientific City," southwest of Paris; Mediterranean France; the Dutch Randstad; northern Belgium; and the suburbs of München, Augsburg, Nürnberg, and several other south German cities (fig. 8.17). In some cases, the older, declining industrial centers have sought to claim a share of high-tech industry, as northeast of Milan and at Turin in Italy, where a "Technocity" has developed, but these efforts remain the exception rather than the rule.

The regions devoted to craft-style manufacturing include, most notably, the "Third Italy," which as early as 1981 claimed 37% of all manufacturing employment in that country; the provinces of Bayern and Baden-Württemberg in south Germany, where conservative state governments fostered such development; the south of France; southern England; central Denmark; most of south-central Sweden; and southwestern Finland (fig. 8.17).

The so-called Third Italy, typical of these new industrial spaces, produces a great array of goods, including luxury automobiles such as Alfa Romeo and Ferrari, silks from Como, jewelry from Venice, tiles from Modena, and fine woolen textiles from Biella. The district is also heavily engaged in manufacturing the precision machines and tools required to make some of these goods, including those used in the manufacture of gold jewelry.

Europe's western industrial heartland, then, contains an odd patchwork of distressed deindustrialized districts alongside prosperous centers of high-tech and craft manufacturing. Eastern Europe's condition is less fortunate, for deindustrialization there has not been accompanied by as noteworthy a rise of new enterprises devoted to sophisticated technology or skilled crafts. The east–west industrial contrast is vivid and alarming. Decades of central planning made it difficult for a culture of individualistic entrepreneurialism to take root.

Nonetheless, economic conditions began to improve in the east by the mid-1990s. Many western firms opened factories in the formerly Communist countries, and some local manufacturers made the transition to a market economy. Poland's Szczecin shipyards have risen to world prominence, and the eastern German toy-making town of Sonneberg in Thüringen regained much of its former fame and vigor, after cutting the Communist-era workforce of 18,000 down to a lean 1,200. In Russia, small private businesses, each employing fewer than 100 workers, numbered over 950,000 by 2004, giving employment to nearly eight million people. Enclaves of relative prosperity have developed in Eurorussia, most notably in Moscow, but also in St. Petersburg and even certain provincial towns, such as Belgorod, which experienced significant economic growth in the late 1990s and early 2000s. Most of the European east has been negatively affected by the global economic downturn of recent years, but the gap between east and west is gradually narrowing.

Before leaving the subject of deindustrialization, it is worth noting that some environmental positives followed in its wake. Deindustrialization, especially in eastern Europe, reduced levels of environmental pollution. Emissions of hazardous atmospheric contaminants decreased by 65% at Moscow and St. Petersburg, and 54% at Volgograd (in the south near the Caspian Sea), between 1992 and 2005. The situation in the Black Triangle also improved, but only in the sense that additional damage to the regional habitat was cut back.

Contemporary Patterns

Both the old and new industrial orders in Europe feature a core–periphery pattern (figs. 8.2 and 8.17). Under the geographical configuration that prevailed before deindustrialization, manufacturing districts lay principally in the European core, with few exceptions. In that pattern, the European periphery housed mainly primary industries that supplied raw materials for the manufacturing core.

In Europe's new industrial order, the core has diminished somewhat in size and the periphery expanded (fig. 8.17). If the stricken manufacturing districts of Britain, northern Spain, and eastern Europe are excluded, then the new core, represented by high-tech and craft-industry concentrations, as well as North Sea petroleum, displays a thinner profile than the old one. Even so, the traditional pattern of a manufacturing core and primary industrial periphery remains in evidence.

The industrial geography of Europe, however, is in flux. The economic downturn that took place at the end of the first decade of the twenty-first century reversed some of the gains in unemployment that had taken place a few years earlier, and Europe found itself struggling with falling investment, decreased consumption, and public-sector cutbacks that had implications for industrial and nonindustrial regions alike. Understanding these developments, as well as other aspects of the contemporary economic geography of Europe, requires consideration of the rise of the service and information sectors of the European economy during the post–World War II era, as well as the role European integration has played in economic development. We turn to these matters in the next chapter.

Sources and Suggested Readings

Agnew, J., M. Shin, and P. Richardson. 2005. The Saga of the "Second Industrial Divide" and the History of the "Third Italy": Evidence from Export Data. *Scottish Geographical Journal* 121 (1): 83–101.

Begg, B., J. Pickles, and A. Smith. 2003. Cutting It: European Integration, Trade Regimes, and the Reconfiguration of East-Central European Apparel Production. *Environment and Planning A* 35 (12): 2191–2208.

Bosma, N., and V. Schutjens. 2007. Patterns of Promising Entrepreneurial Activity in European Regions. *Tijdschrift voor Economische en Sociale Geografie* 98 (5): 675–786.

Bradshaw, M. J. 2009. The Geopolitics of Global Energy Security. *Geography Compass* 3 (5): 1920–37.

Braun, B., and R. E. Grotz. 1993. Support for Competitiveness: National and Common Strategies for Manufacturing Industries within the European Community. *Erdkunde* 47 (2): 105–17.

Carter, F. W., and W. Maik. 1999. *Shock-Shift in an Enlarged Europe: The Geography of Socio-Economic Change in East-Central Europe after 1989.* Aldershot, UK: Ashgate.

Carter, F. W., and D. Turnock, eds. 2002. *Environmental Problems of East Central Europe.* Routledge Studies of Societies in Transition 16. London: Routledge.

Collantes, F. 2009. Rural Europe Reshaped: The Economic Transformation of Upland Regions, 1850–2000. *Economic History Review* 62 (2): 306–23.

Cumbers, A. 1995. North Sea Oil and Regional Economic Development: The Case of the North East of England. *Area* 27 (3): 208–17.

de Smidt, M., and E. Wever. 1990. *An Industrial Geography of the Netherlands: An International Perspective.* Nederlandse Industrie. London: Routledge.

Dobruszkes, F. 2006. An Analysis of European Low-Cost Airlines and Their Networks. *Journal of Transport Geography* 14 (4): 249–64.

Dunford, M., and L. Greco. 2007. Geographies of Growth, Decline, and Restructuring: The Rise and Fall (Privatization) of the State-Owned Steel Sector and the Trajectories of Steel Localities in the Italian Mezzogiorno. *European Urban & Regional Studies* 14 (1): 27–53.

Economist. 2007. Every Last Drop. July 14, 60–61.

Epstein, S. R., and M. R. Prak. 2008. *Guilds, Innovation, and the European Economy, 1400–1800.* Cambridge: Cambridge University Press.

Evans, I. M. 1980. Aspects of the Steel Crisis in Europe, with Particular Reference of Belgium and Luxembourg (Manufacturing). *Geographical Journal* 146 (3): 396–407.

Gregory, D. 1982. *Regional Transformation and Industrial Revolution: A Geography of the Yorkshire Woollen Industry.* Minneapolis: University of Minnesota Press.

Grotz, R., and B. Braun. 1996. *Spatial Aspects of Technology-Oriented Networks: Examples from the German Mechanical Engineering Industry.* Bonner Beiträge zur Geographie H. 3. Bonn: Geograph. Inst., Lehrstuhl.

Hall, P. G. 1987. *Western Sunrise: The Genesis and Growth of Britain's Major High Tech Corridor.* London: Allen & Unwin.

Hassink, R., and D.-H. Shin 2005. The Restructuring of Old Industrial Areas in Europe and Asia. *Environment and Planning A* 37 (4): 571–80.

Hudson, R. 2002. Changing Industrial Production Systems and Regional Development in the New Europe. *Transactions of the Institute of British Geographers* 27 (3): 262–81.

Hudson, R., and D. Sadler. 1990. State Policies and the Changing Geography of the Coal Industry in the United Kingdom in the 1980s and 1990s. *Transactions of the Institute of British Geographers*, n.s, 15 (4): 435–54.

Langton, J. 1979. *Geographical Change and Industrial Revolution: Coalmining in South West Lancashire, 1590–1799.* Cambridge Geographical Studies 11. Cambridge: Cambridge University Press.

———. 1984. The Industrial Revolution and the Regional Geography of England. *Transactions of the Institute of British Geographers* 9 (2): 145–67.

Laux, J. M. 1992. *The European Automobile Industry.* New York: Twayne.

Martin, J. E. 1966. *Greater London: An Industrial Geography.* Chicago: University of Chicago Press.

Morris, J. 1987. Global Restructuring and Region: Manufacturing Industry in Wales, 1972–1982. *Tijdschrift voor Economische en Sociale Geografie* 78 (1): 16–29.

Pavlínek, P., B. Domański, and R. Guzik. 2009. Industrial Upgrading through Foreign Direct Investment in Central European Automotive Manufacturing. *European Urban and Regional Studies* 16 (1): 43–63.

Peterson, D. J. 1993. *Troubled Lands: The Legacy of Soviet Environmental Destruction*. A RAND Research Study. Boulder, CO: Westview Press.

Plahuta, S., and G. Halder. 2006. Wirtschaftliche und Soziale Folgen der Deindustrialisierung—Das Beispiel Stuttgart. *Geographische Rundschau* 58 (6): 32–42.

Pollard, S. 1981. *Peaceful Conquest: The Industrialization of Europe, 1760–1970*. Oxford: Oxford University Press.

Porteous, J. D. 1989. *Planned to Death: The Annihilation of a Place Called Howdendyke*. Manchester: Manchester University Press.

Pounds, N. J. G. 1957. Historical Geography of the Iron and Steel Industry of France. *Annals of the Association of American Geographers* 47 (1): 3–14.

———. 1958. *The Upper Silesian Industrial Region*. Slavic and East European Series 5, 11. Bloomington: Indiana University Publications.

Sadler, D. 1995. Old Industrial Places and Regions: The Limits to Reindustrialisation. In *Europe at the Margins: New Mosaics of Inequality*, ed. C. Hadjimichalis and D. Sadler, 133–48. Chichester, UK: J. Wiley.

———. 2004. Cluster Evolution: The Transformation of Old Industrial Regions and the Steel Industry Supply Chain in Northeast England. *Regional Studies* 38 (1): 55–66.

Sagers, M. J. 2006. Russia's Energy Policy: A Divergent View. *Eurasian Geography & Economics* 47 (3): 314–20.

Scott, A. J. 1988. *Flexible Production Systems and Regional Development: The Rise of New Industrial Spaces in North America and Western Europe*. Research Paper 168. Toronto: Centre for Urban and Community Studies, University of Toronto.

———. 2006. The Changing Global Geography of Low-Technology, Labor-Intensive Industry: Clothing, Footwear, and Furniture. *World Development* 34 (9): 1517–36.

Semple, E. C. 1927. The Templed Promontories of the Ancient Mediterranean. *Geographical Review* 17 (3): 353–86.

Tuppen, J. N. 1980. *France: Studies in Industrial Geography*. Folkestone, UK: Dawson.

Warren, K. 1970. *The British Iron and Steel Sheet Industry since 1840: An Economic Geography*. London: Bell.

Wells, P., and M. Rawlinson. 1994. *The New European Automobile Industry*. New York: St. Martin's Press.

Williams, A. M. 1987. The Western European Economy: A Geography of Post-War Development. Totowa, NJ: Barnes & Noble.

CHAPTER 9

The Postindustrial Economy and the Quest for European Integration

The European economy has undergone sweeping changes since the end of World War II. Two developments are at the heart of those changes: the shift away from an emphasis on industrial production to postindustrial economic activities (producer and consumer services, research and development, and the like), and the European integration movement. These are, to some extent, distinct developments. The rise of the service and information economy was a response to global economic shifts that had little to do with the emergence of the European Economic Community and its successor organizations. And the initial steps that were taken toward integration were focused on facilitating trade in agricultural and industrial products. Nonetheless, in recent decades these two developments have become increasingly intertwined, as we discuss later in this chapter.

The Nature of Europe's Service and Information Economy

Service industries involve neither the extraction of resources nor manufacturing, but instead include a broad range of activities that serve people's everyday needs and facilitate economic transactions. These **tertiary sector** activities include health care, education, transportation, energy production, retailing, wholesaling, and tourism. Activities such as banking, consulting, information processing, legal services, and research are sometimes treated as part of the tertiary sector as well, but these have become so important that many geographers and economists now speak of a **quaternary sector** involved with the collection, processing, and manipulation of information and capital. The term *postindustrial* is sometimes used to denote the rise to dominance of these quaternary-sector industries in contemporary Europe, coincident with the decline of primary and secondary industries. No general agreement exists on how to categorize these diverse enterprises. Some prefer to distinguish market (or private) services from governmental (or public) services. Others suggest that the primary distinction should

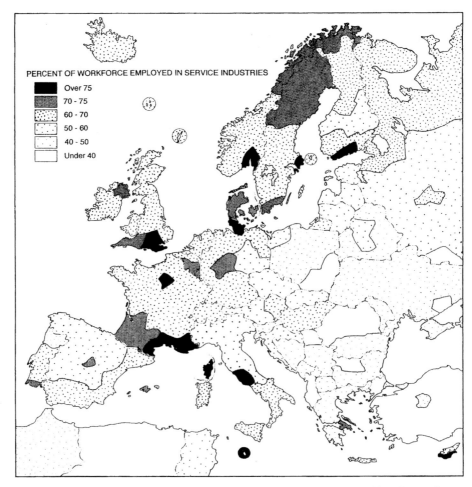

Figure 9.1. Percentage of labor force employed in the service industries. These diverse activities include government, transport, trade, finance, retailing, energy supply, tourism, education, health, and other services. An east–west contrast can be detected within Europe. *Sources:* Eurostat and various national statistical yearbooks.

be between producer and consumer services. Still others continue to label all service industries as tertiary economic activities.

The most outstanding feature of Europe's tertiary- and quaternary-sector industries is their disproportionate growth since about 1950. Service activities have always been present, of course; the blacksmith in the traditional rural village, the road builder in a medieval city, and the engineer at an Industrial Revolution–era steel plant were all part of the tertiary sector. But as recently as the middle of the twentieth century, Europe's economy could still be described primarily as an industrial one. That is no longer the case. In recent decades a postindustrial economy has taken root, particularly in western Europe—and tertiary and quaternary activities now dominate.

Well over half of the labor force in many countries and provinces now finds employment in service industries (fig. 9.1). As recently as 1961, only 30% of the workforce in Austria worked in the services sector; now, two out of three Austrian workers are involved in tertiary- and quaternary-sector activities. Eastern Europe, long shackled by its Cold War industrial economy, lags behind the western part of Europe in this respect, but even there the proportion of the population employed in the service sector is growing rapidly.

What accounts for this transformation? The reasons are multiple and complex, but four interrelated catalysts are of particular importance: rising labor costs in Europe, declining transportation costs, mechanization of the production process, and expanding trade. As European industry became increasingly successful and workers gained more rights and protections as a result of collective action or government regulations, labor costs increased. At the same time, technological innovations and the expansion of transportation infrastructure led to a significant decline in the cost of shipping goods and resources over long distances. These developments meant that labor costs came to contribute much more to the total cost of production than did transportation. As a result, it became increasingly difficult for European industry to compete with industries established in parts of the world where cheap labor and low levels of regulation were the norm. Industries developing in other parts of the world could also take advantage of accelerating global trade to find markets for their products in distant places. Europe thus began to lose its industrial dominance, and many industrial jobs were lost.

The best way to fight back was to make the production process cheaper and more efficient, and that imperative led those European industries that did not close or move overseas to turn increasingly toward the use of sophisticated machines. The result was that many additional industrial jobs were lost. Where Europe could compete was in the development and design of the sophisticated machinery used in industry, as well as in the provision of the technologies and the financial and management services needed to sustain increasingly sophisticated tertiary and quaternary activities. Add to this picture the higher levels of education workers needed to participate in the new economy, as well as the growth in size of a middle class with the time and resources to travel and take advantage of other products of the service economy, and you begin to gain some appreciation of how and why Europe's postindustrial economy developed.

Europe's tertiary and quaternary economy is vast and complex. To understand something of its roots and its current character, it is useful to look at a few key elements that are particularly important either for the role they play in sustaining economic activity or for their overall contribution to Europe's economy. We begin by focusing on communication—for Europe has one of the most extensive communication networks of any region of comparable size in the entire world. We then turn to energy production because of its centrality to sustaining modern ways of living and doing business. We conclude by looking at several activities that are very significant contributors to the overall European economy: tourism, retailing and social services, and the set of quaternary-sector activities that sustain the postindustrial economy.

Communications

Much of Europe has excellent internal communication connections, especially telecommunication, including computer-to-computer data exchange, e-mail, telefax, and cellular phone service. The growth of the European telecommunication system has been particularly rapid in the 1990s and early 2000s. By 2012, over 68 million Germans were using the Internet, as were more than 54 million citizens of the United Kingdom and France. Per capita Internet use is highest in northern Europe (fig. 9.2). The figures are lower for parts of eastern Europe and Turkey.

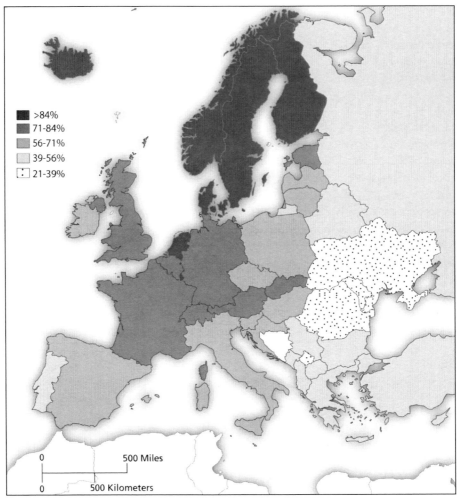

Figure 9.2.   Internet connections, proportional to population, 2012. Northern Europe is the most "wired" region and eastern Europe the least. Italy and France lag far behind the remainder of the European core. *Source:* Based on data from Internet World Stats, http://www.internetworldstats.com/stats4.htm.

By the middle of the first decade of the twenty-first century, Europe led the world in the percentage of the population using cell phones. Today, the number of cell phones in most European countries exceeds the size of the population. Moreover, Europe plays host to leading cellular phone providers.

Energy Production

Europeans consume vast amounts of energy to sustain their high standard of living. A sizable service industry thus exists to supply the needed power. Traditionally, indigenously produced coal provided the greater part of Europe's primary energy, but after about 1950, when consumption levels in Western Europe began rising beyond all expectations, coal gradually lost its dominance. Petroleum and natural gas soon surpassed coal in most of western and southern Europe, though most oil had to be imported, placing Europeans in a vulnerable position. The sharp oil price increase instigated by the Organization of Petroleum Exporting Countries in 1973 sent shock waves through Western Europe, and the Russian turnoff of the subsidized oil flow to its sphere of domination in eastern Europe in the early 1990s had a similarly traumatic impact.

One European reaction to the rapidly growing need for energy and the problem of foreign dependency has been increased development of indigenous sources such as hydroelectric, wind, and geothermal power (fig. 9.3). Denmark pioneered the effort to harness the westerly winds for electric power generation, and tens of thousands of tall, three-bladed wind turbines now line the North Sea, Atlantic coast, and river estuaries from Denmark to France and Spain. Six of the top-ten countries around the world producing *aeolic* power are found in Europe (in order of importance, Germany, Spain, the United Kingdom, Italy, France, and Portugal). Denmark leads the world in terms of per capita wind energy production, and the Danish government is moving forward with an ambitious plan for the construction of five huge offshore wind turbine parks that will boost wind energy production 200% by 2040. Iceland gets over 25% of its electricity from geothermal power, tapping the island's superheated volcanic subsurface.

The far more controversial nuclear power industry also grew in response to rising consumption. The United Kingdom put the first nuclear power plant online in 1956, followed by France two years later and West Germany in 1961. As of 2012, the five countries in the world with the greatest reliance on nuclear plants to meet their power needs were all European: France (75% of all power generated), Slovakia (54%), Belgium (51%), and Ukraine (46%) (fig. 9.3). The largest number of nuclear power reactors in Europe is in France (58), followed by Russia (33) and the United Kingdom (16). Despite the significance of these numbers, the trend in energy production from nuclear plants has been downward. During the 1980s, concerns over safety, the disposal of nuclear wastes, and terrorism led many European countries to curtail production. A particular shock arrived in 1986, when the worst nuclear power accident in world history occurred at the Chernobyl plant in northern Ukraine (then part of the Soviet Union). This meltdown, apparently caused by a low-intensity earthquake,

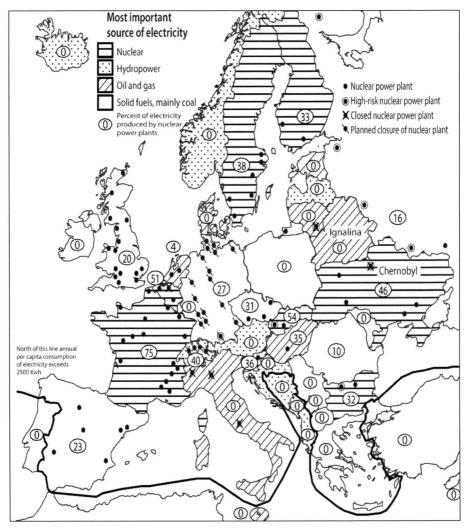

Figure 9.3.   The geography of electrical energy. *Sources:* United Nations, *Energy Statistics Yearbook*; World Bank statistics; *European Marketing Data and Statistics.*

spewed radioactive pollution over much of Europe, causing noteworthy contamination as far afield as northern Scandinavia. Closer to the site of the disaster, five million hectares of farmland were contaminated, and neighboring Belarus had to abandon 20% of its arable land. Over 1,600,000 Belarusians today live in radioactive contamination zones, the vast majority in Homel province, which experienced a 6% decline in population between 1989 and 1999. Children living near the plant experienced an elevated incidence of thyroid tumors, and perhaps 10,000 persons died as a direct or indirect result of the catastrophe.

In the wake of Chernobyl, most countries stopped building new plants; Italy phased out its modest industry, and voters in Sweden demanded that their country follow suit, though that has not happened. Nonetheless, nuclear power started getting a second look in the early 2000s in the wake of growing concern about the role of fossil fuels in global climate change. Even in Germany, where the parliament voted in 2002 to shut down all nuclear plants by 2020, debate was rekindled by those asking if nuclear energy might not be a lesser evil than global warming. In 2008, Italy became the first western European country to conclude that it was—committing to building nuclear power plants by 2013. But then came the 2011 Fukushima Dai-ichi nuclear disaster in Japan, which was brought on by an earthquake and accompanying tsunami. In its wake, opposition to nuclear energy has grown, with opponents pointing out that the problem of waste disposal continues to be unsolved and that no plant can ever be completely safe. In 2012, Germany decided to phase out its remaining nuclear power plants by 2022. But the situation remains fluid, and it is not yet clear how different parts of Europe will respond to the debate over the nuclear industry.

The complex spatial pattern of energy production in Europe (fig. 9.3) reflects the lack of consensus concerning energy—how to provide an adequate supply safely, dependably, and at an affordable cost, while at the same time avoiding significant ecological damage. Europeans must find a solution to this pressing problem if their prosperity and high living standards are to survive. Environmental costs remain high, however, and inefficiencies are not hard to find. For example, pigs from the Netherlands go by truck to Italy for slaughter so that the prestigious label "Parma ham" can be affixed to the meat, yielding a higher price, while Bavarian potatoes journey to Italy for washing, only to be reshipped to Germany to sell, wasting fossil fuel and clogging Alpine highways in order to benefit from less expensive Italian labor.

Tourism

Tourism—the short-term movement of people to destinations away from their place of permanent residence for reasons unconnected to livelihood—forms an integral part of the European lifestyle and of the European economy. In the western half of Europe, tourism experienced very rapid growth after 1950, and especially in the two decades following 1965, during which the number of tourists doubled. Tourism constitutes an important growth sector in the economy and provides one of the reasons why employment in the service sector has grown so large. Prior to World War II, tourism was largely an elitist activity of the upper class. Today, however, most Europeans participate, meaning that the majority of tourists visiting European countries are from other European countries. Today, tourism is directly responsible for some 4% of Europe's GDP and indirectly responsible for 9% of GDP—and additional growth is expected in the years ahead.

Tourism displays a vivid geography in its sources, destinations, and flows. Most tourists come from the wealthier countries of northern and western Europe, and their vacation destinations most often lie to the south. Over half of all European tourists seek out beaches for their holidays. Spain possesses the greatest concentration of southern seaside resorts, grouped in such coastal districts as the Costa del Sol and Costa del Azahar, as well as the Balearic Isles (fig. 9.4). Between 1959 and 1964, the

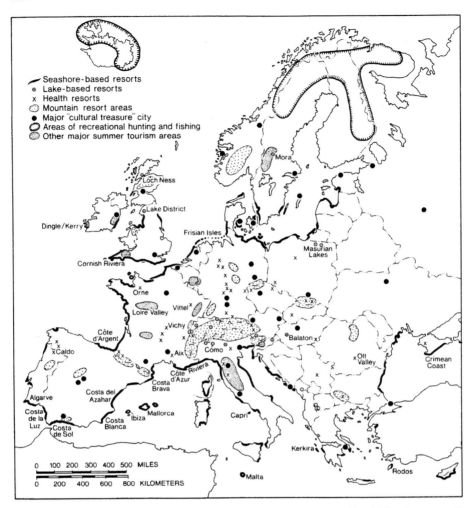

Figure 9.4.   Major tourist destinations in Europe. The most important tourist flow is from north to south, favoring the Mediterranean beaches and Alpine mountain resorts. *Sources:* Ferdinand Mayer, ed., *Diercke Weltatlas* (Braunschweig: Georg Westermann, 1975), 55, 98–99; George Hoffman, ed., *Europe in the 1990s: A Geographical Analysis* (New York: John Wiley, 1989), 184–85.

number of tourists coming to Spain increased from 4 to 14 million, and the country's foreign currency earning grew tenfold, marking the beginning of the Iberian beach resort era. Today, some 55 million international visitors come to Spain each year, and a fifth of all cash receipts derive from tourism, making it the country's largest industry. As is often the case with tourism, the economic impact in Spain remains highly localized in a coastal corridor and a few inland cities. Even today, tourism infrastructure is less well developed in most interior areas, away from the beaches, in spite of the cultural richness of the country.

Many beach resorts also developed in Mediterranean France, northern Italy, the Dalmatian coast of Croatia, the Black Sea shore of Bulgaria, and Ukrainian Crimea.

The tourist industry's main shortcoming is extreme vulnerability to economic down-turns and political unrest, as evidenced by the drop in tourist flows after the global economic downturn of 2009–2010. Also, tourist flows to beach resorts tend to be channelized. Two-thirds of the vacationers in Malta, where the tourist boom began in the 1960s, come from the United Kingdom, in part because the islands were once a British colony. Germans prefer the Italian beaches and also heavily patronize the Dalmatian coast and southern Spain, as well as Greece.

The second most common tourist flow is from lowland to highland. Mountain and hill areas attract abundant visitors in both winter and summer, and the Alps, benefiting from a central location, dominate the highland tourist industry (fig. 9.4). Together, Switzerland and Austria annually receive almost twice as many visitors—31,000,000—as their combined resident population (fig. 9.5).

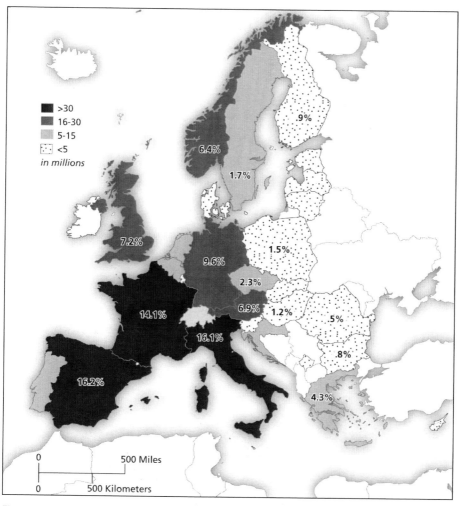

Figure 9.5. Tourism in Europe, 2011–2012. Dependence upon tourism varies widely within Europe, with both north–south and east–west contrasts. *Source:* Eurostat.

At least a quarter of all EU tourists seek out rural areas for their vacations. Many farms in favored districts offer guest accommodations. A third of all farmers in Finland's Åland Islands house vacationers, as do about a fourth of those in the Austrian Alps. In some Norwegian municipalities, the proportion runs as high as 40%.

Cultural tourism also ranks high in Europe, directed to places offering museums, well-preserved medieval or Renaissance quarters, theatrical and musical festivals, notable archaeological sites, and the like. Fifteen million tourists visit Venice each year. Stonehenge in England became so overrun by visitors that protective measures became necessary, as also occurred at the Acropolis in Athens. The very names of certain cities—Paris, Vienna, Florence—connote culture and refinement, attracting many tourists. More bucolic in message and appeal, the numerous open-air folk museums of Europe remind visitors of a romanticized, lost rural past. Such outdoor museums, centered upon collections of traditional farmsteads relocated from the countryside, appeared first in Scandinavia, the prototype being Skansen in Stockholm (fig. 9.6). The concept has spread through most of trans-Alpine Europe, from Kizhi Island in Russian Karelia to the Ulster Folk Museum in Northern Ireland and the Schweizerisches Freilichtmuseum in central Switzerland. Following the Skansen example, many of these open-air displays combine the appeals of folk museum and amusement park.

Figure 9.6. Traditional farmsteads in Stockholm's pioneering open-air museum known as Skansen. Photo by A. B. M., 2012.

European tourists are less likely than their American counterparts to spend their vacations traveling to one place after another. A "tour" differs from a "holiday," and most Europeans prefer the latter. Their normal pattern is to get as quickly as possible from home to the desired destination—no small achievement, given the frequent summer traffic jams on European roads—and then spend the entire holiday there, perhaps making day excursions to other, nearby attractions. Self-contained holiday resorts offering diverse amusements have recently gained in popularity, catering to the European mode of tourist travel.

Linking the penchant for single-destination tourism to the craving of the urban European for the rural countryside led also to the widespread practice of owning vacation homes. Most of these are modest cottages of recent construction, but some are old farmhouses abandoned as the agrarian population left the land and migrated to urban areas. The Dordogne River valley of France, for example, has become a favorite area for British vacationers. In some Spanish provinces, over 30% of all residences are vacation homes—many owned by Germans. The rural environs of Helsinki in southern Finland average more than five vacation cottages per square kilometer. In eastern Europe, where tourism remains a less important activity due to lower living standards, the dacha, or country cottage, has long been common. In Bulgaria, a third of all city dwellers own a dacha in the countryside.

Another distinctly European type of tourism involves "taking the waters" at one or another of a huge assortment of health resorts, a practice most common in Germany and France. The generous health-care systems of such countries make it possible for citizens to receive treatment, at government expense, for real or imagined ailments and afflictions. The road signs posted at the limits of many towns in Germany tell the traveler that the name of the place is *Heilbad-* or *Kurort-*Such-and-Such, treating one or more problem of the lungs, kidneys, joints, stomach, or some other part of the anatomy. Amusements receive abundant attention as part of the cure, and the stay at such a place can be most enjoyable. Visitors spend a pleasant holiday, sometimes drawing full wages from work all the while. Needless to say, spas have prospered and proliferated in this subsidized system of health-related tourism, although in recent years the generous reimbursements from health insurance are no longer as certain as they once were (see Chapter 11).

The removal of most political barriers to travel in eastern Europe has opened up that huge area to mass tourism from the affluent west. Virtually every formerly Communist country benefits from this west-to-east tourist flow, and some places and regions, such as Prague, Budapest, Dresden, the Harz Mountains and Thüringer Forest of eastern Germany, St. Petersburg, Moscow, Riga, and Tallinn are especially popular.

When mass tourism arrives in full force, residents find it a mixed blessing. Economic benefits come with tourism, but so do assorted problems. The experience of the Alps is instructive. As late as 1955, most of that mountain range remained a land of traditional, and in places impoverished, dairy farmers living in picturesque log houses. The elite tourism of the previous century had touched few of these residents and changed little in their way of life. Many young people fled the mountains, seeking a better living in the lowland cities. Then, in a single generation between 1955 and 1975, mass tourism came to the Alps, prompting a pervasive shift from dairy farming to dependence upon winter and summer visitors. Certain isolated, poverty-stricken places became prosperous, highly desirable tourist destinations within the span of two decades. Money injected into the rural Alps by tourism provided a cure for the depressed economy, prompting the construction of an excellent road network and halting the emigration of the young. As a result, most residents of the Alps benefit from tourism and regard it as a good thing.

Even so, they paid a high price. The local mountain culture was disrupted. A folk society based upon mutual cooperation, egalitarianism, and respect for tradition gave way to a popular culture in which neighbors competed for tourist income, and the old ways were largely abandoned. An ancient adaptive system of land use in ecological balance with the fragile Alpine environment yielded to a new one that required massive, and necessarily destructive, habitat modification. Ski runs, cut through protective belts of communal forests on slopes above the valley floors, scarred the mountainsides, caused erosion, and removed natural protection against avalanches. Also, tourism greatly increased the number of people tramping about the Alpine countryside, further damaging the local flora and fauna. Highway construction brought additional massive damage. In short, the people of the Alps lost their traditional culture, and the land suffered extensive ecological modification as a result of mass tourism. A proven, sustainable system of land use gave way to an economically vulnerable one.

The legendary Greek isle of Crete provides another cautionary tale. Home of the ancient Minoan civilization, Crete was long sought out mainly by culturally oriented tourists, who visited its numerous archaeological sites. As recently as 1971, only 15,000 tourists visited the island annually. True, Crete was impoverished and suffering from emigration to the mainland, but it was home to a traditional Mediterranean way of life that possessed both charm and dignity. Then, in the 1980s, came mass tourism—fun-in-the-sun, beach-based, and wildly successful. The number of tourists rose to two million by 1995, and much of the island's beautiful north coast was converted into an unbroken row of hotels—a "vacationer ghetto." Almost no planning was done, and few restrictions on what could be done were imposed. Many inhabitants find work in the hotel industry or other tourist-related businesses (car rental agencies, restaurants, etc.), but the pay is often low, and layoffs are common during slow periods. Most of Spain's best beaches and the Algarve region of southern Portugal have similarly been overdeveloped.

Tourism of any sort has the tendency to destroy the basis of its existence. Mass tourism will certainly do that. Is there an alternative? Intelligently written land-use zoning and building codes can retard the worst excesses of mass tourism. The French Riviera provides an encouraging example, though at the cost of creating an "elitist landscape" that is largely inaccessible to the average tourist. **Ecotourism** offers yet another alternative. Its goal is sustainability, causing little damage to nature or local cultures. Necessarily, ecotourism involves small numbers of tourists willing to "rough it" in less-than-resort-like conditions. But many tourists do not want that sort of vacation, and in any case Europe has few natural habitats or native cultures left.

Retailing and Governmental/Social Services

The remainder, and far greater, part of the service sector consists of retailing and the provision of governmental and social services. Retailing is, of course, ubiquitous. Its distribution largely mirrors the population patterns discussed in Chapter 3, although the size of the retail sector is particularly large in the wealthiest parts of Europe and in tourist areas. Governmental and social services include various public agencies, health care and welfare systems, educational facilities, and other enterprises serving collective and individual needs. The majority of Europeans are employed in the retailing, governmental, and social services sectors. Most hold jobs paying modest wages—often lower than those recently lost in the primary and manufacturing industries. For some Europeans, the postindustrial age has brought diminished living standards. We will look in greater detail at such social issues in Chapter 11.

The Quaternary Sector

Another sector of activity consists of higher-order services catering principally to the needs of business, education, and research. These services include banking, stock and bond exchanges, accounting, legal services, research and development, various types of consulting, and the processing and provision of knowledge and information. Such activities, as well as many corporate headquarters, cluster strikingly in the inner core of western Europe, revealing the dominant economic position of that part of Europe—especially Germany, France, and the United Kingdom (fig. 9.7).

London and Paris early became the financial centers of not just Europe but the world. In the twentieth century, and especially in the 1990s, London eclipsed its rival. Centered in "The City"—the old central part of London—the financial service industry employs hundreds of thousands of workers today. London has scores of banks, many of the world's largest insurance companies, a famous stock exchange, and handles a third of the world's currency trading. Deindustrialization hardly touched London's prosperity due to the city's role as the world's financial leader. Dubbed the "Thames tiger," London's rate of employment in the financial sector expanded steadily during the early 2000s, though it fell off somewhat after 2009–2010. If Greater London, a city of over eight million, were an independent country, it would rank among the top ten largest economies in Europe. Frankfurt, Zürich, and Paris also rank as major financial centers, but far behind London. The United Kingdom's rejection of the EU's common currency, the euro, has not had a notable impact on the city's role as a major international financial center.

The segment of the quaternary sector devoted to the generation, storing, and processing of diverse types of information forms a mainspring in the current age of rapid technological change. It includes an institutionalized research and development component, and subsidiary consultancy firms. This information sector tends to be clustered in the same European inner core that houses financial services (fig. 9.7). Locationally, the information services remain linked to the major centers of high-tech

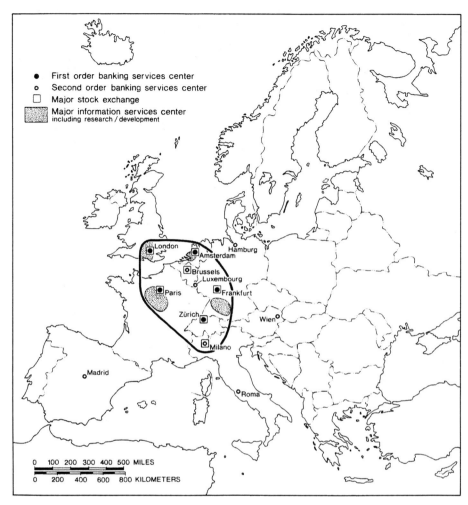

Figure 9.7. Major centers of producer service industry. Banking, insurance, research/development, information processing, stock and bond exchanges, and other producer services are highly concentrated in an inner-core region of Europe.

manufacturing, in particular the western suburbs of London, the southern and southwestern satellite cities of Paris, the Randstad Holland megalopolis, and southwestern Germany (figs. 8.17 and 9.7).

The striking concentration of quaternary activities represents a powerful statement of core–periphery contrasts in Europe. Even though such services, in a time of instant communications, need not be concentrated geographically, the fact is that the core of Europe has, in some respects, grown smaller and more powerful in the postindustrial age. Most of the decisions and innovations that shape and reshape the economy and future of Europe derive from the inner core, from a small, elite group engaged in the quaternary sector.

Europe, then, has evolved into a postindustrial area, in which most people find employment in a diverse array of service and information industries. This development leads Europeans into uncharted waters, just as the original Industrial Revolution did a quarter millennium ago. Particularly in the wake of the recent economic downturn, uncertainties, even pessimism, about the postindustrial future abound among some Europeans, including those living in the wealthiest lands, but change has long been an inevitable constant.

The Trajectory of Integration

Europe's shift from an industrially focused economy to one centered on postindustrial activities came during a time when the European integration project took major steps forward. As we saw in Chapter 6, the roots of the European integration movement can be traced to the 1950s when Europe was rebounding from the devastation of World War II. It was both a political and an economic project from the beginning, but the assumption has generally been that economic integration would pave the way for greater political integration. Even though that assumption is now being called into question (see below and Chapter 12), it certainly held true during the latter decades of the twentieth century.

European integration has involved both "widening" and "deepening"—the former term referencing the growing number of countries that have come within the umbrella of the EEC/EC/EU (see fig. 9.8), and the latter term indicating the growing power and political reach of the supranational bloc's central institutions. Broadly, the integration process has unfolded through six periods. The first period, stretching from the founding of the EEC in the late 1950s through the early 1970s, saw the establishment of basic institutions and remarkable success in eliminating tariff trade barriers between countries. Brussels emerged as the administrative center—a brilliant choice given that the city lies at the center of a country straddling the Romance–Germanic language divide. Designating Brussels as the administrative capital also meant not having to choose between the two major powers in the early EEC: France and Germany. Even though the executive arm of the EEC was located in Brussels, a desire not to concentrate too much power in one place led to a decision to locate the major judicial functions in Luxembourg and to house the parliament, when meeting in general session, in Strasbourg—a city in France that sits along the German border, that was traded back and forth between France and Germany over the centuries, and that has an indigenous population speaking a Germanic dialect.

During the first period of European integration, the economies of the member states became increasingly interlinked. They were joined in the 1960s by Austria, Denmark, Norway, Portugal, Sweden, Switzerland, the United Kingdom, Finland, and eventually Iceland—states that were not members of the EEC at the time but that had founded an organization known as the European Free Trade Association (EFTA), which negotiated a free-trade agreement with the EEC. (Many of the original EFTA members subsequently joined the EC/EU. Only Iceland, Norway, Switzerland,

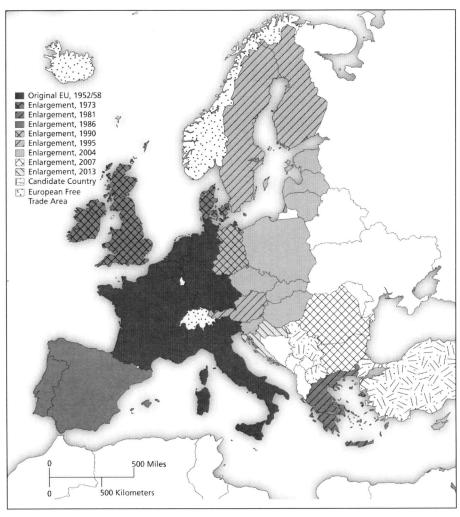

Figure 9.8.   The European Union. From a six-country nucleus in the 1950s, the EEC/EC/EU has grown to include much of Europe.

and tiny Lichtenstein are members today. With Iceland and Norway becoming part of the so-called European Economic Area in 1994, and Switzerland negotiating its own bilateral treaties with the EC/EU covering much the same ground, the EFTA has lost much of its original purpose.)

By the late 1960s, the EEC merged with "communities" focused on atomic energy and coal and steel (see Chapter 6) to form the European Communities—a name soon simplified to the European Community (EC). The success of economic integration and the growing willingness of the founding countries to admit others led to the addition of three new member states in 1973: Denmark, the United Kingdom, and Ireland (fig. 9.8).

The second major period in the European integration project stretched from late 1973 to the mid-1980s. This period was marked by a major global economic recession. With economic growth slowed, countries within the EC began looking for ways to protect their industries. Tariffs were no longer an option, but in violation of the spirit of the European integration project, some turned to nontariff trade barriers (e.g., regulations and taxes that impede the exchange of goods between countries). Many of these regulations were struck down by the administrative and judicial arms of the EC, but the late 1970s through the early 1980s was a period of stasis for the EC in general. No great forward strides were taken, but the institutions were sufficiently robust to keep things from sliding back too far. Only one new country joined the EC during this period: Greece, in 1981 (fig. 9.8). Greece was less well off than the other EC members, but it was an appealing candidate both because of its historical legacy as the crucible of European civilization and because membership was seen as a way to ensure that communism did not gain the upper hand in the country.

The third major period of European integration stretched from the mid-1980s to 1993. This period saw a significant expansion in the administrative competence of the EC and led to the establishment of what could increasingly be regarded as a single economic space. By the mid-1980s, it became clear that something fairly dramatic was needed to end the stagnation that had characterized the late 1970s and early 1980s. A series of meetings culminated in the adoption of the Single European Act in 1986, which called for the elimination of all nontariff trade barriers by 1992 and paved the way for greater political cooperation. Around the same time, a number of member states signed the so-called Schengen Agreement, which eliminated border controls between participating countries (fig. 9.9). Perhaps more than any other step taken in the integration process, this agreement altered the way Europeans thought about the traditional state-based political-geographic order. Moving across international borders became no more difficult than going from Oregon to Washington.

By the early 1990s, the project of eliminating nontariff trade barriers had largely been achieved, and the EC was becoming an increasingly powerful actor. The EC took on growing responsibility, for example, in the environmental policy and regional development arenas. This period also saw further territorial expansion, with Spain and Portugal joining the EC in 1985. Moreover, what had been East Germany came into the fold as part of an enlarged Germany after reunification in 1990 (fig. 9.8).

Building on the momentum of the third period, the fourth period of integration was ushered in by the signing of the Maastricht Treaty in late 1993. Also known as the Treaty on European Union, this treaty transformed the EC into the European Union (EU)—an acknowledgement of the significant deepening of European integration that had taken place. The treaty institutionalized greater cooperation in law enforcement, judicial matters, and immigration; it gave greater power to the European parliament; it expanded the EU's role in social matters; and it paved the way for the introduction of a common currency in Europe (the euro). The treaty was contested in some parts of Europe and was only adopted after two votes in Denmark and special opt-out provisions on social matters were worked out for the United Kingdom. But its general impact was to further the momentum of European integration.

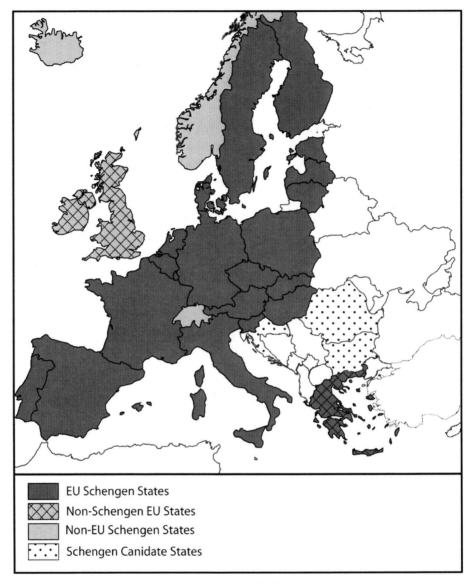

Figure 9.9. Schengen Agreement countries, 2013. The agreement now encompasses most of the EU and EFTA countries, but the United Kingdom and Ireland have not joined.

Within a few years, the Amsterdam Treaty gave the EU a greater role in foreign policy and, by 1998, a European Central Bank had been founded. In the early 2000s, the euro came into use throughout much of the EU; by 2013 the so-called **Eurozone** encompassed all of the members of the EU as of 2000, with the exception of the United Kingdom, Denmark and Sweden, as well as Slovenia and Slovakia, which joined the EU in 2004 (fig. 9.10). Three other states joined the EU near the beginning of this period: Sweden, Finland, and Austria (fig. 9.8).

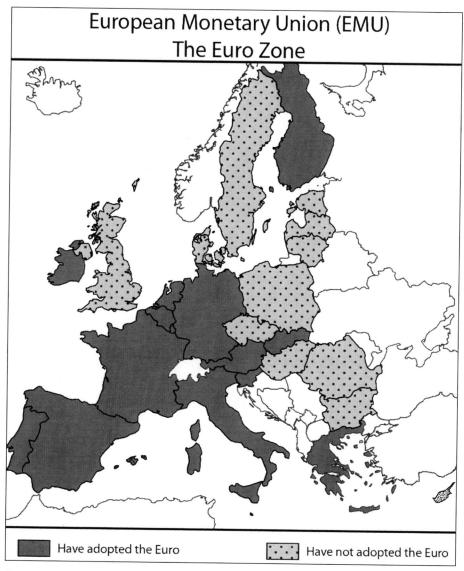

European Monetary Union (EMU) The Euro Zone

Have adopted the Euro

Have not adopted the Euro

Figure 9.10.   The Eurozone in 2013.

The fifth period of European integration is associated with the extraordinary territorial expansion of the EU in May 2004 to encompass eight new member states in the eastern part of Europe (Estonia, Latvia, Lithuania, Poland, Czechia, Slovakia, Hungary, and Slovenia), as well as two Mediterranean islands (Cyprus and Malta)—followed by the addition of two more eastern European countries in 2007 (Romania and Bulgaria) (fig. 9.8). The 2004 expansion alone added 77 million people and over 700,000 square kilometers to the EU. The expansion was driven by a sense of obligation in the European west toward the peoples and countries that had long been under

Soviet domination, and by the desire to promote stability in Europe as a whole. Expansion brought some economic gains—particularly for the new entrants—but it also greatly complicated the integration process. A symbol of how difficult integration had become in an enlarged EU came in 2005, when a proposed constitution for the newly expanded EU suffered defeat at the hands of French and Dutch voters. (The EU has continued to function under a few major treaties, the most recent of which is the so-called Lisbon Treaty, which entered into force in 2009.)

The latest period of European integration unfolded in the wake of a debt crisis that started in Greece near the end of 2009 and was tied to the global economic downturn of the time. This period has been one of considerable difficulty for the EU, as resentments have developed between countries facing divergent economic circumstances. As we will see in our discussion of the crisis below, the "deepening" of the economic integration has greatly slowed during this period, with some even asking whether monetary union was a mistake. Given the difficulties of this most recent period, it is not surprising that the "widening" of the EU has slowed as well. Croatia joined the EU in 2013, and a few other countries have applied for membership (fig. 9.8). But the second decade of the twenty-first century is unlikely to see many new additions to the EU.

Economic Impacts of Integration

It is almost impossible to determine with any precision how much impact integration has had on the European economy because there is no easy way to ascertain what might have happened without the rise of the EEC/EC/EU. What can be said with certainty is that, during the early phases of integration, the elimination of tariff trade barriers spurred considerable intra-European trade in agricultural and manufactured goods. By the 1970s, it was increasingly common to find products from one EC country on the shelves of other EU countries.

Then, as integration took further steps forward in the 1980s and 1990s, not only did intra-European trade continue to accelerate; a growing number of cooperative and joint ventures came into being. Transnational alliances developed in the business, research, and legal sectors, and the EC economies became increasingly interdependent. Mobility increased between EC countries, cooperation along international boundaries within the EC grew, and the European transport network was reconfigured to facilitate interaction among EC states.

The introduction of the euro at the beginning of the 2000s furthered the economic interpenetration of the, by then, 15 EU countries. Nonetheless, the significant territorial expansion of the EU in 2004 brought into the mix a set of national economies facing different challenges from many of the longer-standing EU member states. The remainder of the first decade of the twenty-first century was dominated first by the struggle to cope with the new EU entrants and then by the economic downturn that greatly slowed the pace of economic integration.

The immediate catalyst for the economic downturn in Europe was a debt crisis in Greece. Greece had joined the euro at the beginning of the 2000s. Since the euro was viewed as a safe currency, interest rates on loans fell to unprecedented lows, and borrowing by both private interests and the government accelerated. In the process, levels of debt mushroomed. In late 2009, a new Greek government revealed that the budget data the prior government had been reporting significantly understated the level of public debt. A crisis in investor confidence quickly followed, fueled by fears that there would be a run on the funds held by Greek banks and loan defaults by the Greek government.

Greece is a relatively small economy by EU standards, but fears quickly arose that other European countries with large public and private debts could follow in Greece's footsteps. Attention focused particularly on Ireland, Portugal, Italy, and Spain—countries that have had persistently high government-debt-to-GDP ratios (fig. 9.11). Debts were only part of the problem, however. In the years leading up to the crisis, wages in southern European countries had risen rapidly, even as Germany had held wage increases down and expanded its exports. The result was that the weaker economies were increasingly at a competitive disadvantage with Germany, but they could not adjust to the situation by devaluing their currencies because they had adopted the euro. As a result, economic confidence in these countries eroded further, producing a downward spiral.

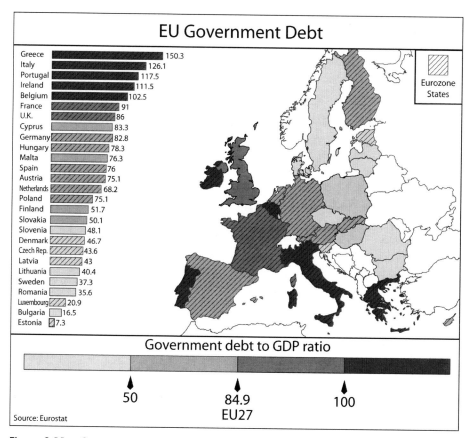

Figure 9.11.   Government debt as a percentage of GDP, 2012. *Source:* Eurostat 2012.

The disintegration of the Eurozone was averted when the EU and the International Monetary Fund approved a financial assistance plan for Greece in May 2010. Assistance was later extended to other troubled countries, and by 2012 a long-term rescue program was established, known as the European Stability Mechanism. Germany in particular insisted that access to rescue funds had to be contingent on economic reforms within recipient countries, which largely took the form of austerity measures (spending cuts, tax increases, and the like) designed to reduce budget deficits. These same measures, however, produced a spike in unemployment, particularly among the young (see Chapter 11), which in turn made it more difficult to address the debt problems.

By 2013 there were signs of improvement in the European—and the global—economy. But the Eurozone crisis has fostered significant divisions within Europe along geographical and political lines that cannot easily be overcome. In geographical terms, it has pitted southern European countries against those in the north—particularly Germany, with the latter viewing the former as profligate and undisciplined, and the former viewing the latter as domineering and hegemonic. In political terms, it has pitted those who view austerity measures as the only long-term solution to the problem against those who contend that draconian austerity measures undermine the ability of economies to recover.

There are also significant differences in opinion concerning the types of institutional arrangements that are needed to address the crisis. Some EU enthusiasts hope to see a banking union and a common fiscal policy for the EU. Others argue that such centralizing approaches are untenable in the face of growing resistance to the loss of local and national control over economic and social matters (see Chapter 12). It will be some time before we know how these differences play out, but it is important not to allow the drama of recent economic events in Europe to dominate our thinking so much that we ignore the larger impacts of integration on the region's economic geography.

We have already seen some of those impacts in our discussion of the history of European integration: an acceleration of trade between member states, an interpenetration of tertiary and quaternary economic activities across Europe, and a rise in transborder interaction, which in turn has spurred the development of many border regions. A couple of other impacts of integration on Europe's economic geography deserve mention as well. One is that integration has likely promoted the development of increasingly large-scale business clusters. When trade costs come down in an increasingly integrated economic space, the incentives for firms to be close to consumers decreases; hence, firms tend to exploit economies of scale—concentrating production in one region and exporting to other regions.

Another economic impact of integration is more indirect. Any country that seeks to join the EU has to meet a variety of economic and political criteria that demonstrate the country's suitability as an EU member. Those criteria spurred significant policy changes in the eastern European countries that joined the EU since 2004, and they continue to drive significant reforms of an economic and political nature in applicant countries such as Serbia, Macedonia, and Montenegro (fig. 9.8).

Just as the development of agriculture over the centuries took place against the backdrop of particular patterns of rural settlement (Chapter 7), the story of Europe's manufacturing, industrial, and postindustrial economies is set within a changing set of urban places. We thus turn to the evolution of the European city in the next chapter.

Sources and Suggested Readings

Amin, A., and N. J. Thrift, eds. 1994. *Globalization, Institutions, and Regional Development in Europe*. Oxford: Oxford University Press.

Arentsen, M. J. 2006. Contested Technology: Nuclear Power in the Netherlands. *Energy and Environment* 17 (3): 373–82.

Ashworth, G. J., and P. J. Larkham. 1994. *Building a New Heritage: Tourism, Culture, and Identity in the New Europe*. London: Routledge.

Bailly, A. S. 1995. Producer Services Research in Europe. *Professional Geographer* 47 (1): 70–74.

Bathelt, H. 2005. The German Variety of Capitalism: Forces and Dynamics of Evolutionary Change. *Economic Geography* 81 (1): 1–9.

Briassoulis, H. 2003. Crete: Endowed by Nature, Privileged by Geography, Threatened by Tourism? *Journal of Sustainable Tourism* 11 (2–3): 97–115.

Brulhart, M., and P. Koenig. 2006. New Economic Geography Meets Comecon—Regional Wages and Industry Location in Central Europe. *Economics of Transition* 14 (2): 245–67.

Bryson, J. R. 2007. The "Second" Global Shift: The Offshoring or Global Sourcing of Corporate Services and the Rise of Distanciated Emotional Labour. *Geografiska Annaler Series B: Human Geography* 89 (Supplement 1): 31–43.

Casado-Diaz, M. A. 2006. Retiring to Spain: An Analysis of Differences among North European Nationals. *Journal of Ethnic and Migration Studies* 32 (8): 1321–39.

Clancy, M. 2011. Boom, Bust and the Changing Geography of Irish Tourism. *Irish Geography* 44 (2–3): 173–90.

Clark, G. L. 2003. *European Pensions and Global Finance*. Oxford: Oxford University Press.

Dicken, P. 2011. *Global Shift: Mapping the Changing Contours of the World Economy*. 6th ed. London: Sage.

Dicken, P., and M. Quevit, eds. 1994. Transnational Corporations and European Regional Restructuring. *Nederlandse Geografische Studies* 181.

Garcia, C., and J. Servera. 2003. Impacts of Tourism Development on Water Demand and Beach Degradation on the Island of Mallorca (Spain). *Geografiska Annaler, Series A: Physical Geography* 85 (3–4): 287–300.

Gibb, R., ed. 1994. *The Channel Tunnel: A Geographical Perspective*. Chichester, UK: Wiley.

Gospodini, A. 2009. Post-Industrial Trajectories of Mediterranean European Cities: The Case of Post-Olympics Athens. *Urban Studies* 46 (5–6): 1157–86.

Green, A. E., and J. R. Howells. 1988. Information Services and Spatial Development in the UK Economy. *Tijdschrift voor Economische en Sociale Geografie* 79 (4): 266–77.

Hall, C. M., and A. A. Lew, eds. 1998. *Sustainable Tourism: A Geographical Perspective*. Harlow, UK: Longman.

Hall, D. R. 1993. Impacts of Economic and Political Transition on the Transport Geography of Central and Eastern Europe. *Journal of Transport Geography* 1 (1): 20–35.

Hall, P. G., and K. Pain, eds. 2006. *The Polycentric Metropolis: Learning from Mega-City Regions in Europe*. London: Earthscan.

Hermelin, B. 2007. The Urbanization and Suburbanization of the Service Economy: Producer Services and Specialization in Stockholm. *Geografiska Annaler Series B: Human Geography* 89 (Supplement 1): 59–74.

Holloway, L., R. Cox, L. Venn, M. Kneafsey, E. Dowler, and H. Tuomainen. 2006. Managing Sustainable Farmed Landscape through "Alternative" Food Networks: A Case Study from Italy. *Geographical Journal* 172:219–29.

Howkins, T. J. 2005. Changing Hegemonies and New External Pressures: South East European Railway Networks in Transition. *Journal of Transport Geography* 13 (2): 187–97.

Kepka, J., and A. B. Murphy. 2002. Euroregions in Comparative Perspective: Differential Implications for Europe's Borderlands. In *Boundaries and Place*, ed. J. Hakli and D. Kaplan, 50–69. Boulder, CO: Rowman & Littlefield.

Kind, H. J., K. H. M. Knarvik, and J. Torstensson. 1999. *What Determines the Economic Geography of Europe?* London: Centre for Economic Policy Research.

Krätke, S. 2007. Metropolisation of the European Economic Territory as a Consequence of Increasing Specialisation of Urban Agglomerations in the Knowledge Economy. *European Planning Studies* 15 (1): 1–27.

Leo, M. D. 2007. Chernobyl Revisited. *Discover*, 68–75.

Marples, D. R. 2004. Chernobyl: A Reassessment. *Eurasian Geography & Economics* 45 (8): 588–607.

Pickles, J., ed. 2008. *Globalization and Regionalization in Post-Socialist Economies: The Common Economic Spaces of Europe.* New York: Palgrave Macmillan.

Rubalcaba-Bermejo, L. 2007. *The New Service Economy: Challenges and Policy Implications for Europe.* Cheltenham, UK: Edward Elgar.

Selstad, T. 1990. The Rise of the Quaternary Sector: The Regional Dimension of Knowledge-Based Services in Norway, 1970–1985. *Norsk Geografisk Tidsskrift* 44 (1): 21–37.

Smith, A. 2013. Europe and an Inter-dependent World: Uneven Geo-economic and Geo-political Developments. *European Urban and Regional Studies* 20 (1): 3–13.

Smith, A., and A. Swain. 2010. The Global Economic Crisis, Eastern Europe, and the Former Soviet Union: Models of Development and the Contradictions of Internationalization. *Eurasian Geography and Economics* 51 (1): 1–34

Ter Brugge, R. 1984. Nuclear Energy in the Netherlands. *Tijdschrift voor Economische en Sociale Geografie* 75 (4): 300–304.

Tranos, E., and A. Gillespie. 2011. The Urban Geography of Internet Backbone Networks in Europe: Roles and Relations. *Journal of Urban Technology* 18 (1): 35–50.

CHAPTER 10

The European City

Cities are relatively large, permanent settlements containing a fairly dense cluster of socially heterogeneous people engaged in specialized, primarily nonagricultural types of work. Cities are distinguished from traditional rural villages by their size, the comparatively high level of **occupational specialization** of their residents, and their relatively elaborate systems of governance, which amass and spend capital for public projects. Virtually all of Europe's most influential innovations, changes, and great ideas discussed in Chapter 1 came out of urban settings, and cities have been the principal incubators of both the industrial and the postindustrial European economy.

Cities also play host to the vast majority of the European population. As recently as the turn of the twentieth century, the majority of Europeans lived in rural areas. But the twentieth century saw a tremendous migration from the countryside to urban areas, and now more than 75% of Europe's population lives in cities and towns. The proportion in Belgium exceeds 97% (fig. 10.1).

To appreciate the nature and significance of the European city, it is useful to look at the development of urbanization over time. We thus look at where and why cities developed, the sites they occupied, and their **morphology** (material form and organization) from ancient to modern times. We then focus on key attributes of the contemporary European city, as well as some of the major differences among cities in different parts of Europe. We conclude with a brief assessment of the overall urban pattern found in Europe today.

The Rise of the European City

The city represents an ancient, vital European institution, but its origins lie elsewhere. The diffusion of urbanism followed the same northwest path from the Near East that brought the Indo-European languages, Christianity, agriculture, and the political state into Europe (fig. 10.2). Many of these innovations were interrelated in that agriculture greatly increased food production per capita, freeing a portion of the population to engage in urban activities, such as trade, crafts, military service, and political

299

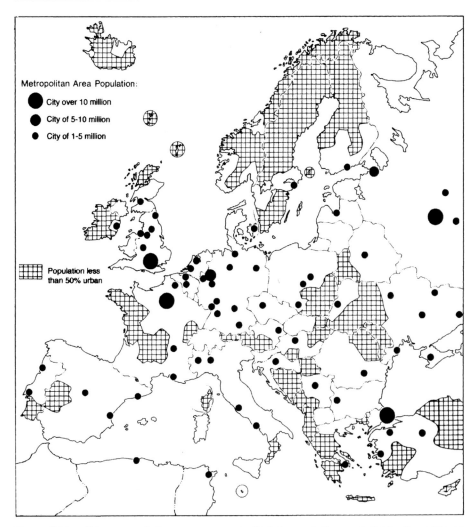

Figure 10.1.   Urban population as a percent of total population and distribution of large metropolitan areas in the early twenty-first century. Countries differ somewhat in their definition of *urban* and *metropolitan area*, but these figures are roughly comparable. For purposes of this map, urban is defined as settlements of 10,000 or more. The core of Europe is more highly urbanized, in general, than the peripheries.

administration. These occupations all became centered in cities and in fact provided the very reason for urban existence. Trade represented the most important single function. Hence, the term ***mercantile city*** best describes European urban centers prior to the eighteenth and nineteenth centuries.

Cities have also served as centers of administration. Rulers found cities convenient bases from which to rule. Many early cities arose as religious sites, centered on temples that were often built in prominent places, for example on hilltops. The priestly class also formed an influential part of the urban population from the time that cities started to develop. Scholars, artists, and philosophers joined the merchants,

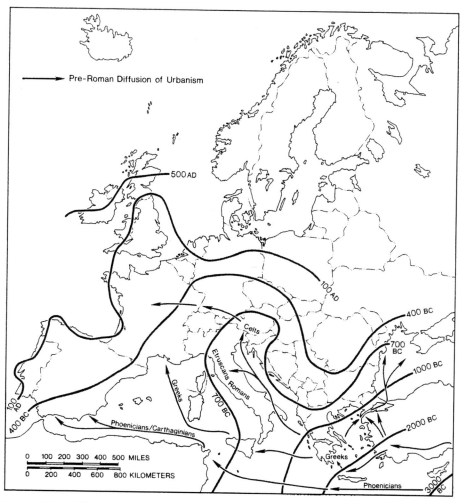

Figure 10.2.   Diffusion of the city. The source and paths of diffusion show striking similarities to the diffusion routes of the Indo-European languages, agriculture, the political state, and Christianity. Just as was probably true in the spread of agriculture and languages, Iberia received its first urban impulse from Afro-Asiatic peoples by way of North Africa. *Source:* Pounds 1969, with modifications.

artisans, rulers, soldiers, and clerics as urbanites, making the city a center of learning and creativity.

The Greeks were the first Europeans to adopt urbanism from the Near East and Anatolia. Small cities began to develop about 2000 BCE, and, within seven centuries, small **city-states**, each ruling a modest-sized tributary rural territory, dotted the Peloponnesus and Aegean shores. The so-called Greek Heroic Age (that is, the age of Homer) played out in these city-states, ending around 1100 BCE. Most of the early Greek cities were small in size and rather unimpressive in appearance. Unlike farm villages, they often boasted a temple, palace, theater, and marketplace. Many of them were eventually surrounded by walls.

Having grown up over time without planning, street patterns were irregular, although the larger streets would tend to wind toward the marketplace, which also functioned as the center of public affairs. After a period of decline following the Heroic Age, the Greeks began their greatest era of city-founding around 850 BCE, culminating in the Hellenic Golden Age. The great city-states of Ancient Greece reached their apex. Rarely did cities exceed 5,000 people, though Athens may have had as many as 300,000 residents in the peak of its classical glory, and Corinth perhaps had 90,000. Only the larger cities acquired importance beyond their local areas. Even at the height of classical urban development, as little as 25% of the Greek population lived in cities.

Ancient Greece's impact on European urbanism was not limited to Greece proper. Greek colonists carried urbanism as far afield as the Black Sea coasts, southern Italy, and the south of France. Syracuse on Sicily and Marseille in Languedoc trace their origins to Greek colonists. Unlike the cities in the homeland, Greek colonial cities were the product of planning. The Greeks would choose a site of strategic or economic importance and then lay out a grid of streets that would shape the development of the city. Their interest in mathematics and geometry led them to adopt a north-south-oriented **rectilinear street pattern**, an approach to urban design that is still with us today. There was no single dominant intersection in the Greek colonial city. Instead, important buildings were simply aligned along streets in the central part of the town. The external perimeter of the town was often irregular, reflecting how far it was feasible to extend the grid.

By about 500 BCE, some 600 cities existed in peninsular Greece and the Aegean Islands. The Phoenicians, a Mediterranean people of the Near East, also founded some cities as trading colonies in Europe, especially in southern Iberia. By that time, peoples who were beyond the Greek realm, but influenced by Greek ideas, had begun establishing cities as well. Beginning about 800 BCE, the Celts established a number of small cities in the Alpine peripheries, most notably at Hallstatt in Austria, and the Etruscans of Italy became active city builders in the same period. Romans, destined to become the greatest of all European city founders, were influenced by both Greeks and Etruscans. They eventually forged a vast empire and brought into being the Pax Romana. At the dawn of Roman greatness, the imperial core districts of Latium (modern Lazio) and Etruria (modern Tuscany) contained some 42 cities. By the midpoint in the Roman Empire's life span under Augustus, 430 new cities existed in Italy alone (fig. 10.3). In its classical grandeur, Rome may have boasted a population of close to a million people, packed into an area of barely 23 square kilometers.

The Roman city was similar in form to the Greek colonial city—planned and with a rectilinear street pattern—although the Romans tended to establish major intersections at the heart of the city where the most important buildings would be located. Central plazas were also common. The Romans speeded the diffusion of urban life through Europe by founding new cities in France, Germany, Britain, and interior Iberia, as well as along the Danube River. Some new towns grew around military barracks or camps, an origin suggested by the British town suffixes of -*caster* and -*chester*, as in Lancaster or Winchester, derived from the Latin word *castra* (army

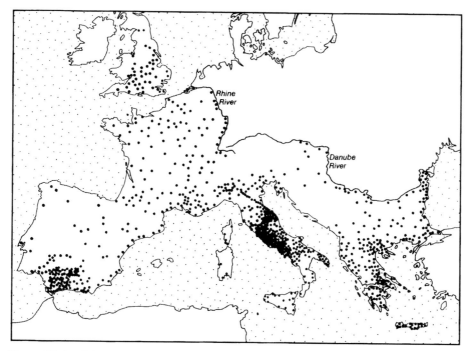

Figure 10.3.   Cities of the Roman Empire by the third century C E. Note the clusterings in central Italy, southern Spain, and Greece. *Source:* After Pounds 1969.

camp). The Romans also took over and expanded fortified villages. Three areas stood out as centers of urban development under Roman rule: central Italy, Greece, and Andalucía in Spain (fig. 10.3). Most of the Roman cities remained small by modern standards. In France, the towns ranged from about 600 to 35,000 people, whereas in the British periphery of the Roman Empire, the size varied from 500 or fewer up to the 17,000 inhabitants of London.

The heritage of Roman urbanization is considerable. Many sites have been continuously occupied since Roman times, for example, the city of Trier in Germany. Other sites were reoccupied after a period of abandonment. Contemporary city names are often corruptions of the original Latin form, such as London (Londinium). One of the most interesting names, Zaragoza, began as the Roman Caesarea Augusta and was corrupted by the Arabic Moorish conquerors to Zarakusta, and again by the Christian "reconquerors" of Spain to its present form.

The Medieval City

After the fall of the Roman Empire, Europe's urban population shrank. Some towns became totally abandoned, particularly north of the Alps; the disintegrating buildings provided stones for rural dwellers building cottages and fences. Europe entered its last great age of city-founding in the Middle Ages, taking advantage of increased security provided by the mature feudal system and greater agricultural productivity as the climate warmed between the ninth and fourteenth centuries. Germanic peoples established most of the new cities during this era. Europe's urban focus shifted to new regions, particularly the Po–Veneto Plain and the Germanic Low Country/Rhinelands in northwestern continental Europe (fig. 10.4).

A combination of factors explains the concentration of cities in these two regions. First, they were both areas of relative political stability. Second, they were agriculturally rich areas, for example, the Po Valley and the rich agricultural lowlands and deltas of the North European Plain. Finally, they were geographically strategic sites for the development of significant trade networks. Northern Italy was in a position to capture a share of trade movements across the Alps and could take advantage of the Po River and the northern Adriatic Sea to build a far-flung trade network. The Low

Figure 10.4.   Distribution of important cities, about 1500 CE. Northern Italy and northwestern continental Europe had become the new urban centers in Europe. Thousands of smaller towns do not appear on the map. *Source:* Norman J. G. Pounds, *Hearth and Home* (Bloomington: Indiana University Press, 1989), 260.

Country/Rhinelands area could take advantage of the great rivers draining northwest-ern continental Europe and their strategic location adjacent to the meeting point of the English Channel and the North Sea. These geographic advantages help explain why some of the largest cities at the time were Bruges, Ghent, Antwerp, and, across the English Channel, London.

Most of the towns in the Germanic Low Country/Rhinelands region grew from fortified preurban cores, sites dominated by the stronghold of a feudal lord. The ninth and tenth centuries had been a major period of castle construction by feudal landowners as they sought to secure the surrounding countryside. The catalysts in changing most preurban cores to towns were itinerant traders, who initially made use of secure marketplaces adjacent to strongholds along transport routes. In time, the desire for safe winter quarters led the traders to establish permanent residences in the preurban cores, creating merchant colonies. Artisans were attracted by the presence of merchants, and the town population grew steadily. In an early stage of development, a town often consisted of several distinct nuclei: the feudal fortress; one or more mar-ketplaces; scattered, fortified houses of merchants; a church; and some farmhouses. The German city of Braunschweig, for example, originated in 1269 through the union of five distinct nuclei, each of which had its own name. In an earlier era, Rome had arisen in a very similar manner as the union of adjacent hilltop villages.

CITY SITES

Geographers study diverse spatial and ecological aspects of urbanization. Perhaps none is more fundamental than an analysis of the specific physical location, or **site**, of a city. An easily defended site was particularly important to feudal lords who built strongholds during the insecure period after the Roman Empire fell. Romans them-selves rarely chose protected sites for their army camps and other settlements because their military force enjoyed superiority to that of neighboring tribes. Roman camps typically possessed offensive advantage along roads and navigable streams rather than on high points. Still, episodes of piracy in the classical and preclassical Mediterranean may well have influenced the defensive siting of Athens and Rome, both of which lie a short distance inland from the coast.

Many types of defensive sites exist. The **river-meander site**, with the city located inside a loop where the stream turns back upon itself, leaves only a narrow neck of land unprotected by the waters. Besançon on the Doubs River in far eastern France provides an example of a river-meander site. Incised meanders proved particularly popular because the river loop became permanent by cutting down to form a steep-sided valley. The city of Bern, capital of Switzerland, on the Aare River, offers a splendid example of an incised river-meander site, as does Toledo in Spain (fig. 10.5).

Similar to the river-meander site, but even more advantageous, the river-island site combined a natural moat with an easier river crossing, the latter an advantage for the merchant trade. Paris began on an island in the middle of a major river (the Île de la Cité in the Seine River), as did Limerick in Ireland and others. Stockholm, the capital of Sweden, occupies a lake-island site, originating on a dozen or so small

Figure 10.5. Toledo, in the central Meseta of Spain, an example of a river-meander urban site. The original settlement, now the core of the city, lay inside the loop of the incised meander of the Tajo River. Such a location provided natural defense on three sides. Photo by T. G. J.-B., 1986.

islands in the area where Lake Mälaren joins the Baltic Sea. Perhaps even more appealing, the offshore-island site combined defense with access to surrounding seas. The classic example, Venice, rests on wooden pilings driven into an offshore sandbar, which separated a coastal lagoon from the open Adriatic Sea. Larch wood imported from Russia serves as Venice's foundations. Defensive concerns were also an ingredient in the choice of sheltered harbor sites, where narrow sea entrances could easily be defended from attack by sea. Oslo, at the head of a fjord in Norway, and the Portuguese capital of Lisbon both occupy sheltered harbors.

High points offered obvious defensive advantages. Many towns lie at the foot of a fortified high point (fig. 10.6). Such cities often derived their names from the stronghold, as is indicated by many place names ending or beginning in *-burg*, *-bourg*, *-borg*, *castelo-*, *-grad*, and *-linna*, all of which mean *fortress* or *castle* in various European languages. Scottish Edinburgh (Edwin's fort), dominated by the impressive Castle Rock, provides a good example, as do Salzburg in Austria and Castelo Branco in Portugal. Other cities sited adjacent to fortified high points include Prague, Vaduz in Liechtenstein, Sion in Switzerland, and Budapest. Closely akin are those towns and cities that, in their formative stage, lay entirely on high ground, often adjacent to the stronghold. Examples include Belgrade (white fortress) on a high bluff overlooking the confluence of the Danube and Sava rivers; Segovia and Zamora in Spain; Laôn in France; Shaftesbury, a Saxon hill town in England; and Castelo de Vide in Portu-

Figure 10.6.   The city of Sion/Sitten, in the Swiss Canton of Valais/Wallis, an example of the high-point urban site. Sion developed at the foot of not one but two fortified high points, secular and ecclesiastical. The beautifully preserved fortresses still dominate the skyline of the city. Merchants who were responsible for creating the original urban nucleus chose to locate adjacent to the fortresses for reasons of security. Photo by T. G. J.-B., 1978.

gal. Often such hill towns in Romance-language lands bear the place name prefix *Mont-* or *Monte-*, as in Monte Corno, Italy.

Mercantalism, largely responsible for the development of cities from preurban cores, generally favored stronghold sites that lay on trade routes. Numerous types of sites possessed advantages for the merchants. In the early medieval period, before bridges became common, river ford sites, where the stream was shallow and its bed was firm, offered good sites. Some cities bear names that indicate the former importance of fords, including the German and English suffixes of *-furt* and *-ford*. Frankfurt (Franks' ford) in Germany lies at an easy crossing of the Main River, where the ancient trade route from the Upper Rhine Plain passes northward toward the North European Plain. Upstream on the Main River from Frankfurt lie the towns of Ochsenfurt (ford for oxen), Schweinfurt (swine ford), and Hassfurt (Hessians' ford). The English cities of Oxford on the Thames, Hertford on the Lea, and Bedford on the Ouse again suggest the former importance of river shallows in urban siting.

A similar function was served by sites where narrowed streams and firm banks and beds facilitated the building of bridges. Town names including *pont, bridge, brück*, and the like signal the centrality of the bridge to the urban area. Good bridge sites help explain the location of many cities founded in Roman times. Historic London Bridge, of which several have existed through history, originally stood at a point on the

Thames River, just upstream from the marsh-flanked estuary, at a site where the banks were firm and the stream was narrow. It served as an important river crossing on the Roman route from the Strait of Dover to the interior of England. Examples of bridge-centered cities from the medieval period include Cambridge (bridge on the Cam River) in England, Pontoise (bridge on the Oise River) near Paris, Bersenbrück (broken bridge) in northwestern Germany, Innsbruck (bridge on the Inn River) in Austria, and Puente-la-Reina (queen's bridge) in Spain.

Many city sites north of the Alps are riverine because navigable streams have long served as trade routes. Confluence sites, where two rivers meet, are common. The German city of Koblenz, at the juncture of the Rhine and the Mosel Rivers, actually derived its name from the Latin word for *confluence*, while Passau in the German province of Bavaria may be the only city where three rivers—the Danube, Inn, and Ilz—meet at precisely the same point. The rise of Paris was facilitated by the convergence of the Marne, Oise, and Seine rivers in the general vicinity of the city, and Lyon profited from its position at the confluence of the Rhône and Saône rivers. Head-of-navigation sites serve as transshipment points, such as Basel on the upper reaches of the navigable sector of the Rhine River in Switzerland. In countries such as Finland, where an intricate network of lakes and rivers provided the major trade routes, fortifications built at strategic narrows sometimes provided urban nuclei, as at Savonlinna (castle in Savo province) and Hämeenlinna (castle in Häme province).

Crossroad sites occur throughout Europe. One of the more famous is Vienna, the Austrian capital, located where an east–west route connecting the Hungarian Plain with southern Germany along the Danube Valley met the ancient north–south route, which skirted the eastern foot of the Alps and passed through the Moravian Gate to Poland and the Baltic Sea. Hanover in Germany stands at the juncture of an old route that runs along the southern edge of the North German Plain and the road that follows the course of the Leine River through the Hercynian hills south of the city. Leipzig was made famous by its trade fair, which occurred there because the city was situated at the intersection of two main trans-European trading roads during the Middle Ages.

Seaport sites often are found at or near the juncture of navigable rivers or estuaries and the coast, for example, London, Hamburg, Bordeaux, and Gdansk. In southern Europe, however, the seasonality of precipitation and short length of many streams rendered rivers less useful for transportation. Great ports usually developed at the juncture of highways and the coast rather than at the marshy, shallow river mouths. Cádiz lies some 30 kilometers south of the mouth of the Guadalquivir River, and Marseille is well to the east of the Rhône delta marshes in southern France. Other Mediterranean rivers such as the Po and Tevere also have no major ports at their mouths, in part because of silting.

Although mercantile activity was by far the most significant of the economic functions served by the medieval city, other economic factors sometimes affected city siting. Extraction of iron ore, copper, salt, silver, and other minerals or metals often gave rise to mining towns. In Germany and Austria, place names, including *salz* or *hall* (salt), *eisen* (iron), *gold*, and *kupfer* (copper), as in Salzburg in Austria as well as Eisenach and Kupferberg in Germany, indicate the present or former importance of mining.

The German city of Halle still has a saline spring in its very center, where the settlement began in Celtic times. Sites with perceived health benefits also developed into towns. Spa towns—some dating back to Roman times—developed around mineral or hot springs. These places typically bear names indicative of their function, including elements such as *bains*, *bad(en)*, or *bagni*, all of which mean *bath*. Examples include Wiesbaden in Germany, Bagnoli (bath) near Naples in Italy, and Luxeuil-les-Bains in eastern France. The English city of Bath, known to the Romans as Aquae Sulis, has an ancient resort tradition. In the Slavic lands, the name elements *-vody* (waters), as in Mineralny Vody (mineral waters), a city near the Caucasus Mountains, and *-vary* (hot springs), as in Karlovy Vary, Czechia, describe resort towns.

CITY ATTRIBUTES

The three essential attributes of most medieval northwestern European city were the charter, town wall, and marketplace. The charter, a governmental decree from an emperor or lesser ruler granting political autonomy to the town, freed its populace from the manorial restrictions of the rural areas that greatly limited individual freedoms. The city became self-governing and responsible for its own defense. Charters were typically requested by colonies of well-to-do merchants, who found that manorial restrictions hindered the mobility and exercise of personal initiative so vital in trading activities. Many cities date their founding from the granting of a charter, though most existed prior to that time. City-states similar to those of classical Greece, legitimized by charter, appeared throughout most of central and western Europe. So important were the charters that the citizens of the cities of medieval Flanders would build great towers to house them and to symbolize their freedoms. These towers dominated the skyline, sometimes even overshadowing the main church (fig. 10.7).

Self-government demanded self-defense, and the castles and fortified houses found in feudal kingdoms gave way to city walls (fig. 10.8). All important parts of the city lay inside the wall, including the mercantile and manufacturing establishments, fortress, church, and homes of the majority of the population. Urban expansion often required the construction of new, more inclusive walls, and some larger cities eventually needed three or four rebuildings. In the period before gunpowder came into widespread use, city walls were usually sufficient to repel invaders.

The marketplace, often supplemented by a trading hall (*bourse*), served as the focus of economic activity in the town, for the mercantile function remained dominant throughout the medieval period. Larger places held annual trade fairs, some of which began in the days of itinerant traders before permanent settlement had transformed the preurban cores into towns. Some of the more famous of these fairs survive to the present day, as at Leipzig, Frankfurt-am-Main, Milan, Lyon, and Lübeck (fig. 10.9).

Many of the cities in the northern Italian realm developed out of towns that could trace their roots to Roman times. There were exceptions. Most notably, Venice developed as a major city between the ninth and twelfth centuries on a series of inauspicious islands in a lagoon off Italy's northwestern coast. From that position, however,

Figure 10.7.   The skyline of Bruges, Belgium. The structures that attract attention are not just the church spires but the tower that housed the charter representing the freedoms of the city. Photo by A. B. M., 1986.

Figure 10.8.   Ávila, on the Castilian Meseta of interior Spain. The city retains its splendid ring of medieval walls. Photo by T. G. J.-B., 1986.

Figure 10.9. The central market square in Lübeck, Germany. An important site for traders when Lübeck was a leading city in the Hanseatic League, the square continues to be used today for weekly markets and annual trade fairs. Photo by A. B. M., 1973.

enterprising merchants were able to build an urban base that, for a time, dominated the exchange of goods between western/central Europe and the Byzantine and Islamic realms to the south and east. Venice was joined by a variety of other northern Italian towns that prospered through a combination of trade, agricultural production, and the manufacture of specialty goods.

Whether north or south of the Alps, most of the towns of the Middle Ages were modest in size. Few exceeded 100,000 in population. The famous textile center of Ghent had only 56,000 inhabitants in the mid-fourteenth century. Paris, the largest European city, and Naples were the only cities with more than 100,000 inhabitants by 1400. Moreover, the vast majority of people continued to live in rural areas. Nonetheless, in global comparative terms, the level of urbanization in Europe by 1400 was greater than any part of the world other than parts of South and East Asia.

MEDIEVAL URBAN MORPHOLOGY

Europe's medieval urban places were characterized by a distinctive morphology, or cityscape. In most cities north of the Alps and Pyrenees, the street pattern was irregular, a function of a lack of planning (fig. 10.10). The city's most important church, marketplace, and civic buildings were often found near the center of the town, but streets met at odd angles, and blocks (to the extent one can use that term) took on the shape of parallelograms or triangles. Many of these cities had walls, which gave rise to an abrupt urban–rural transition. As cities expanded and those walls had to be built farther out, the traces of the former walls were left in the street pattern. Note the inner circle of streets in the urban plan for Nördlingen (fig. 10.10).

In marked contrast to the irregular street pattern of most northern European cities, the cities of the south that could trace their roots to the Romans, Etruscans, or Greek colonists were characterized by a grid pattern. One can still see traces of the ancient pattern today in cities such as Pavia and Naples in Italy, Cologne (Köln) in Germany, Zaragoza in Spain, and Chester in England (fig. 10.11), although later disruptions often make it difficult to detect the original grid. In the late Middle Ages, the gridiron plan experienced a revival and served as the model for new towns founded by the Germans in east-central Europe and by the French kings in southern France. The latter were often fortified towns designed to help extend the control of the monarchy farther south during the thirteenth and fourteenth centuries. Sometimes they started with preexisting settlements, as was the case with the famous walled city of Carcassonne. The older city has an irregular street pattern, but the part constructed in the fourteenth century has a grid street pattern.

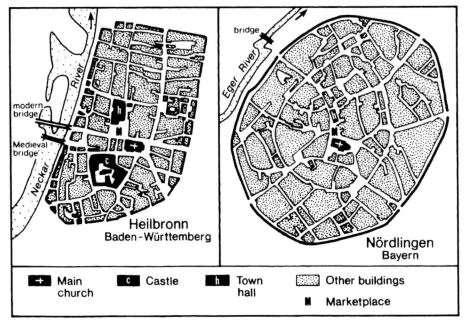

Figure 10.10.   Street plans of medieval towns in Germany. In Heilbronn, the castle-fortress, the Deutschherrenhof, was the successor to an ancient Frankish fortress. The church, town hall, and marketplace shared the center of the city with the fortress. Heilbronn was heavily damaged in World War II. Nördlingen, where the old outer wall is still intact, has the maze of streets typical of medieval towns. An earlier wall that was outgrown is clearly traced by the circular street. *Sources:* Erwin A. Gutkind, *International History of City Development* (New York: Free Press, 1964–1969); Dickinson 1945.

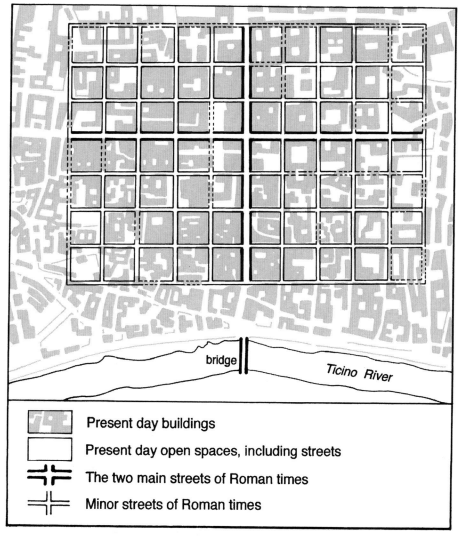

Figure 10.11.   Survival of the Roman grid pattern in Pavia, Italy. To walk in the central section of modern Pavia (Roman Ticinum) is to tread in the footsteps of the ancient Romans. The degree of survival of the Roman checkerboard pattern is quite remarkable, for most of the original streets are still in use after 20 centuries. The two main intersecting streets of Roman times have maintained their dominance. Note how much less regular the streets are outside the old Roman core. Pavia is on the Ticino River south of Milan. *Source:* After Erwin A. Gutkind, *International History of City Development* (New York: Free Press, 1964–1969).

Renaissance–Baroque Urban Development (1500–1800)

After about 1500, the founding of new cities declined markedly, except in the far north. Moreover, only a small portion of the European population was urbanized. In 1600, just 4 million of the 85 million Europeans lived in towns with populations of 15,000 or more, about 5% of the total. The Low Countries and northern Italy, the most highly urbanized areas, could claim only about 12 or 13% of their populations as urban, whereas only 2% of Germans, French, and English lived in large towns at that time.

Nonetheless, a number of noteworthy developments in the urban structure of Europe occurred from about 1500 to 1800. Most notably, this period saw the rise of national capital cities, particularly in western Europe. Fueled by the growing concentration of wealth associated with the increasingly successful European state-building project (see Chapter 6) and by the wealth flowing into parts of Europe from the early period of colonization, some cities exploded in size. In 1400, London had only 50,000 inhabitants, and Bristol, its major rival English port, had 30,000. Three centuries later, London had grown to 700,000 while Bristol remained at 30,000. Cities such as London, Amsterdam, Paris, and Madrid underwent dramatic modifications as they grew, as seen in major public projects that served to enhance their grandeur. In many cases, however, it was a grandeur not just born of internal successes but of an exploitive colonial relationship with other parts of the world.

A related feature of the Renaissance and Baroque periods was the growth of urban planning. Inspired by classical ideas and the field of geometry, Renaissance town builders laid out districts with, for example, radial street patterns focused on a royal palace. Cases such as Palmanova, Italy, provide an extreme case, with a street pattern radiating out in a full circle from a point at the center of the town (fig. 10.12). Not all parts of Europe had the resources or space to devote to such projects, however, and in some places, towns declined during this period. The disruption of trade ties in northern Italy, for example, led to some outmigration from towns and cities.

The Industrial City

European cities changed rapidly after about 1800 as a result of the Industrial Revolution. Manufacturing became the dominant function of many urban centers, putting an end to the age of mercantile cities (see Chapter 8). The hallmark of the industrial phase was a great increase in city size, prompted by the gravitation of the majority of the European population to urban, industrial areas. England and Wales urbanized more than half their population by the 1850s. A half century later, more than three-quarters of the English and Welsh lived in cities, and Germany had become the second country to have over half of its population living in urban areas. Many other countries, especially in northwestern Europe, reached this level by 1930, and the trend continues to spread toward the peripheries (fig. 10.1).

The Industrial Revolution produced new cities in places such as northern England and Germany's Ruhr Valley. It also gave rise to the first European cities to have more than a million inhabitants. London passed the million mark in the first decade of the nineteenth century and exceeded two million by 1850. Paris claimed more than a million by 1846. By the turn of the twentieth century, Berlin, Vienna, St.

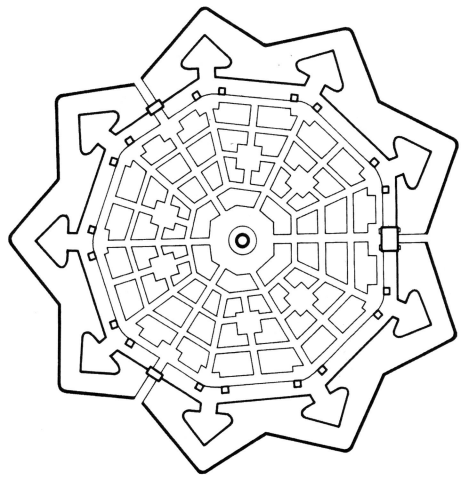

Figure 10.12.   Central part of Palmanova, Italy, in the far eastern Po–Veneto Plain. Founded in 1593 during the Renaissance era, Palmanova displays a highly planned street pattern, as did most of the cities established after the end of the Middle Ages.

Petersburg, and Moscow had reached this level. As people and industry arrived in already established cities, they found a **preindustrial core** that was often relatively densely packed and fairly prosperous. Around that core was a **preindustrial periphery** where more recent, poorer immigrants had concentrated. As industrialization unfolded, this was the area where the railroad stations could be built. The tight clustering of venerated, old structures made it impossible for railroad lines to penetrate the preindustrial core. Large cities such as Paris and London have a circle of rail terminals, and the stations typically bear the name of the major city that lies on their rail route. In Paris, one finds the Gare de Lyon (station of Lyon) at the terminus of the rail line leading out to that city to the south, the Gare St. Lazare, the Gare d'Orléans, and so on. In some instances, one suburban railroad station serves as the main one

Figure 10.13. The Champs Elysées in Paris, a classic example of a nineteenth-century urban development project designed to highlight the glories of France and facilitate movement within the French capital. Photo by A. B. M., 2001.

where trains for all destinations may be taken, but the traveler must sometimes choose correctly among five or more stations to find the right train.

In time, the crowded slums of the preindustrial periphery gave way to more substantial buildings as the city grew, and some prosperous neighborhoods developed. In function, this ring came to be dominated by residences, railroad stations, and retail activity. In capital cities, a nationalist-infused desire to develop visually impressive symbols of greatness (fig. 10.13), and a concern to break up or control worker ghettos, led to plans to build grand, straight ceremonial avenues or boulevards in the preindustrial periphery, sometimes even penetrating into the preindustrial core. Thousands of Parisians, for example, lost their homes through royal decree to make way for a set of *Grands Boulevards* on the right bank of the Seine. These impressive avenues provide a marked contrast to the remainder of the street pattern.

As the preindustrial periphery was made over, the poorer people, the new migrants, and many of the factories were pushed out to another ring around the European city, the **industrial suburb**. This area was often characterized by a dingy halo of factories, large apartment blocks or row houses for the workers, and railroad yards. Yet this became the largest part of the typical European city, dwarfing the older preindustrial core and periphery. It housed the burgeoning population that made Europe dominantly urbanized, as commoners finally became urbanites.

Characteristics of the Mid-Twentieth-Century European City

By the middle of the twentieth century, the effects of industrialization had been felt in most European cities, and some were on the cusp of entering a postindustrial era. Most European cities have experienced significant change since then, but a template was well established by the middle of the twentieth century that still is very much in evidence and that continues to influence what these cities look like and how they function. That template reflected many of the different influences on city development described above. As we review its main characteristics, it may be useful to think about how the identified characteristics differ from the typical North American city, as such an exercise can provide insights into the role urban morphology and social geography play in the life of cities.

The most notable characteristics of the mid-twentieth-century European city were:

1. *A set of more or less concentric rings* with the preindustrial core at the center, surrounded by the preindustrial periphery, surrounded by the industrial suburbs. The preindustrial core encompassed the mercantile city of earlier times, including all districts that formerly lay within the ramparts and walls. Remnants of these walls often survived, marking the outer limits of the core. The famous Porta Nigra (black gate) in the German city of Trier is a Roman survival, while the Holstentor (Holstein gate) at Lübeck survives as a remnant of medieval walls. In some instances, the entire circuit of city walls enclosing the old core remained in place. Still today Lugo in Spanish Galiza retains its Roman walls, and Ávila in the Castilian heartland of Spain boasts a medieval ring of walls and gates that ranks among Europe's finest (fig. 10.8). More often, the walls no longer exist, their place taken by a ring street and a string of parks. Riga in Latvia and Frankfurt-am-Main fit this description, as do many other places.

2. *A low degree of **functional zonation**,* that is, the separation of different functions into different spaces. Each of the rings had a mix of residences, retail establishments, and manufacturing activities. The medieval custom of combining residence and place of work continued on, and most cities never had zoning ordinances such as those common to North American cities. Many bakers, butchers, and restaurant owners lived above their shops, and it was not unusual to encounter small-scale manufacturing and a variety of services activities taking place right next to apartments and retail establishments.

3. *A high degree of compactness.* In comparison to North American urban centers, mid-twentieth-century European cities of comparable population covered less extensive geographical areas (fig. 10.14). A foreign visitor could easily gain the impression that European cities were smaller in terms of population than they actually were. In 1960, for example, single-family detached homes accounted for

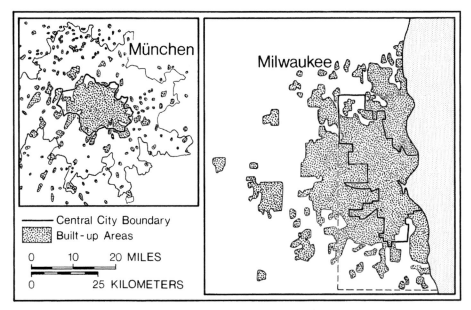

Figure 10.14. Munich (München), Germany, and Milwaukee, Wisconsin, metropolitan areas drawn to the same scale. The two urban areas have similar populations, but notice how much more compact the built-up area of Munich is. *Source:* After Lutz Holzner, in *Research Profile* (University of Wisconsin–Milwaukee Graduate School) 9, n. 2 (1986): 18.

only 16% of all urban residences in West Germany. Throughout Europe, many urbanites preferred to live close to the center of town, where the old city core served as a place to gather after work, to stroll, and to dine. Many city dwellers resided at least within walking or cycling range of their place of employment, though commuting was becoming increasingly common.

4. *An irregular street pattern in the preindustrial core and periphery.* This street pattern was a product of the unplanned development that occurred before the Industrial Revolution, and it was only altered when decisions were made to channel industrial wealth into the kinds of grand urban-planning initiatives described above. But irregularity was the norm. In parts of southern Europe, particularly Iberia, Arabic influence produced a particularly twisted maze of streets with numerous dead ends, as in the old quarters of Toledo, Lisbon, and Seville. As cities industrialized and grew, planners often succeeded in creating more regular street patterns farther from the core, but even there a strict regularity was hard to achieve because of the need to connect the new street pattern with the old, winding pattern of the core. Most of the streets in the core were narrow and ill suited for the age of the automobile, and, in many places, attempts to modify the crazy quilt pattern of streets and render it more suitable for motorized traffic flow were resisted. Wartime destruction leveled as much as 80% of the buildings in some German cities, providing an opportunity to revise street patterns in the central portions. Urban planners wanted to lay out broader and straighter streets, but few West German cities actually acquired thoroughfares in the process of rebuilding. There were exceptions, of course. The Dutch and British reconstructions of

Rotterdam and Coventry produced cities better adapted to the needs of the automobile. But most cities kept their irregular street patterns, leading to traffic problems that have become ever more critical because of the narrowness of thoroughfares and the scarcity of parking space.

5. *A religious building or palace at the symbolic center of the city.* Unlike American urban areas such as Chicago, where an intersection at the center of the commercial district has long served as the focal point of the city, the equivalent in most European cities was (and still is) a building of religious or governmental significance at the heart of the old preindustrial core, often in conjunction with a square or marketplace. Impressive cathedrals are particularly common focal points, bearing witness to the extraordinary importance and vitality of Christianity in the Middle Ages. Even as early as the era of classical Greece, municipal pride in public buildings and religious edifices was one of the traits that distinguished townsfolk from residents of farm villages, and citizens bore the large expense involved in cathedral construction with little complaint. Many of these churches—such as Notre Dame de Paris on the Île de la Cité; San Marco in Venice; St. Stephen's in Vienna; the magnificent cathedral at Chartres southwest of Paris; and Santa María in Burgos, Spain—rank among the great architectural treasures of the world. If the city served as the residence of a royal family, the focal point might have been a palace or fortress. Examples include Edinburgh Castle in Scotland and the Palazzo Ducale in Venice, the latter located right next to the cathedral.

Figure 10.15. Paris, looking westward from the Tour Montparnasse. An American would mistake this as a view toward the center of the city, whereas in reality the modern high-rise buildings stand outside the central city. Photo by A. B. M., 2012.

6. *A skyline with the tallest buildings on the periphery.* Standing in contrast to the North American city, which is dominated by high-rise buildings at the center of the city, most of the commercial skyscrapers and tall apartment blocks in the typical European city were constructed outside the urban core, often in the industrial suburbs (fig. 10.15). This is still true today. The central skyline of most cities will have a few tall structures such as church spires, a venerable hilltop fortress, or a special landmark such as the Eiffel Tower. But the urban core is dominated by historic buildings of considerable age, erected before the elevator and modern structural technology permitted thin-walled buildings to reach great heights. Edifices of more than five or six stories are uncommon. Even when catastrophes destroy the old urban cores, Europeans generally rebuild them as before, keeping the taller buildings on the periphery. Photographs of pre– and post–World War II Munich reveal striking similarities, even though 80% of the city was destroyed by bombing. Perhaps the most remarkable re-creation took place in the former German Baltic port city of Danzig (present-day Gdansk) in Poland since 1945. The German population of the severely damaged city was expelled, but the Poles then proceeded to spend huge sums of money to produce a duplicate of the old German Hanseatic city. Their attention to detail in reconstruction was simply astounding. The end product was a museum town from another age. Yet with time, effort, and money, Poland solidified a valid claim to a city that Germans and Russians had destroyed.

7. *A concentration of significant wealth in the core.* North Americans sometimes think of the inner city (outside the central business district) as a zone of poverty and crime. But the cores of most European cities were very different. Traditionally, the most expensive and prestigious residences had been near the city center, creating a concentration of wealth at the heart of the city that often endured. There were pockets of poverty nearby, and areas where only those of a certain ethnic background or those practicing a particular craft would live (see Chapter 11), but the heart of the preindustrial core was generally a prosperous area with a variety of small retail stores, cafés, restaurants, multifamily residences, and workshop-like factories of craftsmen workers. Guild houses of the medieval crafts still stood in some preindustrial urban cores, as did the old trading hall for merchants. Institutional functions also remained common in the central city, including governmental agencies and museums. By contrast, most recent immigrants and members of the poorer working class moved to the peripheries, where land was cheaper and low-skills jobs were found.

The Late/Postindustrial European City

Sweeping changes have occurred in the European city over the past five to six decades. The principal catalysts for change are:

- The decline of secondary industry
- The rise of tertiary and quaternary activities

- The expansion of public transportation networks
- Growing automobile ownership
- The arrival of new immigrants
- The growing size and prosperity of the middle class

These circumstances helped to bring about suburbanization, counterurbanization, and gentrification—three developments that have had a significant impact on the character of the typical European city over the last 60 years.

Since about 1950, some wealthier Europeans began to move out beyond the industrial suburbs to a newly developing outer ring of **postindustrial suburbs**. The outer ring consists of a loose assemblage of low-density residences dominated by detached single-family houses, modern factories devoted to high-tech industry, and firms specializing in data gathering and processing. Some planned satellite towns also appear in this ring, as do the garden plots and dachas (cottages used sometimes as summer homes, particularly in Russia) of the inner-city population. In spite of the low density of building, the outer ring sometimes contains American-inspired, high-rise commercial structures made of glass and steel. Access to the city center by mass transit is normally available. Typically, the outer ring developed in segments and remains incomplete. In London, where the outer ring lies beyond a zoned, largely open green belt, a high-class residential fringe began taking shape in the western periphery by the 1950s, and it has since spread clockwise around to the northeast.

In other words, **suburbanization** is occurring in Europe. Though it began later than in North America, due in part to a lag in accepting the private automobile to commute to work, suburban development is bringing urban problems very similar to those in the United States, especially sprawl on the peripheries of cities and decay in the center. The suburban shopping mall, another symptom of urban Americanization, made its appearance in Europe's outer rings in the 1980s. France, the United Kingdom, Italy, and Germany now have hundreds of malls. From Lisbon to Budapest and beyond, shopping malls with hundreds of stores have opened over the past twenty years, and they are transforming the retail landscape. Some countries have passed legislation in an effort to control the proliferation of malls, but the retail patterns of most sizable cities have been Americanized to a fairly significant extent.

In the period after about 1965, **counterurbanization**, the movement of population from the largest cities to areas that lie beyond the commuting range of those cities, also became more common. For a time, counterurbanization caused some of Europe's larger cities to stagnate or decline, while villages and smaller urban places grew. This trend, in turn, gave rise to larger second- and third-order cities in Europe. The movement away from cities was typically driven by the more affluent segment of the population, and it often occurred in stages, beginning with the acquisition of a second home for vacation purposes. An author, data processor, or designer came to realize that his or her job could be performed just as well in locations remote from the urban office.

The sudden, rapid decline of such traditional manufacturing industries as textiles and steel also caused many economically specialized cities to lose less well-off segments of the population. Among the hardest hit by manufacturing decline were Glasgow,

Manchester, Belfast, Turin, and many cities in the formerly Communist East. Equally important, waves of foreign immigrant guest workers began arriving in parts of many cities, causing some longer-term residents to flee.

The United Kingdom, the first country to urbanize massively, became the first to feel the effects of counterurbanization in the 1960s. West Germany experienced an almost simultaneous onset of the phenomenon, followed by the Low Countries, France, and Denmark. In France, the period from 1975 to 1982 saw the rural population grow more rapidly than the urban population for the first time in well over a century. France's Atlantic coastal, Mediterranean, and Alpine provinces gained population most rapidly.

Counterurbanization slowed in most countries in the 1980s, leading some urban geographers to label it as a temporary shift. France experienced a resurgence of growth in the largest metropolitan areas by 1990, and only the decaying heavily industrial cities exhibit long-term population losses. Germany, too, saw a slowing down of counterurbanization in the late 1980s, following 15 years during which the trend intensified. Today, counterurbanization is occurring most profoundly in eastern Europe. The cities of the southern Urals region in Russia are among the most severely impacted.

The slowing or reversal of counterurbanization throughout much of Europe can be attributed in part to a recent movement of people back into cities—particularly individuals living alone and couples without children. These people are lured by the proximity of urban amenities and the ease with which they can access their places of work. The **gentrification** of formerly poor areas within major cities has facilitated the move back to cities. Gentrification refers to the rehabilitation of deteriorated or abandoned areas within urban areas in an effort to replace low income with more affluent populations. Gentrification can occur either through the private property market, that is, individuals or firms buying up and converting areas, or it can be a product of urban redevelopment policies. Both are common in Europe, and they have made the cities more attractive places to live for the middle and upper classes. But the less well-off have faced displacement and the prospect of moving to even less desirable areas.

Generous social welfare policies have blunted the social impacts of gentrification to some degree (see Chapter 11), but gentrification can still pose significant challenges for the poor. Perhaps the group most adversely affected consists of urban squatters—homeless people who illegally take up residence in derelict, empty buildings. Called *kraakers* in the Netherlands and *squats* in Britain, this preponderantly young group began moving into abandoned central city buildings in the 1960s. Amsterdam, London, Hamburg, West Berlin, and Copenhagen became the major scenes of urban squatting. The movement peaked in the 1980s, and it has since largely succumbed to police pressure and gentrification.

On a more positive note, the gentrification of abandoned areas in old industrial cities can be a boost to the city at large. The redevelopment of former industrial areas in cities such as Duisburg in Germany's Ruhr Valley is bringing new people into the city and even attracting some tourists (fig. 10.16). Gentrification is also improving the fiscal viability of some cities that were struggling from the loss of tax revenue as people moved out to the suburbs and beyond.

Figure 10.16.   Urban redevelopment in Duisburg, Germany. Middle-class residents, and even some tourists, are being drawn into old industrial districts. Photo by A. B. M., 2001.

These general processes have worked together with the economic, social, and technological developments mentioned at the beginning of this section to change, at least to some degree, the character of the typical mid-twentieth-century European city. But the change has only been partial because many of the characteristics of the industrial city described above could not easily be altered. The best way to see what has remained the same and what has changed is to look at the modern city in terms of its various rings.

THE PREINDUSTRIAL CORE

Changes to the preindustrial core have been comparatively minor. As in the industrial period, this part of the city is generally prosperous and suffers relatively low levels of blight, decay, and crime. In most instances, the preindustrial core is still dominated by compact settlement, low levels of functional zonation, older buildings, and winding streets. Automobile traffic moves with great difficulty, for thoroughfare avenues are rare. Though some European central cities remain choked by automobile traffic, a number have taken major steps to restrict motorist access. Parking space has been drastically reduced, bicycle routes have been provided, and mass transit has been upgraded. Zürich eliminated 10,000 central city parking spaces, and governmental restrictions on automobile traffic in cities such as Amsterdam, Freiburg in Germany, and (most recently) London have led to significant declines in the use of cars in the inner city. In some cities, public bicycle sharing programs have been launched—giving people free access to bicycles for short-distance trips. In cities such as Amsterdam and Heidelberg, bicycles seem to outnumber automobiles. A particularly noteworthy response to the challenges presented by the street pattern has been to designate certain streets or even entire districts as pedestrian zones. Pedestrians in these areas no longer feel intimidated by traffic or repelled by the visual blight of machine space.

Certain well-preserved urban central areas have become virtual outdoor museums, bypassed by the usual range of economic activity. Some central city dwellers complain that they cannot be expected to live in an unchanging, romanticized setting of past times. The crumbling architectural heritage of the past is expensive to maintain and difficult to adjust to the modern age. Venice's core area, largely a historic district, provides an extreme example. Plagued by flooding, decay, and pollution, Venice's historic central area population has declined from 137,000 in 1961 to only 60,000 today.

In an effort to preserve the historic character of central cities while adapting them to the needs of the twenty-first century, **façadism** (the complete gutting and remodeling of the interior of a building while preserving its façade) has become increasingly popular. Outwardly, buildings look much as they did 500 years ago; inwardly, they are a product of the contemporary era.

THE PREINDUSTRIAL PERIPHERY

The preindustrial periphery is a zone where redevelopment and gentrification have been particularly concentrated. As a result, in the typical city, there are fewer pockets of poverty in this zone than in previous times. Much of the urban landscape remains historic in character, but it is more likely to be punctuated by modern structures and developments than is the landscape of the preindustrial core. Former industrial sites are particularly common candidates for redevelopment. Since this part of the city is often redeveloped in chunks, functional zonation is somewhat higher than in the preindustrial core, but it is still low in comparison with the typical North American city. In some cases, major upscale shopping districts have developed in this part of the city, taking advantage of the proximity of many well-to-do consumers and easy-to-use public transportation facilities.

A controlled-access perimeter highway often marks the outer limits of the preindustrial periphery. Inside that highway, regulations often keep buildings at relatively low heights. Street patterns remain fairly irregular, but there are more thoroughfares and arteries than in the preindustrial core. In many cases, the most important of these follow the routes of former roads leading out of the medieval city. Paris's Avenue d'Italie, running through the southern part of the city's preindustrial periphery, is the old road one would have taken out of the old city to go to Italy. Street names can be tricky in Europe, though, as they change frequently, even in places where the street does not take a notable turn. Munich provides an extreme example. Over a length of only six blocks, one reasonably straight street bears the names Maxburgstrasse, Löwengrube, Schäfflstrasse, Schrammerstrasse, and Hofgraben.

THE INDUSTRIAL SUBURBS

Since these areas were not developed prior to the Industrial Era, most buildings are relatively modern, and many are tall. Modern and tall does not necessarily mean nice, however. Many were erected hurriedly and cheaply to house an influx of low-wage workers. Others were developed to meet the industrial needs of the late nineteenth and early twentieth centuries, only to fall into wrack and ruin as the economic tides turned. The industrial suburbs are not uniformly areas of poverty. Some parts developed as middle-class areas with good, quality housing and nice public amenities. Whether the housing is in good shape or not, much of it takes the form of high-rise apartment complexes.

Population density is generally high in the industrial suburbs, but parks and shopping centers are relatively common, and streets are relatively wide. In some places, large tracts of land in particularly poor parts of the industrial suburbs were entirely redeveloped in the post–World War II era. Basically, everything was cleared, and a district of a very different character was planned and built from scratch. In some cases, the goal was to create a middle-class residential area. In others, it was to make room for a postindustrial center for business and commerce. Perhaps the most famous example is La Défense, just outside of Paris proper (fig. 10.17). To the extent that Paris has a downtown reminiscent of something like midtown Manhattan, this is where it is found.

Figure 10.17. La Défense, a hub of Paris's quaternary economy, lies just beyond the preindustrial periphery. Photo by A. B. M., 2001.

THE POSTINDUSTRIAL SUBURBS

On the periphery of most European cities lie the newest suburbs, home to the residences of wealthier people and selected tertiary and quaternary economic activities. We have already reviewed the principal characteristics of these suburbs; they tend to be less compact with a mix of nice apartment blocs, stand-alone houses, and tertiary- and quaternary-sector businesses. Where single-family houses are found, lots tend to be considerably smaller than in the suburbs of Canada or the United States, and front yards are often absent. For apartment dwellers in this zone, as well as in the nicer industrial suburbs, garden allotments serve in effect as backyards. Large tracts of *kleingärten* (small garden complexes) can be found on the periphery of many German cities; indeed, this phenomenon has spread to cities throughout Europe. These allotments were intended as places where urban dwellers could escape their apartments and the unhealthy inner-city environment to the relative solitude of a small hut or garden.

Generally, population densities are much lower in the postindustrial suburbs, and street patterns are more regular, a function of modern planning. Nonetheless, it is much rarer in Europe than in North America to find houses standing off completely by themselves. Instead, they tend to be built adjacent to one another, creating a relatively sharp break between urban and rural. The break may be less abrupt than in the days when city walls were common, but the inertia of a long-standing settlement pattern with a sharp break between urban and rural helps explain why the edges of European cities are so much more distinct than their North American counterparts.

Regional Variations

So far we have emphasized some basic characteristics shared by most European cities, but some generalized regional differences are also worth highlighting. Figure 10.18 identifies a few basic regions in Europe where cities share some broad commonalities. Looking at the characteristics of each of these regions requires us to generalize at a fairly high level, of course, because each city possesses its own distinct character and personality. But such an exercise provides interesting insights into the variable geographic influences that have shaped urban development in different parts of Europe.

The **British city**, more than others in Europe, resembles the urban centers of the United States, although major differences between the two can also be identified. Both British and American cities tend to have a comparatively high rate of owner-occupied housing and detached or semidetached single-family residences, and they are usually surrounded by suburbs that grew rapidly in the post–World War II period. Inner urban decay and blight, coupled with poverty, diminishing services, and crime, afflict many of the major British conurbations. Indeed, concerns over urban decline and crisis have long been heard in Great Britain—fueling suburbanization and counterurbanization. This dispersal also feeds upon the British perception that the real England lies in the countryside and that the city is an anomalous aberration. Suburban expansion causes the British city to be less compact than normal for

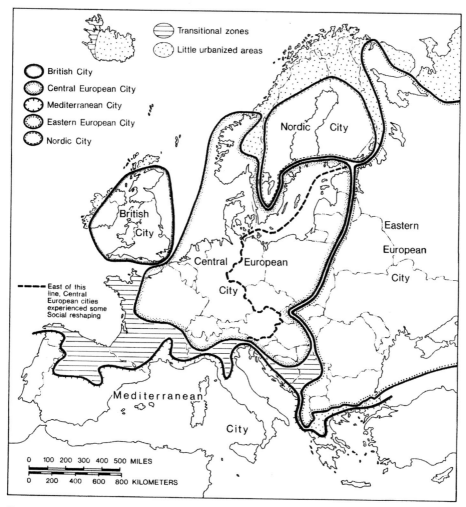

Figure 10.18.   Distribution of European city types. Considerable overlapping of types occurs but is not shown, as for example where socialist influences partially reshaped many central European cities in the Communist era. *Sources:* Leontidou 1990; Hamilton 1978; Ford 1985; Gritsai 1997; Pacione 1997; Sabelberg 1986.

Europe, and it produces a steep population density gradient from core to periphery. Americans find all these British conditions familiar, but continental Europeans are more likely to regard them as odd and generally undesirable.

At the same time, the British city has experienced far more inner-area gentrification than its American counterpart has, and the government has been quite active in the effort to stem decay. In Belfast, for example, the proportion of unfit housing declined from 25% to 8% between 1978 and 1992, largely as a result of public expenditures on urban regeneration. The figure now lies below 5%. The walled inner city of Londonderry (or Derry, as Irish separatists prefer) has undergone refurbishment, the once-blighted East End district of Glasgow became transformed in the

1980s, Newcastle has been undergoing massive urban renewal in recent years, and many similar projects are under way elsewhere.

The **central European city** conforms most closely to what we have been describing as the typical European city (fig. 10.18). In origin, the central European city reflects mainly the period of urban genesis led by Germanic peoples during the feudal Middle Ages. The early attainment of city-state status, which allowed a quasi-democratic form of government to take root in the Germanic cities while the countryside remained under feudal despotism, fostered a sense of urban superiority and a strong antirural bias. One is either a *burgher* (a city dweller) or a *bauer* (a farmer). City governments, visually represented by the town hall, retain considerable importance. Some cities even preserve a vestige of their former independent city-state rule; for example, Hamburg and Bremen enjoy provincial status within Germany, and Luxembourg remains, in effect, a free city-state. Many central European citizens attach great importance to the preindustrial core, the root of urban self-government and democracy. As a result, central city decay has never approached the British levels (fig. 10.19). The preindustrial core, wreathed by parks and remnant walls, remains a prestigious place to live, and historic preservation and renewal projects, including abundant façadism, are common. The central public square usually retains great importance. In World War II, many German preindustrial cores were destroyed by

Figure 10.19.   The preindustrial core of the small Hessian city of Weilburg, on the Lahn River in Germany. A typical central European city, Weilburg perches on an incised meander of the river. The urban core retains its royal palace, cathedral, and town hall. Many people still reside in the central city, though new suburbs appear in the distance. Little evidence of urban decay can be found in such places. Photo by T. G. J.-B., 1991.

bombing, but these old districts, so prized by the citizenry, were lovingly rebuilt, a process still under way today in cities such as Hamburg (fig. 10.20).

Counterurbanism and suburbanization, blunted by the appeal and snobbery of the city and the antirural bias, proved weaker than in Britain. In housing density, the central European city falls between the extremes of the British urban area with its relatively high number of single-family residences and the cities of southern and eastern Europe, where apartment housing prevails. Urban planning and land-use zoning enjoy

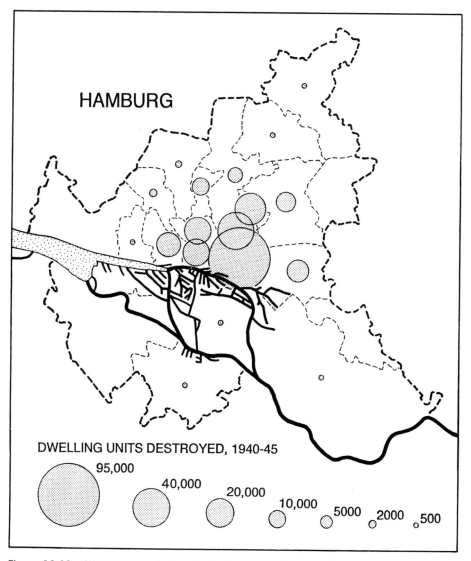

Figure 10.20. War damage to housing in Hamburg, Germany. Destruction was most profound in the old preindustrial core, but the visitor today will not find much evidence of the damage. Most Europeans prize very highly their medieval urban cores. *Sources:* City of Hamburg, *Hamburg in Zahlen*, Statistisches Landesamt 29 (1951): 6.

popular support and have greatly contributed to the renewal, aesthetic appeal, and livability of cities. The pedestrian zone movement began here and still enjoys its greatest acceptance in central Europe.

In some areas, the problems associated with British cities have taken root in central Europe, but they are aggressively combated. Nonetheless, examples of blight and decay can be found in economically depressed industrial cities in Germany's Ruhr area and the coalfields of the Belgian–French border region, as well as in many cities in the east that were long under Communist rule.

Some Central European cities experienced a half century or more of Communist rule, which imposed rigid socialist control over what had been a capitalistic urban structure. Warsaw, Budapest, Leipzig, Prague, and Riga provide examples. These cities all bore the earlier imprint of central European urban culture. Socialist ideals and planning never completely transformed them, though change did come. In Warsaw, for example, an early Communist-directed residential mixing of social groups after 1945 steadily gave way during the following 40 years to a reemergence of class-based neighborhoods. Budapest became an odd amalgamation of central European and Communist urbanism (fig. 10.21). Most of these cities have even more rapidly regained their central European character and identity since the fall of Communism in the early 1990s.

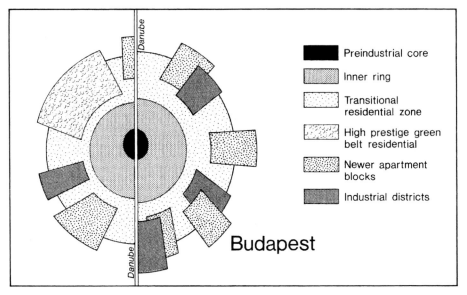

Figure 10.21.   A stylized scheme of modern Budapest. A central European type of city in heritage, Budapest reflects that tradition in its preindustrial core and inner ring. A socialist city from the late 1940s until 1990, Budapest accordingly has peripheral apartment blocks located adjacent to industrial complexes. The high-prestige green belt represents an anomaly for a Communist city and reflects significant new influences on urban development in Hungary, beginning as early as 1970. Source: Enyedi and Szirmai 1992, 99.

In the **Mediterranean city**, a greater spontaneity of growth and development occurred with minimal attention to urban planning or zoning (fig. 10.18). The Germanic rural–urban dichotomy is less common in Mediterranean civilization, and the transition from the city to the countryside is more gradual. Since classical times, many farmers and rural laborers have resided in Mediterranean cities. Less social segregation occurs, and the juxtaposition of good and bad districts is common. A diversity of social classes is found in most parts of the Mediterranean city in mixed neighborhoods, though squatter slums and low-income apartment high-rises dominate many outer peripheries.

Small workshops of self-employed artisans are scattered through the city, and mixed land use reflects the lack of zoning or, more exactly, widespread disregard for zoning regulations. Owners more typically live above their places of business than in the British or central European cities, and most other people live close to where they work. Inhabitants tend to view the city rather than the home as the principal venue for life; as a result, more people are to be seen in the streets, plazas, and shops. A central business district in the British/Germanic sense is not common, and small shops appear even in the finer residential neighborhoods. To the Germanic eye, the Mediterranean city might seem disorderly, but the people of the south instead see their cities as places of light, heat, and spontaneity, a welcome contrast to the more cold, disciplined cities north of the Alps.

Mediterranean cities represent the most compact type in Europe, with very high residential densities and virtually no development of an outer ring. High-status residential areas instead lie in the preindustrial periphery, adjacent to the preindustrial core and linked to it by a fine boulevard (fig. 10.22). While the old, walled part of the town retains great prestige and swarms with life, much of it is given over to institutional functions, especially schools, museums, churches, and convents. A failure to restrict automobile access to the center creates a nightmare of traffic congestion, noise, and air pollution in the preindustrial core, and the pedestrian-zone concept is only beginning to take hold. The periphery of the Mediterranean city is the most stigmatized section. Industries are concentrated there, as are poor people. Many of them live in spartan high-rise apartment blocks.

The **eastern European city** bears the residual imprint of socialism and Communism (fig. 10.18). In fact, this urban type was formerly called the **socialist city**. Eastern Europe was very weakly urbanized prior to the Communist era. In the Soviet Union in 1926, for example, only 18% of the population lived in cities. By 1989, however, the proportion of urbanites reached 66%. In such countries, socialist doctrine shaped urban development in diverse ways, and the legacy will persist long into the future. Under Communism, the government controlled urban development, including the demand for and supply of housing. Land, in effect, had no monetary value.

In its idealized form, the socialist city was suppose to:

- Minimize socioeconomic residential segregation
- Guarantee availability of public services such as child care
- Provide abundant public green space

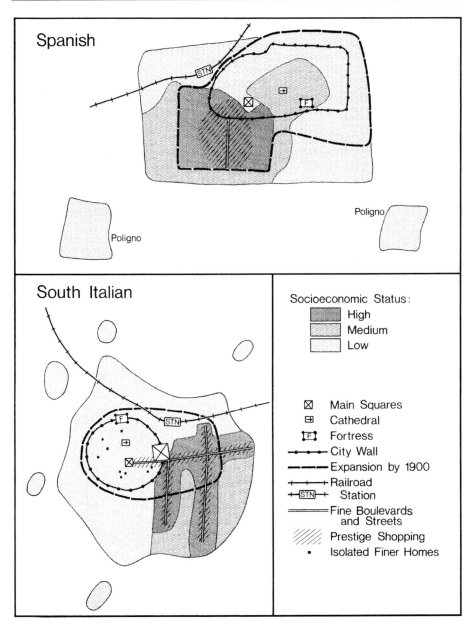

Figure 10.22.   Models of the typical Spanish and southern Italian city provide examples of the Mediterranean city type, but they are sufficiently distinctive to be considered regional subtypes. The outlying clusters, called *polignos* in Spain, are recent laborer apartment blocks or squatter settlements. In the southern Italian type, the core has a maze of dead-end streets and remains largely residential, while in the Spanish type, most of the core is now institutional and has connecting streets. *Sources:* Ford 1985, 268; Sabelberg 1986; Fusch 1994; Pacione 1987.

- Offer equal, if rudimentary, access to all consumer goods
- Create self-sufficient, small neighborhoods where residents lived, worked, and shopped

In many respects, eastern European cities still reflect these socialist goals, particularly in Russia, Ukraine, Belarus, and the Balkans. The eastern European city resembles a collection of separate towns tied together. Population densities remain remarkably high in comparison to cities in most of the remainder of Europe, and the normal gradient toward lower densities on the urban periphery is retarded and, in some cities, even reversed, with an outer rim of higher concentration of people (fig. 10.23). All of Moscow has a population density comparable to that of central London.

Less marked functional zonation occurs within the city than in the west, including a much more even spread of industries throughout the urban area, a phenomenon associated with the former absence of a cash market in land. Social, economic, and ethnic segregation by districts or sectors is diminished. Workers in a particular industry might be segregated in response to a desire to minimize the journey to work. Public mass transportation prevails, though growing prosperity has meant a significant expansion in the use of automobiles. In comparison to the west, a higher proportion of the urban workforce finds employment in manufacturing, construction, and transportation, with lower percentages in trade, administration, and services—though the situation is changing rapidly. Moscow no longer has much of an industrial vocation but is instead dominated by postindustrial economic activities.

Figure 10.23. The northern periphery of Moscow. Huge complexes of high-rise apartments produce dense concentrations of population even on the outer margins of the city, a typical phenomenon in the eastern European city type. Even so, much green space is preserved, catering to the Russian love of the forest. Photo by T. G. J.-B., 1997.

Other socialist ideals will long leave a visible legacy in the European east. During the Communist era, authorities sought to convey the power of the state. Governmental buildings of overwhelming size, reflecting monumentality in architecture, provide one example. Oversized public squares, in which mass political rallies could be held, appear gargantuan, cold, and empty at other times. And the cult of personality associated with some Communist dictatorships, most notoriously in Romania and Albania, allowed megalomaniacal leaders to massively reshape cities, often destroying much of the beauty from earlier eras. The pre-Communist city disappeared from central Bucharest, and the imprint of a personality cult will long linger there.

At the same time, many eastern European cities have had to cope with decaying infrastructure—a product of rapidly constructed and inadequately maintained buildings inherited from the socialist era. But pervasive change has come since the fall of Communism. Moscow, the Russian capital, provides an example, if somewhat atypical. A July 1991 decree provided for privatization of apartments in Russian cities. In Moscow, some 25% of all housing had been privatized by 1993, as had nearly 5,000 businesses, mainly those engaged in consumer services. The socialist city had few shops, but in Moscow today, retail outlets abound, from upscale boutiques to makeshift sidewalk markets. Moscow now has legendary traffic jams. One also finds more light, including neon signs, color, and outdoor advertising (fig. 10.24), but also more litter and crime. Many Communist monuments have toppled, and the socialist slogans that formerly festooned public places have all but vanished. Numerous factories

Figure 10.24. The urban landscape in contemporary Moscow. Commercial developments have greatly changed the city's character since the fall of the Soviet Union. Photo by A. B. M., 2013.

closed, and the proportion of the urban workforce employed in manufacturing plummeted. Service-sector jobs multiplied rapidly, involving everything from clerks and fast-food workers to realtors, banks, lawyers, and stockbrokers.

A less widespread city type, the **Nordic city**, occurs in Scandinavia and Finland. More recent in origin, these cities generally date from the seventeenth and eighteenth centuries, the era of the Swedish Empire, when new cities were laid out by planners. A grid pattern of streets characterizes the core of the Nordic city, though often that pattern breaks down in the suburbs (fig. 10.25). A waterside site was unfailingly chosen for Nordic cities, whether marine, riverine, or lakeside. Of the various European

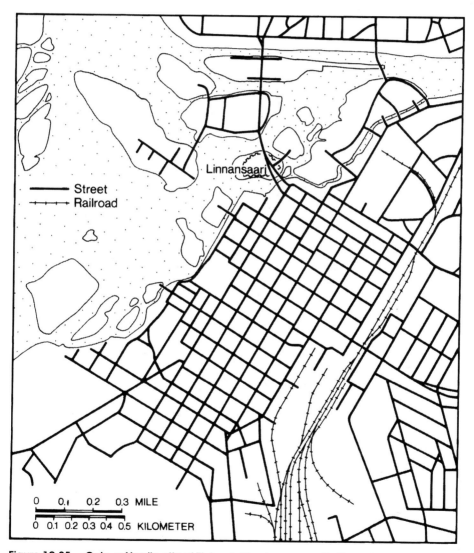

Figure 10.25. Oulu, a Nordic city of Finland. Clearly preserved in its central section are the gridiron plan and public squares laid out by its Swedish founders. The city dates from 1605 and was originally protected by the island fortress on Linnansaari.

urban types, the Nordic city is the least compact, with broad avenues; abundant free-standing, single-family residences; and spacious open areas. In fact, some Nordic cities consist of several different clusters separated by green space or even farmland, heightening the dispersed urban character. Trees grow more abundantly along the urban streets, revealing the strong northern love of forests. Most Nordic cities are modest in size, usually having less than 100,000 inhabitants. Local industries typically consist of small firms manufacturing high-quality, even luxury products, but postindustrial economic activities dominate. In spite of their comparatively small size, Nordic cities offer an impressive array of amenities, from museums, sport complexes, and hospitals to symphony orchestras and bicycle paths.

The Modern Urban Pattern

Site, morphology, and internal cultural/economic patterning, while essential geographical attributes of cities, do not complete the spatial analysis of urbanism. The distribution of cities must also be considered. In spite of the fact that Europe forms the most highly urbanized culture area in the world, **megalopolis** development is not common there. A megalopolis forms when adjacent cities grow until they coalesce, forming a poly-nucleated urban complex. In the United States, the region from Boston to Washington, DC, is a megalopolis. In most parts of Europe, land-use planning and green-belt preservation worked against the development of megalopolises. But megalopolises have developed: Randstad in the Netherlands (fig. 10.26) with a collective population of 7.5 million; the Rhine–Ruhr in western Germany, containing about 11 million inhabitants; Lancs–Yorks in the old industrial heart of England; Donbas in eastern Ukraine; and the somewhat more spread-out Flemish Triangle of northern Belgium. These megalopolises retain more open space than might be expected, thanks to rigorous zoning policies. Randstad Holland, for example, remains doughnut-shaped, due to a largely successful plan to keep the center (the Green Heart) open (fig. 10.26).

The area encompassing Randstad Holland, the Rhine–Ruhr, and the Flemish Triangle contains the greatest concentration of cities in Europe. Moving up in scale, some geographers make reference to a great arc of urbanism stretching from Lancs–Yorks to Rome, sometimes called the "blue banana" because of its shape and because the maps produced by the group of French geographers who first proposed the concept showed the area in blue (fig. 10.27). Since the urbanized "banana" is interrupted by the Alps, it should not be seen as a zone of continuous urbanization, but it encompasses a zone of unusually high levels of urbanization and urban-related economic activities. There are, of course, many important cities outside of the banana, but they tend to be somewhat more widely separated from one another and less intimately interconnected with a hyper-urbanized zone.

Our focus in this chapter has been on the locational, morphological, and economic attributes of European cities. Since the vast majority of Europeans live in urban areas, they play a major role in Europe's social and ethnic geography as well. We turn to these matters in the next chapter.

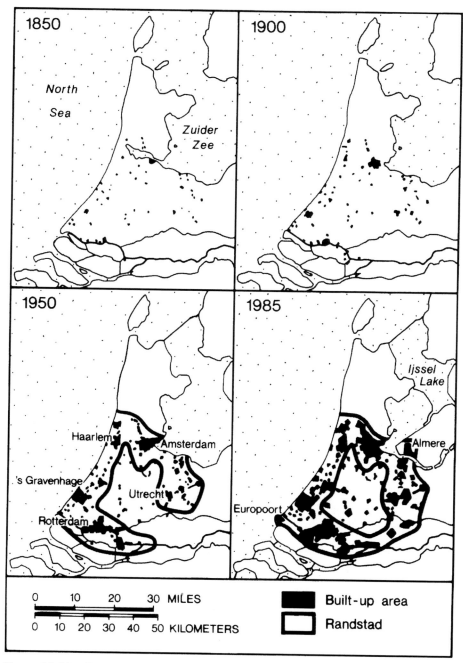

Figure 10.26.   Development of Randstad Holland, a megalopolis in the Netherlands. Land-use planning and zoning are being employed to keep the central area, or "doughnut hole," open, but suburban development is encroaching. Note the use of some reclaimed Zuider Zee polderland for expansion of the Randstad. *Sources: Randstad Holland* (Utrecht and 's-Gravenhage: Centre for the Geography of the Netherlands, 1980), 14; van Wessep et al. 1993.

Figure 10.27. European megalopolises in the "Blue Banana" dominate Europe's core. *Sources:* After van Wessep et al. 1993; Dieleman and Faludi 1998.

Sources and Suggested Readings

Agnew, J. A. 1994. *Rome. World Cities Series.* Chichester, UK: John Wiley & Sons.

Agnew, J., J. Mercer, and D. E. Sopher. 2007. *The City in Cultural Context.* London: Routledge.

Antrop, M. 2004. Landscape Change and the Urbanization Process in Europe. *Landscape and Urban Planning* 67 (1): 9–26.

Argenbright, R. 1999. Remaking Moscow: New Places, New Selves. *Geographical Review* 89 (1): 1–22.

Balsas, C. 2001. Commerce and the European City Center: Modernization, Regeneration and Management. *European Planning Studies* 9 (5): 677–82.

Bater, J. H. 2006. Central St. Petersburg: Continuity and Change in Privilege and Place. *Eurasian Geography & Economics* 47 (1): 4–27.

Beaujeu-Garnier, J. 1986. Urbanization in France since World War II. Research Paper, University of Chicago, Department of Geography, 47–62, 217–18.

Benevolo, L. 1993. *The European City. The Making of Europe.* Oxford: Blackwell.

Bontje, M. 2005. Edge Cities, European-Style: Examples from Paris and the Randstad. *Cities* 22 (4): 317–30.

Brade, I., K. Axenov, and E. Bondarchuk. 2006. *The Transformation of Urban Space in Post-Soviet Russia.* Vol. 4. London: Routledge.

Burtenshaw, D., M. Bateman, and G. J. Ashworth. 1991. *The European City: A Western Perspective.* New York: Halsted Press.

Clark, D. 1989. *Urban Decline.* London: Routledge.

Clark, P., ed. 2006. *The European City and Green Space: London, Stockholm, Helsinki and St. Petersburg, 1850–2000.* Historical Urban Studies. Aldershot, UK: Ashgate.

Clout, H. D., ed. 1994. *Europe's Cities in the Late Twentieth Century.* Nederlandse Geografische Studies 176. Utrecht: Royal Dutch Geographical Society.

Conzen, M. P. 2010. A Cartographic Analysis of Como's Urban Morphology. In *Cartografia di Paesaggi, Paesaggi nella Cartografia,* ed. C. Cerreti, L. Federzoni, and S. Salgaro, 115–31. Bologna: Pàtron Editore, Geografia e Organizzazione dello Sviluppo Territoriale, Studi Regionali e Monografici.

Conzen, M. R. G. (author), and M. P. Conzen (ed.). 2004. *Thinking about Urban Form: Papers on Urban Morphology, 1932–1998.* Bern: Peter Lang.

Cornish, V. 1923. *The Great Capitals: An Historical Geography.* London: Methuen.

Couch, C. 2008. *Urban Regeneration in Europe.* Oxford: Blackwell Science.

Danta, D. 1993. Ceausescu's Bucharest. *Geographical Review* 83 (2): 170–83.

David, T. 1963. London's Green Belt: The Evolution of an Idea. *Geographical Journal* 129 (1): 14–24.

Dekker, K., and R. Van Kempen. 2004. Large Housing Estates in Europe: Current Situation and Developments. *Tijdschrift voor Economische en Sociale Geografie* 95 (5): 570–77.

Dennis, R. 1984. *English Industrial Cities of the Nineteenth Century: A Social Geography.* Cambridge Studies in Historical Geography 4. Cambridge: Cambridge University Press.

Dickinson, R. E. 1945. The Morphology of the Medieval German Town. *Geographical Review* 35: 74–97.

Dieleman, F. M., and A. Faludi. 1998. Randstad, Rhine-Ruhr and Flemish Diamond as One Polynucleated Macro-Region? *Tijdschrift voor Economische en Sociale Geografie* 89 (3): 320–27.

Dingsdale, A. 1999. Budapest's Built Environment in Transition. *GeoJournal* 49 (1): 63–78.

Doherty, P., and M. A. Poole. 1997. Ethnic Residential Segregation in Belfast, Northern Ireland, 1971–1991. *Geographical Review* 87 (4): 520–36.

Dunford, M., and G. Kafkalas, eds. 1992. *Cities and Regions in the New Europe: The Global-Local Interplay and Spatial Development Strategies.* New York: Belhaven Press.

Enyedi, G., and V. Szirmai. 1992. *Budapest: A Central European Capital.* London: Belhaven Press.

Ewan, S., and M. Hebbert. 2007. European Cities in a Networked World During the Long 20th Century. *Environment & Planning C: Government & Policy* 25 (3): 327–40.

Ford, L. R. 1985. Urban Morphology and Preservation in Spain. *Geographical Review* 75 (3): 265–99.

Fusch, R. 1994. The Piazza in Italian Urban Morphology. *Geographical Review* 84 (4): 424–38.

Gomez, M. V. 1998. Reflective Images: The Case of Urban Regeneration in Glasgow and Bilbao. *International Journal of Urban and Regional Research* 22 (1): 106–21.

Graybill, J. K., and M. Dixon. 2012. Cities of Europe. In *Cities of the World: World Regional Urban Development,* 5th ed., ed. S. D Brunn, M. Hays-Mithell, and D. J. Ziegler, 237–80. Lanham, MD: Rowman & Littlefield.

Gritsai, O. 1997. The Economic Restructuring of Moscow in the International Context. *Geo-Journal* 42:341–47.

Gritsai, O., and H. Van der Wusten. 2000. Moscow and St. Petersburg, a Sequence of Capitals, a Tale of Two Cities. *GeoJournal* 51 (1–2): 33–45.

Hall, P. G., and K. Pain, eds. 2006. *The Polycentric Metropolis: Learning from Mega-City Regions in Europe.* London: Earthscan.

Hamilton, F. E. I. 1978. The East European and Soviet City. *Geographical Magazine* 50:511–15.

Harvey, D. 2003. *Paris, Capital of Modernity.* New York: Routledge.

Hermelin, B. 2007. The Urbanization and Suburbanization of the Service Economy: Producer Services and Specialization in Stockholm. *Geografiska Annaler Series B: Human Geography* 89 (Supplement 1): 59–74.

Hoggart, K., and D. Green, eds. 1991. *London: A New Metropolitan Geography.* London: Edward Arnold.

Ioffe, G., and T. G. Nefedova. 2000. *The Environs of Russian Cities.* Mellen Studies in Geography 3. Lewiston, NY: Edwin Mellen Press.

Johnston, R. J. 2013. *City and Society: An Outline for Urban Geography.* London: Routledge.

Jones, E. 1960. *A Social Geography of Belfast.* London: Oxford University Press.

Kearns, G., and C. W. J. Withers, eds. 2007. *Urbanising Britain: Essays on Class and Community in the Nineteenth Century.* Cambridge Studies in Historical Geography 17. Cambridge: Cambridge University Press.

Kunzmann, K. R., and M. Wegener. 1991. The Pattern of Urbanization in Western Europe. *Ekistics—The Problems and Science of Human Settlements* 58: 282–91, 350–51.

Ladd, B. 1997. *The Ghosts of Berlin: Confronting German History in the Urban Landscape.* Chicago: University of Chicago Press.

Leontidou, L. 1990. *The Mediterranean City in Transition: Social Change and Urban Development.* Cambridge Human Geography. Cambridge: Cambridge University Press.

Lichtenberger, E. 1993. *Vienna: Bridge between Cultures.* World Cities Series. London: Belhaven Press.

Light, D., and C. Young. 2010. Reconfiguring Socialist Urban Landscapes: The "Left-Over" Spaces of State Socialism in Bucharest. *Human Geography* 4 (1): 5–16.

McCarthy, L., and C. Johnson. 2012. Cities of Europe. In *Cities of the World: World Regional Urban Development*, 5th ed., ed. S. D Brunn, M. Hays-Mithell, and D. J. Ziegler, 189–236. Lanham, MD: Rowman & Littlefield.

Meijers, E. 2007. Clones or Complements? The Division of Labour between the Main Cities of the Randstad, the Flemish Diamond and the Rhein–Ruhr Area. *Regional Studies* 41 (7): 889–900.

Michael, P. 1987. Socio-Spatial Development of the South Italian City: The Case of Naples. *Transactions of the Institute of British Geographers*, n.s., 12 (4): 433–50.

Nicholas, D. 2003. *Urban Europe: 1100–1700.* New York: Palgrave Macmillan.

Pacione, M. 1987. The Socio-Spatial Development of the South Italian City: The Case of Naples. *Transactions of the Institute of British Geographers* 12:433–50.

———, ed. 1997. *Britain's Cities: Geographies of Division in Urban Britain.* London: Routledge.

Parr, J. B. 2007. Spatial Definitions of the City: Four Perspectives. *Urban Studies* 44 (2): 381–92.

Petsimeris, P. 2002. Population Deconcentration in Italy, Spain and Greece: A First Comparison. *Ekistics* 69: 163–72, 412–14.

Pounds, N. J. G. 1969. The Urbanization of the Classical World. *Annals of the Association of American Geographers* 59 (1): 135–57.

Regulska, J., and A. Kowalewski. 1993. *Warsaw.* World Cities Series. London: Belhaven Press.

Robert, E. D. 1945. The Morphology of the Medieval German Town. *Geographical Review* 35 (1): 74–97.

Rudolph, R., and I. Brade. 2005. Moscow: Processes of Restructuring in the Post-Soviet Metropolitan Periphery. *Cities* 22 (2): 135–50.

Sabelberg, E. 1986. The South-Italian City: A Cultural-Genetic Type of City. *GeoJournal* 13:59–66.

Thomas, D. 1963. London's Green Belt: The Evolution of an Idea. *Geographical Journal* 129 (1): 14–24.

Till, K. E. 2005. *The New Berlin: Memory, Politics, Place*. Minneapolis: University of Minnesota Press.

Turok, I., and V. Mykhnenko. 2007. The Trajectories of European Cities, 1960–2005. *Cities* 24 (3): 165–82.

Van Criekingen, M., M. Bachmann, C. Guisset, and M. Lennert. 2007. Towards Polycentric Cities: An Investigation into the Restructuring of Intra-Metropolitan Spatial Configurations in Europe. *Belgeo* (1): 31–50.

van Wessep, J. 1994. Gentrification as a Research Frontier. *Progress in Human Geography* 18 (1): 74–83.

van Wessep, J., F. M. Dieleman, and R. B. Jobse. 1993. *Randstad Holland*. London: Belhaven.

Van Winden, W., L. Van den Berg, and P. Pol. 2007. European Cities in the Knowledge Economy: Towards a Typology. *Urban Studies* 44 (3): 525–49.

Vance, J. E. 1990. *The Continuing City: Urban Morphology in Western Civilization*. Baltimore, MD: Johns Hopkins University Press.

Western, J. *Cosmopolitan Europe: A Strasbourg Self-Portrait*. Surrey, UK: Ashgate.

CHAPTER 11

Europe's Changing Social and Ethnic Geography

As in all places, wealth is unevenly distributed in Europe, but disparities in socioeconomic well-being are less dramatic there than in almost any other part of the world. Throughout much of European history, the situation was different: prosperity was concentrated in the hands of a small aristocratic class. The last 150 years, however, have seen the rise of a large middle class and a dramatic reduction in the percentage of the population living in abject poverty. Hence the large areas of destitution one can find in the megacities of South Asia or South America, or even on the Appalachian Plateau of the United States, are largely absent from Europe. Geographically, there are differences in levels of **human development**, but the visitor is often struck by the degree of socioeconomic evenness across Europe. Shantytowns on the outskirts of large cities such as Rome and Bucharest exist, but evidence of poverty at a large scale is relatively rare. Crime rates spike in sections of some urban areas, but violent crime in European cities is the exception. And Europeans enjoy some of the highest life expectancies found anywhere in the world.

What explains this state of affairs? The answer lies in part in matters we have examined in previous chapters that contributed to Europe's overall wealth—especially Western Europe's head start on industrialization and a system of colonialism that allowed Europe to extract wealth from afar. But the region's social geography is also the product of a particular social model that has taken root there in the past century and a half. The social model is characterized by a comparatively active governmental role in the provision of education, health care, housing, child care, and other social services, which are among the most generous in the world. The term *welfare state* reflects this state of affairs and signals that state governments are the principal providers of social goods.

A second feature of the European social model—in many senses a corollary of the first—is that Europeans pay relatively high taxes and are generally accepting of those taxes. There is considerable evidence of tax evasion in some countries—notably Greece and Italy—but a comparison of tax rates across substantial-sized countries in different parts of the world shows European countries leading the world in taxation (fig. 11.1). It follows that a larger percentage of the gross domestic product is consumed by the

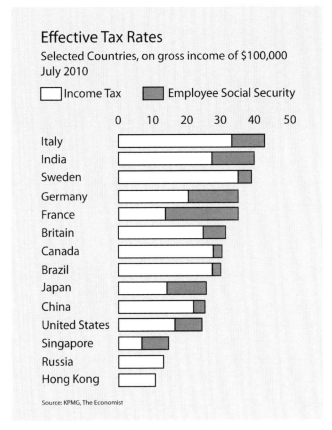

Figure 11.1. Effective tax rates for selected major countries. Note that most of the countries with the highest tax rates are European. *Source: Economist.*

state in Europe than in places such as the United States or Japan. There are pressures for change, however. New market economies in eastern Europe, such as Slovakia and Poland, have attempted to fuel industrial growth by introducing rates of taxation that are lower than western European countries. Meanwhile, there have been successful moves to lower taxes in countries such as Germany, the Netherlands, and the United Kingdom in an effort to stimulate growth. Nonetheless, corporate, income, and consumption ("value added") tax rates in Europe remain among the highest in the world.

Europe's strong tradition of labor unionization is a third element of the European social model. In many parts of Europe, citizens are relatively sympathetic toward workers seeking protections and benefits through their employers and the state. Employees tend to have generous fringe benefits, and many of these benefits are guaranteed by law. The most commonly cited example is vacation time, which in many places in continental Europe accrues at the rate of five weeks or more per year for everyone from the factory worker to the white-collar manager. In addition, European countries have some of the longest maternity and paternity leave periods found anywhere in the world. In Sweden, 18 months' paid leave is legislatively guaranteed—with the government picking up half the cost and the employer the other half. Bulgaria has even more generous maternity leave policies. In the case of Sweden, at least three months out of 18 must be taken by the other parent (usually the father) to ensure both parents play a role in rearing the child.

One particularly interesting example of a social initiative benefiting labor is France's 35-hour workweek. Prior to 2000, the norm had been 39 hours, but a law came into effect at the turn of the twenty-first century establishing the 35-hour figure (meaning that work beyond 35 hours per week is supposed to be considered overtime). Proponents of the law argued that the lower requirement would help reduce unemployment and enhance workers' quality of life. The measure has generated considerable controversy (see below), and various schemes have been developed that allow employers to work around the requirement. But the decision officially to shrink the workweek is suggestive of the degree to which labor conditions continue to influence political decision making in parts of Europe.

The unemployment realm provides yet another example of the benefits accruing to labor. Many countries have laws making it difficult to fire workers—particularly those working in the large civil service sector—and most countries offer comparatively generous unemployment benefits. Labor strife and work stoppages in places such as France and Italy are not uncommon, and not infrequently those actions produce results that are favorable to workers.

Underpinning Europe's social model is a broad social commitment to equality and communitarianism. The phrase inscribed on the façade of almost every public building in France sums up the concept: "Liberté, Egalité, Fraternité" (Freedom, Equality, Brotherhood). There are certainly many instances in which reality does not live up to this ideal, but there is nonetheless relatively broad support for the idea that the responsibilities of the state lie in all three areas. The term *equality* is understood to mean not just that citizens should be equal before the law and enjoy equal opportunities, but that the state should facilitate social and economic equality. This understanding helps explain why the welfare state came into being.

The concept of *fraternité* can best be understood against the backdrop of what geographer Nicholas Entrikin describes as an imaginary continuum of social values, with individualism lying at one end of the continuum and civic communitarianism at the other. European values and ideals, as reflected in politics, media, and other social activities, have historically tended toward the communitarian side of the spectrum. While making generalizations about the views of large, diverse groups of people is inherently problematic, the communitarian impulse is evident when one contrasts Europe at large with places such as the United States and Australia. By most measures, the latter societies tend to emphasize the role of the individual, whereas the European focus is more on the collective.

For all the strength of the communitarian tradition, over the past two decades more and more Europeans have started wondering whether the emphasis is shifting in the direction of the individualistic norms that dominate in the United States and Australia. The pressure to move in this direction reflects the challenge of maintaining the European social model in changing economic and social times (see below). The social model has served to spread wealth relatively widely, but it has also made it difficult for European economies to respond quickly and flexibly to larger economic shifts. Some also argue that it has failed to reward individual initiative and has even promoted a culture of complacency.

In recent years, much of the discussion of the social model has focused particularly on its consequences for the competitiveness of European business and for long-term economic viability of states where debts are running far ahead of revenues (see fig. 9.11). The active involvement of the state in assessing high taxes, as well as mandating generous worker benefits and workplace standards, amounts to a highly effective safety net for employees and their families. Someone laid off from an Italian auto factory need not worry that her immediate needs will not be met, thanks to this social safety net. But such a model makes the car produced in Italy more expensive than one produced in a place with lower social standards. In the process, European businesses can find themselves at a competitive disadvantage and unable to generate additional tax revenue even as the costs of maintaining social welfare benefits rises.

The challenges facing the European social model are further complicated by Europe's aging population (see Chapter 3). Simply put, the working population has been shrinking as a percentage of the total population. This trend raises a whole host of issues, since everything from pension schemes to health care programs are premised on the idea that the population is fairly evenly distributed across different age groups, with the population pyramid weighted toward the youngest age groups. In nearly every European country, the population pyramid is inverted, with elderly retirees making up a larger segment of the population than school-aged children (see Germany's population pyramid in fig. 3.7).

Immigration offers a partial solution to this problem, but it carries with it other challenges to the traditional social model. Rapidly increasing rates of immigration over the last few decades have brought large numbers of new residents into western European countries—some of whom are placing additional strains on welfare resources. Then there are the prejudices and resentments against immigrants that can undermine support for a social model that first developed during the late nineteenth and early twentieth centuries, when the nation-state ideal was at its strongest and most people thought the state's obligation was to the dominant ethnic nation within the state's territory (see the discussion of the nation-state idea in Chapter 6).

To make sense of Europe's changing social and ethnic mix, we turn first to basic patterns of social well-being, health, employment, education, gender roles, and ethnic differences that lie behind the general picture sketched above. We then look in more detail at how changes in economy, demography, and migration are altering the European social scene.

Patterns of Social Well-Being

The European social model traditionally emphasized "cradle-to-grave" care by the state, including parental leave and subsidies to parents with children, universal health care, unemployment insurance and welfare, and old-age pensions. The model's roots lie in nineteenth-century Germany, when Otto von Bismarck was the chancellor. He is credited with implementing the first health insurance scheme for the poor (1883), work accident insurance (1884), and social security for the elderly (1889). This social safety net was introduced partly out of genuine concern for the plight of disadvantaged populations confronting rapid industrialization and urbanization. But most historians agree that Bismarck's initiatives were also pragmatic political responses to an increasingly unruly working class clamoring for social reforms.

By the early twentieth century, other forms of social insurance, such as unemployment insurance, were introduced in Germany. Of course, prior to Bismarck's reforms there was a tradition of charity in Germany and throughout Europe. A poor person who became sick might receive treatment at a charity hospital run by the church, an unemployed worker might have access to handouts through the church or some other charity organization, and an old person might be able to remain housed and fed thanks to family members or municipal homes set up for indigents. What was revolutionary about Bismarck's reforms is that they put a secular, national government in charge of the social safety net. They also made benefits available to most of the population. Like other contemporaneous policies that established the "nation-state" as the focus of identification for people—the establishment of national parliaments, armies, and even post offices—the welfare state was instrumental in shifting people's orientation from their local community, their regional king, or even their church, toward the state. From these beginnings, the social model spread throughout Europe, albeit not immediately or everywhere. As a result, by the latter part of the twentieth century most Europeans came to enjoy social protections that resemble those that began in Germany in the late 1800s.

Nonetheless, within Europe notable regional differences exist in the degree to which states are involved in the provision of social services. Since social welfare programs are so diverse, it is difficult to gain a precise picture of these differences, but the general pattern becomes clear when one maps data on the percentage of gross domestic product devoted to social welfare programs in states belonging to the Organization for Economic Cooperation and Development (OECD) (fig. 11.2). The continental western European countries tend to have the most generous social welfare benefits. By contrast, the welfare state is less well developed in countries lying at the northeastern and eastern peripheries of the "continent."

An indication of more general patterns of socioeconomic well-being can be gained from mapping differences in GDP per capita. The European Spatial Planning Observation Network, an EU program, developed an interesting cartographic representation of differences in GDP per capita in "Europe and its neighborhood" in 2002 (fig. 11.3). The figure shows the gap that exists between western and eastern Europe, as well as contrasts between the EU and surrounding areas. The Mediterranean stands out as a major socioeconomic dividing line, but so does the border between Finland and Russia.

Of course, these state-scale patterns tell us nothing about differences within states. Figure 11.4 shows the differences in per capita GDP within EU member states when this variable is mapped at the scale of first-order substate regions. The figure shows relatively little internal regional variation within wealthier countries such as Finland and the Netherlands, but much greater variation in countries such as Italy and Spain.

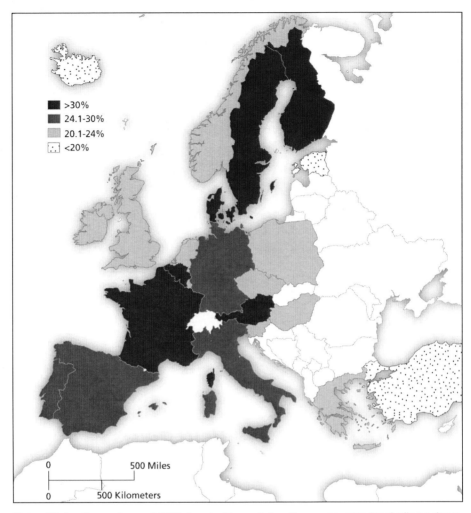

Figure 11.2.   Percentage of GDP devoted to social welfare programs (excluding education) in states belonging to the Organization for Economic Cooperation and Development. The welfare state is most in evidence in the western part of continental Europe, but most European states spend more on social welfare than most other parts of the world. *Source:* OECD 2012.

The continuing challenges faced by eastern Germany are also evident from this figure. Regional differentiation tends to be lower throughout much of eastern Europe, but the overall base is lower. It is interesting to note, however, that the regions around a few of the capital cities stand out as areas of particular prosperity—notably Prague (Czechia) and Warsaw (Poland).

Moving to an even smaller scale (or a larger scale if one is thinking in map terms), the differences in socioeconomic well-being within city regions described in Chapter 10 are a prominent feature of Europe's social geography. Within the preindustrial city, segregation has often occurred along occupational lines. Surviving street

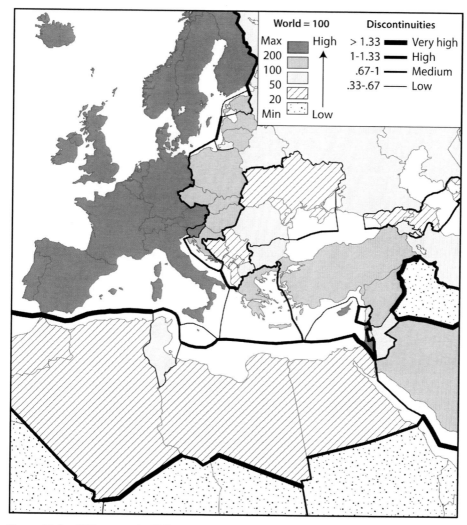

Figure 11.3.   Differences in GDP per capita in Europe and surrounding areas. The old Iron Curtain is still very much in evidence, as are the gaps across the Mediterranean Sea. *Source:* Based on a map in European Spatial Planning Observation Network, *ESPON Synthesis Report III,* October 2006, 35.

names provide clues. In Munich, we find the Ledererstrasse ("Street of the Leather-Workers"), Färbergraben ("Street of the Cloth-Dyers"), Sattlerstrasse ("Street of the Saddlers"), and others. Such names referred to the artisans' places of work and usually also to their residences. In medieval Lübeck, merchants lived to the west of a main north–south street, while artisans resided to the east. Ordinary laborers lived outside the town walls.

Residential neighborhoods in many European cities today remain rooted in class. The clustering of foreign laborers in certain districts speaks of their socioeconomic status as much as their ethnic background. A map of socioeconomic differences in the

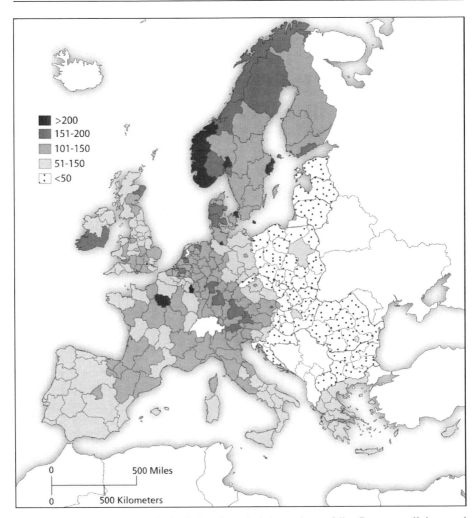

Figure 11.4.   GDP per capita in first-order substate regions of the European Union and European Free Trade Association member states, relative to the EU average (percentage). This map highlights the significant regional differences within countries such as Italy and Germany as well as the comparative prosperity of capital-city regions in countries such as France, the United Kingdom, and Spain. Note also that the poorest areas are heavily concentrated in the former Eastern Europe. *Source:* Eurostat 2010.

Paris metropolitan region shows the extent of the contrasts in a single city (fig. 11.5). The central and western sections of Paris proper are zones of significant prosperity—as are areas immediately to the west where new urban development has taken hold. A notable decline is evident in the northeastern section of Paris, and the inner suburbs to the north, west, and south stand out as zones of considerable distress.

After World War II, a more American-like pattern began to emerge in many European metropolitan areas, with prestigious neighborhoods developing in the outer ring. In present-day Liverpool, England, for example, persons engaged in the profes-

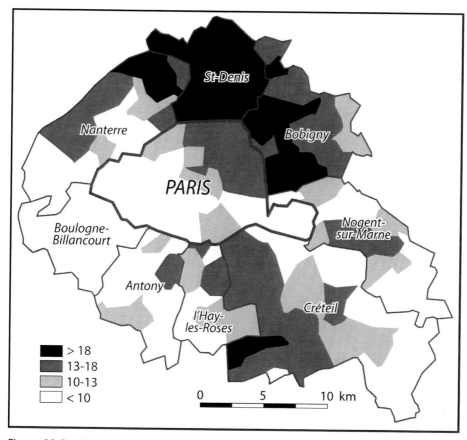

Figure 11.5.   Levels of socioeconomic well-being in the Paris metropolitan area. Unlike many American cities, the poorest parts of Paris and other western European cities are found in the first ring of suburbs. *Source:* IPUMS database.

sions, business owners, and administrators live in residential areas farthest from the city center, whereas unskilled and semiskilled laborers reside in and near the preindustrial core. In Paris, the impact of this trend is evident in the greater prosperity of suburbs lying far from the urban core—notably those that lie southeast of the city (fig. 11.5).

Health

Europe has one of the healthiest populations in the world, as measured by average life span, rates of infant mortality, access to health care, and infection rates of life-threatening communicable diseases. Of the top 20 countries in the world in life expectancy as ranked by the World Health Organization in 2011, 12 were in Europe, including the microstates of Andorra, Luxembourg, and San Marino (the United States' rank was 37). The average infant mortality rate in the EU (i.e., the number of infants per thousand that die before reaching the age of one) is 4.1, compared with 5.9 for the United States, 15.2 for China, 15.8 for Saudi Arabia, and 119.4 for Afghanistan. Within Europe, a clear east–west contrast in the infant mortality rate exists; Romania, Albania, and Bulgaria have the highest rates in Europe, ranging between 11 and 16. But even in eastern Europe, the rate remains low by world standards. Infant mortality rates are so low because government-provided or government-mandated health coverage is available for everyone. Interestingly, despite the costs of the universal health coverage plans in effect in Europe, per capita spending on health care is generally about half of what it is in the United States.

The type of health coverage that is available differs from place to place in Europe. The United Kingdom has a single-payer system of health coverage, with all hospitals publicly owned. Most medical personnel in the UK are employees of the government. England's National Health Service, begun in the late 1940s, is now one of the five largest employers in the world; only the United States Department of Defense, the Chinese military, Walmart, and McDonald's employ more people. Countries in southern Europe such as Greece, Italy, and Spain, as well as the Nordic countries, also have health systems that are primarily financed through taxation at the national level, though in some cases regional or, in the case of Finland, local administrations are involved.

In France and Germany, as well as in many of the former Communist states of central and eastern Europe, the norm is a combination of public and private health insurance (the "social health insurance" model), typically involving complicated formulas of employer, individual, and income tax contributions. Unlike in Britain, French and German doctors are typically not government employees. Instead, they are self-employed and participate voluntarily in government-organized systems. In these countries, patients have the freedom to "shop around" for their doctor or hospital. Regardless of the precise form, European countries typically have virtually universal health coverage for their citizens. The prospect that a person between jobs could be uninsured for a time is unknown in most of Europe.

Although Europeans enjoy generally high life expectancies, there are health problems worth noting. As in all industrialized societies, heart disease and cancer are leading causes of death. Alcohol and tobacco dependency are also chronic public health concerns, particularly in central and eastern Europe—especially in countries that were formerly part of the Soviet Union or were under Soviet influence (fig. 11.6). Some 40% of Russians smoke regularly; as a result, mortality rates in Russia from smoking-related illnesses such as lung cancer and emphysema are high. Some modest tobacco restrictions came into force in 2013, but it will likely be some time before these will have much impact.

The cultural norm in much of Europe emphasizes alcohol consumption as a regular part of the daily routine. Of the top ten countries in terms of beer consumption in the world, only two are not in Europe; in top-ranked Czechia, the average citizen consumes some 132 liters (approx. 39 gallons) of the sudsy liquid per year. Likewise, 14 of the top 15 wine-consuming countries are European, and the average French person consumes 46 liters (approximately 12 gallons) of wine annually.

There is evidence that modest alcohol consumption can have health benefits, but alcoholism is a significant problem in parts of Europe, as are alcohol-related incidents

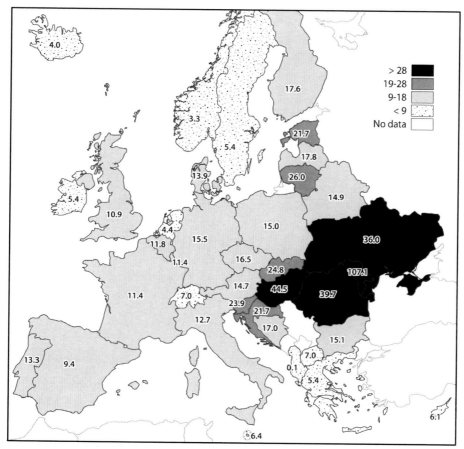

Figure 11.6.   SDR, chronic liver disease, and cirrhosis per 100,000 people. These diseases are primarily associated with the excessive consumption of alcohol. Note the particularly high incidence levels in eastern Europe. *Source:* World Health Organization, Regional Office for Europe.

in the workplace and on roadways. In the United Kingdom, a culture of binge drinking and associated antisocial behavior among young people has become a national topic of concern. A 2006 government report indicated that 40–50% of British 15-year-olds drank alcohol in a given week. The rates of alcohol and drug abuse among British people were consistently among the highest in Europe. By the early 2000s, the street scene in many English town centers on a Friday or Saturday night had become so disorderly that former prime minister Tony Blair declared binge drinking a "British disease" that could only be combated through the intervention of parents, government, and business.

Other drug use is also relatively widespread in Europe. In the Netherlands, a country known for liberal laws on the consumption of marijuana and hallucinogenic mushrooms, a drug tourism industry has emerged in the late twentieth century, drawing people from throughout the continent, and as far away as North America, to Amsterdam's famed "coffeehouses," where cannabis can be legally dispensed. Recently, a movement was launched to curb both the tourist aspect of the trade and drug use among young people. In 2013, for example, non-Dutch residents were banned from cannabis-selling coffeehouses, and many coffeehouses located close to schools are being forced to move. It seems there are growing limits to Holland's famed culture of tolerance.

Two other public health concerns bear mentioning. Although global statistics on suicide are notoriously unreliable (given taboos associated with the subject in many cultures), according to the World Health Organization, nine of the top ten suicide rates in the world in 2011 were found in European countries. The highest four suicide rates in the world were reported in former Soviet republics (Lithuania, Russia, Belarus, and Latvia), with men having much higher rates than women. Obesity is also a growing problem in much of Europe. Decreased physical activity and increasing caloric intake, particularly of fatty and sugary foods, combine to make obesity one of the "greatest public health challenges of the 21st century" in Europe, according to the World Health Organization. Even places with traditionally slender people, such as Norway and France, are seeing a clear upward trend in the number of obese people. Nonetheless, this problem is much less pronounced in Europe than it is throughout much of the United States.

Employment

Despite the generally high level of prosperity found throughout most of Europe, many European countries have been plagued by persistently high levels of unemployment. Currently the worst problems are found in the countries of the European periphery (fig. 8.18). In eastern Europe unemployment is tied to the transition away from the industrial economy, as well as a relatively inflexible labor market in which job transition can be difficult and generous unemployment benefits can undermine the incentive to return to work. Significant parts of eastern Europe also experienced high levels of unemployment in the 1990s, as wrenching economic adjustments were made in the shift from communism to capitalism. Many of these eastern European countries saw falling unemployment rates during the early 2000s, but significant pockets of unemployment remained. Some regions of the Baltic states, for example, have among the highest rates of unemployment in Europe; the same is true for eastern Slovakia, away from the urban economic engine of Bratislava near the Austrian border.

In southern Europe, unemployment swelled in the wake of the economic downturn that began in 2009. The austerity measures that were put into place to address the euro crisis (Chapter 9) produced a dramatic spike in unemployment, particularly among young adults, in Greece and Spain. Even several years after the onset of the crisis, Greece's and Spain's unemployment rates exceeded 25%. Urban growth centers such as Madrid, Barcelona, and Bilbao started in a much stronger position, whereas comparatively high rates of unemployment have long been found in many rural areas of southern and western Spain. Italy exhibits a classic north–south division. In the north, where almost all Italian industry is located around such cities as Turin and Milan, unemployment is relatively low. By contrast, in the Italian south, or Mezzogiorno, high unemployment has been the norm for over a century.

Countries in northwestern Europe, such as the Netherlands and the United Kingdom, as well as the Nordic countries, have had consistently lower unemployment rates in recent time, though they too were affected by the economic downturn. Nonetheless, when viewed over a several-decade time scale, the northern European employment trajectory (with the exception of Ireland) has been positive. Finland, for example, which was facing rather dramatic economic challenges during the early 1990s, had an unemployment rate of just over 15% in 1995. Thanks in part to booming telecommunications and high-technology sectors, the unemployment rate was nearly halved in a decade. In late 2007 it stood at just under 7% and grew by only 1% in the wake of the recent economic downturn. Norway has one of the lower unemployment rates in the world at just under 4%.

Germany struggled with relatively high unemployment rates (between 8 and 11%) in the late 1990s and early 2000s after the post-unification economic boom petered out in that country. In eastern Germany specifically, unemployment rates of 20% were not uncommon in some districts. In recent years, the unemployment rate for the country as a whole has come down, but the east still lags the west.

In the United Kingdom, within-country disparities are particularly notable. Just a few hours by train north of central London, one of the richest places in the EU—and indeed the world—lies Liverpool's derelict river frontage in the center city. Similarly, Düsseldorf and Gelsenkirchen, in Germany's Ruhr Valley, are separated by less than 50 kilometers. Düsseldorf is a wealthy center of finance and industry, but Gelsenkirchen has never recovered from the mining and steel industry bust of the 1970s.

Unemployment may be the most dramatic labor issue facing Europe today, but underemployment is a significant issue as well. An underemployed worker is one who is not employed at a level equal to his or her capacity or training. People stuck in part-time jobs who desire full-time jobs, or those with training and skills that exceed the job they are holding, are underemployed. The underemployment rate in Europe grew in the wake of the financial crisis—reaching particularly high levels in Spain and Ireland. A few eastern European countries bucked the trend—notably Bulgaria, Czechia, and Estonia—but they nonetheless continue to struggle with high rates of unemployment. Addressing the underemployment issue represents a significant social challenge for Europe in an era when a combination of technological developments and outsourcing are shrinking job opportunities in many economic sectors.

Education

Another distinctly European social trait is a high level of formal education. By any measure, Europe possesses among the best-schooled peoples in the world. Access to basic education for the great majority of Europeans came about in the nineteenth and early twentieth centuries, beginning in northwestern Europe and spreading southward and eastward. German peasants learned to read and write in the first half of the

1800s, while most Russians, Italians, and other Mediterranean and Slavic farm folk remained illiterate. Only after the Communist takeover did education become available to the average Russian. In most of Europe, education spread to the masses because of ambitious government-supported education plans. European central governments generally oversee the operation of schools, which do not charge tuition.

The literacy rate offers a crude, but still revealing, measure of basic education. The overwhelming majority of Europeans above the age of 15 can read and write, and in most countries, from Ireland to Russia, the proportion stands at 99% or even higher. Only in Malta and Portugal does the literacy level fall below 96%. The Mediterranean forms an educational fault line along Europe's southern boundary, beyond which literacy rates are far lower, as in Algeria at 73%, Egypt at 72%, and Morocco at 56%.

More revealing than basic literacy is the level of reading proficiency. A survey done in the late 1990s found that the proportion of adults reading at the lowest of five levels stood at only 7% in Sweden, 11% in the Netherlands, 14% in Switzerland, and 15% in Germany. These figures reflect an approach to primary and secondary education that emphasizes fundamental competency in reading, writing, math, history, geography, and general science. In France, for example, it is almost impossible to complete the minimal schooling requirements without having at least a reasonable mastery of basics in these subject areas. Until fairly recently, most schools in France followed a fairly traditional model—separate schools for boys and girls, at least through the early grades, and a considerable emphasis on memorization. Coeducation is now the norm, and the curriculum tends to encourage more creativity (fig. 11.7). Nonetheless, training in the basics is still the emphasis, and standards are high. Some critique the French system for being overly traditional and unimaginative, but the average 18-year-old in France has an impressive grasp of fundamentals.

Book readership in Europe provides further evidence of the emphasis on education and literacy. Northern Europe leads in the number of book titles published each

Figure 11.7. One of the book's authors in front of the former main entrance to the public primary school he attended in 1964–1965. Note the inscription above the door: Ecole de Jeunes Garçons (Young Boys' School). Like other French schools, this one went coed in the 1970s (the main entrance was moved to the side of the building). But many aspects of the traditional French educational system are still in place. Photo by A. B. M., 2012.

year. The United Kingdom ranks first, followed by Germany, Spain, France, Italy, and the Netherlands. On a per capita basis, countries such as Iceland, Denmark, and Finland rank high—a notable achievement given that little or no foreign demand exists for books in the dominant languages of those states.

Universities in Europe are open to qualified students. Traditionally, these were free, but a growing number of countries are now charging students at least a nominal fee (much less than their counterparts in the United States). There is growing concern that these fees will rise significantly as universities cope with enrollment growth and stagnant or declining state funding. There is also concern that relatively few continental European universities are ranked among the world's best anymore. Given that the graduates of European high schools are, by many measures, the best educated in the world, it is surprising not to find more high-ranking universities. Reform movements are under way in several countries, but embedded hierarchies within institutions and pressures on state budgets make significant change difficult.

The Role of Women

The status of women in Europe has improved dramatically since the early twentieth century. In the decades after World War II, most governments implemented legislation mandating the equal treatment of women in the workplace and in public life. Gradually, the pay disparities between men and women decreased, women began assuming positions of greater authority in the private sector, and a growing number of women entered public life.

Despite these advances, women have not achieved parity with their male counterparts. Most parliaments throughout Europe are still dominated by men (fig. 11.8), and there are few women heading major corporations. Even equal pay for equal work is elusive. Most assessments show women earning between 4 and 22% less than their male counterparts who hold comparable jobs. Interestingly, gender pay gaps are less pronounced in Poland (4.5%) and Italy (5.8%) than in the United Kingdom, Germany, and Finland (between 18 and 22%) (fig. 11.9).

Behind these pay gap figures lie some interesting complexities. If one looks at the absolute employment gap (i.e., the difference between the percentage of men and women in the workforce), the Nordic countries stand out as places where the gap is small (fig. 11.10). The low absolute employment gap there may well reflect a low level of discrimination and a high level of support for working women in that part of Europe. In contrast, the absolute employment gap is comparatively high in a few countries that have low gender pay gaps, notably Italy. This apparent anomaly is partially explained by differences in the pay gap between the public and private sectors. Italy's relatively small pay gap is the result of public-sector salaries that put women on a similar footing with men.

There is also evidence that women still face a "glass ceiling" in the private sector. Corporate leadership positions in most European countries are far more likely to be occupied by men than in the United States. A telling study in 2012 found that almost 97% of the boards of major corporations were chaired by men.

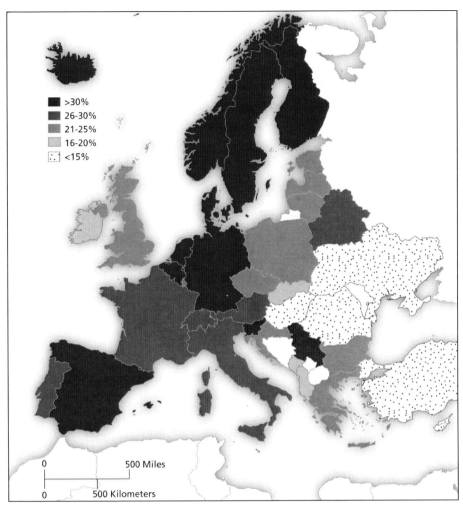

Figure 11.8. Percentage of women occupying seats in the parliaments of EU countries, 2012. The highest numbers are generally found in northern Europe, but Spain and Serbia have a substantial number of female parliamentarians as well. *Source:* Inter-Parliamentary Union.

In national-level politics, the ranks of women in positions of authority are increasing: witness the election of Angela Merkel as the first female chancellor of Germany in 2005. Nonetheless, as of 2013, women still occupied on average less than 25% of the seats in the parliaments of European countries. Regional variations can be found that are somewhat similar to those found in the absolute employment gap, but not in the pay gap (compare figs. 11.8, 11.9, and 11.10). The data on parliamentary representation suggests that women are most visible in public life in the Nordic countries and in northern continental Europe. They are less well represented in parts of eastern Europe and in the British Isles.

Continuing disparities between women and men show the limitations of focusing solely on legislation requiring equal treatment of women and men. Many European

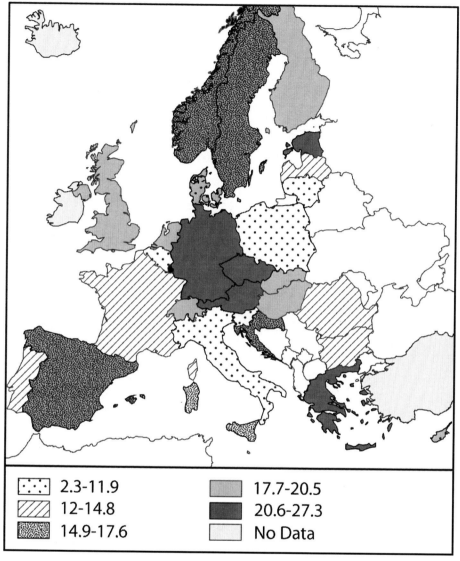

Figure 11.9.   The gender pay gap within the European Union, 2011. The EU average at this time was just over 16%. *Source:* Eurostat.

Legend:
- 2.3–11.9
- 12–14.8
- 14.9–17.6
- 17.7–20.5
- 20.6–27.3
- No Data

countries, and the EU itself, are increasingly recognizing the importance of considering the conditions that can lead to unequal outcomes, and the challenges of overcoming those conditions. Affirmative action programs have been introduced in many places and are supported under EU law. Moreover, networks of experts and advocates in women's rights have sprung up, and governments have taken a more aggressive role in everything from child care to highlighting the accomplishments of women in education. Increasingly, the call is heard for "gender mainstreaming"—the incorporation of gender issues throughout the full range of governmental policies and institutional

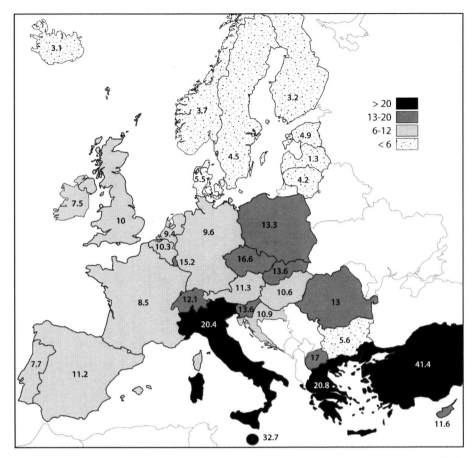

Figure 11.10. The absolute gender employment gap within the European Union, 2011. This map shows the difference between the percentage of men and the percentage of women in the workforce. *Source:* Eurostat 2011.

arrangements. Gender mainstreaming has emerged as a significant EU policy commitment, although there is a lively debate over its direction and effectiveness.

Ethnic Patterns

In Chapter 6, we discussed the division of Europe into historical nations, which both helped to produce and were shaped by the political pattern. But a system of states based on the nation-state idea has never been fully implemented because states have not been entirely successful in forging single nations out of disparate peoples. Even leaving aside the complexities introduced by recent streams of migrants, Europe does not consist solely of Spanish, French, Belgian, and Dutch peoples; it also encompasses Galicians, Basques, Catalans, Walloons, Flemings, Frisians, and many more. These latter groups represent a source of unevenness in Europe's social space that is different from the geographical variability associated with socioeconomic conditions, health, or the role of women.

Most of Europe's historically rooted ethno-cultural groups occupy discrete regions and live in uneasy tension with the dominant political-territorial order (fig. 11.11). It is difficult to generalize about the socioeconomic situation of these groups. Some are located in areas of significant economic prosperity (Basques and Catalans in Spain, Flemings in Belgium), whereas others are found in more economically marginal regions (Galicians in Spain, Bretons in France, Walloons in Belgium). What they share in common is some desire to maintain distinctiveness from the "nation-state" in which they live.

In pursuit of that desire, many members of Europe's long-standing ethno-regional minority communities seek some degree of autonomy from the state in which they are situated, and in certain places the call is for complete independence. The degree of radicalization is directly related to the extent to which state authorities

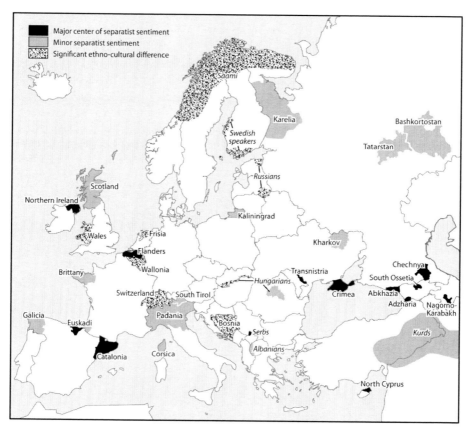

Figure 11.11.   Areas of separatism or significant ethno-cultural difference within states. This map shows only areas that are the object of separatist sentiment or where significant ethno-cultural minorities can be found. More than a dozen new recognized independent states have appeared as a result of separatist movements since 1980, and several others, such as Turkish North Cyprus and Abkhazia, have achieved de facto independence.

seek to impose a single ethno-national norm throughout the territory. When states are actively engaged in such efforts (e.g., Franco's Spain), radicalization usually follows. On the other hand, when states take a more conciliatory and inclusive attitude toward ethno-cultural minorities (such as Finland toward its Swedish-speaking minority, or the Netherlands toward the Frisians), there is less incentive to demand high levels of autonomy or independence.

Of course, Europe's ethnic diversity is not just a function of long-standing ethno-cultural heterogeneity. In recent decades many European countries have been destinations for migrants coming from other parts of the world. Unlike the United States, large-scale immigration is a relatively new phenomenon in Europe. Even Britain's vast colonial empire did not produce a large wave of immigration until, ironically, direct colonial rule came to an end during the middle of the twentieth century. Spain's deep involvement in Latin America, dating to the sixteenth century, likewise did not result in large-scale migration to the Iberian Peninsula.

As we saw in Chapter 3, however, over the past 60 years the wealthiest countries in Europe, almost without exception, have been destinations for large numbers of new immigrants from south Asia, southeast Asia, the Middle East, and Africa. Most of the immigrants have ended up in the western part of Europe, with Switzerland, Belgium, Austria, Sweden, and Ireland taking on a particularly large number in relation to population size (fig. 11.12). Much of eastern Europe has largely missed out on large-scale immigration (Estonia shows up as having a high number of foreign-born people because of the Russian component of the population there), but sizable numbers of eastern Europeans have become migrants themselves. Refugees from the war-torn former Yugoslavia have ended up in Germany and the United Kingdom, while many Romanians (particularly ethnic Roma, or gypsies) have made their way to Italy. More important in numerical terms, workers from poorer parts of eastern Europe have been moving to the west over the past two decades.

The migration streams highlighted above have complicated Europe's social geography, but in a very different way from historical ethno-regionalism. Many of the new migrants have come to Europe to fill particular economic niches—particularly as low-wage, menial laborers. They are thus often at the lower end of the socioeconomic ladder. Moreover, they and their families have settled overwhelmingly in and around cities—making many western European urban areas decidedly heterogeneous.

It is important to remember that European cities have been culturally and ethnically diverse since ancient times, when the first European urbanites often segregated themselves along tribal lines. Religion long acted as one of the most powerful forces segregating people within the towns of Europe. In Roman cities, evidence strongly suggests that Christians occupied certain neighborhoods early in the diffusion of their faith. The term **ghetto**, used to designate a Jewish neighborhood, derives from medieval Venice, and most European towns of the Middle Ages had separate Jewish districts, reminders of which are still seen in names such as the German Judengasse ("Street of the Jews") or Sevilla's Judaría ("Jewish Quarter"). Even today, residential segregation along religious lines can be seen in Belfast and Londonderry, Northern Ireland, where one finds distinct Catholic and Protestant neighborhoods (fig. 5.13).

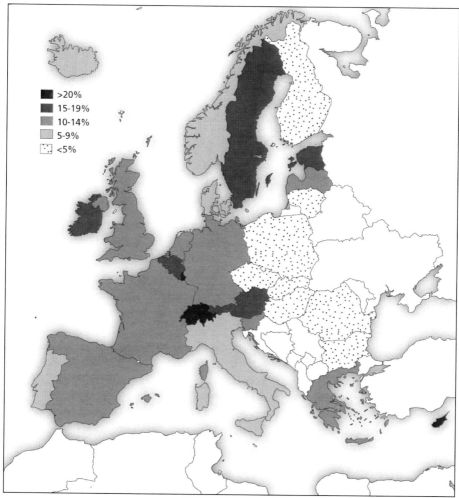

Figure 11.12.   Percentage of the population that is foreign born in European countries.
The relatively high numbers in Estonia and Latvia is a result of migration from Russia to neighboring countries to the west, whereas substantial foreign-born populations in western European countries reflect migration from north Africa and southwest Asia. *Source:* Eurostat 2012 and selected national statistical sources.

The level of denominational segregation in Belfast rose sharply in the 1970s and more gently in subsequent decades, ghettoizing the city's Catholics, who make up a third of the population.

Linguistic differences also traditionally separated people within European cities—most commonly in multilingual areas. Brno, in the Czech province of Moravia, had a medieval residential pattern in which Germans lived in the northern part of the city and Czechs in the south. Towns such as Armagh and Downpatrick in Northern Ireland developed distinct quarters in the seventeenth century, as is indicated by the survival of English Street, Irish Street, and Scotch Street. In medieval Caernarfon, Wales, the portion of the town enclosed by walls housed the English, while Welsh clustered in the area just outside the walls.

Whatever the historical patterns, the recent wave of foreign immigration to western European cities has further transformed the ethnic and racial character of European cities (fig. 11.13). In London, for example, the district of Wembley, where the famous soccer stadium is located, is over 50% immigrants; you are just as likely to see *paan* shops, a Bollywood video shop, African hair salons, or a Muslim-run halal butcher shop there as you are a traditional British pub. Frankfurt-am-Main had a population that was more than 27% foreign born by 2000, as did Vienna. Many of these immigrants found homes in the decaying residences of the preindustrial core and inner ring—often occupying apartments abandoned by natives who had moved to the periphery.

Some ethnic neighborhoods and ghettoes developed from this influx. In Paris, for example, foreigners cluster in the northeastern quadrant, including parts of both the inner and middle rings. Many Muslims live in segregated neighborhoods in Paris and other cities of mainland Europe. Nonetheless, ethnic residential segregation is generally lower in European cities than in American cities. In Europe, foreign ethnic segregation often occurs at the level of individual apartment houses rather than at larger scales; tiny, multiple concentrations of individual foreign ethnic groups are relatively common.

The presence of large numbers of new culturally and ethnically different residents has, perhaps unsurprisingly, created social tensions. Some Europeans express concerns about the social and cultural landscape changes brought by immigrants—

Figure 11.13. Evidence of Middle Eastern immigrants in Brussels. The Arabic language is very much in evidence in sections of the city. Photo by A. B. M., 1986.

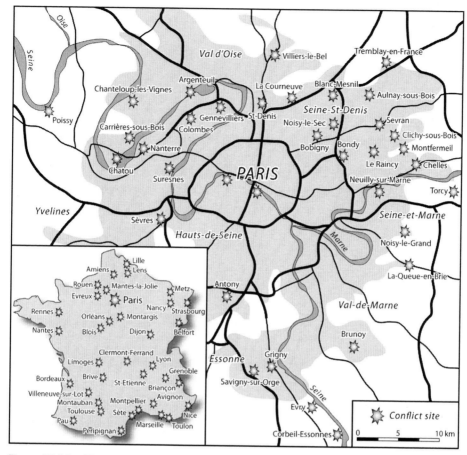

Figure 11.14.   The geography of the 2005 riots in the Paris metropolitan area. The pattern provides a clear reflection of the spatial distribution of immigrants in the city. *Source:* Based on a map in the *Economist,* November 10, 2005.

and prejudice against immigrants is distressingly common. Riots in several Parisian suburbs during 2005, and again in 2007, reflected disenchantment among North African immigrants who felt they were being denied economic opportunities for advancement in France (fig. 11.14). Terrorist attacks on transportation targets in Madrid (2004), London (2005), and Toulouse (2012) by Islamist extremists, meanwhile, have given rise to overtly anti-immigrant sentiments such as those aired by the **xenophobic** British National Party (BNP), which distributed recruitment fliers after the London bombings arguing that the UK had become an "overcrowded multicultural slum." Faith-based hate crimes rose by fivefold in the two weeks after the bombings of public transit in the British capital city.

In Germany, an ongoing debate is simmering about that country's large immigrant population, including more than 2.5 million immigrants from Turkey (of those, slightly over 500,000 have obtained German citizenship). The debate centers on the lack of integration of most Turks into German culture, as exemplified by the failure of a substantial number of Turks to learn the German language. Yet many Turks believe that their isolation within German society is due to an unwelcoming environment by Germans who once desperately needed their labor but who have made little attempt to accommodate their cultural practices and differences. The mere term "guest workers" (*Gastarbeiter*) used to describe Turkish immigrants—in other words, you may stay as a temporary guest—offers some credence to this widespread belief among Turks.

France is home to the largest concentration of Muslims in Europe (some five million). France's Muslims come primarily from Morocco and Algeria; a substantial number end up in the Paris conurbation in subsidized housing complexes on the periphery of the city. Although predominantly Roman Catholic, France, like the United States, has a strong tradition of secularism, which dates from the French Revolution in the late eighteenth century. Government-funded schools (nearly all schools in France) may not teach any particular religion, and religious displays, such as Christian crosses, are banned in classrooms.

When a presidential commission recommended in 2003 that personal attire associated with a particular religion be banned, there was an outcry among Muslims who felt targeted by the measure. Many Muslim girls wore headscarves to cover their hair, ears, and neck, in line with Islamic dictates on proper attire for women. The report also recommended banning Jewish yarmulkes and Sikh turbans, but Muslims in particular felt singled out by the new law. The "headscarf law," which came into effect in 2004, set off a firestorm of protest, but immigrant communities felt largely powerless in the face of a large majority of the French public (as well as school teachers) who supported the ban. Then in 2011, France took another step—banning full face covering in public spaces except under special circumstances. Although the law has not led to the issuance of many citations, it has fueled feelings of discontent among immigrants of the Muslim faith in France, who must balance their precarious socioeconomic status in French society with cultural traditions rooted in their faith.

The French case is an extreme one, but tensions between the dominant culture and immigrant populations play out across Europe. Switzerland, once thought to be comfortable in its insularity, is now a major site of immigration. A 22% foreign-born population gives Switzerland one of the highest nonnative populations in Europe. Obtaining Swiss citizenship is quite difficult, for Europeans and non-Europeans alike. Of the foreign residents in Switzerland, more than half are from EU countries (particularly Italy, Portugal, and Germany), though a sizable number came as refugees and economic migrants from the former Yugoslavia. "Foreigner criminality" (*Ausländerkriminalität*) is an oft-discussed political topic in Switzerland, even though crime rates remain well below those of many other industrialized countries. As in several other countries, nationalist parties have profited at the polls by exploiting this issue. In 2007, for example, the right-wing Swiss People's Party (SVP) won the most votes ever recorded by a party in a Swiss general election (29%), boosted in part by its stance on criminality by foreigners. In a poster ad campaign, the party showed four sheep, three white and one black, with one of the white sheep kicking the black sheep off the Swiss flag. In spite of domestic and international attention to such explicitly racist politics, the party scored well among voters with its promise to clean up what it called "rampant crime" by expelling foreign criminals from the country. It also played a prominent role in pushing a law banning the construction of new minarets in Switzerland (towers built adjacent to Islamic mosques), which went into effect in 2009 (and is the subject of ongoing challenges). The party's support has slipped somewhat in recent years, but it still is a significant force in Swiss politics. As is the case in other places with strong economies and large immigrant populations, such as Germany and Sweden, Switzerland shows that the issue of immigration is not merely an economic one; rather, it goes to the heart of people's conceptualization of their cultural identity.

The Swiss case is but one example of the success that far-right, anti-immigrant parties have experienced in Europe in recent years. The head of France's National Front, Marine Le Pen, won 18% of the vote in the first round of the 2012 French presidential race after expressing strong criticism of recent migrants (albeit somewhat softened from the critiques made by her father, who founded the party). In the Netherlands, Geert Wilders, founder of the Party for Freedom—the third largest party in the country by 2010—has called for a ban on the Koran, the burka, and halal food. As much as European governments like to paint their countries as beacons of tolerance and openness, it would be naïve to think that the opening of their borders to higher levels of immigration during the last several decades has not produced a backlash.

As the first decade of the twenty-first century gave way to the second, anti-immigrant parties in the Netherlands, France, and Switzerland may have lost some support, but the economic downturn of the time fueled the growth of such parties in other places. Greece's ultranationalist Golden Dawn party surged in popularity in the 2012 national elections after making claims that Greeks were being undermined by immigrants and externally driven austerity measures. In Hungary, Jobbik and other far-right parties gained support by arguing that the country's Roma population is undermining the quality of life for Hungarians. None of these parties comes even close to attracting majority support, but they provide clear evidence of the tensions that have developed in the wake of Europe's growing multicultural character.

The Traditional Social Model in Transition

With European businesses, communities, and states struggling to maintain their competitiveness in an era of globalization, the traditional European social model has come under increasing pressure. Moreover, the ability of states to provide for everyone is being challenged by the aging of the population and by migration. It should come as little surprise, then, that a growing number of Europeans are questioning whether they can maintain their relatively high standard of living and preserve the social model that developed during the twentieth century. To understand the dimensions of the problem, it is useful to look at the key challenges that model is currently facing.

MACROECONOMIC CHALLENGES

As we discussed in Chapter 8, production and consumption patterns in the twenty-first century are increasingly global. A visit to any corner of Europe reveals evidence of globalization. In most places, the small-scale manufacture of basic goods for the local market has given way to highly specialized production systems geared toward global markets. Consider, for example, the geographical changes that have occurred over time in the production and use of goods such as dishes. During preindustrial times, the dishes used by a typical European were likely produced within a few miles of his or her home. The town potter, with the help of perhaps a handful of assistants, would have made enough plates and cups to meet the demand of the local community; the practice of shopping around, or of traveling to another place to buy pottery from a distant potter, was a privilege reserved for only the wealthiest in society.

Industrialization—from the late eighteenth century onward—greatly increased the scale of production–consumption patterns. An individual's choice of dishes might have increased to a host of brands carried by the local pottery shop, even though most of those brands still would have come from factories within the same region or country. Some pottery manufacturers during this era even had royal consent to produce in the name of the king or queen, offering evidence of their "national-ness." Although the cost of production might have been cheaper in some distant locale, the cost of transportation, as well as stiff duties assessed on imported goods, worked against goods being imported from afar. It was during this era that the social model in Europe as we know it today began to emerge.

The vast geographical expansion of production during the last century, combined with a dramatic decrease in the cost of transporting goods (through containerization, for example), as well as the lowering of barriers on imports, dramatically altered the scale of the production–consumption relationship. Were you to head today to a major department store in any European city, or surf an online shopping site, you would be confronted by a wide array of dishes with various brand names from around the world. Some might be European, from such well-known brands as Waterford (Ireland), Bernardaud (France), or Rosenthal (Germany)—successor enterprises to age-old manufacturers—but these would be substantially more expensive than most people can afford for normal evening dinnerware. For all its appeal aesthetically and environmentally, pottery produced locally by craftspeople is typically uncompetitive in terms of price with the goods arriving from afar by the container-load at ports such as Rotterdam and Hamburg (fig. 11.15).

The shift that has taken place in the scale and location of production, marketing, and purchasing has had significant social impacts. The European social model developed with the assumption of a national political context, national industries, and minimal in- and out-migration. That model is not easily maintained when businesses can move halfway around the globe in search of more favorable conditions (fewer regulations, less taxation, etc.) and when competitors can offer lower wages and fewer protections. To maintain competitiveness, government and business leaders have increasingly looked at reducing the size of the public sector and exploring ways of making the labor market more flexible by, for example, making it easier to let employees go. Yet many Europeans are understandably uneasy with the proposition that their accustomed standard of living—from long vacations to job security to generous pensions—is being called into question.

Figure 11.15.   Containers being loaded onto a ship in the Copenhagen harbor. Containerization and cheap energy have greatly reduced the costs of long-distance freight transport over the past 60 years. Photo by A. B. M, 2010.

The debate over such issues has been very much in evidence in France, where some people have sharply criticized France's famous 35-hour workweek, saying it shows an inadequate work ethic in France. The argument is that France is falling behind the times because French workers are not spending enough hours working, and it is difficult to fire them if they do not perform well. Not everyone embraces this argument, of course, but even those who want to preserve the 35-hour workweek recognize that the traditional social model will have to change if France is to remain competitive.

Other European countries have struggled with similar issues, and the trend has been toward the adoption of so-called **neoliberal** reforms (that is, reforms aimed at reducing the role of government in the economy, promoting free trade, and reducing expenditures on social services). Nonetheless, reforms have not yet undermined core tenets of the social model. In Scandinavia—particularly Denmark and Sweden—serious economic crises during the early 1990s (high unemployment and massive government debt) led to labor and welfare reforms. These countries are now held up throughout Europe as models of globally fit, socially responsible market economies. As for Germany, during the 1990s and early 2000s, the country's fitness as a business location became somewhat of a national obsession; again, the debates centered largely on the inflexibility of the labor market and a social model that arguably encouraged some able workers to stay at home and collect generous unemployment benefits rather than work menial jobs for less pay. Beginning in 2000, a series of reforms—

corporate and income tax cuts, reduced unemployment benefits, and a liberalization of the rigid system of craft guilds—were introduced under the mantra of "reform or lose out" in the global economy.

The latest set of macroeconomic challenges to the social model came in the wake of the economic downturn, and associated Eurozone crisis, that began in 2009. Germany was much less hard hit than other parts of Europe by the crisis, in part because of a growing Chinese market for its products, but also because of the reforms it had implemented earlier in the decade. As the Eurozone's wealthiest country and the home to the European Central Bank, any effort to address the crisis in a serious way required German involvement. With a German government headed by a chancellor (Angela Merkel) who was a proponent of neoliberal reforms, and a German populous that was loathe to bail out economies that were widely viewed as undisciplined and irresponsibly managed, the Germans tied assistance to the adoption of neoliberal reforms and accompanying austerity measures.

Some of these reforms put governments in a position to implement policies that would have been politically difficult to enact without outside pressure, but as we saw previously, these policies led to higher levels of unemployment and depressed living standards, which in turn made it more difficult for depressed economies to grow. Social unrest followed, and some easing of the neoliberal/austerity approach eventually became necessary. But the struggle goes on to find a reasonable balance between reigning in government expenditures and supporting social services that can help the disadvantaged and make it easier for those who are caught in the crosswinds of economic change to adjust. This struggle will undoubtedly continue for some time to come. There is little doubt, however, that the European social model of the near future will be less expansive than it was a generation ago.

THE DEMOGRAPHIC CHALLENGE

When Bismarck introduced old-age pensions during the 1880s in Germany, the retirement age was set at 70 years old—an age that only 30% of males reached at the time. The retirement age was subsequently lowered to 65, where it remained for many decades. Then during the 1970s, when children born after World War II were entering the labor market in large numbers, there was a surplus of available labor. During this time the idea of "early retirement" was introduced to make room for the new pool of labor. Someone who had worked for 30 years could retire at age 60 and collect a pension until death. The system was financially viable because of the relatively small number of retirees in comparison to the number of workers. The ratio of current workers to retired persons throughout most of Europe was between five and eight to one.

Times have changed, however. The aging of the European population (see Chapter 3) has reduced the ratio of the working population to those collecting pensions to as low as four to one, and in some places the trend is in the direction of even lower worker-to-retiree ratios. Future population growth trends are notoriously difficult to predict, but the potential dimensions of the demographic problem come into focus when one looks at some basic numbers being generated by the European Commission. In 2011, the total fertility rate (TFR) for the EU as a whole was just under 1.6, and no EU country had a TFR above 2.1 (the rate needed for replacement of the existing population). The TFRs in parts of northern and northwestern Europe are high enough that the Nordic countries, the British Isles, the Netherlands, Beligum, and France are not far below the 2.1 level, but most other European countries are well below that figure (fig. 11.16). One European Commission report predicts that the EU's population will continue to grow until 2025, thanks largely to immigration, but thereafter it will begin to decline. Between 2005 and 2030, the working-age population is predicted to decline by 21 million in the EU, a significant figure when one considers that the entire population of the EU is less than 500 million. In eastern

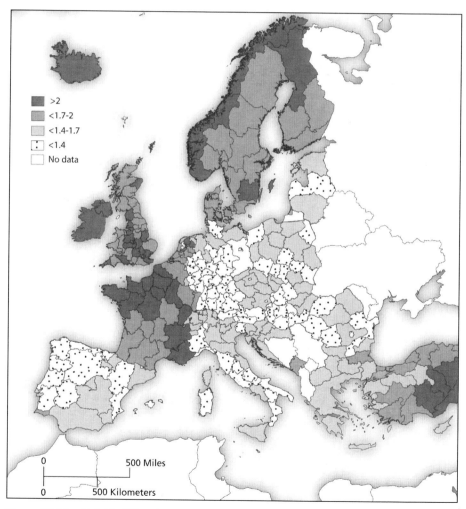

Figure 11.16.   Total fertility rates in first-order substate regions in the EU. In marked contrast to North Africa and southwest Asia, fertility rates in European countries are below replacement levels. *Source:* Eurostat 2011 and selected national yearbooks.

Europe, population declines are predicted to be particularly dramatic. By 2030, Bulgaria and Romania may well lose 21% and 11% of their populations, respectively. Turkey, which is not a member of the EU, is the only country along the eastern border of the EU where the population is likely to increase during that time period.

The share of the world's population living in Europe is also decreasing rapidly. Whereas Europe comprised 12% of the global population in 1970, that figure is expected to shrink by half by 2030, while the share in Africa and parts of Asia will grow. In 2012, Iceland, which had the highest TFR in Europe at just under 2.1, was far behind Niger, the country with the highest TFR in the world at a little over 7.0. In the United States, the rate is 2.1, or just at the replacement level (these figures, of course, do not take into account immigration).

The causes of these demographic changes are complex. Declining fertility rates are broadly correlated with economic growth and gender equalization in the labor market. Moreover, the structure of urban life in the contemporary era often works against larger families, and couples are typically waiting longer to have their first child than was the case in the past. Today, the mean age of mothers when their first child is born is getting close to 30, and many parents wait to have children until they are in their mid-30s or later, when careers are better established and the risks of setbacks are fewer. Societal expectations are also changing. A path that was once seen as natural, or even expected—schooling, marriage, babies, in that order—is no longer the norm. Longer stints in pursuit of higher education, cohabitation without marriage, extended stays abroad, and high mobility are quite typical, particularly among 20-somethings of higher socioeconomic status. In many places, societal and familial pressures toward child rearing have given way, or at least been delayed, in favor of an emphasis on self-exploration, self-expression, and career development.

Many governments are now faced with trying to come to terms with the impacts of these demographic tendencies. How will economies continue to grow as workers retire and fewer and fewer people are present to replace them? Is it possible to implement policies that stop or reverse these trends? Are the potential impacts of demographic change really so bad? Are these trends the inevitable consequence of particular development paths in Europe? Should additional immigration be encouraged to offset declining birth rates?

There is, of course, much debate about questions such as these, but one thing is clear: the social systems of the post–World War II decades cannot be sustained unless changes are made. Immigration has provided a reprieve for a time in parts of Europe, but not in others, and immigration carries with it other social costs. Hence much of the attention is focused on adjusting social benefits and looking for ways to encourage larger families.

On the social benefits side, the trend in recent years has been in the direction of decreases in guaranteed benefits, lengthened periods of service to collect full pensions, and increases in the mandatory retirement age—from 65 to 67, and even higher. As for the issue of population growth itself, many European countries have adopted **pronatalist policies** (i.e., policies designed to increase fertility rates, or at least slow the decline in the birth rate). These policies range from generous maternity leaves and support for women having children to inexpensive daycare and redesigned urban

Figure 11.17.   Park in Paris's 13th Arrondissement. Over the past couple of decades, many of Paris's parks have become more child friendly with the addition of basketball courts, Ping-Pong tables, and the like. Photo by A. B. M, 2012.

spaces that are child friendly (fig. 11.17). Population policies are not without controversy, as some people believe that family planning is not an area that is appropriate for state intervention. But with low population growth presenting states with increasingly significant challenges, governments see few options other than to encourage more births. Four brief case studies illustrate what is happening.

Spain had a moderately high TFR until relatively recently—particularly during the 40-year reign of dictator Francisco Franco, who died in 1975. Under Franco, contraception and abortion were illegal (Spain still has some of the strictest abortion laws in Europe), and women's roles were largely confined to the home. Following democratic reforms, economic growth took off, and employment possibilities for women opened up. These developments led to a precipitous decline in Spain's TFR. It was not until the 1990s that the state began to assume a more active role in encouraging more births, but Spain's fairly decentralized system of governance made it difficult to implement a coordinated set of population policies. Nonetheless, Spain has adopted some pronatalist policies, such as improved maternity leave. In keeping with more traditional views on family in Roman Catholic Spain, however, the overall emphasis has been on creating more favorable overall conditions for families with children. The steps have been modest but include increasing the availability and lowering the cost of preschool education, and increasing the availability of affordable housing (a large percentage of 20- to 29-year-olds in Spain live with their parents, in part because of the high expense of housing). These measures are showing some positive results—particularly in the south (fig. 11.16). Nonetheless, Spain's TFR remains far below replacement level, although the demographic challenge is muted because of the large number of immigrants coming to the country (fig. 11.12).

Sweden has had a more proactive family policy than Spain. In keeping with its liberal reputation, there are fewer taboos on children being born to unwed parents in Sweden, and abortion and contraceptives are readily available. During the 1980s, Sweden showed fairly dramatic gains in fertility rates. These corresponded to the introduction of proactive family policies such as generous family leave; universal, inexpensive child care; and even "speed premiums"—a bonus for parents having babies in quick succession. Gains in fertility in Sweden during the 1980s also corresponded to strong economic growth, while economic stagnation during the 1990s led again to a downward trend in birthrates. As such, some demographers speculate that pronatalist government policies are only one part of the birthrate equation in Sweden. Just as important is the fact that women are highly integrated into the workforce there and are more likely to contribute significantly to overall family earnings. During periods of economic growth, mothers with stable work were more likely to have children, whereas during periods of stagnation, uncertainty and job insecurity may have lowered birth rates.

Population policies in Germany lie somewhere between those of Spain and Sweden. Unlike Sweden, the idea of a traditional nuclear family is still very much a part of German government policy. There is, for example, a German ministry of "Family, Seniors, Women, and Youth" at the federal level, and the German constitution recognizes marriage as a cornerstone of society. Yet there are still taboos associated with government involvement in population policy, because of the history of the Third Reich and Hitler's explicitly pronatalist (and racist) family policy. Since the 1970s, the German government has compensated families for each child, under the assumption that the state has a role to play in assisting families in the costs of child rearing. Until recently, each household received the same basic amount per child, but this was changed as of 2007 to reflect the fact that women who were employed in the workforce were still having fewer children, later in life, than those not in the workforce. Now, rather than a standard rate given to each family with a child, a system of "parents money" replaces a percentage of the income of a stay-at-home parent for a specified period of time. This change was designed to encourage working professionals to have children. It is too early to know whether it will produce a sustained increase in fertility rates, but there was evidence of a spike in births after the date when the generous new benefits went into effect. There have been some criticisms of this program as elitist, however, since its goal is to subsidize well-educated, employed (and therefore better off) individuals having children, while at the same time eliminating the simple "educational" grants to all children regardless of family income.

Poland provides a case study of the demographic challenges to the European social model in the formerly Communist east. With its large agricultural sector and strong Roman Catholic traditions, Poland long had high fertility rates—the highest in Eastern Europe outside the Soviet Union in the period after World War II. Aggressive pronatalist policies during the Communist era kept Poland's fertility rate high for a time (larger, nicer houses went to those with larger families), but the TFR fell to the replacement level of 2.1 in 1989—the year when free-market reforms were first intro-duced in the country. During the 1990s, fertility rates fell even further, as govern-ment benefits to parents were restricted or privatized, and material conditions worsened for segments of the population; the country's current TFR is less than 1.4. Unlike Spain and Germany, Poland's low rate of natural increase is not offset by immigration. This situation poses significant challenges for Poland and most other eastern European countries, which are in a similar situation. It will be a struggle at best to maintain reasonably far-reaching social welfare programs in the face of these highly unfavorable demographic trends.

THE IMMIGRATION CHALLENGE

The welfare state has traditionally been organized primarily at the national scale, and the very notions of mutual assistance and social solidarity have carried with them strong nationalist tendencies (of Italians helping Italians, or French helping French). In the wake of the recent wave of immigrants, many countries are wrestling with how far the social model can and should extend. With the EU now composed of 28 coun-tries, these questions are likewise played out in Brussels and Strasbourg. Is, for exam-ple, a Roma from Bulgaria (an EU member state since 2007) who immigrates to Italy entitled to the rights and privileges of the Italian welfare state? Previously, the answer to that question was unequivocally no, but EU membership theoretically puts Euro-pean citizens on equal footing.

Far more pressing a concern, of course, is the question of immigration from non-European countries. The arrival of large numbers of relatively poor immigrants over the past few decades raises the prospect of increased strains on the European social model. The offset comes in the form of an expanded workforce paying taxes. But in situations where immigrant unemployment is high and where immigrant workers bring with them large families who are not necessarily contributing to the tax base, extending the social support network to immigrants can be a significant challenge. That many of these immigrants came at the invitation of European governments in an effort to address labor shortages presents, in the minds of many, a moral obliga-tion to include them within the social model. But inclusion is difficult in an era of economic struggles, demographic decline, and a growing unease among native-born populations about the changing ethnic makeup of European societies.

Not surprisingly, then, immigration remains a lively topic of discussion through-out Europe, and that discussion itself can serve to undermine some of the core values that have sustained the social model. It seems that populist sentiments are fairly easily mobilized when complex issues involving race, belief systems, taxation, and the provi-sion of services are reduced during election campaigns to questions such as, Are you willing to finance the arrival of yet more immigrants from some of the poorest spots on earth? Can "our" culture afford more new arrivals? Why should immigrants have jobs when so many (Germans, Dutch, French, etc.) are unemployed? These questions are not unique to Europe, of course, and how they are viewed varies widely, with sharp contrasts evident along geographic, class, and educational lines. Clearly, though, immigration has not just been a source of economic dynamism and cultural richness; it has also produced substantial material and psychological strains on the underpinnings of the European social model. How Europe confronts those strains is one of the region's fundamental challenges in the years ahead.

Attitudes toward Europe's changing social trajectory are shaped not just by developments unfolding in individual countries and cities but by the European integration project. We thus turn our attention to the possibilities and prospects of European integration in the final chapter of this book.

Sources and Suggested Readings

Allen, J. T. 2006. The French-Muslim Connection: Is France Doing a Better Job of Integration Than Its Critics? In *Pew Global Attitudes Survey*. Washington, DC: Pew Research Center. Available from http://pewglobal.org/reports/display.php?ReportID=253.

Burgoon, B., and F. Dekker. 2010. Flexible Employment, Economic Insecurity and Social Policy Preferences in Europe. *Journal of European Social Policy* 20 (2): 126–41.

Cinalli, M., M. Giugni, and P. R. Graziano. 2013. The Policies of Unemployment Protection in Europe. *International Journal of Social Welfare* 22 (3): 287–89.

Dingsdale, A. 2002. *Mapping Modernities: Geographies of Central and Eastern Europe, 1920–2000*. London: Routledge.

Dodgshon, R. A. 1987. *The European Past: Social Evolution and Spatial Order*. Houndmills, UK: Macmillan Education.

Entrikin, J. N. 2003. Political Community, Identity, and Cosmopolitan Place. In *Europe without Borders*, ed. M. Berezin and M. Schain, 51–63. Baltimore, MD: Johns Hopkins Press.

European Commission. 2005. Confronting Demographic Change: A New Solidarity between the Generations, 27. Available from http://ec.europa.eu/employment_social/news/2005/mar/comm2005–94_en.pdf.

Foucher, M. 1995. *The New Faces of Europe*. Strasbourg: Council of Europe Press.

Grant, J., S. Hoorens, S. Sivadasan, M. v. h. Loo, J. DaVanzo, L. Hale, S. Gibson, and W. Butz. 2004. *Low Fertility and Population Ageing: Causes, Consequences, and Policy Options*, 152. Leiden: RAND Europe and the European Commission. Available from http://www.rand.org/pubs/monographs/2004/RAND_MG206.pdf.

Häkli, J., and D. H. Kaplan. 2002. Learning from Europe? Borderlands in Social and Geographical Context. In *Boundaries and Place: European Borderlands in Geographical Context*, ed. D. H. Kaplan and J. Häkli, 1–17. Lanham, MD: Rowman & Littlefield.

Hamnett, C. 2003. *Unequal City: London in the Global Arena*. New York: Routledge.

Hudson, R. 2002. New Geographies and Forms of Work and Unemployment and Public Policy Innovation in Europe. *Tijdschrift Voor Economische En Sociale Geografie* 93 (3): 316–35.

Johnson, C. 2011. Mezzogiorno without the Mafia: Modern-Day Meridionalisti and the Making of a "Space of Backwardness" in Eastern Germany. *National Identities* 13 (2): 157–76.

Jonas, A. E. G. 2006. The Globalized City: Economic Restructuring and Social Polarization in European Cities. *International Journal of Urban and Regional Research* 30 (1): 233–34.

King, R. 2002. Towards a New Map of European Migration. *International Journal of Population Geography* 8 (2): 89–106.

Koopmans, R. 2005. *Contested Citizenship: Immigration and Cultural Diversity in Europe*. Social Movements, Protest, and Contention 25. Minneapolis: University of Minnesota Press.

Malheiros, J. 2002. Ethni-Cities: Residential Patterns in the Northern European and Mediterranean Metropolises—Implications for Policy Design. *International Journal of Population Geography* 8 (2): 107–34.

Monzini, P. 2007. Sea-Border Crossings: The Organization of Irregular Migration to Italy. *Mediterranean Politics* 12 (2): 163–84.

Musterd, S. 2005. Social and Ethnic Segregation in Europe: Levels, Causes, and Effects. *Journal of Urban Affairs* 27 (3): 331–48.

O'Loughlin, J., and J. Friedrichs, eds. 1996. *Social Polarization in Post-Industrial Metropolises*. Berlin: Walter de Gruyter.

Organisation for Economic Co-operation and Development. 2003. *Berlin: Towards an Integrated Strategy for Social Cohesion and Economic Development*. Paris: Organisation for Economic Co-operation and Development.

Price, M., and L. Benton-Short. 2007. Immigrants and World Cities: From the Hyper-Diverse to the Bypassed. *GeoJournal* 68 (2): 103–17.

Ray, R., J. C. Gornick, and J. Schmitt. 2010. Who Cares? Assessing Generosity and Gender Equality in Parental Leave Policy Designs in 21 Countries. *Journal of European Social Policy* 20 (3): 196–216.

Rodríguez-Pose, A., and V. Tselios. 2009. Education and Income Inequality in the Regions of the European Union. *Journal of Regional Science* 49:411–37.

Saltman, R. B., R. Busse, and J. Figueras. 2004. Social Health Insurance Systems in Western Europe. In *European Observatory on Health Systems and Policies Series*, ed. J. Figueras, M. McKee, E. Mossialos, and R. B. Saltman, 298. Maidenhead: Open University Press and the World Health Organization. Available from http://www.euro.who.int/document/E84968.pdf.

Samers, M. 2004. An Emerging Geopolitics of "Illegal" Immigration in the European Union. *European Journal of Migration & Law* 6 (1): 27–45.

United Kingdom Home Office, Advisory Council on the Misuse of Drugs. 2006. Pathways to Problems: Hazardous Use of Tobacco, Alcohol and Other Drugs by Young People in the UK and Its Implications for Policy, 100. London. Available from https://www.gov.uk/government/uploads/system/uploads/attachment_data/file/119053/Pathwaystoproblems.pdf.

Van Marissing, E., G. Bolt, and R. Van Kempen. 2006. Urban Governance and Social Cohesion: Effects of Urban Restructuring Policies in Two Dutch Cities. *Cities* 23 (4): 279–90.

Western, J. 2007. Neighbors or Strangers? Binational and Transnational Identities in Strasbourg. *Annals of the Association of American Geographers* 97 (1): 158–81.

White, P. 1984. *The West European City: A Social Geography*. London: Longman.

Wilkes, R., N. Guppy, and L. Farris. 2007. Right-Wing Parties and Anti-foreigner Sentiment in Europe. *American Sociological Review* 72:831–40.

CHAPTER 12

Whither European Integration?

Our discussion of the rise of the EEC/EC/EU in Chapter 9 emphasized economic matters, but European integration is not just an economic undertaking; it is a political project as well. The EEC came about as the result of an intergovernmental agreement, and it led to the creation of political institutions that have expanded their scope of authority over time. These institutions now exercise a good number of functions that are more typically the province of the governments of sovereign states. As such, a new level of governance now exists in Europe, one that exercises considerable power.

Understanding the political dimension of the integration project requires more than just analyzing the administrative functions of EEC/EC/EU institutions; it is also important to consider the impacts of the EU on citizenship in Europe. Most Europeans are no longer simply French, Germans, or Hungarians; they are also citizens of the European Union. What are the implications of European Union citizenship for longer-standing national allegiances? Is Europe headed toward a future that leaves behind the nationalist foundations on which the modern state system was built (see Chapter 6)? The answers to questions of this sort are far from clear, but there is much to be learned from looking at some of the historical and geographical features of the integration process.

Geographic circumstances have influenced European integration from the beginning. As we saw in Chapter 6, the EEC might never have gotten off the ground in the late 1950s if the two core powers behind the initiative—France and Germany—had not had products they wanted to trade with one another. France was a ready market for the output of Germany's rebuilt heavy industries, and Germany was an obvious outlet for French agricultural production and specialty manufacturing. The French–German trading relationship provided a geographic foundation around which early European cooperation could be built. Of relevance as well was the new willingness in the Europe of the 1950s to challenge the traditional role of the European "nation-state" in light of the disastrous conflicts of the first half of the twentieth century and the growing dominance of the United States and the Soviet Union on the global stage.

Over the past half century, more countries have come into the EEC/EC/EU fold, the economies of those countries have become increasingly interdependent, the reach of central governmental and regulatory institutions has expanded, and more and more Europeans have come to think of the EU as part of their lives—and even their identities. With the partial exception of the period of stagnation during the 1970s, from the 1950s through the early 2000s the general trajectory was in the direction of both widening and deepening—with neither occurring at the expense of the other.

In recent years, however, the European integration experiment has been in some turmoil. The May 2004 enlargement of the EU (fig. 9.8) set off a vigorous debate over the advisability of further enlargement. Then in 2005 the voters in both France and the Netherlands rejected a proposed constitution for the EU that was designed both to coordinate the various treaties under which the EU had been operating and to give the EU more administrative power and autonomy over matters such as foreign policy. A subsequent treaty (the Treaty of Lisbon) embodied many of the principles that were contained in the constitution but eliminated references that make the EU sound like a state (including the word constitution) and provided opt-outs for the United Kingdom, Poland, and Ireland on matters deemed to be invasive of national sovereignty by the leaders of those countries. Just as the treaty was coming into force, however, economic turmoil erupted in Europe, which (as we have seen) brought the future of the euro into question and exposed deep rifts among member states.

The EU has continued to grow in recent years—adding Romania and Bulgaria in 2007 and Croatia in 2013. Moreover, the fiscal and monetary authority of EU institutions has grown in the wake of the Eurozone crisis. Nonetheless, serious questions are being raised about what the EU is and where it should be going, and the level of support for the EU has slipped in parts of Europe.

Public opinion is constantly changing and is tricky to gauge, but "Eurobarometer" surveys run by the EU are helpful because they are fairly comprehensive and are administered frequently. They regularly include questions about support for European integration. A Spring 2011 survey asking Europeans whether they thought membership was a good thing for their countries yielded strong positive responses in the Netherlands, Ireland, Luxembourg, Spain, and Belgium, but on average only 47% of the population in EU countries regarded membership as a good thing, and in 17 countries the figure fell below 50% (fig. 12.1). The lowest support came from Latvia (25%), the United Kingdom (26%), Czechia (31%), and Hungary (32%), followed by Cyprus, Austria, and Slovenia. When the question is whether people trust the EU, the picture is even more discouraging for proponents of European integration. On average only 31% of the European population surveyed in 2011 indicated that they trusted EU institutions, and the figures were as low as 13% in Cyprus, 17% in Spain, 19% in Greece, 20% in the United Kingdom, 24% in Portugal, and 25% in Spain (fig. 12.2). These responses came at one of the low points in the economic crisis, but they highlight the challenges the EU faces as it seeks to move forward.

The reasons behind the lack of faith in the EU and its institutions are complex. Many Europeans feel somewhat disaffected from the European integration experiment—particularly in the wake of the financial downturn. Some Europeans resent the loss of local control and are concerned about the social implications of the rapid

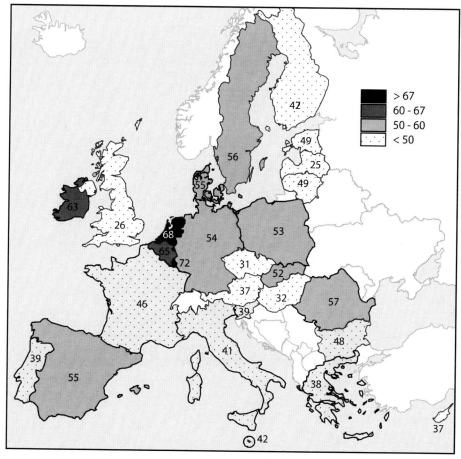

Figure 12.1.   Attitudes toward European integration in 2011. The numbers reflect "yes" responses to the statement, "Membership in the EU is a good thing." *Source:* Eurobarometer.

changes unfolding in Europe. The latter is not just a product of integration, of course; globalization and increased migration play important roles as well. But the EU is clearly implicated in the macroeconomic and social changes that are undermining long-standing arrangements.

Despite the breadth and depth of concern about the EU, few predict its demise. The EU continues to receive relatively strong support among better educated, more economically successful segments of European society—and those are the segments that exert disproportionate influence over political and social affairs. Moreover, the EU tends to be viewed more favorably by younger people than by those who are aged 55 or over. Even more importantly, the impacts of European integration are so pervasive that it would be extremely difficult to abandon the project now.

The question, then, is not so much whether the EU will continue to exist, but what form it will take. At the heart of the discussion are two fundamentally different perspectives on the future of European integration. One perspective views the EU as

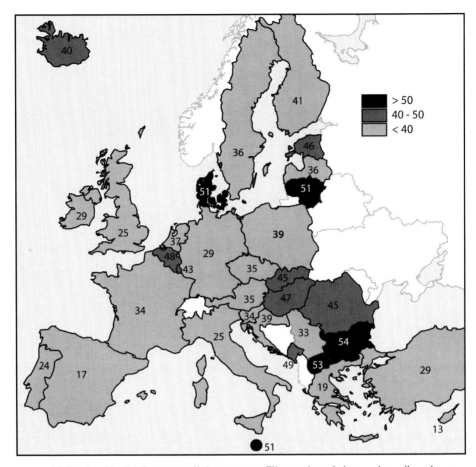

Figure 12.2.   Trust in the European Union among EU member states and applicant countries, 2011. Trust tends to be lowest in northern Europe and a swath of countries through the European center. *Source:* Eurobarometer.

a big state in the making. Proponents of this perspective concede that much power remains vested in individual states and that the EU has some formidable internal divides to overcome, but they note that it took the United States nearly a century to forge a fairly unified state out of a disparate set of colonies. Europe, they argue, is simply engaged in the same drawn-out process.

In opposition to this perspective are those who think the idea of creating a big European statelike entity is infeasible, a mistake, or both. They acknowledge that Europe has taken major strides both in widening and in deepening, but they argue that the great uncertainties unleashed by the recent expansion of the EU, the defeat of the proposed constitution for the EU, and the divisive debate that occurred in the wake of the euro crisis reflect fundamental differences that cannot and should not be resolved through the concentration of ever greater powers in the central institutions of the EU. Instead, they see the future of the EU largely as an economic club that facilitates interstate commerce, but leaves most governmental powers in the hands of national governments.

To make sense of the circumstances that give rise to these different positions, it is useful to look at some of the most important impetuses for integration and disintegration in contemporary Europe. We start on the integration side, but as we review the key catalysts of integration it is useful to keep in mind that some of them can be sources of disintegration as well.

Impetuses for Integration

GLOBALIZATION

As we have seen throughout this book, Europe has been shaped by forces beyond its borders for centuries, if not millennia. But the extent and pace of globalization has greatly accelerated over the past 50 years—most obviously in the economic arena. In the face of rapidly expanding networks of investment and economic exchange, many European economists, businesspeople, and everyday citizens believe that the region will be at a decisive disadvantage if its economies are divided among the more than 45 relatively small-scale territorial units found in Europe. They view the EU as a fundamental source of economic competitiveness—promoting intra-European trade, allowing major economic ventures to develop across state lines (a good example is the European consortium Airbus), and enhancing Europe's clout in international economic and financial circles. Bolstering this view is the great expansion of intra-European trade that occurred as the European integration project moved forward, and the emergence of the euro as an important international reserve currency.

Given the boost to international commerce that is attributed to the EEC/EC/EU, it is not surprising that some of the greatest support for European integration is found in Europe's major business and financial centers. That support became clear when the citizens of the Nordic countries voted on whether to join the EU in the mid-1990s. The Norwegians ultimately rejected EU membership, whereas the Swedes and Finns voted to join. Mapping the vote at the scale of first-order substate regions, however, reveals a pattern that is obscured if the national scale is the sole focus of attention: the people living in the major urban nodes of all three countries supported EU membership, whereas those in rural areas were more hesitant to join (fig. 12.3). Similar geographical differences in support for integration can be found in many other parts of Europe as well.

THE CHANGING GEOPOLITICAL ORDER

As was discussed in Chapter 6, the superpower-dominated Cold War order that took shape after World War II was an initial driver of European integration in the 1950s. Much has changed since, but the idea that larger units are more likely to have influence at the global scale has endured. Thus there are still many Europeans who feel that

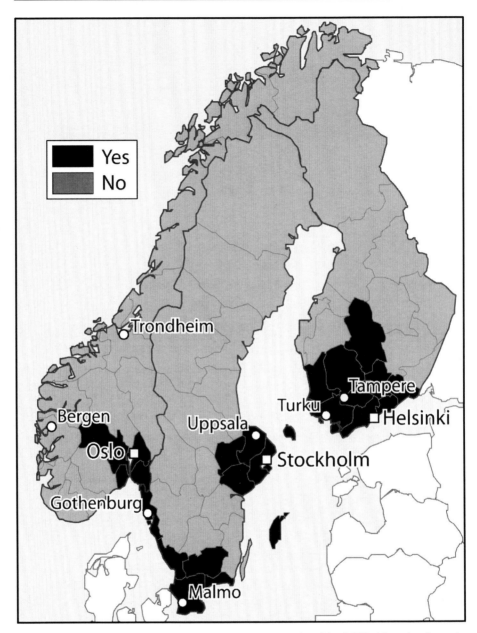

Figure 12.3.   The Nordic vote on European Union membership, 1995. Mapping the vote at the scale of the first-order substate regions highlights the continuities across the three northern European countries; even though the membership vote failed in Norway and succeeded in Sweden and Finland, the yes vote in all three countries was concentrated in the urban-economic core. *Source:* Based on a map in Murphy and Hunderi-Ely 1996, 286.

the region is unlikely to be able to shape global developments, or even to chart its own path, if there is no significant coordination among its peoples and states.

Of course the Cold War is no longer with us, and there is much debate over where the global geopolitical order is, or should be, heading. But growing discussions about the breakdown of the world into competing regions based on religion and history has promoted integrationist impulses in some circles. Perhaps more importantly, the rise of an increasingly assertive, less collaborative United States during the early years of the twenty-first century fostered considerable support for integration in Europe because of a perceived need to provide a counterweight to the United States in the global arena. This argument was made with particular force in the aftermath of the U.S. invasion of Iraq in 2003 when a considerable majority of Europeans (although not all European governments) strongly opposed the U.S. initiative. The argument has become more muted in recent years as the United States has assumed a more consultative posture and as Europe has had to confront its own divisions over foreign policy matters. But the concern over the need for a counterweight to the United States in world affairs still serves as a strong impetus for European integration.

Looking back over the past 50 years, it is interesting to note how the United States has shifted from being a strong advocate of European integration in the 1950s to a more neutral position in recent years. Yet the relationship with the United States is as strong a catalyst for integration as ever, albeit in a different way. Whereas once the impetus for integration came about as a result of U.S. persuasion and foreign aid, now it is produced by the idea that a counterweight is needed to the United States as an economic and geopolitical power.

RELATIONSHIPS WITH SURROUNDING REGIONS

A corollary of the impetus for integration provided by global geopolitical developments is the advantage integration can provide in the effort to confront challenges on the European periphery. A particularly significant moment in this regard came when the Iron Curtain fell and the then EC was confronted with a radically changed political and economic environment immediately to its east. Having long opposed the Soviet presence and championed the cause of democracy and economic liberalization in the eastern part of Europe, many in the EC felt a moral obligation to reach out to their newly liberated neighbors. There were also practical concerns: if the EC did not step in and help what used to be called Eastern Europe get on its feet, the countries in the west could be faced with a set of unstable and potentially dangerous societies on their doorstep.

All of these circumstances produced a move to bring much of former Eastern Europe into the European integration project. The EC/EU provided the umbrella under which west and east could reengage, and the regulatory requirements that had to be met by the eastern countries in order to join the EC/EU were seen by many as critical to the process of reform. Thus, even though the expansion of the EU in the early 2000s introduced a new set of problems, it was also seen as a triumph for the idea of European integration. And European integration continues to be viewed as a force that is producing positive results in parts of southeastern Europe (including Turkey) that are not yet part of the EU because the prospect of membership has fostered what many see as constructive reforms in would-be member states. (Since admission to the EU is premised on meeting a set of political and economic criteria designed to promote democracy, the rule of law, human rights, freedom of the press, and economic competitiveness, applicant countries typically undertake significant reforms in an effort to secure membership.)

Somewhat farther afield, the EU as a bloc engages in negotiations with political entities in the Middle East and Africa over matters ranging from security to trade. Differences among EU countries sometimes turn these negotiations into sources of fragmentation rather than integration, but the ability of the EU to speak for Europe at large is often seen as a source of strength. For example, there is mounting concern that China's economic penetration into Africa is undermining Europe's efforts to promote human rights and democratization in a region that has traditionally fallen principally within Europe's sphere of influence. Many Europeans feel that they are in a poor position to challenge China's approach if Europe cannot speak with one voice.

HEIGHTENED INTERACTION

European integration has clearly facilitated interactions and arrangements that make it difficult to think of Europe simply as a collection of states. Most obviously, integration has served to make it almost inconceivable that the Europe of the twenty-first century will see a repeat of what happened in 1914 and 1939. The magnitude of this achievement should not be underestimated, nor should its importance as a catalyst for integration go unappreciated. A comparable achievement today would be to create the foundations for lasting peace and cooperation between Israelis and Palestinians. The magnitude of what has been achieved in Europe is widely recognized, and it helps explain why so many people are committed to the idea of European integration, even when disagreements arise over the ways integration is being pursued.

The increasing ease and frequency of movement of Europeans from one country to another also works against polarization within the EU. As we discussed in Chapter 9, throughout most of Europe one no longer engages in the long waits to cross international borders that are characteristic of many parts of the world (fig. 9.9). The "Schengen area" in Europe has been steadily expanding, and it is likely to continue to do so—furthering the momentum of the European integration project. At the same time, there are many programs that promote interactions among Europeans. Students, for example, regularly travel to other countries to pursue their studies under an EU initiative known as Erasmus.

The economic interactions that have developed across Europe mean that people's well-being in one European state is closely linked with what goes on in another. People regularly buy products aimed at the EU market as a whole. The packaging on those products reminds consumers that they are part of something larger than the state in which they live. They drive cars with license plates incorporating the EU flag. They carry passports with an EU designation, and they are often surrounded by organizations and businesses with a Europe-wide focus. All of these features of life in contemporary Europe contribute to the sense that the EU represents a more-or-less irreversible process.

ECONOMIC ADVANCES

Considerable support for the integration project in some parts of Europe has come from gains in prosperity after joining the EEC/EC/EU. States such as Ireland, Spain, and Greece have benefited heavily from the EU's "structural funds" (fig. 12.4), and these are states where support for European integration is particularly strong. Similarly, the previously mentioned tendency for those in Europe's key urban-economic centers to support European integration reflects a widespread sense that integration has generally worked in favor of key urban-based sectors of the economy. Also, the development

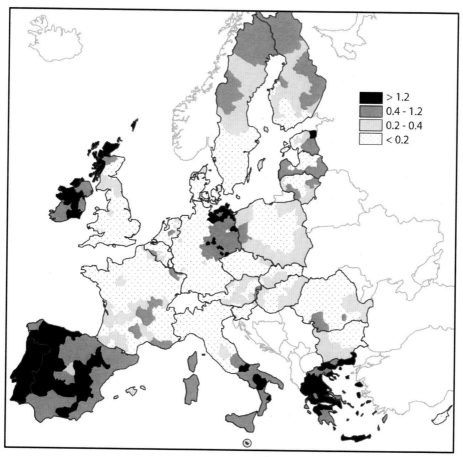

Figure 12.4. Areas benefiting from European Union regional development funds. Regions in newer EU member states are beginning to benefit, but the map shows the long-standing importance of regional assistance funding to Ireland, Portugal, Spain, and Greece. *Source: Based on a map in European Spatial Planning Observation Network, ESPON Synthesis Report III, October 2006, 73.*

assistance that is dispersed by the EU has fostered support for the integration process—both in parts of the EU that have been beneficiaries, and in neighboring countries and regions where EU investment and aid has brought greater prosperity.

Growing prosperity in the newest member states in the European east is also helping to foster support for integration throughout much of that region. As we have seen, the economies of the newest member states lag behind their counterparts to the west (a source of fragmentation, as we will see later), but after joining the EU, growth rates in the east accelerated, foreign direct investment from the western part of Europe grew, and trade with longer-standing EU members increased. Moreover, integration opened a job market in western Europe for those from the east that has helped to reduce unemployment and bring money into some poorer parts of the region. It is thus not surprising that the majority of citizens in countries such as Bulgaria, Romania, Poland, and Slovakia hold favorable views of European integration (fig. 12.1).

The adoption of the euro by many long-standing EU members (fig. 9.10) has also deepened the penetration of the European integration project into people's daily lives. Not everyone is a proponent of the euro, of course, particularly in the wake of the recent financial crisis. But the euro has promoted yet more interaction of people and capital across national boundaries. It has also been accompanied by the establishment of a European Central Bank and a set of related economic arrangements that bring member states' economies and fiscal practices into ever-closer alignment. It has thus made it increasingly difficult even to think about distinctly national economies in contemporary Europe.

THE "IRRATIONALITY" OF THE PATTERN OF STATES

Looking back over the many maps we have examined in this book, it is often easy to see how patterns on one map reflect those on another. Maps of terrain and precipitation help us understand agricultural patterns; population distribution maps reflect the influence of agricultural topographic, and climatic patterns; and so on. When it comes to the political pattern, however, it is almost as if all the other maps were thrown away and a new map was created from scratch. The political map is so different because it is the product of the vicissitudes of conquest and power balances, not underlying environmental or social arrangements. As a result, political boundaries rarely delimit discrete physical or human territories.

Even though the logic for the pattern of states rarely lies in underlying geographic conditions, states can work to change those geographic conditions and try to make them correspond more closely with their boundaries (e.g., by enforcing language policies that create language regions). Nonetheless, many "irrationalities" inevitably remain. States necessarily represent awkward territorial frameworks for dealing with environmental issues, economic development challenges, infrastructure planning, and much more because the spatial character of these problems rarely coincides with the territorial reach of states. Against this backdrop, integration offers the potentially appealing prospect of being able to develop approaches to issues and problems that are more in keeping with the underlying geography of the problems themselves than is possible in a more territorially fragmented world region.

Many Europeans recognize that whether the issue is the construction of a high-speed transit network, the disposal of nuclear waste, the regulation of fisheries in surrounding waters, or the development of poor border areas, the European state system represents an obstacle to coordinated planning that can only be overcome through some kind of supranational institutional initiative. They are thus drawn to the possibilities inherent in EU initiatives that take a non-state-based approach to issues and problems (see, e.g., fig. 12.5). On a more individual level, the ability to take advantage of people, resources, and even job opportunities outside one's country of birth represents an appealing prospect to many

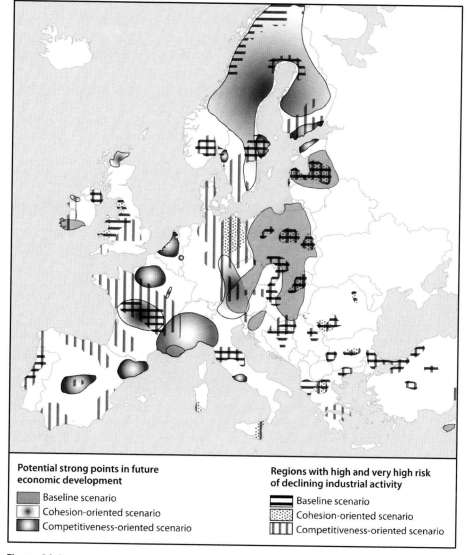

Potential strong points in future economic development

- Baseline scenario
- Cohesion-oriented scenario
- Competitiveness-oriented scenario

Regions with high and very high risk of declining industrial activity

- Baseline scenario
- Cohesion-oriented scenario
- Competitiveness-oriented scenario

Figure 12.5.   Future development scenarios within the European Union: Baseline = focus on widening and deepening, Cohesion-oriented = deepening prioritized, Competitiveness-oriented = widening prioritized. The starting place is not the state but underlying patterns of socioeconomic well-being. *Source:* Based on a map in European Spatial Planning Observation Network, *ESPON Synthesis Report III*, October 2006, 54.

Europeans—particularly those living in towns and villages in border regions that would be cut off from their natural **hinterlands** if borders were to function the way they did during the first half of the twentieth century.

ETHNO-REGIONALISM

Despite the ability of most European states to create large-scale national communities within their borders, many ethno-regional minorities remain within and between European states—and many are looking for some degree of autonomy, or even independence (fig. 11.11). In one sense, Europe's ethnic complexity might be thought of as a source of fragmentation, since ethno-regionalist movements have promoted a substantial **devolution** of authority in several European states over the past several decades—most notably in Belgium, Spain, and the United Kingdom. In all three of these cases, ethno-regionalist groups have managed to wrest considerable power from central authorities—and devolutionary pressures continue. Some Basques and Catalans in Spain, Corsicans in France, and Flemings in Belgium see independence as the ultimate goal.

Despite the disintegrative potential of these movements, they also serve as catalysts to integration because groups with a distinct sense of ethno-regional identity are often too small or vulnerable to go it alone, and the EU offers an appealing, alternative political-territorial framework to that of the traditional state. It is for this reason that some partisans of ethnic autonomist and separatist movements have been proponents of European integration. They see it as a development that ultimately weakens the power of the central governments of countries such as Spain, France, and the United Kingdom and as an alternative locus of power that is not rooted in the nation-state idea (Chapter 6). Many Catalans, for example, can identify more easily with Europe than with Spain.

As we will see in the next section, European integration has not been embraced by all proponents of ethno-regionalism. But the EU offers possibilities for ethno-regionalists that make European integration appealing to many. Regions can have direct access to Brussels, integration can facilitate cooperation among ethnic groups straddling state boundaries, and ethno-regionalists can sometimes bring state governments to account by appealing to the judicial organs of the EU. These possibilities make ethno-regionalism a force favoring integration in a number of corners of Europe—as well as at the very core of the EU, where a substantial number of Flemings, and some Walloons, view Europe as an attractive alternative to Belgium.

Impetuses for Fragmentation

GLOBALIZATION

One of the principal critiques leveled against economic globalization is that it makes it increasingly difficult for local communities, or even states, to control their own economic futures. European integration is implicated in this critique, in that it has facilitated the upscaling of economic decision making and activity. Moreover, the elimination of trade barriers has made it hard for some small-scale farmers and businesspeople to turn a profit. The ease of transacting business across national borders has facilitated the rise of large-scale multinational corporations that can take advantage of economies of scale that are not available to smaller businesses and industries.

All of these developments help make Europe more competitive at the global scale and foster support for European integration among economic and political elites. But they can also foster resentment—particularly where local, traditional, smaller-scale interests are losing out to larger, more impersonal, externally controlled entities. The point is that globalization is a double-edged sword. Yes, it offers economic opportunities for some, but it can also erode the traditional protections offered by individual states and undermine people's quality of life. For the many Europeans who are concerned about the latter issues, European integration is a mixed blessing at best.

The mid-1990s vote on EU membership in northern European countries (noted above) shows that skepticism about European integration is particularly intense in the rural sector (fig. 12.3). Many of the voters outside of the major cities were concerned that joining the EU would undermine the small-scale farming and business activities that are the mainstays of life in significant parts of the rural European north. Many of the areas with high numbers of no votes were eligible for EU regional development aid, but that prospect was not enough to offset voters' concerns over loss of local control and the erosion of traditional modes of livelihood. The view of integration from the Nordic rural areas described above is emblematic of feelings that one finds in many corners of Europe. Moreover, a significant proportion of the European population is concerned about the erosion of the European welfare state (Chapter 11) and about the depersonalization of everyday life in the face of globalization. With the EU looking like the face of globalization to those concerned about the diminishment of local differences and control in the wake of global economic integration, support for the EU suffers accordingly.

THE CHANGING GEOPOLITICAL ORDER

Even though the geopolitical shifts of the past several decades have served as a catalyst for integration, they have also required Europeans to take positions on issues that are viewed in dissimilar ways in different parts of Europe. As such, they have exposed some of the region's more significant internal divisions and highlighted the challenges of creating a more integrated political space in Europe.

The EEC and EC had little authority over questions of international relations, but the EU has played an ever-more-significant and visible foreign-policy role (Chapter 6). Foreign policy decisions often require confronting sensitive, highly charged matters that have traditionally been the prerogative of state governments. On matters ranging from the U.S. intervention in Iraq, to the Iranian nuclear program, to climate change, to the Syrian civil war, differences within the EU have not been easy to resolve. The difficulty of reaching agreement intensified when the new eastern European member states joined in 2004 and succeeding years. These countries were faced with radically different political and economic circumstances during the decades after World War II. As a result, many of their citizens and leaders view foreign policy questions through a different lens than do their counterparts to the west.

The uncertainty of the geopolitical environment of the early twenty-first century heightens the potential for fragmentation. Is the world breaking down into competing regional blocs? To what extent is the rise of China an opportunity or a challenge? What, if anything, can Europe do to reduce turmoil in the Middle East? What role should NATO play in conflicts outside of Europe? Intense differences exist across Europe over questions such as these. When the EU becomes involved, the complexities grow. It is not surprising, then, that critics of the integration project highlight the inability of the EU to function as a strong international actor as an example of the limitations of integration. They further suggest that strengthening the EU's foreign policy competence would lead either to incoherence or to a potentially unpopular imposition of the priorities of a few powerful EU countries, no matter what the governments and citizens of other countries might want.

NATIONALISM

Proponents of the integration process frequently herald the growing tendency for Europeans to identify with Europe. This tendency is well illustrated in public opinion surveys that ask people to indicate whether they consider themselves to be a particular nationality, European, or some combination of the two. A recent poll—conducted in May 2013—showed that over 50% of the population in the majority of EU countries identified with the notion of being "European" as well as being a member of a particular nationality—and the figure exceeded 45% in all countries except the United Kingdom and Ireland (fig. 12.6).

For all the significance of these findings, there is another way to read these surveys. Respondents can choose among European only, European followed by nationality, nationality followed by European, and nationality only. The percentage of people who put Europe ahead of their own nationality (by answering either European only or European followed by nationality) is fairly small. Only in Luxembourg did the percentage exceed 20%, and in more than half the then member states it was 10% or below.

What these survey results suggest is that nationalism is far from dead in Europe. Indeed, it remains a potent force that affects how most Europeans view integration. The bottom-line question for many Danes and Britons is whether integration is working in the interests of Denmark and the United Kingdom. The enthusiasm of Poles and Romanians for joining the western club has been tempered by a desire to ensure that their own distinctive national cultures do not get lost in the mix. Moreover, the loss of the ability within the eurozone to respond to economic crises at the state level by adjusting exchange rates has produced resentments in some countries within the eurozone and has kept other countries—notably the United Kingdom and Denmark—from adopting the euro.

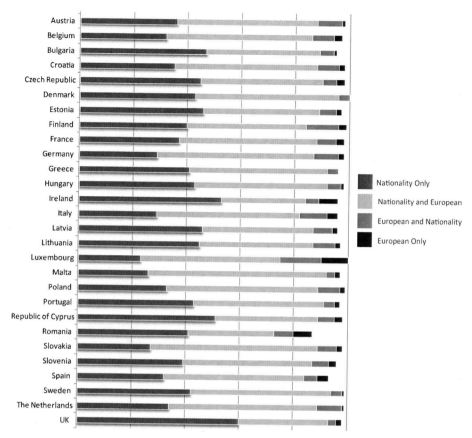

Figure 12.6. Degree of identification with states, the European Union, or a combination of the two, 2013. Even though a substantial number of Europeans identify to some degree with Europe, questionnaires of this sort highlight the continuing importance of nationalism in Europe. *Source:* Eurobarometer.

The greatest problem that comes from comparing the Europe of the last 50 years with the early United States is that, for all the differences that existed among the original 13 U.S. colonies and the states that joined them in the decades following 1776, the people living in those states did not have a sense of identity or territorial attachment that was in any way comparable to the nationalist affinities that have been part of the modern European scene. Europe is clearly no longer in the Age of Nationalism that gave rise to World War I, but for the majority of Europeans, the "nation-state" still comes first. Nationalism thus remains the single greatest source of fragmentation in Europe—making it difficult for the EU to move beyond a system where individual states can veto important decisions or take actions that may be in the collective interest, but that disadvantage a few key states.

BUREAUCRATIZATION

The EU is a large, complicated institution with multiple branches—each accompanied by its own system of administration. A fair degree of bureaucratization is thus an inevitable part of European integration. The EU's reputation for bureaucratization, however, is particularly entrenched because of the way it functions. First, at the heart of the project of creating a common European economic space is the development and enforcement of regulations. As such, many people see the EU primarily as a rule-generating bureaucracy. Second, much of the power in the EU is vested in a Council of Ministers from the various states, the members of which have not been elected, and in a Commission of functionaries appointed by state governments. Substantial power is thus wielded by individuals who are not directly responsive to the electorate, giving rise to concerns that the organization is encumbered by a "democratic deficit"—a deficit that fuels the sense that the EU is a bureaucratic maze.

Not surprisingly, concerns over bureaucratization are a source of fragmentation in Europe. Those opposing further integration frequently argue that Europeans should not delegate control over their fates to a distant, unresponsive bureaucracy in Brussels. This argument has gained traction in an enlarged EU. With ever more peoples and territories gathered under the EU umbrella, it is increasingly difficult for individuals and communities to see the EU as an organization over which they have meaningful control.

Anti-integrationists also express concerns over administrative costs, which are substantial and which many regard as doing little to enhance the well-being or the quality of life of most Europeans. Consider, for example, the cost of language services within the EU. Even before the 2004 enlargement, language services accounted for a significant percentage of the EU's administrative budget (see Chapter 4). With the addition of 13 new countries and multiple new languages since then, those costs have grown considerably. Another area of controversy is the cost of maintaining Strasbourg as the official seat of the European Parliament, even though much of the day-to-day parliamentary business is conducted in Brussels. Every month significant sums are expended shipping people, documents, and equipment back and forth between the two cities. The cost irks many, but there is little incentive for France to allow the European Parliament to move to Brussels.

DIFFERENCES OVER WIDENING AND DEEPENING

From the perspective of those living in Western Europe prior to 1989, the only possible candidates for admission into the EEC/EC were those countries lying to the west of the Iron Curtain. The disintegration of the post–World War II order, however, opened up the question of what exactly constitutes Europe, or at least what areas might or should be eligible for inclusion in the European integration project. In the lead-up to the 2004 expansion of the EU, there was little debate over the first tier of countries abutting former Western Europe's eastern boundary, but the situation beyond that was much murkier. The very process of opening up the question of what might constitute Europe (at least for integration purposes) fostered uncertainty and debate that has not yet been resolved. The EC/EU can no longer define itself in opposition to a Soviet-dominated east; it now needs a different raison d'être.

Confronting the diversity of views on this matter is a major and ongoing challenge for the EU. Some want to see the EU as little more than a loosely linked economic space; they tend to favor widening, but they are not interested in further deepening. Many in this camp see widening as a guarantee against further deepening, as widening makes it more difficult to develop centralized approaches to issues and problems. At the other end of the spectrum are those who want to see Europe emerge as an ever better integrated economic, social, and even political space. Many people holding this view are concerned that widening will undermine the ability of the EU to deepen—making them cautious about admitting new members. In between these two positions are a diversity of perspectives, some of which are based on the idea that widening and deepening need not be oppositional, some of which highlight the advantages of admitting specific countries for particular strategic or economic reasons, and some of which are premised on the notion that some parts of the EU should move faster toward integration than others.

Reconciling these divergent views is not an easy task; indeed, they are at the heart of the current debate over where the EU is headed. Differences in perspective are manifest most clearly in differences over Turkey's potential membership in the EU. Turkey has long been a candidate to join the EU. Some see Turkish membership as a positive step for Turkey and the EU—rewarding Turkey for reforms in recent years, bringing an important new economy into the mix, and undermining the notion that Europe stands in opposition to a purported Islamic regional bloc. Others oppose Turkish membership out of concern that Turkey is too different culturally and economically and that Turkish membership would make further deepening almost impossible. Proponents of this view argue that if Turkey joins the EU, there is no logical basis for denying membership to Ukraine, and perhaps Russia down the line—leading to an EU that stretches from the Atlantic to the Pacific. Former French president Valery Giscard d'Estaing echoed this line of thinking when he headed the group charged with drafting a new constitution for Europe. He suggested that if Turkey were admitted to the EU, Morocco would reasonably expect to follow, and perhaps Lebanon and Israel—leading to the end of the EU as we know it.

It is not yet clear how these debates will be resolved. Opinion polls indicate that Turkish membership does not have broad support among the citizens of current EU member states, but public opinion can be fluid. What lies behind the Turkish debate, though, are the more fundamental differences in how European integration is conceived, which were sketched out at the beginning of this chapter. A considerable majority of Britons are interested in little more than an economic union, whereas most Belgians and Slovaks are looking for much more.

HEIGHTENED INTERACTION

At the heart of the widening-versus-deepening debate are questions about the impacts of growing interactions between places with different socioeconomic and cultural characteristics. As we saw earlier, interaction has been an important catalyst for integration in Europe, but when peoples with substantially different standards and ways of living are joined together in a formal process of integration, interaction can serve as a source of fragmentation as well. The disintegrative tendencies of interaction typically revolve around the difficulties of forging formal linkages among countries in very different economic circumstances and the tensions associated with the movement across international boundaries of peoples from divergent economic and cultural backgrounds.

Difficulties and tensions of this sort have been in evidence each time the EEC/EC/EU has been joined by new states that were clearly less well off and that had been isolated from longer-standing member states (for example, Greece, Spain, and Portugal). The addition of 13 new eastern European countries between 2004 and 2013, however, raised the stakes considerably. The recent enlargements were different from their predecessors both in the number of states and peoples involved and in the economic diversities they brought into the fold. As figure 12.7 shows, the newest EU members in the east are behind their western counterparts in terms of gross domestic product per capita; even with relatively high growth rates, it will take decades for many of them to reach parity with most western European countries.

The difficulty of confronting these differences has raised significant doubts in the minds of many about the future of the European integration project. Exacerbating the problem is the growing movement of people from lesser to better-off parts of the EU. Even before the recent enlargements, concerns were being raised in the United Kingdom and France about the potential for a flood of Polish plumbers (the symbolic example) to come in and swamp local labor markets. Of course, many recognized that migrant laborers could fill important vacant niches in the labor markets of the receiving countries, but there was significant concern that jobs would be taken from locals and that salaries and social protections would be diminished. In the early years after the 2004 enlargement, the movement of peoples from east to west was modest, but mobility has been accelerating, as have concerns over the impacts of growing numbers of migrants on local economies and workers in the west. Those concerns, in turn, translate into negative attitudes toward European integration more generally.

The disintegrative potential of mobility can be the greatest when cultural differences are at play. As was noted in Chapter 11, the movement of Roma peoples into Italy has led to violence and has fostered considerable concern about European integration among segments of the Italian population. To a lesser extent, the growing visibility of Polish, Slovakian, and Bulgarian communities (to reference just three examples) in parts of western European has ignited social tensions that have undermined support for integration among segments of the population.

ETHNO-REGIONALISM

Earlier we noted the interest of some ethno-regionalists in supporting European integration as an alternative to the state. Yet ethno-regionalism must be thought of as a force promoting fragmentation, not just integration. Ethno-regionalist movements

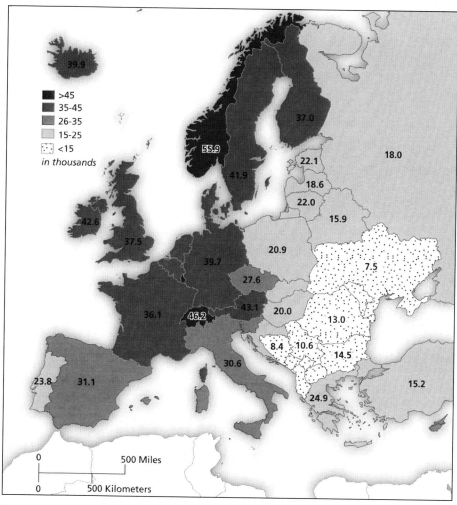

Figure 12.7.   Gross domestic product per capita in the EU, 2011–2012. The impact of Europe's post–World War II division remains very much in evidence. *Source:* CIA, *World Factbook.*

have not been uniformly supportive of integration, and ethno-regionalism carries with it the potential for an increasingly disaggregated Europe that can make integration ever more difficult to achieve.

Turning to the first of these points, integration presents a dilemma for ethno-regionalist leaders seeking to promote greater autonomy. Europe may represent an alternative to the state, but there is little interest in substituting one source of external rule (the state) with another, even more distant source of authority (the EU). With that in mind, some ethno-nationalists are hesitant to support European integration. Those taking this position are not necessarily opposed to a loosely constructed EU, but they do not want to see the EU evolve into a statelike entity.

The ultimate goal of the more assertive ethno-nationalist movements is to create new spaces on the European political map with considerable capacity to control their own affairs. To the extent that such goals are achieved—if there were to be a Flanders and a Wallonia instead of just a Belgium sitting at the EU table, for example—the European integration challenge could become yet more complicated because there would be a growing number of units to accommodate. This issue has not yet received much attention, as there are relatively few ethno-regionalist movements that are likely to give rise to independent or quasi-independent territories in the near future. Nonetheless, devolution cannot be ignored as a potential source of fragmentation in the decades to come.

Where from Here?

In 2006 the international affairs editor of the *Financial Times*, Quentin Peel, made reference to an "underlying concern that the EU has become too big, too distant and, for a growing number, too threatening to their livelihoods." This quote captures much of the concern that is circulating in Europe today about the status of the European integration experiment—particularly in the wake of the recent financial crisis. Predictions are inevitably hazardous, but integration appears to be facing a rocky period in the short-to-medium term because, for all the progress that has been made, recent developments have highlighted the problems facing a Europe where the pace of economic integration has outpaced the development of a Europe-wide sense of political identity.

Moreover, the recent enlargements of the EU have introduced important new differences and complexities. Adding 13 new members in less than a decade (2004–2013) necessitated significant adjustments in the way the EU functions. Important steps are being taken to address the new realities, but a host of fiscal and power-sharing issues will continue to occupy the EU for some time to come, including politically difficult matters such as the degree to which some areas in the EU are willing to subsidize the economic development of other areas. And those adjustments have to be worked out at a time of growing distrust of the EU.

At least for a time, then, the EU is likely to take a cautious approach to admitting new member states. Moreover, it will be difficult to assemble the consensus needed to expand significantly the authority of the EU. There is already much discussion of what some call enlargement fatigue among the populace of the EU's longstanding member states. Despite evidence pointing to the economic advantages that have accompanied integration, many western Europeans question whether the EU, at least in its current form, actually benefits their country. A 2012 Eurobarometer survey showed that only 52% of Europeans responded positively to the statement, "Taking everything into consideration, would you say that (your country) has on balance benefited or not from being a member of the European Community." Positive responses exceeded 60% in only 11 of the 27 EU countries surveyed at the time, and only 35% of respondents in the UK, 40% in Hungary, and 43% in Italy thought the EU had benefited their country.

As for deepening, the depth and extent of the negative attitudes toward the EU in countries such as the United Kingdom, Austria, Sweden, and Finland make it difficult for the EU to assume greater powers. Until the early 2000s, most significant EU decisions had to be agreed to unanimously by all member states. A system of qualified majorities came into play in 2001 with the signing of the Treaty of Nice, but it is still hard to push through major reforms when they are opposed by one or more of the larger states. Unless opinion swings more favorably toward the EU, then, it will be difficult to extend the EU's administrative and judicial competence into new areas.

Whatever the precise configuration of the EU in the years ahead, the challenge of confronting disaffection will likely remain significant. The UK represents a particular challenge because of the low level of support for the EU there (a potential referendum on EU membership there could even pave the way for the UK's withdrawal). Anti-EU sentiment is more muted in other parts of Europe, but it seems increasingly clear that efforts aimed largely at making the EU bigger and more powerful will face strong opposition and may even be counterproductive. With that in mind, the time may be at hand when the EU needs to move away from emphasizing large-scale, statelike projects, such as monetary union, and instead focus greater attention on the sorts of initiatives that can give people a stronger sense that the EU is not just a replacement for the state—but offers possibilities and opportunities beyond the state.

In considering what those possibilities might be, it is important to recognize that even though many Europeans define their interests and their larger identity in European terms, they are not necessarily doing so at the expense of their traditional cultural identities and concerns. By extension, many do not want to see a large, economically oriented bureaucracy assume responsibilities in areas that threaten traditions of local autonomy. Recent developments suggest that the much talked about, but not always followed, EU principle of "subsidiarity"—the idea that decisions should be made at the lowest level and smallest scale appropriate to the issue at hand—needs renewed consideration. They also suggests that the EU, if it is to be successful, should not be a framework promoting homogeneity, but should be a forum that facilitates flexible cooperation across Europe in a variety of ways. Promoting this type of agenda means paying attention not just to the distribution of powers between states and the EU but to regions as well.

The idea that integration could give rise to a "Europe of the Regions" has always been part of the movement for European unity. The regions encompassed by this expression are usually understood to be simply administrative subdivisions of states, but more imaginative regional constructions can be part of the picture as well. One of the most interesting spillover effects of European integration is the development of increasingly important links among and between regions in different countries. Some of these are developing directly across international boundaries (fig. 12.8), whereas others involve geographically dispersed regions (e.g., fig. 12.9). In a potentially significant departure from the state-based perspective that has dominated most decision making in the EU, efforts are now being made to facilitate these regional linkages. Beginning in the early 1990s the EC established a funded program to support cross-border cooperation schemes (INTERREG). Local representatives from border areas

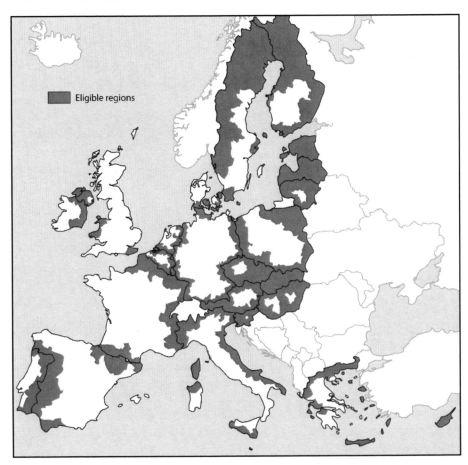

Figure 12.8.   European Union border regions eligible to participate in the EU's INTERREG III program. The program fosters transboundary and transnational cooperation. Some kind of active transboundary cooperation is now taking place across many borders in the EU, as well as between border regions in EU and non-EU states. *Source:* European Union, http://ec.europa.eu/regional_policy/index_en.htm.

may apply for funds to encourage administrative and economic cooperation across the border. The program has expanded over the years, and the EU has adopted new programs aimed at encouraging collaborations among more geographically distant regions. Developments such as these demonstrate the role the EU can play in overcoming problems arising from the fragmentation of Europe into many relatively small states.

As we saw in Chapter 6, the modern state system is premised on the idea that the surface of the earth should be divided up into discrete national territories, each with its own sovereign government. That idea is currently being challenged, yet it continues to shape the way Europeans and others approach the integration process. Too often, progress is equated simply with the transference of powers from the state to the EU level. The current challenges facing the EU highlight the problem with this preoccupation. Although the EU is not likely to disappear, its future is uncertain if it is only envisioned as a big state made up of many smaller ones. Instead, the

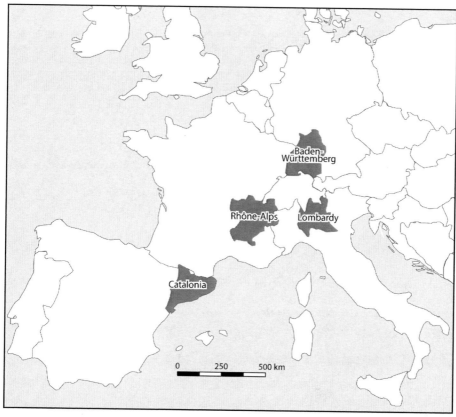

Figure 12.9.   Regions participating in the Four Motors Agreement. The agreement links economically dynamic regions in four core European states. Agreements such as this have the potential to alter the economic geography of Europe and to destabilize the idea that most of what matters in Europe can be captured by the traditional map of states. *Source:* Murphy 1993.

EU's most promising prospects may well lie in arrangements that help Europeans overcome the rigidities of the traditional European state system without sacrificing respect for local interests and identities. If the EU can foster such arrangements, the part of the world that gave birth to the modern state system could be the place that ultimately transcends it.

Sources and Suggested Readings

Agnew, J. A. 2001. How Many Europes? The European Union, Eastward Enlargement and Uneven Development. *European Urban and Regional Studies* 8 (1): 35–38.

Antonsich, M. 2009. National Identities in the Age of Globalisation: The Case of Western Europe. *National Identities* 11 (3): 281–99.

Bachmann, V., and J. D. Sidaway. 2009. Zivilmacht Europa: A Critical Geopolitics of the European Union as a Global Power. *Transactions of the Institute of British Geographers* 34:94–109.

Bauman, Z. 2004. *Europe: An Unfinished Adventure.* Malden, MA: Polity Press.

Brunt, B. M. 1995. Regions and Western Europe. *Journal of Geography* 94:306–16.

Cole, J., and F. Cole. 1997. *The Geography of the European Union*. 2nd ed. New York: Routledge.

Dahlman, C. 2004. Turkey's Accession to the European Union: A Geopolitical and Cultural Assessment. *Eurasian Geography and Economics* 45 (8): 553–74.

Deas, I., and A. Lord. 2006. From a New Regionalism to an Unusual Regionalism? The Emergence of Non-standard Regional Spaces and Lessons for the Territorial Reorganisation of the State. *Urban Studies* 43:1847–77.

Delamaide, D. 1994. *The New Superregions of Europe*. New York: Plume/Penguin.

Hadjimichalis, C. 2011. Uneven Geographical Development, Socio-spatial Justice and Solidarity: European Regions after the 2009 Financial Crisis. *European Urban and Regional Studies* 18 (3): 254–74.

Heffernan, M. 1998. *The Meaning of Europe: Geography and Geopolitics*. New York: Arnold.

Hudson, R., and A. M. Williams. 1999. *Divided Europe: Society and Territory*. London: Sage.

Judt, T. 1996. *A Grand Illusion? An Essay on Europe*. New York: Hill and Wang.

Kepka, J., and A. B. Murphy. 2002. Euroregions in Comparative Perspective: Differential Implications for Europe's Borderlands. In *Boundaries and Place*, ed. J. Hakli and D. Kaplan, 50–69. Boulder, CO: Rowman & Littlefield.

Kramsch, O. T., and B. Hooper, eds. 2004. *Cross-Border Governance in the European Union: Transnationalism*. Routledge Research in Transnationalism. New York: Routledge.

Murphy, A. B. 1993. Emerging Regional Linkages in the European Community: Implications for State-Centered Perspectives on European Society. *Tijdschrift voor Economische en Sociale Geografie* 84 (2): 103–18.

———. 2006. The May 2004 Enlargement of the European Union: View from Two Years Out. *Eurasian Geography and Economics* 47 (6): 635–46.

———. 2008. Rethinking Multi-level Governance in a Changing European Union: Why Metageography and Territoriality Matter. *GeoJournal* 72 (1–2): 7–18.

———. 2013. Trapped in the Logic of the Modern State System? European Integration in the Wake of the Financial Crisis. *Geopolitics* 18 (3): 705–23.

———, and A. Hunderi-Ely. 1996. The Geography of the 1994 Nordic Vote on European Union Membership. *Professional Geographer* 48 (3): 284–97.

———, and C. M. Johnson. 2004. German Geopolitics in Transition. *Eurasian Geography and Economics* 45 (1): 1–17.

Newhouse, J. 1997. Europe's Rising Regionalism. *Foreign Affairs* 76 (1): 67–84.

Paasi, A. 2002. Regional Transformation in the European Context: Notes on Regions, Boundaries and Identity. *Space & Polity* 6:197–201.

Painter, J. 2008. European Citizenship and the Regions. *European Urban and Regional Studies* 15:5–19.

Pedersen, Roy N. 1992. *One Europe/100 Nations*. Clevedon, UK: Channel View Books.

Pfaff, W. 2005. What's Left of the Union? *New York Review of Books* 52 (12): 26–29.

Risse, T. 2012. The Euro between National and European Identity. *Journal of European Public Policy* 10 (4): 487–505.

Schott, M. 2007. Geopolitical Imaginations about the European Union in Recent Political Discussions. *Tijdschrift voor Economische en Sociale Geografie* 98 (2): 284–95.

Sellar, C., and J. Pickles. 2002. Where Will Europe End? Ukraine and the Limits of European Integration. *Eurasian Geography and Economics* 43 (2): 123–42.

Sidaway, J. D. 2006. On the Nature of the Beast: Re-charting Political Geographies of the European Union. *Geografiska Annaler B* 88 (1): 1–14.

Stephanou, C. A., ed. 2006. *Adjusting to EU Enlargement*. Cheltenham, UK: Edward Elgar.

Zielonka, J. 2006. *Europe as Empire: The Nature of the Enlarged European Union*. Oxford: Oxford University Press.

Glossary

Acid precipitation—Rain or snow that has a higher level of acidity because of a chemical reaction between water in the atmosphere and industrial pollutants.

Afforestation—The replanting of forests.

Afro-Asiatic—The language family that dominates much of the Middle East and North Africa. Includes Arabic, Hebrew, and Maltese.

Age of Discovery—The period from the fifteenth to the seventeenth centuries during which European mariners, notably the Spanish, Portuguese, British, Dutch, and French, traveled the world in search of resources, lands, and peoples to claim for their respective crowns.

Agribusiness—Large-scale, commercialized, market-oriented agriculture.

Alluvial soils—Loose, fertile soil deposited by water flowing over flood plains.

Alpine period—Period of significant tectonic activity between c. 100 and 60 million years ago that resulted in the creation of east–west mountain ranges in Europe, such as the Alps and the Pyrenees.

Altaic—A language family thought to have originated around the Altai Mountains of Central Asia. Includes Turkish, Tatar, Azeri, and Gagauz.

Andosols—Rich and porous soils found in volcanic areas.

Animism—Religious practices that imbue objects such as rocks, heavenly bodies, mountains, forests, and rivers with souls.

Anti-empire nationalism—The effort by a national group living within an empire to create a sovereign nation-state of their own.

Arable land—Land suitable for agriculture.

Armenian Orthodox Apostolic Church—Officially a branch of Eastern Orthodoxy, it has an independent status because it never acknowledged the supremacy of the patriarch at Constantinople.

Ashkenazim—Jews who settled primarily in western and southern Germany and the Kingdom of Poland. They often spoke Yiddish, a German-derived language written in Hebrew.

Autocephalic—Self-governing (church), derived from Greek *auto* (self) and *cephalous* (head).

Azores anticyclone—A high-pressure system generally situated in the North Atlantic. Its seasonal movement off the northwest African and southwest European coasts contributes to the Mediterranean climate found throughout much of southern Europe.

Baltic—A subfamily of the Indo-European languages originating west of the Pripyat Marshes. Over time it lost ground to Germanic and Slavic speakers and is now represented by Latvian and Lithuanian.

Bora—A periodic wind that blows from north to south into the Adriatic, Greece, and Turkey, particularly in the winter. It brings cold snaps to parts of southeastern Europe.

British city—The type of city found in the British Isles that generally has a higher degree of semidetached, single-family residences and greater functional zonation than the typical continental European city.

Capitalism—An economic system based on private ownership in which land and goods are exchanged at prices determined by free-market competition.

Caucasic—A language family to the southeast of the Indo-European family in the Caucasus. Includes Georgian.

Celtic—A subfamily of Indo-European that was once dominant throughout Europe but now is mostly confined to the northwestern periphery. Includes Welsh, Breton, Cornish, and Gaelic.

Central European city—The most common type of city found in Europe, characterized by compactness, a low degree of functional zonation, a core that is both historic and relatively prosperous, and surrounding suburbs, some of which are industrial and relatively poor.

Checkerboard village—A village with a relatively rigid rectilinear street pattern, a legacy of the Roman imperial land survey.

Chernozem—A black-colored topsoil rich in organic matter that produces a high agricultural yield. This soil is found only in cool to temperate climates.

City-states—Cities that function as independent political entities. The ancient city-states of Greece are classic examples.

Collective agriculture—The system implemented in Communist states in which fragmented private landholdings were replaced by large communal farms.

Colonialism—Rule by an autonomous power over a subordinate, usually distant people. Because of the scope and scale of European colonialism that began in the sixteenth century, the term is often used to refer specifically to the European colonial project of the last 500 years.

Columbian Exchange—The great exchange of flora, fauna, microorganisms, culture, technology, and people that followed in the wake of Christopher Columbus's 1492 voyage across the Atlantic Ocean.

Composite language—A language whose form was taken from more than one language.

Continent—Conventionally a sizable landmass standing more or less separate from other landmasses. In the case of Europe and Asia the term is stretched to denote major world regions that were once considered to be separate realms.

Coriolis effect—The process by which the rotation of the earth deflects the movement of ocean and atmospheric currents clockwise in the northern hemisphere and counterclockwise in the southern hemisphere.

Cottage industry—Secondary economic activities produced at home using simple technology. Generally confined to farm villages as a sideline to agriculture.

Counterurbanization—The movement of people from the largest cities to smaller towns and cities that lie beyond the commuting range of their former places of residence.

Cuesta—A ridge of tilted sedimentary rock with a gentle slope on one side and a moderately steep drop-off on the other.

Cultural landscape—The visible trace of human presence on the land, consisting of an assemblage of tangible physical and human features found in an area.

Culture area—A region that is thought of as the homeland of a people who hold numerous beliefs, behaviors, and overall ways of life in common, including ideology, technology, social institutions, and material possessions.

Dechristianization—A term used to describe the move toward secularization that has occurred recently in parts of Europe.

Deindustrialization—The decline or abandonment of industrial activity in a region.

Demographic transition—The shift from high birth rates and high death rates to low birth rates and low death rates in the wake of industrialization and urbanization. Because death rates historically fell before birth rates, the demographic transition is associated with a period of rapid population increase followed by low, or even negative, population growth.

Devolution—The transfer of governmental competencies from the state to substate regions.

Dialect net—A linguistic zone of multiple dialects in which the speakers of each dialect can understand the neighboring ones but not those farther away in regions with which they have no regular contact.

Dialects—Variants of standardized languages.

Diaspora—The dispersal of a cultural or ethnic group from a homeland. Originally referred to the dispersal of the Jewish people from ancient Palestine.

Dikes—Human-constructed banks along the edges of water bodies that are designed to protect against flooding.

Eastern European city—An eastern European variant of the central European city characterized by large public spaces, massive public housing projects, and a particularly low degree of functional zonation.

Eastern Orthodoxy—A form of Christianity prevailing in eastern Europe that arose from the church in Byzantine Constantinople.

Ecotourism—Tourism designed to promote sustainability by minimizing long-term damage to nature or local customs.

Esker—Narrow, gravel-lined channel that is produced by a stream lying under an ice sheet.

Ethnic cleansing—The attempt by one ethnic group to eliminate another ethnic group from a place or region.

Eurasia—Term combining Europe and Asia into a single continent instead of two.

Eurocentrism—A perspective that looks at developments around the world through the lens of European circumstances and beliefs. Eurocentrism typically is premised on the idea of European superiority.

Eurorussia—The portion of Russia to the west of the Ural Mountains often regarded as belonging to Europe.

Eurozone—The states that have adopted the European Union's common currency, the euro.

External migration—Migration across national borders.

Façadism—The complete gutting and remodeling of the interior of a building while preserving its façade.

Federal state—A state in which internal states or provinces retain considerable power or even autonomy.

Feudal system—A loosely organized, not strictly hierarchical political-economic system binding nobles, local landowners, and peasants together through a set of reciprocal obligations. The feudal system was found throughout much of Europe in the Middle Ages.

Fjord—A long, narrow inlet between steep cliffs or hills created by glacial erosion.

Föhn—In southern Germany, a warm, dry wind from the south that results when a cyclonic storm moving north of the Alps in the winter draws drier, warmer winds over the mountains from the Mediterranean lands.

Fontanili—An east–west line of springs in the Po–Veneto Plain where the ground-water table reaches the surface.

Functional zonation—The segregation of different functions (retailing, manufacturing, residential) in different areas within a city.

Gentrification—The rehabilitation of deteriorated or abandoned areas and the concomitant replacement of low-income people by those who are more affluent.

Geolinguistics—The study of language changes over space and through time.

Geomorphology—The scientific study of landforms, including the processes that shape them.

Germanic—A major subfamily of the Indo-European languages that arose in Jutland and spread throughout northern and west-central Europe. Includes German, English, Danish, Swedish, Norwegian, Icelandic, and Dutch.

Ghetto—Originally a Jewish neighborhood, in particular the Jewish quarter in medieval Venice. The term now refers to a poor area dominated by minority groups who have little choice but to stay there.

Green village—A compact village in which the houses are grouped around a central green or commons that serves as a marketplace, a festival ground, and a protected enclosure for livestock.

Guest workers—Immigrants invited by national governments to come into a country for a time in response to labor shortages. Many guest workers end up staying more or less permanently.

Guild—A professional organization of free artisans skilled in a particular craft; skills were passed down from generation to generation through an apprenticeship system.

Gulf Stream—A warm ocean current originating in the Gulf of Mexico that influences the climate of the eastern United States and Canada as well as western Europe.

Hanseatic League (Hansa)—A trading union of towns around the shores of the North and Baltic seas in the Late Medieval and Early Modern periods.

Hardscrabble belts—Regions separating and surrounding the favored lands of three-field farming and Mediterranean agriculture, afflicted with broken terrain, excessive cloudiness, or sterile soils.

Heat island—A zone of higher temperatures in cities resulting from the reflective properties of urbanized landscapes.

Heath—Shrubland vegetation found in areas with poor-quality, acidic soils.

Hellenic—A subfamily of the Indo-European languages to which modern Greek belongs.

Hercynian period—Period of significant tectonic activity between c. 280 and 240 million years ago resulting in the uplift of areas along Europe's northwestern fringe and into the main western European landmass (including the Ardennes, Vosges, and Black Forest).

High-tech industry—Industries producing high-technology products such as electronic and microelectronic devices, data processing equipment, and robotics, as well as firms that make use of high-tech products in the manufacturing process.

Hinterland—The zone surrounding an urban area that regularly provides goods and people needed to sustain the urban area.

Holocene—The current interglacial period, which began some 10,000 years ago.

Homo sapiens—Modern humans.

Human development—A measure of human well-being that includes not just economic circumstances but also health, social and psychological well-being, education, and human security.

Hydrogeography—The study of the distribution and spatial character of streams and bodies of water on the surface of the earth.

Ice age—A geologic period characterized by multiple cold episodes, called glacials, interrupted by periodic warmer times known as interglacials. The earth has been in an ice age since at least the beginning of the Pleistocene, some 1.65 million years ago.

Indo-European—One of the major language families of the world, and the dominant language family in Europe. In Eurasia, Indo-European languages are spoken from Europe to India.

Industrial Revolution—The invention of diverse machines and the harnessing of inanimate power that began in Great Britain in the 1700s, leading to countless crucially influential inventions such as the steam engine, railroad, internal combustion engine, automobile, expressway, radio, orbital satellites, manned space flight, and the digital computer.

Industrial suburb—An area immediately outside a city proper—characterized by factories, huge workers' apartment blocks or row houses, and transportation facilities.

Infant mortality rate—The number of children per thousand who do not survive to the age of one year.

Internal migration—Migration within national or state boundaries.

Islam—A religion arising out of the Arabian Peninsula and based on the teachings of the prophet Muhammad, as set forth in the Koran.

Isogloss—A line on a map signifying a linguistic boundary of some sort.

Isostatic rebound—The gradual uplift that occurs when a segment of the earth's surface that has been depressed by the weight of an ice sheet loses the heavy layer of ice that depressed it. As the area rebounds, adjacent areas are sometimes pulled downward.

Karst topography—A landscape dominated by permeable limestone, which has numerous large sinks or troughs caused by water filtering down through the limestone.

Laïcité—the French tradition of secularism going back to the Revolution of 1789 that requires a strict separation of church and state.

Land consolidation—Redrawing property lines to reduce or eliminate the fragmentation of holdings.

Land reform—A process intended to distribute land more equally. Often large land-holdings are broken up to allow more people to own their own land.

Language families—A grouping of languages that share broad similarities in structure and vocabulary.

Latifundia—System in which nobility has control over large estates, which are divided into small units and farmed by indentured peasants.

Lingua franca—A common language that is used as a means of communication among speakers of diverse tongues.

Littoral—The coast or shore of a water body.

Loess—Wind-deposited, fine-textured sediment that was originally produced by glaciers and ice sheets grinding up rock.

Market gardening—Also known as truck farming. Small-scale agriculture, typically orchards, vineyards, and vegetable plots.

Marxism—A body of political, economic, social, and cultural theories based on the writings of Karl Marx and Friedrich Engels. Marxism particularly seeks to explain the economic and social consequences of industrial capitalism.

Medieval Warm Period—Sometimes called the Medieval Optimum, a period between the ninth and twelfth centuries that brought warmer average temperatures to much of Europe.

Mediterranean agriculture—The distinctive agrarian system traditionally practiced in Cyprus, Greece, the eastern Adriatic coast, peninsular Italy, the Languedoc Plain, and southern Iberia.

Mediterranean city—A southern European variant of the central European city characterized by greater spontaneity of growth and development and less segregation by socioeconomic class.

Megalopolis—An immense conurbation resulting from the growing together of several large cities.

Mercantile city—An urban center in which trade is the most important economic activity.

Mercantilism—An economic system based on commercial production and trade.

Milankovitch cycle—A cycle of global warming and cooling cause by changes in (1) the shape of the earth's orbit, (2) the tilt of the earth on its axis, and (3) the earth's position in its orbit at equinox. The Milankovitch cycle has produced repeated glacial advances and retreats during the Pleistocene.

Mistral—A regular wind that blows from north to south down the Rhône–Saône corridor into the Mediterranean, particularly in the winter and spring. The mistral brings cold air into the coastal fringe of France and beyond.

Modernity—A set of ideas and practices set in motion by the sixteenth-century European Enlightenment that was rooted in the idea that reason and scientific rationality would lead to progress.

Monotheism—The religious practice of worshipping a single deity.

Moor—An expanse of open, infertile, poorly drained land, often including areas of heath and peat bogs.

Moraine—Debris scraped up and deposited at the foot of glaciers.

Morphology—The external form, structure, and organization of a thing or place.

Motes—Small hills in Ireland erected as fortifications by invading Normans in the Middle Ages.

Nation—A group of people with a shared sense of culture and history and a desire to control their own affairs.

Nationalism—The glorification of a particular nation and the historic homeland it claims as its own.

Nation-state—Originally a sovereign political territory associated with a group of people with a shared sense of culture and history. In many circles the term has come to be used as a synonym for an independent state.

Neanderthal—A hominid living in Europe between c. 200,000 and 30,000 years ago that became extinct in the wake of the arrival of *Homo sapiens*.

Neoliberal—Policies aimed at reducing the role of government in the economy, promoting free trade, and privatizing social services.

Neolithic revolution—The domestication of plants and animals.

Nomadic herders—People who move with their animals, often in a regular cyclic pattern, to take advantage of multiple natural grazing areas.

Nordic city—The type of city found in Scandinavia and Finland that is relatively recent in origin and that bears more evidence of planning and functional zonation than most other European cities.

North Atlantic Drift—An extension of the Gulf Stream, bringing warm ocean currents to northwestern Europe.

Nucleation—The concentration of some phenomenon in space.

Occupational specialization—Also known as division of labor. A circumstance in which workers perform particular tasks within a production chain, thereby increasing productivity.

Orographic effect—Process by which humid air masses moving from west to east rise over hill and mountain barriers, cooling and decreasing their ability to hold moisture in an evaporated state. This produces precipitation on west-facing slopes.

Othering—Defining one group or area in negative opposition to other groups or areas.

Paganism—A pre-Christian set of beliefs in multiple deities and other supernatural beings governing all spheres of the physical world and human life.

Podsols—An infertile and acidic soil from which minerals have been leached. Podsols are typically found under temperate coniferous woodlands.

Polders—Areas of land that have been reclaimed from the sea by dikes and water-pumping systems.

Polytheism—The religious practice of worshipping multiple deities.

Postindustrial—The rise to dominance of quaternary-sector industries coincident with the decline of primary and secondary industries.

Postindustrial suburbs—The outer ring of suburbs that developed since the 1950s, consisting of a loose assemblage of low-density residences dominated by detached single-family houses, modern factories devoted to high-tech industry, firms specializing in data gathering and processes, and high-rise commercial towers.

Potential support ratio—A measure of the number of persons aged 15–64 years per one older person aged 65 years or older.

Preindustrial core—The densely packed center of a city that was already built up before the Industrial Revolution.

Preindustrial periphery—The part of a city surrounding the preindustrial core into which urbanization was spreading before the Industrial Revolution.

Primary economic activities—Those involved in extracting resources from the earth and seas, such as agriculture, mining, fishing, and lumbering.

Primate city—A city that contains by far the largest population and greatest concentration of economic and cultural functions within a state.

Primogeniture—A system of inheritance found principally in Germanic Europe under which the holdings of one generation pass intact to the oldest male child of the next generation.

Pronatalist policies—Policies designed to increase fertility rates, or at least slow the fall in the birth rate.

Protestantism—A fragmented agglomeration of many denominations such as Lutheranism, Presbyterianism, and Anglicanism that split off from the Roman Catholic Church. Generally concentrated in northern Europe.

Quaternary sector—Economic activities associated with the collection, processing, and manipulation of information and capital, such as education, consulting, and research and development services.

Reconquista—Literally, "reconquest." The term refers to the ultimately successful effort of Christian kingdoms to push the Islamic Moors out of the Iberian Peninsula. The reconquista began with the Battle of Covadonga in 722 and ended with the defeat of the last Moorish stronghold in Granada in 1492.

Rectilinear street pattern—A grid pattern of parallel and perpendicular streets.

Return migration—The return of migrants or their descendants to the historical homeland whence they or their ethnic ancestors originally came.

River-meander site—A piece of land created when a stream turns back upon itself, leaving only a narrow neck of land surrounded almost completely by water. River-meander sites could be easily defended, making them good choices for settlements in unstable regions.

Roman Catholicism—A form of Christianity centered on the pope in Vatican City, dominant in southern and parts of eastern Europe.

Romance—A subfamily of the Indo-European languages derived from Latin, dominating the western and southern edges of Europe that were once part of the Roman Empire. Includes Italian, Spanish, French, Portuguese, and Romanian.

Sclerophyllous—Protective external tissues of plants found in dry areas that serve to retard evaporation.

Secondary economic activities—The processing of resources into finished goods, also known as manufacturing.

Sephardim—Iberian Jews who were expelled from Spain and Portugal following the reconquest and resettled throughout North Africa and northern Europe, particularly Britain and the Netherlands.

Sharecropping—A system in which a landowner allows a peasant to use a piece of land in exchange for a share of what is produced on the land.

Shifting cultivation—Also known as slash-and-burn agriculture, the practice of cultivating crops for a few years in one place and then abandoning that place for another after soil fertility declines.

Siltation—The buildup of sediment in a stream or lake.

Sirocco winds—Hot, humid southeast to southwest winds originating in North Africa and flowing across the Mediterranean.

Site—The physical setting and specific location of a place or phenomenon.

Slavic—A major subfamily of the Indo-European languages spoken throughout much of eastern Europe. Includes Russian, Polish, Czech, Slovakian, Ukrainian, Belarusian, Serbo-Croatian, Slovenian, Bulgarian, and Macedonian.

Socialist city—See **Eastern European city**.

Sovereignty—The idea that independent countries should be free from external interference.

Specialization—A system in which diverse traditional subsistence agriculture is replaced by cash crops that are sold to obtain a profit.

Standardized language—The form of writing and speech promoted by elites to foster communications across a broad area.

Street village—A village aligned along a single road.

Suburbanization—The movement of people from city cores to the outskirts of an urban area.

Terpen—Mounds of earth upon which structures were built to avoid flooding in the Low Countries.

Tertiary sector—The service industries; those that involve neither the extraction of resources nor manufacturing but instead include a range of activities that serve people's everyday needs and facilitate economic activity. Includes health care, transportation, energy production, retailing, wholesaling, and tourism.

Thracian (Thraco-Illyrian)—A subfamily of the Indo-European languages originating from the Stara Planina and Rhodopi Range, but today represented only by Albanian.

Three-field farming—Agricultural system in which land was divided into three segments, one planted with a summer grain, one with a winter grain, and one left fallow. The segment devoted to each of these activities was rotated every year.

Topocide—The deliberate obliteration of a place. Coined by Douglas Porteous in reaction to changes to the physical environment during the Industrial Revolution.

Total fertility rate—The number of children born to women of childbearing age.

Transhumance—Nomadic system in which herds move to high pastures in the mountains in the summer and down to the lowlands during the winter.

Transportation—The movement of people and goods between locations using something constructed by humans.

Tundra—An extremely cold biome known for low biotic diversity and where plant growth is hindered by little precipitation and a short growing season.

Uniate Church—A hybrid of eastern (Orthodox) and western (Catholic) Christianity centered in western Ukraine and surrounding areas.

Unification nationalism—The effort to bring together, within a single state, peoples who are thought to share a common culture and history.

Unitary states—States with executive and legislative power concentrated in a central government.

Uralic—A language family that was pushed to the periphery by Indo-European languages. Includes Finnish, Estonian, Sami, and Hungarian.

Welfare state—Social model under which the state provides services such as health care, education, unemployment insurance, and pensions to its population as a "safety net."

Xenophobia—Fear of the foreign or of foreigners.

Zero population growth—A demographic situation in which the mortality rate is equal to the birth rate, producing a stable, or even declining, population.

Index

Page locators in italics refer to figures and tables

Abkhazia, *190, 361*
Abkhazis, 17, 150
abortion, 77–78
Adriatic Sea, 30, 49, 243
Aegean Sea, 4, 35, 260
Africa, 13, 167, 386
Afro-Asiatic languages, 101, 102, *114,* 115
Afsluitdijk, 53
Age of Discovery, 4, 13, 20, 260
Age of Nationalism, 165, 167–68, 393
agriculture, 17, 73, 105; agribusiness, 222, *223*; cattle/hog fattening, 219; cheeses and butter, 218, 219; collective, *222,* 222–24; cooperatives, 220–21, 224; core–periphery pattern, 226, *227,* 229; dairying, 217–19; environmentally friendly farming, 226–28; fishing and fish farming, 221; hardscrabble herding/farming, 199, *200,* 204; horticulture, 199–200, 199–203, 215–17, *216*; intertillage, 201, *201*; language diffusion and, 98–99; livestock, 199, 201–2, 203–4; major systems, 199, *200*; market gardening, 216, 217; Mediterranean, 199–202, *200,* 211, 217; modern systems, 215–21; neolithic revolution, 197–99, *198*; nomadic herding, 199, *200, 205–6, 206,* 222; orchard trees, 41, 197, 199–201, *202*; pasture, 201–2; percentage of workers employed in, *228*; polders, 52–54; privatization, 224; sheep raising, 220; shifting cultivation, 199, *200,* 204–5, *205,* 222; slow food movement, 227–28; specialization, 215–16, *216,* 219; tenant farmers, 207, 220, 222–23; three-field farming, 105, 199, *200,* 203–4, 207, 211–12, 217; transhumance, 202, 204, 205; two-field rotational system, 199. *See also* crops; rural sector
Ahnström, Leif, 1
air masses, 37, 38, 41
Albania, 47, 113, 150, 184, 257; population pyramid, *79,* 79–80
Albanian language, 113
Aletsch glacier, 58
Alpine period, 27, 29
Alps, 29–30, 34–35, 37, 42, 182; demographics and, 89; glaciers, decrease in, 58; tourism, 283, 285–86
Alsace, France, 170, 243
Alsatian language, 106
Altaic language family, *114,* 115
Amsterdam, 52, 53, 354
Amsterdam Treaty, 292
Anatolia, 115, 199, 301
Andalucía, 179, *180,* 303
Andorra, 103, 160
andosols, 47
Angles, 176
Anglican Church, 127, 131, 137
Anglo-Saxons, 105
animism, 124, 127
anti-empire nationalism, 165–66
anti-immigrant groups, 84
anti-Semitism, 154, 155
Antwerp, 56

Apennine Mountains, 29–30, 34
Appian Way, 249
apprenticeship system, 235, 269
Aquitaine, 172
Arabic, 102, 115
Arabs, 8, 35
Aragon, 179, *180*
Arctic Ocean, 41
Arctic Sea, 17
Ardennes (hills), 33
aristocracy, 207, 222–23
Armenian Orthodox Apostolic Church, 17,
    144–45
artisans, 234, 331
Ashkenazim, 155
Asia (mythological character), 2–3
Assyrians, 2
Athens, 233, 302
Atlantic Ocean, 17
Atlas of World Languages (UNESCO), 109
atmosphere, 56–58, *57*
Attiki, 59
austerity measures, 296, 354, 370
Austria, 167, 175, 283
Austro-Hungarian Empire, 161, 166, 167
automobiles, 243, 250–51, *251,* 323;
    traffic congestion, 253–55, *254,* 285,
    319, 334
Ávila, Spain, *310*
Azores anticyclone, 36, 37, 40

Bacchus (god), 200
Baden (Germany), 170
Balearic Islands, 29, 103
Balkan Peninsula, 9, 30, 35, 109
Balkan war of the 1990s, 82
Balkans, 41, 144; fragmentation, 184–86, *185*
Baltic languages, 99, 113
Baltic Sea, 41
Barents Sea, 42
Baroque period, 313–14
Bartholomew, Apostle, 144
Basel, Switzerland, 243
Bashkortostan, 188
Basin of Aquitaine, 33, 35, 60
Basque Autonomous Province, 115
Basque language, 101, 115
Basques, 172, 179, 390
Bavaria, 146, 175
Belarus, 44, 188–89, 280
Belarusian language, 109, 188

Belgium, 60, 164, 182–84, *183,* 191; languages,
    104, 120
Belgrade, 184
Benelux Customs Union, 191
Berlin, 63, 175
Berlusconi, Silvio, 149
Bética Mountains, 29, 42
Bialowieza Forest, 44
bicycle use, 323–24
bishop of Byzantium, 130
bishop of Rome, 130
Bismarck, Otto von, 347, 370
Black Sea, 1, 3, 31, 34–35; creation of, 99,
    113; language diffusion and, 98, 99, 113
Black Triangle, 67, 248, 271
Black Virgin (Polish Catholicism), 135
Blue Banana, 336, *338*
Bolsheviks, 186
book readership, 356–57
bora, 41
borders: closings, nomadic herding and, 220;
    cultural, 16, 148; efforts to find, 4–5, *5, 6,*
    15–17; European Union, 17; France, 29,
    173; Germany, *174*; human traits and, 8, *9*;
    international, 169–70; "Iron Curtain," 175;
    linguistic, 104, *106,* 180–81, 182; political
    vs. ethnic, 185; proposed culture-based, *11*;
    rivers as, 35; state system and, 169–71, *170*;
    Sweden–Norway boundary, 169, *170*;
    Uralic–Indo-European, 114
Bosnia-Herzegovina, 184–85, *185,* 186, 193
Bosnian Muslims, 149–50, 184
Bosporus, 9, 35, 99, 115
Bourgogne, 172
Brabant province, 60
Brandenburg, 175
Bremerhaven, Germany, *262*
Bretagne (Brittany), 33, 172
Brethren (Czechia), 137
Breton language, *110,* 111, *119*
bridges, 249, 250, 251, 254, 307–8
British Crown Dependency, 161
British Empire, 108
British Isles, 33, 39, 61, 176. *See also* England;
    Great Britain; Ireland; Scotland; United
    Kingdom; Wales
British National Party (BNP), 365
Broder, Henryk, 153
Bruges, Belgium, *310*
Brussels, Belgium, 183, *236,* 289, *364*
bubonic plague (Black Death), 72, 85–86, *86*

Budapest, Hungary, 330, *330*
Bulgaria, 17, 113, 115, 146, 372; agriculture, 215, 217, 224, 227, 248; European Union and, 380, 388; Muslims in, 150; social model, 345; tourism, 286
Bulgarian-Macedonian dialect net, 109
Bundesbahn (Germany), 257
bureaucratization, 394
Burgundians, 172
Burns, Robert, 246
Byzantine Church, 131
Byzantine Empire, 35, 129, 233

Calvin, John, 131
Calvinism, 137, 139
Cambrian Mountains, 33
Campanella, Tommaso, 22
canals, 35, 47–48, 258, 261–62
Cantabrian Mountains (Cordillera Cantabrica), 29, 37, 42
Canterbury Cathedral, 127
Canton Bern, 182
cantons, 165, 182
cap-and-trade schemes, 66
capitalism, 22, 234, 245, 354
Carpathian Mountains, 30–31, 34–35
Carpathian–Stara Planina juncture, 48
Caspian Sea, *2, 3, 3*
Castile, Old and New, 34, *180*
Castilian Spanish, 103
Castilians, 179
Castilla, 179
Catalan language, 103, 115
Catalans, 172, 179, 390
Catalonia, 103
Caucasic language family, *114,* 115
Caucasoid race, 7
Caucasus isthmus, *2*
Caucasus Mountains, 4, 58, 98
Cech/Slovakian dialect, 109
Celtic languages, 109–11, *110*
Celts, 101, 105, 176, 178
Central Sierras, 29
Cesari, Jocelyn, 150
Champs Elysées, Paris, *316*
charcoal burning, 60, 240
charity, tradition of, 347
Charlemagne, 172
Chechnya, 17, 150, 188
checkerboard villages, 210, *210, 211*
Chernobyl plant nuclear disaster, 279–80

chernozem (black earth), 45
China, 22, 386
Christianity, 7–9; Armenian Orthodox Apostolic Church, 17, 144–45; believing without belonging, 155–56; Catholic–Protestant split, 131; charismatic denominations, 156; dechristianization, *145,* 145–47; diffusion of, 123–24, 126–29, *128;* east–west divide, 142–44; edict of toleration, 129; Eucharist, 200; European identity linked to, 123, 146–47; fragmentation of, 123–24, *130,* 130–42; missionaries, 129; pilgrimages, 133–35, *134, 135, 143,* 144; Uniate Church, 144–45, 189. *See also* Eastern Orthodoxy; Protestantism; religion; Roman Catholicism
Church of England, 127, 131, 137
Church of Scotland, 137
Cisalpine Gaul, 178
cities, 34, 56, 299–341, *300;* Arabic influence on, 318; attributes, medieval, 309–11; autonomous, 161; bridge-centered, 307–8; British city, 326–28, *327;* capitals, 168, 314; central buildings, 319; central European city, *327,* 328; under Communism, 330; compactness, 317–18; concentric rings, 317; confluence sites, 308; counterurbanization, 321–22; crossroad sites, 308; diffusion of, *301, 304;* eastern European city/socialist city, 331–35, *333, 334;* functional zonation, 317; gentrification, 322, *323,* 327–28; Germanic Low Country/Rhinelands, 304–5; Greece, ancient, 301–2; on high points, 306; industrial, 244, 314–16; river-meander site, 305–6; late/postindustrial, 320–26, *323, 325;* marketplace, 301, 302, 309, *311;* medieval, 303–13, *313;* medieval urban morphology, 311–12, *313;* Mediterranean city, 331, *332;* mercantile, 300, 307, 317; mid-twentieth-century, 317–20; modern urban pattern, 336, *337, 338;* Nordic city, 335, *335;* offshore-island site, 306; postwar reconstruction, 318–19; preindustrial core, 315, 317, 318, 323–24, *328,* 328–29, *329;* preindustrial periphery, 315–16, 318, 324; primate, 168; public projects, 314, 316, *316;* rail terminals, 315–16; regional variations, 326–36; Renaissance-Baroque development, 313–14; rise of, 299–303; river sites, 308; Roman Empire, 302–3, *303;* seaport sites, 308; segregation along linguistic

lines, 363–64; segregation along religious lines, *139,* 140, 362–63; sites, 305–9; social well-being in regions of, 348–51, *351;* street patterns, 302, 311–12, *312, 313,* 318; urban planning, 314, *316,* 335; walls, 242, 301, 309, *310,* 312, 317, 326. *See also* suburbanization

City of the Sun (Campanella), 22

city-states, 20, 301–2, 309, 328

clearances, 220

climate, 5, 18, 36–42, 66; Alpine, 42: arctic climate zone, 42; cloudiness and sunshine, 40; cold spells, 41; drought, 40: global change, 58; heat waves, 39; humid continental, 41–42; humid subtropical, 42; marine west coast, 39–40; Mediterranean, 40–41; minor types, 42; pan-European warming, 58; population density and, 74; precipitation, 39, 40, 41, 42; regions, 38, *38;* semi-arid, 42; subarctic climate zone, 42; subtypes, 40, 41;

coal use, 56, 237–40, 265; on European mainland, 240–41, *241*

Coalbrookdale, England, 239, 250

coastline, 25

cold spells, 39

Cold War, 10, 383, 385

collective agriculture, *222,* 222–24

Cologne (Köln), 152–53

colonialism, 7, 12–13, 167; ancient Greeks, 302; industrial development and, 234–35; language dissemination, 98; migration and, 362; religion and, 123. *See also* Roman Empire

Columbian Exchange, 215

Columbus, 49

Common Agricultural Policy (CAP), 225–26

communications, 277, *278,* 278–79

Communism, 22, 147, 291, 330, 331; collective agriculture, 222–24

Communist Manifesto (Marx), 245

communitarianism, 345

composite language, 107

confederation, 164, 182

Constantine, 129

Constantinople/Istanbul, 9, 85, 129, 140, 233

consultancy, 287, *288*

continents, 1

contraception, 77–78

cooperative agriculture, 220–21, 224

Cordoba, Spain, 233

core areas, state system, 162–63, *163,* 165, 168; Germany and, 174; Russia, 186, *187;* Switzerland, *181,* 182

core–periphery pattern, *14, 46,* 72–73, *73, 177;* agriculture, 226, *227,* 229; demographics, 72–73; Industrial Revolution, 236–37, 271; migration and, 82; quaternary sector, 288; soils regions, *46;* transportation, 251, *256;* United Kingdom, 176, *177*

Corinth, 233, 302

Coriolis Effect, 37

Cornish language, 109, 111

Cornwall, Great Britain, 176, 259

Corsica, 41, 104, 161

Corsicans, 172, 390

cottage system, 235, 236

cotton textile industries, 237

counterurbanization, 321–22

craft industries, 269–70

Crete (Kriti), 32–33, 223, 286

Crimean Mountains, 31

Croatia, 184, 185, *185*

Croats, 144, 149–50, 184–85

crops: barley, 197, 199, 203; cash, 219, 220, 221; citrus, 217; complexes, 197, 199; cork oak, 201, *202;* genetically modified (GMO), 228; Mesoamerican food complex, 215; millet, 199; neolithic, 197; new introductions, 214–15; oats, 203; olive, 40, 44, 173, 201, *201,* 217; orchard trees, 41, 197, 199–201, *202;* organic, 226–27; potato, 215, 219, 228; rye, *200,* 203; wheat, 197, 199, *200,* 203, 219, 220; wine/grapes, 199–200, 217, *218. See also* agriculture

cuesta, 172

cultural landscapes, 133

cultural-historical approach, 19–20

culture areas, 7

Cypriots, 82, 150, 161

Cyprus, 17, 111, 115, 160–61, 293

Cyrillic alphabet, 109, 129

Czechia (Czech Republic), 34, 57, 64, 224; birth rate, 76–77

Czechoslovakia, 161, 168

dairying, 217–19

Danish Isles, 105

Danish language, 93

Danube river, 30, 34–35, 175; Iron Gate, 34–35, 48

Danubian people, 99–100

Darby, Abraham, III, 250
Dardanelles, 9, 35, 115
Das Kapital (Marx), 245
Davies, Shane, 265
dechristianization/secularization, 123, *145,* 145–47, 150
deindustrialization, 264–67, *266, 268,* 287
Delta Project (Netherlands), *55,* 55–56
democracy, 10, 20
demographic transition, 75, *75*
demographics, 19, 71–93; aging population, *78,* 229, 346, 370; challenges, 370–75, *371, 373*; contraception and abortion, 77–78; core–periphery pattern, 72–73; local variations, 90–91; migration, 75, 80–84; natural increase, 75–80, 89; physical geographical features and, 73–74; population distribution and density, 71–74, *73, 74*; population geography, major influences on, 84–89; population growth rates, 72, 75–84; population policies, 89, 372–73; scale differences, 90–91; socioeconomic and political context, 87–88; warfare, effect on, *87,* 87–88
Denmark, 17, 64, *65,* 156, 161, 251, 279
devolution of authority, 390, 398
dialect net, 98–99, *101,* 109, 112
dialects, 93, *94*
Dickens, Charles, 246
dikes, 52, 53
Dinaric Range, 30, 34, 37, 42, 113, 184
Dinaric–Pindhos mountain region, 104
Dionysus (god), 200
disease, 72, 85–87, *86, 87*
Dolomite mountains, *30*
Dover strait, 35
Drin river, 47
Druids, 147
Dublin, Ireland, 39
Dumas, Alexandre, 15
Dunkerque, 172
Dutch language, 104, 106–7, 172, 182
Dutch Reformed Church, 137

earthquakes, 31, *32, 33*
East European Plain, 1, 33, 41; language diffusion and, 99; Muscovy dominates, 186; pipelines, 263; rivers, 35; Russian dialect net, 109
East Germany (German Democratic Republic), 91, 175, 223, 291; deindustrialization, 267; land reform, 224–25
East Slav Kingdom, 186

Eastern Europe: deindustrialization, 270–71, 276; EU member states, 293–94, 380, 388, 391–92; health, 352; natural population growth, 78; social welfare, 347–48, *348*; tourism, 285
Eastern Hemisphere, 1–2, 13
Eastern Orthodoxy, 7, *124,* 131, 140–42, *141, 142,* 189
East–West geopolitical split, 9
Ebro river, 35
economy, 10–11, *11,* 19; Asian, 13–14; economic integration, 289–90; ethno-cultural groups and, 189; of European Union, 22, 192, 382–83; global economic downturn, late 2000s, 67, 267, 283, 294–95, 354–55, 370; government-debt-to-GDP ratios, 295, *295*; integration, impacts of, 294–97; macroeconomic challenges, 367–70; primary economic activities, 197, 233, 265; quaternary sector, 275, 277, 287–89, *288*; religion and, 133; secondary sector, 230, 233, 248; tertiary sector, 275–77. *See also* postindustrial economy; rural sector
ecotourism, 286
Edinburgh Castle, Scotland, 319
education, 10, 355–57, *356*
EE Macedonia, Georgia, Montenegro, and, Ukraine
EEC/EC/EU, 287, 289–90, *290,* 294, 296, 379–80, 383. *See also* European Community (EC); European Economic Community (EEC); European Union (EU)
Eleusis, 126
employment, 354–55; absolute employment gaps, 357, *360*; gender pay gaps, 357, *359*; retirement age, 370
energy production, 66, 277, 279–81, *280*
engineering industries, 242, 244
England, 176; English Scarplands, 33, 34, 48; as original nation-state, 161; population distribution, 74; railroad development, 256–57. *See also* London
English Channel Eurotunnel ("Chunnel"), 35, 257–58, *259*
English language, 107–8, *119*; as lingua franca, 108, 119–20
Entrikin, Nicholas, 345
environment, 47–65; agricultural pollution, 226–27; atmosphere, 56–58; deindustrialization and, 271; disasters, 248; environmentally friendly farming, 226–28;

EU governance arena, 66–68; Green Europe, 65–68; human impacts on forests, 58–65; industrial pollution, 242, *247*, 248; lands and waters, 47–56; manufacturing and industry impacts, 245–48; Netherlands, 49–56; population geography and, 85–87; soils, 45–47; tourism and, 286; vegetation, 42–47

equality, 345

Erasmus initiative, 387

Erlanger, Steven, 15

Erna (volcano), 31–32

erosion, 27, 65

Erse (Irish) language, *110,* 111, 118

eskers, 34

Estonia, 114, 144, 169–70, 224, 362

Estonian language, 113, 118

ethnic cleansing, 82, 150, 184–85

ethnic geography, 75, 360–67

ethnic nations, 161–62, 168, 189; autonomy, demands for, 189–90, 361–62

ethno-regionalism, 390, 396–98. *See also* separatist movements

Etruria (modern Tuscany), 302

Etruscan forest, 48

Etruscans, 102, 178, 197

eugenics, 89

Eurasia, 1–2

Eurasian plate, *26,* 26–27, *27,* 33

euro, 291, 294, 354, 382, 388, 392

"Eurobarometer" surveys, 380

Europa (mythological character), 2–3

Europe, *2, 3*; 47 independent states, 159, *160*; 130 culturally distinct peoples, 159; aesthetic appeal, 229; attempts to find physical borders, 4–5, *6*; Christianity, historical role of, 123, 146–47; decline in global influence, 13–14; eighteenth century, map, *164*; at end of World War I, *167*; as human entity, 7–15; Islamic influences on, 150–51, 318; new states since 1980, *190*; north–south cultural divide, 131; origins of word, 2–3; as physical entity, 1–6; religious regions, 131; social and economic indicators, 10–11, *11*; terrain regions, *26*; western fringe, 163–64

European Agency on Fundamental Rights, 150

European Atomic Energy Community (EURATOM), 192

European Central Bank, 292, 370, 388

European Coal and Steel Community (ECSC), 191

European Commission, 66, 68, 371

European Community (EC), 192, 290

European Economic Area, 290

European Economic Community (EEC), 191–92, 275, 290, 379; food supply policy, 225–26

European Environment Agency (EEA), 58

European Free Trade Association (EFTA), 289–90

European Monetary Union (EMU; Eurozone), 292, *293,* 296, 370, 380

European Spatial Planning Observation Network, 347

European Stability Mechanism, 296

European Union (EU), 10; challenge to European state system, 159; citizenship in, 379; debt crisis, 294–96, *295*; eastern border, 17; Eastern European members, 293–94, 380, 388, 391–92; as economic club, 192, 382–83; enlargement, 8, 226, 289–90, *290,* 380, 398; environmental governance arena, 66–68; fishing policy, 221; foreign policy and, 194, 292, 380, 385, 391–92; lack of faith in, 380–81, *382,* 398; member states, *18,* 191, 289–92; official language, 118; positive regard for, 380, *381*; proposed constitution, 8, 123, 294, 380, 382, 395; regional linkages (INTERREG), 399–400, *400*; as statelike entity, 381–82; trajectory of, 289–94

European Union Force (EUFOR), 194

Europeanization, 13, *16*

Europoort, 262–63

Eurorussia, 16, 45, 186, 224

Eurozone, 292, *293,* 296, 370, 380

Evelyn, John, 56

façadism, 324

Faeroe Islands, 161

Faeroese language, 93, 107

fallowing, 225

Farben chemical works, 243

Fátima, 135

Federal Republic of Germany, 175

federal states, *169,* 169–70, 182

federalism: Belgium, 182–83; Germany, *174,* 174–76; Russia, 188; Spain, 179–80

Feldheim (Germany), 66

Fenno-Scandian Shield, 34

Fertile Crescent, 47

fertility: decline, 75–76, *76*; total fertility rate (TFR), 78–79, 89, *371,* 371–75

feudal system, 105, 161, 207, 304, 309, 328

Finland, 34; agriculture, 204–5, *205,* 206, 220; climate, 42; deforestation, 64; employment, 355; manufacturing and industry, 243–44; tourism, 284, 286

Finnish-Karelian language, 113

Finnish-speaking people, 188

fishing industry, 133, 248

fjords, 28, 29

Flanders, 52, 182–83, 234

Flemings, 139, 390

Flevo Lacus (Netherlands), 51

flood, Black Sea, 99

föhn (wind), 40

fontanili (springs), 34

foreign policy, 194, 292, 380, 385, 391–92

Forest of Carbonnière, 60

forests: afforestation, 60, 61, 64; broadleaf deciduous, 43–45, 60; in classical times, 58–60; deforestation, 49, *57,* 58–64, *61, 62,* 211; human impacts on, 58–65; mixed broadleaf and coniferous, 44, 62; rejuvenation, 268–69

fracking, 66–67

France, 60, *172, 173,* 322; agriculture, 218–19, *223*; dialects, 103; education, 356, *356*; EEC and, 379; English spoken in, 120; fertility rate, 75–76, 89; health coverage, 352; Île de France, 163, *163,* 172, *173*; immigrants and, 366; Jews in, 154; as military power, 194; nationalism, 22; as original nation-state, 161; pilgrimage sites, 134; plains, 33, 34; population, 72; roads, 250; social policies, 345; tourism, 286; as unitary state, 172–74, *173*; workweek, 345, 369; World War II, *88. See also* Paris, France

Francis, Pope, 135–36

Franco, Francisco, 373

Frankish Empire, 172, 174

Frankish Kingdom of 843 CE, 174

Franks, 172, 212

fraternité, 345

Free Orthodox Church, 140

French language, 108, 172, 182; *langue d'oc,* 104; *langue d'oïl,* 104, 172

French Revolution, 165

French Union of Muslim Associations, 153

French–Catalan road signs, 103

French–German political boundary, 19

French–German trading relationship, 191–92, 379

Friesche Islands, 49–50

Frisian language, 107

Frisians, 53

Friuli language, 104

Fukushima Dai-ichi nuclear disaster, 281

Gagauz language, 115

Galicia, *180*

Galician language, 103–4, 115, *117*

Gallegans, 179

Gazprom, 263

Gdansk, Poland, 320

gender mainstreaming, 359–60

genocide, 153–54

gentrification, 322, *323*

geographical imagination, 159, 191

geographical perspective, 17–19

geolinguistics, 96–97

geomorphology, 25, 45–47, 49

geopolitical order, changing, 383–85, 391–92

Georgian language, 115

Georgians, 150

German Democratic Republic. *See* East Germany (German Democratic Republic)

German Empire, 131, 163–64, 168, 174–75

Germanic language subfamily, 101, 105–8, *106*

Germanic tribes, 13, 29, 100, 175, 304; Christianity and, 129; deforestation, 60, 62, *63*; roots of United Kingdom, 176

Germans, ethnic, 82, 106, 188

Germany: archaic language border, *106*; borders, *174*; climate, 39–40; counterurbanization, 322; east–west division, 175–76; education, 355–56; EEC and, 379; employment, 355; environment and, 64, 66; Eurozone crisis and, 296, 370; federalism, *174,* 174–76; health coverage, 352; immigrants and, 80, 84, 365; Islam in, 152–53; manufacturing and industry, 242–43, 244; neoliberal reforms, 369–70; north–south divide, 175; nuclear power and, 279, 281; population, 72, 374; population pyramid, *79,* 79–80; railroads, 257; religious divide, 175; reunification, 161, 175–76, 291; roads, 251, 254; unification nationalism,

165. *See also* East Germany (German Democratic Republic); Nazi Germany; West Germany

Ghent, 234, 311

ghetto, 155, 362

Gibraltar, 102, 259

Gibraltar strait, 35

Giordano, Ralph, 153

Giralda (tower), 151

Giscard d'Estaing, Valéry, 15, 89

glaciation, 44, 49

glaciers, 27–29, *28,* 33, 58

globalization, 190–91, 367–68, 383; as impetus for fragmentation, 390–91

Golden Dawn party (Greece), 367

Gorbachev, Mikhail, 16

governmental (public) services, 275

Grand Mosque of Paris, 152, *152*

Great Britain, 176, *177*; hills, 33, 34; Industrial Revolution, 21–22. *See also* England; Ireland; Scotland; United Kingdom; Wales

Great European Plain, 35, 241, 261–62

Great Mosque (Seville), *151*

Greco-Roman civilization, 2–3, 13, 199

Greece, 3, 11; climate, 40; economic downturn and, 294–96, 354; islands, *59*; land reform, 223; Muslims and, 150; religion, 144–45, 189; terraced hillsides, 47, *48*;

Greek Heroic Age, 301–2

Greek language, 111–12

Greeks, ancient, 2–3, *125*; cities, 301–2; religion, 125, *125*; rise of manufacturing and, 233; seafaring, 259–60; straits, control of, 35

Green Europe, 65–68

green villages, 209, *210, 211*

Greenland, 17, 161

Gress, David, 12

Griggs, Richard, 159

Guadalquivir river, 102, 204

guest workers, 83, 89, *148,* 322, 366

guild system, 235, 236, 243, 245, 269; charcoal burners, 241, 242

Gulf Stream, 36–37

Haarlemmer Lake, 53

half-timbering, 212, *213, 214*

Hamburg, Germany, *329*

Hannibal, 29

Hanseatic League (Hansa), 260

hardscrabble herding/farming, 199, *200,* 204, 220

health, 10, 89, 351–54, *353*; life expectancy, 351–52; problems, 352–54, *353*

health insurance, 347, 352

health resorts, 285, 309

heat islands, 56–57

heath, 45, 64–65, *65,* 128

heathen, as word, 128

Hecataeus, *2*

Heilbronn, Germany, 311, *312*

Hellenes, 99

Hellenic Golden Age, 302

Hellenic languages, 99

Henniche, Muhammad, 153

Henry VIII, 131

Hercynian period, 26, 29

Hercynian regions, 26, 29, 33, 240, 241

Hessen (Germany), 171

high-tech industry, 269–70, 287–88, 321

hills, 33–34, 47

historical territorial record, 8–9

Hohenzollern family, 63

Holland, 39, 52, 54, 55

Holocene period, 71

Holy Roman Empire, 174

Homer, 49, 59, 259, 301

hominids, 71

Homo sapiens, 71

horticulture, 199–200, 199–203, 215–17, 216

housing, 91, 170; single-family detached homes, 317–18; vacation homes, 285, 321

How Green Was My Valley (Llewellyn), 246

Huguenot faith, 131, 139

human development, 343

human traits, Europe and, 7–15; Indo-European language family, 8, *9*; race, 7, *9*; religion, 7–8, *9*

Hundred Years' War, 60

Hungarian Basin, 34–35, 115; Puszta, 44–45

Hungarians, 114–15. *See also* Magyar

Hungarians, ethnic, 186

Hungary, 41, 129, 165, 167, 192, 224

Hus, Jan, 137

Hussite war, 139

hydroelectric power, 243–44

hydrogeography, 25, 35, *36,* 49

Iberia, 7–9; Arabic place names, 102, *103*; geographical features, 29, 34–35; languages, 102; Moors and, 8–9, 102, 129, *151,* 163, 179. *See also* Spain

Ibérica mountains, 42

ice ages, 27–28, *28*

Iceland, 17, 33, 45, 72, 77; energy production, 66, 279; fishing, 221; glaciers, 58

Icelandic language, 93, 107

identity: ethnic, 185; EU membership and, *12*, 380, 392, *393*; language and, 93; regional, 185; religion-based, 123

Île de France, 163, *163*, 172, *173*

individualism, 345

Indo-European language family, 8, *9*, 95; diffusion into Europe, 98–101, *100*, *101*; east–west divide, 99, 101; Germanic languages, 105–8; Hellenic branch, 111–12; Italic division, 101, 102; major subfamilies, 101–9; minor tongues, 109–13; north–south patterning, 115; origin in Caucasus Mountains, 98; Romance–Germanic language divide, 115, 180–84, 289; Slavic languages, 108–9. *See also* language families; non-Indo-European languages

Industrial Revolution, 20–22, 236–40; canal phase, 261; core–periphery pattern, 236–37, 271; diffusion of, 240–44; railroad development, 256; religion and, 139; woolen mills, 204

infant mortality rate, 10, 351–52

inheritance systems, 89, 171, *171*, 207

integration, European, 275; bureaucratization, 394; economic advances, *387*, 387–88; economic impacts of, 294–97; ethno-regionalism and, 390; fragmentation, impetuses for, 390–98; future prospects, 379–402, *390*; geopolitical order and, 383–85, 391–92; heightened interaction, 386–87, 395–96; impetuses for, 383–90; irrationality of state patterns, 388–90; large-scale business clusters, 296; relationships with surrounding areas, 385–86; trajectory of, 289–94; widening and deepening, 289, 294, 380, 382, 394–95, 398–99. *See also* European Union (EU); postindustrial economy

interglacials, 27–28, 71

international languages, 119

International Security Assistance Force (ISAF), 194

invaders and migrating peoples, 8, 29, 30, 33, 35, 45; language patterns and, 102, 104; Magyars, 8, 35, 102, 114–15; Tatar-Mongol invasions, 186

Iraq invasion, 194, 385, 391

Ireland, *177*; Christianity, 129; deforestation, 60–61; external migration, 80, *81*; nationalism, 139–40, 166; natural population change, 77; Protestant–Catholic divide, *139*, 139–40; Republic of Ireland, 176; total fertility rate, 78. *See also* Northern Ireland

Iron Gate (Danube), 34–35, 48

Islam, 7, 8, *124*, 147–53, *148*; Bosnian Muslims, 149–50; Germany, 152–53; growth of, 13; hostility toward, 149–50; influences on Europe, 150–51; mosques, 150–51, 367; parallel society concept, 153. *See also* Moors; religion

islands, 17, 32–33, 41, *59*; political statuses, 160–61

Isle of Man, 161

isoglosses, 107

isolates, 93

isostatic rebound, 49

Istanbul (Constantinople), 9

isthmuses, 1, *2, 3*

Istria, 185, *185*

Italian language, 104, 182

Italian Peninsula, 29–30

Italic speech, 99, 101, 102

Italy: employment, 354–55; mercantilism, 233–34; nuclear power and, 280; population, 72; Roman legacy, 177–79, *178*; sirocco winds, 41; slow food movement, 228; unification movement, 34, 165, 177–78

Japheth (biblical character), 7

Jews, 8, 128, *154*, 362

John Paul II, 123, 135

Judaism, 128, 153–55

Judeo–Christian–Hellenic heritage, 7

Jura (hills), 33, 182

Jutland Peninsula, 100, 105

kaisers, German, 175

Kaliningrad District, 188

Karelia, 34, 113, 188

karst topography, 30

Kasper, Walter, 155

Katowice (Poland), 67

Kharkov District, 189

Kildrummy Church, Scotland, *127*

King James Bible, 98, 108

Kingdom of the Serbs, Croats, and Slovenes, 168

Kingdom of the West Franks, 172
Kjølen Range, 31, 42, 45, 58
Kollwitz, Käthe, 246
Komi Republic, 113
Kosovo, 113, 150, 184, *185,* 186, 193
Kriti (Crete), 32–33, 223, 286
Krym peninsula, 189

labor costs, 266, 277
labor unionization, 344
Ladinic language, 104
laïcité, 153
Lake Yssel, 53, 54
lakes, 34, 50, 53
land consolidation, 221–22
land divisions: checkerboard pattern, 207, *208;* inheritance systems and, 207; latifundia, 207; strip fields, 207, *209*
land reform, 222–25
land tenure, modern era, 221–25
landmasses, 1; configuration and climate, 26, 37
Land's End (Great Britain), 33
language families, 8, 93–98, *94, 95;* influences on, 97; major subfamilies, 101–9; trees, 95, *96*
language patterns, 19, 93–122; alphabet divide, 109, 129; derived from Roman armies, 35; France, 172; geolinguistics, 97–98; identity and, 93; language families, 93–98; linguistic assimilation, 102; linguistic decline and revival, 116; multilingualism, 118–20; physical geographic obstacles and, 99, *100, 101,* 108; Pripyat Marsh and language diffusion, 99, 108, 113; proto-language, 96–97, 98; Romance speech, 35; sociopolitical and environmental context, 95; standard (standardized), 98, 108; Switzerland/Belgium divide, *181,* 182–84; written, 95, 97–98. *See also* place names
language trees, 95, *96*
Languedoc Plain, 34, 217
Las Marismas (marsh), 204
latifundia, 207
Latin, 13, 97, 102–3, 109, 112, 129, 178
Latium (modern Lazio), 178, 302
Latvia, 114, 169–70, 224
Le Pen, Marine, 367
leaching, 47
Lepanto, 9
Lettish (Latvian) language, 113
Letzeburgish language, 106

Libya (Africa), *2,* 3, 193
Liechtenstein, 160
life expectancy, 10, 89, 351–52
linen textiles, 203, 234, 240, 241, 267
lingua franca, 108, 119–20
linguistic drift, 98, *101*
linguistic revival movements, 111, 115, 120
Lisbon, Portugal, 306
Lisbon Treaty, 294
literacy rates, 10, 356
Lithuania, 129, 131
Lithuanian language, 113
Little Ice Age, 28, 39, 85
littoral, 40
locks, 47, 53
loess, 34, 45
Lombards, 179
London, England, 39, 56; as financial center, 240, 287, *288;* foreign born residents, 364; Industrial Revolution and, 240; population, 314. *See also* England
London bombings, 150, 365
London Bridge, 307–8
longboats, 105
Louis, Herbert, 5, *6*
Lourdes, 135
Low Countries, 33; capitalism, 22; cities, 304–5; confederation, 164. *See also* Netherlands
Lübeck, Germany, *311*
Luther, Martin, 131
Luther Bible, 98, 106
Lutheranism, 137
Luxembourg, 191, 289, 328
luxury industries, 242, 270

Maas river, 46, 49, 50, 262
Maastricht Treaty, 291
Macedonia, 113, 184, *185,* 185–86
Madrid, 179, *180*
Madrid bombings, 150
Maghreb countries, 83
Magna Carta, 20
Magna Mater (goddess), 125, *126,* 127
Magyar people, 8, 102, 114–15
Maine–Danube canal, 47–48
malaria, 86, 90
Malta, 17, 72, 160–61, 283
Maltese language, 115, 118
manufacturing, as term, 236
manufacturing and industry, 233–73, 368; colonialism and, 234–35; concentration of

industries, 237–39, *238*; contemporary patterns, 271; deindustrialization, 264–67, *266, 268,* 287; diffusion of Industrial Revolution, 240–42; east–west contrast, 251, *255,* 270; environmental impacts, 245–48; high-tech industry, 269–70, 287–88, 321; historical overview (pre-eighteenth century), 233–35; hydroelectric power and, 243–44; impacts of industrialization, 244–64; industrial rejuvenation, 268–71; Industrial Revolution, 236–40; pipelines, *263,* 263–64; social impacts, 245–46; spread beyond coalfields, 242–44; traditional systems, 235; transportation, impacts on, 248–64; urban centers, 242

maps, 159; Hecataeus, *2*; Pomponius Mela, *3*; religious-inspired, 3–4, *4*; Roman, 3; "T in O," 3–4, *4*

market gardening, 216, 217

market (private) services, 275

marketplace, 301, 302, 309, *311*

Marranos, 155

Marshall Plan, 191

marshes, 48–49

Marx, Karl, 22, 245

Marxism, 245

Massif Central, 33

maternity and paternity leave periods, 344–45

McAdam, John, 250

mechanization, 236–37, 239, 241–42, 277

Medieval Warm Period (Medieval Optimum), 85

Mediterranean: civilizations, 2–3; forest zone, 44; mercantilism, 233–34; population density, 85

Mediterranean agriculture, 199–202, *200,* 211, 217

Mediterranean Sea, 1, 4, 17, 259

Medjugorje, 135

mercantile city, 300, 307, 317

mercantilism, 233–34

Merkel, Angela, 358, 370

Meseta (Spain), 58, 103, *180*

Mesoamerican food complex, 215

metallurgical industries, 238–39, 240, 308

Mezzogiorno, *178,* 179

microstates, 160, 351

Middle Ages: bubonic plague, 72, 85–86, *86*; Christianity, 7; cities, 303–13, *313*; emergences of states, *162,* 162–63; human alteration of environment, 47; tertiary sector, 276

Middle East, 13, 235, 243, 264, 386

Middle English, 108

migration, 13, 75, 80–84, *83,* 190, 362–63; anti-immigrant backlash, 84; challenges, 375–76; east-to-west, 84; external, 80; forced, 81–82, 89, 184–85, 188; from former Soviet republics, 109; internal, 80–81; to manufacturing areas, 242–43; from outside Europe, 82–84; return, 106; rural-to-urban, 81–82, 229; social model and, 346; south-to-north, 82; Turks, 84, 115, 149, 365–66

Milan, Italy, 243, 270

Milankovitch, Milutin, 27

Milankovitch cycle, 27

milking culture-complex, 204

Milwaukee, Wisconsin, *318*

mires, 44

mistral, 41

Mithras (god), 125

Moldova, 102, 104, 189

Molokans, 140

Monaco, 72, 160

monarchy, 165

Mongoloid race, 7

monotheism, 126

Monte Circeo, 49

Montenegro, 184, *185*

Moors, 8–9, 29, 102, 129, *151, 163,* 179, 233. *See also* Islam

moors, 45, 64

moraines, 34

Morocco, 83

morphology, 299; geomorphology, 25, 45–47, 49; medieval urban cities, 311–12, *313*

Moscow, Russia, 41, *333,* 333–35, *334*

mosques, 150–51, 367

motes, 47

Mount Ólimbos, 104

mountains, 29–33; Alpine period, 27, 29; glacial sculpting, 28–29; Hercynian period, 26, 29; west–east direction, 25, 29

Mozarabic language, 102

multilingualism, 118–20

Munich (München), Germany, *318*

Murmansk, 42

Murzayev, E. M., 6

Muscovy (modern Moscow), 186

Muslim-Croat Federation, 186

Muslims, 13, 17, 149–50, 184, 186. *See also* Islam; Moors

mystery cults, 125, 127
mythology, 2–3, 260

Nagorno–Karabakh Province, 17
Naples, Italy, 311
Napoleon Bonaparte, 165
nation, definition, 161
National Front (France), 367
National Health Service, England, 352
nationalism, 22, 147, 392–93; Age of Nation-
    alism, 165, 167–68; Basque, 115; France,
    22; Ireland, 139–40, 166; Russia, 142;
    types, 165–66, *166*; Ukrainian, 189; World
    War I and, 168
nation-state, 22, 163, 185; challenges to,
    360–61, 379; original, 161–62, 164, 165.
    See also state system
Natura 2000, 66
natural increase, 75–80, 89
Nazi Germany, 89, 147, 153–54, 168, 175
Neanderthals, 71
Near East, 299
Negroid race, 7
neoliberal reforms, 369–70
neolithic revolution, 197–99, *198*
Netherlands, *50*; English as a second language,
    119; environmental agenda, 66; Frisian
    language, 107; human modification, 49–56;
    industrial development of, 234; Menno-
    nites, 131; polders, 52–54; sand dune
    barriers, 49–50, 55; Southern Flevoland,
    54. *See also* Low Countries
Nevsky, Aleksandr, 144
new industrial spaces, 270
New World, 215, 234
New York City, 56
Newbigin, Marion I., 16
Newcastle–Tyneside–Tees district, 239, 265
Nieuwe Waterweg, 55
Noah's Flood (Ryan and Pitman), 99
nomadic herding, 199, 205–6, *206*, 222
non-Indo-European languages, 95, 113–15,
    114; in Germanic languages, 105; Roman
    Empire era, 101; taiga as refuge, 44
nontariff trade barriers, 291
Nordish people, 105
Nördlingen, Bavaria, 311, *312*
Norman French state, 35
Normandy, 172
Normans (Vikings), 31, 47, 85, 107–8, 172,
    176

North Africa, 8, 129
North Americans, 22–23
North Atlantic Drift, 36–37, 42
North Atlantic Treaty Organization (NATO),
    192–94, *193*
North European Plain, 33, 35, 261; air pollu-
    tion, 57; manufacturing and industry, 242;
    population density, 73
North German Plain, 175
North Sea, 49–51, 260
Northern Hemisphere, 25
Northern Ireland, *139*, 139–40, 176, *177*, 240.
    See also Ireland
Northern Ireland Assembly, 140
Northern League (Italy), *178*, 179
Norway, 31, 42, 80, 166; fishing and fish farm-
    ing, 221; Sweden–Norway boundary, 169,
    170; tourism, 284; transportation, 251; vote
    on EU membership, 383, *384*
Norwegian language, 93, 107
nuclear power industry, 279–81
nucleation, 239

Occitan dialect, 104
Occitania, 172, *173*
occupational specialization, 299
Odiel river, 49
Odyssey (Homer), 49
Oguz branch of Turkic, 115
Old English, 107
open-air folk museums, 284
Order of the Solar Temple, 147
Organization for Economic Cooperation and
    Development (OECD), 347, *348*
Organization of Petroleum Exporting Coun-
    tries, 279
Organization on Security and Cooperation in
    Europe, 155
Orlowski, Witold, 15
orographic effect, 39
Oslo, Norway, 306
Osman Turks, 115
Österreich, 175
Ostmark (Eastern March), 175
Ottoman Empire, 161, *163*, 166, 167

Padania, 179
paganism, 124–25, *127*, 127–28
Palmanova, Italy, 314, *315*
Palos de la Frontera, 49
Pangea (supercontinent), 26, 33

Paris, France, *319*; city site, 305; as financial center, 287; Grand Mosque, 152, *152*; kings of France based in, 172; La Défense, 325, *325*; levels of social well-being, *351*; Middle Ages, 311; riots, 365, *365;* roads, 250; suburbs, 91. *See also* France

Paris Basin, 33, 34, 35, 172, *173*

Parker, W. H., 7

Party for Freedom, Netherlands, 367

passes, 104, 182, 250

Patmos, *59*

patriarch of Constantinople, 140, 144

Patrick, Saint, 129

Paul, Apostle, 126

Pavia, Italy, 311, *313*

Pax Romana, 302

Peace of Westphalia, 163–64, 168

Pear Tree Pass, 30

peasantry, 207

peat bogs, 44, 45

Peel, Quentin, 398

peninsulas, 25, 29–31, 33, 37

Pennine Chain, 33

Pentecostal church, 138

permafrost, 45

Peter, Saint, 133

petroleum and natural gas, 243, 263–64, 268

Phoenicians, 2, 3, 302

physical geography, 19, 25–68; climate, 36–42; hills, 33–34, 47; islands, 32–33; mountains, 29–33; plains, 33–35; vegetation, 42–47

pipelines, *263,* 263–64

Pitman, Walter, 99

place names, 17–18, 61, 62, 102, *103,* 127; Celtic, 105; cities, 306, 307, 308–9; religious, 133; roads, 324; Roman influence, 302–3; Slavic, 105–6, *106. See also* language patterns

plains, 33–35

Plato, 59

Pleistocene era, 27

plurals, 95

Po river, 35, 58

podsols, 47

Poland, 34, 44, 155; Christianity and, 129, 135; energy supply, 67, *67;* labor exports, 84; population policy, 374–75

polders, 52–54

Polish language, 109

political boundaries, 18–19, 91, 185, 388

polytheism, 124–25

Pompeii, 31

Pomponius Mela, *3*

popes, 7, 8, 130, 144

population clusters, 31, *31, 33*

population density, 72–73, *74,* 81–82, 84–85, 325–26

population geography: environment and, 85–87; major influences on, 84–89

population growth rates, 10, 14, 75–84; annual change, *77;* birth rate, 14, 76–77, 84, 88; fertility decline, 75–76, *76;* population policies, 374–75; population pyramid, *79, 79–80, 346;* potential support ratio (PSR), 79–80; total fertility rate (TFR), 78–79, 89, *371,* 371–75

population pyramid, *79, 79–80, 346*

Porteous, Douglas, 246

ports, 35, 42, 49, 243, 244, 262–63, 308, 368

Portugal, 8–9, 34, 179, *180;* climate, 40; colonialism, 234; as original nation-state, 161; Roman Catholic Church and, 136. *See also* Iberia

Portuguese language, 102–4

Posavina Corridor, 186

postindustrial, as term, 275

postindustrial economy, 275–89; communications, 277, *278,* 278–79; energy production, 279–81, *280;* quaternary sector, 275, 277, 287–89, *288;* retailing and governmental/social services, 2;87; service and information economy, 275–77; tourism, 281–86, *282, 283. See also* integration, European

potential support ratio (PSR), 79–80

Po–Veneto Plain, 34, 41, 42, 178, *178,* 179; cities, 304; industrial sector, 243

prairies, 44–45

precipitation, 39, 40, 41, 56; acid, 57, *57,* 64

preindustrial core, 315, 317, 318, 323–24, *328,* 328–29, *329*

preindustrial periphery, 315–16, 318, 324

Presbyterianism, 131, 137

primary economic activities, 197, 233, 265

primate cities, 168

primogeniture, 89, 171, *171,* 207

printing press, 97–98

Pripyat Marsh, language diffusion and, 99, 108, 113

production–consumption patterns, 367–68

pronatalist policies, 372–73

Protestant Church in the Netherlands, 137

Protestantism, *124, 130, 136,* 136–40, *138,* 175; fragmentation, 137; neo-Protestantism, 137–38; work, view of, 234
proto-Celtic culture, 99–100
proto-language, 96–97, 98
proto-Slavs *(Sorby),* 108
provinces, *14,* 164, 169, 170, 183
Prussia, *174,* 175
Puritanism, 131
Pyrenees, 29, 33, 37

quaternary sector, 275, 277, 287–89, *288*

race, 7, *9*
Raeto-Romanic group, 104
railroads, 252, 255–58, *256, 258*; rail terminals, 315–16
Randstad, Netherlands, 270, 288, *337*
Ravenna (northern Italy), 49
reading proficiency, 356
recreation areas, 229, 261
Reformation, *130,* 137
Reformed Church, 131
reindeer, 220–21
religion, 7–8, *9,* 19, 123, 362; astronomy-based, 125, 127; Christian fragmentation, 130–42; geography of, 123–58; groups in Europe, *124*; local sense of place, *125,* 133; non-Christian minorities, 147–55; paganism, 124–25, 127–28; pre-Christian Europe, 124–26, 127; saints, *126,* 126–27, 133; sects and cults, 147; words, origin of, 127
religious structures, 133, 319; megaliths, 125; mosques, 150–51; Orthodox, 140–42, *141, 142*; Protestant, 138, *138*; Roman Catholic, 123, *151,* 153, 319; shrines, *126*; templed promontories, *125,* 259, *260*
Renaissance, 179, 313–14
research and development, 269, 287, *288*
Rhine river, 19, 49, 50, 51, 56, 172, 182, 242, 262
Rhine–Maas–Schelde Estuary, 49, 50, *52,* 55
Rhône river, 35, 262
Rhône Valley, 90, *90,* 104
Rhône–Saône corridor, 41
rivers, 35, 74, 240; confluence sites, 308; river-meander sites, 305–6
road signs, 103, 111, *112, 117, 118*
roads, 165–66, *166,* 248–55, *252*; autobahn system, 251; controlled-access expressways, 251, *252,* 324; European highway (E desig-

nation), 252; highway density, 252–53, *253*; right- and left-hand drive systems, 252; Roman, 134, 248–50, *249*; traffic congestion, 253–55, *254,* 285, 319, 334
Rock of Gibraltar, 29
Rodopi Range, 113
Roma (gypsies), 113, 362, 396
Roman Catholicism, *124,* 130, 131–36, *132*; Germany, 175; papacy, 135–36; Ukraine, 189
Roman Empire, 3, 8, 29, 101; cities, 302–3, *303*; collapse of, 72, 97, 105, 109, 129, 172, 177, 250; Germany and, 175; Hellenistic, 130; Jews in, 128; land survey system, 207, *208,* 210; Latin, diffusion of, 97; Netherlands and, 50, 54; northern border, 171; roads, 134, 248–50, *249*; secondary industries, 233; western and eastern halves, 130
Roman law, 89, 171
Romance language subfamily, 101, 102–4, 107–8
Romani ethnic minority, 138
Romania, 30, 35, 89, 102, 104, 113, 189; agriculture, 224; deindustrialization, 267; European Union and, 380, 388; religion, 138
Romanian language, 104
Romansh language, 104, 182
Romany language, 113
Roubaix, France, 153
Ruhr district, Germany, *241,* 241–42
Ruhr river, 174
Rumsfeld, Donald, 15
rural sector, 197–231; building styles and materials, 211–13, *212*; depopulation, 228–29; land tenure in modern era, 221–25; migration from, 81–82, 229; perseveration programs, 229–30; production patterns in modern era, 225–28; traditional land divisions and settlement patterns, 207–13, *208*; villages, 208–9, *210, 211. See also* agriculture
Russia, *3, 187*; agriculture, 224, 226; birth rate, 76; Christianity and, 129; Communism, 22; contested status, 15–16; deindustrialization, 267; energy production, 279; evolution of, 186–88, *187*; federalist form, 188; Jews in, 154; manufacturing and industry, 248; Pechory, monastery at, *143,* 144; pipelines, *263,* 263–64; post-communist, 186–87; tundra, 45. *See also* Soviet Union

Russian dialect net, 109
Russian Empire, 166, 167
Russian Karelia, 34
Russian language, 109
Russian Orthodox Church, 140
Russian revolution, 186
Russians, ethnic, 188
Ryan, William, 99

Saale river, *106*
Sachsen, 175
Saharan winds, 41, 58
Sambre–Meuse–Lys valley, 240
Sami (Lapps), 114, 138, *206*; reindeer ranching, 220–21
San Marino, 160
Santiago de Compostela, *135*
Santorini, 32–33
Sapmi (Lapland), 206
Sardegna, 41
Sardinia, 103, 161
Sardinian language, 104
Saxon invaders, 34, 176
Scandinavia, 7, 22, 45, 74; cold phase, 500 BCE, 105; land consolidation, 221–22
Scandinavian dialect, 107
Scandinavian Peninsula, 31
Schelde river, 49, 50, 56
Schengen Agreement, 291, *292*, 386
Schwarzwald (Black Forest), 33
Schweizerdeutsch (Swiss German), 95, 106
Scotland, 111, 131, 176, 235
Scott, Allen, 270
Scottish Highlands, 33, 61
Scottish Nationalist Party, 176
Scottish-Gaelic language, *110*, 111
Sea of Azov, 1, 4
seas, 16–17, 35, 259–60. *See also* Black Sea; Mediterranean Sea
secondary economic activities, 230, 233, 248
secularism, 123, 156
secularization/dechristianization, 123, *145*, 145–47
separatist movements, 161, 189–90, *190, 361,* 390
Sephardim, 155
September 11, 2001 terrorist attacks, 150, 156, 194
Serbia, *185*, 186
Serbo-Croatian dialect net, 109
Serbs, 144, 149–50, 184–85

service and information economy, 270, 275–77, *276*; energy and, 279–81
settlement patterns: clustering, 207–10; dispersed, 210–11
sharecropping, 222
Sherwood Forest (England), 62
Shetland Islands, 39
shifting cultivation (burnbeating), 199, *200,* 204–5, *205,* 222
shipbuilding, 59, 60, 233–34, 239, 267
Siberia, 109, 186
Sicily, 30, 31–32, *178, 179*
Sidon, 2–3
Sierra Nevada, 29
siltation, 48–49
Single European Act, 291
Sion/Sitten, Switzerland, 306, *307*
sirocco winds, 41, 58
Skansen open-air museum, 284, *284*
Slavic languages, 99, 101, 105–6, 108–9, 115
Slavic peoples, 9, 105–6, 115, 129, 175
Slavs, 62, 102
Slovakia, 30, 224, 388
Slovenia, 184, 185, *185*
Slovenian language, 109
sluice gates, 52
snow, 39, 40, 42, 58
social and economic indicators, 10–11, *11*
social and ethnic geography, 343–77; demographic challenges, 370–75, *371, 373*; employment, 354–55; ethnic patterns, 360–67; GDP devoted to social welfare programs, 347, *348, 349, 350*; health, 351–54, *353*; immigration challenges, 375–76; patterns of social well-being, 346–51, *348, 349, 350, 351*; women, 357–60, *358, 359, 360. See also* social model, European
social model, European: cradle-to-grave care, 346–47; elements of, 343–45; in transition, 367–76. *See also* social and ethnic geography
social security, 347
social services, 287
socialism, 22
Sognefjord, *31*
soils, 33–34, *46, 65*
South Tirol (Alto Adige), 179
sovereignty, 163–64, 168
Soviet Union: collapse of, 142, 161, 186, 224, 385; increasing control in Eastern Europe, 191; satellite states, 192; Word War II, 88. *See also* Russia

Spain, 8–9, 13, 34–35; agriculture, 226; civil war, 179; climate, 41, 42; colonialism, 234, 362; erosion, 65; forests, 58; manufacturing and industry, 67, 243; as multiethnic state, 179–80, *180*; as original nation-state, 161; Roman Catholic Church and, 136; total fertility rate (TFR), 373–74; tourism, 281–82. *See also* Iberia

specialization, 299; agricultural, 215–16, *216,* 219

Srpska Republic, *185,* 186

St. Gotthard Pass, 104, 182, 250

St. Peter's (Vatican City), *132*

standard (standardized) language, 98, 108

Stara Planina, 99, 113

state system, 22, 159–95; Balkans, 184–86, *185*; borders, 169–71, *170*; breakups of states, 161; case studies, 171–89; colonialism and, 167; core areas, 162–63, *163,* 165, 168, 174, *181,* 182, 186–87; emergence of European state pattern, 161–68; empires, 165–67; federalism in Germany, *174,* 174–76; France as unitary state, 172–74, *173*; general picture, 159–61; globalization and, 190–91; internal state, 169; Italy's Roman legacy, 177–79, *178*; microstates, 160, 351; nation-state, importance of, 161–62, 163; political-territorial centers, 166–67; rise of, 97–98; roads and development of, 165, *166*; Russia, evolution of, 186–88, *187*; Spain as multiethnic state, 179–80, *180*; twentieth century, 168–71; types of state, *162, 169. See also* nation-state

steam power, 237, 241

steppe grasslands, 5, *6,* 44–45, 129

Stonehenge, England, 147, 284

Strabo, 49

straits, 35, 99, 148

Strasbourg, France, 289, 394

street villages, 209, *210, 211*

Stromboli (volcano), 32

strongholds, 305–6, 308

structural funds, 387, *387*

suburbanization, 81, 91, 170; industrial suburbs, 316, 325; postindustrial suburbs, 321, 326

sunlight, 42, 90

superpowers, 191, 226

supranational organizations, 66, 191–92, 289, 389

Surtsey, Iceland, 33

Sweden, 31, 166–67; climate, 42; English as a second language, 119; external migration, 80; family policy, 374; manufacturing and industry, 243–44; nuclear power and, 280–81; social policies, 345; Sweden–Norway boundary, 169, *170*; transportation, 251

Swedish Empire, 166–67

Swedish language, 107

Swiss German language, 95, 110

Swiss People's Party (SVP), 366–67

Switzerland, 22, *90,* 165, 180–82, *181*; acid precipitation, 64; Aletsch glacier, 58; cantons, 120, 165; immigrants and, 366–67; Islam, 153; languages and dialects, 93, 95; manufacturing and industry, 243; migration to, 84; multilingualism, 120; snow conditions, 58; tourism, 283

"T in O" map, 3–4, *4*

taiga, 44, 64; shifting agriculture, 199, *200,* 204–5, *205,* 222

Tale of Two Cities (Dickens), 246

Tatar language, 115

Tatars, 189

Tatarstan, 188

taxation, 343–44

technological advances, 20–22, *21*; agriculture, 217, 225; language patterns and, 97, 108; neolithic, 199; plows, 108, 203, 207; population geography and, 74, 85; road construction, 250. *See also* Industrial Revolution

tectonic plates, 25–27, *26, 27,* 29, 31; Eurasian plate, *26,* 26–27, *27,* 33

Telford, Thomas, 250

templed promontories, *125,* 259, *260*

terpen, 51, *51*

terraces, 47, *48,* 207

terrorists, 150

tertiary sector, 275–77

textile industries, 233, 234, 237; deindustrialization, 267; European mainland, 240–41, *241*

Thaddeus, Apostle, 144

Thames river, 39, 307–8

Thirty Years' War, 87, 131, 139

Thracian language, 99

Thraco-Illyrian languages, 113

three-continent concept, 3

three-field farming, 105, 199, *200,* 203–4, 207, 211–12, 217; fallowing, 225

Tiergarten (Berlin), 63
Tito, Josip, 184
Toledo, Spain, 233, 305, *306*
topocide, 246
Toscana (Italy), 48
total fertility rate (TFR), 78–79, 89, *371, 371–75*
tourism, 261, 281–86, *282, 283*; ecotourism, 286; health resorts, 285
trade expansion, 277, 294, 304
Transdnistria, 189
Trans-Europ Express, 257
transhumance, 202, 204, 205
transportation, 294, *369*; air transport, 264; pipelines, *263,* 263–64; postindustrial economy and, 277; railways, 252, 255–58, *256, 258*; roads, 248–55; tunnels, 35, 254, 257–58, *259*; waterway systems, 35, 258–63
Transylvanian Alps, 30
Treaty of Lisbon, 380
Treaty of Nice, 399
Treaty of Rome, 192
Treaty on European Union, 291
tsunamis, *32*
tundra, 45; nomadic herding, 205–6, *206*
tunnels, 35, 254, 257–58, *259*
Turin, Italy, 243, 270
Turkey, 8; contested status, 15; European Union and, 150, 395; immigrants to Europe, 83–84
Turkic language, 115
Turkic Muslim regions, 188
Turkish language, 115
Turkish North Cyprus, *190, 361*
Turks, 9; expulsion from Bulgaria, 17; migration, 84, 115, 149, 365–66; straits, control of, 35
Tuscany, 178, *178*

Ukraine, 15, 109; agriculture, 224, 226; development of, 188–89; religion, 129, 154, 189
Ukrainian language, 109
Ulysses (mythology), 260
unemployment, 267, *268*, 296, 345, 354–55, 388
unequal encounters, 12–13
Uniate Church (Greek Catholic, Ukrainian Catholic), 144–45, 189
unification nationalism, 165
unitary states, 168, *169*; France, 172–74, *173*
United Kingdom, 108; core–periphery tensions, 176, *177*; counterurbanization, 322;

deindustrialization, 265; employment, 355; European Union, stance toward, 380, *381, 392, 393*, 399; free churches, 137; health coverage, 352; Isle of Man, 161; Jews in, 154; land consolidation, 221–22; land reform, 222–23; as military power, 194; nuclear power industry, 279; population, 72; roads, 250
United States, 194, 385, 391
Upper Rhine Plain, 174, 243
Ural Mountains, 4, *5*
Uralic language family, 113–14, *114*
Uralic speakers, 197
urbanization, 10, 76, 88, 215
U-shaped valleys (fjords), 28, 29

Val di Chiana (Italy), 48
Valachian Plain, 35, 129
Valle d'Aosta, 104
Vardar–Morava rift valley, 99
Vatican City, *132,* 133–34, 160
vegetation, 18, 42–47; biotic provinces, 43, *43,* 115; forests, 43–45; treeless areas, 44–45
Venice, 42; city site, 306, 309–10, 324; shipwrights, 233–34
Vesuvius, 31
Vienna (Wien), 9, 175
Vierwaldstättersee (Lake of Four Forest Cantons; Lake Luzern), 182
vik (inlet), 31, *31*
Vikings, 31, 47, 85, 172, 176
villages, 208–9, *210, 211, 213*
Vilnius (Lithuania), 155
Virgin Mary, *126,* 134, 135
Vlakhs, 104
vocabularies, 95
volcanic soils, 45, 47
volcanoes, 31–32, *32,* 90
Volga river, 188
Vosges (hills), 33

Waddenzee (Netherlands), 50
Wales, 33, 109, 111, 116, *138,* 176, 239, 265
Wallonia, 182–83
Walloons, 104, 390
Walser people, 204
warfare, 60, 82, *87,* 87–88, *88*
Wars of Religion, 163–64
Warsaw, 41
waterpower, 53, 237, 243–44

waterway systems, 35, 258–63; canals, 35, 47–48, 258, 261–62

Watt, James, 237

wealth: in core of city, 320; industrialization and, 245

wealth indicators, 10, 76, *396*

Weilburg, Germany, *328*

welfare state, 246, 343, 345, *348,* 375, 391; differences within cities, 348–49; political purposes of, 347

Welsh language, 109, *110*

Welsh Language Act of 1993, 111

Wessex (England), 163, *163,* 176, *177*

West Germany, 91, 191, 229, 279, 318, 322

westerlies, 37, 51, 53

Western Church, 7, 130–31

White Sea, 4

Whitelegg, John, 254

Wieringer Polder, 53

Wilders, Geert, 15, 367

William the Conqueror, 107

William "the Diker," Count, 52

wind energy, 53, 66

women, 357–60, *358, 359, 360*

woolen textile industries, 204, 220, 234, 237

word order, 95

work accident insurance, 347

World War I, 87, 166, 168, 184

World War II, 9, 41, 153–54, 175; destruction of preindustrial cores, 328–29, *329*; forced migration, 82; Nazi expansionism, 168

xenophobia, 365

Yalta, 31

Yugoslavia, 88, 161, 168, 184–86, 193

Zakarpats'ka District, 189

Zeeland (Netherlands), 56

Zeus (mythological character), 3

Zubac, Kresimir, 15

Zuider Zee (Netherlands), 51

Zuider Zee Project (Netherlands), 53–55, *54*

Zwingli, Ulrich, 131

About the Authors

Alexander B. Murphy is professor of geography at the University of Oregon, where he holds the James F. and Shirley K. Rippey Chair in Liberal Arts and Sciences. He specializes in political, cultural, and environmental geography, with a regional emphasis on Europe. Murphy is a member of the Academia Europaea and a past president of the Association of American Geographers. He has served for many years as a coeditor of *Eurasian Geography and Economics*. Murphy is the author or coauthor of more than 100 articles and several books. He has won teaching awards both from his university and from the National Council for Geographic Education. In the late 1990s, Murphy led the effort to add geography to the College Board's Advanced Placement Program. He holds a bachelor's degree in archaeology from Yale University, a law degree from Columbia University, and a Ph.D. in geography from the University of Chicago.

Terry G. Jordan-Bychkov (1938–2003) was the long-standing Walter Prescott Webb Professor of History and Ideas in the Department of Geography at the University of Texas, Austin. Prior to that he spent many years as chairman of the geography department at the University of North Texas in Denton. At the time of his death, he had completed field research in 65 countries, exploring topics as diverse as the origins of livestock ranching, folk architecture, burial customs, forest colonization, agricultural practices, and village life. As one of the most published and cited cultural geographers of his generation, he published a number of lauded books. He was the recipient of numerous professional and teaching awards and served as president of the Association of American Geographers. He earned his Ph.D. in geography at the University of Wisconsin–Madison.

Bella Bychkova Jordan is a lecturer in the Department of Geography and at the Center for Russian, East European, and Eurasian Studies at the University of Texas, Austin. A native of Djarkhan, Siberia, she specializes in the ethnic geography of the region. Her books include *The European Culture Area: A Systematic Geography*, fourth edition (with Terry G. Jordan-Bychkov), and *Siberian Village: Land and Life in the Sakha Republic* (with Terry G. Jordan-Bychkov). She holds a Ph.D. in geography from the University of Texas, Austin.